Age Discrimination

Age Discrimination

James Davies – General Editor

Lewis Silkin
Bethan Carney
Victoria Goode
Lucy Lewis
Hazel Oliver
Emma Perera
Hannah Price
Carolyn Soakell

Sackers
Faith Dickson
Robin Simmons

Tottel publishing
SACKER & PARTNERS
lewissilkin

Tottel Publishing Ltd, Maxwelton House, 41–43 Boltro Road, Haywards Heath, West Sussex, RH16 1BJ

A CIP Catalogue record for this book is available from the British Library.

ISBN: 978-1-84592-459-1

Typeset by Laserwords Private Ltd, Chennai, India
Printed and bound in Great Britain by Athenæum Press Ltd, Gateshead, Tyne and Wear

Foreword

In July 1977, 18 months after the Sex Discrimination Act 1975 came into force, the Court of Appeal decided in *Automotive Products Ltd v Peake* that a rule permitting female employees to leave their factory at the end of a shift five minutes earlier than men did not constitute sex discrimination against men. Lord Denning said: 'it would be very wrong to my mind if this statute were thought to obliterate the differences between men and women or to do away with the chivalry and courtesy which we expect mankind to give womankind. The natural differences of sex must be regarded even in the interpretation of an Act of Parliament.'

We have come a long way since then in understanding sex discrimination, but we are only beginning to go down the same road in respect of age discrimination. There is a view that age discrimination is qualitatively different than other forms of discrimination and that, accordingly, a much more nuanced approach is required to deal with it. When age discrimination in the job seeker's allowance was challenged in the House of Lords on human rights grounds in *R v Secretary of State for Work and Pensions, ex p Reynolds,* Lord Walker contrasted differential treatment on grounds of race, sex or sexual orientation with different treatment on grounds of age. 'Age', he said, 'is a personal characteristic, but it is different in kind from other personal characteristics. Every human being starts life as a tiny infant, and none of us can do anything to stop the passage of the years.'

It may well be that a similarly restrictive view will be taken of the Employment Equality (Age Discrimination) Regulations 2006 when they are first construed by the courts. It is undeniable that we start out young and end up old and that there are differences between people of different ages.

The vital issue, however, is whether these are relevant distinctions for employment decision-making and, even if they are, whether it should be legally acceptable to make assumptions based on these differences.

I am not as dextrous in my 60s as I was in my 20s, but dexterity is not a very important part of my work. And, as it happens, I have no doubt that there are plenty of people in their 60s who are more dextrous than I was in my 20s.

Discrimination specialists recognise that differences between older people and younger people, like differences between men and women, should only be considered as legitimate where they can be shown to be relevant to the particular circumstances. Even where differences overall can be documented, the law should acknowledge the great variations that can exist between people of a particular age group. Not to do so would be to commit the heresy of stereotyping.

Age discrimination legislation may be slightly ahead of the curve in terms of changing social attitudes, but our employment tribunals and courts are a lot more sophisticated about discrimination issues than they were in Lord Denning's time. Most of the discrimination strands have some aspect to them that makes them not precisely comparable with other strands. Sex discrimination has to assimilate discrimination on grounds of pregnancy. In disability discrimination, straight comparisons between a disabled and non-disabled person may not be possible. Whatever the ground for discrimination, however, we know that employment decisions should be made on the basis of merit and not on the basis of an assumption about the person. I have no doubt that before too long age discrimination will be seen as fitting very much into the mainstream of discrimination law.

As we move into that era, this book provides an excellent road map of the issues that are bound to arise under age discrimination legislation and how they should be approached by employers. It systematically analyses the problem areas from recruitment through retirement, in far more detail than has been available hitherto. The authors go well beyond textual analysis, however. The Regulations are placed in the context of discrimination law generally and there are many clear and helpful examples of practical problems and how they are likely to be viewed. The book will be of great assistance to those who have to apply the law and those who have to advise on it.

Michael Rubenstein
Co-Editor, Equal Opportunities Review
August 2006

Preface

My interest in age discrimination began many years ago when I was young and before the spectre of the pale, stale male appeared over my shoulder. It arose from acting for managers dismissed in their fifites in the late 1980s and early 1990s who would look at me bemused when I started asking them about their job plans. It then led to a dissertation on the subject as part of a Master's degree and to a close involvement with the area as first a code of practice and then legislation developed.

My hope is that this book will contribute to the success of these new laws which have the potential to benefit all – old, young and in-between – but have the potential to become side-tracked into the world of unintended consequences. It is already clear that these laws will have a more profound effect on the workplace than perhaps any new laws since the race and sex discrimiantion laws of the mid-1970s.

My thanks go to my co-authors at Lewis Silkin: Bethan, Carolyn, Emma, Hannah, Hazel, Lucy and Victoria and at Sacker & Partners: Faith and Robin, as well as to Kate for her support in making it happen, my fabulous PA, Jane, my colleagues at Lewis Silkin in so far as they have noticed that my attention has been elsewhere whilst I have worked on this book and last but not least to my wife, Priska, for her unfailing support.

James Davies
September 2007

About the Authors

Lewis Silkin LLP, a commercial law firm based in London and Oxford has one of the UK's leading employment law practices with over 50 lawyers specialising in this area (*www.lewissilkin.com*).

Sacker & Partners LLP is the leading specialist pensions law firm in the UK with 47 expert lawyers. Our first-class client base of over 1,000 pension schemes includes around 20 FTSE 100 companies (*www.sackers.com*).

Contents

Table of UK Statutes

References at the right-hand side of the column are to paragraph numbers

Table of Statutory Instruments, Circulars, Codes of Practice etc

Table of European Legislation

Overseas Legislation

Table of Cases

M

N

O

P

Solectron Scotland Ltd v Roper [2004] IRLR 4, (EAT) [illegible] 8.18
Sorensen v Sheffield City Council [illegible] [2004] IRLR 352; [2003] [illegible] EAT [illegible]
Southwark London Borough Council v Afolabi [2003] EWCA Civ 15; [2003] ICR 800; [2003] IRLR 220 [illegible] 14.3
Spring v Guardian Assurance plc [1995] 2 AC 296; [1994] 3 WLR 354; [1994] IRLR 460 HL [illegible]
[illegible] v [illegible] [illegible] ICR [illegible] [illegible]
[illegible] v [illegible] [illegible] IRLR 222 [illegible] [illegible]

T

Tattari v Private Patients Plan Ltd [1998] ICR 106; [1997] IRLR 586 [illegible] (1997) The Times, July [illegible] 3.28

V

Van Gend en Loos v Nederlandse Administratie der Belastingen Case 26/62 [1963] ECR 1; [1963] CMLR 105 [illegible] 4.1(b)
Vaughan v Weighpack Ltd [illegible] 7.5
Vento v Chief Constable of West Yorkshire Police (No 2) [2002] EWCA Civ 1871; [2003] ICR 318; [2003] IRLR 102 [illegible] 14.3
[illegible] [illegible] 12.8
[illegible] [illegible]

W

Waters v Commissioner of Police of the Metropolis [1997] ICR 1073 [illegible] ICR 863; [1995] 2 All ER [illegible] 12.7
Webb v EMO Air Cargo (UK) Ltd [illegible] [illegible] [illegible] EWCA Civ [illegible] [illegible] All ER 1 [illegible] [illegible]
Weathersfield Ltd (t/a Van & Truck Rentals) v Sargent [1999] ICR 425; [1999] IRLR 94 [illegible] 4.2(b)
Whiffen v Milham Ford Girls School [illegible] 11.2.1(a)
Wileman v Minilec Engineering Ltd [1988] ICR 318; [1988] IRLR 144 EAT [illegible] 4.2(b)
Williams v [illegible] [illegible] [1993] ICR [illegible] EAT [illegible] 14.2.1(b)

Chapter 1
History and background

1.1 Age and discrimination law

Law has been used in the United Kingdom as a weapon to tackle workplace inequalities since the sex and race discrimination laws of the mid 70s.[1] Other countries' discrimination laws predated the UK's[2] by many years. In 1996 the United Kingdom added disability discrimination legislation[3] and in 2003, laws outlawing discrimination on grounds of sexual orientation or religion or belief.[4]

The latest and, no doubt not the last, discrimination law[5] – the Employment Equality (Age) Regulations 2006, referred to in this book as 'the Regulations' – covers age.

Age, however, differs from the other strands of discrimination in significant respects.

Despite the evidence that age discrimination is considered as a greater problem than other forms of discrimination,[6] there is not a widespread consensus that age discrimination is as heinous an evil as other forms of discrimination. Indeed, it is unclear whether courts and tribunal will regard it in the same way.[7]

This imposes its own challenges for employers attempting to eradicate ageist prejudices and stereotypes from their workplaces[8] as employers may not readily accept the need to change behaviour that has not been regarded as socially unacceptable. The law, at this point, may be one step ahead of social norms.

Age is also arguably different from other forms of prohibited discrimination as we all grow older and as we serve our time both as members of advantaged and disadvantaged groups. It can therefore be seen as 'fairer'. Generally speaking, members of other groups protected by discrimination laws remain within that group throughout their working lives.

It is also accepted that in some circumstances age can be a legitimate reason on which to base employment decisions. This is recognised in the Regulations by the potential to justify direct discrimination, which does not appear in the other discrimination laws[9], and by the number of exceptions set out in the Regulations.[10]

1 Equal Pay Act 1970, (came into force in 1975), Sex Discrimination Act 1975 and Race Relations Act 1976.
2 Examples include US Equal Pay Act of 1963 and Title VII of the US Civil Rights Act of 1964; equal pay art 119 of the original Treaty of Rome 1957.
3 Disability Discrimination Act 1995.
4 Employment Equality (Sexual Orientation) Regulations 2003 and Employment Equality (Religious or Belief) Regulations 2003.
5 Pressure to introduce laws protecting the overweight eg Observer, 9 July 2006; some US cities and states already outlaw weight discrimination.
6 **Chapter 1, 1.2.2**.
7 **Chapter 4, 4.7.2**.
8 **Chapter 13**.
9 **Chapter 4, 4.2.3**.
10 **Chapter 4, 4.2.5** and **4.3.5** and **4.3.5**.

1.2 Need for age discrimination laws

1.2.1 Tackling the demographic time bomb

Britain is ageing.[1] A demographic time bomb is ticking. By 2004, life expectancy of 65-year-olds has risen to 84.4 for women and 81.6 for men.[2] The average retirement age for workers in employment at 50 is 63.8 for men and 61.6 for women.[3] The birth rate is declining.[4] Something, therefore, has to give. The Pension Commission's recommendations included a rise in the average age of retirement.[5]

With average retirement ages having fallen significantly for most of the second half of the twentieth century and life expectancy increasing rapidly, the length of time spent in retirement has nearly doubled between 1950 and 2004.[6] This has resulted in pressure on pensions, and contributed to the rapid decline in final salary occupational pension schemes.

Retirement ages differ in state pension ages as some workers retire early and others work beyond retirement age.

Currently, men and women are entitled to state pensions at ages 65 and 60 respectively. The state pension age for women will increase gradually from 2010 until it is harmonised at 65 in 2020. The Pension Commission's new recommendation is that it should increase to 68 by 2050.[7]

1 Life expectancy at birth has increased over the twentieth century for men from 45 in 1901 to 76 in 2002 and for women from 49 in 1901 to 81 in 2002 – National Statistics 2004.
2 National Statistics 2006.
3 *Pensions: Challenges and Choices, the first report of the Pensions Commission*, Pensions Commission First Report, 2004, p 34.
4 In the UK, an average of 1.74 children is born to each woman in contrast with a population replacement level of 2.1, Eurostat – 2004.
5 Pensions Commission First Report and see **Chapter 12, 12.4**.
6 Increase for men from 10.8 years to 20.1 years, see Pensions Commission First Report, p 35.
7 *New Pension Settlement for the Twenty first Century*, Pensions Commission 2005.

1.2.2 Tackling ageist prejudices and stereotypes

At the same time we live in a youth obsessed world. Older workers perceive that they face discrimination in the workplace. A University of Kent report in 2005 found that age discrimination eclipsed all other forms of discrimination in the United Kingdom.[1]

Discrimination can be rational or irrational. It might be right that older workers are, on average, less fit than younger workers but it would be unfair on older workers for their age to be used as a proxy for fitness in preferring younger candidates for a job. It can also be not only unfair but irrational such as where an employer sets a retirement age of, say, 60 for a job where there is no reason to believe that the over 60s are less likely to perform adequately than the under 60s.

A report commissioned by the Employers Forum on Age judged that age discrimination costs the United Kingdom between £19 billion and £31 billion annually.[2]

1 29 per cent of respondents had encountered age discrimination in the workplace, more than any other form of discrimination.
2 Employers' Forum on Age.

1.3 Development of age discrimination laws elsewhere in the world

Other countries have had age discrimination laws for some time. These laws can be found in national age discrimination laws, regional laws or broader non-discrimination provisions of human rights or constitutional rules.

The United States introduced federal age discrimination laws in 1967 to address difficulties that older blue-collar workers were facing in finding work.

New Zealand introduced age discrimination laws in 1998. Australia and Canada have also introduced age discrimination laws initially at a state level and then federally.

Continental Europe has had some age laws for some time. Ireland introduced them in 1998 and the Netherlands in 2004.

Detailed information about the age discrimination laws of other countries is outside the scope of this book but can be found on the age discrimination website, *www.agediscrimination.info.*

1.4 Development of UK age discrimination laws

1.4.1 Labour government

In the United Kingdom, there was little impetus for age laws until Tony Blair's election in 1997. The Labour Party went into that election originally proposing comprehensive age discrimination laws. That was watered down in its manifesto to a commitment to introduce 'measures' to combat age discrimination.

This then translated in 1999 to a much-derided Code of Practice,[1] which the Government were not even prepared to give statutory force. It seems likely that this back down arose from behind the scenes compromises with the business community.

Indeed, it may well be that the Government already had one eye on developments in Europe where directives were being discussed extending EU sex discrimination laws to race, disability, sexual orientation, religion and belief. At the same time that the Labour Government was acting lukewarm over age laws, it was clear that the EU would be forcing through a directive obliging the United Kingdom to legislate and, perhaps, deliver a convenient scapegoat for criticism that the laws amounted to unnecessary red tape and additional burdens on business.

1 *Age Diversity in Employment, a Code of Practice,* 1999.

1.5 EU directive

Council Directive 2000/78 establishing a general framework for equal treatment in employment and occupation was adopted on 27 November

2000. This is referred to in this book as 'the Directive'. The Directive not only covered age but also disability, religion and belief and sexual orientation. It set a deadline for Member States, including the United Kingdom, to introduce age discrimination laws of 2 December 2006.

A report was published in 2005 by the European Commission on the implementation of the Directive.[1]

1 *Age Discrimination and European Law,* Colm O'Gineide, European Commission, April 2005.

1.6 Numbers of cases

At the time of writing[1] there had been nearly 1,000 age claims filed with the employment tribunals. It is expected that the number of claims will rise and this has been the experience following the introduction of other discrimination laws.[2]

In the United States, where, as mentioned above, the federal age discrimination laws are much more limited than in the United Kingdom there were 16,548 age discrimination claims filed with the Equal Employment Opportunity Commission (EEOC) in 2006. This was slightly less than the number of race or sex discrimination claims and slightly higher than the number of disability claims.[3]

In Ireland, for example, of the new cases dealt with by the Irish Equality Authority in 2006, 15 per cent related to age discrimination, less than that related to disability discrimination but higher than either sex or race discrimination.

1 July 2007
2 The number of disability discrimination claims rose from 1,430 in 1998/99 to 4,072 in 2005/6.
3 Sex = 23, 247; race = 27, 238; and disability = 15, 575.

Chapter 2

Overview of the Directive and the Regulations

2.1 The Directive

As mentioned in **Chapter 1**[1] Council Directive 2000/78 of 27 November establishing a general framework for equal treatment in employment and occupation obliged EU Member States to introduce age discrimination laws by 2 December 2006.

The Directive includes a preamble of 37 paragraphs and a body of 21 articles. The relevant articles, as far as age discrimination is concerned, are:

- Article 2 which defines the concept of discrimination including definitions of direct discrimination,[2] indirect discrimination[3] and harassment[4] and providing that an instruction to discriminate shall amount to discrimination[5];
- Article 3 defines the scope of the Regulations and as regards age discrimination in particular excludes the armed forces from its application;
- Article 4 sets out the genuine occupational requirements exception[6];
- Article 6 which relates specifically to age discrimination deals with justification[7];
- Article 7 deals with the exception for positive action[8];
- Article 8 permits Member States to introduce laws more favourable than those laid out in the Directive but requires Member States not to reduce the level of protection afforded against discrimination in the fields covered by the Directive on account of the implementation of the Directive;
- Article 10 deals with the burden of proof[9];
- Article 11 covers victimisation[10];
- Article 12 obliges Member States to take steps to bring the new laws to the attention of concerned persons;
- Article 16 requires Member States to amend existing laws which might conflict with the Directive; and
- Article 17 requires sanctions to be effective, proportionate and dissuasive;
- Article 18 set the deadline for implementation of the age parts of the Directive at 2 December 2006.

Paragraph 14 of the Preamble is particularly relevant. It states:

> 'This Directive shall be without prejudice to national provisions laying down retirement ages.'

Nonetheless, as there does not appear to be any general exception for retirement ages in the substantive articles of the Directive, this paragraph appears to have little practical importance.

At the time of writing there has been one European Court of Justice (ECJ) decision and one advocate general's opinion on the age part of the Directive.[11]

1 **Chapter 1**.
2 See art 2(2)(a) and **Chapter 4, 1.4.2**.
3 See art 2(2)(b) and **Chapter 4, 1.4.3**.
4 See art 2(3) and **Chapter 4, 1.4.5**.
5 See art 2(4) and **Chapter 3, 3.4.6**.
6 **Chapter 4, 4.2.4** and **Chapter 5, 5.3.2(a)**.
7 **Chapter 4, 4.7**.
8 **Chapter 5, 5.3.2(b)**.
9 **Chapter 4, 4.6**.
10 **Chapter 4, 4.4**.
11 *Mangold v Helm* [2006] IRLR 143, **Chapter 4, 4.7.3** and *Félix Palacios de la Villa v Cartefiel Servicios SA* Case – 411/05 – **Chapter 12, 12.5**.

2.2 The Regulations

The Employment Equality (Age) Regulations[1] came into force on 1 October 2006. For the reasons set out in **Chapter 1**, the provisions governing pensions were delayed by the Employment Equality (Age) (Amendment) Regulations 2006[2] and introduced with effect from 1 December 2006 by the Employment Equality (Age) (Amendment) (No 2) Regulations 2006.[3]

The Employment Equality (Age) (Consequential Amendments) Regulations 2007[4] came into force on 6 April 2007 and made some consequential technical amendments to various other legislation.

In many respects, many of the concepts and definitions in the Regulations are familiar from other discrimination laws. However, as explored in detail in this book there are many important differences, not least the possibility of justifying direct age discrimination and the numerous exceptions listed below.

The Regulations are broken down into 49 regulations divided into six parts together with nine schedules.

1 SI 2006/1031.
2 SI 2006/2408.
3 SI 2006/2931.
4 SI 2007/821.

2.2.1 Part 1 – (General)

Part 1 sets out the definition of discrimination.[1]

1 See Regs 3–6 and **Chapter 4**.

2.2.2 Part 2 – (Discrimination in employment and vocational training)

This part sets out who bring age discrimination claims and against whom.[1]

1 See Regs 7–24 and **Chapter 3**.

2.2.3 Part 3 – (Other unlawful acts)

Regulations 25 and 26 cover liability for the acts of others.[1]

1 **Chapter 3**.

2.2.4 Part 4 – (General exceptions from Pts 2 and 3)

One important characteristic of the Regulations which distinguishes it from other discrimination laws is the recognition that treating people differently on grounds of age can be legitimate. This is recognised both in the possibility not found in other discrimination laws of objectively justifying direct age discrimination and in the exceptions set out in Pt 4 of the Regulations.

Age-based behaviour which falls within any of the exceptions is lawful and does not need justifying.

These exceptions are:

- exception for statutory authority[1];
- exception for national security[2];
- exception for positive action[3];
- exception for retirement[4];
- exception for the national minimum wage[5];
- exception for provision of certain benefits based on length of service[6];
- exception for provision of enhanced redundancy payments to employees[7]; and
- exception for provision of life assurance cover to retired workers[8]

1 See reg 27 and **Chapter 5, 5.3.2(d)**.

2 See reg 28 and **Chapter 5, 5.3.2(e)**.
3 See reg 29 and **Chapter 5, 5.3.2(b)**.
4 See reg 30, and **Chapter 12**.
5 See reg 31 and **Chapter 6, 6.4.5**.
6 See reg 32 and **Chapter 6, 6.3**.
7 See reg 33 and **Chapter 11, 11.5.3**.
8 See reg 34 and **Chapter 6, 6.5.3(d)**.

2.2.5 Part 5 – (Enforcement)

Regulations 35–42 cover issues of jurisdiction,[1] burden of proof,[2] remedies,[3] questionnaires[4] and time limits.[5]

1 See regs 36 and 39 and **Chapter 14, 14.2**.
2 See regs 37 and 40 and **Chapter 4, 4.6**.
3 See reg 38 and **Chapter 14, 14.9**.
4 See reg 41, Schs 4 and 5 and **Chapter 14, 14.6**.
5 See reg 42 and **Chapter 14, 14.3**.

2.2.6 Part 6 – (Supplemental)

This part is a catch all covering various miscellaneous points in regs 43–49. Regulation 43 incorporates Sch 5 dealing with the validity of contracts, collective agreements and rules of undertakings.[1] Regulations 44–46 apply the Regulations to Crown employees and House of Commons and House of Lords.[2] Regulations 47 and 48 incorporate Schs 6 and 7 which set out the duty to consider requests to stay beyond retirement procedure which is an integral part of the approach the government ultimately decided upon for retirement.[3] Finally, Regulation 49 incorporates Schs 8 and 9 which list the consequential changes to other laws necessitated by the Regulations.

1 **Chapter 14, 14.9.2**.
2 **Chapter 3, 3.3.8**.
3 **Chapter 12, 12.9**.

2.2.7 Schedules

The Regulations incorporate nine schedules:

(i) Schedule 1, for some reason, gives over a page to delineating the part of the Norwegian sector of the Continental Shelf within the Frigg Gas Field covered by the Regulations. Presumably the employment tribunal will not be troubled too often (if ever) by complex jurisdiction issues arising out of Schedule 1.

(ii) Schedule 2, on the other hand, will trouble employment tribunals. It sets the application of the Regulations to pension schemes.[1]

(iii) Schedules 3 and 4 set out standard form questionnaires and replies to questionnaires.[2]

(iv) Schedule 5 deals with the validity of contracts, collective agreements and rules of undertakings.[3]

(v) Schedules 6 and 7 set out the procedure to be followed under the duty to consider requests to stay in employment after retirement age.[4]

(vi) Schedules 8 and 9 list amendments to other laws.

1 **Chapter 8**.
2 See reg 41 and **Chapter 14, 14.6**.
3 See reg 43 and **Chapter 14, 14.9.2**.
4 **Chapter 12, 12.9**.

2.3 Guidance on the Regulations

Guidance on the impact of the Regulations can be found from a variety of helpful official and unofficial sources. Many of these can be found on the age discrimination website, *www.agediscrimination.info*.

2.3.1 Official guidance

The DTI published Notes on Regulations[1] to accompany the Regulations. These Notes have no official status but contain helpful explanations about many of the provisions within the Regulations and are referred to throughout this book.

The DTI also published eight age legislation factsheets, including factsheets on: Objective Justification; Vocational Training; Service-related Benefits; Retirement; and Occupational Pensions. They also produced a document described as 'Clarification of Regulation 33'.

Age Positive, part of the Department for Work and Pensions, has also produced a series of publications – *www.agepositive.gov.uk*.

The Department for Work and Pensions has produced a Guide on the pensions part of the Regulations.[2]

The Advisory, Conciliation and Arbitration Service (ACAS) has also produced a series of guides for employers and employees. The ACAS Guide for employers[3] is referred to in various places in this book.

1 DTI, March 2006.
2 *The Impact of the Age Regulations on Pension Schemes, Guidance on the Employment Equality (Age) Regulations 2006 and their impact on occupational and personal pension schemes*, DWP, December 2006.

3 *Age and the Workplace – Employers' Guide, Putting the Employment Equality (Age) Regulations 2006 into practice*, ACAS, EEL03.

2.3.2 Unofficial sources

The Employers' Forum on Age[1] is, perhaps, the leading source of advice and support for employers on age discrimination and age diversity matters. It has produced a series of guidance material including the *Insider Guide to Age Laws*.

TAEN[2] set up the agebusters website.[3]

The TUC and CIPD also produced a joint guide to the Regulations.[4]

As mentioned above, the *www.agediscrimination.info* website also contains a wealth of information on the Regulations and age discrimination more generally.

1 *www.efa.org.uk.*
2 *www.taen.org.uk.*
3 *www.agebusters.org.uk.*
4 *Managing Age – A guide to good employment practice,* CIPD, February 2007.

2.4 The relationship between the Regulations and the Directive

2.4.1 Interpreting the Regulations

As with all domestic legislation (primary or secondary) introduced to give effect to the UK's European Treaty obligations the primacy of the Directive arises in three ways:

(a) the Regulations must, where appropriate, be interpreted in light of the Directive[1];

(b) in limited circumstances, the Directive can be relied on directly[2]; and

(c) an individual who loses out because the Regulations fail to give effect to the Directive can sue the Government if he cannot rely directly on the Directive.[3]

1 **Chapter 1**.
2 **Chapter 1**.
3 **Chapter 1**.

(a) Interpreting in light of the Directive

The UK courts and tribunals will look at the Directive in interpreting the national law if this is possible.

(b) Direct effect

In certain circumstances a directive can be relied on directly. To start with not all directives are capable of direct effect. They must:

- be clear;
- be precise;
- be unconditional; and
- not give the Member State discretion in their application.[1]

In addition, it has been traditionally accepted that directives only have vertical direct effect.[2] In other words, they can be relied on against the State.[3] The State has been interpreted widely to over any 'emanation of the State'. This includes any organisation with special powers conferred by the State and whose operations are under the control of the State.[4] It would, therefore, include privatised utilities.

The absence of horizontal effect of directives and, in particular, the Directive has been called into question by the ECJ's first age discrimination decision in *Mangold v Helm*[5] (see below).

1 Van Gend en Loos (Case 26/62 [1963] ECR 1).
2 Unlike the articles of the Treaty of Rome which have horizontal direct effect and can be relied on by a person against another private sector person.
3 The basis being that the State should not be able to hide behind its own failings in not properly implementing the directive.
4 *Foster v British Gas* [1991] 2 AC 306.
5 [2006] IRLR 143.

(c) Damages

If the Regulations cannot be interpreted in line with the Directive and it does not have direct effect a person who believes that his rights under the Directive have not been given effect under domestic law has the last resort of suing the Attorney General for his losses in the High Court.[1] Such claims are rare.

1 *Brasserie de Pecheur/Factortame (No 4)* [1996] 1 CMLR 889; *Francovich v Italy* [1993] 2 CMLR 66.

2.4.2 *Mangold v Helm*

The decision in *Mangold v Helm* is important not only because of what it has to say about the test of justification of age discrimination[1] but because it suggests that the Directive could be relied on by individuals against a private sector body (ie horizontal direct effect) and suggests that it could be relied on before the deadline for enacting implementing legislation in Member States.

1 **Chapter 4, 4.7**.

(a) Horizontal direct effect

Previously, it had been accepted that only employees of 'emanations of the State' could rely directly on directives and then only if the directive satisfied the three conditions of being sufficiently clear, precise and unconditional.[1] The ECJ accepted in this case that Mr Mangold could rely on the Directive against his private sector employer, Mr Helm, without any real explanation.

1 See **2.4.1(b)**.

(b) Before expiry of the deadline for implementation

Mr Mangold was able to rely on the Directive even though the deadline for Germany to implement it had not expired. Of particular relevance was that the German law being challenged was introduced after the adoption of the Directive and in the period of implementation. The ECJ commented that the prohibition on age discrimination must be 'regarded as a general principle of Community Law'.[1] It stated that the nondiscrimination principles within the Directive emanated not from the Directive but from 'various international instruments and in the constitutional traditions common to the Member States'.[2]

In the Employment Appeal Tribunal (EAT) case of *Bernard Charles Lloyd-Brides v Worthing College*,[3] the claimant sought to rely on *Mangold* to bring an unfair dismissal claim arising out of a dismissal which pre-dated the coming into force of the Regulations, even though he was above the then age limit to bring such claims. The EAT refused to permit him to use *Mangold* to override the upper age limit. It distinguished this situation from that in *Mangold* as the then upper age limit in unfair dismissal legislation pre-dated the Directive whereas the German law overridden in *Mangold* was introduced after the adoption of the Directive.

1 See para 75, p 159.
2 See para 74, p 159.
3 EAT 0065/07/RN.

2.4.3 Compatibility of the Regulations with the Directive

As mentioned above, the Regulations must be read in accordance with the Directive where appropriate.

It should be noted, however, in considering whether or not national laws which discriminate on the grounds of age might be justified and, nonetheless, lawful that art 6(1) of the Directive states that the test of objective justification should be assessed 'within the context of national law'. This qualification is not normally found in Directives and could be relied on by the United Kingdom to support those domestic laws which might be challenged as being incompatible with the Directive. Nevertheless, if this does establish a lower threshold for Member States than in other cases, it seemed to have little effect on the outcome of the ECJ decision in *Mangold* above.

(a) Heyday judicial review

One judicial review application was brought challenging the compatibility of certain aspects of the Regulations[1]

These aspects are:

- the default retirement age[2];
- the absence of any list of legitimate aims which can be relied on to justify age discrimination[3]; and
- the setting of the same test of justification for direct and indirect age discrimination.[4]

The application was heard on 2 December 2006 and the parties agreed that the matter should be referred to the ECJ. At the time of writing the parties are yet to agree the questions to be put to the ECJ. A decision is not expected until late 2008 or even 2009.

1 *R (on the application of Incorporated Trustees of the National Council of Ageing) v the Secretary of State for Trade and Industry*, EWHC 5485/2000 and **Chapter 12, 12.5**.
2 **Chapter 12, 12.5**.
3 **Chapter 4, 4.7.5**.
4 **Chapter 4, 4.7.3**.

(b) Other possible areas of challenge

Other provisions within the Regulations which appear vulnerable to challenge include:

- the 'business need' justification for service-related benefits where service does not exceed five years[1];
- the lower rates of National Minimum Wage (NMW) for young persons[2];
- certain aspects of the pensions exemptions[3]; and

- the retaining of age bands within the statutory redundancy pay scheme and as a necessary requirement for a scheme to comply with the exception for enhanced redundancy payments.[4]

1 **Chapter 6, 6.3.2(b)**.
2 **Chapter 6, 6.4.5**.
3 **Chapter 8**.
4 **Chapter 11, 11.5**.

2.4.4 Secondary legislation

The Regulations are set out in a statutory instrument.[1] This is a form of secondary legislation rather than Acts of Parliament which are primary legislation. Amongst UK discrimination laws, the Sex Discrimination, Equal Pay, Race Relations and Disability Discrimination Acts are, as their names suggest, Acts of Parliament whereas the laws on discrimination on grounds of sexual orientation and religion and belief are contained in secondary legislation.

All secondary legislation has to be introduced under a power conferred by primary legislation. In the case of the Regulations, the primary legislation is the European Communities Act 1972.

1 SI 2006/1031.

2.5 Future developments

Whatever the outcome of any challenges to the Regulations, in three respects important developments to the Regulations have already been promised:

(i) in 2011, the government has committed to reviewing the default retirement age;

(ii) in October 2007 the Commission for Equality and Human Rights will be launched; and

(iii) the government has already published a green paper into discrimination law reform.[1]

1 *A Framework for Fairness: Proposals for a Single Equality Bill for Great Britain*, June 2007.

2.5.1 Review in 2011

As discussed in **Chapters 1** and **12**[1] after much debate the government set a default retirement age of 65 at or beyond which employers can freely retire employees. However, it committed itself to reviewing this in 2011 with a view to either increasing or abolishing the default age. The most likely outcome will be an increase in the default age, perhaps, to 67 or 68.

1 **Chapter 12, 12.4**.

2.5.2 Discrimination law review

This Review[1] proposes numerous changes to UK discrimination law. The most significant changes to age discrimination law would be its extension to goods and services,[2] the possible extension of the public sector equality duty to cover age[3] and the extension of lawful positive action within the parameters set by European Law.[4]

1 *A Framework for Fairness: Proposals for a Single Equality Bill for Great Britain,* June 2007.
2 **Chapter 9** of the Review, pp 135–145.
3 See paras 5.6.1–5.6.3, pp 97 and 98.
4 **Chapter 5, 5.3.2(b)**.

2.5.3 Commission for Equality and Human Rights

Unlike the sex, race and disability discrimination laws,[1] the Regulations did not have any agency entrusted with their enforcement. This will change in October 2007 with the launch of the Commission for Equality and Human Rights established under the Equality Act 2006. This will bring together the agencies responsible for all other stands of discrimination law into one body under the Chairmanship of Sir Trevor Phillips. Its powers and responsibilities will include:

- to advise employers and service provides on good practice and the promotion of equality and good relations;
- to conduct inquiries and carry out investigations;
- to provide advise and information on rights and equality laws;
- to campaign on issues affecting the diverse groups in society that can suffer discrimination;
- to make arrangements for conciliation to assist with disputes;
- to assist individuals who believe they have been the victim of unlawful discrimination; and
- to provide grants.[2]

1 The Equal Opportunities Commission, the Commission for Racial Equality and the Disability Rights Commission.
2 See ss 13–31 of the Equality Act 2006.

Chapter 3

Scope of the regulations

3.1 Introduction

Although it is statistically the case that most age discrimination claims will be brought by employees against their employers, the scope of the Regulations is far wider and embraces other categories of workers, job applicants and work-related qualifications.

In this chapter, we consider:

- who may bring a claim of age discrimination;
- who may be sued for age discrimination; and
- the geographical scope of the Regulations.

Although the geographical scope of the Regulations is generally quite wide, the express provisions relate only to employees and contract workers leaving open the question of the geographical scope for other groups of protected individuals (for example, partners in international partnerships).

Unlike other forms of discrimination, the Regulations do not extend to the provision of goods and services as this was not required in order to be compatible with the Directive. However, an extension of the Regulations to cover the provisions of goods and services is being considered by the government as part of the Single Equality Act which would draw together all discrimination in the legislation.[1]

1 **Chapter 2, 2.5.2.**

3.2 Against whom can a claim be brought?

3.2.1 Employers *(Regulation 7)*

It is certainly the case that the majority of age discrimination claims will be brought against employers. This is particularly true when you consider the broad definition that the Regulations give to 'employment'. The definition of employment is 'employment under a contract of service or of apprenticeship or a contract personally to do any work'[1] and employer and employee construed accordingly. The inclusion of 'or a contract personally to do any work' is far wider than the definition in the Employment Rights Act (ERA) 1996.[2] This definition will include individuals who do not necessarily consider themselves to be employees in the conventional sense (for example, freelancers or consultants who contract personally to do work) and individuals not taxed as employees.

Claims may also be brought against employers by ex-employees and job applicants.

The areas in which age discrimination claims can be brought are considered in more detail in other chapters,[3] but, in summary, it is unlawful for an employer to discriminate on grounds of age:

(a) in the arrangements made for the purpose of determining who should be offered employment;

(b) in the terms on which employment is offered; and

(c) by refusing to offer or deliberately not offering employment.[4]

Once the employment has started, it is also unlawful for an employer to discriminate on grounds of age:

(a) in the terms of employment afforded;

(b) in the opportunities afforded for promotion, transfer, training or receiving any other benefit;

(c) by refusing to afford or deliberately not affording such opportunities for promotion, transfer, training, or receiving any other benefit; and

(d) by dismissing or subjecting an employee to any other detriment.[5]

The employer's treatment of an employee will not be unlawful if it is covered by one of the exemptions included in the Regulations (for example, an employer can show that the discrimination is as a result of a genuine occupational requirement,[6] or if an employer can objectively justify the treatment).

Finally, it is unlawful for an employer to subject an employee or job applicant to harassment on grounds of age.[7] Further details of harassment are included in **Chapter 4**[8] of this book.

See also **3.3** which deals with the claims by employees and self-employed (**3.3.1**); volunteers (**3.3.2**); contract workers (**3.3.3**); employment agency workers (**3.3.4**); applicants and candidates (**3.3.12**); and relationships which have come to an end (**3.3.13**).

1 See reg 2(2).
2 See s 230 of the ERA 1996 which covers rights such as unfair dismissal, etc.
3 See **Chapters 5–8** and **10**.
4 See reg 7(1)(a–c).
5 See reg 7(2)(a–d).

6 See reg 8.
7 See reg 7(3).
8 **Chapter 4, 4.5.**

3.2.2 Partnerships *(Regulation 17)*

Partnerships will often fall under both the employment protection provisions[1] (in relation to individuals who are employed by them) and the partnership protection provisions (in relation to the partners of the partnership). The protection for partners of a partnership is similar (but not identical) to that afforded to those in employment.

Partnerships of any size are covered as are Limited Partnerships[2] and Limited Liability Partnerships (LLPs).[3]

A partnership cannot discriminate on grounds of age:

(a) in the arrangements made for determining who should be offered partnership;

(b) in the terms on which partnership is offered;

(c) by refusing to offer, or deliberately not offering, partnership;

(d) in the way that a partner is afforded access to benefits;

(e) by refusing to afford or deliberately not affording a partner access to benefits; and

(f) by expelling a partner or subjecting a partner to any other detriment.[4]

There is also a protection against harassment on grounds of age.[5]

The protection in (a) to (c) above, also covers a group of individuals proposing to form a partnership and, as with the employment relationship, there is an exemption if it can be shown that there is a genuine occupational requirement.[6]

As with the employment dismissals, the expulsion of a partner includes the expiry of any term after which the partnership is not renewed on the same terms and also circumstances in which a partner is entitled to terminate without notice because of the conduct of the other partners (similar to a constructive dismissal).[7]

Examples:

Adam and Brenda are employed in a firm of solicitors. They decide to set up a partnership and approached Carly to see if she would like to join them. Adam and Brenda tell Carly that because she is in her late 50s, her share of any profits should be less than theirs to reflect the limited likely future length of her involvement in the partnership. Carly would be able to claim age discrimination and Adam and Brenda would need to objectively justify this profit share, which may be difficult to do.

Abigail is a partner at XYZ LLP. The partnership deed requires that she cease to be a partner at 65. Abigail would be able to bring a claim of age discrimination. Partners are not covered by the default retirement provisions and so XYZ LLP would have to objectively justify this requirement.[1]

Alfie is 3 months away from his 65th birthday. He applies for partnership with a new firm of solicitors. The partners decide to decline Alfie's application because he is within 6 months of 65. Alfie can bring an age discrimination claim whether the partnership has a retirement age of 65 or has abolished it altogether. Because, Alfie is applying for partnership (rather than employment), the exemption in reg 7(4) will not apply to him. The partnership will need to be able to objectively justify their decision.[2]

1 See **Chapter 12, 12.8.5(a)**.
2 See **Chapter 5, 5.3.2(c)**.

Please also see **3.3.5**.

1 See reg 7.
2 See reg 17(5).
3 See reg 17(6).
4 See reg 17(1).
5 See reg 17(2).
6 See reg 17(4).
7 See reg 17(8).

3.2.3 Trade Organisations *(Regulation 18)*

'Trade Organisation' is defined as:

> 'an organisation of workers, an organisation of employers, or any other organisations whose members carry on a particular profession or trade for the purposes of which the organisation exists.'

'Profession' includes 'any vocation or occupation' and 'Trade' includes 'any business'.[1] The Chartered Institute of Personnel and Development, the Royal College of Nursing and the Driving Instructors Association, for example, will all be trade organisations.

Scope of the regulations

It is unlawful for a trade organisation to discriminate on grounds of age:

(a) in the terms on which it admits a member;

(b) by refusing to accept, or deliberately not accepting, an application for membership;

(c) in the way it affords a member access to any benefits;

(d) by refusing or deliberately omitting to afford a member access to any benefits;

(e) by depriving an individual of membership, or varying the terms on which an individuals is a member; or

(f) by subjecting a member to any other detriment.[2]

There is also a protection against harassment.[3]

The definition of trade organisation can be illustrated by two cases on the equivalent definition in other discrimination legislation.

In the case of *Medley v Working Men's Club and Institute Union Ltd*,[4] Ms Medley was a member of Bishopthorpe Social Club. The Working Men's Club and Institute Union Ltd was an umbrella organisation of which the social club was part. By paying a fee to the umbrella organisation, it was possible to get associate status. Ms Medley applied for associate status but was refused because she was a woman. It was held by the Employment Appeal Tribunal (EAT) that Ms Medley did not have jurisdiction to proceed with her claim under the equivalent provisions of the Sex Discrimination Act (SDA). The phrase 'an organisation of workers' was limited in its scope. The membership of clubs was not restricted to *working* men. In fact, there were no minimum qualifications or classifications and there was, therefore, no basis upon which it could be argued that the umbrella organisation was 'an organisation of workers'. Neither was the Working Men's Club and Institute Union Ltd. 'an organisation whose members carried on a particular profession or trade for the purposes of which the organisation existed'. It was held that there were two conditions before an organisation could be regarded as such: (i) the organisation had to consist of members who carried on a particular profession or trade; and (ii) the organisation had to be set up for the purposes of carrying on that particular profession or trade.

In *(1) The Medical Protection Society (2) Dr S Bown (3) Dr J Hickey v Dr Saher Sadek*[5], the Medical Protection Society (MPS) appealed against an employment tribunal decision that it constituted an *organisation of workers* and *an organisation whose members carried on a particular profession for the purposes of which the organisation existed* under the equivalent provisions of the Race Relations Act. Dr Sadek was suspended from his duties by his employer and sought advice from the MPS. He was dissatisfied with the advice that he received and the MPS withdrew its support. The MPS argued that it fell outside the relevant definition because it had a large number of corporate members as well as students who were not carrying on a profession. It also held that the phrase 'for the purposes of which the organisation existed' excluded the MPS because it did not exist for the purposes of any profession. The EAT held that it would be wrong to exclude the MPS simply because some of its members were corporate members and students. The fact that the majority of its members were individuals carrying on a profession was sufficient to bring it within the scope of the definition.

Examples:

Amanda is refused membership of a local golf club because she is under 50 years. Unless Amanda is a professional golfer and the club is an organisation of professional golfers, she would not have an age discrimination claim against the club.

Bob is a builder and a member of an organisation of roofers. He joined the organisation in order to increase his prospects of getting roofing work and because his membership includes insurance against lost earnings in the case of a fall. After a fall, Bob seeks to rely on the insurance. However, he finds that the insurance only covers roofers under 50. Bob is 50 years old. Bob can bring an age discrimination claim against the organisation of roofers based on the discriminatory access to benefits.

---

1 See reg 18(4).
2 See reg 18(1) and (2).
3 See reg 18(3).
4 UKEAT/0782/03.
5 UKEAT/594/03.

3.2.4 Qualifications bodies *(Regulation 19)*

A qualifications body is a body which can confer (including renew or extend) a professional or trade qualification. A professional or trade qualification means 'any authorisation, qualification, recognition, registration, enrolment, approval or certification which is needed for, or facilitates engagement in, a particular profession or trade'. As with the definition of trade organisations, 'Profession' includes 'any vocation or occupation' and 'Trade' includes 'any business'.[1] Both the Law Society and the General Medical Council will be qualifications bodies.

However, the provisions relating to qualification bodies do not include the governing body of an educational establishment which is covered by reg

23 (institutions of further and higher education) or the proprietor of a school.[2]

It is unlawful for a qualifications body to discriminate on grounds of age:

(a) in the terms on which it is prepared to confer a professional or trade qualification;
(b) by refusing or deliberately not granting an application for such a qualification; or
(c) by withdrawing such a qualification or varying the terms on which it is held.[3]

It is also unlawful for a qualifications body to harass on grounds of age a person who holds or applies for a qualification.[4] Unlike in the case of employees, there is no exemption for discrimination if age is a genuine occupational requirement.[5]

The definition of qualifications body can be illustrated by cases under other discrimination laws.

In the case of *Shaw v (1) Shropshire County Premier Football League (2) Shropshire County Football Association*,[6] Mr Shaw argued that amateur football that could lead to semi-professional/professional status was a vocation. However, it was held that Mr Shaw, as an amateur football player, was not engaged in a particular profession, and that neither Shropshire County Premier Football league (SCPF) or Shropshire Country Football (SCF) were qualifying bodies. Neither had granted a *qualification or authorisation* to a person who had satisfied appropriate standards of competence to practice a profession or trade. Both SCPF and SCF had limited powers of organisation and discipline which did not affect Mr Shaw's overall status as a footballer.

However, in the case of *British Judo Association v Petty*,[7] the British Judo Association was held to be a qualifications body under the equivalent provisions of the SDA. In that case, Ms Petty a judo referee was granted a national judo referee's certificate which facilitated her engagement as a coach. Having refereed men's events, Ms Petty was told she should not have done so as she had never been selected to referee men's national competitions. The grant of the certificate to her, in effect on the terms that she was not eligible to referee men's national events, was contrary to the terms of the SDA.

In *Tattari v Private Patients Plan Ltd*[8] it was held by the Court of Appeal that Private Patients Plan Ltd (PPP), a private medical insurance company, was not a qualifying body because it did not have power to confer a professional qualification or other approval to enable an individual to take part in a profession. In that case Dr Tattari was a plastic surgeon with a Greek practicing certificate. The PPP did not recognise the certificate and refused to pay Dr Tattari if he treated a patient under the scheme. The PPP was distinguished from a qualifications body as a profit-making concern which required certain qualifications for a commercial agreement, but which did not prevent Dr Tattari from being able to work or treat patients under the scheme.

In *Arthur v Attorney General*,[9] Ms Arthur had applied to become a justice of the peace. Appointments were made by the Lord Chancellor from recommendations of local advisory panels. Ms Arthur had been interviewed by the Middlesex Area Advisory Committee (MMAC) but was not recommended for appointment. Ms Arthur claimed that the failure to recommend her was discriminatory. It was held by the EAT that MAAC was not a qualifications body under the equivalent provisions of the SDA. It held that to be a justice of the peace was not an occupation within the definition of profession. Further, there was a difference between a group, committee or panel which was sifting job applications (as MMAC was in this case), and a qualifications body conferring an approval. To be a qualifications body required more than performing a filtering function.

Although it is generally the case that a claim against a qualifications body would be brought in the employment tribunal, reg 36(2) creates an exemption if there is a statutory right of appeal against the decision of the qualifications body. Therefore, any qualifying body regulated by statute where there is statutory right of appeal against, for example a decision not to confer a qualification, the statutory appeal process must be used and, if necessary, judicial review rather than the tribunal process.

Examples:

Anne is subject to a disciplinary hearing by the Law Society. She believes that an older solicitor would have been treated more leniently because of his established reputation. Anne would be able to bring an age discrimination claim against the Law Society.

Brian is advised by the General Medical Council that his qualification is to be removed. He believes that the only reason for this is his age. Brian would be able to bring an discrimination claim against the General Medical Council.

---

1 See reg 19(3).
2 See reg 19(3).

3 See reg 19(1).
4 See reg 19(2).
5 **Chapter 4, 4.2.4**; **Chapter 5, 5.3.2(a)**.
6 UKEAT/0272/04.
7 [1981] IRLR 484.
8 [1997] IRLR 586.
9 The Times, 18 March 1999.

3.2.5 Vocational training providers *(Regulation 20)*

It is unlawful for any training provider to discriminate on grounds of age against a person seeking or undergoing training:

(a) in the arrangements made for the purpose of determining who training should be offered to;

(b) in the terms on which access to any training is afforded;

(c) by refusing or deliberately not affording a person access to training;

(d) by terminating training; or

(e) by subjecting a person to any other detriment during training.[1]

There is also a protection against harassment.[2]

Training is defined as:

'(a) all types and all levels of training which would help fit a person for any employment;

(b) vocational guidance;

(c) facilities for training;

(d) practical work experience provided by an employer to a person whom he does not employ; and

(e) any assessment related to the award of any professional or trade qualification.'[3]

A training provider includes any person who provides or makes arrangements for training, but it does not include an employer when the training relates to those employed by him (this is covered by reg 7), the governing body of an educational establishment (this is covered by reg 23) or the proprietor of a school.[4]

The protection does not apply if the training concerned is training for which the employer could rely on the genuine occupational requirement exemption.[5]

If training is organised so that it is undertaken by a third party, the training organiser will be responsible for any act of discrimination by the third party if that third party is acting as its agent. See under liability for agents *(Lana v Positive Action Training in Housing (London) Ltd*[6]).

Examples:

ABC Ltd, is a company specialising in training for administrative posts. It has limited resources and so provides its training free to individuals aged under 30 and charges a £1,000 fee for those over 30. People over 30 will be able to bring an age discrimination claim against ABC Ltd.

Numbers R Us, an accountancy firm, offers summer work experience placements. It limits the limited places to students in university. Graduates will be able to claim against the firm that this requirement indirectly discriminates against them on the grounds of their age, as they will be disproportionately older than students.

---

1 See reg 20(1).
2 See reg 20(2).
3 See reg 20(4).
4 See reg 20(4).
5 See regs 8 and 20(3).
6 [2001] IRLR 501.

3.2.6 Employment agencies, careers guidance providers *(Regulation 21)*

It is unlawful for an employment agency to discriminate on grounds of age against a person:

(a) in the terms on which it offers to provide its services;

(b) by refusing or deliberately not providing any of its services; or

(c) in the way it provides any of its services.[1]

There is also a protection against harassment.[2]

'Employment agency' means 'a person or company (whether or not for profit), which provides services for the purpose of finding employment for workers or supplying employers with workers'.[3]

This covers both:

- agencies which supply contract workers to a client where the contract workers remain employed by the employment agency[4]; and

- agencies which find workers for a client where the workers become employed by that client directly.

The genuine occupational requirement exception[5] can be relied on in appropriate circumstances. Even if there is, in fact, no genuine occupational requirement it will not be unlawful discrimination if the employment agency reasonably relied on an employer's statement that there was a genuine occupational requirement.[6] For example, if an employment agency is advised by an employer that the successful candidate must be aged over 18 in order to be able to work shifts in the bar, it will be able to rely on the genuine occupational requirement even if, in fact, the job involves no bar work at all, provided it was reasonable for it to have relied on the employer's assurance.

An employer who knowingly or recklessly makes a statement that there is a genuine occupational requirement when there is not, can be punished with a fine.[7]

Employment agencies must also be careful to avoid liability under reg 26 (aiding an unlawful act[8]). For example, an employment agency which knowingly agrees to filter candidates by reference to age or some other indirectly criterion (eg years' experience) will be aiding the employer's unlawful act.

Cases in other fields of discrimination law have shown that the definition of employment agency is likely to be widely interpreted. In *Bramble v Clibbens Car Hire*,[9] it was held that Mr Bramble could bring his race discrimination claim against Clibbens Car Hire as an employment agency because it supplied 'employers' (customers) with 'workers' (taxi-drivers).

The provisions of reg 21 also cover those who give career guidance and other services related to employment. The governing body of an educational establishment (covered by reg 23) and the proprietor of a school are excluded.[10]

See also **3.3.4**.

Examples:

An independent careers counselling service operating in a university town only provides its services to students on an undergraduate programme. Those who are denied access to the services may be able to bring an indirect age discrimination claim.

An agency supplying secretaries refuses to take on secretaries in their 30s because they are more likely to have childcare responsibilities and, therefore, be less desirable to clients. Any secretary so refused will be able to bring an age discrimination claim.

---

1 See reg 21(1).
2 See reg 21(2).
3 See reg 21(6).
4 Commonly known as employment businesses.
5 See reg 8.
6 See reg 21(4).
7 See reg 21(5).
8 See **3.4.5**.
9 ET Case No. 16461/78.
10 See reg 21(6).

3.2.7 Government in assisting persons to obtain employment *(Regulation 22)*

This provision prevents the government from discriminating on grounds of age or subjecting a person to harassment on grounds of age in the provision of training under s **2** of the Employment and Training Act 1973.[1]

It does not apply where regs 20 (vocational training) or 21 (employment agencies) applies.

1 See reg 22(2) applies to Scotland.

3.2.8 Institutions of further and higher education *(Regulation 23)*

It is unlawful for the governing body of an institution of further and higher education to discriminate on grounds of age:

(a) in the terms on which it offers to admit a student;

(b) by refusing or deliberately not accepting an application for admission as a student; or

(c) in the way that a student is afforded access to any benefits;

(d) by refusing or deliberately not affording a student access to benefits; or

(e) by excluding a student from the establishment or subjecting the student to any other detriment.[1]

There is also a protection against harassment[2] and it will not be unlawful if the circumstances are such that the genuine occupational requirement provisions would apply.[3]

Scope of the regulations

In England & Wales an institution of further and higher education means:

(a) an institution within the further education sector (within the meaning of s 91(3) of the Further and Higher Education Act 1992);

(b) a university (including a university college and the college, school or hall of a university);

(c) an institution, other than a university, within the higher education sector (within the meaning of s 91(5) of the Further and Higher Education Act 1992).[4]

There are equivalent Scottish provisions.[5]

Examples:

Camford University with limited availability for seats at a pop concert to be held on its premises decides that it will try to limit demand by only extending the reduced student price to students aged under 21. All other students will have to pay the full price. Students aged over 21 will be able to bring an age discrimination claim against the university.

The University also has a policy of declining all applications for places if the prospective student has not passed his A-Levels in the previous two years. This is likely to indirectly discriminate against older candidates and those rejected as a result could bring an indirect age discrimination claim. It is unlikely that the University would be able to justify this restriction.

---

1 See reg 23(1).
2 See reg 23(2).
3 See reg 8.
4 See reg 23(4).
5 See reg 23(5).

3.2.9 Individuals

Claimants need not only sue their employer (or other potentially liable body listed above). They can also sue an individual who is responsible for the unlawfully discriminatory act under reg 26 which covers 'aiding unlawful acts'.[1]

Regulation 26(2) states that:

> 'an employee or agent for whose act the employer or principal is liable under Regulation 25 [vicarious liability] (or would be liable

but for regulation 25(3)) shall be deemed to be aid the doing of that act by the employer or principal.'

This provision is particularly relevant to employment cases where the claimant names not only his employer but also certain employees as respondents. Regulation 26(2) makes it clear that the employee can still be liable even if the employer can escape liability by proving that it took such steps that were reasonably practicable to prevent the employee from discriminating.[2] Indeed, there is no reason why the employer need to be named as a respondent at all and the claimant could, in theory, sue only the guilty individual. As the employer will normally have greater resources, suing the colleague but not the employer will be rare.

Claimants can pressurise employers to settle claims by adding named individuals as respondents as this can add to potential reputational damage of a successful claim.[3] Indeed, in some cases a finding of discrimination against an individual can have serious ramifications.[4] For example, a finding by an employment tribunal that a solicitor has been guilty of discrimination (including age discrimination) is considered by the Solicitors Regulation Authority as evidence of professional misconduct and can even lead to that solicitor being struck off.[5]

Examples:

Esther is 23 years old and works in a team of older colleagues. She claims that she has been subjected to a series of derogatory comments by her boss, Danny. Esther says that he regularly comments unfairly on her immaturity and lack of experience. She believes that this constitutes unlawful harassment and sues both her employer and Danny.

Nick is employed as a creative head by PRD&D Global, an advertising agency. At the age of 50 he is told that he is to be made redundant and replaced by Shane, who is 34. He brings as age discrimination claim against PRD&D and also against the Creative Director, Eric who took the decision to dismiss him, and Cathy, the CEO who dismissed Nick's internal appeal.

1 See **3.4.5**.
2 See **3.4.2**.
3 **Chapter 14, 14.11**.
4 **Chapter 14, 14.11**.
5 Solicitors' Code of Conduct. r 6: Equality and diversity
6.01 Duty not to discriminate

(i) You must not in your professional dealings with employees, partners, members, directors, barristers, other lawyers, clients or third parties discriminate, without lawful cause, against any person, nor victimise or harass them on the grounds of:

(a) race or racial group (including colour, nationality and ethnic or national origins);

(b) sex (including marital status, gender reassignment, pregnancy, maternity and paternity);

(c) sexual orientation (including civil partnership status);

(d) religion or belief;

(e) age; or

(f) disability.

(ii) You must take such steps, and make such adjustments, as are reasonable in all the circumstances in order to prevent any of your employees, partners, members, directors or clients who are disabled from being placed at a substantial disadvantage in comparison with those who are not disabled.

6.02 Evidence of breach
Where there has been a decision of a court or tribunal of the UK in proceedings to which you are a party, that you have committed, or are to be treated as having committed, an unlawful act of discrimination then that finding shall be treated as evidence of a breach of this rule.

3.2.10 Other bodies

The Regulations also set out various other persons who can be liable for age discrimination:

- Occupational pension scheme managers or trustees[1];
- Minister of the Crown, a government department, the National Assembly for Wales or the Scottish Administration (appointments to any office or post other than political office or where otherwise covered by the Regulations[2] and as an employer[3]);
- The Chief Officer of police or police authority[4];
- Serious Organised Crime Agency[5];
- Barristers, barristers' clerks and advocates[6]; and
- House of Commons and House of Lords as employer.[7]

See **3.3.7, 3.3.8** and **3.3.10**. and **3.3.10**

1 See reg 11; **Chapter 8**.
2 See reg 12(8).
3 See reg 44.
4 See reg 13.
5 See reg 14.
6 See regs 15 and 16.
7 See regs 45 and 46.

3.3 Who can bring a claim?

As is the case for those who can be responsible for discrimination claims, the scope of the Regulations extend beyond the traditional employment relationship to cover all those in a work environment. In each case considered below those who can claim protection from discrimination on the grounds of age under the Regulations include former, actual, and prospective members of each category.

3.3.1 Employees and self-employed *(Regulation 7)*

As is considered in more detail above[1] the definition of 'employment' is far wider than the definition in the ERA 1996[2] and extends to self-employed freelancers or consultants who contract personally to do work.

This extended definition is particularly relevant when considering for whom an employer is vicariously liable.[3] An employer is likely to be vicariously liable for individuals who, on an ordinary analysis, it would not consider to be its employees.

It has been held[4] that in order to fall within 'a contract personally to do any work', the *dominant purpose* of the contract must be *personally* to do the work. In the case of *Mirror Group Newspapers Ltd v Gunning*[5], Ms Gunning applied to Mirror Group Newspapers Ltd (MGN) to take over a contract for the wholesale delivery of newspapers. She was unsuccessful and claimed sex discrimination. The Court of Appeal found that it was not a contract *personally* to execute work or labour (the definition in the SDA). As the dominant purpose of the contract was the efficient distribution of the newspapers, there was no evidence of a requirement that be done personally.

The question of 'dominant purpose' will turn on the facts of each individual case. However, it is clear that there does not need to be an express obligation to perform the work personally for the contract to be considered one where the dominant purpose was personally to do the work, this purpose will commonly be implied.

It has also been held that it may not just be individuals who can be deemed to be employees. The definition of employment is sufficiently wide to include certain partnerships. In *Loughton and Kelly v Northern Ireland Housing Exe cutive*,[6] the issue before the House of Lords was whether the application by Ms Loughton and Ms Kelly's firms to be on a panel of advisers was seeking employment under a 'contract personally to execute any work or labour'. Initially, Ms Loughton's position had been distinguished as she was a sole practitioner whilst Ms Kelly was a partner in a two partner firm. However, the House of Lords held that the definition was clearly and deliberately wider than the Employment Rights Act definition so as to include both Ms Loughton and Ms Kelly. What was required was that the dominant purpose of the contract was that the firm undertook to do the work and that one of its partners was responsible for and did the work. Ms Kelly was entitled to complain that she, as a partner in the firm, as well as the firm itself, was subjected to discrimination when the firm was refused appointment. This extension beyond individuals is limited in scope and unlikely to apply to companies as the law treats those as a separate legal entity from the people who work in them.

It has been held that a trainee was not considered to be 'in employment'. Had she been employed under a contract of apprenticeship she would have fallen within the definition of employment.[7] However, in this case there was no contract of apprenticeship and instead Ms Daley worked for a company as a trainee under a work experience scheme arranged as part of the Youth Opportunities Programme. She was paid weekly by the company. Although the company was able to recover that payment under the scheme, attendance for training was optional although if she was absent part of her weekly pay was deducted. It was held that there was no mutuality of obligations between the company and Ms Daley and that even if a contract did exist its primary purpose was to train her rather than establish the relationship of employer and employee and that, accordingly, there was no contract of service or contract personally to execute any work.

However, an individual receiving training in this way but who does not fall under the definition of employment will almost certainly fall under the protection for vocational training.[8]

Example:

Arnaud is a freelance producer. Whilst working on a project for a film company he is subject to ageist harassment. Arnaud is likely to be an 'employee' for the purposes of the Regulations.

In fact, following the news coverage that surrounded the allegations of race discrimination, the contestants on Big Brother may fall within the definition of 'employees' because they contract personally to do work. This is relevant because it would render the production company vicariously liable for any discrimination.

Example:

Arthur, aged 62, is the only contestant on the Little Sister reality TV show over the age of 30. He is engaged by Ephemeral Production to appear on the show it produces. He is subject to ageist abuse by the other contestants. He is employed by Ephemeral Production under a contract personally to work and, therefore, would be covered by the Regulations. Ephemeral Productions would be vicariously liable for the actions of the other contestants.

---

1 See **3.2.1**.
2 See s 230 ERA 1996 for unfair dismissal, rights, etc.
3 See **4.1**.
4 *Mirror Group Newspapers Ltd v Gunning* [1986] IRLR 27.
5 [1986] ICR 145.
6 [1998] RLR 593.
7 *Daley v Allied Suppliers Ltd* [1983] IRLR 14.
8 See **3.2.5**.

3.3.2 Volunteers

Unpaid volunteers are not covered unless the work forms part of a paid employment relationship or a vocational training relationship. Cases such as *South East Sheffield Citizens Advice Bureau v Grayson*[1] have held that the absence of consideration and the lack of any obligation to work means that the volunteer is not employed under a contract of employment (whether under the ERA or under discrimination law). Indeed, with volunteers there is no contract whatsoever. They are also, arguably, not involved in an economic activity amounting to employment or self-employment and, hence, not covered by the Directive. However, someone, for example, doing unpaid teacher training experience in a school would be protected as coming within the definition of a vocational training relationship.

1 [2005] IRLR 345.

3.3.3 Contract workers *(Regulation 9)*

A contract worker is defined in the Regulations[1] as any person who is supplied to another person by that person's employer under a contract between the person's employer and the person who both makes work available, and to whom the person is supplied. This person who makes the work available and to whom the worker is supplied is known as 'the principal'.

Even though a principal does not employ a contract worker, it is unlawful for a principal to discriminate on grounds of age against a contract worker:

(a) in the terms on which he allows the contract worker to do the work;

(b) by not allowing contract worker to do it or continue to do the work;

(c) in the way the principal, affords the contract worker access to any benefits or by refusing or deliberately not affording access to them; or

(d) by subjecting him to any other detriment.[2]

Although this list does not include recruitment, it is likely that contract workers are also protected from age discrimination in recruitment.[3]

There is protection against harassment[4] and an extension of the genuine occupational requirement exemption.[5]

Any claim that a contract worker has against his own employer would be brought under the protection for employees.[6]

In *Harrods Ltd v Remick*[7] it was held that the employees of companies who had concessions within Harrods were 'contract workers' for the purposes of the Race Relations Act and such work could be said to be work for Harrods as the principal. In that case, each employee of the concession had to be approved by Harrods and observe Harrods' rules concerning dress and behaviour. The goods sold were sold by the licensee to Harrods immediately before their sale to the public. Ms Remick worked for Shaeffer Pens in the Harrods' pens department. Harrods withdrew their approval of her for failing to adhere to their dress code. It was held that the concept of work did not require that those doing the work had to be under the managerial control of the principal. What mattered was there was a contractual obligation to supply individuals to do work that could properly be described as 'work for' the principal. It was not necessary that the supply of workers was the primary obligation of the contract.

Examples:

Adam is employed by an employment agency. He is supplied to a building company as a temporary worker to cover paternity leave. Whilst there, he suffers ageist harassment. Adam will be able to bring an age discrimination claim against the building company.

A cleaning company has various contracts throughout the city. It employs its cleaners and sends them on a casual basis to whichever premises it considers most appropriate each night. The cleaners will be protected from age discrimination by each of the companies whose premises they clean.

1 See reg 9(5).
2 See reg 9(1).
3 **Chapter 5, 5.2.2.**

4 See reg 9(2).
5 See reg 8.
6 See reg 7.
7 [1997] IRLR 583.

3.3.4 Employment agency workers *(Regulation 21)*

Employment agencies are defined above.[1] The definition also covers employment businesses which supply workers to clients.

Workers 'employed' by an employment agency can sometimes be employees (employed under a contract of service) or engaged on a self-employed basis. In either case, the worker will be covered by the Regulations and come within the definition of 'employee' in reg 7.[2]

Workers who are employed by the agency have the same protection from discrimination by their employer as any other employee. If the agency supplies one of its employees to another person (the principal) to carry out work, that employee will be a 'contract worker' and will also be protected from discrimination by the principal.[3]

In addition, the Regulations specifically cover the way in which agencies treat their staff by making it unlawful for an agency to discriminate:

> '(a) in the terms on which [it] offers to provide any of its services;
>
> (b) by refusing or deliberately not providing any of its services; or
>
> (c) in the way it provides any of its services.'[4]

It would, therefore, be unlawful for a recruitment agency only to offer its services to older workers (subject to any objective justification for doing so) or to refuse to put someone forward for a position because the employer prefers an employee of a certain age (again subject to any objective justification). In such circumstances, the individual may also have a claim directly against the prospective employer if the agency can be said to be acting as 'agent' for him with his (express or implied) authority.[5]

Agencies that act on unlawfully discriminatory instructions from employers may also be liable for knowingly aiding another person to do an unlawful act.[6]

However, the agency will have a defence if it can show that it relied on a statement from the employer that the instruction would not be unlawful and that it was reasonable for it to rely on the statement. In such circumstances, the employer will be subject to criminal sanctions punishable by a fine if it makes the statement knowing it to be false or reckless as to whether it is false or not.[7]

Of course, the employer instructing the employment agency not to supply an older or younger worker is also potentially liable for age discrimination.

1 See **3.2.6**.
2 See **3.3.1**.
3 See **3.3.3**.
4 See reg 21.
5 See reg 25.
6 See reg 26.
7 See reg 26(4).

3.3.5 Partners *(Regulation 17)*

Partners[1] and LLP members are expressly covered by the Regulations by virtue of reg 17 even though they would seem to come within the definition of 'employee' in reg 2(2) as partners operate under 'a contract personally to do any work'. However, the legal principle of 'generalia specialibus non derogant',[2] is likely to prevent partners relying on the employment parts of the Regulations if they are also covered by reg 17. This maxim provides that even though a set of facts may fall within the literal meaning of a wide provision, a specific provision intended to cover these facts will prevail.[3]

Partnerships can include various types of partner held out to the outside world as 'partner'. They can range from full equity partners to so-called junior or salaried partners. These latter partners may or may not be parties to the partnership deed and may be taxed as self-employed or employees depending on the firm in question. If they are not covered by reg 17 then they will be treated as employees under reg 2(2). It is however, important to identify whether or not they are truly partners as the applicability of the exceptions within the Regulations differs between partners and employees.

It is important to note that the retirement exception does not apply to partnerships. As a result, if a partnership is to fix a retirement age it will have to satisfy the test of objective justification.[4]

Disputes between partners and partnerships are likely to form a significant part of the age discrimination case load. Partners are often highly paid, are not covered by unfair dismissal laws and commonly white men without other realistic discrimination claims.

This is illustrated by the first high profile tribunal claim being brought by former partner Peter Bloxham against law firm Freshfields.[5] In the United States, there is the long-running case of *EEOC v Sidley Austin* arising out of the de-equitisation and retirement of a number of partners by the Chicago-based law firm.[6]

1 In the case of Limited Partnerships and general partners with authority to bind the firm and not limited partners are covered – reg 17(5).

2 General provisions do not derogate from special ones.
3 Bennion, *Statutory Interpretation* (4th edn) 256.
4 **Chapter 12, 12.8.5(a)**.
5 ET/2205086/2006.
6 315 F.3d 699 (7th Cir. 2002).

3.3.6 Office-holders *(Regulation 12)*

In order to come within the definitions of an office-holder for the protection under the Regulations, the officer in questions must:

(a) discharge functions personally under the direction of another person (further defined as being where that person is entitled to direct the office-holder as to when and where he discharges the functions); and

(b) be entitled to remuneration (which must be more than a simply entitlement expenses or lost income as a result of carrying out the functions).[1]

The government's notes accompanying the Regulations suggest that the intention is that office-holders are those not technically in employment but whose position may be similar to that of employees. It gives as examples, company directors (if there is no employment relationship), judges, members of tribunals and ministers of religion.[2]

Not covered are elected posts or political offices because they are not covered by the Directive as these individuals are not considered to be engaged in an economic activity amounting to employment or self-employment.[3]

The Regulations make it unlawful to discriminate on grounds of age in relation to an appointment to an office or post:

(a) in the arrangements for determining to whom the appointment should be offered;

(b) in the terms on which the appointment is offered; or

(c) by refusing to offer the appointment.[4]

This also covers anyone in a position to make representations about who should be appointed to a particular office.[5]

Once appointed it is unlawful to discriminate on grounds of age:

(a) in the terms of the appointment;

(b) in the opportunities afforded for promotion, transfer, training or other benefit, or by refusing to afford him any such opportunity;

(c) by terminating the appointment; or

(d) by subjecting the office holder to any other.[6]

Office-holders are also protected from harassment,[7] and there is the standard genuine occupational requirement exemption.[8]

Examples:

Claire is a Non-Executive Director of a charity and works 2 days a month. She receives no pay other than her travel expenses to the London offices. Claire will not be protected by the Regulations unless she can fall within the definition of 'employee'.

John is the trustee and receives a fixed fee each month for this role and performs his role under the direction of the other trustees. John will be protected by the Regulations.

---

1 See reg 12(9).
2 'Notes on Regulations', DTI, March 2006, para 41.
3 See reg 12(8) and (10).
4 See reg 12(1).
5 See reg 12(2).
6 See reg 12(3).
7 See reg 12(4).
8 See reg 8.

3.3.7 Police *(Regulation 13)*

Although any person holding the office of a police constable is excluded from many other employment rights[1] and usually not governed by a contract of employment, the Regulations specifically provide that police constables shall be treated as being in employment. In this case, the person with control of the force to which the office belongs (usually the Chief Constable) is regarded as the employer unless the discrimination is done by the police authority itself in which case that authority will be liable.

1 See s 200 of the ERA 1996 (though technically within the definition of employee in that Act).

3.3.8 Crown service and House of Commons and House of Lords' staff *(Regulation 44)*

The Regulations apply to the Crown as they do to a private individual and, therefore, apply to Crown Employment as though it were employment in the private sector.[1] This covers employees of a Minister of the Crown, a government department, a statutory body or a person holding a statutory office.[2] It also covers offices or posts to which appointments are made by (or on the recommendation of or subject to the approval of) a Minister of the Crown, a government department, the National Assembly for Wales or any part of the Scottish Administration.[3] It does not cover political office.[4] As mentioned above,[5] the rationale for excluding political office is that they are not engaged in economic activity amounting to employment or self-employment within the meaning of the Directive. House of Commons and House of Lords' staff are also expressly included.[6]

1 See reg 44(1) and (2).
2 See reg 2(2).
3 See reg 12(8).
4 Definition see reg 12(10).
5 See **3.3.6**.
6 See regs 45 and 46.

3.3.9 Armed forces *(Regulation 44)*

Regulation 44(4) states that 'these regulations do not apply to service in any of the naval military or air forces of the Crown'. The DTI's 'Notes on the Regulations'[1] explain that the exemption 'covers all service personnel who may be required to deploy on demand: regular naval, military and air forces and reservists'. It continues that it 'does not extend to civilians working for the Ministry of Defence (MoD), nor to the MoD Police and Guarding Agency or to the MoD Fire Service'.

1 'Notes on Regulations', DTI, March 2006, paras 157 and 158.

3.3.10 Barristers, barrister's clerks *(Regulation 15)* and advocates *(Regulation 16)*

It is unlawful for a barrister or barrister's clerk, in relation to any offer of a pupillage or tenancy, to discriminate on grounds of age against a person:

(a) in the arrangements that it makes for determining who should be offered a pupillage or tenancy;

(b) in respect the terms on which a pupillage or tenancy is offered; or

(c) by refusing, or deliberately not offering, a pupillage or tenancy.[1]

It is also unlawful for a barrister or barrister's clerk, in relation to a pupil or tenant in chambers, to discriminate:

(a) in respect of any terms which apply to the pupil or tenant;

(b) in the opportunities for training, or gaining experience, which are afforded or denied;

(c) in the benefits which are afforded or denied; or

(d) by terminating the pupillage, or by subjecting him to any pressure to leave the chambers or other detriment.

There are similar provisions for advocates in Scotland[2] and also the complimentary protection against harassment on grounds of age.[3]

Interestingly, (d) above (in relation to termination) makes express mention of pupils but not of tenants. Although it is likely that this is just an omission,[4] it remains to be seen how it will be interpreted.

It is also unlawful to discriminate on grounds of age in the giving, withholding or acceptance of instructions to a barrister, or subjecting him to a detriment, or subjecting him to harassment.[5]

Examples:

A firm of solicitors refuses to instruct a particular barrister to act for a media client because it considers that someone younger and, hence, more in touch with the clients business is required. The barrister will be protected by the Age Regulations.

A set of chambers limits applications for pupillages to those within 2 years of graduation. This may be indirectly discriminatory and a claim of age discrimination could be asserted by those declined.

---

1 See reg 15(1).
2 See reg 16 – but only in respect of pupils not tenants.
3 See regs 15(3) and 16(3).
4 'The Notes on the Regulations' issued by the DTI state that it applies to the circumstances in which both tenancies and pupillages are brought to an end, para 48.
5 See regs 15(4) and 16(4).

3.3.11 Others who can claim

Other persons who can sue under the Regulations include:

- Members of trade organisations[1];
- Holders of professional or trade qualifications[2];
- Recipients of vocational training or career guidance[3]; and
- Students of further or higher education.[4]

1 See reg 18; **3.2.3**.
2 See reg 19; **3.2.4**.
3 See regs 20 and 21; **3.2.5** and **3.2.7**.
4 See reg 23; **3.2.8**.

3.3.12 Applicants and candidates

It is not only those in employment or in any of the other relationships mentioned above who can claim under the Regulations. Applicants in any of the above categories can also claim if they believe that they were discriminated against on grounds of their age.

3.3.13 Relationships which have come to an end *(Regulation 24)*

The Regulations protect against an individual suffering either a detriment or harassment after their relationship has come to an end.[1] In order to fall within the protection, it is necessary that:

(a) the relationship is one which is protected under any of the other provisions in the Regulations; and

(b) the discrimination or harassment arises out of and is closely connected to that relationship.[2]

If the relationship ended before 1 October 2006, only discriminatory conduct after that date will fall under the Regulations.[3]

Example:

Jane is 60 years old. Mindful that protection against age discrimination was being introduced on 1 October 2006, her employer dismissed her on her 60th birthday in August (60 being its normal retirement age). On 1 November 2006, Jane applies for a reference that is returned on derisory and ageist terms and which results in her not being offered the job for which she applied. Jane will be able to bring an age discrimination claim.

A clothing company allows ex-employees to continue to benefit from a staff discount after their employment has ended. However, a historical provision of the scheme provides that once an ex-employee reaches 60 years he is no longer allowed to rely on the staff discount. An ex-employee who is over 60 will be able to bring an age discrimination claim.

The following exceptions are relevant to post-termination discrimination:

- pensions[4]; and
- life assurance cover for retired workers.[5]

1 See reg 24(1).
2 See reg 24(2).
3 See reg 24(3).
4 See reg 11 and Sch 2 of the Regulations (see **Chapter 8** for more detail).
5 See reg 34.

3.4 Liability for others' acts of discrimination

The Regulations specifically provide that an employer will be liable for the acts of its employees. In this case, an employer may be able to raise a defence that it took all reasonable steps to prevent the discrimination happening. However, employers may also be responsible for the acts of agents or third parties, in which case they have no defence to a claim. It is also possible to be liable for aiding discriminatory acts.

3.4.1 Employers' vicarious liability for employees *(Regulation 25)*

In common with the law governing other forms of discrimination, the Regulations provide that an employer is liable for the discriminatory acts of employees provided they are done by the employee 'in the course of employment'.[1] This is regardless of whether the employer knew or approved of the acts of the employee. It is important to remember that the definition of 'employee' is wider than the definition in the ERA 1996 and so an employer's vicarious liability extends further than is often appreciated.[2]

Guidance to this meaning can be drawn from cases on other strands of discrimination law.

The Court of Appeal has held[3] that 'in the course of employment' must be given an ordinary layperson's meaning and should be treated as a question of fact to be determined by an employment tribunal. This is a potentially wide interpretation and broadly requires that the tribunal must consider whether the discrimination occurred during work time rather than a more narrow construction of the discrimination being a part of the employee's employment.

The most difficult area is where discrimination occurs away from work, either off the premises or outside work hours (or both). In *Chief Constable of Lincolnshire Police v Stubbs*,[4] it was held that acts of sexual harassment which occurred first in a pub with colleagues after work and then in a pub at a colleague's leaving party were committed 'in the course of employment'. It was held that these functions were an 'extension of ... employment' although it was accepted that it would not always be easy to determine as a matter of fact where the line should be drawn.

However, in *Waters v Commissioner of Police of the Metropolis*[5] it was held that the employer was not be vicariously liable where the conduct fell outside employment. Ms Waters, a police officer, lived at a section house. She went for a walk with a male officer when they were both off duty and returned to the house where it was alleged that Ms Waters was assaulted. Ms Waters reported the assault to her superiors but no action was taken against the colleague. Ms Waters brought a sex discrimination claim, claiming that she was victimised, due to her allegation of sexual assault, by having her name removed from a list of specially trained officers. An employment tribunal dismissed the claim on the grounds that the complaint of sexual assault was not a protected act because the officer could not have been acting in the course of his employment when the alleged assault was committed, so the commissioner could not be vicariously liable for this.

Examples:

XYZ Ltd decides to hold their Christmas party on a saturday at an off-site location. At the party, Arnold subjects Betty to ageist harassment. It is likely that XYZ Ltd will be vicariously liable for Arnold's conduct as the Christmas party is almost certainly an extension of employment.

Avi and Belitta are neighbours. They also work for the same company. Avi has a BBQ to which he invites friends and neighbours. In addition to Belitta, there are four other employees from the company. After the BBQ, Belitta complains that Avi subjected her to ageist harassment. It will be difficult for Belitta to establish a sufficiently close connection to Avi's employment so as to make their employer vicariously liable.

Anthony and Bill are a freelance creative team who are not directly employed. Crystal, who is employed as an account manager, complains that Anthony and Bill have harassed her on grounds of age. The employer is likely to be vicariously liable for Anthony and Bill's conduct because they will fall within the wider definition of employee.

---

1 See reg 25(1).
2 See **3.2.1**.
3 *Jones v Tower Boot Co Ltd* [1997] ICR 254.
4 [1999] IRLR 81.
5 [1997] RLR 589.

3.4.2 All reasonable steps defence

The Regulations provide a defence for employers in the case of an act done by an employee if they can show that they took such steps that were reasonably practicable to prevent an employee from doing the discriminatory act complained of or to prevent more general age discriminatory conduct.[1]

This defence only applies to acts done by employees. Therefore, if a discriminatory act is done by a partner or a contract worker, the partnership or principal will not be able to rely on the reasonable steps defence.

Although what steps are reasonably practicable will vary between employers, it is clear that an employer is required to take some positive action before the discriminatory act complained of occurred. It is also clear that the burden of proof lies with the employer if it wishes to establish the defence.

The most common evidence presented in support of this defence is an Equal Opportunities policy or similar document. However, it has been held that simply producing such a policy, without taking any steps to implement and make employees aware of it, will not be sufficient to amount to reasonably practicable steps.[2]

In *Haringey Council v Al-Azzawi*,[3] it was held that having policies on racial awareness, providing training on those policies and disciplining those who failed to follow the procedures was sufficient to be able to rely on the defence. Equally, in *Davies v Secretary of State for Social Security*[4] it was held that an employer with a comprehensive complaints policy could rely on the defence.

Whilst this is a fact sensitive assessment, it is advisable to assume that the minimum steps likely to be reasonably practicable are:

(a) ensuring that everyone is aware of the policy (it may be sensible to get written confirmation that the policy has been received and read);

(b) training as widely as possible (and certainly managers and decision makers) on age discrimination;

(c) having a mechanism for dealing with complaints of age discrimination;

(d) enabling people to raise concerns about the discriminatory behaviour of others; and

(e) enforcing breaches of the equal opportunities policy (with disciplinary action if appropriate).

Example:

In defending the claim of age discrimination, a company relies on the following to prove that it took such steps as were reasonably practicable to prevent the discrimination occurring:

- an equal opportunities policy;
- a grievance procedure; and
- bi-annual managerial training with a 30-minute session on discrimination in general.

It may be difficult to establish that these steps alone would entitle an employer to rely on the defence. Evidence of promulgation of the policies would almost certainly be required as would evidence that breaches of the policy are properly dealt with.

Taking these steps is also advisable to avoid inferences of discrimination being drawn against an employer which may result because of the burden of proof in an age discrimination claim passing from the claimant to the respondent.[5]

1 See reg 25(3).
2 *Colley v British Road Services* [1994] ET Case no. 4890/94.
3 [2000] EAT 158.
4 [1993] ET Case No 43819.
5 See **Chapter 4**, **4.6**.

3.4.3 Liability for agents

Anything done by a person as agent for another person (a principal) with the authority (whether express or implied) of that other person will be the liability of the principal.[1]

The most common example is where an employer passes to a recruitment agency the responsibility for recruitment for a particular role. If that agency selects candidates for interview in a discriminatory way, the employer will be responsible for that if it has agreed the method of selection.

In fact, it has been held that it may be sufficient for the purposes of passing liability for a principal to have given the agent authority to undertake a particular task even if it has no knowledge that the agent will perform that task in a discriminatory way.

Once again, we can get some assistance from case laws in other areas of discrimination law.

In *Lana v Positive Action Training in Housing (London) Ltd*,[2] Ms Lana was a quantity surveyor. Positive Act Training (PAT) organised by a third party, Walker Management, *would* have Ms Lana for a training placement. Ms Lana advised Walker Management that she was pregnant, which resulted in Walker Management criticising her performance, and stating that the training contract would not be renewed. Accordingly, PAT subsequently terminated Ms Lana's contract for training. The employment tribunal originally found that there was no case against PAT because the placement contract had been terminated by Walker Management for reasons beyond PAT's control, there was no further funding for another placement and there was no alternative placement for Ms Lana because Walker Management was the only quantity surveyor firm on PAT's books.

However, the EAT disagreed and held that Walker Management was PAT's agent and that PAT was liable for any discrimination by Walker Management.

There is no equivalent reasonable steps defence in the case of liability for an agent or any of the other class of individual (for example, a partner or an office-holder).

Example:

A company engages ABC Ltd to search for a new senior executive. ABC Ltd visits the company's premises and (although it is never expressly stated) understands that the company is looking for someone young. An older candidate who does not make it through the initial sift of CVs may be able to claim against both the company and ABC Ltd.

---

1 See reg 25(2).
2 [2001] RLR 501.

3.4.4 Liability for acts of third parties

If a complaint of discriminatory treatment is made by an employee against a third party (ie not an employee or agent of the employer), the employer will not be responsible for that treatment, even if it can be proven that the employer had sufficient control over the circumstances so as to prevent them happening (*Pearce v Governing Body of Mayfield School*[1]). In that case it was held that the school could not be held liable for the discriminatory acts of pupils who were neither employees nor agents of the school. The House of Lords stated expressly that the earlier case of *Burton v De Vere Hotels*[2] had been wrongly decided.

It was held that for a claim of discrimination to succeed against a third party who is not an employee or agent, the failure to act to prevent the discrimination must itself be an act of discrimination. In other words, it must be on grounds of age that the employer fails to take steps to prevent the discrimination.

It should, of course, be remembered that the definition of 'employee' is wide and the practical reality is that a school environment is very different from a corporate environment where the significant majority of people on the premises will fall to be 'employees' or 'agents' for the purposes of vicarious liability even if not actually given those labels within the workplace.

However, it will be helpful to avoid claims which employees suffer at the hands of customers. For example, if a resident in a care home discriminates against a carer because he is perceived to be too young, the carer's employer cannot be responsible for the actions of the resident unless the failure to act to prevent the discriminatory conduct can itself be said to be an act of age discrimination.

In addition, the nature of a partnership is that the firm is responsible for the acts of its partners.[3]

1 [2003] ICR 937.
2 [1997] ICR 1.
3 See s 10 of the Partnership Act 1890.

3.4.5 Aiding unlawful acts *(Regulations 26)*

Although claims are often brought against employers, both employees and agents can still be liable for their own discriminatory acts. The Regulations expressly provide that an employee or agent for whose act the employer or principal is vicariously liable shall be deemed to aid the doing of the act by the employer or principal.[1]

In addition, a person who knowingly aids another to do an unlawful act is treated as though he did that act himself.[2] The only defence is if the individual relied on a statement that the act would not be unlawful and it was reasonable to rely on that statement.[3] It is a criminal offence to knowingly or recklessly make such a statement.[4]

Two House of Lords' cases have given some guidance on who is covered by these Regulations. In *Anyanwu v South Bank Student's Union*[5] it was held that the word 'aids' should be given its ordinary meaning and that a person may 'aid' an unlawful act without inducing the unlawful act or procuring it. In *Hallam v Cheltenham BC*[6] it was held that two police officers had not knowingly aided discrimination when they reported to the Council the difficulties they had experienced with local gypsies. That report led the Council to change unilaterally the terms of hire of a room for a wedding. It was held that a closer connection was required as the police had not been involved in the changes to the conditions and had played no part in that decision.

Examples:

Amelie brings a claim against her employer complaining that a colleague, Bernard, discriminated against her on grounds of age. Amelie can issue proceedings against both her employer and Bernard individually.

Alvin is seconded from Alta Ltd to its parent, Alta Group Plc to assist during a period of maternity leave. Whilst he is on secondment, Alta Group

Plc decides to discipline him. As a result of that Alvin's employment is terminated on notice by his employer, Alta Ltd. If Alvin is successful in proving that the taking of disciplinary action was discriminatory, Alta Group Plc will be liable for aiding an unlawful act.

Other situations which could give rise to claims for aiding an unlawful act might arise in the following situations:

- a client requiring an employee to stop working on its business for a discriminatory reason; and
- a parent company under the terms of whose stock option plan an employee of the subsidiary worked.

Example:

Carl, aged 38, is a creative director with an advertising agency, Spotted Shark. He works on Spotted Shark's key client, Jacquin Jeans', account. Luis, the Marketing Director for Jacquin Jeans account has told, Vikki, Spotted Shark's CEO that he wants Carl off the account. He says he has been happy with Carl's work to date, but going forward believes they need someone younger on the account as he does not believe at Carl's age that he can possibly be sufficiently switched on to Jacquin Jeans' youthful target market. Vikki has no option but to comply with Luis's request. Jacquin Jeans (and potentially Luis personally) would be aiding the unlawful age discriminatory act, Carl's transfer from the key account.

An employee might argue that an insurance company which excludes employees above a particular age or charges a prohibitive premium for that age group aids an unlawful age discriminatory act. However, based on the *Hallam* case mentioned above, the claim is unlikely to succeed. The insurance company is likely to argue that it was the employer's choice not to find alternative cover or self-insure.[7]

1 See reg 26(2).
2 See reg 26(1).
3 See reg 26(3).
4 See reg 26(4).
5 [2001] CR 391.
6 [2001] ICR 408.
7 **Chapter 6, 6.5.3.**

3.4.6 Instructions to discriminate *(Regulation 5)*

It is unlawful for an individual to be subjected to less favourable treatment as a result of his failing to carry out or complaining about instructions to do an act prohibited under the Regulations. See[1] also the discussion on the scope of this protection in the section on the meaning of 'Claimant's Age'.

Examples:

Angie is one of the two HR managers. She is told by the managing director that when recruiting for his secretary she should ensure that the successful candidate is under 40 years. Angie refuses to do so and appoints the best candidate who is 41 years old. In her end of year appraisal, Angie is marked down for failing to follow instructions and her bonus is reduced as a result. Angie can bring a claim of age discrimination.

Aston is told by Ben, the Managing Director, to ensure that when scoring candidates for redundancy, he should ensure that Chris receives the lowest score because at age 50 he is 'past it'. Aston complains to HR about Ben's instructions. Following this, Ben refuses to deal any further with Aston saying that he cannot be trusted because he might report him to HR. Aston can bring a claim of age discrimination.

See in the subsequent text for comment on the position of employees who resign, rather than complain or refuse to comply with the request.[2]

1 **Chapter 4, 4.2.2(d)(i)**.
2 **Chapter 4, 4.2.2(d)(i)**.

3.5 Geographical scope

3.5.1 Employees and contract workers

The scope of the Regulations is far wider than the scope of unfair dismissal protection under the ERA 1996. However, what is often overlooked is that, the express provisions in relation to geographical scope apply only to contract workers and employees. For all other classes of protected individuals there are no regulations which govern the geographical scope.

The Regulations apply to employees and contract workers who:

(a) do their work wholly or partly in Great Britain; or

(b) do their work wholly outside Great Britain and:

  (i) the employer/principal has a place of business at an establishment in Great Britain;

(ii) the work is for the purposes of the business carried on at that establishment; and

(iii) the employee/contract worker is ordinarily resident in Great Britain at:

(A) the time when he/she applies for or is offered the employment/contract work; or

(B) any time during the course of the employment/contract work.[1]

This provision leaves a number of questions unanswered. Most notably, how much work does an employee or contract worker need to do in Great Britain in order to be said to do their work 'partly' in Great Britain? In the absence of guidance to the contrary it seems reasonable to assume that the threshold will be low and will almost certainly cover workers posted to the United Kingdom for a limited period and covered by the Posting of Workers Directive.[2]

Additionally, what does it mean to have a place of business at an establishment in Great Britain? Does this cover a company which has a subsidiary in Great Britain or an overseas subsidiary of a British company? It is likely that the scope of the Regulations will be sufficiently wide to overlap with the protection afforded by other European countries. In which case, an employee or contract worker may have a choice of jurisdiction and is likely to opt to litigate in the country with the most favourable remedy.

In Northern Ireland, the age aspects of the Equal Treatment Framework Directive are implemented in The Employment Equality (Age) Regulations (Northern Ireland) 2006 and the same geographical provisions which apply to Great Britain apply equally to Northern Ireland.

On further consideration in assessing the geographical scope is the jurisdiction of employment tribunals.

An employment tribunal in England or Wales only has jurisdiction to deal with proceedings where:

(a) the respondent or one of the respondents resides or carries on business in England and Wales;

(b) had the remedy been by way of action in the county court, the cause of action would have arisen wholly or partly in England and Wales; or

(c) the proceedings are to determine a question which has been referred to the tribunal by a court in England and Wales.[3]

There are equivalent provisions for Scotland.

Examples:

A sales director is employed by a British company, but is based in Germany. The majority of his work involves visiting German clients but he also travels to London once or twice a month for meetings with colleagues and clients. He carries out his work partly in Great Britain and would therefore probably be covered by the Regulations.

An IT manager works in Paris for a company with offices in Great Britain and France and the work she carries out is for the purpose of business in both countries. She has never been a resident of Great Britain and has never done any of her work in Britain. She would not be covered by the Regulations.

An engineer is employed by a British company and is subjected to age discrimination whilst seconded to its Spanish subsidiary, which is a separate legal entity and has a different kind of business from the British parent. All of his work is for the purpose of the business of the Spanish company and he does all his work there. He would not be covered by the Regulations because his work is not for the purpose carried on at the British company, even though he is employed by the British company. However, if part of the work was still done in Great Britain, he would be covered by the Regulations.

An air steward works for a UK airline and flies on long-haul flights around the world. She lives in Britain but her base airport is in the United States. The airline's aircraft are registered in the United Kingdom. She will be covered by the Regulations. However, if the aircraft was registered in the United States, she would not be covered.

A news agency based in Britain employs a correspondent in Russia. Although he is living in Great Britain when he is offered the job, he moves to Russia immediately afterwards. He will be covered by the Regulations, although he would not be covered if he is living in Russia when the offer is made or if his work is not for the benefit of a British news agency.

1 See reg 10(1) and (2).
2 96/71/EC.
3 See reg 19 of the Employment Tribunals (Constitution and Rules of Procedure) Regulations 2004. There is an addition provision which states that proceedings to which Sch 3 (Levy Appeals), 4 (Health & Safety Appeals against Improvement and Prohibition Notices) or 5 (Appeals against Non-Discrimination Notices) applies, the proceedings relate to matters arising in England and Wales.

3.5.2 Employment on board a ship or hovercraft

If the employment/contract work is on board a ship, the Age Regulations will only extend to it if the ship is registered at a port of registry in Great Britain.[1]

If the employment/contract work is on an aircraft or hovercraft, the Age Regulations will extend to it if the aircraft or hovercraft is registered in the United Kingdom and operated by a person who has his principal place of business, or is ordinarily resident, in Great Britain.[2]

1 See reg 10(3)(a).
2 See reg 10(3)(b).

3.5.3 Employment on offshore oil and gas rigs

There are also specific regulations which cover employment/contract work on offshore oil and gas rigs which provide for the inclusion of:

(a) any area designated under s 1(7) of the Continental Shelf Act 1964 except an area or part of an area in which the law of Northern Ireland applies; and

(b) (in the case of the exploration or exploitation of the Frigg Gas Field), the part of the Norwegian sector of the Continental Shelf described in Sch 1 of the Regulations.[1]

This only applies if the employer/contract worker is:

(a) a company registered under the Companies Act 1985;

(b) an overseas company[2] which has established a place of business within Great Britain from which it directs the exploration; or

(c) any other person who has a place of business within Great Britain from which he directs the exploration.[3]

1 See reg 10(4).
2 Having the same meaning as in s 744 of the Companies Act 1985.
3 See reg 10(5).

3.5.4 Partners and office-holders

It is only in relation to employment and contract work that there are specific provisions that cover the geographical scope of the Regulations. In all other classes of protected individuals, the Regulations are silent on geographical scope. This is particularly relevant for large international partnerships. For example, can a Spanish partner working in Madrid in an international partnership based in the United Kingdom bring an age discrimination claim in the United Kingdom? Can a US partner working in the London office of a US partnership firm bring an age discrimination claim in the United Kingdom?

It seems that tribunals will have three options in determining what the appropriate geographic scope should be in circumstances in which the Regulations are silent:

(a) Apply the geographical scope in reg 10 as though it was expressly stated to cover everyone who is otherwise protect by the Regulations[1]

(b) Simply apply the general tribunal jurisdiction position[2]; or

(c) Apply the cases which have considered the jurisdiction of the ERA 1996 after s 196 of that Act was repealed.

Although there is no certainty in this area, it seems that the most attractive approach is to apply the cases which have considered jurisdiction under the ERA. Had the government intended the jurisdiction provisions of the Regulations to be applied more widely, it would surely have legislated for that. Equally, leaving the question of jurisdiction to the general tribunal jurisdictional rules may be considered to be too narrow a construction and not one that was legislated for.

With regard to the jurisdiction of the ERA, the House of Lords have considered this issue in three combined cases.[3] The House of Lords have held jurisdiction should depend on whether the employee was working in Great Britain at the time of their dismissal, rather than what was contemplated at the time their employment contract was made. Regarding ex-patriated individuals, if this was the approach taken by employment tribunals in age discrimination cases the jurisdiction would only extend in limited cases. As in for example, employees working for a British employer operating within what amounts, for practical purposes, to an extra-territorial political or social enclave in a foreign country; employees posted abroad by a British employer for the purposes of a business carried on in Great Britain; and employees with equally strong connections with Great Britain and British employment law.

Two EAT cases have now applied this approach, one holding that an individual who had been employed outside the United Kingdom for seven years had failed to show a sufficiently close connection with Great Britain or British employment law[4] and the other determining that a individual who had been employed by the Navy, Army and Air Force Institutes (NAAFI) in Germany for 30 years was employed in a British enclave in Germany.[5]

1 See **3.5.1.**

2 Employment Tribunals (Constitution & Rules etc) Regulations 2004, SI 2004/1861, reg 19, this states:

'(1) An employment tribunal in England and Wales shall only have jurisdiction to deal with proceedings (referred to as "English and Welsh proceedings") where –

(a) the respondent or one of the respondents resides or carries on business in England and Wales;

(b) had the remedy been by way of action in the county court, the cause of action would have orders wholly or partly in England and Wales; [or]

(c) the proceedings are to determine a question which has been referred to the tribunal by a court in England and Wales;'

Regulation 19(2) sets out similar provisions for Scottish employment tribunals.

3 *Serco Ltd v Lawson; Botham (FC) v Ministry of Defence; Crofts v Veta Ltd,* [2006] UKHL 3, [2006] IRLR 289.

4 *ADT Fire & Security Plc v Speyer* UKEAT/0126/06.

5 *Cameron v NAAFI* UKEAT/0124/06.

Chapter 4

What is Age Discrimination?

4.1 Introduction

The Regulations set out four different types of age discrimination: direct and indirect discrimination, harassment and victimisation. These categories will be familiar to those with knowledge of other types of unlawful discrimination because they appear in nearly all discrimination legislation.

Direct discrimination is probably what most lay people will be thinking of when they think of discrimination. It occurs when a decision is made because of a person's age or imagined age. For example, direct discrimination occurs when an employer promotes the older of two candidates because it believes the greater age will mean that candidate will have greater authority and inspire more respect than a younger person.

In contrast, indirect discrimination happens when a decision is made on the basis of a factor other than age but which disproportionately affects certain ages or age groups. A good example of indirect discrimination would be a decision only to recruit recent graduates. Such a policy would result, on average, in recruiting younger candidates, who are more likely to have graduated recently, and would disadvantage older applicants.

An employer might be able to avoid claims of direct or indirect discrimination if it can *justify* actions which seem on the face of it to be discriminatory. Age discrimination is unlike other forms of discrimination, as both direct and indirect age discrimination are capable of justification. With other discrimination laws, only indirect discrimination is capable of being justified. The circumstances in which age discrimination will be justified and the extent to which the tribunal's reasoning will mirror that under other discrimination laws remains uncertain. The first Employment Appeal Tribunal (EAT) cases on this point are eagerly awaited.

The Regulations contain various statutory exceptions. If otherwise directly or indirectly discriminatory conduct falls within one of these exceptions that conduct is not unlawful and it is not, therefore, necessary to consider whether or not it satisfies the justification test.

Harassment is conduct that violates a person's dignity or creates a hostile environment. Finally, victimisation occurs when you treat someone badly because he has alleged discrimination. In this chapter, we will consider these different types of discrimination, how the burden of proof operates in age discrimination cases and the possibility of justification in more detail.

In this chapter we consider:

- the different types of discrimination;
- the way in which the burden of proof operates in age discrimination cases;
- the test for the justification of age discrimination; and
- the exceptions within the Regulations.

4.2 Direct discrimination

The term 'direct discrimination' is not used in the Regulations, nor, indeed, in any discrimination legislation. However, it is the commonly used name for the first type of discrimination, outlawed by reg 3(1)(a) of the Regulations. This provides that:

> 'a person ("A") discriminates against another person ("B") if on grounds of B's age, A treats B less favourably than he treats or would treat other persons [. . .] and A cannot show the treatment, [. . .] to be a proportionate means of achieving a legitimate aim'.

The key parts of this definition are, first, there is *less favourable treatment*. Secondly, this treatment is *on grounds of age*. And finally, this treatment is not *a proportionate means of achieving a legitimate aim* (commonly referred to as 'justification'). This section breaks down the definition and considers each part in turn.

Significantly, there does not need to be an intention to discriminate – it could be unintentional, perhaps because of a sub-conscious prejudice or assumption.[1] For example, a manager might not invite an older staff member to play in the inter-departmental football competition because he assumed that he did not play football without actually seriously thinking about his age. Nonetheless, this would amount to discrimination.

The distinction between direct and indirect discrimination has been blurred by the development of case law on what constitutes being 'on the grounds of' age.[2] This is an area ready for clarification by the higher courts. Age discrimination, in particular, highlights the issue.

In, say, race discrimination law, if an employee is not hired because of the racial prejudices of his employer, this clearly amounts to discrimination 'on grounds of' race. If, however, an employee is not hired because an insurer wants to charge more to provide health cover on account of the person's age, is this direct age discrimination? It could be argued that the rejection is on the grounds of cost and not age. This interpretation is supported by the recent amendments to UK disability laws, where previously discrimination was covered if it was 'for a reason which relates to a disabled person's disability'. But now the Disability Discrimination Act 1995 has been amended[3] to add the claim of direct age discrimination 'on the grounds of' a disability.[4]

If this is right, how far does it extend? If an employer believes that a candidate over 40 will be out of touch with today's youth on account of his age, is he treating him differently on the grounds of age or on the grounds of his being out of touch with the youth of today? But if that did not constitute direct age discrimination, it would drive a coach and horses through established sex discrimination law, where employers discriminate against women on account of stereotypical assumptions about their abilities.

The interpretation of 'on the grounds of' cannot be entirely disassociated from the need in direct discrimination to compare the claimant with a person whose circumstances are not materially different.[5] In the above example of the increased cost of insurance, could the employer argue that the appropriate comparator is someone of a different age in respect of whom the insurance company is charging the same insurance premium, perhaps on account of his pre-existing medical conditions? This argument would be supported by the judgment of Judge Jeremy McMullen QC in *High Quality Lifestyles Ltd v Watts*.[6] In this case, it was held that the appropriate comparator for the HIV positive claimant was someone with an equally infectious disease who was not disabled. It remains to be seen whether or not this restrictive interpretation will be followed in the future.

In all these examples, the employer will be indirectly discriminating on grounds of age if he is not guilty of direct age discrimination. In both types of discrimination, the employer's actions are capable of justification. The most significant difference will be in the comparison exercise.[7]

Equally, the distinction between direct and indirect discrimination is often unclear where the employer is using a characteristic as a proxy for age. Take the example of maturity. If an employer rejects a candidate on the basis of lack of maturity, is he really using maturity as a proxy for age – is the reason in reality age, but the employer is consciously or unconsciously confusing age and maturity because of his prejudice that to be mature the person has to be above a particular age? This would amount to direct age discrimination. Alternatively, is a lack of maturity the real reason for the decision? This would amount to indirect discrimination and the question would be – can the employer justify the need for the level of maturity required for the post?

1 *Bahl v Law Society* [2004] IRLR 799, CA.
2 See **4.2.1(c)**.
3 By Disability Discrimination Act 1995 (Amendment) Regulations 2003, SI 2003/1673.
4 Disability Discrimination Act 1995, s 3A.
5 See **4.2.1**.
6 [2006] IRLR 850.
7 See **4.2.1, 4.3.2** and **4.3.3**.

4.2.1 Less favourable treatment

Regulation 3(1)(a) states that A discriminates against B if A treats B less favourably than he treats or would treat 'other persons'. This requires an assessment of how A treats other persons, in other words, a comparison needs to be made between A's treatment of B and how A treats or would treat people other than B. In order to allow a tribunal to conduct this assessment, a claimant alleging age discrimination should identify a comparator – someone whom the claimant believes would have been treated more favourably.

(a) Similar circumstances comparator

Regulation 3(2) states that:

> 'a comparison of B's case with that of another person under paragraph (1) must be such that the relevant circumstances in the one case are the same, or not materially different, in the other.'

This wording is found in other discrimination legislation and we can therefore look to some of the cases brought about other types of unlawful discrimination for guidance on what it means.

The leading case is a sex discrimination case: the House of Lords decision in *Shamoon v Chief Constable of the Royal Ulster Constabulary*.[1] In this case, Lord Scott said that the comparator must 'be in the same position in all material respects as the victim save only that he, or she, is not a member of the protected class'. The background to Chief Inspector Shamoon's claim lay in her superior officer's decision to deprive her of responsibility for conducting staff appraisals. Two constables had complained to the superintendent about the manner in which Chief Inspector Shamoon had conducted their appraisals and one of them had taken his complaint to the Police Federation. The Federation's representatives had then asked for a meeting with Superintendent Laird and had pointed out that, although it had become customary for chief inspectors to carry out constable appraisals, under the terms of the scheme, appraisals should have been done by the superintendent himself. The superintendent agreed that he would abide strictly by the terms of the scheme in future, despite the fact that it was common knowledge that those terms were due to change in two months' time, so that chief inspectors would in future have formal responsibility for appraisals. Chief Inspector Shamoon was very unhappy about this decision and brought a claim for sex discrimination, naming two other chief inspectors within the same branch who were still doing appraisals as her comparators. However, the other chief inspectors differed from Shamoon in two significant ways. The first was that they had not had any complaints made against them. The second was that, although they worked in the same branch, they were in different divisions and Superintendent Laird had no managerial responsibility over them. There are five separate decisions from the House of Lords but they all agree that the two male chief inspectors named by Shamoon were not appropriate comparators because like was not being compared with like.

Example:

Two employees doing the same work have the same qualifications, skill level and experience as each other. When both are considered for promotion, the older candidate is selected. The younger candidate could cite his colleague as a comparator in a claim that the failure to promote him was on the grounds of his age as his colleague's circumstances are the same as his.

The difficulties with this test in the context of age discrimination are explored in the introduction to this section on direct discrimination.

1 [2003] ICR 337, HL.

(b) Hypothetical comparators

In some circumstances, there will be no one in the workplace suitable as a comparator because there will not be anyone whose position is sufficiently similar to that of the victim to make an effective comparison. This does not mean that the victim is without redress, because a comparator need not be a real person, someone in the same workplace who is actually treated better, it could instead be a hypothetical comparator who *would* be treated better, if there.

It is undoubtedly more difficult for a tribunal to assess how a hypothetical comparator would have been treated than a real comparator, because it will have to make assumptions about the way in which it believes the employer would have behaved. To do this, the tribunal will look at all the circumstances, including the way in which the employer approaches diversity issues and the way in which it treats that protected group and other employees not within the group. From these facts, the tribunal may be able to deduce how the employer would have treated a hypothetical comparator.

If an 'actual' comparator is named but his circumstances (other than age) are materially different from those of the claimant, would the claim fail? Claimants might be well advised to plead a hypothetical comparator in the alternative, as well as any named comparators. However, in a race discrimination case, *Balamoody v United Kingdom Central Council for Nursing, Midwifery and Health Visiting*,[1] it was held that if the claimant does not identify an effective comparator, the tribunal is still under a duty to consider how a hypothetical comparator would have been treated and to compare that treatment to the treatment of the claimant. The tribunal will make an error of law if it does not do this.

It is not clear whether or not this principle is still good law following the House of Lords decision in *Shamoon*. In that case, their Lordships unanimously thought that the original tribunal had been wrong to accept the named comparators as valid and believed that the correct approach would have been to construct a hypothetical comparator and use the other chief inspectors as relevant evidence as to the treatment the hypothetical comparator would have received. However, they were not directed to this case and they do not explicitly state whether or not the tribunal's failure to consider a hypothetical comparator (which had not been pleaded by the claimant) was an error of law.

Evidence about how the employer treated others in the workplace might still be relevant even if their other circumstances are too different from that of the claimant to make them effective comparators because it could help to establish how a hypothetical comparator would have been treated. Identifying the correct comparator becomes more difficult if the claimant alleges that he was treated less favourably because of *perceived* age and this is considered in more detail later in the chapter.

1 [2002] ICR 646, CA.

4.2.2 Grounds of age

(a) Actual age

To succeed in a claim of direct age discrimination it is necessary to show that the less favourable treatment is on *grounds* of the claimant's age. At one stage, tribunals considered that the test of direct discrimination must be a rigid two-stage test: the first step being consideration of whether there had been less favourable treatment than the actual or hypothetical comparator and the second being whether that treatment was on the grounds of the claimant's protected status. However, the House of Lords in *Shamoon* held that it was possible to look at the reason for the treatment before deciding whether or not there had been less favourable treatment.[1] As Lord Nicholls points out:

> 'it is impossible to decide whether Chief Inspector Shamoon was treated less favourably than a hypothetical male chief inspector without identifying the ground on which she was treated as she was.'

To put this in the context of that case, if the reason the Superintendent stopped Chief Inspector Shamoon from conducting appraisals was her sex, that would undoubtedly be less favourable treatment than would have been given to a male comparator in her position. If, however, the reason was because of the complaints made against her, a male comparator would not necessarily have been treated more favourably.

1 *Shamoon* [2003] ICR 337, HL.

(b) Apparent age

Regulation 3(3)(b) of the Regulations specifies that a reference to the claimant's age includes *apparent* age. It is therefore possible to discriminate against individuals on the grounds of age, even when you do not know their age or because they appear older or younger than they are.

Examples:

A female newsreader is sacked and replaced by someone who is the same age as her but appears younger, because the employer believes younger looking women are more attractive and that audiences will respond better to a woman who looks younger.

A company is recruiting for senior management grades. It rejects Bob's application as he looks much younger than his 36 years (the lower end of the age range for managers in the company) the company believes that he will not have the necessary gravitas and respect from clients who will question his experience.

Gill applies for a new job in a bar. The company rejects her application as she looks to be in her 40s. In fact she is 31 – the same age as other bar staff. Gill can still bring a discrimination claim even though the reason for her rejection is her employer's mistaken belief that she is older than she is.

If a claim is being brought because of discrimination on the grounds of perceived age, this will complicate the question of the correct comparator. Normally, the correct comparator would be someone who is the same in all material respects, other than age, as the claimant. However, where the case is based upon *apparent* age, the correct comparator will be someone who is the same in all material respects other than the way in which his or her age is perceived.

Example:

An accountancy firm employs an accountant aged 35 who looks as though he is still in his 20s. The firm makes four accountants in their mid-thirties up to partner but refuses to make up the individual who looks younger than his age, believing he is too young for the responsibility. If he were to bring a claim that the failure to make him a partner was age discrimination, he could compare himself with a hypothetical comparator who is the same as him in all material respects but is not perceived by the firm to look as if he is still in his 20s.

Age (or perceived age) need not be the only reason for the less favourable treatment in order for there to be age discrimination. It simply has to be an important factor. This principle was established in the race discrimination cases of *Owen and Briggs v James*[1] and *Bahl v Law Society*.[2] In addition, there does not have to be a significant difference between the age of the claimant and the comparator for there to be age discrimination, although it might prove harder to establish that the treatment was on the grounds of age if there is not much difference.

(c) On grounds of

The proper test when considering whether treatment was on grounds of the claimant's age, is to consider 'what was the reason for the treatment, whether conscious or unconscious' (*Chief Constable of West Yorkshire Police v Khan*).[3] This is not a 'but for' test in which the question asked is whether 'but for' the claimant's protected status she or he would have been treated differently.[4] Rather it asks for the reason for the treatment to be identified as a protected ground.

This is more easily understood in the context of the facts of the *Khan* case. Sergeant Khan had claimed race discrimination for a failure to promote him. Whilst the claim was ongoing, Mr Khan applied for a job in another police force, which asked Mr Khan's current employer for a reference. The chief constable refused to supply a reference for fear of prejudicing his position in the race discrimination claim and Mr Khan alleged that this was an act of victimisation. If a 'but for' test had been applied, Mr Khan would have succeeded in his victimisation claim because but for the fact that he had brought a claim, the reference would have been supplied. However, the House of Lords said that the real reason for the refusal to supply a reference was not because Mr Khan had brought proceedings, but because his employer temporarily wanted to preserve its position in the failure to promote case and would have supplied a reference once the proceedings had been completed.

If a treatment does not satisfy the test of being 'on the grounds of' age, it may well nevertheless constitute potentially indirect discrimination.

Example:

Cicada Restaurants rejects an application for a kitchen job from Carl, who is 25 years old, as it wants to recruit someone under 22, so that it can pay the person below the adult National Minimum Wage (NMW) (see section **4.7** and **5.3.3** for more detailed consideration of the justification of such a practice). Under the old 'but for' test this would have been an example of direct discrimination. However, under the new 'on grounds of' test, arguably, this amounts to indirect and not direct discrimination. The real reason for Cicada Restaurants' rejection of Carl is not his age but the requirement to pay him adult NMW. In practice, unless the courts and tribunals adopt a different test for the justification of direct rather than indirect discrimination[5] this distinction will normally be more academic than of practical significance in age claims.

The distinction between direct and indirect discrimination may be important in determining the correct comparator or comparator pool. In direct discrimination cases, the claimant can select a real or hypothetical comparator of a different age (see above). In indirect discrimination cases, the claimant must compare the effect of the provision, criterion or practice on all those outside his chosen age group.[6]

1 [1982] ICR 618, CA.
2 [2004] IRLR 799, CA.
3 [2001] IRLR 830, HL.

4 The test in discrimination cases used to be a 'but for' test – see *James v Eastleigh BCl* [1990] ICR 554, HL.
5 See **4.7.3**.
6 See **4.2.1** and **4.3.3**.

(d) Claimant's age

It is worth noting that the definition of direct age discrimination is limited to less favourable treatment on grounds of ***the claimant's*** age, and does not extend to less favourable treatment on age grounds more generally. This is similar to the definition of sex discrimination (which refers to less favourable treatment on the grounds of ***her*** sex). In contrast, the definition of race discrimination is less favourable treatment on 'racial grounds' ***not*** on grounds of the claimant's race and this extended definition is also found in the Employment Equality (Sexual Orientation) Regulations and the Employment Equality (Religion or Belief) Regulations 2003.[1]

1 'Notes on Regulations', DTI, March 2006 explain this difference by reason of the possibility of justifying direct age discrimination which is not possible under the other discrimination laws – para 8.

(i) Instructions to discriminate

Under the Race Relations Act 1976, the broader definition of 'racial grounds' covers a detriment suffered for refusing to comply with any instructions to discrimination. As explained below, it is unclear whether the specific provisions in the Regulations covering instructions to discriminate extend so far.

In the case of *Showboat Entertainment Centre Ltd v Owen*,[1] the EAT held that the words 'on racial grounds' covered 'any reason for an action based on race, whether it be the race of the person affected by the action or of others'. This could include less favourable treatment for refusing an instruction to discriminate against someone on racial grounds (which is what happened in *Showboat* when a white manager was dismissed for refusing to exclude black customers from an entertainment centre) or discrimination for associating with someone of a particular race.[2] It is easy to imagine a scenario similar to the *Showboat* scenario which involves discrimination on the grounds of age. For example, it is relatively common to see notices on shop doorways saying that only a limited number of children are permitted in the shop at one time. This is based upon the assumption that children are more likely to steal than adults. A shop manager who is dismissed for refusing to enforce this injunction would be able to argue that he was discriminated against 'on grounds of age' but not that he was discriminated against on grounds of ***his*** age. He would not be able to bring a claim of direct age discrimination because of the way it is defined.

In a similar case, *Weathersfield Ltd t/a Van and Truck Rentals v Sargent*,[3] a white employee succeeded in a race discrimination claim after she resigned because she was instructed to discriminate against black and

Asian customers. When Mrs Sargent started to work for Weathersfield Ltd (a car and van rental business) she was told 'we do have a special policy regarding coloured and Asians. We have got to be careful who we hire the vehicles to. If you get a telephone call from any coloured or Asians you can usually tell them by the sound of their voice. You have to tell them that there are no vehicles available'. Mrs Sargent did not say anything but was so upset by the policy that she resigned. She wrote to the employers a few days later explaining in full why she had resigned. The facts of this case can be distinguished from that of *Showboat* because Mrs Sargent was not dismissed for refusing the instruction to discriminate, she resigned before matters came to that stage. The Court of Appeal accepted that Mrs Sargent had been constructively dismissed on racial grounds and held that an employee is treated less favourably on racial grounds if required to carry out a racist instruction (regardless of the race of the claimant).

Example:

A manager is instructed to sack an older employee because he is 'past it'. The manager does not complain but resigns rather than carry out the discriminatory instruction. This does not appear to be direct age discrimination on the face of the Regulations.

The Regulations, however, contain specific protection against discrimination connected with being instructed to discriminate in reg 5, which says that:

> 'a person ("A") discriminates against another person ("B") if he treats B less favourably than he treats or would treat other persons in the same circumstances, and does so by reason that:
>
> (a) B has not carried out (in whole or in part) an instruction to do an act which is unlawful by virtue of these Regulations, or
>
> (b) B, having been given an instruction to do such an act, complains to A or to any other person about that instruction.'

Example:

The same manager does not resign, but refuses to carry out the instructions. He is dismissed as a result. This would amount to unlawful discrimination under reg 5.

It is interesting to note that this does not actually outlaw instructions to discriminate on grounds of age, which are outlawed in other discrimination legislation. For example, s.30 of the Race Relations Act 1976 says that 'it is unlawful for a person:

> (a) who has authority over another person; or
>
> (b) in accordance with whose wishes that other person is accustomed to act,
>
> to instruct him to do any act which is unlawful [race discrimination].'

Race, sex and disability discrimination laws also prohibit inducing or attempting to induce discrimination. The Regulations (like the Religion or Belief Regulations and Sexual Orientation Regulations) do not contain similar provisions. Instead, the Regulations simply outlaw discriminating against those who refuse or complain about instructions to discriminate on grounds of age. It is doubtful that this implements the Directive adequately, as the Directive states that 'an instruction to discriminate against persons on [age] grounds . . . shall be deemed to be discrimination'.[4] This may be open to challenge in the European Court of Justice (ECJ).

It is questionable whether the facts in *Weathersfield* (above) would be covered by this provision because in that case the employee simply resigned on being given the instruction to discriminate, she did not refuse the instruction nor complain about it until after her resignation. Under this reg 5, the claimant would have to be treated less favourably because of her refusal to carry out the act or because of her complaint about it. So, it is possible that, even with the provision, the protection against instructions to discriminate does not go as far in the Regulations as it does in the race discrimination legislation.

There are other odd implications of this provision. Firstly, the motivation in complaining about the instruction does not seem to be relevant – the claimant might have complained because he or she would have preferred to be given a different instruction to discriminate and, on the face of it, would still have this protection. For example, a manager instructed not to promote an employee on grounds of her age could complain about the instruction because he himself would like to dismiss the employee because of her age, not merely refuse to promote her. This would be a complaint about the discriminatory instruction and the employee would, apparently, be protected from discrimination for voicing that complaint. Secondly, there does not seem to be any time limit on the complaint – it could occur years after the instruction is given. Furthermore, the complaint may be to anyone, even outside the organisation and there is no requirement that it be made in good faith. But it does have to be true – a complaint based upon a genuine belief that an instruction to discriminate has been given would not be sufficient if it turns out that actually the instruction was not discriminatory (perhaps because the instruction was on the face of it discriminatory but could be justified).

1 [1984] ICR 65.
2 See *Wilson v TB Steelwork Co Ltd* ET Case No 23662/77 where a white woman won a race discrimination claim after being refused a job because her husband was black.
3 [1999] IRLR 94, CA.
4 Council Directive establishing a general framework for equal treatment in employment and occupation (2000/78/EC), art 2(4).

(ii) Associating with people of a certain age

There is no protection in the Regulations against discrimination for associating with people of a certain age.

Example:

A 38-year-old man has many close friends who are in their 20s. His employer believes that people in their 20s are unreliable and anti-social in their behaviour and sacks him because of these associations. This is not unlawful under the Regulations because it is not on the grounds of his age but on the grounds of his friends' age.

The Department of Trade and Industry (DTI) said that the narrower definition of age discrimination was used 'to avoid covering discrimination on grounds of association with persons of a particular age in order not to create confusion with "family friendly" legislation'.[1] It is not clear what this means but may perhaps be to avoid people being able to claim that they are being discriminated against because they have young children. The definition of 'harassment', however, goes wider than that of direct discrimination and includes harassment because of someone else's age – see section on 'Harassment' below.[2]

It is arguable that the Directive has not been properly implemented by this restriction to discrimination on the grounds of the claimant's age because the Directive says protection should be given against less favourable treatment on grounds of age.[3] If this is the case, public sector employees may be able to argue that they are employed by emanations of the State which failed to implement the Directive properly and that the Directive is sufficiently clear and precise for them to rely on directly.[4] Private sector employees would not have any such recourse against their employers.

A similar question has arisen under the Disability Discrimination Act. In the case of Coleman v Attridge Law[5] a woman claimed that she was discriminated against because of her son's disability. The wording in the Disability Discrimination Act 1995 is similar to that in the Regulations and does not permit such an allegation to be the ground for a claim. The point has been referred to the ECJ to determine whether the Directive prohibits disability discrimination by association with a disabled person.

1 *Notes on Regulations*, DTI, March 2006 para 9.
2 See **4.5.3**.
3 See art 2.
4 See **4.1**.
5 ET Case No 2303745/2005.

4.2.3 Justification

Unlike all other forms of discrimination, it is possible to justify direct age discrimination. This means that it is possible to treat people less favourably on the grounds of their age provided that one can show that the treatment is a 'proportionate means of achieving a legitimate aim' (reg 3(1)(b)).

The justification defence also potentially applies to indirect discrimination claims and is discussed in a separate section later.

4.2.4 Exceptions

The exceptions within the Regulations most relevant to direct age discrimination are:

- exception for recruitment of employees within six months of or over the employer's retirement age *(reg 7(4))*;
- exception for genuine occupational requirement *(reg 8)*;
- exception for certain rules and practices in or relating to pension schemes *(reg 11(3)(b))*;
- exception for statutory authority *(reg 27)*;
- exception for positive action *(reg 29)*;
- exception for retirement *(reg 30)*;
- exception for the national minimum wage *(reg 31)*; and
- exception for provision of enhanced redundancy payments to employees *(reg 33)*.

The genuine occupational requirement exception applies to aspects of recruitment, promotions, transfers, the provision of training and dismissals and is considered in more detail in **Chapter 5**.[1]

The recruitment of employees close to and over retirement age, the statutory authority and positive action exceptions are also considered in **Chapter 5**.[2]

The, national minimum wage, pensions, enhanced redundancy payments and retirement exceptions are considered in **Chapters 6**,[3] **8, 11**[4] and **12**[5] respectively.

1 **Chapter 5, 5.3.2** (a).
2 **Chapter 5, 5.3.2** (c), (d) and (b) respectively.
3 **Chapter 6, 6.4.5.**
4 **Chapter 11, 11.5.3** (a).
5 **Chapter 12, 12.6.**

4.3 Indirect discrimination

As with the term 'direct discrimination', the Regulations do not use the words 'indirect discrimination', which is the name usually given to the second type of unlawful discrimination. The definition is the same as for most other current discrimination legislation. However, care should be exercised when relying on old case law about indirect discrimination in other contexts because the definition of indirect race discrimination was different until 2003 and the definition of indirect sex discrimination was different until 2005. In fact, there have been three different definitions of indirect sex discrimination since the Sex Discrimination Act (SDA) first came into force. The original definition was changed once in October 2001 to implement the Burden of Proof Directive, then again in October 2005 to comply with the Equal Treatment Directive.[1] The definition in the Race Relations Act 1976 was amended to bring it into line with the requirements of the Racial Equality Directive.[2]

The distinction between direct and indirect discrimination is not always clear cut.[3]

The definition for indirect sex discrimination in employment and most types of race discrimination are now in the same terms as that for age discrimination, as follows:

> 'A person ("A") discriminates against another person ("B") if [. . .] A applies to B a provision, criterion or practice which he applies or would apply equally to persons not of the same age group as B, but:
>
> (i) which puts or would put persons of the same age group as B at a particular disadvantage when compared with other persons, and
>
> (ii) which puts B at that disadvantage,

and A cannot show [. . .] the provision, criterion or practice to be a proportionate means of achieving a legitimate aim.'[4]

In simple terms, this means that apparently neutral practices which are applied to all ages equally could still be discriminatory if they adversely impact on certain ages or age groups. Like direct discrimination, indirect discrimination does not need to be intentional. It can be a more insidious form of discrimination than direct discrimination because it is less obvious and easier to overlook.

Example:

An employer looks more favourably upon job candidates who have taken time off to travel or gain other types of life experience rather than those going straight from school to university and then work. This preference is not directly related to age but for jobs requiring experience, it will tend to disadvantage older people because taking 'a year out' between school and university has become a much more common practice in the last 20 years. It will also indirectly discriminate against 18/19 year olds in jobs not requiring past experience as they would not have had the opportunity to take time off. It is, therefore, indirectly discriminatory unless it can be justified.

We consider the relevant parts of this definition in more detail below.

1 Council Directives 97/80/EC and 2002/73/EC respectively.
2 Council Directive 2000/43/.
3 See **4.2**.
4 See reg 3(1)(b).

4.3.1 Provision, criterion or practice

The words 'provision, criterion or practice' are not defined but are generally considered to be broad. Until a few years ago, the definition of indirect discrimination in race and sex discrimination law was limited to 'requirements or conditions' that had a discriminatory effect.

The new definition is wider in that it can cover informal practices, as well as formal requirements or conditions. It might include a practice that is generally adhered to but which is not a universally applied requirement. For example, it might generally be the case that an employer only recruits graduates for certain positions even though it does not make this a requirement in the person specification and it does exceptionally take on nongraduates. This could be sufficient to be a 'practice' and it might be indirectly discriminatory because more people now go to university than used to be the case. Older people are therefore statistically less likely to have degrees. Of course, it might well be possible to 'justify' this practice, as a proportionate means of achieving the legitimate aim of ensuring candidates have the requisite skills, knowledge and aptitude for particular positions.[1]

The word 'provision' can encompass a discretionary, one-off management decision which is not applied to others, according to the EAT in the case of *British Airways plc v Starmer*.[2] In this case, a female pilot who wished to work part time for childcare reasons objected to British airways' (BA) decision that she had to work at least 75 per cent of full-time hours. British Airways argued that there was no 'provision, criterion or practice' that pilots had to work at least 75% of full-time hours – some pilots worked 50% of the hours; it was a decision that BA had made in respect of that individual for business reasons. The EAT held that 'there is no necessity for the impugned PCP [provision, criterion or practice] actually to apply or be applied to others' what is required is to extrapolate it to others using the proviso 'would apply equally to a man' contained in the statutory test.

1 See **4.7**.
2 [2005] IRLR 862.

4.3.2 Disadvantage

In this section we consider the meaning of 'particular disadvantage', what is meant by disadvantaging people of the same age group, and how the claimant must be personally disadvantaged.

(a) Particular disadvantage

The phrase 'particular disadvantage' in the test for indirect age discrimination is different from the old (pre 2003/2005) wording for indirect race and sex discrimination which stipulated that the requirement or condition be 'to the detriment of a considerably larger proportion' of one group compared to the other.[1] In the past, statistical evidence was necessary in indirect discrimination cases in order to demonstrate the impact on the 'considerably larger proportion'. In contrast, statistics will be less important under the new definition (including in age-related cases) because there is no longer a need to illustrate 'proportions'. However it will still be necessary to show that members of a group will suffer a particular disadvantage.

Cases under the old definition have held that requirements which seemed to have quite a small disparate impact on the disadvantaged group could still amount to indirect discrimination. For example, in the case of *London Underground Ltd v Edwards* (No 2[2]) a new shift pattern for tube train drivers could be worked by all 2,023 male drivers and by 20 out of the 21 female drivers but was still held to be indirectly discriminatory. The Court of Appeal held that, even though only one woman had problems complying with the new arrangements, 'a considerably smaller proportion of women could comply than men'. The tribunal was entitled to take into account the fact that not a single man was disadvantaged by the requirement, despite the preponderance of men within the group. Also, it was entitled to infer from the small number of women employed compared with men that it was either difficult or unattractive for women to work as train drivers and that the figure of 95.2 per cent of women able to comply was likely to be a minimum rather than a maximum figure.

In another case under the old definition, *R v Secretary of State for Employment ex parte Seymour-Smith and Perez (No 2)*,[3] the House of Lords considered whether or not the (then) requirement for two years' service to bring an unfair dismissal claim was indirectly discriminatory against women. It found that over a period of seven years, the ratio of men to women qualifying for unfair dismissal protection was 10:9 and that this (subject to justification) was enough to amount to indirect sex discrimination. This comparatively small differential was apparently significant enough to fulfil the definition. In the words of Lord Nicholls:

> '[A] persistent and constant disparity of the order just mentioned in respect of the entire male and female labour forces of the country over a period of seven years cannot be brushed aside and dismissed as insignificant or inconsiderable'.

These cases suggest that, even under the old definition, the proportionate disadvantage could be determined in different ways, either by looking at differences in the absolute numbers affected (*Seymour-Smith and Perez*) or at percentages affected (*Edwards*).

The Burden of Proof Directive nonetheless refers to a measure which 'disadvantages a substantially higher proportion of them members of one sex'. This suggests that a comparative approach is still relevant.

It is necessary to compare the disadvantaged not the advantaged.[4]

At the time of writing there are no cases on the new definition of indirect discrimination and what is needed for a protected group to be suffering a 'particular disadvantage' but it seems likely that the new test will be an easier one for a claimant.

1 See pre-2003 definition of indirect race discrimination and pre-2005 definition of indirect sex discrimination.
2 [1998] IRLR 364, CA.
3 [2000] IRLR 263, HL.
4 *Rutherford v Secretary of State for Trade and Industry (No 2)* [2006] IRLR 551.

(b) Disadvantaging people of the same age group

The provision, criterion or practice must disadvantage people of the 'same age group'. Regulation 3(3)(a) says that 'age group' means a group of persons defined by reference to age, whether by reference to a particular age or a range of ages. These apparently straightforward definitions cause some uncertainty in practice. For example, what is meant by age? Would a 28-year-old person whose birthday is in January be 'the same age' as someone who is 28 and 11 months? If the comparison is made a month later when the second individual has turned 29 – are they no longer the 'same age'?

It also gives any claimant a lot of scope to define a claim how he or she wishes. For example, a 28-year-old claimant might wish to say that a particular practice disadvantages 28 year olds. That would be to define her claim very narrowly. Instead, the same claimant could choose to argue that the practice disadvantages everyone in their 20s – or everyone below the age of 30 – or below 40 or even everyone between the ages of 28 and 33. There are a great number of possible permutations, which the claimant might try to exploit to bring a claim in the most effective way. Furthermore, the way in which the claim is pleaded might affect the employer's chance of successfully arguing justification. A practice which disadvantages a large number of people in absolute terms or a significant percentage of the workforce may be harder to justify, as less likely to be proportionate.

The Regulations do not themselves give any guidance on how one determines that an age group has been *particularly disadvantaged.* What sort of evidence is required to show that the disadvantage is suffered by a sufficient number in that age group? What would be a sufficient number in that age group? What would be a sufficient disadvantage? According to the European Commission, statistical evidence is not necessary. In its Proposal for the Directive the Commission said that liability for indirect discrimination 'may be proven on the basis of statistical evidence or by any other means'.[1] It will be up to the UK courts to determine how a 'particular disadvantage' can be shown and, until then, we cannot be certain how it should be done. A claimant could use statistics to support a claim, if available. He or she may be able to get statistical evidence about the impact of the provision within a particular workplace by using a questionnaire. Other more general statistical evidence might be available from employment statistics complied by bodies such as the Commission for Equality & Human Rights, pressure groups such as Age Concern, Heyday or Help the Aged or benchmarking done by bodies such as Human Resource Consultancies. Expert evidence might also help to establish disproportionate impact on certain age groups.

1 *Proposal for a Council Directive Establishing A General Framework for Equal Treatment in Employment and Occupation* (Brussels Nov 25, 1999) p 8.

(c) Disadvantaging the claimant

Besides disadvantaging people in the particular age group, any claimant would have to show that the provision, criterion or practice put him or her at the same personal disadvantage. It is generally thought that this is a less stringent test than under the old definition of indirect discrimination which required claimants (then called applicants) to show that they could not comply with the particular requirement not merely that they were disadvantaged by it. However, the DTI has said about the equivalent wording in the definition of indirect sexual orientation discrimination that it has the same effect as the old definition.[1] It would appear then that the DTI does not believe that this aspect of the law has changed. This is not the view of the majority of commentators and we shall have to see how the case law develops. The DTI's 'Notes on Regulations' do not address this point.

1 DTI Explanation of the Provisions of the Employment Equality (Sexual Orientation) Regulations 2003 and Employment Equality (Religion or Belief) Regulations 2003.

Example:

A 35-year-old might be able to show that a practice requiring employees to work in the evenings disadvantaged the under 50s, as they were more likely to have young children requiring care and therefore not be able to work those hours. If that particular employee was not disadvantaged by evening work, he would not succeed in a claim. However, it would be enough that he was disadvantaged rather than completely unable to comply.

4.3.3 Pools for comparison

As with direct discrimination, indirect discrimination requires a comparison to be made. In this case, the comparison will be between those who are and those who are not disadvantaged by the provision, criterion or practice being applied. Under the old definition of indirect discrimination this comparison involved identifying the 'pool' of people to be compared and then identifying the proportions of those within that pool who could comply with the requirement and those who could not. As explained, statistical evidence was necessary to show that the proportion who could comply was 'considerably smaller'.

It is likely that a tribunal will still identify a pool and assess the proportions of those within the pool who are disadvantaged when applying the new test but, at the date of writing, we do not yet have any court guidance on how tribunals should approach the new definition.

The selection of an appropriate pool is like the selection of an appropriate comparator in a direct discrimination claim. It is to ensure extraneous considerations do not affect the comparison; to enable like to be compared with like. Regulation 3(2) of the Regulations provides that:

> 'a comparison of B's case with that of another person under paragraph (1) must be such that the relevant circumstances in the one case are the same, or not materially different, in the other.'

This was mentioned above in the context of direct discrimination but it applies equally to indirect discrimination.

But, how do you determine what are the 'relevant circumstances' and therefore who should be in the pool? The pool should consist of all those who would qualify for the job or benefit in question if the provision, criterion or practice were not taken into account. As Lord Justice Potter said in *Edwards (No 2)*:

> 'the identity of the appropriate pool will depend upon identifying that sector of the relevant workforce which is affected or potentially affected by the application of the particular [requirement or condition] in question and the context or circumstances in which it is sought to be applied.'[1]

So, once the provision, criterion or practice has been identified the next step is to consider who would be affected by it.

According to Lord Justice Sedley in the case of *Allonby v Accrington and Rossendale College*[2] the identification of the pool should be 'a matter neither of discretion nor of fact-finding but of logic'. But the problems that tribunals and higher courts have had in identifying the correct pool suggest that this process will not always be obvious or clear cut and there may be more than one possible pool.

Example:

Techfast seeks an IT Manager who has graduated in the last five years. Techfast makes this a requirement because it wants up-to-date skills in new information technology. This is likely to disadvantage older applicants. The appropriate pool for comparison is everyone in the job market who has the appropriate skills in new technology and other necessary skills or qualifications to do the job. A 45-year-old applicant would have to identify the age group to which he belonged for the purposes of a claim (eg he might use everyone over 35). The tribunal would then consider the proportion of the over 35s in the pool that had graduated in the last five years compared to the proportion of under 35s in the pool. It is likely that there would be a significantly smaller proportion of over 35s that could comply with the requirement to be recent graduates and therefore people of that age group would be at a particular disadvantage. Of course, it is possible that the employer might be able to justify the criterion in this example.

This example shows the care that an applicant will need to take when deciding what age group to plead. Consider what would have happened if the applicant had pleaded that her age group was 45-year-olds. The tribunal would then consider the proportion of 45 year olds who could comply with the requirement to be recent graduates compared to the proportion of all other ages in the pool who could comply. Everyone above the age of 45 would be likely to suffer the same disadvantage as the applicant. It is possible that the 45 year olds would not appear to be particularly disadvantaged if compared against a group that contained people aged 46 and over as well as those aged below 45 and even more likely that the 45-year-old would be unable to produce evidence of this, whether or not it was so.

In a recruitment case, the pool includes by necessity people outside the relevant organisation who might wish to apply for the job. In other circumstances, the pool *might* be limited to those within the organisation. Where the allegedly discriminatory provision, criterion or practice is being applied to existing employees, the pool is more likely to be confined to those within the business. For example, let us take the case of 'last in, first out' as a redundancy selection criterion. An employee at risk of redundancy might wish to argue that this indirectly discriminates against younger employees because they are less likely to have longer service. On the face of it, the pool of affected individuals should be made up of those within the organisation from whom the selection for redundancy is going to be made. The comparison would then be made between those in that pool. However, this leaves a potential claimant in a difficult position if, for whatever reason, the composition of the workforce does not reflect national averages.

In any particular workplace it could be that those with longer service happen to be, on average, younger than those who joined the organisation more recently – would this leave the affected individuals without a remedy? In the case of *Edwards (No 2)* mentioned above, the tribunal took account of considerations other than the pure statistical composition of the 'pool' when reaching its decision.[3] First, the tribunal attached significance to the fact that there were so many more male train drivers than female in the pool (2,023 to 21) and suggested that this showed that it was difficult or unattractive for women to be train operators and therefore that the figure of 95.2 per cent of women able to comply with the new roster was likely to be a minimum figure rather than a maximum. Secondly, the tribunal took account of the 'common knowledge' that females are more likely to be single parents than men. The Court of Appeal upheld the tribunal's decision and said that it was entitled to use its general knowledge and expertise in the industrial field; to take account of the small number of women in the pool and the fact that more women are single parents.

We, therefore, have at least one case under the old law that suggests that a tribunal is not completely constrained by the 'pool' statistics and can look more widely at national statistics. However, in this case there still was a statistically greater detrimental impact on the women in the pool than on the men. The question was whether the proportionate difference was significant enough. It is not clear authority for the proposition that a pool with a completely atypical composition, which does not show any detrimental impact on the protected group, should be ignored and national statistics used.

That anyway is the position under the old law. But things may now be different. The old wording was that the requirement or condition must be such that 'the proportion of [the protected group] *who can comply* with it is considerable smaller than the proportion of [others] who can comply with it' (our italics). The new test says that the provision, criterion or practice 'puts or *would put*' persons of that [age group] at a particular disadvantage (our italics). Is there a possible argument here that the comparison should not necessarily have to be limited to those who are actually within the workplace pool but could include those who *would* be affected if they were in the pool? This is simply a matter for speculation until we receive the first decisions on the new definition of indirect discrimination.

One aspect of comparator pools is clear. The appropriate comparator group is all relevant people outside the allegedly disadvantaged group. An employee cannot pick another age group and claim that his age group is at a particular disadvantage when compared to that other age group.

Example:

Clearhills, a dairy company, has a redundancy policy that bases redundancy pay on length of service (see **Chapter 11** for a detailed consideration of the legality of such schemes). Paul is 52 and has 18 years' service. To bring an age claim, Paul have to use the group of, say, those under 53 compared to those over 53- or 52-year-olds compared to all those who are not 52. He could not claim, say, that 53-year-olds were treated less favourably than those over 53.

---

1 *Edwards (No 2)* [1998] IRLR 364, CA.
2 [2001] IRLR 364, CA.
3 *Edwards (No.2)* [1998] IRLR 364, CA.

4.3.4 Justification

Like direct age discrimination, indirect discrimination can be 'justified' if it is a proportionate means of achieving a legitimate aim. Justification is considered below.[1]

1 See **4.7**.

4.3.5 Exceptions

The exceptions within the Regulations most relevant to indirect discrimination are:

- exception for certain rules and practices in or relating to pension schemes *(reg 11(3)(b))*;
- exception for certain benefits based on length of service *(reg 32)*; and
- exception for provision of enhanced redundancy payments to employees *(reg 33)*.

The service-related benefits, pensions and enhanced redundancy payments are considered in **Chapters 6**,[1] **8** and **11**[2] respectively.

1 **Chapter 6, 6.3**.
2 **Chapter 11, 11.5.3 (a)**.

4.4 Victimisation

Discrimination by victimisation is another type of unlawful discrimination. This is not a form of discrimination on the grounds of someone's age but occurs when an individual is treated detrimentally because he or she *alleged* age discrimination in some way. The definition is as follows:

> 'a person ("A") discriminates against another person ("B") if he treats B less favourably that he treats or would treat other persons in the same circumstances, and does so by reason that B has –
>
> (a) brought proceedings against A or any other person under or by virtue of these Regulations;
>
> (b) given evidence or information in connection with proceedings brought by any person against A or any other person under or by virtue of these Regulations;

(c) otherwise done anything under or by reference to these Regulations in relation to A or any other person; or

(d) alleged that A or any other person has committed an act which (whether or not the allegation so states) would amount to a contravention of these Regulations.'[1]

This provision is designed to shield employees who make allegations of discrimination or want to bring claims or to assist others in bringing claims (generally known as 'protected acts'). Without such protection it is likely that individuals would be very reluctant to make or assist with allegations of discrimination whilst their employment is ongoing, for fear of reprisals. Note that the individual is protected from victimisation committed because A knows that B *intends* to perform one of the protected acts or *suspects* that B has or intends to do so, as well as because A knows that B has already done so.

This regulation refers throughout to acts done in relation to A or 'any other person'. This reflects the fact that someone might be victimised by someone other than the person he or she has made an allegation against.

Example:

Oz brings a successful age discrimination claim against his employer. He subsequently leaves that employment and tries to get a job with a different employer in the same industry. The prospective employer has heard on the grapevine about the claim and refuses to employ Oz because it believes he is a troublemaker. This is less favourable treatment because Oz brought a claim against another person and is unlawful discrimination by way of victimisation.

As with direct discrimination, the definition refers to 'less favourable treatment' than that given (or would be given) to other persons. As with direct discrimination then, this section requires a comparison with either a real or hypothetical comparator. The comparator should be someone who is the same in all material respects as the claimant other than that she or he has not performed a protected act.[2]

There is one exception to the rule against victimisation, which covers the situation where the allegation (or evidence or information) of discrimination was false and not made in good faith. In such circumstances, the individual has no protection and the employer would be able, for example, to discipline the employee for making a false allegation. However, it must be emphasised that for this exception to apply there must have been both a false allegation *and* it must have been made in bad faith. If an individual makes a false allegation genuinely believing it to be true, he or she is still protected from victimisation and any disciplinary proceedings would give the individual genuine grounds for a claim. Or, if an individual makes a true allegation but with some ulterior motive (for example, to try to force the employer to pay him or her off) that individual is protected from victimisation.

There is, however, a lacuna in the protection offered against victimisation. In a sex discrimination case it has been held that, to succeed in a victimisation claim where the protected act is an *allegation* of discrimination, the protected act must refer to something that could amount to a genuine contravention of the discrimination legislation – if the alleged act is not potentially an act of discrimination – there is no protection. In this case[3] because the alleged discrimination had not taken place 'in the course of employment' it could not be a contravention of the SDA. Therefore, she did not make an allegation of conduct capable of amounting to a contravention of the Act and the claimant was not protected from victimisation for the allegation she did make. This is a very narrow construction of this section. Note that this decision only relates to victimisation claims following less favourable treatment because of allegations of discrimination; it does not deal with allegations of victimisation after bringing proceedings (where an allegation found to be outside the SDA could still amount to a protected act) or doing other protected acts.

The test for establishing whether or not an act has been done 'by reason of' the claimant's protected act is considered in the section 'On Grounds of Age' above.[4]

The case of *Nagarajan v London Regional Transport*,[5] is authority for the fact that the claimant does not have to show that the motivation of the respondent was conscious – an unconscious motivation is sufficient.

It is worth highlighting that many respondents fall foul of the victimisation provisions and it is relatively common for individuals to fail in their primary claim of discrimination but to succeed in a victimisation claim. Sometimes this is because the employer or other employees deliberately target the claimant but it can also occur because it is difficult to keep treating people exactly the same as before once they have made some kind of allegation of discrimination, particularly if they consider the allegation unfounded. Discrimination is very socially unacceptable in our society at this time and people (and organisations) react badly to an accusation of discrimination; in doing so, they can victimise the claimant.

Example:

Glynis is employed as a secretary by Alabama Plastics. Her Manager believes that she is under performing and has spoken to her about this. Glynis is much older than the other secretaries and believes she is being picked on by reason of her age. She brings a tribunal complaint complaining of age harassment by her Manager and the other secretaries. The company declines Glynis's proposal that if they pay her off she will leave. She loses the case. In the course of the hearing she made some hurtful allegations about her colleagues. The tribunal did not accept her evidence but did not find that the claims were made in bad faith. She returns to work. Alabama Plastics finds itself in a difficult position as, if the Manager or the other secretaries treat Glynis differently, they may be guilty of unlawful victimisation. In the end, the company finds it all too difficult and pays off Glynis to leave.

Glynis leaves and applies for a job with Montana Plastics. They recall the publicity surrounding Glynis's claim and reject her. They tell her this. Glynis would now have a victimisation claim against Montana Plastics.

1 See reg 4.
2 See **4.2.1**.
3 *Waters v Metropolitan Police Commissioner* [1997] IRLR 589, CA – cross refer to vicarious liability section for a summary of the facts of this case.
4 See **4.2.2**.
5 [1999] IRLR 572, HL.

4.5 Harassment

4.5.1 Definition of harassment

Another distinct type of age discrimination is harassment. Regulation 6 defines harassment as follows:

> 'A person ("A") subjects another person ("B") to harassment where, on grounds of age, A engages in unwanted conduct which has the purpose or effect of –
>
> (a) violating B's dignity; or
>
> (b) creating an intimidating, hostile, degrading, humiliating or offensive environment for B.'

The component elements of this definition are considered below. Typical types of age-related harassment might include making jokes about a person's age, name-calling, teasing or bullying someone because of his age. In extreme cases it may include age-related physical abuse.[1] As might be expected, there is no possibility of defending harassment claims by saying that the behaviour was justified. And because harassment claims do not rely on showing 'less favourable' treatment, there is no need to identify a comparator in harassment claims.

Age harassment claims may be quite common in the first years of the Regulations. Jokes about a colleague's age are still commonplace in many workplaces and it remains a challenge for many employers to ensure their employees do not harass unlawfully on the grounds of age when it is still not universally regarded as socially unacceptable in the same way as racist, sexist or homophobic harassment.

1 See **4.5.7**.

4.5.2 Contrast with directive

This definition differs in two ways from the definition in the Directive. In one respect UK law is narrower than the Directive. In another, its scope is broader.

First, art 2(3) of the Directive refers to unwanted conduct *related to* age rather than on the *grounds of age*. The Directive's wording could be construed as wider than that of the Regulations, for example, 'related to age' might include conduct where age is not the reason or an important reason for the behaviour but it just plays some part – possibly even a minor part – in the conduct. Tribunals may take this difference of wording into account when deciding harassment claims and interpret the Regulations in line with the wording of the Directive.

In a judicial review brought by the Equal Opportunities Commission (*Equal Opportunities Commission v Secretary of State for Trade and Industry*,[1]) Mr Justice Burton recently concluded that similar wording in the SDA did not properly implement the Equal Treatment Directive, that the Directive's wording could not be read in and the provision should be recast. It is yet unclear how the government will react and whether it will amend all the discrimination legislation.

Secondly, the Directive defines harassment as conduct violating dignity *and* creating an intimidating, hostile etc. environment, whereas under the Regulations only one limb of the definition needs to be satisfied to succeed in a claim. In practice, of course, conduct which violates someone's dignity may well also create an intimidating, hostile, degrading, humiliating or offensive environment – there will be significant overlap between the sections. However, where there is no overlap, the test under the Regulations is an easier test than that contained in the Directive.

The government decided to implement the Directive in this way because it considered that the old UK case law on sexual and racial harassment had come up with a broader test of harassment than that in the Directive. That case law had developed before there was a free-standing definition of harassment and was based upon the concept that harassment was a type of less favourable treatment related to sex or race and was consequently a type of direct discrimination. Because these were direct discrimination claims the old cases on sexual and racial harassment did require a comparator to be identified, either real or hypothetical, with whom the treatment of the claimant could be compared. The SDA 1975 and Race Relations Act 1976 both now contain the stand-alone definition of harassment in the same terms as the definition in the Regulations, which does not require a comparator.[2]

1 [2007] IRLR 327, HL.
2 For an example of the implication of the change, *Gravell v London Borough of Bexley* (2007) IDS Employment Law Brief 830, 3.

4.5.3 Grounds of age

This term is used both in the definition of direct discrimination and harassment. Indeed, as mentioned above, the first sexual or racial harassment claims were brought as direct discrimination cases as no separate claim of harassment existed. The meaning of 'grounds of age' in the context of direct discrimination claims is considered above.[1]

In the recent *Equal Opportunities Commission* (EOC) case, the EOC criticised the use of the words 'grounds of' because it necessitated *causation*; it suggests that the protected ground is the *reason* for the treatment. The EOC suggested (and the Judge, Justice Burton, accepted) that only an association with the protected ground was needed in harassment cases.[2]

Example:

A workplace bully targets an older colleague rather than younger ones because he thinks the younger workers will respond physically to the bullying and he is scared of them. He chooses to focus on the older man as an easier victim but he does not bully him *because of* his age. It is not clear that this would be conduct 'on grounds of age'. However, it would certainly be 'related to age' and ought to be covered in order to implement the Directive properly.

The Court in the *EOC* case has directed the government to redraft the SDA to implement the directive properly. The government may take the opportunity to amend all the equality legislation.

As mentioned above, the definition of harassment, as currently drafted, is less restrictive than that of direct age discrimination. We discussed above how direct age discrimination must be less favourable treatment on grounds of the *claimant's* age and could not be on grounds of anyone else's age, such as an associate of the claimant. In contrast, harassment is generally just on grounds of age. It could therefore include harassment of someone because of associations with persons of a certain age. It could also include harassment for refusing to carry out an age discriminatory instruction or harassment because of the perpetrator's perception of the claimant's age.

Examples:

A 25-year-old employee is married to a much older man. Her work colleagues tease her about this with comments about her husband's pipe and slippers.

A manager refers to a 60-year-old employee as 'past it'.

A 45-year-old manager is instructed by other managers not to promote a 28-year-old employee, as she is deemed to be too 'light weight' without the necessary 'gravitas' for the role. When he complains about this instruction, he is marginalised within the management team.

All of the above may amount to harassment.

Of course, it is possible to harass someone because of their age without using derogatory age-related language. For example, staff in a particular department might isolate someone who is much older than the rest of the team because of this person's age but without making overt references to it. They could fail to include the individual when going to lunch or socialising in the evenings, exclude him from chats round the coffee machine and fail to send him emails that were sent to the rest of the department. Such behaviour might result in the individual feeling marginalised and excluded, resulting in an intimidating or hostile working environment. The issue for the claimant in these circumstances would be establishing that the conduct was on grounds of age – rather than simply because colleagues did not like him. In order to do this, the claimant would try to establish evidence from other circumstances that suggests that age was a factor in the behaviour – perhaps by looking at the way people of different ages were treated. If the claimant could show facts from which the tribunal could conclude discrimination if given no other explanation, the burden of proof would shift to the respondent to prove that the behaviour was *not* age discrimination – see section on 'The Burden of Proof and Inferences'.[3]

Could an alleged harasser argue that he or she had used derogatory age-related language because he or she did not like the victim for other reasons – so the treatment could not really be said to be 'on grounds of age'? It seems unlikely. In a case about sexual harassment, *Porcelli v Strathclyde Regional Council*,[4] it was argued that men had made sexually abusive comments to a female colleague because they did not like her, rather than because she was a woman. The court believed that the reason for the treatment was that the victim was not liked. However, it held that a man who was not liked would have been treated differently and therefore the conduct was on grounds of the claimant's sex. This claim was brought before there was a free standing definition of harassment in the SDA, but there does not seem to be any reason for thinking that it would be decided any differently under the new harassment provision. Furthermore, it seems likely that behaviour such as this would also shift the burden of proof to the employer.[5]

Contrasting with the decision in *Porcelli* is an EAT case called *Brumfitt v Ministry of Defence*.[6] In that decision, a woman was found not to have been sexually harassed by an instructor who used offensive and obscene remarks (of a sexual nature) during a training day. The EAT found that the remarks were directed at men and women (and both would have found them offensive) and therefore that there was no harassment. This differs from the *Porcelli* case because in that case it was found that a man would have been treated differently, whereas in *Brumfitt* men and women were treated the same. Given the arguments that the definition should encompass all harassment *related to* age, it is our view that any abusive language which uses ageist terms will probably give grounds for a claim of harassment, whatever the motives of the person responsible.

1 See **4.2.2**.
2 *Equal Opportunities Commission* [2007] IRLR 327, HL at [6]–[40].
3 See **4.6**.
4 [1986] ICR 564, Ct Sess (Inner House).
5 See **4.6**.
6 [2005] IRLR 4, EAT.

4.5.4 Unwanted conduct

The definition of harassment requires that the conduct is 'unwanted'. This means that, for example, jokes about an individual's age will not amount to harassment if the individual genuinely does not mind and they cannot be said to be 'unwanted'. Does this mean that the individual has to complain before the behaviour can be said to be 'unwanted'? The answer, is no. There is no requirement that the individual has to complain.

In a sex discrimination case, *Reed and anor v Stedman*,[1] the EAT held that 'unwanted' meant 'unwelcome' or 'uninvited' and that it would give a licence to one-off acts of harassment to say that an act had to be done and then rejected before it could be known to be 'unwanted'. So, a one-off act, can amount to harassment. Furthermore, even if there is a series of acts and the individual has not complained about the earlier conduct, the behaviour could still be deemed to be 'unwanted'. An individual who appears not to mind could just be reluctant to make a fuss or be afraid that a complaint might make the situation worse. There is strong social pressure on people to 'keep a sense of humour' when jokes are made at their expense and other pressures not to 'rock the boat' in the workplace, all of which might inhibit people from complaining about harassment, even when it is unwanted. The government said in its consultation document that a victim of ageist harassment does not have to make it explicit that the behaviour is unwanted.[2]

Example:

Ernest is 50 and plays for his company's football team. His colleagues are continuously joking and teasing him about his age. He says nothing as he really enjoys the games and wants to be 'one of the lads'. Even though Ernest hasn't complained, this may well amount to ageist harassment.

Mary works for RP PR and is the oldest member of staff by some way. She is very sensitive to this. On her 50th birthday her colleagues joined together to buy her a weekend to Paris and all signed a card. Mary is upset about this as it only reminds her of how she stands out by reason of age. Although Mary complained once about a colleague asking if she was looking forward to being a grandmother at the time her son got engaged, her colleagues are not aware how sensitive Mary is to her age. Even if she is genuinely upset, the birthday gift and card are unlikely to amount to harassment. However, after having complained, if her colleagues buy her a card the following year, believing she is making a fuss about nothing, then this might amount to harassment as they are aware of her sensitivity.

---

1 [1999] IRLR 299, EAT.
2 'Equality and Diversity: Coming of Age', DTI, 2006, para 3.3.4.

4.5.5 Purpose or effect

The definition of harassment refers to conduct which has *either* the purpose *or* the effect of violating dignity, etc. This means that harassment is not limited to situations where the perpetrator *intended* to violate dignity or create a hostile environment. Intentional behaviour is covered but provided the conduct had the necessary *effect*, the perpetrator could have been quite oblivious to the recipient's feelings and still be guilty of harassment. Presumably the majority of alleged harassers will deny that they intended to create an unpleasant environment or to violate the victim's dignity.

In some cases, the tribunal will no doubt find on the facts (perhaps inferring from the circumstances) that this was their intention and that they are trying to cover it up. However, in more borderline cases where intention is unclear, or even where the perpetrator's motives are clearly innocent, claimants will be able to argue that, whatever the intention, the *effect* was to harass.

Regulation 6(a) provides some further guidance on how one might determine that conduct has had a certain 'effect'. It says:

> 'conduct shall be regarded as having the effect specified in paragraph (1)(a) or (b) only if, having regard to all the circumstances, including in particular the perception of B, it should reasonably be considered as having that effect'.

There are several things to notice about this definition. The first is that B's perception is particularly significant when determining whether or not harassment has occurred. However, there is still a requirement that it must have been 'reasonable' for the behaviour to have had that effect. So, the test has both a subjective and an objective element. A tribunal will probably consider first what was B's perception about the conduct before considering whether B's perception was a reasonable one. A paranoid claimant who thinks that a colleague saying 'hello' each morning is age-related harassment will not succeed in a claim (even if he or she genuinely believes that this conduct was on grounds of age and created an intimidating environment) because it was not reasonable for that behaviour to have had that effect. However, a harasser will not be able to escape liability by saying that it was only a joke, or that he or she had not intended to cause offence, or even by saying that the victim was wrong to believe that an intimidating environment had been created, provided that the conduct could reasonably be considered as violating dignity or creating that environment.

The question of whether the conduct had the purpose or effect of violating dignity, etc. is closely linked with the need for the conduct to be unwanted (above).

The EAT considered the subjective and objective elements of the test in the case of *Moonsar v Fiveways Express Transport Ltd*,[1] a sex discrimination case. This case was brought before the new stand-alone definition of harassment was introduced and was decided as a direct discrimination case. However, it considered the same issue of whether conduct 'objectively' amounted to harassment and whether the claimant 'subjectively' experienced it as harassment. Ms Moonsar's male colleagues' downloaded and viewed pornography in the office they shared (although they did not distribute it to her) and she claimed that this amounted to harassment. The EAT held that this conduct was 'objectively' degrading to a female employee and that the claimant 'subjectively' found the behaviour unacceptable. The fact that she had not complained to her employer until after her dismissal did not matter because the behaviour was 'so obvious'.

The 'objective' part of the test was part of the EOC's recent challenge to the SDA harassment definition. The EOC contended that there should not be any objective element to the test at all – it should be purely about the perception of the claimant. However, the Judge failed to find for the EOC on this point and a similar challenge to this part of the Regulations seems unlikely – the inclusion of an objective element appears to be in line with the Directive.

1 [2005] IRLR 9, EAT.

4.5.6 Violating dignity or creating an intimidating, hostile, degrading, humiliating or offensive environment

As explained earlier in this section, harassment is defined in the Regulations as conduct which violates dignity *or* creates an intimidating, hostile, degrading, humiliating or offensive environment, whereas under the Regulations both of these limbs need to be satisfied. The government's 'Notes on the Regulations' (March 2006) state that, although the government chose to use 'or' instead of 'and', 'conduct which violates a person's dignity almost invariably also creates an offensive (etc) environment for that person, and vice versa; it is difficult to envisage a practical example of harassment which involves one but not the other, because each element has such a broad definition.' It is difficult, but perhaps not impossible. For example, an isolated incident of ageist abuse by a temporary colleague may violate a person's dignity, but may not have the effect of creating an offensive working environment.

4.5.7 Examples of harassment

Harassment can take a number of forms and the definition encompasses a wide range of behaviour. Examples include:

- derogatory or degrading comments about age or matters associated with age or aging;

- jokes about age or matters associated with age;
- ostracising someone on grounds of age;
- unwanted physical conduct on grounds of age (eg patting a younger employee on the head);
- derogatory stereotyping based on age;
- talking down to, humiliating or patronising younger or older workers; and
- bullying someone by excessive workloads, impossible deadlines or constant criticism on age grounds.

4.5.8 Liability of employer and individual

As dealt with more fully above, an employer is liable for discriminatory acts done by employees in the course of their employment even if such acts are done without the employer's knowledge or approval.[1] This includes acts of harassment. Employers could therefore find themselves responsible for harassment committed by employees of which they were completely ignorant and which they would have forbidden, if they had known about it. The only way employers can escape liability for acts committed by employees in the course of their employment is for the employer to show that it took such steps as were reasonably practicable to prevent the employee from doing that act.[2]

All employers should have well publicised diversity and harassment policies and give diversity training to all employees which make it clear that age discrimination and harassment are not acceptable. This is particularly important in the context of age discrimination because discriminating on the grounds of age and ageist harassment are still often quite socially acceptable forms of behaviour, similar to the way in which sex and race discrimination were quite socially acceptable when the SDA and Race Relations Act were brought into force. It will take some time before changes in attitudes filter through into the workplace and employers might well find themselves liable for age discrimination by employees who thought such behaviour would be tolerated. This potential defence, of having taken all steps as were reasonably practicable to prevent the harassment, is considered in more detail in **Chapter 3**, Scope of the Regulations.[3]

It would be a mistake for employees not to worry about the consequences of their discriminatory acts just because their employer is vicariously liable, as they will not necessarily escape liability themselves. Regulation 26(2) states that 'an employee or agent for whose act the employer or principal is liable under reg 25 (or would be so liable but for reg 25(3)) shall be deemed to aid the doing of the act'. And 'knowingly aiding' an act of discrimination is itself an unlawful act. The effect of this regulation is that an individual could be named as a respondent in an age discrimination claim in addition to the employer, could have a declaration made against him or her and could become personally liable for an award of damages to the claimant. If the employer was able to rely on the 'reasonable steps' defence, the employee would be the only one potentially liable for the act of discrimination. If the employer was not vicariously liable because the harassment had not been done 'in the course of employment' the employee could not be said to be aiding an unlawful act because no unlawful act would have taken place. In these circumstances, neither the employee nor employer would have any liability. These areas are covered in more detail in **Chapter 3** above.[4]

So, what does it mean that an act has to be committed in the course of employment? Can an employer escape liability because the harassment was committed, for example, at the pub after work? Whether something is done 'in the course of employment' is ultimately a question of fact for the tribunal to determine. Acts committed in the workplace and during work time are generally held to be done 'in the course of employment' but social events held after work are a more difficult area. An office Christmas party is arranged by the employer for the purpose of rewarding and incentivising staff, ultimately for the benefit of the business, it is therefore very likely that anything that occurs then will be in the course of employment. But how about more informal work-related social events, which might not even be organised by the employer? In a sex discrimination case, *Chief Constable of Lincolnshire Police v Stubbs*,[5] it was held that acts which had taken place in a pub after work when socialising with work colleagues were 'in the course of employment'. This is a particularly important decision when you bear in mind that harassment often does take place at social events when people become less inhibited because they have been drinking or merely because they are not on work premises and are no longer performing their work tasks. However, not everything that happens outside working hours will be deemed to be in the course of employment. In *H M Prison Service v Davis*[6] (another sex discrimination case) an incident which happened off-duty and at an employee's home was not deemed to be in the course of employment. These issues are considered in more detail in **Chapter 10**.[7]

What about harassment by a customer or client of the employer? Is the employer still liable? It is not clear whether an employer would be liable for harassment of its employees committed by a third party. An EAT decision in 1996 on the old harassment law had held that employers could be responsible for the acts of third parties. This was the case of *Burton and Rhule v De Vere Hotels* in which two black waitresses brought race discrimination claims against their employer when they were racially harassed by guests at their workplace who had been listening to a comedy act by Bernard Manning.[8] The EAT held that the employer had been liable because it had allowed the harassment to happen in circumstances in which it could control whether it happened or not; it did not have to anticipate the discrimination to be liable. However, the House of Lords subsequently disapproved this decision and said that an inadvertent failure to protect an employee from third-party harassment (where the failure was not related to the protected ground) would not make the employer liable.[9]

But the issue of third-party harassment is one of the matters that came up in the recent challenge by the EOC to the SDA.[10] In that case, Mr Justice Burton held that amending the definition of harassment to read unwanted conduct 'in relation to sex' rather than 'on the ground of her sex' would mean that the definition of harassment encompasses a failure to take steps to prevent continuing and/or regular objectionable conduct. If he is right about this and the definition of age harassment is recast in the terms he suggests, an employer would similarly be liable for a knowing failure to prevent age-related harassment by a third party.

In any event, if the employer does not investigate or take action against third-party harassment *because* of the employee's age, whereas it would have done in another case, that in itself could amount to discrimination.[11] And an employer who knowingly *aids* a third party to discriminate will also be liable.[12]

1 See 225 reg 25 and **4.3.1**.
2 See reg 25(3).
3 See **3.4.2**.
4 See **3.4.1**.
5 [1999] IRLR 81, EAT.
6 EAT 1294/98.
7 See **3.4.1**.
8 *Burton* [1996] IRLR 596.
9 *MacDonald v AG for Scotland; Pearce v Governing Body of Mayfield Secondary School* [2003] ICR 937, HL.
10 *Equal Opportunities Commission* [2007] IRLR 327, HL.
11 *Home Office v Coyne* [2000] ICR 1443, CA.
12 See reg 26(1).

4.6 Burden of proof and inferences

The issue of the burden of proof – or who has to prove their case, the claimant or the respondent – is highly significant in discrimination claims, because it can be so hard for a claimant to prove that he has been discriminated against and not always straightforward for the respondent to prove that he has not discriminated. In this section, we consider the development of the burden of proof in discrimination law before examining the current tests. This is one area of employment law that seems to be continuously developing with new case law.

Example:

Cilla, 30, applies for a job and is not selected. The successful candidate, Caroline, is 50. Both candidates have similar qualifications and experience. Cilla suspects that the reason she did not get the job is because of her age; in particular, she thinks that the employer had concerns that she might take time off to have or to look after children because she is at an age when she may have young children. However, the employer had not referred to children or families at all in the interview and Caroline was not obviously a poorer candidate. Cilla might be right that there was an element of discrimination in the selection procedure but employers in these circumstances are unlikely to admit to it. Cilla would face an uphill struggle to prove discrimination. However, she would be in a much stronger position if it was up to the employer to prove that it had *not* discriminated.

As with other forms of discrimination, the Regulations include provisions dealing with how the tribunal should approach the question of the burden of proof. Regulation 37(2) states:

> 'Where, on the hearing of the complaint, the complainant proves facts from which the tribunal could, apart from this regulation, conclude in the absence of an adequate explanation that the respondent:
>
> (a) has committed against the complainant an act to which regulation 36 applies; or
>
> (b) is by virtue of regulation 25 (liability of employers and principals) or 26 (aiding unlawful acts) to be treated as having committed against the complainant such an act,
>
> the tribunal shall uphold the complaint unless the respondent proves that he did not commit, or as the case may be, is not to be treated as having committed, that act.'

Even before discrimination legislation codified this partial reversal of the burden of proof (see below), the courts were grappling with it. The usual rule in litigation is that it is up to the claimant to prove his case. But, in discrimination cases, the courts have long acknowledged the fact that it is rare for an employee to be able to produce direct evidence of overtly discriminatory words or actions when bringing a claim of discrimination (the so-called 'smoking gun' to prove the discrimination). Accordingly, a number of cases have considered when it is proper for a tribunal to be able to draw inferences of discrimination from all the surrounding circumstances, coupled with a failure by the respondent to provide a good explanation.

In *King v Great Britain-China Centre*,[1] a race discrimination case decided before the introduction of the current test in the legislation, the Court of Appeal gave the following guidance on inferences and the burden of proof:

- It is for the claimant who complains of racial discrimination to make out his case. Thus if the claimant does not prove his case on the balance of probabilities he will fail.
- It is important to bear in mind that it is unusual to find direct evidence of racial discrimination. Few employers will be prepared to admit such discrimination even to themselves. In some cases the discrimination will not be ill-intentioned but merely based on an assumption that 'he would not have fitted in'.
- The outcome of the case will therefore usually depend on what inferences it is proper to draw from the primary facts found by the tribunal. These inferences can include, in appropriate cases, any inferences that it is just and equitable to draw in accordance with s 65(2)(b) of the Race Relations Act 1976 from an evasive or equivocal reply to a questionnaire.
- Though there will be some cases where, for example, the non-selection of the claimant for a post or for promotion is clearly not on racial grounds, a finding of discrimination and a finding of a difference in race will often point to the possibility of racial discrimination. In such circumstances the tribunal will look to the employer for an explanation. If no explanation is then put forward or if the tribunal considers the explanation to be inadequate or unsatisfactory it will be legitimate for the tribunal to infer that the discrimination was on racial grounds. This is not a matter of law but, as May LJ puts it in *North West Thames Regional Health Authority v Noone*,[2] 'almost common sense'.
- It is unnecessary and unhelpful to introduce the concept of a shifting evidential burden of proof. At the conclusion of all the evidence the tribunal should make findings as to the primary facts and draw such inferences as they consider proper

> from those facts. They should then reach a conclusion on the balance of probabilities, bearing in mind both the difficulties which face a person who complains of unlawful discrimination and the fact that it is for the claimant to prove his case.

This much quoted guidance provided that, if the claimant proved facts from which the tribunal could draw inferences, it would be 'legitimate' for the tribunal to infer that unlawful discrimination had occurred in the absence of an adequate explanation for the discriminatory treatment from the respondent. However, the guidance did not *require* the tribunal to infer discrimination in such circumstances.

The *King* case was approved by the House of Lords in *Glasgow City Council v Zafar.*[3] The issue of the burden of proof had however, also prompted scrutiny throughout Europe and the Burden of Proof Directive (Council Directive 97/80/EC) was introduced in December 1997, particularly dealing with the burden of proof in cases of sex discrimination. The Preamble to the Burden of Proof Directive reflects the concerns already identified in the UK courts in relation to the issue of the burden of proof:

> '(17) Whereas plaintiffs could be deprived of any effective means of enforcing the principle of equal treatment before the national courts if the effect of introducing evidence of an apparent discrimination were not to impose on upon the respondent the burden of proof that his practice is not in fact discriminatory.
>
> (18) Whereas the Court of Justice of the European Communities has therefore held that rules on the burden of proof must be adapted when there is a prima facie case of discrimination and that, for the principle of equal treatment to be applied effectively, the burden of proof must shift back to the respondent when evidence of such discrimination is brought.'

Article 4 of the Burden of Proof Directive provides:

> '1. Member States should take such measures as are necessary, in accordance with their national judicial systems, to ensure that, when persons who consider themselves wronged because the principle of equal treatment has not been applied to them establish, before a court or other competent authority, facts from which it may be presumed that there has been direct or indirect discrimination, it shall be for the respondent to prove that there has been no breach of the principle of equal treatment.'

In the light of the provisions of the Burden of Proof Directive, s 63A of the SDA 1975 was introduced, together with s 54A of the Race Relations Act 1976 and s 17A(1C) of the Disability Discrimination Act 1995. Provisions concerning the burden of proof were also included in the Employment Equality (Religion and Belief) Regulations 2003 (reg 29) and the Employment Equality (Sexual Orientation) Regulations 2003 (reg 29). Regulation 37(2) of the Regulations is in the same terms as these sections.

The EAT provided guidance on these new burden of proof provisions in *Barton v Investec Henderson Crothwaite Securities Ltd.*[4] Essentially, the *Barton* guidance built upon the guidance set out in *King* and provided that under the amended law, the courts should adopt a two-stage process. At the first stage, the claimant must prove facts from which inferences *could* be drawn that the respondent has committed an act of discrimination. In deciding whether or not the claimant has proved such facts, the outcome will usually depend on what inferences it is proper for the tribunal to draw from the primary facts at that stage. Once the claimant has established facts that on first appearance seem to show discrimination, ie a prima facie case, the burden of proof will then shift to the respondent. To discharge the burden of proof the respondent must prove, on the balance of probabilities, that the treatment was in no sense whatsoever on the grounds of (age). If the respondent cannot discharge the burden of proof then the courts are required to find that the claimant's claim is successful. This guidance, in light of the statutory amendments, arguably goes further than the original *King* decision which provided that, in such circumstances, it would be 'legitimate' for the courts to find discrimination (rather than being required to find discrimination). The *Barton* guidance was approved with some revisions by the Court of Appeal in *Igen Ltd v Wong*.[5]

The guidance as amended by *Igen* is as follows:

- It is for the claimant who alleges discrimination to prove, on the balance of probabilities, facts from which the tribunal could conclude, in the absence of adequate explanation, that the respondent has committed an act of discrimination.
- If the claimant does not prove such facts the claim will fail.
- In deciding whether the claimant has proved such facts it is important to bear in mind that it is unusual to find direct evidence of sex discrimination. Few employers would be prepared to admit such discrimination, even to themselves. In some cases the discrimination will not be an intention but merely based on the assumption that 'he would not have fitted in'.

- The outcome at this stage of the analysis will usually depend on what inferences it is proper to draw from the primary facts found by the tribunal.
- The tribunal does not have to reach a definitive determination that such facts *would* lead it to conclude that there was sex discrimination – it merely has to decide what inferences *could* be drawn.
- In considering what influences or conclusions can be drawn from the primary facts, the tribunal must assume that there is no adequate explanation for those facts.
- These inferences could include any that it is just and equitable to draw from an evasive or equivocal reply to a questionnaire.
- Inferences may also be drawn from any failure to comply with a relevant code of practice.
- When the claimant has proved facts from which conclusions could be drawn that the respondent has treated the claimant less favourably on the ground of sex, the burden of proof moves to the respondent.
- It is then for the respondent to prove that he did not commit or, as the case may be, is not to be treated as having committed, that act.
- To discharge that burden it is necessary for the respondent to prove on the balance of probabilities that his treatment of the claimant was in no sense whatsoever on the ground of (age), since 'no discrimination whatsoever' is compatible with the EC Burden of Proof Directive.
- The respondent must not only provide an explanation for the facts proved by the claimant, from which the inferences could be drawn, but that explanation must be adequate to prove on the balance of probabilities that (age) was no part of the reasons for the treatment.
- Since the respondent would normally be in possession of the facts necessary to provide an explanation, the tribunal would normally expect cogent evidence to discharge that burden of proof – in particular, the tribunal will need to examine carefully explanations for failure to deal with the questionnaire procedure and/or any code of practice.

Despite the detailed guidance laid down in *Barton*, as amended by *Igen*, the burden of proof and the circumstances in which it should shift from one party to the other, continues to be an issue for judicial comment. In the EAT decision of *Laing v Manchester City Council*,[6] Elias J stated that courts should not be unduly constrained by the two-stage test laid down in the *Barton* guidelines. He said that there was no single right answer to explain when the inference of possible discrimination becomes justifiable '... and tribunals can waste much time and become embroiled in artificial distinctions if they always feel obliged to go through these two stages'. The fact that a tribunal does not always have to go explicitly through the two-stage process was confirmed in *Brown v London Borough of Croydon* which was heard with *Madarassy v Nomura Plc*,[7] the most recent case on this area at the time of writing.

In the *Madarassy* case, Mummery LJ confirmed that the *Igen* guidance was clear and certain and did not need amending. As he put it 'repetition is superfluous, qualification is unnecessary and contradiction is confusing'. He therefore confirmed that, rather than amending the guidance, he would utilise the *Madarassy* case to demonstrate how the burden of proof should work. In this case, Mummery LJ clarified a number of issues in relation to the burden of proof:

- The burden of proof does not shift simply because the claimant is able to show a difference in status (eg sex/age/race etc) and a difference in treatment. Such differences only indicate a 'possibility of discrimination'. Taken alone, these facts do not amount to sufficient material from which a tribunal 'could conclude' that, on the balance of probabilities, the respondent had committed an unlawful act of discrimination.
- In determining whether the claimant has successfully shifted the burden of proof to the respondent, the tribunal will need to consider all of the evidence relevant to the discrimination complaint; for example, evidence as to whether the act complained of occurred at all; evidence as to the comparators relied upon by the claimant; whether the comparisons being made were of like with like; and available evidence of the reasons for the differential treatment.
- The absence of an adequate explanation by the respondent for the differential treatment only becomes relevant if a prima facie case of discrimination is proved by the claimant. The tribunal then moves on to the second stage and the burden is on the respondent to prove that it has not committed an act of unlawful discrimination.
- Although, the provisions concerning the burden of proof contained in the discrimination legislation involves a two-stage analysis of the evidence, the tribunal does not in practice hear the evidence and the argument in two stages. The tribunal will hear all of the evidence in a case before it embarks on the

> two-stage analysis in order to decide, first whether the burden of proof has moved to the respondent and, if so, whether the respondent has discharged the burden of proof.

It is debatable whether or not, in the light of this case law, the law on the burden of proof and inferences has changed since the *King* case. It is true that in that case it was said that the tribunal could infer discrimination in the absence of an adequate explanation from the respondent, not that it was *required* to do so. Whereas, under the burden of proof provision, without an adequate explanation, the tribunal 'shall' uphold the complaint unless the respondent proves it did not discriminate. However, it seems unlikely that, in practice, a tribunal would not have upheld a complaint under the old *King* guidelines if the claimant had shown facts which suggested discrimination and the employer did not have an adequate explanation.

There is one matter, however, which has not been completely cleared up by the decision in *Madarassy*. This is whether 'the absence of an adequate explanation' can be taken into account by a tribunal when considering whether or not a prima facie case has been made out. *Madarassy* says it cannot – the absence of an adequate explanation only becomes relevant *after* the prima facie case has been established. But the previous decision of *Igen* (approved in *Madarassy*) had held that a tribunal *may* take account of the *absence* of the employer's explanation at stage one (whilst it should not take account of the explanation itself until stage two).

There is also some specific judicial guidance on drawing inferences. The case of *Anya v University of Oxford*,[8] predated the burden of proof provisions but the EAT has confirmed that it is still good law.[9] In *Anya*, the Court of Appeal said that inferences can be conclusions in respect of circumstantial evidence drawn from primary facts, as well as legal conclusions drawn from these primary and secondary findings. As stated earlier, this might include inferences drawn from a failure to respond properly to a questionnaire. The tribunal must make findings of fact *before* it can draw any inferences.

One discreet point about lack of documents was established by the Court of Appeal in *EB v BA*.[10] Once the burden of proof has shifted, the absence of documents can only be adverse to the employer, as the failure to produce them was not a failure of the claimant.

The burden of proof provision applies to all forms of age discrimination: direct, indirect, victimisation and harassment. It is difficult to see quite what it will add to indirect discrimination cases. However, it is likely to be relevant to direct discrimination, harassment and victimisation claims, in all of which the respondent may well deny that the grounds for the less favourable treatment were age, leaving the tribunal to try to infer the reasons.

Examples:

An employer considers three candidates for promotion: a man and a woman in their 30s and a man in his 50s. The promotion is offered to the man in his 30s. The candidate in his 50s questions why he was not promoted and suggests it was because of his age. All candidates had equivalent qualifications, skills and experience and received equally good appraisals the previous year. The employer claims the younger candidate was promoted because he had better people skills, which is denied by the older candidate. Neither candidates' appraisals mention their people skills. The older candidate submits a questionnaire which asks, amongst other matters, about the age diversity in the organisation (generally and by grade) and asks about ageist banter in the workplace. The employer fails to reply in time and its ultimate reply is evasive. A tribunal could draw inferences about the failure to reply properly when considering if a prima facie case had been made out. If all other evidence is neutral – this may help to establish such a case and shift the burden of proof, so that the employer is required to prove that it did not discriminate.

John, a senior accountant in his 50s, works for an accountancy firm, Numbers R Us. He is dismissed, ostensibly on grounds of his performance. However, the firm fails to follow a clearly defined performance management programme with John and instead holds a number of undocumented meetings with him at which he is informed that he isn't up to the job. John cannot conclusively prove that he has been discriminated against on grounds of age. However, at the tribunal, John is able to demonstrate that he has been excluded from training opportunities while younger employees have not. He is also able to prove that senior management has made a number of ageist comments towards him. Furthermore, none of the senior management team, to whom he reports, has received training on equal opportunities or age discrimination.

These facts, taken together, could well be sufficient for the tribunal to find that the burden of proof should shift to Numbers R Us. If the firm is then unable to show a detailed and documented appraisal and performance management programme, which can be used as clear evidence to demonstrate the performance concerns which led to John's dismissal, then it will be found to have discriminated against John.

---

1 [1991] IRLR 513, CA.
2 [1988] IRLR 195.

3 [1998] IRLR 36, HL.
4 [2003] IRLR 332, EAT.
5 [2005] IRLR 258, CA.
6 [2006] IRLR 748, EAT.
7 [2007] EWCA Civ 33, CA.
8 [2001] IRLR 377, CA.
9 *Dattani v Chief Constable of West Mercia Police* [2005] IRLR 327, EAT.
10 [2006] IRLR 47, CA.

4.7 Justification

4.7.1 Introduction

As already mentioned, under the Regulations, unlike other forms of discrimination, it is possible for a respondent to 'justify' direct and indirect discrimination. This means that, provided the measure which would otherwise be discriminatory is 'a proportionate means of achieving a legitimate aim', the respondent can defeat a claim.[1]

Under the Directive, indirect discrimination is capable of being justified under the standard justification test in art 2(2)(b)(i) 'that provision, criterion or practice is objectively justified by a legitimate aim and the means of achieving that aim are appropriate and necessary'. Both indirect and direct age discrimination is justified under a separate provision in art 6.

Article 6(1) of the Directive states:

> 'Notwithstanding Article 2(2), Member States may provide that differences of treatment on grounds of age shall not constitute discrimination, if, within the context of national law, they are objectively *and reasonably* justified by a legitimate aim, including legitimate employment policy, labour market and vocational training objectives, and if the means of achieving that aim are appropriate and necessary.
>
> Such differences of treatment may include among others:
>
> (a) the setting of special conditions on access to employment and vocational training, employment and occupation, including dismissal and remuneration conditions, for young people, older workers and persons with caring responsibilities in order to promote their vocational integration or ensure their protection;
>
> (b) the fixing of minimum conditions of age, professional experience or seniority in service for access to employment or to certain advantages linked to employment;

(c) the fixing of a maximum age for recruitment which is based on the training requirements of the post in question or the need for a reasonable period before retirement.'

There is an interesting difference in the justification definitions in the Directive and in the Regulations.

The Regulations set out the same test of justification for both direct and indirect discrimination, namely 'the treatment [ie direct discrimination] or, as the case may be, provision, criterion or practice [ie indirect discrimination] [is] a proportionate means of achieving a legitimate aim'. Case law has already held that 'appropriate and necessary' under the Directive means 'proportionate' as used in the Regulations.[2]

However, there is another difference. Article 2(2)(b)(i) talks about objective justification. These words are not found in the Regulations but are used to describe the test in the Regulations[3] which is derived from the Article 2(2)(b)(i) wording. Article 6(1), however (which is the only basis for justifying direct age discrimination) refers, as set out above, to treatment being 'objectively *and reasonably* justified'. It is unclear whether the addition of the words 'and reasonably' adds anything. If not, why are they there?[4]

The government's consultation document about the first draft age discrimination regulations, 'Coming of Age',[5] explained that:

> 'the Directive allows more scope for justifying direct age discrimination than other strands because age may genuinely be a relevant factor for certain aspects of employment and vocational training.'

Nevertheless, an employer may be unwise to seek to rely heavily on justification arguments. Advisory, Conciliation and Arbitration Service argues that treating people less favourably because of their age will only be justifiable in exceptional circumstances:

> 'Remember that different treatment on grounds of age will only be possible exceptionally for good reasons.'[6]

This echoes what was said in the government's 'Coming of Age' consultation paper:

> 'The principle remains that different treatment on grounds of age will be unlawful: treating people differently on grounds of age will be possible but only exceptionally and only for good reasons'.[7]

One of the most important unanswered questions regarding the Regulations will be the courts and tribunals approach to justification.

There are three particular issues which are explored below:

(i) Should age discrimination be more easily justified than other forms of discrimination?

(ii) Should direct discrimination be more difficult to justify than indirect discrimination?

(iii) Is the test of justification the same for a Member State justifying a discriminatory law and for an employer justifying a discriminatory practice?

This section then goes on to examine the legitimate aims which could potentially be relied on; the test for proportionality; the time at which justification should be assessed; and the interrelationship between justification and the exceptions in the Regulations.

1 See reg 3(1).
2 See 'Notes on Regulations', DTI, March 2006, para 14.
3 eg 'Notes on Regulations', DTI, March 2006, para 13.
4 See **4.7.3**.
5 'Equality and Diversity: Coming of Age', DTI, July 2003, p 31, para 4.1.10.
6 ACAS Guidance, *Age and the workplace: Putting the Employment Equality (Age) Regulations 2006 into practice* (ACAS) p 30.
7 'Equality and Diversity: Coming of Age', DTI, 2006, p 32.

4.7.2 Age v other forms of discrimination

The justification definition mirrors that in other UK discrimination laws. We must await, however, decisions of the appellate courts in order to see if they approach the test less stringently for age discrimination than for other prohibited forms of discrimination.[1]

We are given a possible insight into the UK courts' approach to the Regulations by its attitude under human rights law and by the approach of the ECJ and overseas courts to age cases.

1 See Swift, 'Justifying Age Discrimination' (2006) 35(3) ILT, 228.

(a) European convention on human rights

The House of Lords considered the justification of direct age discrimination in the joined cases of *R v Secretary of State for Work and Pensions, ex p Carson and, ex p Reynolds.*[1] *Reynolds* concerned age discrimination. Ms Reynolds was under 25 and lived alone in a council flat. She received jobseeker's allowance (JSA) and income support (IS) at the weekly rate of £41.35. If she had been over 25 she would have received £52.20.

She unsuccessfully claimed that this age-based difference of treatment breached the nondiscrimination provisions of art 14 of the European Convention on Human Rights. Of particular interest is their Lordships' acceptance that this direct age discrimination was justified.

The secretary of state justified the discrimination on the following grounds:

> '(1) People in the 18–24 age group in general earn less than those 25 or over, and may legitimately be regarded as having lower earnings expectations.
>
> (2) The majority of those 18–24 do not live independently and may legitimately be regarded as having lower living costs than the group of claimants aged 25 or over.
>
> (3) The payment of lower rates of JSA and IS to those between 18–24 may be expected to have the effect of discouraging them from living independently, and encouraging them to live together with others, notably parents or other family members, which may be seen to have wider social benefits.
>
> (4) Other aspects of the social security system serve to prevent any resultant hardship to the minority of persons in the position which was that of the claimant who are aged between 18–24 and do live independently.
>
> (5) It is important from the point of view of good administration for the social security system to be based upon clear, easily applicable rules, rather than attempting to cater for the individual situation of every claimant.'

Their Lordships considered the comparative seriousness or potency of age discrimination compared to some other forms of discrimination such as sex, race or sexual orientation discrimination.

Lord Walker of Gestingthorpe considered this in some detail.[2] He did not accept that age discrimination was equivalent to the more 'suspect' grounds of discrimination such as sex, race or sexual orientation. He drew upon US discrimination law to support this.[3] And whilst he accepted that 'these distinctions are not so clearly signalled in the jurisprudence of the European Court of Human Rights' he was satisfied that the equivalent doctrine is to be found there. Lord Walker referred to Lord Nicholls of Birkenhead's comments in *Ghaidan v Godin-Mendoza*[4] in which he stated:

> '... where the alleged violation comprises differential treatment based on grounds such as race or sex or sexual orientation the

court will scrutinise with intensity any reasons said to constitute justification. The reasons must be cogent if such differential treatment is to be justified.'

He did not accept age to come within one of these 'suspect' grounds. He states[5]:

> 'Age is a personal characteristic, but it is different in kind from other personal characteristics. Every human being starts life as a tiny infant, and none of us can do anything to stop the passage of the years.'

He suggests that unlike the more suspect grounds of discrimination he does not regard age discrimination as being 'intrinsically demeaning'.

Although the test of justification under the European Convention on Human Rights appears to be the same as under the Regulations and other discrimination laws, it remains to be seen whether the ECJ will accept this distinction between suspect and less suspect grounds of discrimination.

The test of justification for Convention cases adopted by the Lords and derived from the Court of Appeal's decision in *Wandsworth London BC v Michalak*[6] is:

> 'did the difference in treatment have an objective and reasonable justification: in other words, did it pursue a legitimate aim and did the differential treatment bear a reasonable relationship of proportionality to the aim sought to be achieved?'

This mirrors the definition of justification in the Regulations (see above).

Of potential relevance to justification under the Regulations, the Lords accepted these arguments notwithstanding:

- the arbitrary nature of the age 25 threshold; and
- that the difference of treatment was not targeted at those not living independently.

The Lords accepted that 'a line must be drawn somewhere'[7] in order to meet the need for legal certainty and the need for a workable rule. Lord Walker of Gestingthorpe[8] referred to the US Supreme Court decision of *Massachusetts Board of Retirement v Murgia*[9] in which it was observed 'drawing lines which create distinctions is peculiarly a legislative task and an unavoidable one. Perfection in making the necessary classifications is neither possible nor necessary'.

The Lords also noted that these social security regulations had originally distinguished between householders and nonhouseholders but that this had proved unworkable and had been replaced with the age qualification.[10]

1 [2005] UKHL 37.
2 *Ex p Carson and Reynolds* [2005] UKHL 37 at [55]–[60].
3 *San Antonio School District v Rodriguez* (1973) 411 US 1 and *Massachusetts Board of Retirement v Murgia* (1976) 427 US 307.
4 [2004] 2 AC 557, 568 at [19].
5 *Ghaidan* [2004] 2 AC 557, 568 at [60].
6 [2003] 1 WLR 617, 625 at [20], Brooke LJ.
7 *Ex p Carson and Reynolds* [2005] UKHL 37 at [41], Lord Hoffmann.
8 *Ex p Carson and Reynolds* [2005] UKHL 37 at [56].
9 *Murgia* (1976) 427 US 307.
10 Ex p Carson and Reynolds [2005] UKHL 37 at [56]. Lord Hoffmann para 39 and Lord Walker of Gestingthorpe para 87.

(b) Overseas laws

It is not only in the United States where the courts have accepted that age discrimination is less of an evil than other forms of discrimination.[1] The Canadian Supreme Court has adopted a similar approach.[2]

1 *Murgia* (1976) 427 US 307.
2 *McKinney v University of Guelph* (1990) 13 CHRR D/171 (SCC).

(c) European court of justice

Nonetheless, whatever the correct position under the Convention and overseas laws, the only ECJ case on the age provisions of the Directive gives little support to the contention that there should be a less stringent approach to justification under the Regulations than under other discrimination laws such as the Sex Discrimination or Race Relations Acts.

Mangold v Helm[1] concerned the lawfulness of German laws which exempted workers over 52 years from limits on the use of fixed-term employment contracts.

The ECJ accepted that the purpose of this law was to meet a legitimate aim, namely the vocational integration of older workers but that it did not represent a proportionate means of doing so and was hence unlawful.

The ECJ in the *Mangold* effectively accepted that the German Government was justified in considering reduced employment protection rights for older workers to encourage employers to employ them. However, the way in which Germany had sought to achieve this aim was disproportionate as it applied to:

> 'all workers who have reached the age of 52, without distinction, whether or not they were unemployed before the contract was concluded and whatever the duration of any period of unemployment.'[2]

The implication here is that the German Government could have exempted those over 52 years from the restrictions on the use of fixed-term contract provided they had limited it to those in this age group who were having difficulty in finding work. It is interesting to contrast this with the House of Lords approach in *Carson* above.

There is nothing in *Mangold* to support the Lords' view in *Carson* that age discrimination was less suspect than other forms of discrimination and, hence, easier to justify.

It is also worth noting that the examples of legitimate aims contained in the Directive, the original draft Regulations and the government's consultation papers did not include the promotion of diversity. If age discrimination was to be regarded as less suspect than other forms of discrimination, it would be expected that employers would be able to rely on the promotion of race and sex diversity to justify age discrimination. However, it does not seem that they will be able to do so.

Example:

Heavenly Corner Chocolates has a predominantly white male workforce. It is committed to improving its race and gender diversity and, therefore, wants to create opportunities for a more diverse workforce. It, therefore, sets a retirement age at 50. It seems highly unlikely that this will be regarded as lawful as it suggests that age discrimination is less wrong than sex or race discrimination.

---

1 [2006] IRLR 143.
2 *Mangold* [2006] IRLR 143 at [64].

4.7.3 Direct v indirect discrimination

Although the wording in the Regulations indicates the test of justification is the same, whether it be direct or indirect discrimination, there is still some uncertainty as to whether or not the courts will impose a more stringent standard for justifying direct discrimination. This would reflect the fact that permitting justification of direct discrimination is exceptional and not reflected in any other discrimination legislation. It would also reflect that in balancing the discriminatory impact of a measure against the need to address the legitimate aim by that means, the discriminatory impact of direct discrimination is normally likely to be greater than discriminatory impact of indirect discrimination. As mentioned in the section on 'Justification',[1] there is a subtle difference in the Directive in the articles governing justification aimed at indirect and direct age discrimination. The first cases on this are eagerly awaited. The Heyday judicial review[2] challenge also argues that the UK Government is in breach of the Directive for treating the justification of direct and indirect discrimination in the same way in the Regulations.

1 See **4.7.1**.
2 *R (on the application of Incorporated Trustees of the National Council of Ageing) v the Secretary of State for Trade and Industry*, EWHC 5485/2000.

4.7.4 Member State v Employer

A further question is whether the test of justification is the same for a Member State justifying age discriminatory domestic laws and for an employer justifying age discriminatory practices.

In *Mangold* the ECJ acknowledged that 'Member States unarguably enjoy broad discretion in their choice of the measures capable of attaining their objectives in the field of social and employment policy'.[1]

It is not clear that the ECJ would confer the same broad discretion on employers in their means of achieving their legitimate aims as they permit Member States in setting their domestic laws.

We now go on to consider the two parts of the definition of justification separately; thinking firstly about what might amount to a 'legitimate aim' and then looking at what is meant by 'proportionality'.

1 *Mangold* [2006] IRLR 143 at [63].

4.7.5 Legitimate aims

As mentioned above, the Directive gives three examples of possible legitimate aims, which might justify direct age discrimination:

(a) special conditions on access to employment and vocational training for young people, older workers and persons with caring responsibilities, in order to promote their vocational integration or to ensure their protection;

(b) fixing minimum age, experience or seniority for access to employment or advantages linked to employment; and

(c) a maximum recruitment age based on the training requirements of the post or the need for a reasonable period before retirement.[1]

In the first example, the aim is promoting the vocational integration of and protecting younger and older people. In the second example, the aim is unclear. It is possibly ensuring that staff are suitably experienced. In the third example, the aim is presumably ensuring the employer has a reasonable return on his investment.

'Age Matters', the government's first consultation document produced before draft Regulations were published, suggested that the Regulations should set out a finite list of specific aims that would be capable of justifying direct age discrimination.[2] However, after receiving responses to the consultation paper, the government decided that it would be 'too restrictive and prescriptive' to have an exhaustive list of legitimate aims for justifying direct discrimination.[3]

Having retreated from the position that there should be a finite list, the government still proposed to have a nonexhaustive list of examples of legitimate aims that might justify direct discrimination and it included such a list in the first draft Regulations and in the 'Coming of Age' consultation paper.[4] But the response to this in the consultation exercise was unfavourable and the final form of the Regulations contained the same general test of justification for both direct and indirect discrimination, without any examples or any definitive test of permissible aims.

As mentioned above, the absence of an exhaustive list of permissible aims is one of the subjects of Heyday's judicial review.[5] This has been referred to the ECJ but it is difficult to see the basis of this element of their challenge.

Article 6(1) of the Directive sets out examples of circumstances where a difference in treatment on grounds of age might be justified. As mentioned above, the potential legitimate aims listed in the Article are not totally clear but at the minimum, include:

- the vocational integration of young or older workers;
- the protection of young or older workers;
- the training requirements of job; and
- the need for a reasonable period of employment before retirement.

The 'Age Matters' consultation paper[6] referred to:

- health, welfare and safety, for example the protection of younger workers;
- facilitation of employment planning, for example where a business has a number of people approaching retirement at the same time;
- the training requirements of the post;
- encouraging and rewarding loyalty; and
- the need for a reasonable period of employment before retirement.

The later 'Coming of Age' consultation paper[7] added, without explanation, an additional potential aim of recruiting or retaining older people. This aim would, nevertheless, be consistent with the examples in art 6 of the Directive listed above.

As mentioned above, the final Regulations declined to set out a definitive list of legitimate aims.

Example:

An employer with a normal retirement age of 65 advertises a permanent position as an HR Manager. Edith, aged 64 and 4 months, is rejected because of her age. It is likely that this could be justified because of the legitimate aim to have a reasonable period of employment before retirement. If the job requires a two-year training period, this employer may also be justified in not recruiting Ethel who is 63. However, if the job was a short-term contract for six months with no training period, it would not be justified in rejecting Ethel.

The aims listed above in the 'Age Matters' consultation paper are only examples. It is important to remember that even the examples in the government consultation document may be challenged, as that document is not itself legally binding – it is just the government's view of the law, which may prove to be wrong.

Other possible legitimate aims include:

- cost;
- recruiting and retaining older workers;

- business needs/profitability;
- customer preference;
- 'fitting in' with the employer;
- vocational integration;
- promotion of diversity;
- complying with legal or regulatory rules;
- demands of fitness or stamina; and
- preserving dignity.

We say a few words below, about the particularly contentious aims of cost and recruiting and retaining older workers. The other examples are explored in more detail in **Chapter 5** on 'Recruitment',[8] save for preserving dignity which is considered in the **Chapter 12** on 'Retirement'.[9]

1 Council Directive establishing a general framework for equal treatment in employment and occupation (2000/78/), art 6.
2 'Equality and Diversity: Age Matters', DTI, 2003, para 3.19.
3 'Equality and Diversity: Coming of Age', DTI, 2005, para 4.1.5.
4 'Equality and Diversity: Coming of Age', DTI 2005, p 31, para 4.1.7 and p 33, para 4.1.17.
5 *R (on the application of Incorporated Trustees of the National Council of Ageing) v The Secretary of State for Trade and Industry* [2000] EWHC 5485.
6 'Equality and Diversity: Age Matters', DTI, 2003, para 3.15.
7 'Equality and Diversity: Coming of Age', DTI, 2006, para 4.1.17.
8 **Chapter 5, 5.3.3**.
9 **Chapter 12, 12.8.1(a)**.

(a) Cost

Experts dispute whether or not cost can ever be a 'legitimate aim' and capable of justifying otherwise discriminatory treatment. The 'Coming of Age' consultation paper stated that 'economic factors such as business needs and considerations of efficiency' could be 'legitimate aims' but that 'discrimination will not be justified merely because it may be more expensive not to discriminate'.[1] It is hard to see what an economic factor might be if not expense, so this is a confusing statement. One explanation is that the clue is in the word 'merely' and that expense could be part of an argument about justification, provided the argument was not only about cost.

This distinction would be supported by the leading authority on cost as a potential legitimate aim, namely the EAT case of *Cross v British Airways Plc*.[2] *Cross* concerns the justification of indirect sex discrimination. However, in the absence of any other higher level cases, *Cross* has become the main source of perceived wisdom about cost and justification. This may turn out to have been a blind alley into which many have ventured.

For this reason it is worth considering the case in some detail. The facts are complex but in essence concerned the retirement age of BA's pilots and cabin crew. The sex discrimination claims were essentially secondary claims brought by three of the women claimants in litigation involving a large group of employees who transferred from British Caledonian to BA in 1988. British Airways had a contractual retirement age of 55 and British Caledonian had a contractual retirement age of 60. British Airways' staff who joined before 1971 also had a contractual retirement age of 60. There was a dispute (which is not relevant to the discrimination law case) as to whether the change in retirement ages from 60 to 55 at the time of transferring the British Caledonian employees was valid. At that time, the lower retirement age with fully funded pension offered to the British Caledonian staff was seen as a benefit and the improved pension for the transferring employees cost BA a significant sum.

However, over the years the advantage of the change to retiring at 55 years with a fully funded pension over their previous right to work up to 60 years became less clear.

The three women claimants showed that the pre-1971 BA staff still employed were predominantly male whereas the post-1971 staff (approximately 96 per cent of the staff) were predominantly female. 98.55% of women were disadvantaged by this distinction compared with 90.28% of men. The women therefore claimed that the retirement age of 55 applying to all but a few of the BA workforce was indirectly discriminatory against women. The EAT accepted that there was a provision, criterion or practice which applied to the detriment of a considerably larger proportion of women than men. The discrimination claims then turned to BA's argument of justification.

The employment tribunal had accepted two of the various aims advanced by BA for the change in retirement ages, namely:

(i) minimising costs, particularly in the financial situation it had found itself in; and
(ii) maintaining the existing terms and conditions of employment so far as they relate to retirement and access to pensions.

The claimants argued that costs as a justification was impermissible. The EAT decision considered the ECJ and domestic authorities which contain considerable ammunition for both the argument that cost cannot amount to a legitimate aim justifying discrimination and, for the contradictory argument that cost can justify discrimination.[3]

The EAT faced with this conflict sided with the employment tribunal in deciding that cost alone could not justify discrimination, but that cost was a relevant factor where it was not the sole justification.

In *Cross* the EAT accepted BA's second justification namely the effect on its pension scheme of raising the contractual retirement age to 60. This would not have merely been a cost to BA but would have called into question the Inland Revenue approval of the BA scheme and would have been unpopular with many BA employees. As a result, the EAT considered that the cost to BA could be taken into account in deciding whether the indirect discrimination was justified. This is sometimes referred to as the 'Cost plus' justification.

This leaves many questions unanswered and is surely not the last word on the matter. As mentioned above, we must wait to see if:

- courts will adopt the same approach to justifying age discrimination as justifying sex and other forms of discrimination; and
- courts will adopt a stricter test for justifying direct discrimination than they have adopted for indirect discrimination.

In addition, no doubt courts and tribunals will be asked how cost can truly be distinguished from other economic factors?

However, in other places in the 'Age Matters' and 'Coming of Age' consultation papers it suggests that cost could potentially be used as justification for a failure to provide insurance cover (such as medical or permanent health insurance) to some employees.[4] When one assumes that the principal reason for an employer not providing medical insurance to all employees is likely to be the extra cost in giving it to older employees, this seems to come back to a cost-related justification. This contradicts what the consultation paper says elsewhere about discrimination not being justified merely because it is expensive not to discriminate.[5]

Another relevant point in this debate is that a number of factors come down to cost at heart, even if that is not the name given. So, for example, efficiency gains are really about reducing costs. The ACAS guidance for employers on age discrimination says that 'economic efficiency may be a real aim but saving money because discrimination is cheaper than nondiscrimination is not legitimate'.[6] Again, this begs the question about the difference between economic efficiency and saving money. All in all the position as to whether cost can be used to justify age discrimination is fairly confused and case law to clarify the point is urgently needed. Until we have such case law, the safest position an employer can take would be not to rely on cost alone as sufficient justification.

It can be difficult to distinguish between business needs/profitability, cost (see above) and customer preference (see below). It might be that a tribunal will be more sympathetic to justification defences if the employer can show not only that avoiding discrimination would increase costs or run counter to customers' preference but also that it would impact on the business' profitability or viability. This is supported in DTI Minister Jim Fitzpatrick's letter to the Employers' Forum on Age[7] in which he states:

> 'For individual employers faced with costs that have an adverse impact on their business there remains the possibility of objective justification . . . I believe that, where the evidence and their particular circumstances support it, employers will be able to argue that limiting the availability of benefits was objectively justified, if it meant that they would otherwise have insufficient funds for the research and development necessary to keep the business competitive or if it came down to a choice between providing benefits rather than jobs.'

Mr Fitzpatrick's apparent view that improved profits would not be enough but that cost could be a legitimate aim if the business' future was at stake might seem attractive at first glance. However, it brings with it problems including what the legal basis for such view might be and where the line should be drawn between the need for investment/job preservation and the simple desire to improve profits.

1 'Equality and Diversity: Coming of Age', DTI, 2006, para 4.1.16.
2 [2005] IRLR 423.
3 *Jenkins v Kingsgate Ltd* [1981] IRLR 228 (ECJ); *Bilka-Kaufhaus v Weber von Hartz* [1986] IRLR 317 (ECJ); *Rainey v Greater Glasgow Health Board* [1987] IRLR 26, HL; *Allonby* [2001] IRLR 364 CA; *Roks v Bestuur van de Bedrijfsvereniging voor de Gezondheid* (*'Roks'*) [1994] ECR 1–571; *Hill v Revenue Commissioners* [1998] IRLR 466 (ECJ)l; *Kütz-Bauer v Freie und Hansestadt Hamburg* [2003] IRLR 368 (ECJ); *Steinicke v Bundesanstalt für Arbeit* [2003] IRLR 892 (ECJ); *Schöneit v Stadt Frankfurt am Main, C-4/02 and 5/02* [2004] IRLR 983 ECJ.
4 'Equality and Diversity: Age Matters', DTI, March 2003, pp 45–46, paras 7.8, and 7.9; 'Equality and Diversity: Coming of Age', DTI, July 2005, para 4.4.6, p 43.
5 **Chapter 5, 5.3.3.**
6 ACAS Guidance, *Age and the Workplace: Putting the Employment Equality (Age) Regulations 2006 into practice* (ACAS) p 31.
7 Letter of 6 November 2006 from Jim Fitzpatrick MP, Minister for Employment Relations and Postal Services, responding to representations about insured benefits.

(b) Recruiting and retaining older people

Another potential issue is the question to what extent a reason that itself has an age-discriminatory element could amount to justification? As mentioned above, the government's 'Coming of Age' consultation paper suggests that the aim of 'recruiting and retaining older people' can amount to justification.[1] This seems a little unlikely, given the fact that this aim itself is directly discriminatory on grounds of age. It also contradicts the government's advice later in the consultation paper that a legitimate aim 'cannot be related to age discrimination itself'.[2]

It is well known that the government sees public policy advantages in having a greater number of older people in work because of the perceived pension crisis and an aging workforce. However, these are issues for society at large, rather than a particular workplace.

An employer could always take permitted 'positive action' if older people are under- represented in the business rather than discriminate (see **Chapter 5, 5.9.2(b)** for more information about positive action). Intending to recruit older workers is a form of positive discrimination. The 'Coming of Age' paper, therefore, suggests that positive discrimination could potentially be justified. However, this seems to us to be unlikely; it seems difficult to believe that an employer could justify discrimination because its aim is to recruit older people, despite the fact that the government appears to consider this acceptable. An employer would be wise to consider carefully any justification arguments where the proposed justification is itself directly discriminatory.

When suggesting that 'recruiting and retaining' older people might be a legitimate aim, the government is presumably relying on the example in the Directive which says that:

> 'the setting of special conditions on access to employment and vocational training, employment and occupation, including dismissal and remuneration conditions, for young people, older workers and persons with caring responsibilities in order to promote their vocational integration or ensure their protection.'[3]

It is worth pointing out that the example in the Directive refers to protecting young and old – it is not limited to older people (unlike the Government's example mentioned above in the 'Coming of Age' consultation paper).

Further, the example in the Directive is given immediately after a reference to 'legitimate employment policy, labour market and vocational training objectives'.[4] This would imply that the Directive envisages a policy which is addressing issues at a societal level rather than at the level of an individual business.

It may be that this aim is more relevant to Member States' arguments about justifying laws than employers' best practices.[5]

The idea of 'promoting vocational integration' also makes more sense in the context of a nation's concerns than those of one organisation. Finally, surely the real aims in the Directive's example are those of 'promoting vocational integration' and 'ensuring the protection' of certain categories of workers rather than crudely aiming to recruit more of a certain age group. The Directive reflects a difference in approach to the discussion about positive discrimination on the continent. In some other European Union (EU) Member States there is greater scope for positive discrimination than our own rather limited concept of 'positive action'.

Article 141(4) of the EC Treaty explicitly allows member states 'to adopt or maintain measures providing *specific advantages* in order to make it easier for the under-represented sex to pursue a vocational activity or to prevent or compensate for disadvantages in professional careers'. Similarly art 2(4) of the Equal Treatment Directive states that the Directive 'shall be without prejudice to measures to promote equal opportunity for men and women, in particular by removing existing inequalities which affect women's opportunities in the areas referred to in art 1(1)'

Some other EU Member States have positive action legislation that allows an employer to select the person from the under-represented gender where two candidates are equal in all respects. The ECJ has ruled in favour of such an approach.[6]

The cases above (all relating to sex discrimination) effectively state that a woman, where women are under-represented, may be granted preference over a competitor of the opposite sex if they are in all respects equivalent in terms of merit. Such an approach would amount to unlawful discrimination under UK law.

1 'Equality and Diversity: Coming of Age', DTI, 2005, p 33, para 4.1.17.
2 'Equality and Diversity: Coming of Age', DTI, 2005, p 34, para 4.1.18.
3 See art 6.1(a).
4 See art 6.1.
5 See **4.7.4**.
6 *Marschall v Land Nordrhein-Westfallen* (EOR 77) [1998] IRLR 39; *Application by Badeck & others v Hessischer Ministerprasident* (EOR 92) [2000] IRLR 432; *Abrahamsson and Anderson (applicants) v Fogelqvist (respondent)* [2000] IRLR 732.

4.7.6 Proportionality

The second half of the justification test is that of proportionality. Proportionality requires a consideration of whether or not the same legitimate aim could be achieved without the same discriminatory impact. If the aim could be achieved in another manner without discrimination, or with less discrimination, this should be preferred.

Example:

An employer limits its recruitment for manual labourers to those under 55 years. It seeks to justify this on the basis that it is a physically demanding job and it is essential that those employed are fit, healthy and able to do the job properly without endangering health and safety. Although these are likely to be legitimate aims, the assumptions are based on a stereotypical view of people over 55 years. It may be true as a generalised statement that people under 55 years will be, on average, more physically fit. However, there will be many exceptions on an individual basis. The employer's aims can be achieved in a less discriminatory manner by testing fitness levels. An employment tribunal would almost certainly expect the employer to make a case-by-case assessment of health and fitness.

Proportionality also requires a balancing exercise between the respondent and claimant, which considers whether the benefits of the legitimate aim significantly outweighs the discriminatory effect. And lastly, it requires that the discriminatory treatment actually does achieve or contribute towards the aim. It is no good an employer trying to argue that it is justified in paying more to shelf-stacking staff with 10 years' experience than those with five years' experience in order to reward their greater expertise if that extra five years' experience does not actually increase expertise.

Example:

Ace Airlines wants to have a retirement age of 40 for flight attendants. It has two reasons. The first is that it thinks it will make its business more attractive if it has younger, 'better-looking' flight attendants and more people will book flights. The second is for health and safety reasons, as flight attendants are responsible for the health and safety of passengers. It says that it needs to be sure that the flight attendants are sufficiently physically fit to be able to help passengers if there is an emergency. The aim of preserving health and safety is legitimate and the aim of meeting customer needs, a more contentious one.[1] But, in any event, is a retirement age of 40 a proportionate way to achieve them?

Almost certainly it is not. When balancing the benefits of the legitimate aim against the discriminatory effect, it is likely that a tribunal would think that health and safety is of greater importance than the business benefits of employing younger people. However, the health and safety objectives could probably be met by a different measure that has a smaller discriminatory effect, like testing applicants' physical fitness. In any event, the cut-off age of 40 is very low if the aim is to ensure physical fitness – it is difficult to see why, for example, a 50-year-old would not have sufficient physical fitness to do the job. Finally, if Ace Airlines does want to attempt to justify the retirement age on this basis it will need some evidence that the retirement age of 40 actually contributes to the aim. So, it would need to show that having younger flight attendants does improve business performance and safeguards health and safety. It may well be that it would struggle to show this.

1 **Chapter 5**, **5.3.3(c)** and **(h)**.

4.7.7 Timing of justification

Employers will often find themselves called upon to justify age discriminatory rules or practices that were introduced long before the Regulations came into force. In many cases, there will be no records of the reasons for the rule or practice and those responsible for them will have long since left.

However, it is clear that the employer is free to justify the rule at the time of the challenge even if its justification may well differ from the reasons of those originally responsible for the rule or practice.

The ECJ held in *Schönheit v Stadt Frankfurt am Main*[1]:

> 'However, a difference in treatment between men and women may be justified, depending on the circumstances, by reasons other than those put forward when the measure introducing the differential treatment was adopted.
>
> It is for . . . the party to the main proceedings who invokes it, to establish before the national court that there are objective reasons unrelated to any discrimination on grounds of sex such as to justify the measure concerned . . .and they are not bound in that respect by the intention expressed when the measure was adopted.'

The EAT decision in *Secretary of State for Trade and Industry v Rutherford (No 2)*[2] is another example of assessing the justification of allegedly discriminatory measures at the time of the claim and not the time the measure was originally introduced.[3]

There would, therefore, seem no reason why, in justifying the rule or practice, the employer cannot justify it not merely by the importance of the rule or practice in achieving its legitimate aim but also by the detrimental consequences of having to change a rule or practice that predated the Regulations. Often the detrimental consequence of removing the discrimination will be costly[4] but it could go further. In *Cross*[5] the employment tribunal accepted 'maintaining the existing terms and conditions of employment so far as they relate to retirement and access to pensions'[6] as a legitimate aim and this went unchallenged at the EAT.[7]

Example:

Silvermeadows Ltd has an enhanced redundancy policy which provides for redundancy payments to be calculated on the basis of a month's pay for each year of service. This is challenged as being indirectly age discriminatory as it disadvantages younger staff (for a detailed consideration of the justification of enhanced redundancy schemes see **Chapter 11**). The scheme was set up in 1963 and nobody who was around at that time still remains in employment. Unsurprisingly, there are also no records explaining the rationale of those who had drafted the scheme. In justifying the scheme, Silvermeadows Ltd would be entitled to rely on its reasons in not amending the scheme at the point of challenge. It would, it seems, be entitled to take into account the expectations of those in employment. Levelling up would be unrealistic as all payments would then be calculated on the maximum years of service. Any other approach would result in winners and losers and longer serving staff losing out on payments they would have expected upon redundancy.

1 [2004] IRLR 983, at [86] and [87].
2 [2003] IRLR 858.
3 *Secretary of State for Trade and Industry* [2003] IRLR 858 at [159] and [167]–[170].
4 See **4.7.5(a)**.
5 [2005] IRLR 423 – see **4.7.5(a)**.
6 *Cross* [2005] IRLR 423 at [58].
7 *Cross* [2005] IRLR 423 at [58] and [59].

4.7.8 Justification standard and exceptions

The Regulations contain various exceptions[1] Courts and tribunals will be called upon to assess the justification of otherwise age discriminatory rules or practices which correspond closely to rules or practices which would fall within one of the exceptions and thus be lawful but which do not satisfy all the conditions.

It could be argued that the government has carefully set out the conditions to be satisfied to fall within one of the exceptions and that, if the conditions are not satisfied, it should be assumed that the rule or practice should not be justified as otherwise the exception would have been drafted widely enough to encompass it.

On the other hand, the opposite could be argued, namely that the government considers rules or practices that come within the exceptions as legitimate. A rule or practice which almost falls within an exception is, therefore, likely to be justified and an employment tribunal would be entitled to take the proximity to an exception into account.

It is, however, contended that neither of these approaches is correct. An employment tribunal faced with a challenge to a rule or practice that nearly satisfies the conditions to come within an exception should consider its justification on the normal basis – does it represent a proportionate means of achieving a legitimate aim? It is quite likely that an employer would be able to satisfy this test if the rule or practice resembles one which would come within the exception but it would be wrong to take into account the proximity to the exception in coming to this conclusion.

Example:

Again, using Silvermeadows as an example. It decides to amend its redundancy schemes so that it mirrors the statutory scheme in all respects save that it decides not to cap the calculation at 20 years' service.[1] The scheme does not, therefore, come within the enhanced redundancy exception. Should a tribunal considering the justification of this scheme say: (a) that it is so close to the exception that it must be justified; (b) that as it falls outside an exception covering enhanced redundancy payment, it is unlikely to be justified; or (c) that the exception is irrelevant and the discriminatory impact must be balanced against the employer's legitimate aims in the normal way? It is suggested that the third analysis is correct and, on these facts, the scheme is probably lawful.

1 See **Chapter 11, 11.5.3(b)**(iii) for specific discussion of this point.

---

1 See regs 27–34.

Chapter 5

Recruitment

5.1 Introduction

Effective antidiscrimination laws must, of course, protect those seeking work as well as those already working and the Regulations, like all other UK antidiscrimination legislation, make it unlawful for employers to discriminate in relation to recruitment.[1]

This protection covers not only prospective employees, but also those seeking work in other capacities, such as self-employment, as a partner or office holder, as a contract worker or via an employment agency.[2]

The Directive makes it clear that the age laws that Member States must introduce must extend to:

> '... conditions for access to employment, to self-employment or to occupation, including selection criteria and recruitment conditions whatever the branch of activity and at all levels of the professional hierarchy ...'[3]

In the context of age discrimination, the Directive sets out particular aims of the age laws including the 'social and economic integration of elderly ... people'[4] and 'encouraging diversity in the workforce'.[5]

The Preamble to the Directive emphasises that it does not require 'the recruitment ... of an individual who is not competent, capable and available to perform the essential functions of the post concerned ...'[6] Whilst there is no express statement to this effect in the Regulations, they do make it possible for an employer to argue that both direct and indirect age discrimination in recruitment are legally justified.

In this chapter we consider:

- the types of workers who are covered by the Regulations relating to recruitment;
- the circumstances in which age limits in recruitment might either come within one of the exceptions within the Regulations or be justifiable;
- aspects of recruitment which might be indirectly discriminatory;
- how age discrimination laws might affect different stages of the recruitment process; and
- how age limits might be covered by other discrimination laws.

1 **Chapter 3, 3.3.12.**
2 **Chapter 3, 3.3.12.**
3 See art 3.
4 Preamble para 6.
5 Preamble para 25.
6 Preamble para 17.

5.2 Scope of the regulations

Chapter 3 considers the scope of the Regulations in detail. We consider in the following text, their scope in the context of recruitment.

5.2.1 Recruitment of employees

In relation to the recruitment of employees[1] the Regulations state:

> 'It is unlawful for an employer, in relation to employment by him at an establishment in Great Britain, to discriminate against a person:
>
> (a) in the arrangements he makes for the purpose of determining to whom he should offer employment;
>
> (b) in the terms on which he offers that person employment; or
>
> (c) by refusing to offer, or deliberately not offering, him employment.'[2]

The meaning of 'arrangements' in this context is considered below[3] and the issue of age discrimination in the terms on which employment is offered is covered in **Chapter 6**.

1 **Chapter 3, 3.3.1** for definition of employee.
2 See reg 7(1).
3 See **5.6**.

5.2.2 Recruitment of contract workers

The Regulations also prevent discrimination based on age by a 'principal' (a person to whom the contract worker is supplied by his employer) against a contract worker.

The Regulations expressly prevent age discrimination against a contract worker by a principal in relation to:

- the terms on which the principal allows the contract worker to work;
- the termination of the relationship;
- access to benefits; or
- subjecting him to any other detriment.[1]

They do not, however, specifically prevent discrimination by the principal in respect of the recruitment of contract workers. Nonetheless, the case of *BP Chemicals v Gillick*[2] suggests that the laws preventing discrimination against contract workers are not limited to those who are actually working. This means they may also cover discrimination in the recruitment of contract workers.

Ms Gillick had been supplied by a recruitment agency to work at BP. She stopped work due to pregnancy and when she asked to return to work, BP refused to give her the job back. The Employment Appeal Tribunal held that she was a contract worker under the terms of the Sex Discrimination Act 1975 (SDA) and that the laws protected her even though she was not working for BP at the time. In the (EAT's) view, it would be wrong to construe these provisions of the SDA as 'a prohibition against discrimination against a woman contract worker who is actually working but not prohibiting discrimination in refusing to let her get her foot in the door at all.'

Since the provisions relating to contract workers in the Regulations are similar to those under the SDA it is likely that they too will be held to apply to the recruitment of contract workers.

1 See reg 9 – **Chapter 3, 3.3.3** for definition of contract workers.
2 *BP Chemicals v (1) Ms M Gillick* and (2) *Roevin Management Services Ltd* [1993] IRLR 437.

5.2.3 Recruitment of officeholders

Regulation 12 covers the recruitment of officeholders. Regulation 12(1) states:

> 'It is unlawful for a relevant person, in relation to an appointment to an office or post to which this regulation applies, to discriminate against a person:
>
> (a) in the arrangements which he makes for the purpose of determining to whom the appointment should be offered;
>
> (b) in the terms on which he offers him the appointment; or
>
> (c) by refusing to offer him the appointment.'

Regulation 12(2) covers government appointments.[1]

The meaning of 'arrangements' is considered below[2] and the issues of age discrimination in the terms on which the appointment is offered is considered in **Chapter 6**.

A 'relevant person' is defined as:

> '(i) any person with power to make or terminate appointments to the office or post, or to determine the terms of appointment,
>
> (ii) any person with power to determine the working conditions of a person appointed to the office or post in relation to opportunities for promotion, a transfer, training or for receiving any other benefit, and
>
> (iii) any person or body referred to in paragraph (8)(b)[3] on whose recommendation or subject to whose approval appointments are made to the office or post'.

1 Any office or post to which appointments are made by (or on the recommendation of or subject to the approval of) a Minister of the Crown, a government department, the National Assembly for Wales or any part of the Scottish Administration.
2 See **5.6**.
3 Government appointments.

5.2.4 Recruitment of other workers

Specific provisions within the Regulations cover the offering of pupillage by barristers, barristers' clerks or advocates or the offer of a tenancy by barristers or barristers' clerks[1] and the offer of partnership by firms.[2]

1 See regs 15 and 16.
2 See reg 17.

5.3 Direct discrimination in recruitment

5.3.1 Introduction

Direct age discrimination occurs when someone is treated less favourably, on the grounds of their age (or their apparent age) than others would be treated in similar circumstances.[1] The distinction between direct and indirect discrimination is not always clearcut.[2]

In the context of recruitment, direct discrimination tends to occur where:

(a) an age limit is specified for a particular role; or

(b) there is no express age limit specified, but the claimant asserts that the employer applied one in practice.

These issues are explored in more detail in this section. Indirect discrimination in recruitment is considered in the next section.

Age limits are sometimes used overtly, where an upper or lower age limit (or an age range) is specified for appropriate candidates or, more often, covertly as an unwritten rule or policy. The ACAS Guidance[3] encourages employers to base decisions about recruitment on the skills and abilities required to do the job.

Unlike in other UK discrimination laws, direct age discrimination in recruitment will not be unlawful if either:

- one of the exceptions to the Regulations applies[4]; or
- the employer can objectively justify the discriminatory treatment.[5]

1 For a more detailed explanation of direct age discrimination, see **Chapter 4**, **4.2**.
2 **Chapter 4**, **4.2**.
3 ACAS Guidance, *Age and the Workplace: Putting the Employment Equality (Age) Regulations 2006 into practice* (ACAS) p11.
4 See the overview in **Chapter 2**; **5.3.2**.
5 See **5.3.3**.

5.3.2 Exceptions

Direct discrimination will not be unlawful and will, therefore, not have to be justified if it falls within one of the exceptions in the Regulations. The exceptions relevant to recruitment are that:

(a) age is a 'genuine occupational requirement' of the post (reg 8);

(b) the employer is taking positive action (reg 29);

(c) the candidate is within six months of the employer's normal retirement age or is over the normal retirement age (reg 7(4));
(d) the employer's actions are done in order to comply with a statutory requirement (reg 27); and
(e) the employer's actions are done for the purpose of safeguarding national security (reg 28).

(a) Genuine occupational requirements (Regulation 8)

The Regulations contain a specific exception which allows an employer to discriminate against a person in recruitment where:

> 'having regard to the nature of the employment or the context in which it is carried out:
>
> (a) possessing a characteristic related to age is a genuine and determining occupational requirement; and
> (b) it is proportionate to apply that requirement in the particular case; and
> (c) either:
>   (a) the person to whom that requirement is applied does not meet it; or
>   (b) the employer is not satisfied, and in all the circumstances it is reasonable for him not to be satisfied, that the person meets it.'[1]

This is known as the genuine occupational requirement (GOR) exception. The GOR exception is also contained in other UK discrimination legislation and is expressly permitted under the Directive.[2] It is most likely to apply where having a particular characteristic related to age is needed for the purposes of authenticity, for example in fields of modelling or acting.

Example:

A television company recruiting for a pensioner in a soap opera rejects a person on audition who looks younger than 65.

This is direct discrimination on grounds of apparent age. However, an employment tribunal is likely to accept that this kind of scenario falls within the GOR exception, ie that appearing to be over 65 years is a genuine and determining occupational requirement bearing in mind the nature of the rôle. The requirement seems proportionate in the circumstances, particularly as the television company has restricted the rôle to those who look over 65 years, rather than those who are actually over 65 years.

The television company may even be able to reject a candidate before audition if, in all the circumstances, it is reasonable for it to be satisfied that the candidate does not meet the requirement. For example, it may be reasonable to reject a candidate whose CV says he is 30 years. If it says he is, say, 58 years, it is less likely to be reasonable to reject him based on his age without first seeing him and assessing how old he looks.

It is possible for an employer seeking to defend a directly discriminatory recruitment practice to claim both that he has an objective justification and, in the alternative, that there is a GOR exception.[3]

The ACAS guidance on the GOR exception says that it will only apply in 'very limited circumstances', although it cites an example which is wider than the 'authenticity of roles' case referred to above:

> 'An organisation advising on and promoting rights for older people may be able to show that it is essential that its chief executive – who will be the public face of the organisation – is of a certain age. The age of the holder of the post may be a genuine occupational requirement.'[4]

Whilst employment tribunals may interpret the GOR exception as widely as this, it would seem to be contrary to the principles of the Directive to do so. Certainly, the government in its consultation paper, 'Coming of Age', said it considered age will only be a genuine occupational requirement in very few cases.[5]

The Race Relations Act contains analogous genuine occupational requirement provisions.[6] These provisions were only introduced in 2003.[7] The Act also contains similar 'genuine occupational qualification' (GOQ) provisions.[8] These provisions lists situations in which being of a particular racial group can be a lawful requirement for a job. These include certain jobs where being of a racial group is necessary for reasons of authenticity and where:

> 'the holder of the job provides persons of that racial group with personal services promoting their welfare, and those services can most effectively be provided by a person of that racial group.'[9]

It seems uncontroversial that demands of authenticity can potentially amount to a GOR under the Regulations. It seems less clear whether tribunals will accept a GOR analogous to the personal services GOQ in the Race Relations Act.

Example:

An inner city youth club that aims to keep the local youth out of trouble recruits a youth centre manager. It believes that if it recruits a manager much older than the people it is aiming to attract, they will be less likely to attend as they will not consider an older worker as being in tune with their culture. It is possible, but far from sure, that the youth club might be able to show that the age limit represents a genuine occupational requirement. It therefore argues that being under 30 years is a genuine occupational requirement for the post.

The GOR exception only applies in relation to recruitment arrangements and recruitment decisions – it does not apply to the terms on which employment is offered. This means that even if an employer is legally allowed to recruit someone based on age (because it is a genuine and determining requirement of the post) he must not apply detrimental terms to that person because of this, unless there is an objective justification for doing so.

1 See reg 8.
2 See art 4.
3 See also example in **5.3.3(b)**.
4 ACAS Guidance, *Age and the Workplace: Putting the Employment Equality (Age) Regulations 2006 into practice* (ACAS) p 35.
5 'Equality and Diversity: Coming of Age', DTI, July 2005, p 36.
6 See s 4A of the Race Relations Act 1996.
7 By the Race Relations Act 1996 (Amendment) Regulations 2003, SI 2003/1626, reg 7 to comply with EC Directive 2000/43 implementing the principle of equal treatment between persons irrespective of racial or ethnic origin.
8 See s 5 of the Race Relations Act 1996.
9 See s 5(2) (d) of the Race Relations Act 1996.

(b) Positive action (Regulation 29)

The Regulations specifically allow employers to take positive action to try to encourage applicants of a particular age to apply for positions where this age group is under represented – a practice which might otherwise be direct age discrimination. The Directive states that:

> 'with a view to ensuring full equality in practice, the principle of equal treatment shall not prevent any Member State from maintaining or adopting specific measures to prevent or compensate for disadvantages linked to [age].'[1]

Recruitment

This has been incorporated into the Regulations as a specific exception for positive action[2] which applies to recruitment and to training.[3]

In the context of recruitment, the exception makes clear that the Regulations do not make unlawful:

> 'any act done in or in connection with . . . encouraging persons of a particular age or age group to take advantage of opportunities for doing particular work where it reasonably appears to the person doing the act that it prevents or compensates for disadvantages linked to age suffered by persons of that age or age group doing that work or likely to take up that work.'[4]

Example:

Telejet has customer services staff who are generally young and it wants to take steps to improve age diversity within this group of employees. It decides to state on its job advertisement that, whilst it will recruit based on merit, it would particularly encourage those over the age of 40 to apply. Although Telejet receives more applications from older candidates than it has on previous occasions, it still recruits based on merit, ie on who has demonstrated that they have the skills necessary for the role and performed best at interview.

Placing an advertisement which encourages older people to take advantage of the opportunity to apply for a customer services position is likely to fall within the positive action exception. It may otherwise have been an age discriminatory arrangement which would have had to be objectively justified.

To fall within the exception Telejet must reasonably believe that this kind of action will improve the lot of people in the disadvantaged age group. This appears to be the case here, as Telejet has evidence which demonstrates that its customer service staff are generally young. Placing an advertisement encouraging applicants over the age of 40 is likely to help it redress this imbalance.

In this example, Telejet takes positive action by stating in the job advertisement that they encourage applications from the over 40s. Other options might be to advertise in websites or publications which target that age group or in places where they meet. For example, advertising in broadsheet newspapers may target older applicants more effectively than advertising on the web.

'Positive action – not positive discrimination'

Positive action is allowed under this exception, positive discrimination is not. Positive discrimination means compensating for the disadvantages suffered by a particular age group by giving a candidate in that age group preferential treatment because of their age.

The UK courts and tribunals have adopted a narrower definition of positive action than in many continental jurisdictions.[5]

The Directive contains as an example of potentially justified direct age discrimination:

> 'the setting of special conditions on access to employment and vocational training, employment and occupation . . . for young people, older people or persons with caring responsibilities in order to promote their vocational integration or ensure their protection.'[6]

This was replicated in the draft Regulations but removed from the final version. Whilst promoting greater diversity is a legitimate and admirable aim, positive discrimination is still discrimination and not something the UK Courts and Tribunals are likely to accept. An employer will be acting unlawfully under UK law if it recruits an older worker in preference to a better qualified younger one, in order to promote greater diversity.

Example:

Following on from the example above, Telejet decides that the steps it has taken to carry out positive action have not done enough to redress the age imbalance in its customer service staff. In its next recruitment round the company limits applications to those over the age of 40.

This is positive discrimination and will be unlawful direct age discrimination unless it can be objectively justified, which is very unlikely.

The Directive gives another example where different treatment based on age might be justified, namely 'the fixing of minimum conditions of age, professional experience or seniority in service for access to employment . . .'[7] The Directive does not identify what the employer's possible aim might be in setting 'a minimum condition of age' for a post. The juxtaposition with professional experience or seniority suggests the drafter had in mind situations, where being older makes one better equipped to do the job.

However, it is difficult to envisage any example where this is likely be considered an objective justification for a minimum age limit under UK law.

1 See 333 See art 7.
2 See reg 29.
3 **Chapter 7, 7.2** on training opportunities in employment and **Chapter 13, 13.7**.
4 See reg 29(1).
5 **Chapter 4, 4.7.5(b)**.
6 See art 6(1)(a).
7 See art 6(1)(b).

(c) Proximity to or over the age of retirement (Regulation 7(4))

The Regulations contain a specific exception allowing employers to reject, on the grounds of age, certain applicants who are near or over retirement age.

It is not unlawful for an employer to discriminate against a person in relation to the arrangements made for determining to whom he should offer employment or refusing to offer or deliberately not offering employment to that person if:

- the person's age is greater than the employer's normal retirement age or, if the employer does not have a normal retirement age, the age of 65[1]; or
- the person would, within a period of six months from the date of his application to the employer, reach the employer's normal retirement age, or, if the employer does not have a normal retirement age, the age of 65.'[2]

Example:

An employer has a normal retirement age of 68. An individual applies for a job with the employer and at the time of making his application he is aged 67 and 8 months.

The employer is entitled to reject the candidate as he would reach the employer's normal retirement age within six months from the date of his application.

The employer decides to abolish its retirement age. The same individual applies for a job. The employer can still safely reject the application as, in the absence of a retirement age, the employer can reject anyone within six months of or over their 65th birthday.

The advantage of this exception is that it allows employers to reject candidates who are close to or beyond its normal retirement age without the need to objectively justify such treatment.

It also ties in with the statutory duty to consider whether employees should be allowed to work beyond retirement – if employers were to recruit a candidate who will reach their normal retirement age within six months, they would automatically be in breach of their statutory duty as they would have failed to notify the employee of their intended retirement date between 12 and 6 months before retirement[3]

If the employer believes that it is reasonable to reject candidates who have longer than six months to go until retirement, for example because of the training requirements of the post or the need for a reasonable period in employment before retirement, then the normal principles of objective justification will apply. This is considered below.[4]

Employers are allowed to reject candidates who are within six months of its normal retirement age without the need to objectively justify such treatment even if:

- it regularly allows employees to work beyond retirement;
- it regularly employs staff on contracts of less than six months; or
- there is a high turnover of staff so that many leave within their first six months.

In each of these examples, it might be difficult for the employer to have objectively justified rejecting the candidate with, say, five months to go before he reached the employer's normal retirement age if it would not have relied on the exception.

Example:

A department store has a normal retirement age of 65. It recruits additional employees on fixed-term contracts for six weeks over the busy Christmas and New Year period.

The department store would be entitled to reject a candidate who will reach the age of 65 within a period of six months from the date of his application, even if he could have worked for the entire period of the fixed-term contract whilst under the age of 65.

This exception only applies to an applicant who is within a period of six months of retirement at the date of his application. 'Date of application' is not defined in the Regulations.

If 'the date of his application' means the date on which an application form or CV is received by the employer, then an individual could apply for a position with an employer who was a retirement age of 68 when he is aged 67 and 5 months and the employer would not be able to rely on the exception even if the individual would be aged 67 and 8 months by the time he is interviewed.

It may be that the employment tribunals will interpret the date of application broadly and will include the decision-making process as part of the application process. If they do not, then an employer in the situation described above will have to objectively justify any rejection on the application based on a reasonable period before retirement[1].

1 See **5.33(f)**.

This exception relating to proximity to retirement age and post-retirement age candidates was not in the first draft of the Regulations but was inserted into the final version. This eliminated the anomaly highlighted during the consultation process that the draft Regulations allowed an employer to retire an employee lawfully at the age of 65 (or its normal retirement age if higher) but left him exposed to an age discrimination claim if, after being retired, the employee reapplied for his or her job and was rejected.

Example:

Sara is approaching the age of 65, which is the employer's normal retirement age. Sara is notified (within the correct time limits) of her right to request to stay on beyond retirement. She applies to stay on but her application is refused and her appeal against this is rejected. One of the reasons for refusing her request is that her retirement is seen as an opportunity to reduce headcount as she will not be replaced. The employer retires her and is safe from claims of age discrimination and unfair dismissal as it has complied with the retirement procedure.

Six months after her lawful retirement, Sara sees an advertisement for her position. She is upset about this and applies for the position.

The employer is entitled to reject her application simply because she is over its normal retirement age. The fact that the employer may have lied about the reasons for retiring her is irrelevant – it does not affect the validity of her retirement (assuming it was not discriminatory for a reason other than age), nor does it give her any right to be given her old job back.[1]

1 For further detail on the retirement procedure see **Chapter 12, 12.9**.

This proximity to retirement/post-retirement age exception only applies in relation to recruitment arrangements and recruitment decisions – it does not apply to the terms on which employment is offered. An employer with a normal retirement age of 65 could not, therefore, offer employment to a 68 year old on the condition that he agrees to less favourable terms of employment than those on offer to the under 65s. This would be direct age discrimination outside the scope of the exception and, as such, would be unlawful unless objectively justifiable (which is very unlikely).

The exception only applies to the recruitment of employees and not to the recruitment of people who contract personally to do work, eg the self employed, contract or agency workers or partners. In relation to these individuals, a refusal to recruit on grounds of age would have to be justified in each case. This is because the exception applies only to those who, should they be recruited, would be covered by the exception for retirement,[5] an exception which only applies to employees as defined in the Employment Rights Act 1996.[6]

An astute employee might suggest he continues after retirement in a self-employed capacity. If the employer rejects this on the grounds of age, the employee might, nonetheless, be able to claim under the Regulations.

Example:

Kate reaches her company's normal retirement age of 65 and her request to stay on is rejected. The company has some self-employed consultants working for it and so Kate applies to return on a self-employed basis. The company rejects her application as she has passed its retirement age.

Kate would seem to have a strong age discrimination claim as the company's only reason for rejecting her is her age. It cannot rely on the reg 7(4) exception (relating to applicants who are over, or within six months of, retirement age) as this only covers employees and not the self-employed.

Of course, if the company rejects Kate because the work cannot be done on a self-employed basis rather than because of her age, this would not amount to age discrimination.

The exception only applies where the employer's normal retirement age is 65 or over or if it does not have a normal retirement age. If the employer adopts a retirement age which is below the age of 65, then a refusal to employ a person who is less than six months from or is over that retirement age would be unlawful unless the employer could objectively justify that refusal.

A practical issue for an employer who wants to rely on this exception is how to find out the applicant's age. This is considered below.[7]

1 See reg 7(4)(a).
2 See reg 7(4)(b).
3 **Chapter 12, 12.9.2**.
4 See **5.3.3(f)**.
5 See reg 7(5).
6 See reg 30 and ERA, s 230(1).
7 See **5.6.4**.

(d) Statutory authority (Regulation 27)

The Regulations contain an exception allowing an employer to discriminate on age grounds, if they are required by law to do so.[1] This includes age discrimination in relation to recruitment.

Example:

A restaurant chain states in a job advertisement for bar staff that applicants must be over the age of 18. This is direct age discrimination. However, it will not be unlawful as the requirement is being adopted by the employer in order to comply with a statutory provision, namely the prohibition on under 18s selling alcohol.

This exception only applies in relation to statutory provisions made under UK law. Therefore, if the employer makes recruitment decisions based on the laws of other countries, it will have to objectively justify any detrimental age-based treatment.

Employing children under the age of 16

There are complicated rules governing the employment of children (ie those under the age of 16) and any employer who discriminates on the grounds of age by complying with the rules is protected by the statutory authority exception.

There is a basic set of rules set out by statute,[2] but local authorities are permitted to issue bye-laws which deviate from them in certain respects. Employers will therefore need to check with their local council to find the laws applicable to them.

The laws relate to:

- the age at which children can do any work at all (whether paid or unpaid);
- the kind of work they can do;
- the number of hours per week (which varies according to whether it is during or outside of term time);
- the number of hours per day;
- the timing of those hours;
- the length of time between rest breaks; and
- the timing and length of holidays.

Examples of other rules relating to children and young people include restrictions on:

- under 18s serving and selling alcohol on licensed premises[3] or working in betting shops, casinos and other premises where betting takes place[4];
- under 21s driving certain types of vehicles, such as minibuses and buses; and
- under 18s working on seagoing ships.[5]

1 See reg 27.
2 The Children and Young Persons Act 1933 as amended.
3 Licensing Act 2003, s 153.
4 Gambling Act 2005, Pt 4.
5 Merchant Shipping Act 1995, s 55(1A).

(e) National security (Regulation 28)

The Regulations contain an exception allowing employers to discriminate on grounds of age for the purposes of safeguarding national security. In practice, such an exception is likely to be rarely, if ever, used.

5.3.3 Justification

In order to justify the use of age limits in recruitment the employer must demonstrate that the age limits represent a proportionate means of achieving a legitimate aim. This is considered in more detail in **Chapter 4**.[1] In practice, many of the situations in which an employer might seek to justify age discrimination will arise in recruitment. In this section, we consider the potentially legitimate aims an employer may put forward in order to justify the use of age limits[2]:

(a) cost;

(b) business needs/profitability;

(c) customer prejudice/preference;

(d) insurance costs;

(e) 'fitting in' with the team;

(f) training requirements of the post and a reasonable period before retirement;

(g) facilitation of employment planning;

(h) vocational integration;

(i) health and safety;

(j) promotion of diversity;

(k) employment-related insurance; and

(l) compliance with the law.

Many of these aims have been taken from examples given either in the Directive and/or by the government in its 'Coming of Age' consultation paper.[3] It is worth emphasising that, although the Directive and consultation papers provide some guidance in relation to justification and legitimate aims, each individual case will be decided on its own facts and circumstances and on the general principles of objective justification.

1 **Chapter 4**, **4.7**.
2 **Chapter 4**, **4.7.5**.
3 'Equality and Diversity: Coming of Age', DTI, July 2005, p 33, par 4.1.17.

(a) Cost

An employer may seek to justify direct age discrimination on the basis that it would be more expensive not to discriminate. This is considered in more detail in **Chapter 4**.[1] Case law suggests it is unlikely that cost alone will be accepted by tribunals as a sufficient justification.

As mentioned in **Chapter 4**, it is far from clear, however, that tribunals will adopt such a narrow view in age claims, particularly as the distinction between the aim of saving cost and other aims is often illusory – many other aims really amount to an effort to save costs. Further, it might be quite easy in practice to introduce secondary legitimate aims to legitimise the use of costs as an aim.

Examples:

An employer decides not to recruit drivers under the age of 25, as it will have to pay higher premiums on its car insurance to cover them. It is unlikely that the employer will be able to justify this discriminatory treatment simply because it may be more expensive not to discriminate.

An employer is entitled to pay young persons (18–21) less than over 21 year olds under the national minimum wage exceptions (reg 31[1]). A restaurant appoints a 19-year-old candidate in preference to a 23 year old only because they will be able to pay the 18 to 21 year olds less. On the face of it, the employer's aim would be cost and its legitimacy questionable. However, one would expect the decision to be lawful, particularly as the government's aim in maintaining a lower national minimum wage rate for young people is to encourage employers to recruit them (vocational integration). Perhaps the restaurant's best approach would be to cite both cost and vocational integration as its stated aims, although it is perhaps unlikely that a tribunal would believe that the latter was a genuine factor in its decision.

1 **Chapter 6, 6.4.5** for further details.

This issue can be illustrated by teachers' pay scales. Teachers' pay is governed by a six point pay spine largely linked to teaching experience. A school rejects a teacher with seven years teaching experience in favour of a less experienced teacher who will be at a lower point on the pay spine and cheaper. It does not enquire of the more experienced teacher if she will work for the pay of the less qualified teacher as it must adhere to prescribed pay scales. The more experienced teacher could bring an indirect age discrimination claim against the school and allege that its aim in selecting the less experienced teacher was purely to save costs. Both more and less experienced teachers might be able to challenge pay scales linked to experience: the less experienced teacher on the grounds that he is at least as competent as the more experienced teacher but is being paid less and experience disadvantages capable young teachers; the more experienced teacher on the grounds that he or she is being priced out of jobs by reason of age, when he might well be happy to work for the pay being offered to the less experienced teacher.

The argument that this policy is unjustifiable indirect age discrimination is supported by the US Supreme Court decision in *Markham v Geller*.[2]

1 **Chapter 4, 4.7.5(a)**.
2 [1981] 451 US 945.

(b) Business needs/profitability

The position is even less clear when the justification is not based on costs but on business needs or profitability. As stated in **Chapter 4**, 'Economic factors such as business needs and efficiency may be legitimate aims, but arguing that it could be more expensive not to discriminate will not in itself be a valid justification'.[1]

As also mentioned above, it is not always straightforward to distinguish cost from other economic justifications.

In the European Court of Justice (ECJ) case of *Jenkins v Kingsgate Ltd*,[2] the Court held that maximising the use of expensive machinery and encouraging productivity justified indirect sex discrimination. Leading counsel for the unsuccessful claimants in *Cross v British Airways*[3] sought to distinguish this from the aim of saving costs by arguing that it amounted to the aim of the efficient use of capital and labour. It is difficult to see any legitimate justification for this semantic distinction.

In the end most justifications come down to cost. The aim of a reasonable period before retirement, for example, represents little more than allowing the employer a fair return on his investment.

1 **Chapter 4, 4.7.5(a)**; 'Equality and Diversity: Coming of Age', DTI, July 2005, p 33, para 4.1.16.
2 [1981] ICR 592] – this case concerned a part-timer who was paid a lower hourly rate than a full timer doing the same work.
3 [2005] IRLR 423 – **Chapter 4, 4.7.5** for detailed consideration of the case.

(c) Customer prejudice/preference

There may be situations where an employer wishes to use an age limit when it feels under pressure from clients or customers to do so or when it believes that doing so will help attract or retain its target client base. In practice, justification of such treatment is likely to be closely linked to that of business needs and/or loss of profitability (for more on which, see the section (a) an cost and (b) an Business needs profitability above).

Examples:

In practice, although an employment tribunal may believe that maintaining profits and avoiding redundancies in the face of customer prejudice are legitimate aims, it is unlikely to find that they justify discriminatory treatment. This issue is considered in more detail in the example below.

An employer rejects a candidate for a job of door-to-door sales person because it discovers at the interview that he looks like a teenager even though he is in his early 30s. The employer believes that its customers will not buy its services from someone who looks this age, and employing the applicant would result in a loss of sales. A street-wear designer label wishes to recruit sales staff to work in its stores who are young and 'live the image'. They believe that this attracts the young people who wear their clothing to their stores. They restrict applications to those who are between the ages of 18 and 24.

An advertising agency rejects a 38-year-old applicant for a job on a particular client team because the client has specifically said it only wants young designers working on its projects. The employer directly discriminated against the candidate and it is unlikely that an employment tribunal will be sympathetic to a justification based simply on the assertion that it was carrying out client instructions. However, the agency may try to argue that if it did not comply with the client's discriminatory requirement of young designers the client would go elsewhere, resulting in significant loss of profits and potential redundancies. Presumably, the client may also be liable for aiding an act of discrimination.[1]

1 **Chapter 3**, **3.4.5** and reg 26.

This example raises various questions:

- Can the store argue that being young is a genuine occupational requirement?
- If not, what is its legitimate aim?
- Is the aim attracting younger customers?
- Or is the aim selling clothes?
- If it is the latter, is this in reality a cost or profitability/business need?
- Could the store add a second aim of having clothes modelled well, which needs younger people?

An employer in this situation might conceivably seek to rely on the genuine occupational requirement exception and argue that possessing a characteristic relating to age is a genuine and determining requirement of the role for example, because it is necessary for the shop assistant to be able to model the clothes they are selling.

The government has said that trying to attract a young target group cannot be a legitimate aim because it has an age-discriminatory aspect[1]. This came from an example in its 'Coming of Age' consultation paper very similar to the one above which stated:

> 'A retailer of trendy fashion items wants to employ young sales assistants because it believes this will contribute to its aim of targeting young buyers. Trying to attract a young client group will not be a legitimate aim because this has an age-discriminatory aspect.'

This example has attracted much comment. It is not too clear what is meant by the illegitimate aim having an age-discriminatory aspect. It cannot be right that targeting a product at a particular age group is now an illegitimate aim. It may well be that pandering to the customer prejudice is impermissible but that is not quite the same thing. It may well be that the example is designed to show that recruiting young people simply to attract a young clientele would not be justified. However, it leaves open the question of the aim of selling more clothes. As mentioned in **Chapter 4**[2], the degree of financial need on the part of the employer might be relevant. The 'Coming of Age' consultation paper has also suggested that economic factors such as business needs and considerations of efficiency may be legitimate aims.[3] Whilst it might seem difficult to reconcile these apparently contradictory statements in the situation faced by the retailer in our example, it may be possible to justify an aim which is not simply to attract younger buyers but to increase sales, particularly if it could show that if it does not do so it will go out of business with resultant job losses.

However, as stated above in the context of justifying indirect sex discrimination, the Employment Appeal Tribunal held that costs alone cannot constitute a legitimate aim. However, they did go on to find that it is appropriate to take costs into account in the balancing exercise in deciding whether or not the employer's discriminatory treatment is a proportionate means of achieving a legitimate aim.[4]

The company may be in a stronger position if it could argue that being able to model the clothing effectively is a second legitimate aim so that cost is then only one factor to be considered.

As stated above although an employment tribunal may believe that maintaining profits and avoiding redundancies are legitimate aims, it is unlikely to find that they justify discriminatory treatment where customer prejudice is involved. Certainly, customer prejudice would never be accepted as an excuse for other forms of discrimination, for example in relation to sex or race. Whilst direct age discrimination is different – in that direct age discrimination can be legally justified (whereas direct race or sex discrimination never can be) – it seems uncertain that the employment tribunals will allow a defence based on customer prejudice to succeed.

The existence of customer prejudice is highlighted by the callers into Radio 5 on the Friday before the Regulations came into force, whose principal concern seemed to be the likely impact of the Regulations on lap dancing clubs. It is submitted that an artificial age bar would be difficult to justify even here. Though in practice the demands of fitness and agility would dictate that most dancers will be young. Indeed, without some clear evidence a club might be at risk in making broad assumptions about the impact of recruiting older dancers on business.

A celebrated American case illustrates the potential for claims. In 1995, one of America's best known broadcasters, Janet Peckinpaugh, was dismissed from her newsreader post at the age of 44. Her employer, WFSB-TV, had organised viewer focus groups which identified a customer preference for older male newsreaders to be accompanied by younger female colleagues. Her employer felt obliged to respond to these findings in a competitive market and dismissed her. Whilst strictly speaking Ms Peckinpaugh won under sex, rather than age, discrimination laws the issues of gender and age were inextricably intertwined in the case. A jury awarded her US $8.3 million.

The issue of TV presenters is newsworthy at the time of writing, with allegations of ageism being reported in the press with the BBC's decision to replace Nick Ross as presenter of the celebrated Crimewatch TV programme, following on from the decision to replace other long-standing BBC presenters such as Anna Ford and Moira Stewart. In 2003 there were well-publicised allegations of ageism when Italy's public broadcaster RAI replaced 'continuity announcer' Alessandra Canale with a younger woman. Ms Canale was 38.[5]

1 'Equality and Diversity: Coming of Age', DTI, July 2005, para 4.1.18.
2 **Chapter 4, 4.7.5.**
3 See para 4.1.16.
4 *Cross v British Airways*, above.
5 The Guardian, 22 September 2003.

(d) 'Fitting in' with the employer

The use of age limits based on assumptions that candidates of a particular age or age group will or will not 'fit in' with the employer's business is unlikely to be viewed as a legitimate aim which can justify discriminatory treatment.

Example:

A small telesales company, Petittélé, has eight employees, all of whom are under the age of 30, are good friends and socialise together after work. This results in a stable workforce with high morale which translates into a productive team. Petittélé advertise for an additional member to join the team and decide not to shortlist any applicants over the age of 40, as they don't think older people will fit in with the team.

It is highly unlikely that Petittélé would be able to justify the age discrimination in its recruitment practice if it were to be challenged by an unsuccessful older candidate.

Even where there is no overt reference to age, an employer who uses the concept of 'fit' will also be vulnerable to claims that this is a mask for age discrimination.

(e) Training requirements of the post

Article 6 of the Directive gives Member States some flexibility to implement the Directive in a way which treats people differently on the grounds of age, provided that such differences of treatment can be objectively and reasonably justified by a legitimate aim. One example cited in art 6 of a difference in treatment that may be justified is 'the fixing of a maximum age for recruitment which is based on the training requirements of the post or the need for a reasonable period of employment before retirement . . .'.

Other than the exemption entitling the employer to disregard candidates within six months of the employer's retirement age,[1] there is no specific exception relating to the training requirements of a post in the Regulations. However, the examples in the Directive suggest that employers will be able to rely on training needs as a legitimate aim justifying the use of age limits in recruitment. This also appears to have been the view of the government, which cited the particular training requirements of the post in both of its consultation papers, 'Age Matters' and 'Coming of Age', as a legitimate aim which might justify differences in treatment.

Justifying the rejection of a candidate on the grounds that he is too old to meet the training requirements of the post will be particularly relevant where specific training requirements are set externally, for instance by a professional body.

Example:

The Law Society requires a person who wishes to become a solicitor to work as a trainee solicitor for two years.

A law firm with a retirement age of 65 should be able to objectively justify restricting trainee applications to those under the age of 63 based on the training requirements of the post.

Similar professions where age limits on recruitment may be justified include those, where employment and training are combined such as architects, doctors, accountants and air traffic controllers.

This justification may also be relevant where there are no training requirements for the post set by a professional body.

Example:

A manufacturing company is recruiting a trainee manager. It believes that it will take at least three years for the successful candidate to become sufficiently familiar with the business' various operations to enable him to fulfil a managerial role in the business.

If this is correct, it might be justifiable to reject a candidate who is within three years of his retirement age of 65.

---

1 See **5.3.2(c)** above and reg 7(8).

(f) A reasonable period before retirement

As mentioned in section (e) an the training requirements of the post above, art 6 of the Directive specifically gives the need for a reasonable period before retirement as an example of a legitimate aim, which could justify age limits in recruitment.

No doubt the government had in mind the aim of 'a reasonable period before retirement' to justify the specific exception (added to the final draft of the Regulations) allowing the rejection of an applicant who has passed or will reach the employer's retirement age within six months of the date of his application.[1] In this situation, 'retirement age' means either the employer's normal retirement age (which must be over 65) or, if there is no normal retirement age, the age of 65.[2]

However, there are also cases where it could be justifiable to reject candidates who are more than six months away from their normal retirement age, on the basis they will not have a reasonable period of work before retirement.

For example, an employer who provides costly and time consuming training will want to see a return on that investment. To achieve this, it may wish to set an upper age limit for applicants based not only on the training requirements of the post but also on them getting a reasonable period of work from them before they retire. The government, in its first 'Age Matters' consultation paper, acknowledged that:

> 'there are circumstances – usually to do with the return on investment in training and development – when the length of time a potential recruit would have with a company would not make business sense.'[3]

Examples:

Continuing the law firm example cited above, the same law firm may seek to limit applications to those under the age of 60 on the basis that they wish trainees not only to complete their training before retirement, but to work with them for a reasonable period before retirement. This latter requirement may be more difficult for the law firm to justify if, in practice, many trainees are not given the chance to stay with the firm on qualification.

Continuing the example of the management trainee, the company may well be justified not only in rejecting those over 62 years but those approaching this age. However, it will not always be easy to draw the line – a 60 year old? A 55 year old? A 50 year old? In making the case for this, the length of time the managers normally stay with the company will be relevant.

A call centre rejects a 64 year old as she will retire in 12 months' time at the company's retirement age of 65. In practice, however, there is a very high turnover of staff and few employees stay in the business for much longer than 12 months. In this case the company will probably struggle to justify rejecting the candidate by relying on the aim of 'a reasonable period before retirement'.

An employer will find it much easier to defend a claim based on a reasonable period before retirement or, indeed, the training requirements of the post if they have established, before a recruitment exercise, where they will draw the line. Without this, a claimant will find it easier to argue that, in reality, his rejection was due to unjustified age prejudice.

1 See reg 7(4).
2 See reg 7(5); **5.3.2**.
3 'Equality and Diversity: Age Matters', DTI, March 2003, p 43, para 7.3.

(g) Facilitation of employment planning

'Employment planning' means making decisions based on projections as to which positions are likely to need filling, at what level, when and how they will be filled. 'Facilitation of employment planning' may, in exceptional circumstances, be a specific aim which justifies different treatment, according to the government in its 'Age Matters' and 'Coming of Age' consultation papers.[1] It goes on to cite, by way of example, the situation where a business has a number of people approaching retirement age at the same time.

It seems reasonable that an employer in this situation should be allowed to prefer younger recruits to its workforce. However, in practice, determining the age limit to use will not be easy.

Example:

A small business has a number of senior employees who are over the age of 60 and are likely to retire in the next two to five years at the employer's normal retirement age of 65. It therefore wishes to recruit a number of younger employees to ensure that goodwill in the business is remaintained and client relationships are maintained and developed.

This may be a legitimate aim. However, setting an appropriate age limit may be difficult. If the employer were to set it at 40, a 41 year old is likely to be able to persuade an employment tribunal that he would have been able to contribute value to the organisation for over 20 years if he had not been prevented from applying on grounds of age. A limit of say 55 may be easier to justify.

The need for succession planning, which refers to the highest ranking jobs within an organisation, may also justify the use of age limits.

Example:

The CEO of a business will retire in two years' time when he reaches the company's normal retirement age of 65. There is no suitable internal candidate to take his place, so the business is planning to recruit externally someone who will be able to take over the reins of the company. Clearly the employer will need the successor to be younger than the current CEO – but how much younger? A requirement that the successor must be under the age of 60 will be easier to justify than a requirement that he be under the age of 50, with shades in between. In this case, the aim of succession planning might be difficult to differentiate in practice from aim of allowing a reasonable period before retirement.

It is not clear how far (if at all) employment tribunals will permit age limits in recruitment to be used for the purposes of employment or succession planning. The old model of younger recruits eventually filling the shoes of their older, more senior colleagues may now be obsolete with workers more likely to move jobs, retire early, be made redundant etc. Strong evidence to the contrary will be required to justify using age limits on recruitment for reasons relating to the structure of the workforce.

1 'Equality and Diversity: Age Matters', DTI, March 2003, p 16, para 3.15; 'Equality and Diversity: Coming of Age', DTI, July 2005, p 33, para 4.1.13.

(h) Vocational integration

Article 6 of the Directive gives another example of a situation where age limits may be justified, namely 'the setting of special conditions on access to employment ... for young people, older workers and persons with caring responsibilities in order to promote their vocational integration ...'.

As mentioned above, this is likely to be of less relevance to employers than to the government in setting its employment policy.[1]

The wording of art 6 suggests that it should be possible for an employer, in certain circumstances, to rely on vocational integration as a legitimate aim justifying the use of age limits. In the first draft of the Regulations, the government included 'the setting of requirements as to age in order to promote the vocational integration of people in a particular age group' as an example of treatment which an employment tribunal may find to be a proportionate means of achieving a legitimate aim, depending on the circumstances. However, the examples were removed from the final version of the Regulations. In practice, we expect that the employment tribunals will be reluctant to allow a justification based on vocational integration and will, instead, expect an employer who wishes to encourage it to take positive action rather than to positively discriminate.[2]

It is not entirely clear what is meant by 'vocational integration'. One obvious example is in the context of graduate recruitment. For example, an employer may perceive that graduate recruitment should be limited to those in their 20s on the basis that this gives younger people the opportunity to start their careers. However, the government's comments on graduate recruitment, namely that age limits should not be applied to such schemes, suggests that using age limits for this reason would not be justified.[3]

1 **Chapter 4, 4.7.4**; *Mangold v Helm* [2006] IRLR 143 – see **Chapter 4, 4.7.2**.
2 See **5.3.2(b)**.
3 See **5.4.3** and also 'Equality and Diversity: Coming of Age', DTI, March 2006, para 4.3.7.

(i) Health and safety considerations/demands of fitness or stamina

Another example given in art 6 of the Directive of a difference in treatment which may justify a Member State discriminating on grounds of age is 'the setting of special conditions on access to employment ... for young people, older workers and persons with caring responsibilities in order to ensure their protection ...'.

The government is likely to rely on this exception in relation to its provisions to protect the health and safety of younger workers.

In the 'Age Matters' and 'Coming of Age' consultation papers the government gave 'health, welfare and safety – for example, the protection of younger workers' as an example of a specific aim which may justify differences in treatment.[1] This was then included in the draft Regulations, with 'the setting of requirements as to age in order to ensure the protection ... of people in a particular age group' being cited as an example of treatment which, depending on the circumstances, a tribunal may find to be a proportionate means of achieving a legitimate aim. However, the examples were eventually removed from the final version of the Regulations.

In practice, clear medical evidence is likely to be necessary in order to justify the use of an age limit on grounds of health, safety or welfare. An employer will not be able to rely on assumptions or generalisations about the health, fitness or stamina of older workers.

If, on the other hand, an employer rejects a candidate on the basis of a *statutory requirement* which is designed to protect the health and safety of older or younger workers, there will be no need for objective justification – the employer will be able to rely on the specific statutory authority exception.[2]

Example:

An employer does not want to employ older staff to work at its factory. It believes that, in general, those over 50 years will be slower and make more mistakes which will, as a result, pose a health and safety risk to the applicant as well as to other employees.

The protection of employees on health and safety grounds will no doubt be a legitimate aim. In considering whether this aim justifies the use of age limits, an employment tribunal will consider whether age limits actually contribute to the pursuit of the aim. In the absence of strong medical evidence, it is unlikely that the employer will be able to show that this is the case.

Further, whilst the protection of the health and safety of employees is an important aim, the age limit has a high discriminatory impact – all those over the age of 50 are excluded, regardless of individual capability.

Finally, an employment tribunal will consider whether the aim can be adequately achieved by means which have a less discriminatory impact. One obvious alternative would be to carry out regular health checks for all staff.

An employer might also wish to consider using age as a proxy for fitness and stamina demands. An employer is even less likely to be able to rely on setting age limits as a proportionate means of achieving this aim than it is where health and safety issues arise.[3]

Example:

Get Fit Gyms imposes an age limit of 40 for a vacancy as a fitness instructor. It considers that the instructor will need to be fitter than its clients and that candidates over 40 are unlikely to have the required fitness for the job. This requirement is unlikely to be justified. Although the aim of fulfilling the reasonable demands of the job is legitimate, a more proportionate response would be to test fitness rather than use age as an unreliable proxy.

---

1 'Equality and Diversity: Age Matters', DTI, March 2003, p 16, para 3.15; 'Equality and Diversity: Coming of Age', DTI, July 2005, p 33, para 4.1.17.
2 See subsection **5.3.2(d)**.
3 **Chapter 9**, **9.3.1** and **9.5**.

(j) Promotion of diversity

Employers may wish to adopt age limits in order to promote diversity within its workforce. In the draft Regulations, the government cited the 'fixing of a minimum age to qualify for certain advantages linked to employment or occupation in order to recruit or retain older people' as an example of treatment which, depending on the circumstances, an employment tribunal may find to be a proportionate means of achieving a legitimate aim. This example was repeated from the Directive.[1]

It is also mentioned by the Home Office and the Association of Chief Police Officers as one of the aims justifying retirement ages for the police.[2]

However, this example, along with all the others, was removed from the final version of the Regulations and it is likely that tribunals will expect employers wishing to promote diversity to rely on the positive action exception. It seems unlikely that positive discrimination will be lawful under the Regulations. For consideration of the differences between positive action and positive discrimination, see above.[3]

See the consideration of whether age is a less serious ground of discrimination than other forms above at **4.7.1** of **Chapter 4**.

1 See art 6(2).
2 **Chapter 12**, **12.8.1(b)(i)**.
3 See **5.3.2(b)**.

(k) Employment-related insurance

There are a small number of occupations where compulsory insurance is necessary in order to carry out the job. For example, for a driving job car insurance will be required and many professions require professional indemnity insurance such as architects, solicitors and accountants.

In its 'Age Matters' consultation paper the government stated that where compulsory insurance is not available because of the applicant's age, employers would be justified in not recruiting him.[1] However, it went on to state that if the insurance is available but is more expensive for a particular age group then employers would have to 'refer to a real business need before they could justify discrimination on the basis of increased cost'.[2]

Employment-related insurance is referred to in **Chapter 6**.[3]

1 'Equality and Diversity: Age Matters', DTI, March 2003', paras 7.8 & 7.9.
2 See **5.3.3(a)**.
3 See **Chapter 6, 6.6.1**.

(l) Compliance with the law

There is a specific statutory authority examination which allong employers to discriminate if they are required by law to do so.[1] Employers should also be able to impose age limits in the rare cases where, to do otherwise would breach similar regulatory rules.

In many cases, the age limit will be an indirect consequence of a necessary qualification to do the job. For example, in order to have a licence to drive a larger goods vehicle, the individual must be 21 years. The requirement of the job is not to be 21 years old but to have the LGV licence. However, the minimum age limit is an indirect consequence of this requirement.

Similar rules apply with pilots of helicopters and small planes as the Civil Aviation Authority still imposes an upper age of 60 for solo pilots and 65 if flying with another pilot on board.[2]

1 See **5.3.2(d)**.
2 **Chapter 10**, **10.2.2**; **Chapter 12**, **12.8.1(b)(ii)**.

5.4 Indirect discrimination in recruitment

Indirect discrimination takes place when the employer applies an apparently age-neutral provision, criterion or practice to everyone, which in practice puts applicants of a particular age or age group at a particular disadvantage. For example, requiring a certain number of years experience may indirectly discriminate against younger candidates. Like direct discrimination, indirect discrimination may be justified if the employer can show that the provision, criterion or practice adopted is a proportionate means of achieving a legitimate aim. This is discussed in more detail in **Chapter 4.**[1]

Indirect discrimination in the context of recruitment may arise in the following circumstances (amongst others):

- vocational training;
- apprenticeship schemes;
- graduate recruitment and graduate training schemes;
- minimum experience requirements;
- maximum experience requirements; or
- requirements for 'flexibility'.

These are discussed in more detail below.

1 **Chapter 4**, **4.3**.

5.4.1 Vocational training

The provisions which make it unlawful to discriminate in the provision of vocational training are similar to those which apply to the recruitment of employees.

> 'It is unlawful . . . for any training provider to discriminate . . . :
>
> (a) in the arrangements he makes for the purpose of determining to whom he should offer training;
>
> (b) in the terms on which the training provider affords him access to training,

(c) by refusing or deliberately not affording him such access;

(d) by terminating his training; or

(e) by subjecting him to any other detriment during his training.'[1]

Training is defined widely in the Regulations so that it covers:

> '(a) all types and all levels of training which would help fit a person for any employment;
>
> (b) vocational guidance;
>
> (c) facilities for training;
>
> (d) practical work experience provided by an employer to a person whom he does not employ; and
>
> (e) any assessment related to the award of any professional or trade qualification.'[2]

It covers employers who provide any form of training including vacation placements or work experience schemes.

There is obviously scope for some uncertainty about what training would help fit a person for any employment. It is arguable that this could extend to most adult education classes such as language courses or pottery classes. It will be unlawful (direct discrimination) to place age limits on such schemes without an objective justification for doing so. It will also be unlawful to have pre-conditions for entry to such schemes which are unjustifiably indirectly discriminatory, for example by requiring applicants to be in their final year of university or recently graduated. The concerns about applying such conditions are considered in the following section.

Example:

FMCG Ltd operates a vacation placement scheme to graduates who are in their final year of university. Those who perform well during the vacation placement are likely to be offered a position on the employer's graduate recruitment scheme.

The requirement in relation to the vacation placement is indirectly discriminatory – whilst there may be some older students in their final year of university, the majority will be in their early 20s.

FMCG Ltd may seek to justify the requirement by saying it has the legitimate aim of vocational integration, namely giving those with little or no work experience the opportunity to gain experience in their industry. Even if an employment tribunal accepts this, it will need to balance it against the discriminatory impact of the requirement, which not only deprives older workers of the opportunity to gain experience with the employer but also has the knock-on effect of disadvantaging them in relation to the graduate recruitment scheme.

The tribunal will also consider whether FMCG Ltd's aim could have been achieved in a less discriminatory manner, for example by limiting applications to those who have not worked in the sector before. This would allow older workers who may be considering a career change the opportunity to apply.

It will also be unlawful to discriminate unjustifiably in the terms on which vocational training is provided.

Examples:

Barchester Adult Education Centre provides training courses. They provide discounted rates to the over 60s. This discriminates on the grounds of age. Assuming the training came within the definition of vocational training under the Regulations, this would be unlawful unless it could be justified. It is unlikely that the Centre could rely on assumption of the reduced income of the over 60s to justify the discount. They could try to rely on the vocational integration aim but this, too, is likely to be problematic. It is not targeted and would mean that the highly paid CEO of Barchester Industries would benefit from the discount in the same way as an unemployed 60-year-old.

---

1 See reg 20.
2 See reg 20(4).

5.4.2 Apprenticeship schemes

The government funding for apprenticeships is currently limited to those who are over 16 years and under 25 years on the date the apprenticeship begins. The government may well argue that this is justified by reference to the legitimate aim of vocational integration. The discriminatory impact will be lessened once the 'adult apprenticeships' come into operation, which the Learning and Skills Council are currently developing for people over 25 years. There is no exception in the Regulations allowing employers to limit candidates for apprenticeship, to those who are eligible for government funding (ie the under 25s) and to do so would be direct age discrimination.

5.4.3 Graduate recruitment and graduate training schemes

Historically, employers have applied age limits to graduate recruitment schemes. However, the government stated in its 'Coming of Age' consultation paper that such age limits would not be justified.[1]

Requiring applicants to have certain educational or academic qualifications for a role may be indirectly discriminatory. For example, requiring applicants to have three GCE A levels or equivalant may disadvantage older applicants, since the numbers gaining qualifications have increased significantly. For example, the numbers gaining two or more GCE A levels or equivalent has increased from 30 per cent in 1995–06 to 39 per cent in 2001–02.[2] Further, requiring a degree will exclude most applicants under the age of 21. Requiring an employee to be a graduate will similarly disadvantage older candidates, as the proportion of students graduating from tertiary education has also increased significantly in recent years. In the last 10 years the number students in further education in the United Kingdom increased from 1.72 million to 2.46 million.[3]

Similarly, requiring qualifications which were rare or did not exist when older candidates graduated may well be discriminatory.

Example:

24/7 News requires its graduate trainees to have Media Studies degree. Henry, 50-years-old, has worked in media for many years but graduated at a time when Media Studies degrees were rare. He should be able to show that this requirement places people over 50 years at particular disadvantage compared to those under 50 years. 24/7 News would then have to objectively justify this requirement which might prove difficult.

The number of students studying Media Studies increased between 1996–07 and 2005–06 from 4,888 to 26,820.[4]

The ACAS Guidance gives the following example:

> 'A local engineering company is looking for a new Personnel Officer and asks for applicants to be graduates and hold the IPD [now called the CIPD] qualification. As many more people attend university today than say 25 years ago, there is a lower chance that older Personnel Officers will be university graduates even though holding the IPD qualification and having considerable practical experience. This graduate requirement might thus be

> indirect age discrimination if the employer is unable to justify. Remember also that the [CIPD] qualification was formerly the IPM qualification.'[5]

Employers will need to consider whether these kinds of qualifications are really necessary and, if so, why. An applicant without a degree may still have the skills and abilities required for the post either through experience or a mix of experience and other types of qualifications. At the very least, it would be prudent to require a 'degree or equivalent qualification' to show that the absence of a degree is not a bar to a post.

With, as mentioned above, the number of high grades at A level having increased significantly in recent years, older candidates who do not have the grades for a particular post might argue that the requirement to have certain grades is indirectly age discriminatory opening up the debate about whether or not the examinations have become easier.

Example:

Bowman James, solicitors, require candidates for a post as a junior employment lawyer to have a minimum of 2 As and a B at A level. Jimmy, 45 years old, is not considered and has an A and 2 Bs claims that this requirement unlawfully indirectly discriminates on the grounds of age. He claims that his grades are the equivalent of 2 As and a B as the examinations are easier nowaday. The firm disputes this. In any event, Jimmy counters that even if they are not easier, the requirement puts those over 40 years at a particular disadvantage and, statistically, they are less likely to have the grades. The firm argues that the requirement is justified as they have scores of applicants, and so cannot interview them all and that this represents an objective and fair means of shortlisting. One would think that an employment tribunal would be sympathetic to Bowman James but one can see Jimmy's argument.

Similarly, many large employers who have in the past operated a 'graduate recruitment scheme' as a way of recruiting to positions which require a certain amount of technical and/or analytical skill are removing the word 'graduate' (for example, renaming them management training schemes) and opening them to those without degrees.

Another requirement that has historically been applied to these types of schemes is to require applicants not to have any previous work experience. This may exclude otherwise eligible older candidates who are seeking a career change and, therefore, be indirect age discrimination.

Some employers are keen to recruit only recent graduates, who they perceive will have the most up-to-date knowledge and skills. Obviously, this is likely to discriminate against older people. It might be possible to justify it in very fast moving areas such as IT, but it would be much safer to test each applicant in relation to their actual knowledge in certain areas rather than making assumptions based on date of graduation.

Examples:

A company runs a graduate recruitment scheme for managers. It limits candidates to those who graduated within the last three years which it says is to ensure that the candidates have up-to-date knowledge. As it does not stipulate in which subjects candidates must have their degree, it would be difficult for it to justify this requirement.

An IT company requires candidates to have graduated within the last two years so as to limit candidates to those with 'up-to-date technical skills'. This would be a legitimate aim but it might well be able to achieve this in a less discriminatory way, namely by testing candidates.

Many employers use 'the milk round' – targeted recruitment days at universities – to advertise their graduate recruitment schemes. If this is their main or only method of attracting recruits, it could amount to an indirectly discriminatory recruitment arrangement. It would be safer to use it as one component of a more open graduate recruitment strategy and certainly the ACAS Guidance recommends that employers use other avenues to capture a wider pool of applicants of differing ages.[6]

Inferences of age discrimination may also be drawn from graduate recruitment scheme brochures and web pages. Imagery or wording which is discriminatory, or which might portray the organisations as insufficiently age diverse, should be removed.

Another popular route into graduate training schemes is via vocational training schemes (see above[7]) such as 'vacation schemes'. As the name of these schemes implies, they are often designed for university students to take up during the holidays. This again may give rise to an inference that the employer intends to discriminate in favour of younger applicants and many employers are now renaming these schemes, for example as 'work placement schemes'.

1 'Equality and Diversity: Coming of Age', DTI, March 2006, p 41, para 4.3.7.
2 Office for National Statistics: *Social Trends 34.*
3 Higher Education Statistics Agency.

4 Higher Education Statistics Agency.
5 ACAS Guidance, *Age and the Workplace: Putting the Employment Equality (Age) Regulations 2006 into practice* (ACAS) p 14.
6 ACAS Guidance, *Age and the Workplace: Putting the Employment Equality (Age) Regulations into practice* (ACAS) p 14.
7 See **5.4.1**.

5.4.4 Minimum experience requirements

Employers often limit applications to those with a minimum number of years experience, a requirement which is potentially indirectly discriminatory. For example, a requirement for applicants to have at least five years' experience will disproportionately disadvantage younger workers as they will be less likely to be able to comply with the requirement than older workers.

Example:

Picton Ltd urgently wishes to recruit an administrative assistant. It wants somebody familiar with general administrative work who can hit the ground running as there will not be time to train them up. Therefore, they advertise the position to candidates with 'at least one year's experience'. The legitimate aim for adopting the experience requirement would be to ensure that they identify candidates who are immediately able to carry out the job at the level required. However, the experience requirement will be indirectly discriminatory, as certain younger age groups are less likely to have one year's experience. In deciding whether the requirement is justified, an employment tribunal will consider:

- whether the importance of the aim (recruiting a candidate who can do the job) outweighs the discriminatory effect of the experience requirement (the discriminatory impact of a requirement of one year's experience will be limited); and
- whether the requirement will actually achieve the aim. It is quite likely that it will in this case, since the difference between someone with a year's experience and someone with no experience at all will be significant.

Bearing in mind these factors, an employment tribunal may find that the requirement is a proportionate means of achieving the aim, even though the aim could be achieved equally well by means which have a less discriminatory effect, such as advertising by reference to types of experience rather than years of experience.

Further, where the period of experience required is short it is likely to be difficult to produce evidence that a particular age or age group has been disadvantaged. A requirement of a longer period of minimum experience will be more vulnerable.

Example:

Picton Ltd now wishes to recruit a Diversity Officer to work in its HR department. It needs somebody who already has experience of initiating diversity programmes as there is no one with sufficient experience internally to train the successful recruit. It, therefore, advertises for a Diversity Officer with 'at least seven years' experience'.

In deciding whether the requirement is justified, an employment tribunal will again consider whether the importance of the aim outweighs the discriminatory effect of the experience requirement. Here the balancing exercise is less favourable to the employer. Whilst, the aim is of importance to the employer, the discriminatory impact is quite high as a relatively high proportion of the candidates will be excluded by reason of their age from applying for the role. In this example, a larger age group is likely to be placed at a particular disadvantage. Assuming candidates are likely to be graduates, they will probably be 28 years old before they have seven years experience and may be older, as many will not have specialised as Diversity Officers until well after graduation.

The tribunal will then consider whether the requirement will actually achieve the aim of identifying candidates with suitable experience for the role. It is not clear in this example that it will. The correlation between years experience and ability to do the job eventually becomes less clear – a person who has worked in the sector for six years may have gained more valuable experience than somebody who has worked for eight years. In our example, a tribunal is much less likely to find that the requirement is justified, particularly as the aim could have been achieved equally well by means which have a less discriminatory effect, ie advertising by reference to knowledge or experience rather than years of experience.

Although in some circumstances a 'term of years' experience requirement may be justified, the safest course of action for the employers will be to remove such requirements wherever possible and instead recruit by reference to the actual experience required.

5.4.5 Maximum experience requirements/overqualified

Employers sometimes apply a maximum as well as a minimum experience requirement, eg that applicants must have between 7 and 10 years' experience, on the basis that the employer does not want to recruit a person who is 'overqualified'. A maximum experience requirement is likely to indirectly discriminate against older workers and will need to be objectively justified. This is likely to be more difficult than justifying minimum levels of experience.

'Overqualified' can often be used as a proxy for 'too old' and mask preconceptions about those with more experience such as that they:

- demand higher rates of pay;
- expect earlier promotion;
- will be less motivated in less demanding jobs;
- will leave within a short period; or
- are unwilling to take instructions from somebody with less experience.

These stereotypical assumptions underpin the need for age discrimination laws. Where there are genuine and reasonable concerns, an employment tribunal may expect the employer to put those concerns to the more experienced applicant at interview, rather than to exclude them from the recruitment process altogether.

In the Irish case of *Noonan v Accountancy Connections*[1] the applicant, an accountant in his 50s with 20 years experience, applied for the position of 'Senior Financial Accountant' which he had seen advertised on a recruitment website. The job advertisement specified that the post required candidates with a minimum of 2–3 years' experience. He was rejected on the basis that he was 'too senior' and was told that the employer was pitching the role at recently qualified candidates with around two-years' post-qualification experience. Shortly afterwards he applied for the position of 'Senior Financial Analyst' through the same website. No age limit was specified in the job advertisement. He was again rejected on the basis that they wanted someone with 2–3 years' post-qualification experience and, was also told that he would be more senior than the person he would be reporting to and that would be a problem.

Mr Noonan brought claims of direct and indirect age discrimination in the Equality Tribunal. His direct discrimination claim was based on the argument that 'too senior' in fact meant 'too old'. The company argued that it referred not to his age but to the length of his post-qualification experience. The Equality Tribunal held that whilst 'senior' could be interpreted as a reference to age, and therefore that Mr Noonan had raised the inference of age discrimination, it was actually intended by the company to refer to the length of his experience. This meant that the presumption of direct age discrimination had been rebutted by the company and this claim failed.

The indirect discrimination claim was based on the assertion that anyone over the age of 30 would almost certainly have more than 2–3 years' experience. Setting that as the maximum, therefore, discriminated against the over 30s. The Equality Tribunal accepted this so that, again, Mr Noonan had raised the inference of discrimination and it was up to the respondent to rebut it.

The company argued it had been a genuine requirement for both positions that the candidate should only have 2–3 years' experience because someone with more experience might be less satisfied in the job, would not have the same career path as a less qualified person, would not fit in, would outgrow the role and have no learning curve. It was held that the company's arguments were generalisations which were unsupported by any objective evidence. The requirement that any applicant should be no more than 2–3 years qualified, indirectly discriminated the applicant on the grounds of age and was not justified.

The safest course for employers is to avoid the use of minimum or maximum years' of experience wherever possible and instead to specify the kind and level of experienced required.

The use of post qualification experience (PQE) by professions such as lawyers in both recruitment and pay is discussed in **Chapter 6, 6.4.2(b)**.

In Ireland again the Irish Equality Authority to action when an advertisement was published for lawyers with maximums of five and six years' PQE.[2] This resulted in the Law Society banning further job advertisements containing PQE limits.

1 DEC-E2004/042.
2 *Equality Authority v Law Society Gazette Lawrence Simons International Legal Recruitment*, Equality Authority Annual Report 2006, 48.

5.4.6 Requirements for 'flexibility'/full-time work

The requirement that an employee be 'flexible' can be a euphemism for being prepared to work long hours, unpredictable house, to socialise after work, to travel with the job etc.

It is well established that, under sex discrimination laws, such requirements can indirectly discriminate against women, who are less likely to be able to comply because of their childcare responsibilities.[1]

Similarly, the requirement to work full-time potentially discriminates indirectly against women who are less likely to be able to comply with this requirement because of childcare responsibilities.

Childcare also falls disproportionately on certain age groups. Particularly, men with child care responsibilities find it problematic to bring equivalent claims to women with childcare responsibilities. They might well have to consider if age discrimination laws provide alternative rights.

Another impact of the ageing population is that more and more people are becoming carers.

A requirement to work 'flexibly' or to work full-time is problematic for people workers with these responsibilities. Responsibility for caring for those, usually relatives, with caring needs also falls disproportionately on certain age groups. These carers may also want to consider their rights under age discrimination laws.

It is worth considering whether such requirements will amount to indirect age discrimination. It will be necessary to show that those with caring responsibilities (both male and female) are likely to be within a particular age range. If so, the employer may have to justify them by identifying a potentially legitimate aim and showing that the requirement is a proportionate means of achieving that aim. Whilst those with childcare responsibility are more likely to be in the 25–40 age range, the peak age for carers is the 50–59 age group.[2]

In considering indirect age discrimination and those with caring responsibilities, it is important to remember the correct test for pools of comparison.[3] A claimant would have to show that the provision, criterion or practice complained of put a particular age group at a disadvantage. It is not enough to show that a group of people who share a characteristic which disadvantages them are predominantly within a particular age group.

Example:

Kerry PR require their staff to work flexibly and stay late at short notice if workload demands. Clive is 30 years and a single father with two young children. He cannot organise his childcare around this requirement. He claims that the majority of workers with childcare responsibilities are between 25 and 35 years and, that Kerry PR's requirement for flexibility from all staff discriminates against this age group and is unjustified as he believes there will always be plenty of other staff who will want the overtime.

Clive is using the wrong comparison. In order to get this claim off the ground, he would have to show that 25–35 year olds were placed at a particular disadvantage compared to those outside this group by the requirement to be able to work flexibly. He would have to compare the proportions of the two groups who could and could not comply with this requirement for whatever reason: childcare, care for elderly relatives or other reasons. He might be able to do this but would probably struggle to produce the evidence to support this.

---

1 See eg *London Underground v Edwards* [1995] IRLR 355.
2 Young, Grundy and Jitlal, *Care Providers, Care Receivers: A longitudinal perspective* (Joseph Rowntree Foundation, 2006).
3 **Chapter 14, 14.6.**

5.5 Proving discrimination in recruitment

The burden of proof and the rôle of inferences are of vital importance when considering whether or not discrimination in recruitment can be proved. They are also considered in detail in **Chapter 4.**[1]

Example:

Two candidates are interviewed for a position. One candidate is aged 35 and the other 55. The 55 year old is unsuccessful and the job is offered to the younger candidate. The 55 year old discovers that this younger candidate has much less relevant experience than he does and brings a claim that he was discriminated against on grounds of his age.

If the employer can show that the younger candidate was better qualified, and/or produces evidence, such as interview notes which explain the difference in treatment, it will have satisfied the burden of proving that there was no discrimination. If it is unable to produce the necessary evidence, then the employment tribunal must conclude that discrimination took place.

The burden of proof will shift to the employer if the claimant can point to facts which suggest that age discrimination might have taken place. Unsuccessful candidates can use the questionnaire procedure which is common to all forms of unlawful discrimination to find this kind of evidence.[2]

Recruitment

The Australian case of *Hopper and others v Virgin Blue Airlines Pty Ltd*[3]. is helpful in showing the kind of evidence which will be relevant to these types of claims.

Eight women aged from 36–56 years who had been rejected by airline Virgin Blue for jobs as cabin crew, complained of age discrimination in the Antidiscrimination Tribunal of Queensland.

The women alleged that the discrimination took place not at the application stage, but when they were invited by Virgin Blue to attend a group assessment. This stage of the process involved attending Virgin Blue's premises with 60 other candidates where they were assessed by, on average, 1 assessor per 10 candidates.

The selection process involved assessing candidates for certain 'behavioural competencies' to see if they demonstrated an underlying characteristic that would result in effective or superior performance at work. The particular characteristics assessed in the group session were 'assertiveness', 'team work', 'communication' and 'Virgin Flair'. 'Virgin Flair' was defined as '. . . a desire to create a memorable, positive experience for customers. The ability to have fun, making it fun for the customer'. To assess these characteristics, Virgin Blue asked candidates to prepare for and perform a dramatic routine.

The tribunal hearing the case accepted that assessing for 'behavioural competencies' was a recognised recruitment technique and that this kind of testing was intended to produce an age-neutral result. The claimants argued that the subjective assessment process Virgin Blue had adopted had a (conscious or unconscious) age bias that prevented them being fairly considered for employment.

To prove their case, they asked the tribunal to draw inferences of age discrimination from evidence including an article in the Australian edition of FHM magazine entitled 'Branson's Angels' which featured five female employees posing in leather bikini tops, high boots and miniskirts. They also pointed to the Virgin Blue in-flight magazine 'Voyeur' that contained pictures of employees who were or appeared to be young. In addition, they gave evidence that the assessors made a 'beeline' for the young, blond attractive candidates and were more interested in looks than ability.

In this case, the tribunal was not persuaded by this evidence. Instead, it drew inferences from statistical evidence alone which showed that only 1 out of the 750 candidates who were offered a job by Virgin Blue during the relevant period was between the age of 36 and 56 (and that person was, in fact, aged 36).

The tribunal concluded that this statistical evidence showed that the 'behavioural competencies' technique adopted 'did not work as it should have' and demonstrated that the assessors must have been unconsciously discriminating on grounds of age. It therefore, upheld the women's complaints and awarded them damages.

In coming to its decision, the tribunal took into account various factors including the fact that the assessors had little training on the assessment procedure (in particular on assessing 'Virgin Flair') and that the assessors were all relatively young.

On appeal to the Supreme Court of Queensland, Virgin alleged, amongst other things, that the tribunal had taken into account irrelevant considerations when coming to its decision. In particular, Virgin alleged that the tribunal had acted unreasonably and illogically in deciding if there was direct discrimination at the assessment stage as the statistical evidence that was relied upon, related to the age of applicants who were offered a job (and not to applicants who had passed the assessment stage). Virgin also argued that the statistical analysis by the tribunal failed to take into account the individual circumstances of each of the claimants compared to successful applicants under the age of 36. The Supreme Court rejected these arguments and upheld the tribunal's conclusion based on the statistical evidence that the selection process favoured younger applicants.[4]

In the context of recruitment, the kind of evidence which may give rise to an inference that discrimination took place include:

- job advertisements which suggest that the employer is seeking applicants of a certain age or age group;
- the adoption of informal recruitment methods such as recruitment by recommendation;
- promotional materials which suggest that the employer may have an age bias;
- asking for a date of birth or other unnecessary information which suggests age in the application form;
- absence of written guidelines for those recruiting as to the requirements of the post or transparent, objective and nondiscriminatory criteria for assessing suitability for the post;
- a lack of interview notes or reasons for rejection of candidates;
- asking questions relating to age during the interview process;
- a lack of equal opportunities and interview training by those involved in the recruitment process;
- a lack of age monitoring by the employer; and/or

- statistical evidence which shows an age-skewed workforce and no attempt by the employer to take steps to redress this imbalance.

These are considered in more detail below.

1 **Chapter 4, 4.6**.
2 **Chapter 14, 14.6**.
3 [2006] QADT 9
4 [2007] QSC 075.

5.6 The recruitment process

It is unlawful for an employer to discriminate against a person 'in the arrangements he makes for the purpose of determining to whom he should offer employment'.

'Arrangements' in this context is likely to be construed widely. It will include job advertisements (or other methods of seeking applicants, such as by word of mouth), application forms, the job description and person specification, the criteria for short listing and selection and the interview itself.

It has generally been accepted that discriminatory recruitment arrangements, such as advertisements or selection criteria, may in themselves be unlawful. For example, that a person could bring a claim of age discrimination against an employer where, as a result of a discriminatory age limit or indirectly discriminatory conditions stated in a job advertisement, that person did not apply for the position. However in one of the first tribunal decisions under the Regulations, it was held that the placing of a job advertisement is not an arrangement made for determining, who the employer should offer employment.[1] Even if this decision is not followed in future cases, the value of such claims are wizely to be small–in order to get substantial damages the individual would have to show that, but for the age restriction he would have applied for and been offered the position. If he is not able to show this, his damages are likely to be limited to a proportion of this loss, based on the likelihood we would have been offered the job if the discrimination had not concerned and, to an injury to feelings award.

The more likely consequence of a discriminatory recruitment arrangement is that it will give rise to an inference of age discrimination where an application is rejected. For example, an unsuccessful older applicant who is rejected in favour of someone younger and less qualified, may point to wording in the job advertisement which suggests that younger applicants were being targeted. The tribunal may draw inferences of age discrimination from this evidence.

1 *Clarke v Gap*, ET, see Employers, Forumon Age, *Legal News 008*, May 2007.

5.6.1 Job advertisements

Not so long ago, age limits were commonplace in job advertisements. Employers considered reasonable to advertise along the following lines:

ADVERTISING – Executive Assistant/PA £30,000–32,000

You will need first class advertising experience at senior management level, have exemplary organisational/admin/secretarial skills, are between 27 and 38 years old and earning not less than £27,000 – please fax your CV on . . .[1]

1 *Campaign*, 24 September 1999.

Employers advertise for positions in a variety of ways: advertisements in newspapers and magazines, on notice boards, on television, on radio, on the internet, by distributing flyers and by email.

Under UK sex and race discrimination legislation it is unlawful to publish or cause to be published an advertisement that indicates or might reasonably be understood to indicate that the employer intends to discriminate either directly or indirectly. An individual cannot bring a complaint but special powers are granted to the Equal Opportunities Commission and the Commission for Racial Equality, as applicable, to enforce these laws.

There is no equivalent provision in relation to age discrimination so there is no immediate breach of any law where an employer publishes an advertisement which contains, either directly or indirectly, age discriminatory requirements.

As mentioned above, in one of the first tribunal cases under the Regulations it was held that the placing of a job advertisement is not an 'arrangement made for determining to who the employer should offer employment'. This suggest that a person has to apply for a job and be rejected in order to claim although this was a tribunal decision only so another tribunal is not bound to follow it.[1] In contrast, under Irish age discrimination laws it appears the position is different in the case of *Ruddy v SDS*, Mr Ruddy succeeded when his employer excluded those of 60 years from the opportunity to participate in an 'owner-driver scheme'. He succeeded with his case even though he did not apply to join as he considered this 'futile'.[2]

Job advertisements should be carefully worded. Indirectly, discriminatory criteria such as age limits, experience requirements and wording which suggests the employer is looking for candidates of a particular age, should be avoided unless they can be objectively justified.

Recruitment

In the Irish case of *Equality Authority v Ryanair*,[3] Ryanair placed an advertisement in the Irish Times in which it was stated that the 'ideal candidate will be young and dynamic'. Ryanair defended the claim stating that their reference to the word 'young' was a state of mind and not a chronological age. The Equality Officer found that the use of the word 'young' indicated an intention to exclude applicants who were not young and that the use of the word amounted to clear age discrimination.

Other job advertisements in Ireland referring to 'creative and professional young graphic designer'; 'outstanding young ACAs/MBAs/COMAs/ Consultants', 'young enthusiastic chef departie'; and 'young ambitious solicitor' resulted in action by the Irish Equality Authority.[4]

The ACAS Guidance provides the following examples of job advertisements which may suggest the employer is looking for a younger or older employee:

> 'We require an enthusiastic person, flexible enough to fit in with our fast moving market place, not afraid to challenge the status quo and in touch with latest thinking.
>
> Our ideal candidate will need to manage competing demands. He or she should be reflective, and have boardroom presence and gravitas.'[5]

Some examples of words which may be associated with youth are:

active	high flier
animated	hot-shot
bubbly	innovative
dynamic	keen
eager	lively
energetic	quick learner
enthusiastic	self-motivated
fresh	sparkling
full of life	spirited
fun	vibrant
go-getter	vivacious

The use of a word such as 'dynamic' is unlikely, in itself, to be problematic, but coupled with other indicative words or images could well be enough for an inference of discrimination to be drawn, so that the burden of proving that there was no discrimination would pass to the employer.

Examples of words that may be associated with older age are:

accomplished	mature
boardroom presence	reliable

dependable	responsible
developed	serious
established	stable
gravitas	trustworthy
in your prime	young at heart

It is important when framing any job or person specification not to fall into a lazy trap of using a characteristic as a proxy for an essential criterion. If the characteristic disadvantages a particular age group, the employer is likely to have to explain its use.

A group of managers[6] asked in 2006 to identify the positive and negative attributes of younger and older workers came up with the following:

	Positive points	**Negative points**
Young people	Ambitious	Immature
	Cheaper	Irresponsible
	Energetic	Less committed
	Enthusiastic	Less experienced
	Faster	More likely to take time off sick
	Fitter/healthier	No respect
	Flexible	Unreliable
	Good looking	
	Long-term employment	
	Trainable	
Old people	Experienced	Boring
	Grateful	Resistant to change
	Hard-working	Set in their ways/inflexible
	Level headed	Technologically illiterate
	Loyal	Tired
	Mature	Unhealthy/health problems
	Reliable	Unsociable
	Responsible	
	Thorough	

Junior/senior

There has been much debate as to whether the use of the words 'junior' and 'senior' should be eliminated by employers.

Use of the word 'senior' to denote a role requiring more experience is unlikely to be problematic on its own, eg the use of 'IT analyst' and 'Senior IT analyst'. It becomes more of an issue where these words are used to describe the individual and not the role, for example, 'A senior manager required for the post of Head of Sales . . .' Whilst this can be a convenient way to describe experience, it could be misinterpreted as indicating an intention to prefer an older candidate.[7] A better approach would be 'Candidates with management experience required for the position of Head of Sales. The ideal candidate will have experience of . . .' Whilst it is more time consuming for the individual drafting a more descriptive advertisement, it helps to avoid inferences and should help to attract the right level of candidate.

The use of the word 'junior' is perhaps more of an issue. It is more strongly associated with youth than 'senior' is with older age and is best avoided – it is rarely likely to be justifiable to reject a candidate because they have too much experience.[8]

Where words which imply a particular age range, such as 'senior' or 'junior' are used, a written record should be kept of what is meant by them in that particular context. This could be a useful reference in any future allegation of age discrimination.

1 *Clarke v Gap*, ET, see Employers Forum on Age, *Legal News 008,* May 2007.
2 *Ruddy v SDS (An Post),* DEC – E2007–020.
3 DEC-E2000-014.
4 Equality Authority Annual Report 2006, 47.
5 ACAS Guidance, *Age and the Workplace: Putting the Employment Equality (Age) Regulations (2006) into practice* (ACAS) p 13.
6 Identity of company is confidential
7 See *Noonan* DEC–E2004–042 – see **5.4.5** for facts of case.
8 See **5.4.5**.

5.6.2 Informal methods of attracting applicants

Informal recruitment methods may also be adopted, for example unsolicited applications or recommendations from staff, clients, friends etc. These kinds of informal recruitment methods can perpetuate a lack of diversity in a workforce. The ACAS Guidance recommends that employers tap into the diverse skills of their local community and advertise in a way that will be accessible to a large audience.[1]

It is possible that a discriminatory informal recruitment policy could give rise directly to a claim from someone who can show that he has suffered a detriment because of it for example.

Example:

A media company employs 10 staff, the oldest of whom is 30. It seeks to avoid paying for recruitment advertising or agency costs by encouraging its staff to introduce friends in the industry to fill vacancies. This recruitment method is likely to reinforce the lack of age diversity within the company as the friends of the existing staff are most likely to be of a similar age. Whilst this practice has a potential to discriminate indirectly on grounds of age, any legal challenge is unlikely as the older person who did not get the opportunity to apply is unlikely to be aware of the missed opportunity. The media company might, in any event, seek to justify the practice. This again raises the issue of cost as an aim.[1] The company might argue that cost is but only one aim and another is to minimise the risks involved in recruiting unknown candidates. The company's position will be stronger if informal recruitment methods are accompanied by more formal ones, giving candidates who are unknown to existing staff other opportunities to apply for jobs.

1 **Chapter 4, 4.7.5(a).**

It is more likely that this kind of practice would cause problems for the employer indirectly – where a person who complains of some other form of age discrimination, points to it as evidence of a lack of commitment to equal opportunities and diversity.

1 ACAS Guidance, *Age and the Workplace: Putting the Employment Equality (Age) Regulations 2006 into practice* (ACAS) p 12.

5.6.3 Promotional materials

Corporate brochures, handbooks, websites and other promotional materials can all contain words and imagery which suggest an age bias. Graduate recruitment scheme brochures and websites for example, are often full of pictures of young people. The ACAS Guidance advises employers to think about the 'hidden message' that may be present in any promotional literature, particularly the pictures.[1]

Imagery should suggest diversity and it is also sensible to include an equal opportunities statement.

1 ACAS Guidance, *Age and the Workplace: Putting the Employment Equality (Age) Regulations 2006 into practice* (ACAS) p 13.

5.6.4 CVs, application forms and dates of birth

Where employers ask applicants to apply by CV, they will often provide irrelevant information about their age (eg date of birth) or which may suggest their age (eg dates of qualifications, education, employment, etc.). Even if the employer did not ask for this information, it will be vulnerable to a claim that it was influenced by it. For this reason, it is usually better not to invite the submission of CVs, but to use application forms which ask only for the information which is necessary to identify the strongest candidates.

Many employers have removed questions about age or date of birth from their application forms, as recommended in the ACAS Guidance.[1] However, there may be circumstances where an employer does need this information at the application stage.

1 ACAS Guidance, *Age and the Workplace: Putting the Employment Equality (Age) Regulations 2006 into practice* (ACAS) p 11.

(a) Proximity to retirement

An employer who wishes to rely on the proximity to retirement exception does not necessarily need to ask the applicant's age or date of birth. It could, for example, require him to tick a box on his application form confirming that at the date of the application he is not over or within six months of the employer's normal retirement age.

(b) An age limit is objectively justifiable, or is necessary to comply with a statutory requirement

In these situations, the employer could simply ask applicants to tick a box confirming they are not over or under a certain age. Although, requesting even this information in an application form could amount to a discriminatory arrangement, it will be lawful if the appropriate exception is deemed to apply, or if imposing the age limit is found to be justified.

(c) For monitoring purposes

If an employer wishes to monitor the age of applicants, this information should be collated in a separate, anonymous diversity monitoring form that is not seen by those involved in the recruitment decisions. Many employers already use these forms to monitor other forms of diversity such as race and sex. Age or an age range can simply be added to the list.

See below for further consideration in relation to monitoring.[1]

1 See **Chapter 13, 13.6**.

(d) For administrative purposes

Information about a successful candidate's age or date of birth can be needed for administrative purposes such as identifying when he will reach normal retirement age (if it has one) or for the providers of insured benefits (such as private healthcare or personal health insurance). As this is only relevant once employment has been offered, there is no need to ask for date of birth on an application form.

If an employee refuses to give information about his age, and the employer has a nondiscriminatory reason for requesting it, a job offer may be retracted or an employee disciplined or even dismissed. However, the employer would have to show not only that it had reasonable grounds for requesting the information but also that it acted reasonably in the taking the action it took. If, for example, the information could have been passed directly to a third party (such as an insurer) by the employee, it is unlikely that an employer would be justified in insisting on seeing the information itself.

(e) Dates of education and dates of employment

In most cases employers will not need to know the dates of education or qualifications. However, it could be legitimate to ask for these dates where the employer requires up to date knowledge and shifts. Whether such a requirement can be justified is considered at **5.4.3** above.

The situation is different in relation to dates of employment. By knowing when an applicant was employed, employers can assess how much and what kind of experience the applicant has had, whether there are gaps in employment and whether he has frequently moved jobs. For most positions, this kind of information will be relevant to the selection process which will usually outweigh any inference of discrimination.

Some employers prefer not to have any information relating to age on the application form and instead wait until employment is offered to ask employees to confirm their age/date of birth. Uncertainty about an employee's age at the interview stage can lead to inappropriate questions, however, and interviewers should be trained to avoid this.

5.6.5 Job descriptions and person specifications

Job descriptions (setting out the main duties of the job) and person specifications (describing the skills, abilities and qualifications necessary to do the job) can be extremely helpful in avoiding discrimination claims so long as they are not themselves tainted by discrimination. They:

- give the candidate good information about the role he is applying for;

- ensure that the shortlisting process is based on ability to do the job;
- help exclude irrelevant considerations and personal preferences; and
- provide a means of focussing interviewers on the requirement of the job.

Some elements of the person specification will be considered essential and others merely desirable. Both can be included, but their relative importance should be made clear so that candidates who do not have the essentials can be excluded at the shortlisting stage.

If there are any requirements which have the potential to be discriminatory, for example age limits or experience requirements, these should be considered at this stage and the basis on which they are believed to be objectively justifiable or to fall within an exception to the Regulations should be recorded in case they are subjected to future challenge.

5.6.6 Short-listing

Each CV or application form should be judged objectively and consistently against the person specification. The way in which the criteria are applied in each case, and decisions about selection and nonselection, should be recorded in writing. This not only helps to ensure that the recruitment process is fair but will make it easier to prove to any future employment tribunal that there was no discrimination.

5.6.7 Interviewing

The job description and the person specification will be crucial documents in an interview. They can be used either as they are or as the basis for developing a standard set of questions to use as the framework for the interview. This helps ensure consistency and makes it easier to keep a good record.

The questions asked at interview should be designed, amongst other things to:

- check important information such as whether a candidate has a particular qualification;
- investigate the range and depth of previous relevant experience;
- assess relevant skills and personal qualities such as the ability to work in a team, to lead a team, to communicate with the public, etc.

Questions which are designed to find out someone's age or which imply that age might be a factor in the selection decision should be avoided unless they can be objectively justified. Questions related to length of experience should be avoided unless this is genuinely relevant and emphasis put instead on type, breadth and quality of experience.

Notes of interviews, as well as written evidence of the reasons for selection or rejection of candidates, should be made and retained for at least six months after the recruitment exercise. In fact, the ACAS Guidance recommends that such documentation is to be retained for ideally 12 months.[1]

1 ACAS Guidance for employees, *Age and the Workplace: Putting the Employment Equality (Age) Regulations 2006 into practice* (ACAS) p 15.

5.6.8 Training of recruiters

Increasingly employment tribunals expect employers not only to have an equal opportunities or diversity policy covering all forms of unlawful discrimination, but also to be able to show that they have given recent equal opportunities training to those shortlisting and interviewing.

Interview training is particularly important to avoid ageist questions and assumptions. This is demonstrated in the following two Irish cases:

Hughes v Aer Lingus[1]

A 53-year-old woman who had previously worked as a senior cabin attendant applied for the position of junior cabin attendant at Aer Lingus. During her interview she was asked how she would cope with younger people being in charge and how, being older, she would feel about starting at the bottom rung of the ladder. She was not offered the position on the basis that she was overqualified and as a result brought a claim of age discrimination.

The Equality Officer found that her nonselection was not based on age. Aer Lingus provided evidence to show that they did recruit three junior cabin attendants who were over the age of 50. Further, the Equality Officer found it was reasonable for Aer Lingus to explore with her how she would cope being a junior cabin attendant after having been a senior one.

However, it was held that the line of questioning suggested that age was an issue and that the questions could have been put in a way that avoided unnecessary reference to age. For example, Aer Lingus could have asked 'how would you cope with people with less experience than you being in charge?' rather than 'how would you cope with younger people being in charge?' As such, the Equality Officer found that the applicant had been discriminated against in her interview in that she had been subjected to a discriminatory line of questioning, but not in the failure to appoint her to the position.

She was awarded £5,000 for distress and, as her performance at interview may have suffered as a result of the discriminatory questioning, Aer Lingus was ordered to either offer her a new interview for a cabin crew position with a different panel of interviewers or to offer her such a position.

O'Neill v The Board of Management, St Gabriel's National School[2]

In this case the applicant was a 48-year-old teacher who applied for the position of deputy principal. She was unsuccessful both at her initial interview and on appeal. The successful candidate was under 30 years and had only 7 years' experience, whereas, the applicant had 27 years' experience. One of the questions asked in the first interview was 'considering that you have been teaching for 27 years, why would you be bothered with the hassle of the job of deputy principal?'[3]

The Equality Officer in this case found that this question was discriminatory and therefore that she has been discriminated against at the time the question was asked. The normal order in such a case would be that the school should offer her another interview by a different panel. However, since she had been second interviewed by a panel which included two individuals who were not at the first interview, the second interview had been conducted in a nondiscriminatory way. The Equality Officer concluded, as with Ms Hughes, that the decision not to recruit her was not discriminatory but the questions posed to her at the first interview were discriminatory. Like Ms Hughes, Ms O'Neill was awarded €5,000 for compensation for the distress she had suffered.

1 DEC – E2002 – 049.
2 DEC–E2005–007.
3 See **5.4.5**.

5.6.9 Selection

Similar considerations apply in relation to selection as they do to shortlisting (see above).

5.6.10 Monitoring and statistics

The ACAS Guidance[1] advised employers to monitor its recruitment programmes, including the age profile of applicants as well as those shortlisted, appointed and interviewed. In addition, employers who have not done so may wish to survey their current workforce for diversity and consider ways of improving diversity, such as taking positive action. An employer who fails to monitor, risks a tribunal drawing inferences of discrimination.

Employers can be compelled to make data collated through monitoring available to individuals bringing age discrimination claims through use of questionnaires (similar to the questionnaires used in sex, race and other discrimination claims) and/or by way of disclosure in the tribunal proceedings.[2] Inferences of age discrimination may also be drawn if such data is unfavourable. However, if transparent, consistent, well-documented, nondiscriminatory recruitment practices are adopted, the employer will be in a much stronger position to rebut any presumption of discrimination from unfavourable data, particularly if it can show it is taking steps to improve diversity.

The ACAS Guidance also recommends that employers monitor each particular recruitment process, so that before moving from the shortlisting to the interview stage the employer checks that 'no bias, deliberate or unintentional, has influenced decisions'. It suggests that this check be carried out by someone who has not been involved in the shortlisting.[3] It also recommends that decisions are again checked for bias at the final selection stage.

1 ACAS Guidance, *Age and the Workplace: Putting the Employment Equality (Age) Regulations 2006 into practice* (ACAS) p 3.
2 **Chapter 14, 14.6** and **14.8**.
3 ACAS Guidance, *Age and the Workplace: Putting the Employment Equality (Age) Regulations 2006 into practice* (ACAS) p 15.

5.7 Age limits and other forms of discrimination

In addition to amounting to direct age discrimination, age limits can also be indirect sex or race discrimination. For example, in the case of *Price v Civil Service Commission*[1] the EAT held that limiting applications for the post of Executive Officer to those aged 28 or over was indirect sex discrimination since 'knowledge and experience suggest that a considerable number of women between the mid-20s and the mid-30s are engaged in bearing and minding children'.

Further, in *Perera v Civil Service Commission*[2] an upper age limit of 32 for Administrative Trainees was held to be indirect race discrimination. On the statistics at that time, the proportion of ethnic minority Executive Officers (of which Mr Perera was one) who could comply with the requirement were significantly smaller than the proportion of white Executive Officers who could comply.

Outside of the area of recruitment, sex discrimination laws were used to challenge the upper age limits for unfair dismissal and redundancy pay rights in the long-running *Rutherford v Secretary of State for Trade and Industry* case.[3]

1 [1977] IRLR 291.
2 [1982] IRLR 147.
3 See summary of facts, **Chapter 12, 12.4**.

Chapter 6

Pay and benefits

6.1 Introduction

In common with other anti-discrimination legislation, the Regulations prohibit age discrimination in relation to the terms of employment offered to employees. The potential impact of the age discrimination legislation on pay and benefits is perhaps greater than that of other anti-discrimination laws. In this chapter we consider:

- how discrimination will arise and when it will be unlawful;
- the use of service-related benefits and the exemptions employers can rely on;
- the impact of the Regulations on pay, including setting starting salaries, pay increases and pay scales;
- the difficulties employers will face in relation to health benefits and particularly those benefits provided under insurance policies;
- how the provision of company cars to employees might be affected; and
- the impact on share plans and other awards.

This chapter does not deal with pensions or redundancy payments, which are considered in **Chapters 8 and 11**, respectively.

In addition, the Regulations do not cover the provision of benefits if the employer provides those benefits to the public, or to a section of the public which includes the employee, unless the provision to the public is materially different than that provided to the employee or the benefit is regulated by the contract of employment or relates to training.[1] This prevents a claim where a benefit is provided by a company which coincidently also employs the individual to whom the benefit is provided. For example, if an employee is employed by a private medical company and, outside his employment, the employee makes arrangements to be covered by private medical insurance by the company which employs him, the provision of that cover will be excluded from the Regulations, provided it has nothing to do with the employment. This is consistent with the fact that the Regulations currently cover employment and similar relationships and do not extend to the provision of goods and service.

1 See reg 7(6).

6.2 When discrimination will arise

There are many aspects of pay and benefits schemes, which may give rise to direct discrimination, or which will place certain age groups at a disadvantage and are therefore potentially indirectly discriminatory. Both direct and indirect age discrimination are potentially justifiable in relation to pay and benefits.[1] In addition, the Regulations set out several exceptions where otherwise direct or indirect age discrimination will be lawful.

1 **Chapter 4**.

6.2.1 Direct discrimination

Decisions on policies that distinguish between employees based on their age will be directly discriminatory. Examples include:

- provision of private medical insurance to only those employees under the age of 65;
- provision of company cars to only those aged 21 or over.

These examples are explored in more detail later in this chapter.

6.2.2 Indirect discrimination

Pay and benefits schemes may give rise to indirect discrimination if the terms are the same for all employees regardless of age, but the effect of the scheme is to place employees of a particular age group at a particular disadvantage compared to others. Examples include:

- pay increases based on length of service or experience may disadvantage younger workers. Younger workers are less likely than older workers to have long service or experience, and therefore less likely to receive higher pay;
- provision of life assurance subject to employees' passing a medical examination may put older workers at a disadvantage, as they may be less likely than younger workers to pass the examination.

These examples are explored in more detail later in this chapter.

6.2.3 Justification

Direct or indirect age discrimination in pay and benefits will be unlawful unless the employer can rely on one of the exceptions listed below or the employer can show objective justification.[1] Objective justification is a particular issue where pay and benefits give rise to discrimination.

Employers who need to change their benefit schemes to remove discriminatory elements are likely to find that there is an additional cost in operating their benefits in a less discriminatory way. However, as mentioned in **Chapter 4**, avoiding increased cost on its own may not amount to objective justification.[2] In many cases, cost is likely to be the sole reason that benefits are not already provided to all employees on a non-discriminatory basis. If employers' benefit schemes result in discrimination, they will find it difficult to show that continuing to provide benefits in that way is justified, even if eliminating the discrimination results in a substantial expense. This is considered in more detail in the following text.

1 **Chapter 4, 4.7**.
2 **Chapter 4, 4.7.5(a)**.

6.2.4 Exceptions

The exceptions within the Regulations most relevant to pay and benefits are:

- exception for provision of certain benefits based on length of service[1];
- exception for the National Minimum Wage[2]; and
- exception for provision of life assurance cover to retired workers.[3]

The exception for provision of enhanced redundancy payments to employees is covered in **Chapter 11** on 'Redundancy'.[4]

1 See reg 32.
2 See reg 32.
3 See reg 34.
4 **Chapter 11, 11.5.3**.

6.3 Service-related benefits

6.3.1 Introduction

Many employers use length of service as a basis for determining pay and benefits. Salary increases are sometimes related to service and other benefits that are often based on length of service include company sick pay, additional holiday entitlement and enhanced maternity pay. Use of length of service in benefits may well place younger workers at a disadvantage compared to older workers, as younger workers are less likely to have long service. Therefore, the use of service-related criteria in providing benefits and determining pay may be indirectly discriminatory. Service-related criteria should not be confused with experience-based criteria, which are also potentially indirectly discriminatory.[1]

Length of service is typically taken into account in relation to benefits in one of the following ways:

1 See **6.4.2**.

(a) Benefits provided after a qualifying period of service

Certain benefits may be provided only after completion of the probationary period, or after, say, one or two years' service. It is unlikely that potential claimants will be able to show easily that such short qualifying periods place a particular age group at a disadvantage when compared to others. Longer qualifying periods may be used for long service awards, but are unusual for other types of benefit. The longer the period taken into account, the more likely it is that there will be an indirectly discriminatory impact.

There is also a possibility that qualifying periods could indirectly discriminate against older workers approaching retirement. This may be the case in relation to share options, for example, where often a particular period of service is required before employees are entitled to exercise their options. If employees have to retire before they are able to exercise their options, this will place them at a disadvantage.[1]

1 See **6.7.3(a)**.

(b) Enhancement of benefits with longer service

This may include, for instance, service-related pay increases, or increased holiday entitlement with each year of service. Depending on the age profile of an employer's workforce, this may well have an indirectly discriminatory impact, as employees with shorter service will tend to be younger, and will be at a disadvantage when compared to older workers.

Where benefits have an indirectly discriminatory impact, employers would ordinarily need to show objective justification for their practices. With service-related benefits, this would place a very large burden on employers, in terms of assessing the existence of any discriminatory impact in the first place, and then attempting to justify a potentially large number of service-related benefits within their organisations. It was recognised during consultation on the Regulations that there is widespread use of service-related criteria with regard to pay and benefits in the United Kingdom and that the Regulations were not designed to eradicate this.[1] During the consultation period the government came under pressure to exempt service-related benefits entirely. The government would not go this far but acknowledged that it would be unnecessarily bureaucratic for employers to justify all of their service-related benefits individually.

1 See eg 'Equality and Diversity: Coming of Age', DTI, July 2005, p 47.

6.3.2 Exception for provision of certain benefits based on length of service

The Regulations, therefore, include an exception for service-related benefits, which does not exempt the employer entirely from justifying the indirectly discriminatory impact but makes it easier for him to do so.

Regulation 32 provides:

> '(1) Subject to paragraph (2), nothing in Part 2 or 3 [of the Regulations] shall render it unlawful for a person ("A"), in relation to the award of any benefit by him, to put a worker ("B") at a disadvantage when compared with another worker ("C"), if and to the extent that the disadvantage suffered by B is because B's length of service is less than that of C.
>
> (2) Where B's length of service exceeds 5 years, it must reasonably appear to A that the way in which he uses the criterion of length of service, in relation to the award in respect of which B is put at a disadvantage, fulfils a business need of his undertaking (for example, by encouraging the loyalty or motivation, or rewarding the experience, of some or all of his workers).'

The exception for service-related benefits, therefore, falls into two parts:

- a blanket exception for benefits based on service of five years or less ('five-year exception'); and
- an exception for all other service-related benefits provided that the employer reasonably believes that awarding benefits in this way fulfils a business need ('business need exception').

The exception covers only benefits which are based on length of service – not differentials on grounds of age. In addition, the exception does not extend to other criteria – such as experience-based criteria – which may also indirectly discriminate, and which employers will still need to justify objectively.

Importantly, the service-related exception does not apply to service-related benefits arising as a result of termination of employment, for example redundancy pay.[1]

The exception applies to the broad definition of 'worker' in the Regulations, including not only employees, but also office-holders, police constables, partners and members of LLPs, Crown employees and members of staff of the House of Commons and House of Lords.[2]

On a strict reading of the exception, the service-related benefit exception applies only where the comparator is a real person and not a hypothetical one. It must, however, be assumed that the exception applies equally to comparisons with hypothetical comparators.

1 **Chapter 11**, **11.5.2** in relation to continuous service and redundancy payments.
2 See reg 2(2).

(a) Five-year exception

Benefits based on length of service are automatically exempt from the Regulations where the service taken into account is five years or less.

Example:

An employer's holiday scheme provides basic holiday entitlement of 20 days a year, but a service-related element entitles employees to one extra day's holiday per complete year of service, up to a maximum of five days after five years' service. This would fall within the five-year exception.

In addition to increased holiday entitlement, the five-year exception will be used in relation to qualifying periods of service for access to certain benefits, such as health insurance. Qualifying periods for benefits of this type tend to be well under five years. It is also common for employers to permit employees to join benefit schemes only after completion of their probationary period – this would also fall within the five-year exception as probationary periods invariably only last several months.

(b) Business-need exception

Where the length of service taken into account exceeds five years, the automatic exemption does not apply. Employers will not be required to justify the service-related benefit objectively using the justification test set out in reg 3(1). However, an employer will benefit from the statutory exception only if it reasonably appears that providing the benefit in this way fulfils a business need.

The Regulations give the following examples of business needs:

- encouraging loyalty;
- encouraging motivation; and
- rewarding experience.

These are likely to be the most common reasons for employers to use service criteria in the provision of benefits. However, they are given as examples only, so employers should be able to use service-related benefits to fulfil other business needs.

These examples raise two questions:

(i) Is 'rewarding' loyalty also a legitimate aim? If so, why is it not listed when rewarding experience is?

(ii) Is rewarding experience really a legitimate aim? Experience in itself is inexorably linked to age and is not necessarily always an appropriate indicator of competence or skills. In any event, if the intention is to reward experience then relevant service with other organisations should also count, not just service with the current employer.[1]

In the original draft of the Regulations, the example of 'rewarding loyalty' was given, as opposed to 'encouraging loyalty', now in reg 32(2).[2] Arguably, it would be harder to show that a benefit encourages loyalty, rather than merely rewards it. Why the change? The DTI's 'Notes on Regulations' which accompanied the final version of the Regulations shed no light on this.

It seems likely that employment tribunals will be sympathetic to employers which consider they have a business need to reward loyal service of employees, provided they have addressed their minds to using service-related benefits as a means to achieve this. This may well have the result of effectively exempting all service-related benefits if an employer can show it took an active decision to use or continue using the relevant benefit for this purpose.

It is interesting that the government has chosen to include rewarding experience as a business-need employers can rely on, without having to show it as a proportionate means of achieving their aim (ie to justify it objectively). The European Court of Justice (ECJ) decision in *Cadman v Health and Safety Executive* (an equal pay case),[3] would tend to support the inclusion of rewarding experience. The ECJ determined that use of length of service as a criterion is an appropriate way to reward experience, which enables a worker to perform his or her duties better. There is no need to justify specifically why this is appropriate for a particular job, unless the employee produces evidence which raises serious doubts about the appropriateness. Despite this decision, it seems that there may be many cases where longer service does not equate to better experience (and the better performance of duties) in a particular role. This may well be an area of dispute in the coming years.

On the face of it, the business-need test should be easier to satisfy than the objective justification test. An employer will be not required to show that use of the service-related criterion is a proportionate means of achieving the aim in question, or that there is a less discriminatory way of achieving the aim. The employer will, however, need to show that it 'reasonably appeared' to it that the service-related benefits fulfilled the business need identified.

This means that it will not be sufficient for an employer simply to assert, when defending a claim, that it had a particular business need. Employers will be expected to demonstrate that they have given consideration to whether they have the business need relied on. They will also need to be able to show an employment tribunal why they believed the service-related benefit was effective in fulfilling that need.

It is not clear what kind of evidence employers will be required to produce to persuade an employment tribunal that they believe their service-related benefit fulfils a business need. Evidence which employers could try to collect includes:

- responses to employee satisfaction surveys covering pay and benefits;
- information from exit interviews relating to pay and benefits;
- information on benchmarking benefits packages within the employer's industry or sector; and
- data on staff turnover within the employer's organisation and within the market sector.

It will be difficult to gather evidence which is measurable in an accurate way and it is unlikely that employment tribunals will expect a 'scientific' analysis. No doubt, cautious employers will seek to gather evidence, at least until the expectations of tribunals are clearer.

As with the standard test of justification, employers should be able to assess their belief in their business need post introduction of the Regulations and not at the time the benefit was introduced. It will not be necessary to look back many years into the intentions of decision makers who have long since left the organisation.[4] However, defending a claim by relying on the business-need exception is likely to be easier for an employer which has addressed its mind to the issue before a challenge is made.

Example:

Flower Power Kombi Hire provides for increased holiday entitlement after 2, 5, 10 and 15 years' service. This has been the case since time immemorial (or, at least since Rita, in the accounts department, joined 30 years ago). The first two increases are definitely lawful. However, Flower Power Kombi Hire must show a reasonable belief in the business benefits of the increases after 10 and 15 years' service. The current HR Manager, Scott, believes that employees have come to expect the benefit and whilst it probably isn't a major consideration, he believes that it contributes to the feel of a company that values its long-serving staff. Scott has no empirical evidence to show this. However, it is likely that a tribunal will accept that he had a reasonable belief in the business benefit of the holiday increases.

Employers will also be reassured by the decision of the ECJ in *Cadman*.[5] This decision related to a claim brought under the Equal Pay Act 1970, where the difference in pay between the claimant and her comparators was due to the longer service of the comparators. The ECJ decided that employers do not need to justify specifically the use of length of service to determine pay, even where this results in disparate pay between men and women employed in equal work or work of equal value.

The ECJ said that employers had a legitimate aim in rewarding experience, acknowledging that employees with greater experience would tend to perform their duties better. As a general rule, the ECJ, therefore, determined that employers could base pay on length of service to reward experience (confirming the decision in *Danfoss Handels- og Kontorfunktionaerernes Forbund i Danmark v Dansk Arbejdsgiverforening* (*acting for Danfoss*)).[6]

The court went on to hold that specific justification would be required where a worker provided evidence that raised serious doubts that length of service is appropriate to attain that objective with regard to their particular job. Whilst this case considered the requisite threshold for establishing objective justification of the use of service, the decision suggests that the courts and tribunals are not likely to scrutinise service-related benefits too closely, particularly where an exception applies.

1 See **6.4.2**.
2 See also 'Equality and Diversity: Coming of Age', DTI, July 2005, para 5.1.8, p 46 which refers to the business benefit of rewarding staff loyalty.

3 [2006] IRLR 969, ECJ.
4 **Chapter 4, 4.7.7**.
5 [2006] IRLR 969, ECJ.
6 [1989] IRLR 532 ECJ.

(c) Counting service

In relation to how service is to be counted, reg 32 states:

> '(3) In calculating a worker's length of service for these purposes, A shall calculate –
>
> (a) the length of time the worker has been working for him doing work which he reasonably considers to be at or above a particular level (assessed by reference to the demands made on the worker, for example, in terms of effort, skills and decision making); or
>
> (b) the length of time the worker has been working for him in total;
>
> and on each occasion on which he decides to use the criterion of length of service in relation to the award of a benefit to workers, it is for him to decide which of these definitions to use to calculate their lengths of service.
>
> (4) For the purposes of paragraph (3), in calculating the length of time a worker has been working for him –
>
> (a) A shall calculate the length of time in terms of the number of weeks during the whole or part of which the worker was working for him;
>
> (b) A may discount any period during which the worker was absent from work (including any period of absence which at the time it occurred was thought by A or the worker to be permanent) unless in all the circumstances (including the way in which other workers' absences occurring in similar circumstances are treated by A in calculating their lengths of service) it would not be reasonable for him to do so;
>
> (c) A may discount any period of time during which the worker was present at work ("the relevant period") where –
>
> (i) the relevant period preceded a period during which the worker was absent from work, and
>
> (ii) in all the circumstances (including the length of the worker's absence, the reason for his absence, the effect his absence has had on his ability to discharge the duties of his work, and the way in which other

workers are treated by A in similar circumstances) it is reasonable for A to discount the relevant period.'

Employers therefore have a choice under reg 32(3) about how they count employees' length of service for the purpose of the exception:

- count only service at or above a particular level; or
- count employees' total service.

If the employer chooses to count service at or above a particular level, it must count service which it 'reasonably believes' to be at a particular level. The level is assessed by reference to the demands made on the worker in terms of the 'effort, skill and decision-making' required of him. These are given as examples only, but mirror the examples of factors to be taken into account when determining job value for the purpose of an equal pay claim based on work of equal value.[1] It is not clear how employment tribunals will assess this in practice.[2]

Regardless of which method employers choose, they are also allowed to discount certain periods from the calculation if it is reasonable to do so under reg 32(4). These periods are:

- periods of absence (including absence that was thought to be permanent at the time)[3]; and
- periods of work that preceded a period of absence.[4]

Employers will probably need to treat employees consistently in discounting these periods in order for it to be reasonable for periods to be discounted.

Discounting periods of absence could discriminate in ways which are not related to age. For example, if periods of maternity or parental leave, or periods of sickness absence that relate to a disability, are not counted towards employees' service, the employer may face other claims of discrimination.

The provision in reg 32(4) allowing employers to count 'total service', and to disregard periods of employment prior to an absence from work, means that employers are permitted (but not obliged) to count only continuous service. This means that an employer would not need to count the previous service of an employee who had left the organisation and returned at a later date. The employee's 'absence' from work when he or she initially left would count as an absence which was thought to be permanent at the time.

This effectively allows employers, if they so wish, to reset the clock if someone leaves and rejoins the organisation at a later date. However, it needs to be applied consistently to all employees.

Example:

An employer awards three extra days' holiday after five years of service. An employee worked for the employer for three years until his resignation in 2003. He then starts working for the employer again in 2006. The employer will be permitted, if it wishes, to discount the period of 'permanent absence' between 2003 and 2006, as well as the period of work prior to the 2003 resignation as it treats other employees in this way. The employee will, therefore, be awarded the extra holiday in 2011, when he has accumulated five years' continuous service.

Total service for the purpose of reg 32(3)(b) may need to include service with another employer. Regulation 32(5) states:

> '(5) For the purposes of paragraph (3)(b), a worker shall be treated as having worked for A during any period during which he worked for another if –
>
> (a) that period is treated as a period of employment with A for the purposes of the 1996 Act by virtue of the operation of section 218 of that Act; or
>
> (b) were the worker to be made redundant by A, that period and the period he has worked for A would amount to "relevant service" within the meaning of section 155 of that Act.

This means that service with a different employer must be counted for the purpose of the exception where there has been a change of employer falling within the scope of s 218 of the Employment Rights Act (ERA) 1996, including a move from one associated employer to another[5] or a transfer under the Transfer of Undertakings (Protection of Employment) Regulations 2006. Service must also be counted if it would be counted for the purpose of qualifying for a redundancy payment under s 155 of ERA 1996.[6]

1 See **1(5)** Equal Pay Act 1970.
2 In equal value claims under the Equal Pay Act 1970, special Equal Value Procedure Rules apply (Sch 6, Employment Tribunals (Constitution and Rules of Procedure) Regulations 2004, SI 2004/1861). Among other things these rules provide for the relevant jobs to be evaluated by a tribunal-appointed job evaluation expert.
3 See reg 32(4)(b).
4 See reg 32(4)(c).
5 See ERA 1996, s 218(7).
6 Calculated in accordance with s 214 of the ERA 1996.

6.3.3 Types of service-related benefit

Set out below are examples of common service-related benefits, and how the exemption in the Regulations would apply. Employers may provide other service-related benefits which are not covered here. Consideration needs to be given in each case to whether the benefit will meet the requirements of the five-year or business-need exception. Service-related pay is dealt with below in **6.4.1**.

(a) Entitlement to participate after completing probationary period

Many employers' benefits schemes are only available to employees once their probationary period has been completed. This can include access to:

- private medical insurance;
- income protection insurance;
- pension scheme;
- life assurance;
- sick pay;
- season ticket loan; and
- flexible benefits schemes (which may include some of the benefits outlined above).

Probationary periods are usually three or six months in duration. Using the probationary period as a qualifying period will therefore fall within the scope of the five-year exception.

Some employers provide for probationary periods to be extended if performance has not been entirely satisfactory during the initial period. In that case, if the probationary period is extended and the employee is not given access to the scheme until the end of the extended period, permission to join the scheme is arguably not service related, but performance related. The service-related exception in the Regulations is unlikely to apply in those circumstances. However, given that probationary periods would only very rarely be extended beyond a year, it is unlikely that this would give rise to a disproportionate impact on a particular age group which would require the employer to justify the practice.

(b) Increasing holiday entitlement

Holiday entitlement is commonly increased according to length of service. There are a number of ways in which such a scheme could operate:

- a gradual increase, providing an extra day per year of service (usually up to a maximum number of extra days) – eg as set out in the example in **6.2.1** (a) above);
- a gradual increase, but commencing only after a certain amount of service – eg after five years' service, an extra day per year of service up to a maximum of five days after ten years' service;
- a number of extra days awarded in a block after a certain number of years' service – eg five extra days after ten years' service; or
- extra days awarded in stages – eg two extra days after five years' service, then another three days after ten years' service.

Some employers also give extra holiday after very long periods of service, for example 20 years. This is less common.

If an employer only awards extra holiday according to service of five years or less, the position is very straightforward and the five-year exception will apply. If extra holiday is awarded after more than five years' service, the business-need exception is likely to apply. The employer would need to show that it had a business need and that giving extra holiday in this way fulfilled that need.

It is likely that an employment tribunal would be persuaded that awarding extra holiday according to length of service rewarded loyalty, and probably also that it encouraged loyalty. Once an employee has earned his or her extra holiday entitlement, there may well be a disincentive to move to a job where the employee would have to start again with the basic holiday entitlement (all other things being equal). It is also likely that extra holiday encourages the motivation of employees. However, if challenged, employers would need to show that their particular holiday scheme fell within an exception and may possibly need to produce evidence to demonstrate that the business-need exception was satisfied.

(c) Sabbaticals/career breaks

Many employers now operate sabbatical policies. Sabbaticals are usually only available to employees with a certain length of service. Normally, employees will be eligible to apply for sabbaticals once they have the requisite length of service. Whether a sabbatical is then granted is usually at the employer's discretion, taking into account the requirements of the business.

If the service criterion is five years or less, the five-year exception will apply and the service-related eligibility criterion will be automatically permitted by the Regulations. It is fairly common for sabbaticals to be given only to employees with relatively long service, so the service qualification may well exceed five years in many organisations. Sabbaticals are typically unpaid, although some employers do offer paid sabbaticals.

Less commonly, some employers provide an extra block of 'holiday' after a certain period of service – eg after ten years' service, an employee is entitled to a one-off block of four weeks' additional holiday. Usually these are designed so that the employee can take a long break, effectively a 'mini-sabbatical'.

Employers whose sabbatical policies require service of more than five years will need to show that their policy fulfils a business need. It seems reasonable that sabbaticals could be said to reward loyalty and encourage the motivation of employees who take them, but employers may be required to produce some evidence of this. Given that many sabbaticals are unpaid, it is perhaps unlikely that this is an area in which many challenges will be made as there will not be any financial loss.

(d) Increasing sick pay entitlement

Many employers provide a basic sick pay entitlement which increases according to service. There are many different variations in how sick pay is increased.

Example:

An employer's sick pay policy provides the following entitlement to company sick pay:

Length of service	**Sick pay**
Less than 2 years	4 weeks
More than 2 years, but less than 10	3 months' full pay plus 3 months' half pay
10 years or more	6 months' full pay plus 6 months' half pay

For increases based on five years' service or less, the five-year exception will automatically exempt such increases. In the example above, the increase in sick pay at two years would be covered by the five-year exception, but the increase at 10 years could only fall within the business-need exception.

Where sick pay is increased based on service of more than five years, it would need to be determined whether the employer reasonably believed that this fulfilled a business need. It seems a reasonable proposition that increasing sick pay rewards and encourages loyalty, but it is not clear what, if any, evidence an employer might be required to produce.

(e) Notice entitlements

Some employment contracts provide for longer serving employees to be entitled to (and obliged to give) longer notice to terminate their employment. It is also common for notice to increase after completion of the probationary period. The right to receive longer notice based on service could be argued to be a service-related 'benefit', particularly where there is also a contractual right to receive pay in lieu of notice if notice is not given.

If notice and notice pay could be argued to be a benefit in this way, there is an interesting question as to how the exception applies. The right to a payment in lieu of notice arises 'by virtue of [the employee] ceasing to work for [the employer]' and reg 32(7) would, as a consequence, exclude it from the exception. The use of service in determining notice requirements for the purpose of a payment in lieu would therefore need to be justified objectively. The right to receive notice itself arguably does not, however, arise by virtue of the employee ceasing to work for the employer, as it is a right which crystallises before the employment ends.

This distinction between how notice itself and payments in lieu of notice might be treated is illogical and it seems unlikely that the service-related benefit exception was intended to have this effect. In any event, it may well be relatively easy for employers to justify giving longer notice to long servers, particularly in light of the *Cadman* decision. Where the notice to be given by the employee also increases by service, it is likely that this would also be justifiable. Employers have a legitimate interest in having a longer period to effect handovers and transfer knowledge of long-serving employees, who are likely to have greater experience of the organisation in question.

An employer which sticks to the service-related statutory minimum period of notice should be able to rely on the statutory authority exception. Employers which link notice to service but are more generous than the statutory minimum may need to justify their practices.

Example:

Marina Developments' standard terms provide for one month's notice for employees with less than one year's service; three months for those with one to three years' service and six months for those with over three years' service. They reserve the right to pay in lieu of notice. This disadvantages younger employees who are more likely to have joined recently and is, hence, potentially indirectly discriminatory. Marina Developments cannot rely on the statutory authority exception. It is not clear whether or not they can rely on the service-related benefit exception. This depends on whether it is taken outside of the exception by coming within the definition of a 'benefit awarded to a worker by virtue of his ceasing to work for [the employer]'.[1] On the face of it the variable payments in lieu of notice are more likely to come within the natural meaning of that definition than the right to notice. This outcome, however, is problematic in its implications. In any event, if it is not covered by the service-related benefit exception there must be a fair chance that Marina Developments will be able to justify it as a proportionate means of achieving a legitimate aim, such as rewarding loyalty or giving the company adequate protection from departing employees who will be more embedded within the organisation after a longer period of employment. The issues are similar to those regarding service-related enhanced redundancy payments which are considered in detail in **Chapter 11**.[2]

1 See reg 32(7).
2 **Chapter 11**, **11.5.3(b)(i)**.

(f) Long-service awards

Employers give long-service awards in a multitude of different ways. Awards may include bonus-type payments, gifts, gift vouchers or simply certificates recognising service. Additional holiday is sometimes awarded (see **6.3.2(b)** and **6.3.2(c)** above).

The number of years' service which tends to be rewarded varies greatly from employer to employer. However, most long-service awards will be given for more than five years' service, so would fall outside the scope of the five-year exception.

The question would then be whether a particular long-service award fulfils a business need of the employer so as to come within the ambit of the business-need exception, and what evidence is available to show this. The aim behind such awards is clearly to reward loyalty, although it is questionable whether such awards also *encourage* loyalty (the example relating to loyalty now contained in reg 32 – see above). Such awards will probably contribute to increased motivation as they are likely to enhance employees' feelings of well-being within the organisation.

(g) Service-related retirement gifts

Retirement gifts are sometimes also linked to length of service. These gifts would not fall within the scope of the service exception as they relate to the termination of employment.[1] This means that an employer may have to justify objectively the use of service criteria in awarding the benefit, as well as justifying the direct discrimination which arises as a result of only awarding the benefit to employees who are old enough to be retiring (see **6.6** below in relation to retirement gifts more generally). Such gifts are usually of a relatively low value. It is also questionable whether the service element of these benefits gives rise to any age discrimination in any event, as they will usually only be available to employees who have reached normal retirement age or thereabouts.

1 See reg 32(7).

(h) Other benefits linked to qualifying periods

Benefits relating to family leave (over and above statutory entitlements) are often linked to service. For example, company maternity pay and paternity pay. Given that such qualifying periods tend to be short, they are unlikely to have a disproportionate impact on any particular group and will usually fall within the five-year exception.

6.4 Pay

In most organisations, age does not directly influence pay. However, the factors taken into account in determining pay may result in indirect age discrimination.

Length of service and experience are often taken into account in fixing pay, even where employers do not have structured pay scales. Experience is often a factor in setting starting salaries. Length of service or seniority, is often an integral part of an employer's pay scale. Using length of service or experience as pay criteria potentially indirectly discriminates against younger workers, as they are less likely to have built up many years of experience or service.

Besides having an impact on pay arrangements employers put in place for their employees, the Regulations affect some partnership remuneration arrangements in a similar way.

Although few pay decisions are directly based on age, the national minimum wage (NMW) is an exception to this and is dealt with specifically in the Regulations.

6.4.1 Service–related pay

Many pay scales provide for pay increases based on each successive year of service, even if this is simply one of several factors. Pay arrangements will often be structured so that a particular pay scale applies to a particular grade, and pay is based on service within that grade.

It is possible for service-related pay to result in large and persistent discrepancies. In many cases, an employee entering a new grade at the bottom of that grade may never be able to 'catch up' with employees who have longer service in that grade, even if the 'new' employee is able to perform the job as well or better than the longer-serving employees.

(a) Applying the service exception to pay

Service-based pay is likely to fall within the exception for service-related benefits in reg 32. The exception refers to the 'award of *any* benefit' (emphasis added)[1] and the only exclusion is for benefits payable by virtue of the worker ceasing to work for the employer. Pay has therefore been widely accepted as falling within the scope of the exception. The Explanatory Memorandum to the Regulations makes it clear that it was intended to cover pay- and non-pay benefits.[2]

Pay based on five years' service or less will benefit from the five-year exception in the normal way. Where service-based pay increments continue beyond five years, the issue will be whether the employer can show that it believes service-related pay fulfils a business-need of its organisation.

'Rewarding experience' is one of the examples in reg 32 of a business need an employer may seek to rely on, and this is particularly relevant to pay. In light of the ECJ's decision in *Cadman*,[3] employers are likely to have a relatively straightforward task in persuading employment tribunals that they reasonably believe service-related pay fulfils the business need of rewarding experience.

The *Cadman* decision leaves open the possibility, in equal pay claims, for employees to challenge length of service as a valid reason for pay differentials, if there is good evidence why the employer should not be able to rely on it. The same possibility exists in relation to age discrimination, although the employer's reliance on the business-need exception of rewarding experience would, on the face of it, be an easier test to satisfy than the objective justification test considered in *Cadman*. There must, however, be some scope to argue that any derogation from the test for justifying the indirectly sex discriminatory impact of service-related pay by an employment tribunal in considering whether or not it unlawfully discriminates on grounds of age would be incompatible with the Directive.

If, for example, an employee had some evidence that employees with longer service performed no better (or, perhaps, performed less well) than those with shorter service (perhaps they became stale after a while), the employer may struggle to show that it reasonably appeared that service-related pay fulfilled the business need of rewarding experience. It may still be open to the employer to argue that it believed service-related pay fulfilled another business need, such as rewarding loyalty.

1 See re 32(1).
2 See p 5, para 7.15 of the Explanatory Memorandum.
3 [2006] IRLR 969, ECJ – see **6.3.2(b)**.

(b) Counting service

The way service is counted for the purpose of the service exception is likely to be particularly important for pay issues. As mentioned above, employers have the choice of counting employees' total service, or counting service at or above a particular level.[1] It is entirely up to the employer which method to use. However, in relation to pay, counting service at or above a particular level or grade is likely to be more appropriate.

Given the way in which work at a particular level should be assessed by the employer (see **6.3.1 (c)** above) it is possible that service could be incorrectly counted in some cases, where the employee is working at a certain level, but the employer treats him as working at a lower level. This may result in the exception not applying in that particular case.

Example:

An employee, Mustafa, works as an Assistant Sales Manager of Batsford Ltd. His immediate manager, Malcolm, is the Sales Manager. Malcolm is absent from work due to illness. During his absence, Mustafa is asked to 'act up' in the Sales Manager role. He undertakes all the duties of that post and is paid a salary supplement to reflect his extra responsibilities. After six months, the company learns that Malcolm will not be able to return to work.

Mustafa is then offered a promotion to the role of Sales Manager, which he accepts. This is a higher grade than the Assistant Sales Manager post and now on the Managers' pay scale. Upon promotion, Mustafa starts at the bottom of the Managers' pay scale. One of the elements of the pay scale is length of service in the Manager grade. Mustafa's service is counted from the time he was promoted.

Arguably, Batsford Ltd should have counted his service from the time they asked him to 'act up' in the Sales Manager role. From that time, he was carrying out work at the same level as the Manager grade, even though he had not formally been promoted. By failing to count that service, Batsford Ltd may have lost its right to rely on the service exception in relation to Mustafa's service-related pay, in the event of a challenge on age grounds.

In a situation such as the example above, in order for an employee to be able to bring a successful claim, he would first of all need to show that the service-related pay arrangements placed his particular age group at a disadvantage. Even if the employer was not able to rely on the exception, because of the way service was counted, they may still be able to objectively justify service-related pay. The *Cadman*[2] decision suggests that it will not be easy for employees to challenge service-related pay arrangements.

As mentioned above, amongst the examples listed in art 6(2) of the Directive which might amount, in appropriate circumstances, to justification of age discrimination is 'the fixing of minimum conditions of .. seniority in service for access to ... certain advantages linked to employment'.[3] This reinforces the view that service-related pay will normally not amount to unlawful indirect age discrimination.

1 See reg 32(3).
2 [2006] IRLR 969, ECJ.
3 See art 6(2).

6.4.2 Experience and pay

Unlike service, there is no exception in the Regulations relating to the use of experience in pay decisions. Basing pay on years of experience is likely to place younger workers at a disadvantage and employers will need to justify experience-related pay objectively where such a disadvantage arises.

Experience is often taken into account when setting starting salaries and differences, which arise at the recruitment stage and can persist into the future. It is less common for experience to be used directly in pay scales or decisions about pay increases in the same role. However, there are some sectors in which experience is used in this way.

(a) Using and justifying experience in pay decisions

The desire to attract, retain and reward experienced staff will be a legitimate aim for employers to pursue. The government appeared to recognise this by including 'rewarding experience' as an example of a business need in the service-related benefits exception in reg 32. The *Cadman* decision also reinforces the position that it is legitimate for an employer to pursue such an aim.[1]

Article 6(2) of the Directive also lists among its examples 'the fixing of minimum conditions of . . . professional experience . . . for access to . . . certain advantages linked to employment.'[2] It remains to be seen whether this reference to *professional experience* is important and that it will be easier to justify pay scales linked to experience in professional jobs than in others.

Using experience as a factor in pay may result in younger workers being disadvantaged in terms of pay, in relation to the same or similar rôles, or jobs of the same value within an organisation. As there is no specific exception for experience, the question is then whether the use of experience in an employer's pay decisions is a proportionate way of achieving the aim of attracting and rewarding experienced staff.

Linking pay to a specific number of years' experience is likely, in most cases, to be hard to justify. For example, it may be difficult to demonstrate a significant difference between even 10 and 15 years' experience in a particular job, in terms of the extra value the additional five years would bring to the role. Employers are more likely to be able to justify taking into account the particular type and quality of experience they are looking for, rather than numbers of years, even if there is a discriminatory impact. Asserting that a certain number of years' experience is necessary, without reference to the actual experience gained during those years, is unlikely to be sufficient to justify a discriminatory impact in pay.

Any discrepancy in pay based on experience needs to be proportionate in order to be justified on an objective basis. Proportionality will include the amount of the extra salary awarded mirroring the amount of extra experience. Employers paying a large premium to some employees who are only slightly more experienced than others, may find this difficult to justify if it can be demonstrated that a particular age group is put at a disadvantage as the resulting discrimination might not be considered proportionate to the employer's aim.

1 *Cadman* [2006] IRLR 969, ECJ.
2 See art 6(2)(b), Council Directive, establishing a general framework for equal treatment in employment and occupation (2000/78/EC).

(b) Experience/Post-qualification experience – based pay scales

Most employers do not base their pay scales on experience. However, in the legal and accountancy sectors, amongst others, it is common for the salaries of professional staff to be based on experience. Salaries are normally fixed by reference to the number of years of post-qualification experience (PQE) of employees. There has been much debate regarding the use of PQE in both recruitment and reward and the impact that the Regulations may have and the legal press has reported a number of solicitors firms moving away from a direct link between pay and PQE.

Basing pay on years of PQE is potentially indirectly discriminatory, as younger employees are less likely to have as many years of experience as older employees. However, it is potentially justifiable. Employers have a legitimate aim in rewarding and retaining competent experienced staff. The question is, therefore, whether basing pay on PQE is a proportionate means of achieving that aim.

Firms operate their PQE-based pay scales in a variety of ways, for instance:

- a fixed point salary scale, increasing with each year of PQE;
- a salary range for each year of PQE, with performance taken into account to determine where in the range a particular employee should be placed; and
- a salary scale (usually fixed point), but with flexibility to 'deem' a particular employee to have a different level of PQE than their actual level – for instance, where a lawyer has worked in another jurisdiction before qualifying in the United Kingdom, or where a particular level of performance demands that an employee should be treated as having a higher or lower level of PQE.

Salaries ordinarily increase in regular intervals for each year of PQE. This is also normally related to an increase in the rate the firm charges clients for work done by its employees, which, in turn, should determine the complexity or difficulty of the work the employee carries out. Most firms' salary scales reach a plateau at around seven to nine years' PQE, after which salary increases are largely based on cost of living and become smaller.

Although the system appears to be based solely on economic factors, ie the profitability of the firm based on the business model of paying higher salaries to employees whose charge-out rates are higher, it is likely that in most cases PQE-based pay can be justified. Inevitably, there will be anomalies arising from individual performance, but the level of experience and ability to undertake more difficult work broadly correlates with years of PQE.

In assessing the justification of a pay scale of this type, it is relevant to consider whether or not there might be an alternative less discriminatory means of achieving the employer's aim. For example, it is quite difficult to envisage an appropriate means of setting lawyers or accountants charge-out rates other than by reference to professional experience.

The *Cadman* decision supports this, in holding that employees with more experience will, generally speaking, be better able to perform their duties. Awarding regular pay increases according to PQE does therefore seem to be proportionate, particularly if increases become smaller at a stage where one extra year of PQE makes less difference. In addition, if experience or PQE-based pay is also accompanied by a separate performance-related bonus, it is likely that this will be easier to justify.

6.4.3 Performance and pay

Most pay decisions and pay scales will include factors other than service or experience. Performance is frequently taken into account in the assessment of pay increases. If service and/or experience are only part of a wider assessment that includes performance, any discriminatory impact resulting from service/experience is likely to be smaller and easier to justify.

However, it is possible that some aspects of performance assessment could also give rise to age discrimination. This may be because specific performance criteria are discriminatory, or because the criteria are applied in a discriminatory way. In addition to affecting pay increases, performance will often have an impact on bonus awards.[1] Examples of potentially discriminatory performance criteria are set out below.

The considerations here are similar to those involved in selecting and applying redundancy selection criteria. These are considered in **Chapter 11**.

1 **Chapter 7**, **7.4**.

(a) Attendance/sickness absence

Health issues can affect performance, in terms of both absence and quality of work. Sickness absence may be taken into account directly, or may have an effect on overall productivity. An employee may also under-perform generally if suffering from an illness.

Indirect age discrimination issues may arise if older workers tend to suffer more health problems than younger workers. Employers will also need to take into account potential obligations under the Disability Discrimination Act 1995 (DDA), where a medical condition amounts to a disability. In particular, employers have a duty to make reasonable adjustments to prevent their arrangements placing a disabled employee at a disadvantage compared to other employees who do not have that disability. This would include adjustments to enable the employee to perform their job duties – eg allowing an employee to work at home when they might otherwise not be able to travel to work.

The interrelationship between age and health issues is explored in more detail in **Chapter 9**.

(b) Potential

Employers sometimes take into account potential for development when assessing performance. This may be included as a specific criterion in appraisals or other performance assessments, but this is relatively uncommon.

It is more likely that an employer would make assumptions about the potential of an older worker nearing retirement, in terms of the development opportunities they are willing to pursue. In practice, this will probably arise when younger employees are being actively developed by their managers, and older workers are overlooked. This may mean that older employees are denied training and development opportunities, which has a subsequent impact on their performance assessments and promotion opportunities.

Such assumptions about the potential of older and younger workers are discriminatory and likely to lead to claims, particularly where there is an impact on pay.

(c) Flexibility

The issues arising in relation to indirect sex discrimination may be just as relevant for indirect age discrimination. For example, employees with young children are more likely to find it more difficult to undertake significant travel or to work long or unsocial hours. In some organisations, this may have an impact on their performance assessment.

Employees with childcare responsibilities are statistically more likely to fall within a particular age range, and those employees may be put at a disadvantage if there is an expectation that employees will work long hours, or undertake a large amount of travel. Justification will be required for any practice that places a particular group at a disadvantage in this way, as for indirect sex discrimination.

Besides childcare, there is a potential impact on employees with responsibilities for looking after elderly relatives. Again, those with elder care responsibilities are statistically more likely to be in a particular age group. They may similarly find it more difficult to undertake travel and work long/unsocial hours.

Employees bringing indirect age discrimination claims based on the impact of childcare/elder care responsibilities will need to identify their pools for comparison and show that their particular age group is, in fact, placed at a disadvantage. This is likely to be far from easy. Once this is established, however, it will be for the employer to show objective justification. This is considered in more detail in **Chapter 5**.[1]

1 **Chapter 5**, **5.4.6**.

6.4.4 Partnership profit share and the lockstep

There are various ways in which partnerships arrange how to share profits among their partners, including a very simple system of all partners taking equal share of the profit. The most common arrangements in professional partnerships (such as law firms, accountancy practices) are:

(a) seniority – commonly referred to as a 'lockstep';
(b) performance; and
(c) a combination of seniority and performance – a 'modified lock-step'.

These arrangements have the potential to be indirectly discriminatory on grounds of age and will, therefore, breach the Regulations unless objectively justified or covered by one of the exceptions.

(a) Lockstep

Under a lockstep system, a partner takes an increasing proportion of the profits available for distribution with each year he is a partner, regardless of performance. The lockstep normally has a 'ceiling' at which point an individual partner's percentage share stops increasing.

Although a seniority-based system is indirectly discriminatory, the service-related benefits exception in reg 32 applies to partners and partnerships as well as to employees.[1] A profit-share scale which increases profit according to seniority will fall under the five-year exception for the first five years, and is capable of coming within the scope of the business-need exception after that. The partnership would need to show that it reasonably believed that its profit-share arrangements based on seniority fulfilled a business need. It is likely to be relatively straightforward to show that such a system encourages loyalty.

In some systems, the percentage share may decrease as a partner reaches a particular level of tenure or moves closer to retirement. This would discriminate against older partners and would need to be objectively justified. Where the reason for the reduction relates to long tenure, it should be noted that the service-related benefits exception in reg 32 would not apply. The exception only applies to the receipt of enhanced benefits with increasing service.

In some pure seniority-based systems, it may be possible for partners who are hired from outside the organisation to enter the lockstep at a level above the very bottom. Therefore, in a claim involving a lateral hire (whether as the claimant or a comparator), the difference between the profit share of the relevant partners may not be due to service and the exception would not apply. Assuming the claimant could show potential discrimination, the normal test of objective justification would then apply.

The partnership might be able to satisfy this justification test by referring to the aim of attracting and fairly remunerating a partner with a strong client base or key skills. The partnership would have greater problems if its aim was to reflect the experience of the incoming partner as it would then be tacitly admitting that its pay scale was not designed to encourage and reward loyalty (which is not necessarily linked to performance), but to reflect either experience or skills and performance. Here, experience is being used as a proxy for performance in circumstances where the evidence might demonstrate it to be a poor proxy particularly if the shorter-serving partners often have higher personal or client fees.[2] See **6.4.2** above for more detail on the use of experience as opposed to service as a justification for pay scales.

Pure lockstep systems may also cause problems in connection with retirement. The retirement exception in reg 30 applicable to employees[3] does not apply to partners. Therefore, if a partnership wishes to retire any partners purely on age grounds, this would need to be objectively justified, which is likely to be quite difficult. Once a partner reaches the lockstep ceiling, he will continue to receive a profit share at that highest level, regardless of performance. In the past, in cases where a partner has been under-performing at that level, partnerships have often simply waited until the partner could be retired at the retirement age under the partnership deed. This will no longer be a safe option, and partnerships will need to deal more proactively with performance issues if they want to avoid under-performing partners drawing profits at the highest level.

Further, if the partnership's business need or legitimate aim underpinning lockstep is rewarding and/or encouraging loyalty (or even experience), the partnership that expects the longer-serving partner to be performing at a higher level to justify his higher pay may be in trouble. The pay differential is not being explained by the firm by performance but loyalty (or experience).

1 See definition of 'worker' in reg 2(2).
2 See discussion on *Cadman* linked to experience/service in **6.3.2(b)**.
3 **Chapter 12**, **12.8.5(a)**.

(b) Performance

Some profit-share arrangements are based purely on performance, with no reference to seniority. The performance criteria used vary widely according to the needs of the business. In many cases, the criteria used will be age neutral. However, care must still be taken to avoid indirectly discriminatory criteria, and to ensure that age-neutral criteria are not applied in a discriminatory way, as the assessment of performance often entails subjective judgments. (see **6.4.3** above).

(c) Modified lockstep

Many professional partnerships use a combination of seniority and performance to determine profit share, often referred to as a modified lockstep.

Example:

The Law Partnership has a seven point scale. New partners start at scale point one. However, they don't automatically go up a scale point each year. At the end of each financial year there is consideration of which partners' performance justifies a move up the scale. If a partner performs very badly he can move down a scale point but this is rare.

Some, more recently appointed (and largely younger) partners will find that they are performing better than other partners who are higher on the scale and, therefore, paid more. This arises from the higher paid partner having been with the partnership longer and also having performed well in previous years. This should come within the service-related exception to the extent that it is explained by the greater period of service as a partner and, would probably satisfy the objective justification test insofar as it reflects high performance in past years.

6.4.5 National Minimum Wage

The NMW Act 1998 and the NMW Regulations 1999[1] provide for the NMW to be paid according to different age bands.

1 SI 1999/584.

(a) Exception for National Minimum Wage

The NMW rates in place from 1 October 2007 are[1]:

- £5.52 for workers aged 22 and over (the 'Adult NMW');
- £4.60 for workers aged 18 to 21; and
- £3.40 for workers under 18 years of age.

The age bands directly discriminate on age grounds. In the consultation paper 'Coming of Age', the government stated that they considered the NMW age bands were consistent with the Directive and objectively justified on the basis that:

- the bands make it easier for young people to secure employment, as many employers would be unwilling to pay the higher Adult NMW to younger workers; and
- the age bands encourage young people to remain in education.[2]

The Regulations provide for the age-related NMW bands to remain, under a specific exception in reg 31:

'(1) Nothing in Part 2 or 3 shall render it unlawful for a relevant person ("A") to be remunerated in respect of his work at a rate which is lower than the rate at which another such person ("B") is remunerated for his work where –

(a) the hourly rate of the national minimum wage for a person of A's age is lower than that for a person of B's age, and

(b) the rate at which A is remunerated is below the single hourly rate for the national minimum wage prescribed by the Secretary of State under section 1(3) of the National Minimum Wage Act 1998.'[3]

This permits employers to continue to pay the NMW according to an employee's age, without committing an act of unlawful age discrimination.

The exception for the NMW is not limited to circumstances where the employer pays only the minimum wage to all employees doing a particular kind of work. Under the exception, employers will be able to pay:

- employees aged 22 and over more than those aged 18 to 21 doing the same job, as long as the 18 to 21 age group is paid less than the Adult NMW rate; and
- employees aged 18 to 21 more than those under 18 doing the same job, as long as those under 18 are paid less than the Adult NMW.

In either case, all employees must be paid at least the NMW applicable to their age group. Different rates of pay for employees in the same age group, doing the same job, are not permitted by the exception.

Example:

- A-Z Ltd pays employees aged 18 to 21 and under at £4.60 per hour, while paying employees aged 22 and over at a rate of £10.00 per hour for the same work. This is permitted under the legislation, even though the differential is significant, as the employees aged 21 and under are paid less than the Adult NMW.

  A-Z Ltd increases pay for the 18 to 21 age group to £7.00 per hour. This arrangement would not be permitted by the exception because the 18- to 21-year-olds would be paid more than the Adult NMW, despite the fact that they would be better off under the new arrangement. The company could only pay these rates if it could objectively justify them.

– It would not be permissible under the exception for the company to pay 18- to 20-year-olds £5.00 an hour and 21-year-olds £5.25 per hour, as different pay rates within the same age band are not allowed. A-Z Ltd would need to objectively justify these rates to avoid unlawful discrimination.

There has been widespread criticism of the effect of the exception in reg 31, as it appears to allow for potentially unfair treatment of younger workers.

Some employers have responded to the Regulations by removing pay differences based on age.

It must be arguable that retaining different age bands for NMW purposes is incompatible with the Directive. It is quite difficult to distinguish the UK's aims behind these age bands and the German Government's aims behind the relaxing of the rules on fixed-term contracts for older workers which were struck down by the ECJ in *Mangold v Helm*.[4]

The Government, however, set out its rationale for retaining the different rates in the DTI's 'Notes on Regulations'.[5] They refer to other Member States which maintain different rates and to a Low Pay Commission Report which considered that applying the adult NMW rate to young people would have adverse labour market consequences.

It should be noted that the exception only expressly covers pay. It does not cover choosing to hire young workers because the employer can pay them at a lower rate, or dismissing workers once they reach the age at which they become eligible for adult NMW. These issues are covered in **Chapters 5 and 10** respectively.[6]

1 NMW Regulations 1999 (Amendment) Regulations 2007, SI 2007/2318.
2 'Equality and Diversity: Coming of Age', DTI, March 2006, para 5.2, p 52.
3 The hourly rate is prescribed in reg 11 of the NMW Regulations 1999, (SI 1999/584) and that rate has most recently been amended by the NMW Regulations 1999 (Amendment) Regulations 2007, SI 2007/2318.
4 [2006] IRLR 143 and see consideration of *Mangold* in **Chapter 4, 4.7.2(c)**.
5 See paras 104–105, pp 18 and 19 of the Note.
6 **Chapter 5, 5.3.3(a)** and **Chapter 10, 10.2.2**.

(b) Apprentices

Regulation 31 also provides that apprentices who do not qualify for NMW can be paid less than those who do.

> '(2) Nothing in Part 2 or 3 shall render it unlawful for an apprentice who is not a relevant person to be remunerated in respect of

his work at a rate which is lower than the rate at which an apprentice who is a relevant person is remunerated for his work.

(3) In this regulation –

"apprentice" means a person who is employed under a contract of apprenticeship or, in accordance with regulation 12(3) of the National Minimum Wage Regulations 1999,[1] is to be treated as employed under such a contract;

"relevant person" means a person who qualifies for the national minimum wage[2] (whether at the single hourly rate for the national minimum wage prescribed by the Secretary of State under section 1(3) of the National Minimum Wage Act 1998 or at a different rate).'

Apprentices under age 19 or in the first year of apprenticeship are not covered by NMW rules. This provision ensures these apprentices cannot rely on the Regulations to claim equivalent pay with older or longer-serving apprentices.

1 NMW Regulations 1999, SI 1999/584, to which relevant amendments have been made by NMW Regulations 2000, SI 2000/1989 and NMW Regulations 2004, SI 2004/1930.
2 A person qualifies for the NMW if he is a person who – (a) is a worker; (b) is working, or ordinarily works, in the United Kingdom under a contract; and (c) has ceased to be of compulsory school age: see s 1(2) of the NMW Act 1998.

(c) Changes to other National Minimum Wage provisions

Other changes have been made to the NMW Regulations 1999 as a result of the Age Regulations:

- Apprentices in the first 12 months of government apprenticeships do not qualify for the NMW. Previously, apprentices in those circumstances would qualify for the NMW once they reached the age of 26. This has been removed, so that an apprentice in the first 12 months will not qualify for the NMW simply by reaching their 26th birthday.[1] Apprentices under the age of 19 still do not qualify for the NMW, even after the first 12 months of their apprenticeship.[2]
- The NMW Regulations previously provided for payment of the 18-21-year old rate to be paid to workers over the age of 21 undertaking accredited training in the first six months of their job. These provisions have now been revoked.[3] Those workers are now entitled to the Adult NMW.

1 See reg 12(2)(a) of the NMW Regulations 1999, revoked by para 58(2), Pt 2 of Sch 8 of the Employment Equality (Age) Regulations 2006.

2 See reg 12(2)(c) of the NMW Regulations 1999.
3 See reg 13, para (2) to (6) of the NMW Regulations 1999, revoked by para 58(3), Pt 2 of Sch 8 of the Employment Equality (Age) Regulations 2006.

6.5 Health benefits

The impact of the Regulations on the provision of health-related benefits is significant. These benefits are often provided under insurance policies. As the Regulations only apply, at least for the time being,[1] to the field of employment, insurance companies are free to include policy terms which discriminate on the grounds of age, either directly or indirectly.

Age is a factor which insurance companies frequently take into account in their actuarial assessment of risk, in the same way as specific medical factors and gender are taken into account. Both the Sex Discrimination Act 1975 ('SDA 1975') and the DDA 1995 have specific provisions relating to insurance.

The SDA 1975 allows discriminatory treatment on grounds of sex in relation to an annuity, life assurance policy, accident insurance policy or 'similar matter involving the assessment of risk' where the discriminatory treatment arises from reliance on actuarial or other data, from a source that it is reasonable to rely on and where it is reasonable to rely on the data in all the circumstances.[2] Gender is often taken into account in the assessment of health risks.

Under the DDA 1995, insurance providers (under the goods and services provisions) must not treat a disabled person less favourably than someone without the disability in question.[3] They also have a duty to make reasonable adjustments for disabled people, where a policy, practice or procedure makes it impossible or unreasonably difficult for a disabled person to make use of a service which is otherwise available to the public. Less favourable treatment or a failure to make adjustments will be unlawful unless justified. However, there is a specific provision setting out when the justification test will be met in relation to insurance. Less favourable treatment will be justified if it is based on information, such as actuarial data or a medical report, which is relevant to the risk to be insured, and from a source it is reasonable to rely on and where it is reasonable to rely on the information in all the circumstances.[4]

In the absence of a similar exception in the Regulations, employers using policies containing age discriminatory terms will need to justify those terms objectively in order to avoid unlawful discrimination. This may be difficult as employers have little control over the decisions insurance companies make, or the factors they take into account in reaching those decisions.

Benefits schemes which may be affected by the Regulations include:

- private medical/dental insurance;
- health checks;
- income protection insurance (IPI) – sometimes also referred to as permanent health insurance (PHI) or long-term disability benefit;
- life assurance/death in service benefit;
- critical illness cover; and
- personal accident cover.

The uncertainty regarding insured benefits has resulted in a campaign to exempt them. The Employers Forum on Age, the Association of British Insurers and GRiD (Group Risk Development) have joined forces in highlighting that this uncertainty is causing employers to decline requests from employees to work beyond 65 years when they would otherwise be happy for them to stay on, or to remove insured benefit schemes.[5]

1 See **Chapter 2, 2.5.**
2 See s 45 of the SDA 1975.
3 See s 19 of the DDA 1995.
4 See reg 4 of the Disability Discrimination (Service Providers and Public Authorities Carrying Out Functions) Regulations 2005, SI 2005/2901.
5 More details are available from the age discrimination website, *www.agediscrimination.info*.

6.5.1 When discrimination will arise

There are a number of ways employers provide health benefits that may result in age discrimination.

(a) Minimum and maximum ages for entitlement to benefits

Most health benefit schemes have a maximum age for membership, beyond which an employee will no longer be entitled to the benefit. This is part of the policy terms agreed between the employer and the relevant insurer. The maximum age is usually the same as the employer's normal retirement age (alternatively, sometimes the pension age under the employer's pension scheme where this is different from the normal retirement age).

Maximum ages in existing policies are potentially problematic for employers who have had to raise their retirement age in line with the default retirement age, or who will now have employees staying on past the normal retirement age. It will be unlawful for employers to continue to operate maximum ages in their health benefit schemes, unless this can be justified.[1]

Example:

Julia's Fashions had a retirement age of 60 before the Regulations came into force. This was aligned with the pension age under its occupational pension scheme. It also provided medical and income protection insurance to employees up to retirement. With the introduction of the Regulations, Julia's Fashions increased its retirement age to 65 but left its pension scheme unchanged. It is faced with Iain who is 59 and wants assurance that he will be covered by the schemes after 60 and Naomi who is 66 and was allowed to work beyond retirement when she reached 60 a couple of years ago. The insurers want a significant increase in premiums to cover staff up to 65 years and won't cover Naomi. It seems unlikely that Julia's Fashions will be able to stop coverage at 60 years for Iain. They will be expected to look at other insurers for Naomi. If the premiums are excessive for Naomi, they might wish to self-insure.

Although it is commonly assumed that it is only older workers who are disadvantaged by the way health benefits are provided, some benefits have minimum age requirements and therefore disadvantage younger workers. For example, health assessments are sometimes only provided to employees over the age of 40 or 50. This is considered in more detail below.[2]

1 **Chapter 12, 12.10.2**.
2 See **6.5.3(b)**.

(b) Cost of benefit varying with age

Premiums for insured health benefits can increase according to the age of the workforce or an individual employee, sometimes dramatically. This is based on a tendency for medical problems to increase with age.[1] The way in which premiums are allocated to individual employees varies between different employers and policies.

In many group schemes, particularly for medical insurance, an overall premium is calculated by reference to periodic profiles of the workforce and divided equally among the employees who are members of the scheme to give a flat rate per employee. Where the employer meets the cost of the scheme, that flat rate is the sum on which the employee will be taxed. Alternatively, where the employer passes on the cost to the employee for the benefit, the employee will simply pay the flat rate for the benefit.

However, in some schemes, individual rates are calculated according to actuarial data, including age. An older employee would, therefore, have to pay a higher premium (or be taxed on a higher sum where the employer meets the cost of the benefit). This will usually be the case where benefits are provided through flexible benefits schemes and the cost to each employee of each benefit is calculated according to actuarial factors including his age.

Having to pay a higher premium clearly places the older worker at a disadvantage in these circumstances and amounts to unlawful direct age discrimination unless the employer can objectively justify it. It is arguable that having to pay more tax (where the employer provides the insurance as a taxable benefit) also results in the employee being discriminated against. This seems, however, to come within the statutory authority exceptions, as the tax charge is being levied by reference to the cost to the employer by reason of HMRC rules. When considering justification, a key issue is whether the employer could operate the scheme in a less discriminatory way. Where it is an option to allocate premiums within a group policy to individuals on the basis of a flat rate (which should often be possible other than within a flexible benefits scheme), employers may be expected to do so.

However, a potential problem with operating a scheme in this way is that, in some cases, younger employees will not take up the benefit, as they will be able to secure personal cover more cheaply than the tax on the flat rate. If only older employees were members of the scheme, this would have the result of increasing even the flat rate premiums. For the same reasons, it has been argued that a flat rate discriminates against younger workers as they will have to pay more than an open market actuarial calculations suggests they should. It is, however, less likely that this argument would win favour with a tribunal given that it is the older workers who are clearly disadvantaged in relation to insured health benefits.

1 **Chapter 8**, **8.1**.

(c) Requirement for medical assessments

In some cases, employees are required to undergo medical assessments before being accepted into a health benefit scheme. There are two different ways in which the requirement may be applied:

- (i) Only workers over a certain age are required to have a medical assessment, as a condition of cover. This is directly discriminatory, and will be unlawful unless justified. It seems unlikely that an employer could justify this. However, the employer could obtain cover for those employees over the age threshold who pass the assessment and seek individual cover for the others. The only discrimination would be the need to undergo the assessment and not the potential withdrawal of the benefit. The discriminatory impact would be much smaller and the employer is much more likely to justify its actions.
- (ii) All employees have medical assessments as a condition of cover. This may indirectly discriminate against older workers, as it is

possible that older workers would be less likely to 'pass' the medical, depending on exactly what is assessed. However, if the only factors are then taken into account in deciding whether to provide cover related to the actual health of the employee, this is more likely to be justified. On the other hand, if the only reason for not providing the benefit is cost, justification may prove more difficult. It will be directly discriminatory if older workers have to demonstrate better health than younger workers in order to be admitted into the scheme, and harder for employers to justify not providing the benefit in those circumstances.

Example:

- BBB Ltd provide life insurance cover to all employees, subject to employees over 55 years passing a medical check-up. Mr D is 60 years old. He undergoes a medical assessment, but does not pass due to having had a heart attack two years earlier. He is refused cover.
- Requiring only those employees over 55 years to undergo a medical check-up is directly discriminatory, and unlawful unless justified. To avoid discriminating, BBB Ltd could require all employees to have the assessment.

Even if all employees have the assessments, failure to provide cover to Mr D may still be indirect discrimination, as older employees are more likely to have had heart attacks, excluding them from cover. A less discriminatory way of providing the benefit would be to provide cover to Mr D, but exclude from the cover death due to a heart attack, or possibly other heart or related conditions (depending on the particular circumstances).

See **6.5.3** below for further discussion on particular types of health benefit.

6.5.2 Justification

Where an employer discriminates in the provision of health benefits, this will be unlawful unless justified. An employer would therefore need to demonstrate that the discriminatory treatment was a proportionate means of achieving a legitimate aim in the usual way.[1] This would apply both to failure to provide a benefit to a particular employee, and to less favourable treatment of an employee in terms of the cost of the benefit in question (or, possibly, the tax payable on a benefit funded by the employer, as set out above).

It is unlikely that employers will be genuinely unable to find policies to cover the majority of their older workers in respect of most health benefits at least up to the age of 70. Even if an employer is unable to find a policy to cover all its workers, it may be required to self-insure to avoid unlawful discrimination. The main issue will be additional expense – either in relation to higher premiums, or potential self-insurance.

The difficulties in relation to health benefits has led to suggestions that many employers will refuse requests to stay on past retirement, to avoid encountering problems in the provision of these benefits.[2]

1 **Chapter 4, 4.7**.
2 **Chapter 12, 12.10.2.**

(a) Cost as justification

It is not clear to what extent cost and economic factors will be accepted by employment tribunals to justify discrimination in relation to health benefits. The government's view, which corresponds with sex discrimination case law, is that employers may not rely on cost as the sole justification for any age discrimination. This is explored in detail in **Chapter 10**. As the case law stands at present, if the sole aim of the employer is to avoid increased cost, this is unlikely to be sufficient to amount to objective justification. However, the aims of employers providing the benefit, and the means of achieving those aims, are more complex that mere cost, and differ depending on the type of benefit offered and how it is provided.

In the *Cross v British Airways*[1] sex discrimination case, relating to a difference in treatment in pension benefits, the aim of the employer was not just cost, but also the maintenance of existing terms of employment relating to retirement and pensions. This case is considered in detail in **Chapter 4**.[2] It was held that this could amount to objective justification. Similar principles may apply where, for instance, health benefits are provided as part of a flexible benefits scheme.[3]

For instance, the main aim behind income protection insurance is to provide employees with replacement income if they are incapacitated and unable to work. It is, therefore, potentially justifiable to cease cover for employees at retirement age, on the basis that providing replacement income for a period when the employee would not ordinarily be working is not an aim of the scheme.[4] If an employer passes on the higher cost of providing benefit to older workers, cost is clearly a factor. However, the employer may also have a legitimate aim of making the benefit available to employees, without requiring some workers to subsidise others.

The employer might also be in a stronger position when it comes to justifying an existing benefit than justifying the discriminatory aspect of a new scheme.[5]

The same aims are likely to apply to age-related premiums for medical cover. But the underlying aim behind the provision of medical cover in general is to give employees access to prompt and high quality medical care, possibly with the additional aim of reducing the amount of time an employ is likely to be out of the office due to illness and associated medical treatment. Applying a maximum age for entitlement does not help to achieve that aim, and would seem to be related entirely to cost. Cost-effectiveness for the employer is clearly a factor in relation to these benefits, but it is not the sole consideration in every case.

As it appears that cost cannot be used as sole justification, the question remains unresolved in relation to whether it can ever be justified to refuse to provide the benefit where the employer considers that the cost of the premiums is prohibitive, or does not consider it is in a position to self-insure. While it is likely that a large organisation could support the extra cost in the short term, it may result in some employers deciding to review the range of benefits that they offer. In smaller organisations, it may become impossible for a particular benefit to be provided to the workforce at all.

Again, this is explored in more detail in **Chapter 4**.[6]

1 [2005] IRLR 423.
2 See **Chapter 4**, **4.7.5**.
3 See **6.5.3(f)** for details about flexible benefits scheme.
4 See **6.5.3(c)**.
5 By reference to the aims accepted by the EAT in *Cross* which included maintaining existing employment terms.
6 **Chapter 4**, **4.7.5(a)**.

(b) Payment in lieu of benefits

One question to be considered is whether employers could provide cash payment in lieu of insured benefits, where these become prohibitively expensive for older workers. The cost-neutral position would be to provide a cash payment equivalent to the value of the benefit provided to other employees. It is not clear whether this would be permissible under the Regulations, as it would still amount to less favourable treatment of the older workers – they would not receive the actual benefit and it is unlikely that the amount paid would purchase an equivalent benefit in the open market. However, the employer may have a better chance of justifying the difference if the overall value of the benefits package is the same, and this approach has a less discriminatory impact than simply not providing the benefit at all. It will ultimately be for the employment tribunals to decide on a case-by-case basis whether this approach can be justified.

A cash alternative is not without its own problems even if it provides potential justification. If a payment in lieu is offered to the older age group only, younger employees may complain that they are being discriminated against by not being given a choice between the benefit and the cash allowance.

6.5.3 The impact on particular benefits

Part of the difficulty employers now face stems from the fact that the insurance market has been slow to react to the implications of the Regulations. Most health benefits policies are renewable annually and many employers have adopted an approach of waiting until the renewal date before considering changes. Insurers have not in most cases at the time of writing, therefore, had to address their minds to the impact of the Regulations on the decisions employers may need to make about their health benefit provision. It is likely that the way some benefits are currently provided under insurance policies will change over time.

(a) Private medical insurance

Private medical insurance is usually provided by employers under a group scheme. As mentioned above, premiums for each employee may be calculated on the basis of a flat rate (distributing the total premium among all the members of the scheme), or according to individual factors. Employees may need to undergo medical assessments prior to cover being provided. Eligibility for cover normally ceases at the same age as the employer's normal retirement age and many employers have needed to raise their retirement age where this was lower than the default retirement age. There are, therefore, several aspects of the schemes which can give rise to issues of age discrimination.

(i) *Increase in retirement age*

Where an employer has previously had a retirement age of less than 65, the maximum age for membership of the private medical scheme is also likely to have been that lower age. The employer is likely to have had to increase its retirement age to the default retirement age of 65.

It is unlikely that the employer would be able to justify not extending medical cover to all employees, including those over its previous retirement age, notwithstanding that premiums for the cover are likely to increase.

(ii) *Staying on past retirement*

In many cases, employees staying on past their normal retirement age will not ordinarily be eligible for private medical cover under the normal rules of the scheme. It is likely that employers would be able to secure cover relatively easily for employees up to the age of 70, (although this would be more expensive) and therefore it would be difficult to justify not providing cover to those employees. For employees aged over 70, employers may be able to justify not providing cover if they are genuinely unable to obtain cover from insurers, but they will need to demonstrate that they have made reasonable attempts to find suitable cover.

It might be argued that employers of the over 70s should self-insure and with the insurer administering the claims (see age-related premiums below). This would, however, seem unlikely.

It seems more likely that employment tribunals will be sympathetic to employers in this case (notwithstanding the argument that the employers' aim could be seen as 'cost alone'). If not, employers are likely to be very reluctant to employ the over 70s, at least where they operate insured benefit schemes.

(iii) *Age-related premiums*

Where premiums are calculated on an individual basis, they are likely to increase with age. It is likely that employers could agree with their insurers, or obtain different policies, to have the premiums calculated on the basis of a flat rate. This is a less discriminatory way of providing the benefit, and it is likely that the requirement of proportionality means that an employer should consider this approach where it is an option. Another option in many cases will be for the employer to provide group cover for all but the most expensive employees and then take out separate equivalent cover individually for them. The issues become more difficult within a flexible benefits scheme (see **6.5.3 (f).**). Most insurers will also offer a policy under which they administer claims but the actual costs of the medical cover are borne by the employer. Premiums for cover under such a policy should not vary with age. It is likely that such schemes will become more popular as a result of the uncertainty created by the Regulations.

(iv) *Pre-cover medical assessments*

Requiring only older employers to undergo medical assessments prior to providing cover is directly discriminatory, but may be proportionate if the alternative is that no cover can be obtained at all. A requirement for all employees to undergo assessments is likely to be justified. As mentioned above, the key issue is the consequence of the medical assessment (see section above on requirements for medical assessments). If cover is denied altogether on the basis of certain medical conditions, this may not be proportionate. It is more likely to be justified to provide cover but with pre-existing medical conditions excluded (which would include any conditions identified in the assessment). As long as all employees are treated in the same way then such exclusion of pre-existing conditions should not be discriminatory.

(b) Health check-ups

Health checks are sometimes provided as a benefit (this is different from compulsory medicals, as dealt with in **Chapter 8** or pre-cover assessments for medical cover above). These usually provide general check-ups, and screenings for certain kinds of medical conditions. In some cases, employers only provide health checks to the over 40s or over 50s, or provide them more frequently to those age groups (for example, every year, instead of every two years for younger employees). Where checks are provided to all employees, some specific tests are only available to employees over a particular age (eg mammograms for women).

The aim behind treating older workers more favourably in relation to health checks is the protection of older workers, on the basis that they are more likely to develop health issues or specific medical problems. This is very common and potentially justifiable, but an employer wishing to rely on this would need to produce evidence demonstrating the greater risks to older workers. The organisations providing health checks or the employer's medical advisers will be able to provide advice to employers on how risks increase with age. However, views on the age at which workers become more at risk varies from provider to provider. Nonetheless, one would expect employers to be given a degree of leeway by tribunals provided that they have some medical advice to substantiate their approach. Providing the same health checks to all employees who wished to take them up would avoid any risk of unlawful discrimination.

(c) Income protection insurance

Income protection insurance (IPI) is designed to provide an income if an employee suffers an illness or injury, which prevents him working for a long period of time. Benefits are normally fixed at a percentage of salary (eg 75 per cent) and also cover employer's national insurance contributions and employer's pension contributions in respect of the employee in question.

Employers take out insurance policies, which provide for payments to be made to the employer in respect of an employee who meets the relevant definition of disablement or incapacity and, therefore, qualifies for benefits under the scheme. There is usually a deferral or waiting period, typically six months, before any benefits become payable. There is then a duty on the employer to pay to the employee any benefits received from the insurer. There is no contract directly between the employee and the insurer.

Benefits are normally payable up to a maximum age, usually the employer's normal retirement age. Under some policies, benefits are payable for a fixed number of years, although there is typically a cap of retirement age, if the employee would be due to retire before the end of the fixed payment period. Under all policies, benefits will cease to be payable if the employee recovers to the extent that he no longer meets the definition of disablement under the policy terms.

Unlike other insured benefits, the cost in respect of an individual rises initially and then decreases as he gets towards retirement age. For the youngest employees the unit cost increases as they get older as the risk of the employee claiming increases. However, as the employee gets closer to his retirement, the unit cost decreases as the reduced potential cost of paying the employee to retirement starts to override the increased likelihood of a claim as the employee gets older.

The main age discrimination issues for IPI are the variation in premiums according to age and the cessation of benefits at retirement age:

(i) *Ceasing benefits at retirement age*

The cessation of benefits at retirement age creates two main problems:

(i) the provision of cover to employees who stay on past normal retirement age; and

(ii) whether ceasing payment of benefits at retirement age (for someone already in receipt of them) and normally retiring that person in the normal way will give rise to claims.

As with other health benefits, where employers have raised their retirement age and therefore need to extend cover to the group of employees over the old retirement age, it is likely to be difficult to justify not extending the cover at least until the new retirement age.

A maximum age in the policy terms is directly discriminatory. As mentioned above[1], it is potentially justifiable on the basis that the policy is designed to provide a replacement income up to the point that the individual would ordinarily have retired or could have been required by his employer to retire. There may be further justification if the employee can draw an unreduced occupational pension at that age. The question of whether it will be justifiable to use an upper age limit tied to pension age under an occupational scheme, or even state pension age, is very unclear. However, it seems unlikely that this could be used to justify an upper age limit which was lower than the employer's normal retirement age. In any event, it is also unlikely that pension benefits will be as high as IPI benefits, which reduces the scope for justification still further.

It may be difficult for employers to secure cover for employees who stay on past retirement age. Even if this is possible, it is likely that policies will limit cover to another maximum age and premiums could be disproportionately expensive for the cover provided. This may influence employers' decisions about granting requests to stay on past retirement. At the very least, employers are likely to consider that allowing employees to stay on for only a short fixed period presents a smaller risk as, presumably, any claim would be restricted to lost income for that period.

The position of an employee who has been receiving IPI benefits and who reaches retirement age and is 'retired', is a tricky one. Provided the duty to consider procedure is followed properly, the employee would not be able to bring an unfair dismissal claim, although there is still the potential for a disability discrimination claim.[2]

There is a further question of whether an employee could bring a breach of contract claim in respect of the termination of employment depriving him or her of IPI benefits, in accordance with *Aspden v Webbs Poultry & Meat Group (Holdings) Ltd*.[3] This case established that, where an employee's contract entitled him to benefits during a period of incapacity as long as he remained in employment, a term would be implied into the contract that the employer would not dismiss the employee during the period of incapacity so as to deprive him of those benefits. In the case of cessation of benefits on retirement, there is no right or expectation to continuing benefits beyond that date under the policy terms, so arguably the *Aspden* principle could not apply. No doubt, employees may argue that in these circumstances the reason why they are deemed only to remain until retirement amounts to disability discrimination. This argument is stronger if the employer allows a significant number of employees to work beyond retirement age.

(ii) *Age-related premiums*

Premiums for IPI vary with age but do not simply increase as an individual's age increases. The risk of developing a disabling condition increases with age. However, if an older individual becomes disabled and entitled to benefits, the period of time until they are due to retire is shorter. This means that the insurer only has to pay out a total sum that is smaller than that payable to someone who starts to receive IPI benefits at a younger age. Therefore, premiums start by increasing with age, but after a certain point, start to decrease again.

Employers do not usually pass on the cost of premiums for IPI to employees and are likely to find it difficult to justify refusing to provide the cover based on the cost of premiums alone. Many organisations have already reviewed their IPI cover and are considering choosing fixed-term cover in the future, rather than cover until the normal retirement age. If this approach is adopted, the problems outlined above may still arise if the employee is retired during the fixed benefit period.

1 **Chapter 6, 6.5.2(a)** and see also **Chapter 4, 4.7.5(a).**
2 **Chapter 12, 12.6.1(c).**
3 [1996] IRLR 521 1995 WL 1083888.

(d) Life cover/death in service benefit

Many employers provide some kind of life assurance cover or death in service benefit. The level of cover is normally a multiple of an employee's salary. Life cover becomes more expensive for older employees.

Life cover is sometimes provided under an occupational pension scheme, in which case the pensions exceptions may apply to it.[1]

For other life cover policies, obtaining cover for employees up to the age of 65 should be relatively straightforward. Therefore, problems will mainly arise in relation to employees who remain in work beyond the normal retirement age or in organisations where there is no retirement age at all or a retirement age higher than 65. As for other health benefits, employers may find it difficult to justify not providing the benefit to all employees, merely on the basis of more expensive premiums.

However, it is potentially justifiable for older employees not to receive the same level of cover as younger employees. The purpose of life cover is to provide dependants of the deceased employee with a sum of money to replace the income the employee would have earned while at work. In the case of an employee reaching retirement, their earning potential is much less than an employee at the start of their career.

Group life assurance policies only benefit from exclusion from tax charges provided that benefits can only be paid to those aged 75 or younger.[2] Employers with staff over 75 years will have to justify not providing cover or pay for an individual policy (if available) or self-insure.

There is a limited exception in relation to life cover, where this is provided to a former employee who has retired on ill-health grounds. This allows employers to cease the cover when the employee reaches normal retirement age (or, where there is no normal retirement age, 65).[3]

1 **Chapter 8**.
2 s 481(2) of the Income Tax (Trading and other Income) Act 2005 for income tax purposes and s 539A (2) of the Income and Corporation Taxes Act 1988 for corporate tax purposes.
3 See reg 34.

(e) Critical illness cover

Critical illness cover provides payment of a lump sum if an individual suffers a serious illness or injury such as total blindness, various cancers, heart attack, loss of limbs, multiple sclerosis, Alzheimer's Disease, or stroke among others. The specific illnesses or conditions covered by a particular policy will be defined in the policy terms.

Premiums increase according to employees' ages. The same justification issues arise as for private medical insurance (see **6.5.3(a)**). Employers may find it difficult to refuse to provide cover simply because of the higher levels of premiums for older workers. The position is more difficult where employees are able to opt for critical illness cover (or additional cover) as part of a flexible benefits scheme (see **6.5.3(f)**).

Critical illness cover is usually only available to employees under a certain age, normally the employer's normal retirement age. This creates problems where employees stay on past retirement. As for life assurance, there is a justification argument that older employees do not need the same cover as younger employees, as they would have been due to retire (or already retired) and draw a pension in any event.

However, the purpose of critical illness cover is not only to replace lost income when an individual is no longer capable of working. It is also designed to provide a sum that can be used to mitigate other consequences of critical illness, such as care, medical treatment and modifications to the home or a vehicle. Therefore, although an individual past normal retirement age may not need the same replacement income as a younger worker, they may well need similar levels of care, treatment or modifications which their pension would not cover. This may make it harder to justify not providing the benefit to older workers.

(f) Health benefits within flexible benefits schemes

Under flexible benefits schemes, employees are allocated a fixed sum that they can use to 'purchase' benefits from the range offered by the scheme, which may include health benefits. On the face of it, this seems like an age-neutral provision, as employees at the same level in the business will receive the same amount in their 'flex pot' and are free to choose whether to take any health benefits.

However, health benefits will normally cost more for older workers, leaving them with less of their flex pot to spend on other benefits. In some cases, the premium may exceed the benefits sum the employee has been allocated. As the cost of the health benefits will vary according to age, this will be direct age discrimination. It will be unlawful unless justified, which will include consideration of whether the benefits can be offered in a less discriminatory way.

Under group schemes generally, it will often be possible to calculate individual premiums by dividing the total premium among the members of the scheme, regardless of age (see **6.5.3(a)** above). This is more difficult within a flexible benefits scheme. At the time employees make their selection, they need to know how much they will need to pay for each benefit. In addition, the benefits provider does not know how many employees will take up a particular benefit until after they have made their selection. If an employer wanted to fix a flat rate in advance, this would inevitably be set by the provider at a high level as the insurer would (probably rightly) expect primarily higher risk older employees to take the cover and the cost may, therefore, be prohibitive. It remains to be seen what approach the tribunals will take to justification in these circumstances. However, there is a reasonably strong likelihood that tribunals will acknowledge that flexible benefit schemes probably could not operate effectively without the cost of benefits varying with age and that the employer's aim is much more than cost alone.

6.6 Company cars

Company cars may be provided to employees because they are required to drive as part of their job (eg a salesperson). However, they are also commonly provided as benefits.

6.6.1 Insurance cover

Car insurance premiums usually take age into account, with premiums being higher for drivers aged under 25 or over 60. The policy excess for these higher risk drivers may also be higher. In addition, many companies' car insurance policies also limit insurance to drivers over a particular age, which is often relatively high, for example, 25 years. In some cases, this may mean that company cars are only available to employees over a particular age.

If the insurer is costing employees individually, then this may deter an employer from providing company cars as a benefit or, at least, covering the insurance cost. Employers would have to justify passing this additional cost on to the employee, which might not be easy.

Company cars are often provided as benefits to more senior employees only. As such employees tend to be older, the issue of insurance is likely to be less of a problem, generally speaking. Where a car would otherwise be provided to a younger employee, but the company is unable to obtain insurance cover under its existing policy, this will be direct age discrimination and will need to be justified. Employers will be expected to search for alternative insurance policies. It will be particularly important for employers to find alternative insurance where the car is required by the employee as part of their job, as without the car, they may be unable to take up the role in question. At the very least, a money equivalent could be provided as a car allowance. Again, this raises its own issues of discrimination if the option of a monetary allowance is only offered to the younger employees where insurance cover is costly. In many organisations, employees can choose between a company car and a car allowance.

Where employers are able to obtain insurance for all age groups (subject to the minimum driving age), it is likely that the premiums and/or policy excesses for younger drivers will be higher, and in some cases disproportionately high. Employers may find it difficult to justify not providing a car solely on that basis. Justification will be even more difficult if other employees attract higher premiums for other non-age-related reasons (such as accidents or speeding offences).

6.6.2 Minimum age for driving

In the United Kingdom, a driving licence can only be held by a person aged 17 or over. Statistically, it may be more likely that younger workers do not hold valid driving licences. A company could justify not providing a company car to someone who did not hold a valid driving licence, even if this amounted to age discrimination, on the basis that it would not be legal for them to drive the car. However, if the car is a benefit and can be used by family members, it may not necessarily be justified to refuse it to an employee who did not hold a licence.

However, if a car could not be provided, the company may be required to provide a car allowance instead (bearing in mind the potential problems if the cash alternative is effectively only offered to one age group). If a car was required for the employee to carry out the job in question, it would only be justified not to offer the role if there was no other reasonable way of carrying out the role and undertaking travel (eg by public transport). Bearing in mind that it is likely only to be employees in their late teens and perhaps early 20s who might realistically show an indirectly discriminatory impact on their age group this is unlikely to arise very often.

6.7 Retirement gifts

Some employers provide retirement gifts when employees retire. This may be at normal retirement age, or if the employee decides to retire at an earlier age. In addition to gifts, employers will sometimes pay for leaving parties for retirees.

This potentially amounts to discrimination against younger workers who leave an employer for reasons other than retirement. If the gifts are given only to employees who retire at normal retirement age (or normal pension age), this will be direct discrimination against workers below that age. In the case of other reasons for the younger workers leaving, there is potential indirect discrimination. Arguably, in many cases, those who are departing for a reason other than retirement may not be able to establish less favourable treatment or disadvantage on age grounds, as their material circumstances will not be the same as the retiree – for example, they may be leaving to join a competitor.

Applying rules relating to the length of service of the retiree is considered in the section on service-related retirement gifts above.[1]

Retirement gifts and leaving parties are likely to be of relatively low value, and it is perhaps unlikely that much litigation will take place in this area. Employers who are challenged may well have a good justification argument that they want to say 'thank you' for the contribution of the retiring employee and wish them well for their future. There is obviously less of a rationale for such genuine well wishes if an employee is leaving to pursue a career elsewhere.

It also remains to be seen whether practices of giving retirement gifts continue, given that many employees may be retired against their wishes under the new retirement procedures (see **Chapter 12**).

1 See **6.3.3(g)**.

6.8 Share plans and awards

6.8.1 Introduction

Share plans are common features of employee reward packages. They are used as a mechanism for attracting and retaining employees and as a means of aligning the interests of employees and shareholders by giving employees an 'ownership' stake in the business. In many cases, the value delivered through share plans forms a substantial part of an employee's reward package.

The structure of share plans varies significantly. Plans may be structured so that employees do not acquire shares immediately but instead are promised, or awarded a right to acquire, shares in the future on the satisfaction of certain performance and/or employment conditions, for example, under a share option plan. Alternatively, share plans may be structured so that employees are awarded shares immediately but lose those shares if certain performance or employment conditions are not satisfied within a specified period, for example under a performance share plan. In both cases the performance period is typically at least three years.

Share plans and the policies governing their operation frequently contain age-related provisions (see below). Given the potential value of share awards it is important that these provisions are reviewed to ensure that they do not expose the employer to age discrimination claims. The Regulations apply not only to those plans implemented and those awards granted on or after 1 October 2006, but also any plans implemented and awards granted prior to this date.

This section examines:

- the common age-related provisions within share plans and awards;
- potential exceptions and justification for those provisions;
- possible ways forward where the exceptions and justifications do not apply;
- the impact of the Regulations on existing rules and awards; and
- issues to consider when amending existing share plans and awards.

6.8.2 Potential age discrimination in share plans and awards

The more common age-related provisions contained in share plan rules and awards are set out in the table below. Many of these provisions/policies potentially give rise to age discrimination.

Provision or policy	Potential age discrimination
Basis of participation	
Eligibility to participate in the plan may be dependent on the employee having served a specified number of years' service.	Indirect discrimination against younger employees; it is more common for older employees to have served a specified number of years.

Provision or policy	Potential age discrimination
The value of the awards may be dependent on length of service.	Indirect discrimination against younger employees; arguably it is more common for older employees to have served a specified number of years.
The value of the awards may be dependent on the employees' positions.	Indirect discrimination against younger employees; arguably older employees will have more senior positions.
An employee may not be allowed to participate in the plan if he is within a specified number of years of retirement age.	Direct discrimination against older employees.
Position on leaving	
Employees who retire at normal retirement age are often treated more favourably than those employees who retire early or leave for reasons other than retirement. Employees who retire at normal retirement age are often treated as 'good leavers'. The awards of good leavers will vest (ie the employee will become unconditionally entitled to the underlying shares) in whole or in part either immediately or in accordance with the original vesting schedule. Employees who retire early are often only treated as good leavers with the consent of the employer or the remuneration committee. Employees who leave for reasons other than retirement are often treated as 'bad leavers' (unless they leave because of redundancy, ill-health or disability). The awards of bad leavers normally lapse. Employees are considered good leavers if they meet different combination of age and length of service thresholds (eg see example below in **6.8.5(c)(iii)(A)**.	Direct age discrimination against younger employees. The age element is direct discrimination against younger workers and the service element is potentially indirect discrimination against younger workers.

6.8.3 Exceptions

The age-related provisions listed above will not be unlawful age discrimination if it is possible to objectively justify them or they come within one of the exceptions in the Regulations.

The exceptions that are relevant to share plans are:

(a) benefits based on length of service[1]; and

(b) compliance with a statutory requirement.[2]

1 See reg 32.
2 See reg 27.

(a) Length of service

The service-related benefit exception might be of use. As mentioned above,[1] benefits linked to service of up to five years are lawful and those linked to service in excess of five years are lawful if the employer shows a reasonable belief that they meet a business need.

Where the basis of participation is linked to service this exception will apply. However, where the position on leaving is linked to service, it is less clear. As mentioned above,[2] the exception does not apply to benefits awarded to a worker by virtue of his ceasing to work for the employer. This would seemingly take awards on leaving employment outside the exception and mean that the service-related element will need objective justification.

1 **Chapter 6, 6.3.2**.
2 See reg 32(7) and **Chapter 6, 6.3.2**.

(b) Compliance with a statutory requirement

In deciding whether the 'compliance with a statutory requirement' exception is available for share plans, a distinction should be made between approved and unapproved shares plans.

Share plans which are approved (or recognised as qualifying) by Her Majesty's Revenue & Customs ('HMRC') benefit from tax advantages for both the employer and the employee. However, in order to benefit from that advantageous tax treatment, the plans must satisfy certain statutory requirements. Some of those requirements are age-related as set out in the table below.

Approved or qualifying plan	**Length of service**	**Treatment of leavers**
Company Share Option Plan ('CSOP')	No	The legislation allows the rules to treat a participant who retires at an age specified in the plan ('the Specified Age') as a good leaver. The Specified Age for these purposes is age 55 or above.[1]
Save As you Earn Option ('SAYE') Plan	The legislation *allows* the rules to specify a length of service requirement provided it is not longer than five years.[2]	The legislation *requires* the rules to treat a participant as a good leaver if he retires at the Specified Age or at any other age at which the participant is bound to retire in accordance with their employment contract.[3] The legislation also *requires* the rules to allow a participant who reaches the Specified Age to exercise his option if he wishes to do so even if he does not retire.[4] The Specified Age for these purposes is any age between 60 and 75 (inclusive).[5]
Share Incentive Plan ('SIP')	The legislation *allows* the rules to specify a length of service requirement provided it is not longer than 18 months for free shares and not longer than either 6 or 18 months for partnership shares and matching shares depending on how the plan is structured.[6]	The legislation *requires* the rules to provide that an employee who retires at the Specified Age is a good leaver and shall keep any free shares or matching shares.[7] The Specified Age for these purposes is age 50 or above.[8]

Approved or qualifying plan	Length of service	Treatment of leavers
Enterprise Management Incentive ('EMI') Plan	No	No

[1] See paras 24 and 35A, Sch 4 of the ITEPA 2003.
[2] See para 6(2), Sch 3 of the ITEPA 2003.
[3] See para 34, Sch 3 of the ITEPA 2003.
[4] See para 33, Sch 3 of the ITEPA 2003.
[5] See para 31, Sch 3 of the ITEPA 2003.
[6] See paras 15 and 16, Sch 2 of the ITEPA 2003.
[7] See para 32(2), Sch 2 of the ITEPA 2003.
[8] See para 98, Sch 2 of the ITEPA 2003.

In contrast, share plans which are unapproved do not benefit from HMRC approved tax advantages and therefore do not have to comply with any statutory requirements.

6.8.4 Basis of participation

This section examines the exceptions and/or defences that may be available in respect of the provisions governing the basis on which employees participate in share plans.

(a) Eligibility to participate or value of the award dependent on a number of years' service

The service-related benefit exception means that restricting eligibility for awards or determining the value of awards, by reference to length of service will not be age discrimination, provided the period of service used is either five years or less or there is a business need for using a longer period of service.

(b) Value of the award linked to seniority of position in company

The service-related benefit exception will not be available, therefore such a provision will have to be objectively justified.

(c) No eligibility to participate if within a specified period of retirement date

Many share plans restrict (either completely or partially) awards to employees who are within a specified period of their anticipated retirement date.

This policy originated from the institutional investor guidelines issued by the Association of British Insurers ('ABI'). The ABI guidelines do not have legislative force and compliance with them is not mandatory. However, they set out 'best practice' for listed companies.

Prior to December 2005, the ABI guidelines recommended that awards should not be made to employees within six months (previously two years) of their anticipated retirement date. In practice, many companies continued to grant awards to employees within six months of their anticipated retirement date but provided those awards would lapse if employees actually retired within the six month period. The guidelines were amended in December 2005 to remove this restriction entirely.

Retaining the restriction will be difficult to objectively justify, therefore companies should remove such restrictions and rather scale back shares received on vesting if the employee actually retires before the end of the performance period.[1]

1 See **6.8.5(c)**.

6.8.5 Treatment of leavers

(a) Exceptions

As indicated in the table at **6.8.2** above, the tax legislation *requires* the rules of SAYE plans and SIPs to treat an employee who retires at the specified age as a good leaver. However, the tax legislation allows the company to choose the specified age within a certain range (for SAYE plan between 60 and 75 years (inclusive) and for SIP any age of 50 or above).

Where the company has chosen the lowest age in the range (ie 60 years for SAYE plan and 50 years for SIP) the compliance with a statutory requirement exception will apply.

Where the company has chosen a higher age, the compliance with a statutory requirement exception will not apply and objective justification will be required. This is because the exception only applies where the company has chosen the least discriminatory way of implementing the legislation.

The SAYE legislation *requires* the plan rules to allow an employee who reaches the age at which he is 'bound to retire' under his contract of employment to exercise his options if he so wishes. Accordingly, such provisions are within the compliance with a statutory requirement exception. However, the effect of the Regulations is that employers now have a duty to consider requests to stay on, so there is no age at which an employee is 'bound to retire'. As a result, companies should amend SAYE Plans to add a definition of 'bound to retire' (for example, if the company has a retirement age of 65, this could be defined as the age at which he is 'bound to retire').

It is worth noting that the compliance with a statutory requirement exception is not available for the retirement provisions in CSOPs since the tax legislation does not *require* companies to include such provisions in their rules.

Although the tax legislation refers to retiring at the specified age, it does not define 'retirement'. As explained in **Chapter 12**[1] defining retirement is not always straightforward.

Is it retirement:

- If the employee resigns and joins his employer's major competitor (presumably not)?
- What if he joins the competitor in a less demanding part-time training role?
- What if he starts work in an entirely different field?
- Does it matter if it is full-time or part-time?
- What if he sets up his own business importing French wine?
- What if he moves to Tuscany and sells his home grown product at the local market?

There is no authority on the meaning of retirement for these purposes and it has not posed a problem in practice to date. With the advent of the Regulations this might change.

1 **Chapter 12, 12.2.**

(b) Objective justification

As stated above, for SAYE plans and SIPs objective justification is required if the specified age is set at an age higher than the lowest age permitted under the tax legislation. Similarly, for all plans (other than SAYE or SIP) objective justification is required for any retirement provisions, which treat retirees more favourably than other leavers.

Often the commercial rationale for retirement provisions is that they reward loyalty (ie length of service) and, therefore, aid staff retention. This will not be sufficient to amount to objective justification for setting an age above the lowest permitted, since there is no objective reason why an employee who has worked for the company for five years from the age of 60 to 65 should be treated more favourably than an employee who has worked for the company for 15 years from the age of 25 to 40.

A possible justification is that the retirement provisions help companies with succession planning, ie it gives employees who are at retirement age an incentive to retire 'freeing up' positions for the next level of employees.

The argument is that, unless these positions are free, employees at the next level down may resign. For such a defence to succeed, however, there will need to be evidence that the company has a hierarchal 'up and out' structure. This is explored in the chapter on 'Retirement'.[1]

It should be easier for a company to justify not making changes to a plan which existed before the Regulations came into force than one established since 1 October 2006.[2]

1 **Chapter 12, 12.8.1**.
2 **Chapter 4, 4.7.7**.

(c) The way forward

Where the objective justification defence and exceptions are unavailable, the company should consider whether to amend its share plans and awards and, if so, how. This section summarises potential ways forward.

(i) *Do nothing*

Share plan rules often contain a general discretion for the company or the remuneration committee to decide whether a participant's shares should vest on leaving employment. If there is such a discretion, the company may decide to retain the retirement provisions and use the discretion to ensure that those who leave the company for reasons other than retirement are not discriminated against on the basis of their age.

Whilst this approach may have the attraction of simplicity, it will be important to make sure that any discretion is exercised in a non-discriminatory way. It is essential that the reasons for the exercise of the discretion are recorded in writing at the time.

Where the rules do not contain a general discretion, the company may prefer to retain the retirement provisions and settle claims on an individual basis as and when they arise. This approach is potentially very costly if a number of claims have to be settled. In addition, listed companies may run into corporate governance issues if they have not dealt with age discrimination properly and are simply settling claims.

(ii) *Remove retirement as a good leaver provision*

A similar approach to that described in (i) above would be to remove the retirement and early retirement provisions and to rely on, or replace them, with the general discretionary power referred to in (i) above.

As with approach (i) above it will be important to ensure that any discretion is exercised in a nondiscriminatory way and that the reasons for the exercise of discretion are recorded in writing. If this is not done, this approach will not have removed the risk of age discrimination claims but simply moved the focus of such claims from the plan rules to the exercise of discretion.

The other difficulty with this approach is that employees are familiar with retirement being a good leaver reason and the removal of those provisions from the plan may meet with some resistance particularly where there are 'older' participants who will be personally disadvantaged by its removal. Accordingly, this may not be practical for existing awards where participants would have to agree to the removal of the provisions.

(iii) *Redefine retirement*

(A) *Define retirement by reference to length of service*

One approach is to define retirement by reference to a combination of length service and age factors. For example the rules may provide that an employee will be treated as good leaver if:

- at the date of termination the employee has completed 20 years' service;
- at the date of termination the employee has completed 10 years' service and is over the age of 45; and
- at the date of termination the employee has completed 5 years' service and is over the age of 50.

Such provisions discriminate on the basis of age. Why should an employee aged 44 have served for 20 years, whereas an employee aged 45 only has to have served 10 years? The length of service element could also be challenged as being indirectly discriminatory. It will not come within the exception above as it relates to a termination benefit.[1]

An alternative approach is to use only a length of service provision, in place of an age-related provision. For example, it would be possible to provide that in order to be treated as a good leaver the employee must have completed 15 years' service, irrespective of their age. This approach is still likely to constitute potentially indirect age discrimination and, as mentioned above, will not benefit from the service-related benefit exception. However, it may be easier to objectively justify such a provision on the basis that it rewards loyalty, irrespective of age, and so encourages staff retention.

(B) *Define retirement in a manner which is not age-related*

Rather than linking retirement to age or length of service, another approach would be to define retirement by reference to the employee's circumstances on leaving the company. For example. retirement could be defined as:

- termination of employment in circumstances where the employee was not joining a competitor; or
- termination of employment in circumstances where the employee was ceasing work permanently or full-time perhaps with an exception for career changes.

Such an approach gives rise to a number of practical problems:

- The approach involves a different 'mind-set' for the company. Companies tend to view retirement provisions as rewarding loyalty/good service, whereas to define retirement in a non-age/length of service way may be seen as also rewarding those individuals who want to leave the company.
- There is still a risk of indirect age discrimination since it is more likely that older people will 'cease working permanently' than younger people.
- It is difficult to define what plans would constitute ceasing to work permanently/full-time.
- It will be difficult for the company to enforce such a provision:
  - Restrictions on working for a competitor may be an unlawful restraint of trade.
  - What happens if the employee's circumstances change? The employee may begin working full-time or may even join a competitor.

A possible solution to the last issue would be to ensure that in all cases the number of shares that the employee receives is adjusted to reflect the period over which the employee actually worked and the extent to which the performance conditions were satisfied during that period. In addition, vesting of the shares could be delayed in accordance with the original vesting schedule or perhaps for a longer period giving the company an opportunity during which, if it wishes, it could monitor the employee's activities. Vesting in accordance with the original vesting schedule depending on time served and the extent to which the performance conditions had been satisfied would also be in accordance with the latest ABI guidelines (issued in December 2006).

(C) *Define retirement as retirement at the mandatory retirement age*

The best approach may be to define retirement as retirement at the mandatory retirement age where either the employee did not want to continue working beyond that age or the employer did not allow the employee to continue working beyond that age.

The advantage of this approach is that it fits in with the commercial objective – rewarding loyalty/length of service – and should be possible to justify it on the basis that the employee was still working for the company 'at the end'.

Companies which have abolished their mandatory retirement age could set this at 65 years as this is the age at which they can retire employees under the Regulations.

1 **Chapter 6, 6.3.2.**

6.8.6 Additional tax consideration in the case of CSOP

If CSOP rules contain a specified age CSOP options exercised within six months of retirement at the specified age will keep the CSOP tax advantages even if the option has been held for less than three years (normally the tax advantages are only available where the option has been held for three years or more).[1] It has been confirmed by HMRC that if the CSOP rules do not contain a specified age then no tax relief will be available if the option has been held for less than three years.

It seems unlikely that the Company will be held responsible for the effects of the HMRC's tax rules.

1 s 524 of the ITEPA 2003.

6.8.7 Impact on existing plan rules and awards

It is clear that the age discrimination legislation applies to all share plans implemented and all awards made on or after 1 October 2006.

The Regulations also apply to any actions or omissions of a company after 1 October 2006 if they affect any existing share awards in a discriminatory way. Therefore, a company is at risk of an age discrimination claim relating to share awards granted before 1 October 2006 if, for example, a company failed to:

- amend an age discriminatory plan rule even though it was in the company's power to do so; or
- exercise discretion in a way which would mitigate or reverse the discriminatory effects of such a rule; and
- an employee was adversely affected as a result.

It will make no difference that the plans are implemented by a parent company and not the employing company. These are benefits derived from employment and any claim would be against the employing company.

To avoid these uncertainties, company should consider amending existing plan rules and awards prior to any claims for age discrimination being brought.

6.8.8 Amending existing share plan rules and awards

Before amending share plan rules or awards the company will need to analyse its powers of amendment and ascertain what (if any) procedures must be followed.

The four main issues to consider are:

(i) Is shareholder approval required? Generally amendments can be made to plans without shareholder approval if (a) the amendments are to comply with legislative developments; or (b) the amendments do not result in the participant being treated more favourably or acquiring new rights. Where shareholder approval is required, this will have to be obtained at the next annual general meeting or at an extraordinary general meeting.

(ii) Is participant approval required? Plans normally require participant approval where the amendment is to the detriment of the rights of the participants – for example, removing retirement as a good leaver reason. Consideration should be given as to whether it is likely that participant approval will be obtained.

(iii) Will any amendments to the rules apply to options already granted? If not, this will also need to be changed. Any retrospective amendments to existing options will require the consent of those affected.

(iv) Amendments to approved plans require *prior* approval from HMRC (see **6.8.9** below).

6.8.9 Additional considerations for amending approved share plans

As noted above, an employer may want to amend its:

- SAYE plan to lower the specified age to the minimum age (60) and to add a definition of 'bound to retire';
- SIP to lower the specified age to the minimum age (50); and
- CSOP to remove the retirement provisions or reduce the age.

The views of HMRC on the impact of age discrimination on approved share plans[1] are:

- Plans do not need to be amended to reflect the Regulations to maintain HMRC approval.
- If a company wishes to make amendments to the approved plans to comply with the Regulations, they must be approved in advance by HMRC in the usual way.
- Amendments made to comply with the Regulations will generally be acceptable to HMRC.
  - HMRC will approve retrospective amendments to reduce the specified retirement ages in SIPs, SAYE plans and CSOPs.
  - HMRC will not approve a change to take rights away unless *all* affected participants agree to it otherwise HMRC expect to see a 'levelling up' where the amendments are for the benefit of participants.
- Amendments can apply to new as well as existing options or share awards.

1 Share Focus Newsletter, March 2007.

Chapter 7

Opportunities during employment

7.1 Introduction

Age discrimination claims are likely to arise, not only at the time of hiring and at the ending of the relationship but also, in some cases, during the relationship. **Chapters 4** and **6** deal with age harassment during employment[1] and age discrimination in pay and benefits respectively.

This chapter considers other circumstances in which age discrimination claims can commonly arise during the relationship. It includes:

- access to training;
- promotion;
- the award of bonuses;
- work allocation; and
- transfers.

In addition, issues of age discrimination could arise in relation to access to other opportunities, for example secondments overseas.

1 **Chapter 4, 4.5**.

7.2 Training

Access to vocational training is covered elsewhere.[1]

However, employers must ensure that they are not guilty of unlawful discrimination in the training that they provide to their staff.

Opportunities during employment

Regulation 7 specifically extends the Regulations to opportunities for training.[2]

In particular, assumptions should not be made that older workers are likely to have a shorter future with the employer in circumstances where the employer will gain less from that training or that older workers are more likely to be stuck in their ways and less likely to respond to training.

Indeed, older workers may often be more loyal to their employer than younger workers who, in many cases, will be trained by their employer before leaving to pursue their career with one of that employer's competitors.

Example:

Elena is a 53-years-old sales executive. She is the oldest in her team and keeps getting overlooked for training on the company's new products. Her sales figures are better than many of her colleagues'. No reason has been given to her for not being hired. When she questions her manager about this, he dismisses her quickly with vague assurances that it will be her turn next time. Last week, Anoushka joined fresh from college. Anoushka was preferred to Elena for training on the company's new product. This is the last straw for Elena who suspects that in the absence of any other explanation she is being discriminated on grounds of her age. She suspects that they believe she will take longer to pick up new products. Indeed, she overheard her manager once using the phrase 'you can't teach an old dog new tricks'. If Elena is able to persuade a tribunal to draw inferences of discrimination,[1] the company faces having to show why Elena has not been given training opportunities.

1 **Chapter 4, 4.7**.

The Genuine Occupational Requirement exceptions specifically apply to training opportunities[3] so an employer would act lawfully if he provided training to people of a particular age group where to benefit from the training 'possibly a characteristic related to age is a genuine and determining occupational requirement, and it is proportionate to apply that requirement'.[4]

1 **Chapter 3, 3.2.5.**
2 7(2)(b).
3 8(1)(b).
4 8(2).

7.3 Promotion

Similar issues arise at the time of promotion as with recruitment. The Regulations also specifically cover discrimination regarding opportunities for promotions.[1]

In practice, employers may be more likely to face discrimination claims arising out of promotion decisions than out of recruitment decisions. With recruitment decisions the unsuccessful candidate is normally unaware of the comparative strengths of the successful candidate. In a promotion situation, the unsuccessful candidate will often have been overlooked in preference to one of his peers. It is, therefore, critical that the employer is basing his promotion decisions on transparent, consistent and objective criteria.

The way in which the burden of proof in discrimination cases and the use of inferences operate is discussed in **Chapter 4**.[2] If the unsuccessful promotion candidate can persuade an employment tribunal to draw inferences of discrimination, then the employer will have to justify its decision.

Older or younger candidates may challenge the stereotypical assumptions that they might claim is influencing the employer's decision making. The younger candidate might assert that a lack of years of experience or a perceived lack of gravitas influenced the decision. An older candidate might challenge assumptions of lack of dynamism or a shorter period before retirement as influencing the decision.

This is illustrated by the Irish case of *Meehan v Leitrim County Council*.[3] In this case, Mr Meehan, a firefighter, was unsuccessful in his application for the post of Sub-Fire Officer. He was 48 years old and the successful candidate was 32 years old. As his qualifications and experience were significantly greater and there was no evidence to support the employer's argument that the successful candidate had performed better at the interview, Mr Meehan succeeded with his claim of age discrimination.

Examples:

Sîan is a high flying young solicitor. She is her firm's expert on a new equity derivative product and has brought in several valuable new clients. She works long hours and her profile, client billings and personal billings exceed many of the firm's partners. She is only 28 and looks younger than this. She applies for partnership and is rejected. The firm makes noises about her needing more experience and to cut her teeth a little longer. An older solicitor with demonstrably less strong performance is promoted. Sîan may well have an age discrimination claim unless the firm can show clear evidence of objective and nondiscriminatory reasons for rejecting her application.

Consequently, the employer must be in a position to show why it made its decisions. In deciding on its criteria for promotion, similar issues arise for the criteria being used to recruit employees.[4]

If the employer requires a minimum period of service to be eligible for promotion, then the same issues as those relating to service-related pay and benefits would apply.[5] However, it is more likely that minimum levels of experience would be required for promotion than for service-related pay increments and employers may well be required to objectively justify this.

Example:

Sîan decides not to take any action but to wait patiently and apply the following year. In the meantime the firm decides to introduce some clearer criteria by which partnership applications are judged. One of these is that candidates must have practised as solicitor for at least seven years. Sian has only six years post-qualification experience. She has now come to the end of her tether and sues, arguing that the experience requirement indirectly discriminates against the under 30s. She is likely to have a strong case.

As with training opportunities and recruitment, the Genuine Occupational Requirement exception also applies to promotion decisions.[6]

1 7(2)(b).
2 **Chapter 4, 4.7**.
3 DEC – E2006 – 014.
4 See **Chapter 5**.
5 **Chapter 6, 6.3**.
6 8(1)(b).

7.4 Bonuses

Similar issues arise with the award of bonuses as they do with promotion decisions and employers need to be in a position to objectively justify their decisions by reference to consistent, transparent and well-documented procedures.

Employers would also be prudent to consider ensuring that the age profile of those being offered training, being promoted and being given bonuses is monitored as part of a diversity monitoring programme. This is discussed in more detail in **Chapter 13, 13.6**.

7.5 Work allocation

Employers are getting better at ensuring that they are not vulnerable to discrimination claims in the major employment decisions – recruitment, promotion, pay, dismissals. But claimants and their lawyers are now looking at the myriad of smaller decisions that are made every day and which are not documented or made according to clear and objective criteria – whom to give a new piece of work to, whom to invite to a client lunch, whom to take on the pitch for new work.

This is highlighted by the sex discrimination case of *Sinclair Roche & Temperley v Heard and Fellows* case.[1] In this case, two junior partners at a law firm were denied promotion to senior partner. They challenged this as being sex discriminatory. They had fees from work referred by other partners of £22,105 and £7,569, whereas their two male comparators who were promoted had fees from referrals of £368,456 and £473,179 respectively. They claimed that they were discriminated against in the referral of work, effectively a combination of small, allegedly discriminatory decisions. The employment tribunal upheld their complaint. The EAT subsequently upheld an appeal but remitted the case back to the same tribunal. As nothing was subsequently heard, it is assumed that the case was settled.

Example:

Lloyd is a management consultant. His team is paid based on assignments which they bid for internally. Lloyd is older than his colleagues and rarely succeeds. His appraisals and client feedback have always been positive. He believes that the directors who assign projects are reluctant to award them to him as he believes they think his age runs counter to the trendy modern image that the firm has invested in. If the firm cannot explain why Lloyd is not being awarded his fair share of assignments, it is vulnerable to an age discrimination claim.

1 [2004] IRLR 763.

7.6 Transfers

The Regulations also expressly extend the protection afforded by the Regulations to opportunities for transfers.[1]

1 7(2)(b).

Chapter 8

Pensions

In this chapter we consider:

- the main forms of pension provision in the United Kingdom, to set the requirements of the Regulations in context;
- how the Regulations apply to benefits provided by pension schemes, including who is protected, who is a comparator and from when the Regulations apply;
- the non-discrimination rule imposed by the Regulations and 'levelling up';
- the key pensions exemptions – the Regulations contain an extensive list;
- the key pensions omissions – the real impact areas for most schemes;
- objective justification in a pensions context;
- how claims can be made – employment tribunals and the Pension Ombudsman; and

- issues when amending a pension scheme to comply with the Regulations.

8.1 Introduction

Pension provision is, by its very nature, age-related – at its core lies the principle of providing, and in many cases incentivising employees to provide for themselves, an income in retirement. It is perhaps then unsurprising that the application of the Directive's non-discrimination requirement to the varying forms of pension provision in the United Kingdom is uneasy.

Helpfully, the Directive expressly refers to certain aspects of pension provision that Member States can exempt from the requirement not to discriminate on the grounds of age. Article 6(2) refers in this context to the fixing of ages for admission or entitlement to retirement benefits, and the use of age criteria in actuarial calculations (provided in both cases this does not result in sex discrimination).

The Regulations, however, recognise that there are many other aspects of pension provision in the United Kingdom that could, in the absence of an express exemption or a successful objective justification defence, amount to unlawful discrimination. Schedule 2 to the Regulations sets out a long list of exemptions from the requirement in the Regulations not to discriminate on the grounds of age. In this chapter, we analyse the key exemptions in Sch 2 of the Regulations and identify commonplace elements of benefit design that are not exempt.

As art 6(2) of the Directive is narrow in its scope, there remains the risk of a claim that the United Kingdom has failed properly to implement the Directive as the exemptions in Sch 2 to the Regulations are far more extensive. The government will no doubt have been mindful of this risk and presumably it considers that it would be able to defend such a claim. It is, however, worth keeping this in mind, in particular for those employers, such as emanations of the State (and possibly also those carrying out public functions in the private sector), against whom the Directive could be enforced directly.[1]

1 **Chapter 2.**

8.2 Guidance on the regulations

The Department for Work and Pensions ('DWP') has issued guidance[1] on the impact of the Regulations on occupational and personal pension schemes ('Pensions Guidance'). This explains how pension schemes may be affected by the Regulations and provides practical examples of how schemes and employers can make use of the exemptions. However, as the DWP has no specific power under the Regulations or otherwise to issue legally binding guidance in relation to the anti-age discrimination legislation, its Pensions Guidance is expressly stated as having been 'designed to provide general information only'.[2] It is therefore likely to carry limited weight in an employment tribunal and/or before the Pensions Ombudsman.

1 December 2006 guidance available at *www.dti.gov.uk/employment/discrimination/age-discrimination/index.html*. Note that this replaced guidance issued by the Department of Trade and Industry in April 2006.
2 See p 3.

8.3 Different forms of pension provision

There are differences in the application of the Regulations to different forms of pension provision. It is a vital first step, then, to identify through what type of pension scheme benefits are being provided. In general, schemes will be one of either:

- an occupational pension scheme; or
- a personal pension scheme.

8.3.1 Occupational pension schemes

An occupational pension scheme is, for most purposes in the Regulations, a pension scheme that is established under trust by an employer for the purposes of providing benefits for its employees (or the employees of other employers participating in the scheme).[1] Most occupational pension schemes are established under trust.

Occupational pension schemes will generally provide benefits on either (or both) of the following bases:

- a defined benefit basis – that is, where the ultimate benefit to be provided to or in respect of members is defined at the outset. Traditionally, in the United Kingdom, occupational pension schemes that provide benefits on a defined benefit basis calculate the benefit by reference to a proportion of the member's final pay or salary. Increasingly, schemes are providing benefits by reference to each member's average salary over their career with the employer (often known as 'career average revalued earnings' or 'CARE' arrangements); or
- a defined contribution basis – that is, where the contributions payable by the employer and the employee are defined at the outset, but the ultimate benefits are not (these depend on the

contributions paid in, investment return and annuity cost at retirement). These schemes are often known in the United Kingdom as 'money purchase' schemes.

Most occupational pension schemes are pre-funded, but some (mainly public sector and some executive arrangements) are unfunded.

A scheme that is established by an employer for the purposes of providing only life assurance cover can still be an 'occupational pension scheme' within the meaning of the Regulations.

When reviewing benefits provided by an occupational pension scheme for potentially age discriminatory rules and practices, it is important to check all applicable documents, which may include:

- trust deed and rules (as amended from time to time);
- member booklets;
- member announcements;
- discretionary practices; and/or
- the terms of employees' contracts of employment.

1 See para 1 of Sch 2 of the Regulations.

8.3.2 Personal pension schemes (including stakeholder schemes)

These tend to be contract (rather than trust) based. At their simplest, they are a contract between an individual (the member) and the product provider (in most cases, an insurance provider). The employer may operate a group personal pension scheme (often shortened to the acronym 'GPP'), which is essentially a group of individual personal pension schemes covered by an umbrella policy. The employer's obligations will be restricted to a payment obligation, through a commitment (usually in the employee's contract of employment) to contribute at a certain rate to the personal pension scheme.

Stakeholder pension schemes (a specific type of low cost personal pension scheme) fall within the scope of personal pension schemes for the purposes of the Regulations.

The key documents to review for potentially age discriminatory rules and practices in relation to personal pension schemes are:

- the terms of employees' contracts of employment; and
- any information (such as a 'key features' document) provided to employees describing the terms on which they can join, and receive benefits from, the scheme.

8.4 The scope of the Regulations

8.4.1 The pensions prohibitions

Regulation 11 renders it unlawful for any employer in relation to an occupational pension scheme to discriminate against a member or prospective member of that scheme 'in carrying out any of their functions in relation to it'. A 'member' for this purpose means an active member, a deferred member or a pensioner member (but does not include a member whose only rights in the scheme are attributable to pension credits awarded pursuant to a pension sharing order on divorce).

A 'prospective member' means a person who, either under the scheme rules or the terms of his employment contract:

- is able, at his own option, to become a member;
- will become a member if he continues in that employment for a set waiting period;
- will automatically become a member unless he elects otherwise; or
- may be admitted to the scheme subject to any person's consent.

The Regulations extend this prohibition to the trustees or managers[1] of occupational pension schemes. Indeed, the Regulations impose on every occupational pension scheme a non-discrimination rule containing a requirement that the trustees refrain from doing any act which is unlawful by virtue of reg 11.[2] Trustees are therefore required by the Regulations to ensure compliance, which in practice means that employers and trustees will need to engage with each other in addressing potential discrimination issues in connection with an occupational pension scheme.

The Regulations also prohibit an employer from discriminating against a person 'in the terms on which he offers that person employment'[3] and, in relation to its employees, 'in the terms of employment which he affords him'.[4] It is the combination of these prohibitions that captures employer contributions (including access to those contributions) to personal pension schemes within the scope of the Regulations.

8.4.2 1 December 2006 (and 1 October 2006)

The pensions prohibition in reg 11 for occupational pension schemes applies only to pensionable service on or after 1 December 2006. This means that discriminatory practices relating to pensionable service before that date should not as a general principle fall foul of the Regulations. Similarly, the requirements of the Regulations in relation to personal pension schemes apply only to service on or after 1 December 2006. An example of how a member's service may need to be 'split' to address this is as follows:

Example:

If a scheme provides defined benefits with an accrual rate of 1/60th for members who are below age 45, increasing to an accrual rate of 1/45th for those aged 45 or above, this is unlawful direct age discrimination (unless it can be objectively justified). Those members below age 45 could claim that they ought to be entitled to accrue benefits at the (better) 1/45th rate.

If such a claim succeeded, it could only relate to their pensionable service on or after 1 December 2006. So, if a member reaches age 40 having completed a total of 10 years' pensionable service which commenced on 1 December 2002, his accrual rate for the first four years (up to 1 December 2006) would continue to be 1/60th, but his accrual rate for the remaining six years would need to be 1/45th.

Although the coming into force of the pensions part of the Regulations was pushed back from 1 October 2006 to 1 December 2006, the Regulations[5] delaying implementation apply to arrangements for the payment of pension contributions, admission to a pension scheme and the provision of any benefits relating to pensions. It is not entirely clear whether life assurance provided through a pension scheme is a benefit 'relating to pensions' in this context. The safe approach is that it has been unlawful since 1 October 2006 to discriminate on the grounds of age in providing life assurance cover through a pension scheme.

1 We will refer simply to 'trustees' for the remainder of this chapter. 'Managers' are those responsible for the management of an occupational pension scheme that is not established under trust.
2 See para 2(1) of Sch 2 of the Regulations.
3 See reg 7(1)(b).
4 See reg 7(2)(a).
5 See the Employment Equality (Age) (Amendment) Regulations 2006, SI 2006/2408, reg 2(2).

8.4.3 Direct discrimination

Direct age discrimination occurs when someone is treated less favourably on the grounds of their age (or their apparent age) than others would be treated in similar circumstances.[1]

An example of direct discrimination on the grounds of age in a pensions context is as follows:

Example:

A company operates an occupational pension scheme which provides members with a defined benefit pension based on an accrual rate of 1/60th of final salary for each year of their pensionable service. However, from age 60 (the scheme's normal retirement date), the member is no longer able to accrue additional pension if they remain in the service of the employer.

The employee who is aged 61, for instance, is unable to accrue additional pension in circumstances where an employee below age 60 can do so. This is unlawful direct age discrimination for which there is no applicable exemption.

Many of the exemptions applicable to pension schemes in Sch 2 of the Regulations apply to forms of direct discrimination. It may also be possible to objectively justify direct discrimination if the employer can demonstrate that retaining it is a proportionate means of achieving a legitimate aim.[2]

1 **Chapter 4, 4.2.**
2 **Chapter 4, 4.7.**

8.4.4 Indirect discrimination

Indirect discrimination takes place where an apparently age-neutral provision, criterion or practice is applied equally across all ages, but which in practice puts scheme members of a particular age or age group at a particular disadvantage.[1] Indirect age discrimination in a pensions context can be very tricky to identify. Two examples are as follows:

***Example** 1:*

A company operates an occupational pension scheme which provides members with a defined benefit pension based on an accrual rate of 1/60th of final salary for each year of their pensionable service. However, 'pensionable service' is restricted to 35 years.

The restriction to 35 years could be indirect discrimination because, although it does not apply to members based on their age, older members are more likely to be affected by the restriction than younger members. This is because the older workers are more likely to have worked for the employer for 35 years. However, this indirect discrimination is not unlawful under the Regulations as it is exempt.[2]

Example 2:

A company operates a similar pension scheme to that in **Example 1** above. On the death of a member in service, a spouse's pension is payable. The spouse's pension is 50 per cent of what the member's pension would have been, assuming the member had continued in pensionable service through to the scheme's normal retirement date (that is, calculated by reference to the member's 'prospective service').

The prospective service element of the benefit could amount to indirect discrimination against older members. The spouse's benefit payable on the death of an older member will have a smaller prospective service element attached to it than is the case on the death of a younger member. However, this is not unlawful as an exemption applies.

Like direct age discrimination, indirect age discrimination may be justified if the employer can show that the provision, criterion or practice imposed is a proportionate means of achieving a legitimate aim.[3]

1 **Chapter 4, 4.3.**
2 See para 21 of Sch 2 of the Regulations.
3 **Chapter 4,4.7.**

8.4.5 'Levelling up' – the effect of unlawful discrimination

The Regulations impose on every occupational pension scheme a non-discrimination rule containing a requirement that the trustees refrain from doing any act which is unlawful by virtue of reg 11. Personal pension schemes also fall within the scope of the Regulations.

Where a pension arrangement is changed to eliminate age discrimination for future service, it can be changed to level up or level down future benefits. However, case law suggests that during any period when unlawful age discrimination has already occurred, this can only be remedied by 'levelling up' benefits. That is, the pension arrangement must provide the person being discriminated against with the higher benefit that would have applied but for the discrimination. An example of the 'levelling up' principle in a pensions context is as follows:

Example:

A company operates a defined contribution scheme. Members with 10 years' service benefit from an employer contribution of 15 per cent of pensionable salary, whereas members with less than 10 years' service benefit only from a 5 per cent employer contribution. This is indirect age discrimination. The employer in the example is unable to rely on an exemption in the Regulations permitting the imposition of this service criterion because he cannot demonstrate the requisite business need for imposing it. The employer is also unable in the circumstances to establish successfully an objective justification. The discrimination is therefore unlawful.

The effect of 'levelling up' is that all members, regardless of their length of service with the employer, are entitled to an employer contribution at the higher, 15 per cent rate.

We discuss later in this chapter[1] the powers of the employment tribunals and the Pensions Ombudsman under the Regulations in this context.

1 See **8.8**.

8.4.6 The importance of the comparator

Persons claiming discrimination on the grounds of age must be able to demonstrate that their own circumstances are either the same as, or not materially different from, those of their comparator.[1]

In a pensions context, issues that appear at first sight to be potential age discrimination may not actually be so. It may be that differences in treatment between different employees or scheme members are based on their status, rather than their age. An example is employee grade. Many pension schemes will provide higher benefits for executives or senior management, when compared to the level of benefits provided to other staff. There may even be distinctions between staff at different levels, below executive or management level. At first sight, such differences may appear to be indirect discrimination on the grounds of age (eg senior employees may tend to be older). However, an employer ought first to consider whether, in fact, its defence is that the difference arises because different benefits are being provided to employees doing different jobs. In essence, the employer would be saying that differences in pay between employees relates to their grade/role, not their age.

It is important nonetheless to bear in mind that the Regulations do not require a claimant to identify an *actual* comparator – a hypothetical comparator can be used.

1 See reg 3 in **Chapter 4, 4.2.1**.

8.5 The key pensions exemptions

Many aspects of pension scheme benefit design are covered by the wide-ranging list of exemptions contained in Sch 2 of the Regulations. These apply to both occupational pension schemes (Pt 2 of Sch 2 of the Regulations) and personal pension schemes (Pt 3 of Sch 2 of the Regulations). We explore the key exemptions in this section – and the key omissions in the next section.

8.5.1 Service-related benefits

Employers can impose a waiting period for benefits (eg for access to the scheme or before qualifying for a particular benefit) whether the scheme is an occupational or a personal pension scheme.[1] In order to fall within the exemption, the waiting period must operate by reference to the employee's length of service with the employer. If the waiting period is five years or less, an exemption applies automatically.

Employers can impose a waiting period of more than five years but only if certain conditions required by the Regulations are satisfied. Those conditions are:

- the scheme's trustees – who are entitled to rely on the confirmation provided – are required by the Regulations to ask the employer to confirm whether the length of service criterion reasonably appears to the employer to fulfil a business need of the employer's undertaking. The Regulations give examples (but not an exhaustive list) of such a 'business need' – such as encouraging the loyalty or motivation of some or all of the employer's workers; and
- in providing this confirmation, the employer must calculate the length of service of the disadvantaged member(s) and provide this information to the trustees within a reasonable time of their request. The Regulations specify[2] how this calculation should be undertaken, including factors relating to the employee's level of work and periods of absence.

An example of service-related benefits (in this case, service-related contributions) is as follows:

Example:

Employer contributions to a defined contribution occupational pension scheme are based on the following bandings:

Member's years of pensionable service	% employer contribution
Below two years	5%
Two years or more but less than five years	7.5%
Five years or more	10%

The contributions that are tied to a service requirement of less than five years are exempt. The five years' service criterion may be exempt if the employer can demonstrate, in the manner required by the Regulations, that it fulfils a business need. If the employer is unable to do so, active members with less than five years' pensionable service can claim entitlement to the 10 per cent employer contribution.

1 See para 3A of Sch 2 of the Regulations.
2 See paras 3A(3) and 3A(4) of Sch 2 of the Regulations and the cross-referenced paras (4) – (7) of reg 32.

8.5.2 Admission to a scheme

In addition to waiting periods, in relation to occupational pension schemes, employers can restrict admission by reference to[1]:

- a minimum age, including different ages for different groups/categories of worker;
- a maximum age, including different ages for different groups/categories of worker; and/or
- a minimum level of pensionable pay within certain limits linked to the value of State pension provision.

An example of a pensionable pay restriction on admission is as follows:

Example:

A company operates an occupational pension scheme but employees are only permitted to join if their pensionable pay exceeds £5,000.

This is likely to be indirectly discriminatory, as younger employees are more likely to be affected by the restriction than older, higher earning employees. However, the Regulations permit restricting admission by reference to a minimum level of pensionable pay where that minimum does not exceed one and a half times the lower earnings limit.[2] On current figures, the £5,000 restriction would not, therefore, amount to unlawful discrimination.

There is an important distinction between occupational pension schemes that provide pension benefits and those that do not. An occupational pension scheme that does not provide pension benefits[3] – essentially, a life assurance only scheme – is unable to benefit from the exemption in the Regulations[4] permitting the use of a minimum or maximum age for admission. It is therefore unlawful discrimination, in the absence of objective justification, to impose an admission age in relation to such schemes.[5]

In relation to personal pension schemes, although there is no exemption covering admission, there are exemptions that allow employers to set a minimum age for the commencement of payment of employer contributions,[6] including different minimum ages for different groups/categories of worker.[7]

Example:

An employer contributes in respect of its employees to a GPP scheme at the rate of 5 per cent of each employee's basic salary. All of its employees are eligible to join the scheme, but the employer's contributions are only payable in respect of its employees who are aged 25 or over. The employer employs a number of workers who are below age 25 who do not benefit from the employer's contribution (although they are entitled to make their own contributions to the scheme).

The age 25 restriction, although direct discrimination, does not amount to unlawful discrimination under a personal pension scheme as the exemption applies.

---

1 See para 7 of Sch 2 of the Regulations.

2 The lower earnings limit for the tax year 2007–08 is £4,524 per annum. It is the minimum level of earnings that an employee needs to qualify for certain State benefits, such as jobseekers allowance. If an employee's earnings reach or exceed this level, but do not exceed the "earnings threshold", they will not pay National Insurance contributions but will be treated as having paid them when claiming benefits.

3 The test under the legislation is that the scheme does not carry on 'retirement benefit activities' within the meaning of s 255(4) of the Pensions Act 2004.

4 See para 7(a) of Sch 2 of the Regulations.
5 **Chapter 6, 6.5.3(d)**.
6 See para 34 of Sch 2 of the Regulations.
7 See para 35 of Sch 2 of the Regulations.

8.5.3 Contributions to a scheme

Different (and indeed equal) rates of employer and member contributions to a pension scheme are exempted by the Regulations. The exemptions that apply depend on: (a) whether the scheme is an occupational pension scheme or a personal pension scheme; and (b) within the spectrum of occupational pension schemes, whether the scheme provides benefits on a defined benefit or defined contribution basis.

(a) Defined benefit occupational pension schemes

Under the Regulations, member and employer contribution rates can:

- differ in respect of different members, to the extent that the difference is attributable to any differences in their pensionable pay[1];
- be age-related, provided that members accrue pension at the same rate during each year of pensionable service and the 'aim' in setting the different rates is to reflect the increasing cost of providing benefits in respect of older members[2]; and/or
- be restricted to a maximum level of pensionable pay.[3]

Example:

An employer's defined benefit occupational pension scheme provides that members whose pensionable pay is £15,000 or less pay contributions at a rate of 5% of pensionable pay, but members whose pensionable pay exceeds £15,000 pay contributions at a rate of 7% of pensionable pay.

This is permitted by the Regulations even though this could be indirect discrimination if, for example, older employees are more highly paid.

(b) Defined contribution occupational pension schemes

The Regulations permit member and employer contributions that:

- differ in respect of different members, to the extent that the difference is attributable to any differences in their pensionable pay[4];

- are age-related, provided that the 'aim' in setting the different rates is to equalise (or to make more nearly equal) the ultimate benefit 'in respect of comparable aggregate periods of pensionable service'[5];
- are equal across all ages[6]; and/or
- are restricted to a maximum level of pensionable pay.[7]

Example:

Employer and member contributions to a defined contribution occupational pension scheme are based on the following bandings:

Member's age	% contribution
Below 31	5%
31–45	7.5%
45 and over	10%

Provided that the employer can demonstrate that the aim in setting these age-banded rates is to make the ultimate benefit equal or more nearly equal as required by the Regulations, this will not amount to unlawful direct age discrimination.

(c) Personal pension schemes

The list of exemptions included in the Regulations[8] was expanded substantially following industry consultation in the run-up to their implementation. The Regulations exempt:

- a minimum age for the commencement of employer contributions,[9] including different minimum ages for different groups/categories of worker[10];
- equal employer contributions across all ages;
- age-related employer contributions, provided that the 'aim' in setting the different rates is to equalise (or to make more nearly equal) the ultimate benefit derived from contributions made each year by the employer;
- different employer contribution rates, to the extent that the difference is attributable to any differences in the employees' remuneration; and
- the restriction of employer contributions to a maximum level of remuneration.

(d) The need for an 'aim'

Where an employer is seeking to rely on an exemption which requires there be an 'aim' in setting the different contribution rates, the employer needs to be able to demonstrate, if challenged, that the age-related contribution structure does in fact have the 'aim' required by the applicable exemption. In practice, this will involve some work at an early stage from the employer's actuarial advisers to determine whether in fact the age banding satisfies the relevant test. An untested, aspirational aim is unlikely to find favour with an employment tribunal or with the Pensions Ombudsman.

The Regulations do not prescribe how the test needs to be satisfied. In relation to defined contribution occupational pension schemes, for instance, the Regulations do not (either expressly or by implication) require there to be a minimum or maximum number of age bands in order to satisfy this test.

1 See para 9 of Sch 2 of the Regulations.
2 See para 11 of Sch 2 of the Regulations.
3 See para 11A of Sch 2 of the Regulations.
4 See para 9 of Sch 2 of the Regulations.
5 See para 10(a) of Sch 2 of the Regulations.
6 See para 10(b) of Sch 2 of the Regulations.
7 See para 10(c) of Sch 2 of the Regulations.
8 See Pt 3 of Sch 2 of the Regulations.
9 See para 34 of Sch 2 of the Regulations.
10 See para 35 of Sch 2 of the Regulations.

8.5.4 Minimum age for entitlement to benefits (occupational pension schemes only)

At the beginning of this chapter, we observed that pension provision is, by its very nature, age-related and that at its core lies the principle of providing an income in retirement. The essence of this principle is the setting of a 'normal retirement date' – that is, the age at which a member can expect to be entitled to their full benefits. The Regulations permit schemes to set a minimum age, including different ages for different groups/categories, when members are entitled to their full benefits – that is, without consent or reduction for early payment.[1]. The Regulations define this age as the 'early retirement pivot age'.

It is important to note that a member's 'normal retirement date' (for pension scheme purposes) need not be, and often is not, the same as their retirement age for the purposes of their employment contract.[2] There is no requirement in the Regulations, for instance, for a scheme's normal retirement date (ie for pension purposes) to be age 65, to match up with the default retirement age under the Regulations for employment purposes, or any other age set by the employer as its retirement age.

1 See para 14 of Sch 2 of the Regulations.
2 **Chapter 12, 12.7**.

8.5.5 Early retirement benefits (occupational pension schemes only)

Current tax legislation allows benefits from occupational pension schemes to be paid from age 50 (though this minimum age will increase automatically to 55 with effect from 6 April 2010 for most members[1]), or even earlier in circumstances of ill-health. This means that members may be able to draw their benefits earlier than their scheme's normal retirement date.

Where benefits can be drawn early, there is scope for the entitlement to payment and/or the level of benefit to amount to unlawful age discrimination. Potential age discrimination can appear in many guises, but the key elements of early retirement benefits that may be discriminatory are:

- unreduced benefits;
- enhanced benefits; and
- consent requirements.

Let us consider unreduced benefits, for example. Usually, a pension paid early from an occupational pension scheme will be reduced to account for early payment (the scheme rules will usually prescribe how the reduction is calculated and by whom). The reduction is applied to reflect both the present value of money and the fact that (all other things being equal) the pension will be paid for longer. However, if an early pension is not reduced for early payment, it may be discriminatory on the grounds of age, because the unreduced pension is in fact of greater value than the pension would have been at normal retirement date.

The Regulations[2] contain a range of exemptions relating to the early payment of benefits from an occupational pension scheme. The main exemptions are:

(a) imposing at a particular age a consent requirement to the early payment of benefits, provided that: (i) the benefit is actuarially reduced to reflect early payment; and (ii) it is not enhanced (by the crediting of additional periods of pensionable service or additional benefits);

(b) providing certain enhanced early retirement benefits (eg adding extra years of pensionable service to the calculation of the benefit, or applying a lower or no reduction for early payment) from a specified age to active or prospective members who were entitled to the enhancement on 1 December 2006. The purpose of this exemption is to protect entitlements to certain enhanced early retirement benefits that existed when the age discrimination legislation came into force. Note though, that it only applies if the member retires early from active membership of the scheme – it does not apply if the member retires from deferred membership, even if he or she were an active member on 1 December 2006;

(c) providing certain enhanced early retirement benefits (of the types mentioned above) on redundancy (within the meaning of the Employment Rights Act 1996), whether or not subject to any consents;[3] and

(d) providing certain enhanced early retirement benefits from a particular age on the grounds of ill-health (eg adding additional years by reference to the years the member would have been able to work if he or she had not retired on ill-health grounds), whether or not subject to any consents.

1 Schemes can phase in the change from 50 to 55 over the period running up to 6 April 2010. In addition, some transitional protections apply.
2 See paras 12 (general), 13 (protection of rights applicable at 1 December 2006), 13A (ongoing protection of those rights), 13B (redundancy) and 15 (ill-health) of Sch 2 of the Regulations.
3 See **Chapter 11, 11.5.3(d)**.

8.5.6 Late retirement benefits (occupational pension schemes only)

Most occupational pension schemes will provide that if members do not draw their benefits when they first become entitled to do so, they can defer receipt, but the benefit will be actuarially enhanced to reflect late payment. The Regulations permit the setting of an age above which such an enhancement applies – known as the 'late retirement pivot age', including different ages for different categories/groups of members.[1]

Note that the enhancement must be an 'actuarial enhancement' in order to fall within the exemption. Actuarial input is therefore needed in applying the enhancement. Scheme rules generally require trustees or employers who have power to determine the enhancement, to consult an actuary in any event. However, where the enhancement is at a prescribed rate in the rules, confirmation should be obtained from an actuary that the enhancement falls within the scope of the exemption.

There is no exemption in the Regulations for imposing a consent requirement on a late retirement facility. Any consent requirement is likely to be direct age discrimination and can only continue to be imposed if the employer can objectively justify its retention – which in practice is likely to be difficult.

1 See para 14 of Sch 2 of the Regulations.

8.5.7 Death benefits with a prospective service/payment element (occupational pension schemes only)

Most occupational pension schemes will provide benefits on the death of a member that have a potentially discriminatory element. The two most common are:

(i) benefits calculated by reference to prospective service; and

(ii) benefits payable during a 'guarantee' period after a pension starts.

The Regulations exempt the calculation of any death benefit payable in respect of an occupational pension scheme member using either:

- all of the member's prospective service to the date they would have become entitled to take their pension;
- some of the member's prospective service to this date; or
- a fixed number of years of prospective service.

Where a benefit is calculated by reference to prospective service, this could amount to indirect discrimination. An example is as follows:

Example:

A company operates a defined benefit occupational pension scheme. On the death of an active member, a spouse's pension is payable. The pension is equal to 50 per cent of the pension the member would have received, but calculated on the assumption that the member continued in pensionable service until the age he or she would have become entitled to take his or her pension (65 years in this example). John is an active member and dies at 35. His spouse's pension will be enhanced by reference to an additional 30 years' service, because the benefit assumes that John had remained in service all the way through to age 65.

James is an active member and dies at 63. His spouse's pension will only be enhanced for the two years between age 63 and age 65.

The difference in this enhancement could amount to indirect discrimination against the member on the grounds of age. However, it is not unlawful discrimination as the prospective service enhancement is exempt.

Where a scheme provides an enhancement that does not fall within one of these exempt categories, it is worth considering whether the enhancement could be objectively justified. The purpose of a prospective service enhancement, for example, is to recompense the member's dependants for the loss of financial support that the member would have provided if he or she had remained alive. It may be that the employer could establish that an enhancement which does not fall squarely within the exemption meets a similar (social) aim.[1] However, only time will tell if this argument will find favour with the employment tribunals and/or the Pensions Ombudsman.

Many occupational pension schemes will provide a 'guarantee' period in relation to the payment of pensions – that is, if a member dies within a certain number of years of the pension starting, the balance of what would have been paid to the member during those years will be paid. Under current tax legislation, this balance can be paid either as pension (perhaps to supplement a spouse's or dependant's pension) or in lump sum form, although the guarantee period cannot exceed 10 years. There is an argument that the payment of this type of 'guarantee' amounts to indirect discrimination (eg because it is more likely to be paid in respect of people who retire older). However, the Regulations exempt death benefits calculated by reference to such a pension guarantee period.[2]

The Regulations also specifically exempt any difference in the level of death benefits payable in respect of deferred members who die before normal pension age[3] and those payable on the death of a deferred member after normal pension age.[4]

1 **Chapter 4, 4.7.8**.
2 See para 15A(2) of Sch 2 of the Regulations.
3 Note that this exemption operates with reference to 'normal pension age' as defined in s 180 of the Pension Schemes Act 1993, which may differ from the scheme's normal retirement date.
4 See para 15A(4) of Sch 2 of the Regulations.

8.5.8 Level of increases to pensions in payment (occupational pension schemes only)

There are (fairly complex) statutory requirements regarding the application of increases to pensions once they are in payment. Scheme rules, however, may provide increases over and above the statutory requirements and, in doing so, could give rise to potential age discrimination issues. The Regulations[1] exempt the following:

- increases made to members over age 55 but not to those below that age;
- age-related increases where the aim in setting the different rates is to maintain, or more nearly maintain, the relative value of members' pensions; and
- applying different increases depending on how long the pension has been in payment, where the aim of doing so is to maintain, or more nearly maintain, the relative value of members' pensions (eg where inflation has eroded the value of older members' benefits).

As with the exemptions for differing contribution rates,[2] where an employer is seeking to rely on one of these exemptions that requires the aim of the difference to be linked to the relative value of members' pensions, the employer needs to be able to demonstrate, if challenged, that the different rates of increases do in fact have that 'aim'. In practice, this will involve some work from the employer's actuarial advisers to determine whether in fact the differences have that effect. Again, an untested, aspirational aim is unlikely to find favour with an employment tribunal or with the Pensions Ombudsman.

1 See paras 26, 27 and 28 of Sch 2 of the Regulations.
2 See **8.5.3(d)**.

8.5.9 Bridging pensions (occupational pension schemes only)

A scheme's normal retirement date will not necessarily be the same as the State pensionable age – that is, the date when workers are entitled to payment of a State pension. At present, State pensionable age is 65 for men and 60 for women, although legislation is already in force to equalise this for men and women over a period of 10 years starting in 2010. In addition, further legislation is envisaged which will raise the State pensionable age over time.[1]

Often members of an occupational pension scheme will receive their scheme pension before their State pensionable age. Their State pension will then start at a later date, supplementing the scheme pension. In order to ensure that members have a level income stream from the date their scheme pension commences, some occupational pension schemes provide a 'bridging pension'. Essentially, the aim is to 'bridge' this income gap in the period before State pensionable age. Once the member reaches State pensionable age, the 'bridging pension' stops.

The fact that a bridging pension stops at State pensionable age means that it is directly discriminatory – those below State pensionable age are entitled to the benefit, but those above that age are not. The payment of such pensions should not be unlawful, however, as they are exempt under the Regulations.[2] In practice, bridging pensions take many forms and schemes must check whether their particular scheme design actually falls within the exemption.

1 The Pensions Act 1995 includes provision for the equalisation of the State pensionable age between men and women over a 10-year period starting from 6 April 2010. Legislative changes are expected to increase the State pensionable age (once equalised) from 65 to 68 by 2046. See also **Chapter 1**.
2 See para 16 of Sch 2 of the Regulations.

8.5.10 Caps (occupational pension schemes only)

There are a variety of 'caps' that can be included as part of an occupational pension scheme's benefit design. The Regulations exempt the following:

- limits on employer contributions by reference to a certain level of pensionable pay[1];
- limits on benefits calculated by reference to a certain level of pensionable pay[2];
- limits on benefits by reference to a maximum number of years of pensionable service; and
- limits on benefits by reference to a fraction, proportion or multiple of members' pensionable pay.

***Example** 1*:

A company operates a defined benefit occupational pension scheme which has a normal retirement date of 65. The scheme provides members with a pension based on an accrual rate of 1/60th of final salary for each year of their pensionable service. However, 'pensionable service' is restricted to 40 years.

Julia joins the scheme at age 20. By age 60, she has hit her 40 years' pensionable service. She can remain an active member of the scheme, but she will not be able to accrue any additional years of pensionable service above 40 years. (She might remain an active member so that her benefits are calculated by reference to her salary at normal retirement date, and to continue to benefit from any death in service cover that the scheme provides.)

Claire joins the scheme at age 40. She can continue accruing years of pensionable service right up to (and indeed beyond) her normal retirement date (because the 40 years cap will not affect her until she is 80!).

Julia may try to claim that the 40 year cap discriminates against her on the grounds of her age when she joined the scheme. However, this is exempt under the Regulations and is therefore not unlawful.

Example 2:

A company operates a defined benefit occupational pension scheme. Although members accrue pension on an accrual rate of 1/60th of final salary for each year of pensionable service, benefits are limited to two-thirds of the member's pensionable pay at age 65.

The two-thirds restriction is exempt under the Regulations.

Example 3:

A company operates a defined contribution occupational pension scheme. The employer contributes 8 per cent of each member's pensionable pay, regardless of their age. However, the employer does not contribute in respect of pay that exceeds £75,000.

Although the £75,000 is not directly discriminatory, it may be indirectly discriminatory if those who earn above this threshold (and therefore do not enjoy the benefit of employer contributions on part of their pay) are predominantly in a different age group to those earning below the threshold. However, even if such discrimination could be established, it is not unlawful as it is exempt under the Regulations.

1 See paras 10(c) (defined contribution schemes) and 11A (defined benefit schemes) of Sch 2 of the Regulations.
2 See para 24(b) of Sch 2 of the Regulations.

8.5.11 Closure of a scheme (or section) to new members (occupational pension schemes only)

It is increasingly common for employers to close their defined benefit schemes to new joiners as a means of addressing the volatility and expense of funding them. New employees after the closure date will often be offered membership of a scheme providing benefits on a money purchase basis (either through a defined contribution occupational pension scheme or a personal pension scheme) or using a career average (rather than final pay) defined benefit formula.

Over time, there may be scope for a claim for indirect age discrimination. This would be on the basis that those employees who are accruing pension on a (probably more valuable) defined benefit basis are predominantly older than those who are in the post-closure defined contribution scheme. Any such claim should fail, however, as the Regulations exempt the closure of a scheme from a particular date.[1] There is also an exemption that applies if an employer closes its defined benefit scheme to new joiners, but provides the new basis of pension provision through a separate section of the same scheme.[2]

Example:

Hybrid Ltd operates a defined benefit occupational pension scheme, the Hybrid Staff Pension Scheme. It decides to close the scheme to new joiners with effect from 1 January 2008. All new employees after 1 January 2008 will instead be able to accrue pension on a defined contribution basis. The company decides that it will establish a new section of the Hybrid Staff Pension Scheme to provide the benefits for new employees. The existing benefit structure of the Hybrid Staff Pension Scheme will become a defined benefit section.

The closure of the defined benefit section to new employees is not unlawful discrimination as it is exempt under the Regulations. New employees after 1 January 2008 cannot, therefore, claim that they are being discriminated against unlawfully by being denied access to the defined benefit section of the Hybrid Staff Pension Scheme.

---

1 See para 25 of Sch 2 of the Regulations.
2 See para 25A of Sch 2 of the Regulations.

8.5.12 Different benefit structures within a scheme (occupational pension schemes only)

Occupational pension schemes are often made up of a range of different sections, providing benefits on different bases for different employees. Differing benefit designs within a single scheme may have developed over time – for example, because people have historically enjoyed different levels of benefits. The fact that people have different benefits because of historical circumstances does not of itself protect against a discrimination claim.

Differing levels of benefits could amount to age discrimination where those employees with the better benefits are predominantly older. This is not always going to be the case in practice, so an important first step is to assess whether the membership profile of the scheme lends itself towards such a claim being made (now or in the future).

Where there is a risk of such an indirect age discrimination claim, it may nonetheless be possible to rely on an exemption in the Regulations[1] which covers the closure of a 'section' of a scheme. A 'section' for this purpose can be made up of a group of members who became eligible to join (or who joined) the scheme:

- on, after or before a particular date, on the basis that particular benefits/contributions would be provided; or
- as a result of a bulk transfer of members or a business transfer.

By extension, this exemption in practice means that 'cross-section' claims cannot be made where a 'section' is closed. An example is as follows:

Example:

Fabulous Food Group Plc operates an occupational pension scheme with three levels of benefits, as follows:

(i) employees who joined prior to 1 January 2004 accrue defined benefit pensions with an accrual rate of 1/60th;

(ii) employees who joined on or after 1 January 2004 are provided with 5 per cent employer contributions towards a defined contribution pension; and

(iii) employees who transferred to Fabulous Food Group Plc on 1 March 1991 as part of a TUPE transfer,[2] accrue defined benefit pensions with an accrual rate of 1/45th.

The employees accruing defined benefits (both at the 1/60th and the 1/45th rates) constitute different 'sections' for the purposes of the Regulations. This means that the employees accruing benefits in the probably lower value defined contribution section should not be able to claim successfully that they are being discriminated on the grounds of their age by comparison to those employees in the defined benefit sections. Equally, those in the lower accrual rate of 1/60th defined benefit section should not be able to bring a successful age discrimination claim by reference to those in the 1/45th defined benefit section.

However, if the scheme had a fourth section which was still open to new joiners from the confectionaries division of the group, giving 8% employer contributions on a defined contribution basis, an employee who is receiving only the 5% employer contribution might be able to bring a successful age discrimination claim by reference to an employee benefiting from the 8% contribution. The claimant would need to demonstrate that the age profile of the membership is such that there is, in fact, indirect discrimination on the grounds of age. A successful claim, however, would mean that those receiving only the 5% employer contribution would be entitled to the 8% employer contribution in respect of their pensionable service on and from 1 December 2006. Such a claim may, however, be capable of objective justification by the employer, eg if there is a business need to remunerate employees in different parts of the business differently.

---

1 See para 25A of Sch 2 of the Regulations.
2 The Transfer of Undertakings (Protection of Employment) Regulations 1981 (SI 1981/1794), which applies to transfers prior to 6 April 2006.

8.5.13 Compliance with legislation

The Regulations provide that any act done to comply with a statutory provision is not unlawful discrimination. In addition, where an occupational pension scheme is a 'registered pension scheme'[1] for tax purposes, an exemption applies to any discriminatory rule, practice, action or decision where its purpose is to secure any tax relief or exemption, or to prevent any tax charge arising, under the Finance Act 2004.

The most common examples of how these provisions operate in practice are as follows:

- benefits provided by a registered pension scheme cannot start before age 50 (rising to age 55 for most members from 6 April 2010) other than on grounds of ill-health – as required by the Finance Act 2004;
- benefits provided by a registered pension scheme must come into payment by age 75 – as required by the Finance Act 2004;
- a child's pension payable on the death of a member of a registered pension scheme generally must stop when the child reaches age 23 – as required by the Finance Act 2004; and
- members only being entitled to benefits relating to contracted-out rights[2] from State pensionable age – under the Pension Schemes Act 1993.

All of these examples are potentially discriminatory, but they are not unlawful under the Regulations.

1 That is, registered with Her Majesty's Revenue & Customs under Pt 4 of the Finance Act 2004 (as amended), benefiting from the tax advantages afforded to such schemes. A scheme that was 'approved' by the Inland Revenue prior to 6 April 2006 was automatically grandfathered into the new registered schemes system (unless it opted not to become a registered scheme).

2 Contracting-out is the process of using a pension scheme (occupational or personal) to provide benefits instead of the additional State pension. The additional State pension was known as SERPS (State Earnings Related Pension Scheme) up to 6 April 2002, when it became the State Second Pension (S2P). Contracted-out rights can take the form of guaranteed minimum pensions, protected rights or s 9(2B) rights.

8.6 The key pensions omissions

The Regulations contain a long list of exemptions covering most aspects of pension provision through occupational and personal pension schemes. Inevitably, however, there are elements of a scheme's benefit design that may be discriminatory and do not clearly fall within one of the exemptions. Whether problem areas exist will depend on each scheme's benefit design.

There are, however, a number of common features to watch out for that are not exempt under the Regulations. We have touched on some of these already in the section above relating to the key pension exemptions, including:

- service conditions exceeding five years.[1] The test is the same for all service conditions, whether relating to waiting periods or otherwise;
- imposing a minimum or maximum age for admission to a scheme providing life assurance only benefits;
- age-related contributions that fail to meet the 'aim' required by the Regulations;
- providing enhanced early retirement benefits on retirement from deferred membership, even if the individual was an active or prospective scheme member on 1 December 2006;
- consent requirements to late retirement; and
- a scheme with two or more different benefit sections that are open to new joiners.

We consider below some of the other key omissions, namely:

- providing benefits after normal retirement date;
- so-called 'golden numbers'; and
- flexible retirement.

1 See **8.5.2**.

8.6.1 Providing benefits after normal retirement date

Treating an employee who happens to have reached (or passed) his scheme's normal retirement date differently from employees who are below normal retirement date, is potentially unlawful discrimination. There is no exemption for preventing an employee who reaches a scheme's normal retirement date from continuing in active membership of that scheme. This means that it is potentially *unlawful* (before age 75[1]) to:

- stop (or reduce) accrual in a defined benefit occupational pension scheme simply because the employee has reached his normal retirement date;
- stop (or reduce) employer contributions to a defined contribution occupational pension scheme at normal retirement date;
- stop (or reduce) employer contributions to a personal pension scheme when an employee reaches a certain age (usually the employee's contractual retirement age); or
- stop providing (or reduce the level of) life assurance cover for employees above a certain age, whether through an occupational pension scheme, a stand-alone life assurance only scheme or otherwise.[2]

We say 'potentially' unlawful as, of course, it may be possible for an employer in some circumstances to objectively justify these forms of discrimination.[3]

These requirements may have a significant impact on an employer's deliberations about continuing to employ people after their contractual retirement age (or the default retirement age of 65[4]). Where employees do remain in service with their employer beyond the age at which benefit provision or contributions will cease, careful thought needs to be given to facilitating continued benefits/contributions.[5] As part of this, attention will need to be focused on considering the benefits that will be payable on the death of such an employee – and the need to extend any relevant insurance cover where death benefits are insured.

It may be possible, for example, to offer members of a defined benefit occupational pension scheme the option either: (a) to continue accruing benefits after normal retirement date; or (b) to leave the scheme at normal retirement date and benefit from a late retirement enhancement over the period until benefits are drawn. If, having considered the options, a member chooses not to opt for continued accrual, it should make it difficult for him to succeed in a claim that he is being discriminated against on the grounds of his age. However, employers and schemes must ensure members are given sufficient information to make an informed choice. There is no requirement in the Regulations to offer options in this way.

Where the employer contributes to a defined contribution occupational pension scheme or to a personal pension scheme, the simplest and safest stance for employers to take is to offer continued contributions (although legally members retain the right to opt out).

In all cases, the employer, affected employees, trustees (where relevant) and administrators will need to be very clear on exactly how the provision of benefits after normal retirement date will work in practice.

1 Applicable tax legislation imposes a ceiling of age 75 on the provision of pension and ancillary benefits.
2 Note that there is an exemption where life assurance cover provided for ill-health retirees stops at normal retirement date – see reg 34 and para 18 of Sch 2 of the Regulations.
3 **Chapter 4, 4.7**.
4 **Chapter 12 8.6.1**.
5 **Chapter 12, 12.10.2**.

8.6.2 'Golden numbers' (occupational pension schemes only)

This refers to occupational pension scheme rules that provide certain benefits with reference to an 'age plus service' formula. For example, benefits are paid unreduced when a member's age plus service equals 85. Applying such a formula appears to be unlawful age discrimination, unless it can be objectively justified.

Where used, this type of formula operates to establish the date when a member is entitled to enhanced early retirement benefits. It is a common feature of public sector pension schemes and, because of government policy on protecting pension rights of public sector employees who transfer to the private sector, it is also a common feature of private sector occupational pension schemes that have ex-public sector members.

'Golden numbers' generally discriminate because the date a member can retire is set by their age when they join the scheme. There is no applicable exemption (apparently deliberately on the government's part) for such provisions. Indeed, in one of the few court cases to date touching on the pensions part of the age discrimination legislation, the High Court concluded in a 2006 judicial review (regarding the proposed changes to the Local Government Pension Scheme) that the 'rule of 85' formula used in the scheme was unlawful age discrimination.[1]

Example:

A company operates a defined benefit occupational pension scheme. At normal retirement date, members are entitled to draw their full pension. The scheme rules define 'normal retirement date' as the earliest of:

(a) age 60 or the date when the member's age and service equals 85 (the 'rule of 85' age), if later; and (b) age 65.

Adrian joins the scheme at age 25. His 'rule of 85' age is 55, and he can take his pension at age 60.

Martin joins the scheme at age 41. His 'rule of 85' age is 63, and he can take his pension at age 63.

Paul joins the scheme at age 55. His 'rule of 85' age is 70, and he can take his pension at age 65.

The difference in treatment between the three members is triggered by their age when they joined the scheme. This appears to be direct age discrimination for which there is no exemption in the Regulations.

---

1 *R (on the application of UNISON) v First Secretary of State* [2006] IRLR 926. The 'rule of 85' in the Local Government Pension Scheme provided that members would be entitled to enhanced early retirement benefits when their age plus their years of scheme service (which included deferred membership) equalled 85.

8.6.3 Flexible retirement

Prior to 6 April 2006, most members of occupational pension schemes could not draw their pension from an employer's scheme until they left the service of that employer. The tax rules were then changed with effect from 6 April 2006 and this restriction was lifted. Schemes could (but were not required to) offer this 'flexible retirement' facility, allowing people to take their pension while they were still working.

The government has been keen to encourage flexible retirement, reflecting various social aims, such as the retention of skills gained by older workers within the economy. However, in its Pensions Guidance, the DWP comments that employers 'should take advice as to whether their proposals as regards flexible retirement could amount to indirect age discrimination and if so whether they can be objectively justified'.[1]

The government's intentions in this area, however, do not appear to be reflected in the legislation. A failure to offer a flexible retirement facility does not appear to fall foul of the Regulations.

The risk for schemes is that, where flexible retirement is made available to some employees but not to others (for example, because employees are only given the choice at a specified age), it may be that those who are not able to benefit from the facility could legitimately claim unlawful age discrimination. For example, if members of an occupational pension scheme are offered the option of drawing all or part of their accrued pension only when they reach normal retirement date while continuing to work for that employer, those members who are below normal retirement date could claim that they are being discriminated against on the grounds of their age.

1 See of the DWP's Pension Guidance, p 36.

8.7 Objective justification in a pensions context

Chapter 4 analyses in detail the concept of 'objective justification' in the context of the Regulations.[1] Two areas worth particular consideration in the context of age discrimination in a pension scheme are:

(i) the role of the trustees (where the scheme is trust based); and

(ii) whether a 'legitimate aim' is actually met by the discrimination.

1 **Chapter 4, 4.7.**

8.7.1 The role of the trustees (trust based schemes only)

Employers looking to rely on objective justification as a means of operating (or continuing to operate) a discriminatory practice should expect to be challenged by the scheme's trustees. Properly advised trustees ought to do more than simply accept an employer's purported objective justification at face value (except where the employer seeks to rely on a business need within the service conditions exemption in the Regulations, where the trustees are expressly permitted to rely on the information provided by the employer[1]).

The trustees' interests are driven by the fact that the Regulations impose on every occupational pension scheme a non-discrimination rule which requires the trustees to ensure compliance with the Regulations. However, given that objective justification is in most cases likely to be driven by an employer-related need, it is in general accepted that the employer will need to put to the trustees its intended objective justification for continuing with a discriminatory practice.

1 See **8.5.1**.

8.7.2 Does the discrimination actually achieve the 'legitimate aim'?

Although it did not have to decide the point, comments made in the High Court's judgment in *Unison v Secretary of State*[1] provide a useful example of some of the difficulties schemes could face in making out a defence of objective justification in the age context. The case related to the 'rule of 85' in the Local Government Pension Scheme. This rule enabled members to enjoy enhanced early retirement benefits if the sum of the following three factors equalled 85 or more:

- (i) age when employment ended;
- (ii) total years in the scheme; and
- (iii) the period between the end of employment and the early retirement date (which would be nil if someone retired directly from service).

The inclusion of (iii) – essentially a period of deferred membership – meant that a member's eligibility for the enhanced benefit was not in practice dictated by the number of years they were employed in local government. It was driven more by their age on joining. For example, a member who joined the scheme at age 25 could enjoy a full pension at age 55, regardless of how many years he remained employed in local government,[2] whereas a member who joined at, say, age 48, would never be able to meet the 'rule of 85' conditions before the scheme's normal retirement date of 65.

The government was trying to abolish the 'rule of 85'. Unison attempted to argue that the government could have objectively justified continuing it on the premise that the benefit 'rewards loyalty and encourages people to join the local government workforce at an early age'. However, as the benefit in the Local Government Pension Scheme did not distinguish between those who remain in local government and those who did not, the court concluded that this was 'not a system which rewards loyalty'. The court recognised that the 'rule of 85' may have encouraged people to join local government at a young age, but that advantage was marginal (in the context of objective justification) where there was no related incentive for people to remain in local government employment.

The case demonstrates the need to assess carefully whether a purported objective justification will stand up to scrutiny when challenged. This will require employers to ask themselves the right questions in the circumstances. Here is an example:

Example:

A firm of accountants provides higher pension benefits to certain (predominantly older) employees. The difference amounts to indirect age discrimination. The firm considers that it can objectively justify the difference by reference to an 'aim' of retaining staff that are critical to the business.

The employer in these circumstances ought to consider questions such as:

- Does the higher pension provision actually help to retain the relevant employees?
- Is there higher staff turnover amongst those not receiving the higher benefit?
- How devastating would it be for the business to lose the employees with the higher benefits?

---

1 *R (on the application of UNISON) v First Secretary of State* [2006] IRLR 926.
2 Where a member joined at age 25, by the time he reaches age 55, the total of factors (ii) and (iii) will be 30, regardless of the number of years of scheme service undertaken (assuming the member did not opt out of scheme membership). As 55 plus 30 equals 85, the 'rule of 85' condition will be satisfied at age 55.

8.7.3 DWP's Pensions Guidance

The DWP's Pensions Guidance comments that 'legitimate aims' might include business needs, efficiency, reducing staff turnover or providing promotion opportunities to retain good people.[1] That does not, of course, preclude other 'aims' from being sufficient for the purposes of objective justification, but these are useful indicators.

There is one other comment in the DWP's Pensions Guidance in this context that is worthy of mention. One of the pillars of objective justification under the Regulations is that the discrimination must be a 'proportionate' means of achieving the relevant legitimate aim. The guidance states that 'a measure may not be proportionate if an alternative exists that achieves the same aim as effectively but is less discriminatory.[2] This emphasises the need for the discriminatory effect of the provision/practice to be balanced against the perceived legitimate aim. Interestingly, this wording in the guidance was softened in the final version from earlier wording which stated that a measure 'will' not be proportionate if a less discriminatory alternative exists.

1 See the DWP's Pensions Guidance, p 7.
2 See the DWP's Pensions Guidance, p 7.

8.8 Jurisdiction for bringing pensions-related claims

8.8.1 Employment tribunals

A worker can bring a claim before an employment tribunal in the context of a pension scheme in the same way as for any other age discrimination claim.[1] A member (or prospective member) of a pension scheme could in the alternative bring his or her claim against the trustees of the scheme. This may be by reference to an act of the trustees which is unlawful under the Regulations, or on the premise that the trustees are to be treated as having undertaken such an act either in their capacity as the employer's agent[2] or by unlawfully aiding the employer.[3] In those circumstances, the employer will automatically be treated for procedural purposes as a party to the complaint against the scheme's trustees, and will, therefore, be entitled to appear and be heard.[4]

The Regulations empower an employment tribunal to make an order (but not in relation to any time before 1 December 2006):

- declaring that the complainant has a right to be admitted to a scheme on the terms and/or capacity the tribunal considers appropriate[5];
- declaring that the complainant has a right to membership of the scheme without discrimination on the terms and/or capacity the tribunal considers appropriate[6]; and
- for compensation (except for injury to feelings), although there is no power for the tribunal to increase that compensation by reference to a failure to comply with the tribunal's recommendations.[7]

1 **Chapter 14**.
2 See reg 25.
3 See reg 26.
4 See para 5 of Sch 2 of the Regulations.
5 See paras 6(2)(a) and 6(3) of Sch 2 of the Regulations.
6 See paras 6(2)(b) and 6(3) of Sch 2 of the Regulations.
7 See para 6(4)(b) of Sch 2 of the Regulations and para (3) of reg 38.

8.8.2 Pensions Ombudsman

As an alternative to the employment tribunal route,[1] an individual may seek to invoke the jurisdiction of the Pensions Ombudsman.[2] One reason for this may be the applicable time limits[3] – in general, a complaint or dispute must be brought before the Pensions Ombudsman within three years of the act or omission to which it relates occurring. This can be extended by the Pensions Ombudsman to a period of three years from the date when the person knew or ought to have known of its occurrence.

The Pensions Ombudsman has the power in relation to both occupational and personal pension schemes to 'investigate and determine':

- allegations of maladministration; and
- disputes of fact or law.

A complaint or dispute can be brought against the scheme's trustees and/or the employer. It is not only a member who can bring a complaint or dispute before the Pensions Ombudsman, rather 'any actual or potential beneficiary' can do so. This is wide enough to include the pension scheme member, any surviving dependant (including spouses and civil partners) and an ex-spouse of the member entitled to a pension credit in the scheme by virtue of a pension sharing order on divorce.

For the purposes of his investigations, the Pensions Ombudsman has wide powers (akin to those of a court) to call for information to be furnished and documents to be provided.[4]

The Pensions Ombudsman has powers to require any person responsible for the management of a scheme (which can include the employer) to 'take or refrain from taking such steps as he may specify',[5] including awards for compensation.[6] Appeals from a determination of the Pensions Ombudsman are limited to points of law only – there is no route to appeal a determination by reference to the facts.

1 The Pensions Ombudsman will not consider a complaint if a claim has been made to an employment tribunal, unless that claim is discontinued.
2 The Regulations expressly permit this – see reg 35(2).
3 The Personal and Occupational Pension Schemes (Pensions Ombudsman) Regulations 1996, SI 1996/2475 (as amended), reg 5.
4 Pension Schemes Act 1993, ss 149 and 150.
5 Pension Schemes Act 1993, s 151(2).
6 In practice, the compensatory awards granted tend to be small – in the region of up to £1,000.

8.9 Amending pension schemes to comply with the Regulations

Where a provision, practice or criterion amounts to unlawful age discrimination, the employer ought to consider how to go about amending it. This will depend on whether the scheme is an occupational or a personal pension scheme.

In addition to any employment law driven consultation requirements, employers should note that there is a specific pensions law obligation on them to consult for no less than 60 days when making certain changes to future pension benefits.[1] However, these do not apply if a change is being made in order to comply with a legislative requirement – such as the age discrimination legislation.

1 The Occupational and Personal Pension Schemes (Consultation by Employers and Miscellaneous Amendment) Regulations 2006, SI 2006/349. Note that the implementation of the consultation obligation has been staggered for small employers (with less than 150 employees) over a two-year period from 6 April 2006.

8.9.1 Occupational pension schemes

The starting point is to check the power of amendment under the scheme's governing documents. This will determine the answers to two key questions:

(i) Who can exercise the power? In most cases, there will be a role to play for the scheme's trustees, although in some cases the power is vested in the employer alone; and

(ii) Are there any relevant restrictions on the power?

If the trustees of the scheme do not have the power to amend the scheme under the scheme's documents, the Regulations step in to grant them a power to make changes by resolution. The Regulations also enable trustees to make amendments where there are procedural impediments to the exercise by them of a power under the scheme's rules.[1] There are, though, important restrictions on the scope of this statutory power, some of which have the effect of protecting the employer's position. They are as follows:

- if the amendment could not be made under the scheme's rules without the consent of the employer, the statutory power is subject to that consent;
- the statutory power can have retrospective effect, but not in relation to any time before 1 December 2006 (being the date when the pensions part of the Regulations came into force). However, although the power is expressed to have retrospective effect in this way, the government's view[2] is that, where any reduction to benefits is to be made, it can only be exercised so as to take effect from the date of change; and
- the power is expressly stated to be a power to make alterations 'as may be required to secure conformity with the non-discrimination rule.'[3] If an element of scheme design, for example, is not clearly discriminatory on the grounds of age, this statutory power cannot be used by the trustees.

It will also be important to check affected employees' contracts of employment to see whether any proposed amendment to the scheme could amount to a change to their terms and conditions of employment.

1 If the procedure for doing so is likely to be unduly complex or protracted; if it involves obtaining consents which cannot be obtained; or if it involves obtaining consents that can only be obtained with undue delay or difficulty – see para 2(3) of Sch 2 of the Regulations.
2 The DWP's Pensions Guidance, p 36.
3 See para 2(3) of Sch 2 of the Regulations.

8.9.2 Personal pension schemes

In relation to personal pension schemes, the employer is unlikely to be at liberty to change the terms on which an insurance provider provides the benefit. However, employers do need to consider the terms of affected employees' contracts of employment, and look to amend those terms as necessary to comply with the Regulations, in accordance with applicable legal obligations (including consultation requirements) and restrictions.

Chapter 9

Ill-health, disability and age

9.1 Introduction

It is generally assumed to be a fact of life that people tend to suffer from increased medical problems as they get older. Ill-health and disability issues in the workplace already create many challenges for employers, and this can only increase when these issues are combined with potential age discrimination claims. In this chapter, we look at various areas where ill-health and age overlap under the Regulations:

- What assumptions are there about health and age, and are they correct?
- What happens when older workers suffer direct age discrimination because of assumptions about their health, and can this be justified?
- If older workers are more likely to be unwell than younger workers, in what circumstances might there be indirect age discrimination, and can this be justified?
- Can older disabled employees who are compulsorily retired still bring a disability discrimination claim, and how can this be avoided?
- Can employees who have a disability related to old age require reasonable adjustments to be made to accommodate them?

– Can health and safety be a good reason for discriminating against older workers?

9.2 Physiology and age

Both physical and mental capabilities are thought to decline with increasing years. Obviously this is not true for everyone. Workers of all ages may be disabled, or become ill at any time during their employment, and older workers may remain healthy until retirement or beyond. However, this is a widely held belief, even among older people. Research by the Employers Forum on Age from August 2004 reported that nearly one third of people in their 60s believe that you cannot work as well when you get older.[1] Whether this is true or not, such generalised assumptions may well lead to discrimination against older workers.

It is certainly possible that there are stereotyped views about older people, particularly in relation to mental capabilities. In many cultures there is great respect for the wisdom of the old. However, in the United Kingdom workplace there can be negative assumptions about the mental abilities of older workers – such as their ability to think quickly and innovatively, and to adapt to new technologies and ways of working. Age Concern research from 2005 reported that one in three respondents interviewed thought that the over 70s are viewed as incompetent and incapable.[2] These assumptions may well be based more on stereotyping than fact. They also fail to recognise that older workers are likely to have more experience and well developed interpersonal skills, as well as different rather than inferior ways of working, which may actually improve rather than harm productivity.

It is somewhat less controversial that physical abilities tend to decline with increasing age, although again it should not be assumed that this equates to a decline in productivity in many types of jobs.[3] Medical problems will tend to increase as people get older. According to a 2002 study of ageing, one in five people aged 50 or over reported a long-term illness or disability that restricted their daily activities.[4] This rose to two in five for those over 80. The incidence of serious medical conditions such as heart disease, high blood pressure, diabetes and many types of cancer is well recognised to increase with age. This is also borne out by the actuarial calculations made by insurance companies, leading to their unwillingness to provide health and life insurance to those over 65 or 70 (see **Chapter 6**).

However, although older workers may have more medical problems, this does not necessarily equate to an increased number of days off work. In fact, a Labour Force Survey from 2004 found that older workers were, on average, likely to have fewer days off work than younger workers.[5] The percentage of workers taking at least one day off sick in the week dropped from 3.2% of 16 to 24 year olds, to 3.0% of 25 to 35 year olds, and only

2.8% of those over 50. On average, it was women aged 25 to 34 who had the highest rate of sickness absence, at 3.6 per cent. Although this survey looks at days off work rather than the length of absences, this seems to contradict the assumption that older workers are more likely to be unable to attend work due to illness. The specific group with the highest rate of absence was lone mothers, at 4.4 per cent. Again, this group is likely to comprise younger rather than older workers.

The position is somewhat different in relation to self-reported illnesses that are either caused by or related to work. Statistics from the Health and Safety Executive for 2005/20–05 indicate that those over 45 lose the most days off work due to work-related illness, at an average of 1.7 days, as compared to 0.87 days for those aged 25 to 34, and 1.2 days for those aged 35 to 44. For men over 55, this increases to 2.1 days. Taken together, these sets of statistics suggest that older workers are in general less likely to take days off work, but more likely to suffer from a work-related illness – a rather more complicated picture than the general assumption that older workers are the most likely to be unwell.

The potential link between age and ill-health does mean that there may be age discrimination against older workers. Although older workers may not actually be the most likely to take time off sick, assumptions may well be made about their actual or likely health which can lead to direct age discrimination. Older workers may also be disproportionately disadvantaged by an employer's policies or practices related to health issues, leading to potential claims for indirect age discrimination. Many medical conditions that are more prevalent in older people may also be a disability under the Disability Discrimination Act 1995 (DDA 1995), and the overlap between age and disability discrimination is likely to cause some particularly complex issues.

Although it is currently quite unusual for employees to work past 65, demographics suggest that this will become more common. This is likely to cause increasing problems for employers. In particular, the approach of insurers to those over 65 suggests that this age group is significantly more likely to suffer from health problems. The effective insurance cut-off of 70[6] indicates that this age group is even more likely to suffer from significant ill-health. Although the statistics are complicated and suggest that older workers do not necessarily take the most time off sick, serious and long-term ill-health issues do cause particularly complex problems for employers. The possible issues relating to the health problems of older workers may be a reason for employers to continue to insist on a retirement age of 65.

1 See *www.efa.co.uk/age/facts.asp*.
2 Age Concern Research Services/University of Kent, January 2005.
3 P Meadows, *Retirement Ages in the UK: A Review of the Literature*, Employment Relations Research Series No 18 (London: DTI, 2003), 18, which considers evidence that productivity in many jobs in the UK does not decline with age.
4 English Longitudinal Study of Ageing, 2002.

5 The Office for National Statistics – Labour Market Trends, April 2005.
6 **Chapter 6**, **6.5.1(a)**.

9.3 Direct and indirect age discrimination

Direct and indirect discrimination are considered in detail in **Chapter 4**.

9.3.1 Direct discrimination

Direct age discrimination that is related to ill-health and disability issues is most likely to arise where assumptions are made about the health of older workers. Less favourable treatment on grounds of age under the Regulations will arise whenever it is assumed that older workers are more likely than younger workers to become unwell.

Key examples of direct age discrimination include:

(a) **Refusal of health insurance and life assurance benefits to workers over a certain age, or a requirement for older workers to pay higher premiums**
This is a clear example of direct age discrimination, and the issues arising from this (including the possibility of justification) are discussed in more detail in **Chapter 6**.[1]

(b) **Compulsory health check-ups for workers over a certain age**
This may be done to check that a worker is fit to carry out a particular job – either with health check-ups only being required for those over a certain age, or additional tests being carried out for older workers. Although in some ways this could be seen as a benefit if it is paid for by the employer, being required to undergo a health assessment simply because of age may also be seen as intrusive or degrading. Conversely, if workers over a certain age are offered a voluntary health check-up, younger workers may claim they have been discriminated against.

(c) **Age limits on specific jobs**
In some types of job, there is an upper age limit, on the grounds that the job requires a certain level of health or physical fitness. This might be based on health and safety concerns and/or a requirement to be able to fulfil the demands of the job effectively.

This is discussed in more detail later in this chapter in **9.5** as well as in **Chapter 5**.[2] Again, this is a clear example of direct age discrimination, where an individual is denied a job altogether simply because of his or her age.

Age discrimination is unique in that it is possible to justify direct (as well as indirect) age discrimination. However, it is questionable whether direct age discrimination that arises from concerns about ill-health can be justified, because it will be difficult to show that it is a 'proportionate' means of achieving the employer's aim in accordance with reg 3.

The test of proportionality requires the employer to consider using alternatives that would have a less discriminatory effect. The problem here is that age is effectively being used as a 'proxy' for other issues that the employer is concerned about. The employer's real concern is the employee's health and so capability to do the job. However, an upper age limit is being used as a short-cut for assessing capability, on the basis of an assumption that older workers are more likely to be unwell. This is effectively stereotyping of older workers, which is a large part of what discrimination law seeks to prevent. A more proportionate approach is likely to be one that focuses on the real issue, and recognises that workers of all ages might be unwell. For example, it would be less discriminatory to carry out health check-ups on all workers who are in jobs where good health is important. It may be unreasonably expensive or onerous to test all workers in this situation, as discussed further below in relation to health and safety issues. However, as a general rule, the use of age as a proxy in this way is unlikely to find favour with employment tribunals.

Schedule 2 to the Regulations which sets out the pension exceptions includes at paragraph 15 an exception in relation to the provision of certain enhanced early retirement benefit from a particular age on the grounds of ill-health.[3]

1 **Chapter 6, 6.5.3(b).**
2 **Chapter 5, 5.3.3(i).**
3 **Chapter 8, 8.5.5(d).**

9.3.2 Indirect discrimination

Indirect age discrimination connected with health is most likely to arise where an employer has a policy or practice that affects employees who are unwell or disabled. Unlike direct age discrimination, where the problem arises because of assumptions about older workers, indirect discrimination can occur because older workers may in fact be more likely to be unwell. Such claims may arise in connection with an employer's policies on ill-health, or requirements for particular levels of fitness or performance.

The first hurdle for a potential claimant is to show that there is a link between age and ill-health. Indirect discrimination operates where a particular provision, criterion or practice is applied equally to everyone, but this tends to disadvantage a particular age group. In order to make a claim in relation to ill-health issues, a worker will need to show that a particular age group is disadvantaged because that age group is more likely to be unwell. Although this does not require detailed statistics, a claimant will need to provide some evidence to support a claim of age-related disadvantage, showing that there is an actual adverse impact on the age group to which he belongs. Where the policy complained about relates to ill-health absence, this may be particularly difficult, in the light of the statistics discussed above about absence rates from work for different age groups.[1] This may be easier to show in relation to fitness requirements, but a general assertion that older workers tend to be less fit that younger workers may not be enough.

Key examples of potential indirect age discrimination connected with ill-health include:

> **(a) performance and capability procedures that adversely affect employees who are suffering from ill-health, and so under-performing;**
>
> **(b) a practice of dismissing employees after a specific length of absence due to ill-health;**
>
> **(c) limits on the amount of sick pay that is payable to employees who are absent from work on grounds of ill-health; and**
>
> **(d) particular requirements relating to levels of fitness, strength or coordination.**

All the above examples are likely to put older workers at a particular disadvantage as compared to younger workers, if it can be shown that older workers are more likely to suffer from ill-health.

Again, it is possible for the employer to justify the indirectly discriminatory effect of such policies and practices. The employer must first show that its practice fulfils a legitimate aim. In relation to performance and capability issues, and fitness requirements, this aim will presumably be that the worker can actually do the job. For absence dismissal policies and sick pay, the aim is more likely to be controlling the costs of dealing with workers who are unable to attend work.

Once a legitimate aim has been established, the key question is whether the employer's actions are 'proportionate'.

It is likely that this form of indirect discrimination will be easier to justify than the examples of direct age discrimination already discussed. To begin with, the discriminatory impact is less – instead of a rule that adversely affects everyone of a certain age, there is a practice that may affect an older age group more than a younger age group. Unlike direct age discrimination, where there is often an alternative approach that focuses on the employer's real concerns, it may be difficult to find a suitable alternative to the types of performance and ill-health management practices set out above.

An employer could make allowances to accommodate older workers who are unwell, such as by relaxing the rules for those over a certain age. However, this would simply give younger workers a potential claim for direct age discrimination, which would be more difficult to justify; for example, if an employer implemented less strict rules for sickness absence and pay for older workers or less stringent fitness requirements. In relation to fitness, strength or coordination requirements the employer will need to ensure that these requirements are genuinely necessary to perform the role so that they do not create a disproportionate barrier to older workers.

There is an analogy here with the requirement to make reasonable adjustments to accommodate a disabled employee under the DDA 1995.[2] Although the wording of the test for reasonable adjustments is different from the test for indirect discrimination under the Regulations, the DDA test is designed to cover the concept of indirect discrimination in accordance with the requirements of the relevant European Directive.[3] The main difference between disability and age discrimination is that nondisabled employees will have no claim if a disabled person is treated more favourably, while the age discrimination rules apply to everyone. As explained above, this means that it is not possible to adjust workplace practices to assist older workers if younger workers lose out, such as by adopting less strict rules for older workers.

However, despite this key difference, even the developing DDA case law has placed limits on what can be required of an employer by way of reasonable adjustments. In particular, recent decisions have confirmed that there is generally no requirement to continue paying full sick pay to a disabled worker in circumstances where pay would have expired for nondisabled workers.[4] If this is the case under the DDA, where disabled workers can be treated more favourably, it is very likely to be the case for similar indirect discrimination arguments related to age.

Example:

An employer's sickness absence policy specifies that employees with more than two months of continuous sickness absence may be dismissed. Sally is 61, and has been absent for two and a half months with a work-related injury. She is dismissed in accordance with the employer's policy, and claims indirect age discrimination.

Sally will first need to show that the policy tends to disadvantage older workers. To do this, she will need to show that employees in her age group tend to suffer from long-term illness absences more than younger employees. First, she will have to identify the pools for comparison – what age group is she in, and what age group is she comparing herself with? She will then have to show that employees in her age group are more likely to suffer from this type of illness-related absence.

If Sally can show this, the employer will need to justify the policy. The employer can argue that the policy has a legitimate aim, such as the need to cease paying and employing workers who are unable to perform their duties. The employer must also show that the policy is a proportionate way of meeting this aim. This will involve showing that the employer has considered alternatives, and has applied the policy consistently to all of its employees.

In summary, it is likely to be difficult to win an indirect discrimination claim of this type. As discussed, the claimant would need to show that individuals of a certain age are more likely than younger workers to suffer from ill-health and so be placed at a disadvantage by a particular policy. This may not be easy to do in many cases and a generalised assertion on the basis of assumptions about older workers and their health is unlikely to be enough. Even if this hurdle is overcome, it seems likely that an employer will be able to justify such policies in many cases. So long as the employer has a clear reason for the policy, and applies it in a consistent way to everyone, its decision to do so is likely to be proportionate.

1 See **9.2**.
2 See s 4A of the DDA 1995.
3 Council Directive 2000/78 establishing a general framework for equal treatment in employment and occupation.
4 *O'Hanlon v Revenue & Customs Commissioners* [2006] IRLR 840.

9.4 Disability

So far the discussion has focussed on general ill-health and age discrimination. However, many medical conditions that are related to age, or more likely to arise in old age, may also in themselves be a disability under the DDA.

The DDA contains a specific definition of 'disability', which must be met before an individual will be covered by the legislation. This requires someone to have a 'physical or mental impairment which has a substantial and long-term effect on his ability to carry out normal day-to-day activities'.[1] The test is essentially one of severity, requiring a certain degree of actual impairment. However, many age-related medical conditions are likely to fall within this test. In addition, progressive conditions which do not meet this test are covered if they are likely to become more severe in time, which is likely to be the case with medical conditions that deteriorate with increasing age.

The fact that age-related conditions which are a disability for the purposes of the DDA are likely to get worse rather than improve over time as the individual's age increases also raises some particularly complex questions about the interrelationship between age and disability discrimination.

1 See s 1(1) of the DDA.

9.4.1 Disability and retirement

One key question is whether a disabled employee who is retired at the employer's normal retirement age could still have a disability discrimination claim, if the disability is a factor in the employer's reasoning for not allowing the employee to stay on after retirement.

Normally, the employer's reasons for retiring an employee will not be questioned, so long as the correct procedures have been followed. This is dependent on the employer's normal retirement age and proposed actual date of retirement and whether the employee has been informed correctly of the right to request to stay on after retirement.[1] However, if these tests are satisfied, retirement is deemed to be the only reason for dismissal. In addition, even if an employee's request to stay on after normal retirement age is rejected, the employer is immune from an unfair dismissal claim if the statutory procedures have been followed.

However, what if the employer's underlying reason for not wanting the employee to remain after retirement is because the employee is disabled? Can the fact that retirement is deemed to be the only reason for dismissal under the Regulations prevent the employee from bringing a claim under the DDA?

Looking at the general scope of discrimination law, it seems very unlikely that the employee would be prevented from bringing a disability discrimination claim in these circumstances. The provisions in the Regulations which provide that retirement can be the only reason for dismissal are a key part of enabling the employer to show that the dismissal is fair for the purposes of unfair dismissal law. However, this says nothing about other types of claim relating to dismissal, such as discrimination claims.

Although employees who were dismissed at or above normal retirement age could not bring unfair dismissal claims before the Regulations came into force, discrimination claims could still be brought, and there is no reason to think that the Regulations will have changed this. Obviously, the DDA was in force before the Regulations. In addition, disability is included alongside age in the Directive that led to the Regulations being implemented in the United Kingdom.[2] The Regulations cannot lead to another area of discrimination law simply being set aside when an otherwise lawful retirement takes place. It seems quite obvious that a decision to retire an employee would be unlawful sex discrimination if the decision was made simply because the employee was a woman and the same principle will apply if disability is the employer's motivation. Even if this was the intention behind the Regulations, this is unlikely to be compatible with the requirements of the Directive.

If the disability is a factor in the employer's reasoning, it may still be possible to justify the retirement decision. However, this will depend on the type of discrimination under the DDA.

It is not possible to justify direct discrimination under the DDA – less favourable treatment *on the ground of* an individual's disability.[3] As this is a relatively recent amendment to the DDA, the width of this test is not yet clear. However, it will certainly cover decisions that are made on the basis of a prejudice or assumption about a particular disability. For example, an employer believes that it is not desirable to keep an older employee with heart trouble, and decides to retire the employee on this basis. Or, an employer may assume that an older employee with heart trouble is incapable of performing to the required standard, on the basis of a stereotype about this medical condition rather than actual evidence of substandard performance.

It is possible to justify the other main form of discrimination under the DDA, which is discrimination for a reason *related to* an individual's disability.[4] This form of discrimination arises where an employee is treated unfavourably for a reason that is connected with the disability, rather than simply because of the disability itself. For example, an older employee's heart trouble may have led to an actual decline in performance, and the employer decides to retire the employee because of these performance concerns. The employer is not prejudiced against people with heart disease, but is simply removing someone he perceives to be under-performing. The test for justification is the same as under the Regulations and at first sight it would seem that failing performance would be a justification for enforced retirement, even though this was caused by a potential disability. However, justification is only possible if reasonable adjustments to accommodate the employee's disability would make no difference (discussed further in this chapter).[5] This means that, in order to avoid a DDA claim, the employer may well be expected to try to assist performance and accommodate the employee's disability, rather than proceeding straight to a retirement dismissal.

This does not mean that it will be impossible for an employer to retire a disabled employee. However, in order to avoid a potential DDA claim, the employer will either need to be clear that the employee's disability is not the reason for retiring the employee, or show that the dismissal would be justified under the DDA after all reasonable adjustments have been considered. Ideally, the disability should not be a factor in the employer's reasoning at all. This will be easier to show if the employer rarely departs from a particular retirement age, and applies exactly the same policy to the disabled employee. In practice, this means that what is often thought of as the more 'dignified' exit of retirement for older employees who are under-performing because of illness may not be an attractive option for employers, due to the risk of DDA claims. It would be unfortunate if the Regulations actually lead to fewer people being allowed to work beyond retirement due to these concerns. However, although this was already the case before the Regulations came into force, it is likely that there will be a higher risk of claims now due to increased awareness of age discrimination and the requirement on employers to follow a retirement procedure.

Example:

Alex, who suffers from age-related diabetes, is retired by his employer at the normal retirement age of 65. His employer often allows employees to stay on beyond this age. However, the employer refused Alex's request to stay on because it feel his diabetes will affect his performance.

Alex may have a claim for disability discrimination. Although the employer applied its normal retirement age to Alex, its refusal to allow him to stay longer is connected with his disability. Alex will first need to show that his diabetes is serious enough to be a 'disability' under the DDA.

If Alex is disabled, he could try and claim that he was discriminated against on grounds of his diabetes – ie the employer was prejudiced against him simply because of his specific illness. If this succeeds, the employer will be unable to justify the discrimination.

Alex could also claim that he was discriminated against for a reason related to his disability – ie he was retired due to failing performance that was due to his illness. The employer is able to justify this type of discrimination. Genuinely failing performance may be a legitimate reason for requiring a disabled employee to retire. However, the employer will also need to show that this was proportionate. This requires the employer to have considered alternatives, and also made any reasonable adjustments that could have helped Alex to perform better in the light of his illness. If the employer has not considered whether anything can be done to accommodate Alex's diabetes, it is unlikely that it will be able to justify the discrimination.

---

1 See Sch 6 of the Regulations and s 98ZA to 98ZF of the Employment Rights Act 1996.
2 **Chapter 2**.

3 See s 3A(5) of the DDA.
4 See s 3A(1) of the DDA.
5 See s 3A(6) of the DDA.

9.4.2 Disability and reasonable adjustments

As already mentioned above, the DDA includes an obligation to make reasonable adjustments. The test is as follows:

'Where:

(a) a provision, criterion or practice applied by or on behalf of an employer; or

(b) any physical feature of premises occupied by the employer

places the disabled person concerned at a substantial disadvantage in comparison with persons who are not disabled, it is the duty of the employer to take such steps as it is reasonable, in all the circumstances of the case, for it to have to take in order to prevent the provision, criterion, practice or feature having that effect.'[1]

Obviously this applies to age-related disabilities as much as to any other type of disability – meaning that an employer with an older workforce may have increasing obligations to make adjustments to accommodate increasingly disabled workers. Such adjustments can cover a wide variety of things, including alterations to hours and duties, adjustments to premises and even the requirement to offer alternative work.

As already discussed, the requirement to make reasonable adjustments may make it difficult to justify a retirement that is actually based on ill-health or failing performance due to illness. If reasonable adjustments could have made a difference to the situation, these need to be tried first before a disabled employee is dismissed.

The key question is what is 'reasonable' in relation to a disabled older employee. Although not always the case, it is generally assumed that disabilities related to old age are likely to get worse over time as the person's age increases, rather than remain stable or improve. This is somewhat different from many other types of disability, which may improve or even disappear altogether.

It is one thing to make temporary adjustments to accommodate a disabled worker who is being integrated back into the workplace and quite another to accommodate an older worker whose condition is deteriorating over time with an on-going impact on performance. This may also be coupled with the fact that an older worker may not have a long period of time before his expected retirement. An employer may argue that it is not worth making potentially expensive adjustments for a worker who is likely to remain at work for only a short period, whether due to retirement or a deteriorating condition. This is particularly the case where the adjustment involves a large one-off expenditure, as opposed to an ongoing cost. But can these factors be taken into account under the DDA?

Section 18B(1) of the DDA provides a nonexhaustive list of matters to be taken into account in determining whether a particular step is reasonable or not. This list includes the extent to which the step will prevent the effect, the extent to which the step is practicable, and the financial and other costs of taking the step. Although there is no specific mention of the time for which the individual is likely to remain in employment, this may be something that could be taken into account in assessing whether the step is reasonable, and possibly also in judging the financial costs in the light of the likely benefit to the employer. In addition, if an individual suffers from a deteriorating condition, it may be arguable that the step will not prevent the effect for long enough to make the investment worth taking. Obviously, the reasonableness of an adjustment will always turn on the facts of a particular case. An alteration to hours or minor reallocation of duties may be a step that should be taken, irrespective of the progression of the condition or pending retirement. However, an employer may be able to argue that a potentially costly adjustment of premises may not be reasonable for a worker who is due to retire in a relatively short period of time.

Of course, some of these issues are based on a potentially flawed assumption that older workers are not only more likely to be disabled than younger workers, but disabled in a way that leads to deteriorating performance. In individual cases, an employer may well obtain medical advice to this effect and be able to act accordingly. However, this will not necessarily be a general problem. In reality, the impact of individuals tending to remain at work for a few years longer than they do now may not be particularly significant in terms of new and burdensome disability discrimination requirements. However, if these issues do arise, they are potentially complicated and costly if not handled correctly.

Example:

Liz is 64, and has 8 months until she reaches the employer's normal retirement age of 65. She suffers from arthritis, which is getting worse with age. She is struggling to perform her job, and has asked for a specially adapted desk and keyboard, which will help her arthritis. This will cost £ 3,000. She has also asked for shorter working hours as she finds commuting in the rush hour difficult.

If Liz's arthritis is serious enough to be covered by the DDA, the employer has an obligation to make reasonable adjustments to accommodate her disability. The key question is, what is 'reasonable' in the circumstances?

The desk and keyboard is a one-off expenditure which may not be of any use for the employer after Liz retires in eight months. This may mean it may be reasonable to refuse to make the adjustment – although this will depend on a number of factors, including the employer's size and financial resources. Even if the employer cannot make this adjustment, it should look at other alternatives that might help Liz. If Liz was planning to remain in employment after her normal retirement age, her employer will have to take care that its decision-making is not influenced by any refusal to consider Liz working beyond retirement because of her disability. The employment position will be safer if it rarely allows staff to work beyond retirement.

The shorter working hours is more likely to be a reasonable adjustment, unless the change is such that the employer is unable to cover Liz's work, as this is a temporary change. If appropriate, Liz's pay can be reduced to reflect her shorter hours.

---

1 See s 4A(1) of the DDA 1995.

9.5 Health and safety

There are some types of work that raise particular health and safety concerns in relation to older workers. These tend to be jobs that involve particular physical requirements, or which require an unusually high standard of physical fitness to be performed safely. Again, this is based on the assumption that older workers tend to have declining health and fitness, which makes the performance of particular jobs unsafe for them or others.

Employers have a number of health and safety duties in relation to their employees, both under common law[1] and statute. At first sight, compliance with these duties would seem to give a particularly strong justification for potential age discrimination. This would certainly be the case if an employer was seeking to justify a policy that had an indirectly discriminatory effect on older workers, such as a requirement to pass particular physical tests. Although these tests may disadvantage older workers, the need to comply with health and safety requirements is likely to be both a legitimate aim and a proportionate way of achieving these aims – so long as the tests are set at the level genuinely required to do the job, and applied consistently to everyone.

Example:

An employer conducts fitness tests for work in a warehouse, requiring all employees to be able to lift a certain weight. The employer justifies this by its concern over the health and safety of its staff. The weight is heavier than any of the items in the warehouse. The employer does not bother to test workers who look like they can lift the weight.

John, who is 63, fails the test and is dismissed. He claims indirect age discrimination.

The policy tends to discriminate against older workers, who are less likely to be able to lift the weight. The employer needs to justify the policy. The employer is likely to be able to establish a legitimate aim, which is to ensure that workers can carry out their job safely. However, the employer is unlikely to be able to show that this is proportionate – the weight is heavier than the job requires, and the test is not applied consistently to everyone.

However, some employers may wish to use health and safety concerns to set a maximum age limit on particular jobs, on the assumption that workers over this age are unlikely to meet the fitness requirements. As already discussed above, this will be much more difficult to justify as being a proportionate response to the employer's concerns. Age is being used as a proxy for physical fitness, and this is based on assumptions about and stereotyping of older workers rather than consideration of individual circumstances. Although this may often be framed as a retirement age, it will be below 65 and so require objective justification.[1]

1 See **9.3.1**.

There are some jobs in the United Kingdom where it has been common to have a maximum cut-off age for employment. This includes employment in the armed forces and the police, fire-fighters and airline pilots. Retirement ages for pilots and firefighters have been increased. However, police constables, police sergeants, inspectors or chief inspectors still have a maximum retirement age of 60. Employment in the armed forces is actually exempt from the Regulations.[2] However, maximum ages and/or early retirement ages for other types of employment will need to be justified.

British Airways announced in 2006 that it was raising its retirement age for pilots and cabin crew from 55 to 60 initially and then to 65. This was on the basis that health and safety concerns are not a good justification for requiring an earlier retirement and actual tests of abilities will be used instead. There is pressure in other countries to raise the retirement age for pilots, with the American pilots' union recently announcing its support to this increase.

In the absence of any domestic decisions on this issue so far, there is some guidance from other countries. A case about the maximum age for employment as a referee by the Royal Dutch football association suggests that use of a cut-off age may be justifiable in circumstances where individual assessment is not possible.[3] In this case, however, the claimants were successful because it would have been possible to test each individual referee, and so the fixed age limit was not proportionate. In a similar case from Belgium, the court also found that a requirement for football referees to retire at 45 was illegitimate age discrimination.[4] Although the requirement for fitness was an adequate professional condition, this could have been tested objectively. In the United Kingdom, there is actually no age limit for football referees, the only requirement being an adequate level of fitness.

However, there may be other circumstances where it would be disproportionate to require actual testing of physical abilities. An employer may be able to argue that it simply has too many employees to carry out constant testing. This argument is likely to be more compelling if the potential consequences of an accident are severe, such as in the case of an airline pilot. The argument would also be stronger if there are concerns that any lack of ability might not be picked up quickly enough, rather than simply a reluctance to take on the burden in time and costs of carrying out the tests.

In the United Kingdom, one issue that has generated some interest is that of the practice of offering Premiership footballers shorter contracts if they are over 30. This is on the basis that older players are more likely to be injured and have their performance decline over a set period. Although this may seem a health and safety measure, in reality it is less about the safety of the employee than the risk to the club of an injured, or less highly performing, player. In this case, in relying on the injury risk, the employer may be able to establish a legitimate aim of not committing itself to employing a player who is more likely to be injured. However, it is questionable whether this assumption about players over 30 is, in fact, correct.

Although health and safety may sound like a good justification for setting age limits on particular jobs, as the purpose is to protect the worker, in practice employers may well find their assumptions about older workers being questioned. Employers will need to be clear that they have real evidence of the health and safety dangers, and that the age bar has been set at an appropriate level.

1 Law developed through decisions in cases rather than legislation.
2 See reg 44(4).
3 Amsterdam Court of Appeal, 13 January 2000, JAR 2000 at 42.
4 *Vandevenne v Belgian Soccer League.*

Chapter 10

Terminating employment

10.1 Introduction

This chapter considers the impact of the Regulations at and after termination of the employment relationship, including:

- the types of dismissal likely to give rise to claims of age discrimination;
- the issue of which party bears the burden of proving discrimination on the termination of employment, particularly where the reason for dismissal is disputed;
- the interplay between unfair dismissal legislation and age discrimination;
- concentrating on performance-related dismissals which are particularly susceptible to allegations that the dismissal was in fact age-biased;

- the phenomenon of the 'pale stale male', in view of experience of age discrimination legislation in the United States; and
- issues following the termination of employment, in particular, the provision of references.

Redundancy and retirement are dealt with separately in **Chapters 11** and **12**.

As with other forms of discrimination, it seems likely that the majority of claims in relation to age discrimination will arise following the termination of employment. At this point, the employer/employee relationship will have broken down and a disgruntled former employee may well seek legal advice and crystallise his claims. Since 1 October 2006 any employee who is dismissed in his 50s or 60s (even his 40s, or younger in some cases) will now consider (or will be advised by his legal representative to consider) whether his age might have been a factor in the decision to dismiss him.

There are, of course, no age limits set down in the Regulations and so any dismissed employee, regardless of age, could claim that his dismissal was influenced by his age. For example, in certain 'young industries' a relatively young person could have grounds for a claim of age discrimination if he is dismissed. A 38-year-old web-designer, working for an innovative design company, who is dismissed ostensibly because his technical skills are rusty, might be able to bring a claim of age discrimination. Conversely, and perhaps more unusually, an employee might also be dismissed on account of his youth. For example, a younger person, who had been asked to step-up to a senior position within a company, could find that his employment is terminated on the grounds that he does not have the requisite 'boardroom gravitas'. Again, this could be grounds for the employee bringing a claim of age discrimination.

Although the terms 'employee' and 'employer' are used throughout this chapter, the Regulations apply not only in circumstances where an employer terminates its relationship with an employee, but also extend to other categories of workers, rendering it unlawful to discriminate against, amongst others, contract workers, office-holders, pupils and tenants in barristers' chambers, pupils of advocates, partners, and agency workers.[1] The scope of the Regulations is considered in more detail in **Chapter 3**. Accordingly, individuals who are not afforded protection under unfair dismissal legislation may still have recourse to the employment tribunal if they consider that their working relationship ended for reasons relating to their age.

1 See regs 9, 12, 15, 16, 17 and 21 of the Employment Equality (Age) Regulations 2006.

10.2 Types of potentially discriminatory dismissals

There are three categories of dismissal which could give rise to an employee claiming that his termination was unlawful by virtue of the Regulations. These are as follows:

(i) Where the employee disputes the reason for the dismissal – the employer argues that the dismissal was by reason of performance, redundancy, or one of the other potentially fair reasons for dismissal,[1] but the employee contends that the real reason was discriminatory (be it direct discrimination, indirect discrimination or victimisation).

The employee might either argue that the reason given by the employer is completely bogus or that the reason is tainted by discriminatory prejudices.

Examples:

Gemma, in her 40s, working in a youth-orientated clothing shop, is dismissed for misconduct having been late for work on three occasions in the previous six months. Gemma claims that younger employees are not disciplined if they arrive late for work and contends that the dismissal was, in fact, on grounds of age as she does not fit in with the shop's youthful image. Here the reason is bogus.

Beatrice, also in her late 40s, is dismissed from her job as a receptionist at an advertising agency as it is claimed that she no longer suits the image of the agency. Here the reason is not bogus but it is potentially age discriminatory as it is tainted by discriminatory prejudices – that to be the face of the agency you need to be young (or at least look young).

(ii) Where the employee accepts that the reason for the dismissal is age. In cases of direct discrimination, this will normally be retirement and is considered in more detail in **Chapter 12**.

(iii) Where the reason for the dismissal is not disputed, but the employee argues that the reason was unlawfully indirectly discriminatory.

Example:

A company seeks to make redundancies from amongst a pool of office administrators. One of the selection criteria used is 'potential within the business'. Leroy, who is in his 50s, scores poorly against this criteria and consequently is selected for redundancy. Leroy, while acknowledging that the dismissal was by reason of redundancy, might bring a claim of age discrimination on the grounds that the selection criterion used was indirectly discriminatory. The use of indirectly discriminatory criteria in redundancies is explained in **Chapter 11**.

Dismissals include constructive dismissals[2] and the nonrenewal of a fixed term on its expiry.[3]

Example:

Lena is 56 years old and believes she has been continually overlooked for promotion in favour of younger colleagues. Her grievance about this treatment is rejected and she resigns. She would be able to claim that her constructive dismissal amounted to direct age discrimination.

As the definition of employee under the Regulations includes the self-employed and other categories of workers,[4] dismissals in this section include the termination of the contracts of any of these other categories of worker.

1 See s 98(2) of the ERA 1996.
2 See reg 7(7)(b).
3 See reg 7(7)(a).
4 **Chapter 3, 3.3.1**.

10.2.1 Disputed reasons for dismissal

(a) Inferences and burden of proof

Who bears the burden of proof is often critical in determining the outcome of a discrimination claim. It will often be difficult for the claimant to produce the 'smoking gun' direct evidence that he was dismissed for age-based reasons. Equally, it will often be difficult for the employer to prove that the employee's age was not a factor in the dismissal.

This is considered in detail in **Chapter 4**.[1]

In brief, if the claimant is able to prove facts from which the courts could draw inferences of discrimination, then the respondent will need to be able to provide clear and conclusive evidence to rebut the inference of discrimination. This will require employers to document clearly their decision-making process and the detailed, nondiscriminatory, reasons behind their decisions.

The concept of the shifting burden of proof in age discrimination dismissal cases may be best explained by way of an example.

1 **Chapter 4, 4.6**.

(b) Unfair dismissal and age discrimination

Section 98 of the Employment Rights Act (ERA) 1996 provides that an employer can fairly dismiss an employee if the dismissal is for one of five 'fair' reasons.[1] The Regulations also provide a new fair reason for dismissal, namely retirement at or after the age of 65.[2] Provided that the employer follows the statutory retirement procedures set out in Sch 6 of the Regulations, then a dismissal on grounds of retirement will be held to be fair. This is covered in detail in **Chapter 12**.

Disregarding this new fair dismissal on grounds of retirement, if the employer is able to establish that the dismissal was for one of the five other 'fair' reasons, the tribunal will then consider whether or not the dismissal was fair in all the circumstances, as determined in accordance with equity and the substantial merits of the case.[3] The employer should also ensure that it follows the statutory dismissal procedures.[4]

A dismissed employee, with one year's continuous service, can request a written statement from his employer giving particulars of the reasons for his dismissal.[5] Such written particulars are admissible in evidence.

In the light of the introduction of age discrimination legislation, employers will have to be increasingly cautious about the reasons they give for terminating an employee's employment. Not only will employers have to demonstrate that the dismissal fell within one of the five fair reasons for dismissal but they will also have to ensure that the dismissal, is not in any way tainted by discrimination. Any element of the dismissal or the procedure adopted, that could be deemed to be discriminatory, will be likely not only to render the dismissal unfair in accordance with the ERA 1996, but will also lead to a successful claim of age discrimination.

It seems likely that dismissals which are ostensibly on the grounds of capability or redundancy will be particularly susceptible to challenge on the basis that the dismissal was in fact age-biased. The subject of redundancies is covered in detail in **Chapter 11** while performance-based dismissals, and the impact of age discrimination, are discussed in greater detail later in the chapter.

Of course, in the majority of circumstances, only employees with one year's continuous service are able to bring claims of unfair dismissal.

This requirement does not extend to age discrimination claims, however. Employers are often tempted to by-pass their normal dismissal procedures when dismissing employees with less than a year's service. However, a failure to follow a fair procedure could leave an employer vulnerable to claims of age discrimination by all employees, regardless of length of service.

1 See s 98(2) of the ERA 1996.
2 See s 98(ba) of the ERA 1996; **Chapter 12**.
3 See s 98(4) of the ERA 1996.
4 See Pt 1, Sch 2 of the Employment Act 2002.
5 See s 92 of the ERA 1996.

(c) Performance management/appraisals

As set out above, it seems likely that many former employees will argue that a dismissal which their employer claims was fair on grounds of capability (or performance) was in fact motivated by age.

'Capability' is defined as meaning, in relation to an employee, his capability assessed by reference to skill, aptitude, health or any other physical or mental quality.[1]

An employer facing claims of unfair dismissal and age discrimination might either argue that dismissal was on the grounds of capability alone and was wholly unrelated to the employee's age. In the alternative, the employer might admit that dismissal was indirectly age discriminatory but seek to argue that such discrimination can be objectively justified.

Example:

Silicon Valley Computers (SVC) has concerns about the performance of Katie, one of its engineers, who is in her 40s. Katie is failing adequately to resolve problems raised by clients both because she does not seem to pay enough attention to their instructions and because she does not have up-to-date knowledge of the latest technological advances. SVC begins a performance management programme with Katie, particularly concentrating on her ability to follow instructions and attempting to tackle her technological shortcomings. Katie's performance does not improve and she is eventually dismissed. Katie launches a claim of indirect age discrimination on the basis that the requirement for her to have up-to-date technical knowledge indirectly discriminates against older employees. SVC might seek to defend such claims by arguing that the performance objectives had nothing whatsoever to do with the engineer's age. In the alternative, they might also argue that while the requirement for employees to have up-to-date technical skills does indirectly discriminate against older employees, this requirement is so fundamental to their work that any discrimination can be objectively justified, particularly taking into account the fact that SVC provided Katie with additional training.

In the example given above, the company followed a performance management procedure. In discrimination cases, perhaps even more than in unfair dismissal cases, it will be important for the employer to follow a clear and defined performance procedure in order to ensure that the burden of proof does not transfer from the employee to the employer, or if the burden does shift the inferences of discrimination can be rebutted.

Without the benefit of case law demonstrating how tribunals will approach the interplay between age discrimination and unfair dismissal, it can only be assumed that it will apply a similar approach as it has taken to the relationship between disability discrimination and unfair dismissal.

The case of *Jones v Post Office*[2] concerned a postman who drove a delivery van on a rural route and who suffered from diabetes. Having worked for the post office for 20 years, and having managed his diabetes through diet and tablets, Mr Jones suffered a heart attack. Following his heart attack Mr Jones was prescribed insulin. The post office, therefore, removed Mr Jones from driving duties. Following a review, the post office offered to allow Mr Jones to return to limited driving duties not exceeding 2 hours in any 24 hour period. The issue before the Court of Appeal in this case concerned the correct application of s 5 of the Disability Discrimination Act (DDA) 1995 (now s 3A) which states:

> '... a [person] discriminates against a disabled person if:
>
> (a) for a reason which relates to the disabled person's disability, he treats him less favourably than he treats or would treat others to whom that reason does not or would not apply; and
>
> (b) he cannot show that the treatment in question is justified.'

Section 3A(3) goes on to state:

> 'Treatment is justified for the purposes of subsection 1(b) if, but only if, the reason for it is both material to the circumstances of the particular case and substantial.'

The Court of Appeal in this case considered how the tribunal should approach the question of whether or not the respondent could justify the discriminatory treatment. In his judgment, Pill LJ concluded that the tribunal is confined to considering whether the reason given for the less favourable treatment can properly be described as both material to the circumstances of the case and substantial.

Pill LJ goes on to state that this function should not be unfamiliar to the tribunal; 'it is different but not very different from the task Employment Tribunals have to perform in cases of unfair dismissal.' In determining whether an employer's treatment of a disabled person is justified the tribunal's task is to consider the reasonableness of the employer's response. They must respect the opinion of the employer and, adopting language much more familiar in unfair dismissal cases, consider whether the employer's response falls within the range of reasonable responses.

Whilst it is acknowledged that the language of justification in the DDA 1995 is quite different from the language of objective justification in the Regulations, it seems likely that, when assessing whether or not an employer can objectively justify a discriminatory dismissal, the tribunal will have regard to similar factors as it might consider when deciding whether or not a dismissal is fair on grounds of capability. The tribunal is most likely to have regard to whether the employer's action fell within the range of reasonable responses. The test for objectively justifying age discrimination is likely however to be more stringent and might well involve additional considerations (such as medical evidence and the possibility of alternative employment) which might not always be considered in cases of unfair dismissal.

In order for a dismissal to be fair on grounds of capability, the employer must adopt a fair procedure. This should include, as a minimum:

- appraisal of the employee's performance, particularly highlighting areas of concern;
- warning the employee of the likely consequences if his performance does not improve; and
- giving the employee a sufficient opportunity to improve his performance.

Employers are often lax in ensuring that long-serving, senior employees receive regular appraisals and, if performance issues are identified, seeing that such issues are adequately managed. Case law has confirmed that the senior status of an employee will not negate the need to warn such an employee of the need for him to improve his performance.[3] Furthermore, the employer is also likely to need to demonstrate some quantifiable failings on the part of the employee. Criticisms often levelled at older employees such as 'slowing down' or 'taking a backseat' will not be adequate either to establish a fair dismissal or to provide an objective justification for a dismissal for age-related reasons.

While the tribunal has accepted that it is difficult to assess 'such imponderables as the quality of management' and that doubts of the employer as to the abilities of a manager can provide 'some' evidence of his incapacity, further tangible evidence is also likely to be required by the tribunal.[4]

An employer must also provide a failing employee with a reasonable opportunity to improve his performance, by way of structured objectives which the employee can try to achieve. In the case of *Winterhalter*,[5] the EAT held that three months would have been adequate time within which to monitor the employee's performance prior to dismissal. However, the reasonable length of a period of improvement will depend on the circumstances of each case, particularly bearing in mind the employee's length of service. In certain cases, an improvement period of up to three years has been held to be appropriate.[6]

Even if an employer does provide adequate appraisals and a structured performance management programme, it should be cautious in ensuring that assessments do not include ageist terminology. Indicators such as 'stagnant' or 'over-the-hill' may well be regarded as convincing evidence that the assessment was tainted by age prejudices and was thus discriminatory. Assessments might also be tainted by stereotypical views of younger employees.

Assumptions that younger employees will be immature and inexperienced but enthusiastic and willing to work long hours could equally indicate ageist prejudices. These concerns could become particularly relevant if the employee successfully manages to shift the burden of proof onto the employer. An employer will be unable to explain adequately that their treatment of the employee was nondiscriminatory if their evidence contains these kinds of words and phrases.

Whilst the emphasis has mostly been on adequate performance management of older employees in order to avoid them successfully bringing claims of unfair dismissal and age discrimination, such clear and defined appraisal structures will also avoid younger employees bringing successful claims of age discrimination. If a younger employee can demonstrate that he is subject to vigorous performance management processes while similar performance issues are overlooked in older employees, the younger employee may have grounds to bring a claim under the Regulations.

Example:

Two members of a sales team aged 23 and 63 are under-performing and have consistently failed to meet targets. Their manager decides to performance manage the younger employee, but does nothing in relation to the older employee on the basis that he is slowing down and will be retiring in the next couple of years. Following dismissal the younger employee could have grounds for claiming age discrimination.

1 See s 98(3)(a) of the ERA 1996.

2 [2001] EWCA Civ 558.
3 *Winterhalter Gastronom Ltd v Webb* [1973] IRLR 120.
4 *Cook v Thomas Linell & Sons Ltd* [1977] IRLR 132.
5 *Winterhalter* [1973] IRLR 120.
6 *Sibun v Modern Telephones Ltd* [1976] IRLR 81.

(d) The 'pale stale male'

Claims of age discrimination can, of course, be brought by individuals of all ages, races and genders. However, for the reasons outlined in this section, the most common types of claims, and the claims that are likely to have the most significant impact, are likely to be claims brought by white males in their late 40s and 50s – the so-called 'pale stale male'.

The recent spate of 'Sexism in the City' cases, where highly paid female executives have raised complaints of sex discrimination claiming (and in some cases being awarded) compensation often in excess of £1,000,000, have received a lot of media attention. However, in reality, most female executives who feel that they are disadvantaged because of their gender do not raise complaints for fear of being branded a trouble maker, and because of the perceived effect that raising such complaints may have on their future career.

Male executives, in their 50s, who are nearing the end of their career, are unlikely to be hampered by such concerns. An older male executive whose employment is terminated will have little to lose in launching a claim of age discrimination. He will have time on his hands; his losses will be significant and it is likely that he will have been given little to no performance management (see previous section). Furthermore, compensatory awards for unfair and wrongful dismissal are limited and there is little prospect of a pale stale male bringing any other discrimination claim (for example, on grounds of sex, race, etc).

In the United States, where age discrimination has been unlawful for around 40 years, legislation[1] was initially introduced to protect older blue collar workers who, unable to keep up with the demands of production, were dismissed and then unable to find alternative employment. However, in reality, the vast majority of claims have been filed by highly paid white males in their 50s who have been dismissed from executive positions ('the juiciest monetary rewards of bias law in verdicts, settlements and buyouts go to middle-aged white males, especially those in executive and management posts. Did someone say ironic?'[2]).

Whilst the US federal legislation is only applicable to those aged 40 and over, it looks likely that the United Kingdom will follow the pattern of the United States, with the Regulations being mostly utilised by older, white male executives. Prior to the introduction of the Regulations, as mentioned above, white male employees who were dismissed were limited in the claims that they could bring against their employer. If the employee did not have beneficial contractual terms (for example, a long notice period, contractual bonus entitlement, share options, etc.) and the employer had complied with its contractual obligations, a pale stale male would commonly only be able to bring a claim for unfair dismissal. The compensatory award for unfair dismissal is currently capped at £60,600. For a highly paid senior employee, even one who is able to recover the maximum unfair dismissal award, this would be unlikely to adequately compensate for future loss of earnings in circumstances in which it would be likely to be difficult to find comparable alternative employment.

With the introduction of age discrimination legislation, the 'pale stale male' can now launch proceedings arguing that his dismissal was by reason of his age. If he brings a successful claim of age discrimination he can potentially recover unlimited compensation.[3] A successful claimant in his early 50s could, therefore, argue that he is entitled to his full salary (or a significant proportion of his salary) and benefits from the date of dismissal to normal retirement age, on the grounds that he will not be able to find an equivalent senior position. Of course, such arguments will presumably become less persuasive as the new age discrimination laws take effect – when opportunities for older employees become more readily available and employees are better able to mitigate their loss. A successful claimant will also be entitled to an award for injury to feelings.

Example:

Mark, a senior executive who is 53 years old and works in a large city institution, is dismissed without any kind of performance management process being followed, on the basis that the company needs 'new blood'. The company intend to agree a settlement package with Mark. Mark is paid £250,000 per annum and is entitled to a three month contractual notice period. He has no contractual bonus entitlement although for the previous five years he has received bonuses in excess of £100,000. He is also entitled to a five per cent employer contribution to a money purchase pension scheme.

Prior to the introduction of the age discrimination legislation, the company would be likely to have been able to agree a termination package with the executive comprising a payment *in lieu* of his three months notice period, plus a sum of approximately £60,000 (representing the maximum amount he might be awarded if he brought a claim of unfair dismissal in the tribunal) plus perhaps an additional pro-rated sum to compensate for any bonus payment that he might have received for that financial year. Now, however, that same executive will be able to demand a vastly larger termination package. If the executive can successfully argue that he will find it impossible to find a similar position with the city (both by reason of his age and the limited number of senior positions available to him) he might claim compensation equating to his annual salary to the date of retirement at 65 (being £2.75 million). Furthermore, based on his historic bonus awards, he could claim a further £1.1 million in relation to unpaid bonuses plus pension contributions until retirement age. (All the sums would be subject to some reduction on the basis that Mark could find some alternative work in order to mitigate his loss.)

In the example set out above, where the company has simply stated that they want 'new blood', it is not clear whether the company's decision to dismiss the executive was age-related or not. The company may well have had genuine concerns about the executive's performance that it failed to address adequately with him. Equally the company may have simply come to the conclusion that the executive was too old for the job and had outlived his usefulness to the company. Although in some cases it will be obvious that the claim of age discrimination is well-founded, and others where it will be immediately evident that the claim is without merit, where the issue in question is the termination of a senior executive, it seems likely that there will be many cases where the matter is unclear. The executive will not be informed as to why he was dismissed or will not accept that the reasons given by the company are valid.

As set out above, the pale stale male may also be more inclined to bring tribunal proceedings against his former employer than other would-be claimants. An older employee is more likely to have the financial resources often necessary to run on-going tribunal proceedings. In addition, he may also be less concerned about any detrimental effect that the proceedings might be perceived as having on his future career opportunities. Accordingly, a pale stale male is likely to prove to be a determined adversary for employers facing a claim of age discrimination.

1 The Age Discrimination in Employment Act 1967.
2 Walter Olsen, 'Age-Bias Law Backfires on Boomers', US Today, 26 August 1997.
3 See reg 38.

10.2.2 Directly discriminatory dismissals

A directly age discriminatory dismissal where the employer does not dispute that age was the reason for dismissal will normally amount to a retirement. The reason for the dismissal would be the employee having reached his retirement age. Retirement is considered in detail in **Chapter 12**.

It is difficult to envisage many other situations where the employer will acknowledge that age is the reason for dismissal.

An employer might dismiss at a given age if for the employee to continue to perform his duties and responsibilities beyond that age would breach the law.[1] In such a case the employer would have to distinguish between a dismissal by reason of retirement and a dismissal justified by statutory restrictions as the procedures the employer must follow are different.

Examples:

Another example might be where the employer's cost in employing the individual increases when he reaches a particular age. This will be rare but would be the case where the employee reached the age thresholds in the National Minimum wage (NMW) legislation.[1]

Campden Café employs a number of 18- to 21-year-old kitchen and waiting staff to whom they pay the young person's NMW. When they reach 22 they have to increase their pay to the adult minimum rate. The Café likes to let go staff at this age and replace them with younger staff whom they can pay less.

The NMW exception does not exempt this dismissal in the same way that setting an age limit to recruit younger cheaper staff is also unlawful.[2] The Café could try to justify their practice by reference to the aim of cost (but as mentioned before[3] cost alone may not be a legitimate aim upon which an employer can rely to justify discrimination) or the combined aims of cost and vocational integration. Though, as mentioned in the context of recruiting staff to whom an employer can pay the lower rate NMW, the employer's aim is unlikely to be any concern about the welfare of younger workers but a desire only to keep cost down.

1 **Chapter 4, 4.7.5(a)**.
2 **Chapter 5, 5.3.3(a)**.
3 **Chapter 6, 6.4.5**.

---

1 See example of solo pilots, **Chapter 5, 5.3.3(k)** and **Chapter 12, 12.8.1(b)(ii)**.

10.2.3 Indirectly discriminatory dismissals

Indirect age discrimination is considered in more detail in **Chapter 4**.[1]

Examples of dismissals which might give rise to indirect age discrimination claims include:

- redundancy selection[2]; or

- performance or capability dismissals where the demands of health, fitness or stamina disadvantage older employees and cannot be justified.[3]

Example:

Megan Removals requires all its staff to pass tests of physical strength and stamina. Mark who works in the office is 57. He has worked for the company for 10 years and fails the test. He claims that the test indirectly discriminates against people of his age who are less likely to meet the fitness standards demanded by the company. Mark acknowledges that the removal staff need to meet fitness standards, but claims that it is not proportionate to require the office staff also to pass the test. The company believes that it is justified as they might require the office staff to stand in if one of the removal staff is unexpectedly absent.

The employment tribunal upholds his claim noting that Mark has only been asked to deputise twice in 10 years and that there are other office staff who meet the fitness standards.

---

1 **Chapter 4, 4.3.**
2 **Chapter 11, 11.4.**
3 **Chapter 9, 9.3.2.**

10.2.4 Justification and exceptions

An otherwise indirectly or directly discriminatory dismissal will not be unlawful if the employer is either:

- able to objectively justify the dismissal; or
- rely on one of the exceptions within the Regulations.

(a) Justification

Unlike all other discrimination legislation in the United Kingdom, the Regulations provide that direct discrimination (as well as indirect discrimination) can potentially be justified. In order to objectively justify discriminatory treatment (or a discriminatory provision, criterion or practice in the case of indirect discrimination) a respondent will have to demonstrate that such treatment or practice was a 'proportionate means of achieving a legitimate aim'.[1]

As discussed in greater detail in **Chapter 4**,[2] it seems likely that the occasions on which an employer will be able to justify direct discrimination will be relatively limited. Department of Trade and Industry's guidance on the question of objective justification has stated that:

> 'the discriminatory effect of any age-based practice should be significantly outweighed by the importance and benefits of its legitimate aim, and the employer should have no reasonable alternative.'[3]

An employer seeking to objectively justify routine dismissal at a particular age will have an uphill struggle. The company will have to produce conclusive evidence to demonstrate that employees of a given age are no longer able to perform the tasks demanded of them. This is likely to be very difficult and the tribunal will almost certainly find that all employees, regardless of age, should be assessed on an individual basis to see if they are fit for the rôle in question. If an employee is no longer able to perform the more physically demanding aspects of their rôle then the employer should also consider what redeployment opportunities there might be for the employee.

1 **Chapter 4, 4.7**.
2 **Chapter 4, 4.7**.
3 'Age Legislation Fact Sheet No 2', Objective Justification, DTI, March 2006.

(b) Exceptions

In addition to providing employers with scope to attempt to objectively justify discrimination, the Regulations contain certain specific exceptions, which permit discriminatory treatment or practices in certain limited circumstances. These exceptions are set out in Pt 4 of the Regulations.

The most relevant exceptions to dismissals are:

- (i) the genuine occupational requirement exception (reg 82)
- (ii) the retirement exception (reg 30); and
- (iii) the service-related benefit exception (reg 32).

(i) Genuine occupational requirement exception

The genuine occupational requirement exception applies to dismissals as it does to recruitment.[1]

Example:

Myfannwy has played the part of the young single mother in a famous sit-com for the last 10 years. She now looks much older than when she first started. The production company should be able to rely on the genuine occupational requirement exception to justify her dismissal.

---

1 Chapter 5, 5.3.2(a).

(ii) Retirement exception

Regulation 30 which permits the dismissal of employees (although not the other categories of workers covered by the Regulations) at or over the age of 65 where the reason for dismissal is retirement.[1]

1 Chapter 12.

(iii) Service-related benefit exception

It should be noted that the exception concerning certain benefits based on length of service does not extend to any payments or benefits awarded to an employee on termination.[1]

1 Chapter 6, 6.3.2.

10.2.5 Discriminatory events occurring prior to dismissal

An employee who suspects that he may have been dismissed for an age discriminatory reason may also seek to raise further claims of discrimination, relating to actions which took place during his employment. Allegations of ageist harassment, which taken alone might not have prompted an employee to raise a claim of age discrimination, might take on a greater significance following dismissal and prompt the former employee to raise additional claims.

As with all other forms of discrimination, a tribunal will not consider a complaint of age discrimination unless it is brought before the end of the period of three months beginning when the act complained of was done, unless in all the circumstances it considers it just and equitable to do so.[1] Employers should not, however, assume that events that took place more than three months before the date of the claim will be ignored by the tribunal. Allegations of discrimination stretching back in time may be regarded as an 'act extending over a period' within the meaning of the time limit provisions, such that a series of acts can be regarded as one continuing act. In one leading case,[2] the claimant was allowed to raise allegations of sex discrimination which extended over a period of 11 years. By way of an example, an older employee who is dismissed from a senior management position and is replaced with a younger manager might, as well as claiming that his dismissal was discriminatory, raise additional claims of harassment based on ageist jokes and comments that were made to him by his colleagues over the course of recent years.

Even if a former employee does not raise distinct claims in relation to acts or omissions arising prior to dismissal, he may seek to use such earlier events in order to try and persuade the tribunal that it could draw inferences such that the burden of proof should shift to the employer. The subject of drawing inferences and shifting the burden of proof is discussed in greater detail in **Chapter 4**.

1 See reg 42 of the Employment Equality (Age) Regulations 2006.
2 *Henricks v Commissioner of Police for the Metropolis* [2003] IRLR 96.

10.2.6 Termination payments

Employers must not discriminate in the terms they offer to departing employees.

Redundancy payments are considered in detail in **Chapter 11**.

It is otherwise rare for termination payments to be based on age. There is one issue of which employers should be aware, namely the potentially indirectly age discriminatory nature of notice periods and payments *in lieu* of notice calculated on length of service. This is referred to in more detail in **Chapter 6**.[1]

1 **Chapter 6, 6.3.3(f)**.

10.3 References

The scope of the Regulations extends beyond the end of the employment relationship. Regulation 24 provides that when a 'relevant relationship' (meaning a relationship during the course of which an unlawful act of discrimination against, or harassment of, one party by the other party took place) comes to an end, it is unlawful for the employer to discriminate against its former employee by subjecting him to a detriment or harassment. Accordingly, if a former employee is bringing, or could potentially have brought, a claim of discrimination against the former employer, he might have a separate cause of action against his former employer under reg 24 if it provided a potential new employer with a negative reference.

It is important to note that the provisions of reg 24 can pre-date the coming into force of the Regulations on 1 October 2006. If an unlawful act of discrimination took place prior to 1 October 2006 the employee would not have a direct claim in relation to that unlawful act. If, however, his former employer subjected him to a detriment or harassment before 1 October 2006 then he could launch a claim under Regulation 24.

A series of cases have determined that employers will be negligent if they fail to provide references which are true, accurate and fair. However, the reference does not have to be full and comprehensive.[1] Furthermore, in providing references, the employer owes a duty of care not only to the prospective employer receiving the reference, but also to the subject of the reference.[2]

In circumstances where an individual has already raised, or intimated, claims of age discrimination against his employer, and the employer subsequently provides the employee with a negative reference, the employee might have a further, free-standing claim of victimisation against the employer pursuant to Regulation 4.[3]

Example:

Samantha, a solicitor in her 20s, is made redundant from the law firm at which she works. One of the selection criteria used is length of service, against which she scores poorly as compared to her older colleagues. Samantha's appraisal for the previous year used phrases such as 'immature' and 'inexperienced'. In addition, her colleagues including the partner for whom she works, have often made ageist comments about her, referring to her as the baby of the team, and on occasion telling clients that she is 'wet behind the ears'.

Samantha brings a claim of age discrimination. She then seeks new employment with another law firm, who ask her former employer for a reference. Her previous employer commonly provides only a factual reference stating dates of employment and job title. However, they provide a detailed reference in relation to Samantha, stating that her attendance has been poor (a matter which has never been raised with the employee) as well as again referring to her immaturity and inexperience. In addition to having a possible negligence claim against her former employer, Samantha could launch additional claims for age discrimination, arguing that the reference was both directly discriminatory (reflecting the ageist prejudices of the employer) and victimisation (in response to the complaint.

---

1 *Bartholomew v London Borough of Hackney* [1999] IRLR 246 CA.
2 *Spring v Guardian Assurance Plc [1994]* IRLR 460.
3 **Chapter 4, 4.4**.

Chapter 11

Redundancy

11.1 Introduction

The Regulations have a significant impact on dismissals for redundancy and the calculation of redundancy pay, and these are likely to be among the most challenging aspects of the new law for many employers.

In this chapter we consider:

- What happens when employees nearing retirement volunteer for redundancy.
- How the Regulations affect the criteria used for selecting employees for redundancy, for example the use of 'LIFO' (last in, first out), 'experience' and 'potential'.
- How those criteria should properly be applied.
- How redundancy payments – both statutory and enhanced – must be calculated in order to comply with the Regulations.
- What is the legal position when a dismissal satisfies the statutory definition of both a redundancy and a retirement. Is there an entitlement to a statutory and/or enhanced contractual redundancy payment?

11.2 Meaning of redundancy

Redundancy is defined in s 139 of the Employment Rights Act (ERA) 1996 as where:

> 'the dismissal is wholly or mainly attributable to
>
> (a) the fact that [the] employer has ceased or intends to cease –
>
> (i) to carry on the business for the purposes of which the employee was employed by him, or
>
> (ii) to carry on that business in the place where the employee was so employed, or
>
> (b) the fact that the requirements of that business
>
> (i) for employees to carry out work of a particular kind, or
>
> (ii) for employees to carry out work of a particular kind in the place where the employee was employed by the employer have ceased or diminished or are expected to cease or diminish.'

Employers are often tempted to give redundancy as the reason for a dismissal when the true reason is quite different. It may be that they want to spare the employee's feelings, to avoid stigmatising him in the job market or to avoid a difficult and drawn out poor performance or misconduct procedure. This has always been a risky strategy. Where the true reason is hidden, the employee is often more easily able to challenge the dismissal as unfair because the facts simply do not support the reason given, which often in turn means that the wrong pre-dismissal procedures have been followed. In addition, the fact that the employer has not acted properly in legal terms can even, in some cases, give rise to the inference that the true reason was some form of discrimination.

The advent of age discrimination laws obviously gives employees who are made redundant a new angle for investigating and attacking their dismissal, and is another reason for employers to ensure that:

- redundancy is only given as the reason for a dismissal when it is genuine;
- redundancy procedures are fair and objective insofar as possible; and
- proper records are kept evidencing the reasons behind selection decisions.

If a Tribunal is persuaded that there is not a genuine redundancy, it may draw from that the inference that the age of the employee was a factor in the decision and, therefore, that the dismissal was discriminatory.

11.3 Voluntary redundancy

The Regulations also apply to voluntary redundancies, where employees are invited to indicate a wish to be considered for redundancy. Some redundancy policies oblige employers to invite volunteers before making compulsory redundancies. In other circumstances, an employer may decide to invite volunteers in a given case. Some voluntary redundancy schemes are limited to employees of a certain grade or from a certain department or group within the organisation.

11.3.1 Discrimination

Employers must ensure that a voluntary redundancy policy is not directly discriminatory on the grounds of age and that the way in which it operates in practice is not indirectly discriminatory (unless there is objective justification). For example, the policy must not exclude workers of a certain age group from being considered and must not give preference to workers of a certain age group unless the employer can justify such age-based preferential treatment, which would seem highly unlikely.

11.3.2 Voluntary redundancy and enhanced pensions

Older employees may be persuaded to volunteer for redundancy because of the consequent entitlement to an enhanced early retirement pension under their occupational pension scheme. This enhancement is normally available for employees over the age of 50 who are eligible under current Revenue rules to draw a pension. In some cases the employer sets a higher age (eg 55) at which the entitlement to an enhanced pension on redundancy is triggered.

Because pensions are inherently linked to age, the Regulations deal with the potential discrimination arising from the provision of pensions by providing a number of exceptions.

Part 2, Sch 2 of the Regulations (which sets out implications for pension schemes) lists various exceptions. In particular, para 13(B) provides the following exception in relation to enhanced early pensions paid on redundancy:

> '(1) A minimum age for any member of a scheme for payment of or entitlement to a particular age related benefit on the grounds of redundancy where it is enhanced in accordance with sub-paragraph (2) and paid either with or without consent (whether of an employer, the trustees or managers of the scheme or otherwise).
>
> (2) The enhancement of any age related benefit payable to or in respect of a member on the grounds of redundancy where the enhancement is calculated in one or more of the following ways –
>
> (a) by reference to the years of prospective pensionable service a member would have completed if he had remained in pensionable service until normal pension age;
>
> (b) by reference to a fixed number of years of prospective pensionable service;
>
> (c) by making an actuarial reduction which is smaller than if early retirement had been on grounds to which paragraph 12 applied; or
>
> (d) by not making any actuarial reduction for early retirement.
>
> (3) Sub-paragraph (1) shall also apply to different minimum ages for different groups or categories of members.'

The effect of this exception is that employers can safely offer early retirement with an enhanced pension on redundancy to members of occupational pension schemes. The pension exceptions set out in Sch 2 were amended significantly from those originally published and which only allowed enhanced pension on redundancy to those employees who were active or prospective scheme members on 1 October 2006.

Some employers seek to compensate those under 50 who are ineligible for a pension by enhancing their redundancy payment or increasing the cap on their redundancy payment. However, these steps only bring their own problems as this will often take the enhanced scheme outside the exceptions provided by the Regulations which allow enhanced redundancy payments to take account of a worker's age. For more on this, see **11.5.3(d)**.

11.4 Redundancy selection

In order to avoid a complaint of unfair dismissal, employers who are selecting employees for redundancy must use objective selection criteria and apply them fairly. In addition, the selection process must not discriminate on protected grounds (eg sex, race, religion, disability, sexual orientation). With the coming into force of the Regulations, discrimination on the grounds of age must be added to this list. Besides directly using age as a factor in the redundancy selection decision, indirect age discrimination can be present in a redundancy process in many ways.

11.4.1 Selection criteria

(a) LIFO

'Last In First Out' (selecting the most recent recruits for redundancy) has long been a common method for redundancy selection. Its potentially discriminatory effect on female employees (who are more likely to take time out of the labour market to have children) has led many employers to treat it with caution. The anti-age discrimination laws may be the final nail in its coffin.

Younger employees are likely to have shorter periods of service so using LIFO as a way of selecting for redundancy is likely to indirectly discriminate against them. An employer might try to justify this discrimination by arguing that it has a legitimate aim of rewarding loyalty, and that LIFO is a proportionate way of achieving that aim. Tribunals are unlikely to agree, however, and the Advisory, Conciliation and Arbitration Service (ACAS) Guidance states that LIFO is 'likely to be age discriminatory'.[1]

It might be that LIFO can be used with more confidence as one of several criteria or as a 'tie break' between two employees with otherwise equal scores. In these cases, any discriminatory impact is lessened. Further, its use is likely to be more acceptable where there are limited alternative criteria available such as where it is difficult to distinguish skills and competences within a group.

Regulation 32 sets out certain circumstances in which employment benefits can vary according to length of service without contravening the Regulations.[2] This, however, is highly unlikely to apply to redundancy selection based on length of service as it would be stretching the word 'benefit' beyond its natural meaning to include the 'benefit' of keeping your job in a redundancy exercise.

The appropriateness of LIFO selection has been considered in a series of unfair dismissal cases. In *Westland Helicopters Ltd v Nott*[3] the EAT decided that it would be unreasonable to ignore length of service in selecting for redundancy. This case was decided in 1988 and it may well be, particularly with the advent of the Regulations, that it would not be decided the same today. More recently the EAT reviewed the use of LIFO.[4] The Employment Appeal Tribunal (EAT) overturned a tribunal decision that LIFO was an unreasonable criterion to use in redundancy selection. It held that there was no rule that LIFO was either inherently reasonable or unreasonable and each case needed to be looked at on its facts. Again, this case preceded the introduction of the Regulations and cannot be regarded as authority that it would reasonably be justifiable.

1 ACAS Guidance, *Age and the Workplace: Putting the Employment Equality (Age) Regulations into practice* (ACAS), p 20.
2 **Chapter 6, 6.3.2**.
3 EAT 342/88.
4 *Blatchford Solicitors v Berger* EAT 207/00.

(b) Experience

Most employers carrying out a redundancy process will want to retain the most competent employees and/or those with the most relevant experience. However, like 'service', 'experience' is not always a good indication of competence and may disproportionately disadvantage younger employees who are likely to have less of it. Where certain experience gives an employee an advantage in the selection process, the employer should ensure that it can show that it will be of genuine value to the business going forward.

(c) Attendance/sickness absence

Attendance is another common criterion used in redundancy selection procedures. Again, this is a criterion which needs to be applied carefully in order to avoid discrimination claims – historically on the grounds of disability or pregnancy, but now also on the grounds of age.

Perhaps surprisingly, it is not older workers who have the greatest number of absences. For men, it is the age group of 16–24 and for women the 25–34 age group. Indeed, the most important factor in the number of absences is having young children. It is women with children aged between 5 and

10 and men with children between 0 and 4 who have the most absences.[1] Please see **Chapter 9**.[2]

However, where it is used carefully as one of several criteria, absence is unlikely to give rise to age discrimination claims. This is also considered in **Chapter 6**.[3]

1 Labour Force Survey, Office for National Statistics, May 2006.
2 **Chapter 9**, **9.2**.
3 **Chapter 6**, **6.4.3(a)**.

(d) Proximity to retirement

Care should be exercised in selecting employees for redundancy on the basis that they are entitled to a pension or are approaching retirement. Similarly, voluntary redundancy should not be offered to this group in preference to others.

It is likely, however, that an employer would be able to justify doing so if it can show that the employee in question would not have asked to stay on beyond retirement, or that any request to stay on was likely to have been declined. In order for this justification to succeed, other employees in a similar position must have been treated in a consistent way.

In support of this, art 6 (1) (c) of the Directive states that the need for an employee to have a reasonable period of employment before retirement is an example of a legitimate aim which might justify age-based treatment. The DTI consultation documents also gave this as an example of a legitimate aim.[1]

It is unclear, however, how close to retirement age a worker must be in order for proximity to retirement to be a legitimate factor and will probably depend on the particular circumstances of each case (for example, if an enhanced redundancy scheme will cushion the financial impact of the job loss). It will certainly be risky to use proximity to retirement as a reason for selecting those with more than a year or two to go, particularly as their prospects of securing alternative employment will be worse than those of younger redundant employees.[2]

1 'Diversity and Equality: Age Matters', DTI, 2003, para 3.15(e) and 'Diversity and Equality: Coming of Age', DTI, 2005, para 4.1.17.
2 See statistics on *www.agediscrimination.info*.

(e) Potential

'Potential' is occasionally used in redundancy selection matrices. As well as having the disadvantage of being a subjective criterion, and therefore very difficult to apply fairly and consistently, it is also often used as a euphemism for youth and therefore now carries the added risk of giving rise to an inference of age discrimination. There is often an assumption that young people are more open minded, quicker and keener to learn and better able to develop new skills compared with older people who in contrast are assumed to be either less interested in developing or less able to do so. This is also considered in **Chapter 6**.[1]

'Potential' should not be used as a selection criterion unless the employer can demonstrate that it has been evaluated objectively and without discrimination.

1 **Chapter 6, 6.4.3(b)**.

(f) Flexibility

'Flexibility' is another common criterion fraught with risks. This is also considered in **Chapter 5**.[1] Flexibility often means being able to work outside normal hours. This is likely to discriminate on grounds of sex, as women with primary childcare responsibilities are less able to comply, and also on the grounds of age.

Age discrimination is not just about discrimination against older or younger workers and a practice which disadvantages any age group has the potential to be indirectly discriminatory. Employees in their late 20s to early 40s are more likely to have childcare responsibilities, which make it less easy for them to be flexible in their working hours.

This does not mean that flexibility will always be discriminatory and where ability to work outside normal hours is a necessary part of the job then it might well be a justifiable criterion.

Also, if the flexibility the employer needs is actually about the range of tasks an employee can fulfil rather than the hours he works, the criterion is unlikely to be discriminatory.

1 **Chapter 6, 6.4.3(c)**.

(g) Cost

The rationale for making redundancies is often cost savings. Employers, therefore, often select the highest paid employees who cost the most to achieve these savings.

The highest paid employees in many organisations will be the most experienced who will be older. Can the higher paid employee challenge his selection as being indirectly age discriminatory?

Clearly, the employer's selection criterion puts older workers at a disadvantage. However, in most cases, one would expect this to be justified.

No doubt, the employee might argue that the employer's aim is reducing cost which is not legitimate[1] but one would expect the employer to argue that even if 'cost alone' cannot justify age discrimination their aims were a combination of cost and reducing the impact of the cost saving on other parts of the business.

The EAT has held that a cost savings criterion in a redundancy selection exercise was not fair and objective[2] In this case, salespeople were selected for redundancy on the basis of who cost most in terms of overheads but generated least in terms of revenue.

Examples:

Widgets and Bodgets Plc needs to reduce cost due to increasing competition for Far Eastern manufacturers. They employ 10 widget cutters whose pay is based on experience. They believe that they can operate with only five. In order to save as much as possible they select the five highest paid workers. These are the five most experienced and, unsurprisingly, the five oldest. They claim that the selection criterion is unfair and indirectly age discriminatory. If the company can show that they need to make the additional savings created by selecting the higher paid employees they would have a good chance of showing that their selection basis was justifiable.

Wahaaa, an advertising agency, decides to make redundant 50-year-old Nicola, a long-serving, highly-rated and highly-paid Account Director. The agency will not recruit but reallocate her accounts amongst other Account Directors. They tell Nicola that they have chosen her because they need to improve margins and she is paid £250,000, appreciably more than more recently recruited colleagues.

Nicola claims that this amounts to indirect age discrimination. She claims the response of selecting a highly-paid and highly-rated executive to save these costs over, for example, two more junior but less capable colleagues is a practice which disadvantages the older executives, many of whom are highly paid.

If the agency cannot show that it considered alternative means of making the relative savings and also took into account the negative effect of dismissing a highly regarded executive, it could be vulnerable.

---

1 **Chapter 4, 4.7.5(a).**
2 *KGB Micros Ltd v Lewis* EAT 573/90.

11.4.2 Applying the criteria

Even where nondiscriminatory criteria are used, the employer must ensure that there is no unlawful discrimination in the way in which those criteria are applied. Good practice, including the recording of the evidence on which the scoring has been based, will help to keep age prejudices out of the assessment and scoring process, inferences of discrimination will not be drawn and the nondiscriminatory basis for the decision can be shown.[1]

In large-scale redundancies, employers may wish to analyse the age profile of those selected to ensure that, even if the criteria are not on the face of it discriminatory, there is no unconscious age bias.

In the United States, challenges to redundancies ('reductions in force') on the basis that they are discriminatory are common. At the time of writing, Boeing and two other companies, Onex and Spirit AeroSystems, are being sued by 100 former employees for US $3 billion following the sale of one of Boeing's operations. The former employees allege that age bias is illustrated by, amongst other things, a claim that 13.9 per cent of employees over 50 were not made offers of re-employment, whereas only 4 per cent of those under 40 were not made such offers.

1 **Chapter 4, 4.6.**

11.5 Redundancy payments

If a redundancy policy, or some element of it, risks falling foul of age laws it is necessary to consider whether it falls within the exception in reg 33 or, if not, whether it can be objectively justified. In considering objective justification, the first question for a tribunal will be whether the employer was trying to achieve a legitimate aim; and the second will be whether what it did was a proportionate means of achieving that aim.[1]

1 **Chapter 4, 4.7.**

11.5.1 Aims of a redundancy payment

This section considers the first of these issues: the aims of a redundancy payment.

In the case of *Barry v Midland Bank*,[1] the House of Lords held that the principal aim of redundancy payments is to compensate workers for the adverse financial implications of unemployment but that rewarding loyalty was a legitimate secondary aim. The various Lords in that case commented on the purpose of redundancy payments as follows:

Lord Slynn stated:

> 'The purpose of the [redundancy] payment is to provide support for lost income during the period immediately following redundancy. As the industrial tribunal put it, "it is to cushion employees against unemployment and job loss". It is not to remunerate for past service... even if the payment takes account of years of service to reflect loyalty to the employer'.

Lord Hoffmann agreed:

> 'the main purpose of a redundancy payment is to cushion the employee against the hardship of a sudden cessation of his salary, whatever it may have been. On the other hand, the inclusion of past years of service in the calculation recognises that the employer may feel a greater duty to provide such a cushion to those who have worked for him for a longer time.'

Lord Nicholls had a slightly different take on service:

> 'Severance pay is, or may more properly be treated as, compensation for loss of a job. Loss of a job entails loss of the actual salary then being paid. The longer the employee held the job, the greater the disruption.'

It is not clear on what Lord Nicholls based this conclusion and it is certainly arguable that, in fact, those with shorter service will suffer a greater disadvantage in the job market as prospective employers shy away from candidates with a less stable career history.

The purpose of a redundancy payment has also been considered by the European Court of Justice (ECJ) in the cases of *Barber v Guardian Royal Exchange Assurance Group*[2] and *Kowalska v Freie und Hansestadt Hamburg*[3]

In *Barber*, the ECJ stated:

> 'Compensation granted to a worker in connection with his redundancy constitutes a form of pay to which the worker is entitled in respect of his employment, which is paid to him upon termination of the employment relationship, which makes it possible to facilitate his adjustment to the new circumstances resulting from the loss of his employment and which provides him with a source of income during the period in which he is seeking new employment.'

Redundancy

In *Kowalska* it stated:

> 'As regards in particular the payments made to the worker upon the termination of the employment relationship, it must be noted that such payments constitute a form of deferred remuneration to which the worker is entitled by virtue of his employment, but which is paid to him at the time of the termination of the employment relationship, with a view to facilitating his adaptation to the new circumstances which are the result of this termination.'

The DTI's first consultation document, 'Age Matters', discussed at some length the use of service as a factor in the calculation of statutory redundancy payments. Paragraphs 6.12 and 6.13 stated:

> 'Paragraph 6.7 [of the document] explains that the primary purpose of the scheme is to ensure that employers compensate qualifying redundant employees for the loss of expected continued employment in the job. It does not compensate for 'loss of rights in the job'. However, the weighting of payments in favour of more senior employees appears to be a widely supported aspect of the scheme.
>
> We have, therefore, taken this opportunity to review the rationale for the scheme itself. We have concluded that it should henceforth have the supplementary purpose of ensuring that employers recognise, in the amount of any payment to which a redundant employee is entitled, the extent of that employee's past commitment to the business. We believe that, by reference to this supplementary purpose, the use of length of service as a factor in the payment calculation remains justified and appropriate. We propose, therefore, to retain this provision. Other changes to the scheme will take place at the same time as the legislation implementing the age strand of the Directive.'

However, no mention was made of this supplementary purpose in the second consultation paper, 'Coming of Age', and no amendment has been made to the redundancy legislation regarding the purpose of redundancy payments. Arguably, this would be unnecessary, bearing in mind the comments of their Lordships in *Barry v Midland Bank*. However, it is interesting to note that, at least at this point in the consultation process, the government considered such clarification necessary.

The purpose of a redundancy payment is key both in determining whether the government can justify any potentially age discriminatory elements of the statutory scheme and whether employers can do the same for their enhanced schemes.

The aim of statutory redundancy payments was also considered by the EAT in *Secretary of State for Trade and Industry v Rutherford (No 2)*.[4] Stephen Walker[5] testified for the government that:

> 'The basic objective of the statutory redundancy payments scheme is to ensure that where employees who have demonstrated commitment to their employer (by completing at least two years' continuous service) are dismissed through no fault of their own, they are compensated for the loss of expected continued employment.'[6]

1 [1999] IRLR 581.
2 [1990] IRR 444.
3 [1990] IRLR 447.
4 [2003] IRLR 858 at [146]–[148], 877.
5 Then assistant director, responsible for redundancy payments in the employment relations directorate of the DTI.
6 See para 146.

11.5.2 Statutory redundancy pay

The ERA 1996, which sets out the basis for calculating statutory redundancy pay (SRP), contained various provisions which discriminated directly or indirectly on the grounds of age. The Regulations (at Sch 8) make a number of changes to those provisions.

These are:

- the removal of the upper age limit to receive SRP, which was basically the lower of the employer's normal retiring age of 65[1];
- the removal of a relatively obscure provision in s 158 which removed the right to SRP in certain circumstances where the employee was also entitled to receive a pension[2];
- the removal of the tapering of SRP after the employee's 64th birthday set out in s 162[3];
- the removal of the lower age limit of 18 years in calculating continuous employment for calculating SRP previously set out in s 211.(2) of the ERA 1996.[4]

However, not all the age-related factors have been removed. SRP will still be calculated on the basis of age in the following ways:

- each year of employment up to the age of 21 will count as 0.5 × week's pay (capped, currently at £310[5]);
- each year of employment between the ages of 22 and 41 will count as 1 × week's pay (capped);

- each year of employment over the age of 42 will count as 1.5 × week's pay (capped);
- a minimum of two years' service is required; and
- a maximum of 20 years' service can be counted.

This leaves various elements of the calculation of SRP which could potentially discriminate on the grounds of age, namely:

(a) the age bands;

(b) the use of length of continuous employment;

(c) the cap at 20 years' continuous employment; and

(d) the need for two years' continuous employment.

Each of these is discussed subsequently.

1 Repealed by para 30 of Sch 8 of the Regulations.
2 See para 31 of Sch 8.
3 See para 32 of Sch 8.
4 See para 35 of Sch 8.
5 To 31 January 2008.

(a) Age bands

The government was in a dilemma about whether to retain the age bands used in calculating SRP. It announced on 2 March 2006, only days before the final Regulations were published, that the age bands would remain unchanged. The draft Regulations and previous consultation exercises had left blank SRP proposals and there were suggestions that one multiple would be chosen to apply irrespective of age.

Clearly, using age as a factor in the calculation of SRP disadvantages younger employees and discriminates directly on the grounds of age. In order to see off a legal challenge to this, the government will have to show that the age bands represent a proportionate means of achieving a legitimate aim.

It is likely to argue that its legitimate aim is to ameliorate the financial impact of unemployment for older employees. As mentioned earlier,[1] this will almost certainly be considered an acceptable aim.

The government is more likely to struggle with proving that the continued use of age bands is a proportionate means of achieving that aim. The ECJ in *Mangold v Helm*[2] highlights the relatively high threshold which must be cleared in order to demonstrate proportionality. If followed more widely, this case suggests that any law which is directly age discriminatory must be narrowly targeted so that it clearly benefits the workers it is aimed at helping.

The financial impact of redundancy is a combination of the time it takes the redundant employee to secure another job and any consequent cut in pay in that new job. Statistics show that the time taken to secure alternative employment increases steadily from the 16–19 age band to the 35–39 age band, but then reduces for the 40–44 age band before increasing again steadily, with the 50–54 age band taking slightly longer than the 35–39 age band.[3] This might well support the argument for higher payments for older redundant employees but also illustrates the complexity of showing a correlation between age and the financial impact of unemployment.

One cannot help but wonder whether the real aim behind retaining the age bands was political – aimed at avoiding the Regulations cutting some (older) employees' redundancy payments or increasing employers' redundancy costs.

As stated above, the government was rumoured during the consultation process to be considering introducing a single multiple which would be applied to years of service, but irrespective of age. Levelling this up to an across-the-board multiple of 1.5 would have increased employers' costs. A cost-neutral multiple of 1.2 or thereabouts, on the other hand, would have cut older employees' redundancy pay. In the end, a decision was made to avoid the unattractive consequences of changing the calculation method by continuing to link the multiple to age.

It may be that a court asked to consider whether the use of age bands is a proportionate means of achieving the government's likely legitimate aim would conclude there was a fairer way of doing it – by applying an age-related multiple to the payment (as opposed to each year of employment). In this way, the payment would reflect in the level of SRP the varying financial impact of job loss with age. An advantage with this solution would be that these multiples could be varied periodically as the labour market statistics changed.

If the Regulations have the desired impact and reduce age prejudice, then one would expect older workers to experience less difficulty in finding employment. The age-related impact of redundancy would then diminish over time and the government's justification for the current bands (insofar as it exists) would begin to erode.

1 See **11.5.1**.
2 [2006] IRLR 143; **Chapter 4, 4.7.2(c)**.
3 Office for National Statistics January – March 2006 – see *www.agediscrimination.info* website for full chart.

(b) Continuous service

Statutory redundancy pay is based on years of continuous service with one's employer. This indirectly discriminates against younger employees who will, on average, have shorter periods of service than older ones.

The government clearly believes that the service-related element of the redundancy pay calculation is justifiable. As mentioned above, rewarding loyalty has been established to be a legitimate secondary aim of a redundancy payment.[1]

On the face of it, and bearing in mind the exceptions for certain benefits based on length of service in reg 32, linking redundancy pay to service might seem relatively uncontentious.

However, the definition of 'benefit' in reg 32(7) expressly excludes 'any benefit awarded to a worker by virtue of his ceasing to work for [his employer]'. It is not, therefore, possible to rely on the reg 32 exception for service-related benefits with regard to redundancy payments. It is unclear why the government thought it necessary to exclude termination payments from the length of service exception. This exclusion was not in the draft Regulations published for consultation in 2005. If this stemmed from a concern that service-related termination payments were incompatible with the Directive then this concern should logically extend to the use of continuous employment in calculating SRP.

Service-related benefits might, in any event, fall foul of sex discrimination laws. Just as rewarding long service generally disadvantages younger workers, these rewards generally disadvantage women. The approach taken by UK and European courts to justification under gender equality laws is illustrative of the likely approach under age laws (where the discriminatory impact is likely to be greater). The ECJ decision in *Danfoss*[2] had for many years been an authority for the proposition that service-related benefits will always be justified. The court there said:

> 'Even though the criterion of seniority, like that of vocational training, may result in less favourable treatment of female workers than of male workers, seniority goes hand in hand with experience which generally places a worker in a better position to carry out his duties. Therefore, it is permissible for the employer to reward it without the need to establish the importance which it takes on for the performance of the specific duties entrusted to the worker.'

The decision was reviewed by the ECJ more recently in *Cadman v Health & Safety Executive*.[3] The ECJ appear to have watered down the principle but still hold that service-related benefits are generally legitimate. The court said:

> 'rewarding, in particular, experience acquired which enables the worker to perform his duties better constitutes a legitimate objective of pay policy. As a general rule, recourse to the criterion of length of service is appropriate to attain that objective. Length of service goes hand in hand with experience, and experience generally enables the worker to perform his duties better. The employer is therefore free to reward length of service without having to establish the importance it has in the performance of specific tasks entrusted to the employee.'

This implication is that there is a rebuttable presumption that employers need not justify service-related benefits. It remains to be seen under what circumstances the employees will be able to require the employer to justify the indirectly discriminatory impact of service-related benefits.

Of course, *Danfoss* and *Cadman* are decisions on European sex discrimination laws. However, there would seem to be no reason not to expect the approach to justification to apply equally to age discrimination laws.

For a consideration of the justification for using continuous service as a factor in the calculation of *enhanced* redundancy payments, see **11.5.3**.

1 See **11.5.1**.
2 *Handels ug Kontorfunktion Wrernes Forbund I Danmark v Dansk Arbejdsgiverforening, acting on behalf of Danfoss* [1989] IRLR 532.
3 [2006] IRLR 969.

(c) 20 years' service cap

The limit on taking 20 years' employment into account in calculating SRP would not appear to discriminate on the grounds of age. If anything, it limits the discriminatory impact of the use of service in calculating SRP. The argument that it disadvantages older workers with more than 20 years' service as these employees are not having each year of service recognised appears to be ill-founded.

(d) Qualifying period

Excluding employees who have less than two years' service from the right to claim a SRP could be indirectly discriminatory, on the assumption that a certain age group (perhaps younger employees probably in their early/mid-20s) would be particularly disadvantaged by it.

The argument would be as follows: if the principal aim of SRP is to ameliorate the financial disadvantage of the loss of employment, employees with shorter service (who are likely to be younger) should not be excluded. The financial impact of the loss of a job can be particularly significant for an employee who has short periods of employment. His inability to demonstrate a stable career history could stigmatise him in the workplace and make it more difficult to find equivalent alternative employment.

The counter argument is that the aim of redundancy payments is (or includes) to reward and encourage loyal service so that excluding relatively new recruits is justified.

In putting forward the government's case for the upper age limit for redundancy payments that applied before the coming into force of the Regulations, they argued that the two-year service threshold was intended to ensure redundancy payments rewarded those employees who had demonstrated commitment to their employer.[1]

In any event, an employee looking to show that this provision has a discriminatory impact must first identify a disadvantaged age group and then adduce evidence to show that he is placed at a particular disadvantage. This is likely to be very difficult, and until he does so, the issue of justification does not arise. It would seem, therefore, that whilst excluding employees with less than two years' service might be considered to be unfair, it is not likely to be incompatible with the Directive.

1 *Secretary of State for Trade and Industry v Rutherford (No 2)* [2003] IRLR 858 at [146], 877.

11.5.3 Enhanced redundancy pay schemes

Many employers operate enhanced redundancy schemes which pay more to redundant employees than SRP. A wide range of schemes is in operation. These schemes usually take into account the employee's length of service and may also take into account his age.

These schemes are often set out in employee documentation and form part of the employees' contract of employment. Many have been negotiated over time with trade unions. Others are not documented but nonetheless may well have become incorporated into the employment contract by way of custom and practice, because they have been applied in a consistent way over time, giving rise to an expectation from the employees that they will be applied in that way again. In some cases, enhanced redundancy pay may be calculated on an ad hoc basis.

Whatever the basis for making an enhanced redundancy payment, the age discrimination rules will now apply.

An employer will have to show that any potentially age discriminatory element in its scheme either comes within one of the exceptions in the Regulations or otherwise is justifiable.

In the aftermath of the publication of the Regulations enhanced redundancy pay has perhaps caused more problems than any other aspect of the Regulations. This might be due in part to the fact that the provisions relating to SRP in Sch 8, and enhanced redundancy pay in reg 33, did not appear in the draft Regulations and, therefore, did not have the benefit of the rigorous consultation applied to much of the rest of the Regulations.

This section considers:

(a) the exceptions for certain enhanced redundancy pay schemes[1];

(b) schemes which are not covered by the exceptions;

(c) a suggested model scheme; and

(d) augmentation of benefits for those ineligible for enhanced pensions.

In considering schemes not covered by the exceptions, we look at various examples and consider their likely justification and the implications of successful challenge under the Regulations.

1 See reg 33.

(a) Exception for certain enhanced redundancy pay schemes (reg 33)

Regulation 33 provides an exception from the age discrimination laws for 'enhanced redundancy payments to employees'. However, it is very narrow in scope and only covers a small minority of schemes.

Under reg 33(1), it will not be age discrimination:

'(a) to give a qualifying employee an enhanced redundancy payment which is less in amount than the enhanced redundancy payment which he gives to another such employee if both amounts are calculated in the same way; or

(b) to give enhanced redundancy payments only to those who are qualifying employees.'

A 'qualifying employee' is defined in reg 33(2) as an employee who:

- is entitled to SRP[1]; or
- who would have been entitled to SRP but for the fact that he has less than two years' continuous employment[2]; or

- who accepts voluntary redundancy but otherwise would have been a qualifying employee.[3]

Employers can, therefore, rely on the exception even where their schemes cover those with less than two years' service or those who accept voluntary redundancy, neither of whom are entitled to SRP.

On the face of it, this exception would appear only to cover claims of discrimination based on an actual comparator. The wording of the exception ('to give a qualifying employee an enhanced redundancy payment which is less in amount than the enhanced redundancy payment *which he gives* to another such employee . . .') contrasts with the wording of the antidiscrimination provisions of the Regulations which clearly permit a hypothetical comparator (on grounds of B's age, A treats B less favourably than he treats *or would treat* other persons). Since the discrimination provisions permit hypothetical comparators, it must be assumed that the exception is also designed to cover claims based on hypothetical as well as actual comparators.

Regulation 33(3) and (4) impose a very significant limitation on the usefulness of this exception for employers with enhanced redundancy schemes. In order to come within the exception the enhanced scheme must mirror the SRP scheme.[4] In order to do this it must be based on the calculation of SRP set out in s 162 of the ERA 1996.

The only two departures from this which are permitted by the Regulations are set out in reg 33(4), namely:

- the employer can set a higher limit, or no limit, on a week's pay[5];
- the employer can multiply either the multiple for each year of employment or the total amount of the payment by a common multiple.[6]

Example:

An employer calculates redundancy pay by using the SRP age bands and length of service but deviates from the statutory scheme by not capping a week's pay and multiplying the total payment by four.

Under this scheme:

- an employee aged 50 with 5 years' continuous employment with weekly pay of £500 would be entitled to 5 (years of continuous employment) × 1.5 (age multiple) × 500 (weekly pay) × 4 (multiple) = £15,000.

– an equivalent employee aged 40 would be entitled to 5 × 1 × 500 × 4 = £10,000.

This difference, albeit age-based, would fall within the reg 33 exception and be lawful.

A scheme based on a month's pay for each year of service but otherwise mirroring SRP would be lawful as a month's pay will always be a fixed multiple (52/12) of a week's pay.

Had the employer chosen to include employees with less than two years' continuous employment in this scheme, the exception would also still apply as not only would these employees be 'qualifying employees' but their pay would still be calculated pursuant to s 162 of the ERA 1996 (though for those with less than a year's service the payment would be nil as the years of continuous employment would be zero).

1 See reg 33(2)(a).
2 See reg 33(2)(b).
3 See reg 33(2)(c).
4 See reg 33(3).
5 See reg 33(4)(b)(i).
6 These two methods give the same result but apply the multiple at different points in the calculation.

(b) Schemes which are not covered by the exception

Save for the two exceptions mentioned above, schemes which do not mirror the SRP calculation method in the ERA 1996 are excluded from the exception.

Enhanced redundancy schemes vary, but we consider below some of the most common types:

(i) a scheme based on multiples of years of service but without any age bands;

(ii) a scheme which uses age bands which are different from those in the SRP scheme;

(iii) a scheme which does not include the cap on 20 years' service;

(iv) a scheme which calculates a week's pay differently; and

(v) a scheme which limits the payment to the salary the employee would have earned to retirement.

In each case the scheme does not mirror the SRP scheme so as to come within the reg 33 exception, but represents a termination benefit so as to fall outside the reg 32 exemption for certain service-related benefits.[1]

We consider below whether each type of scheme is likely to satisfy the normal test of objective justification. With no case law to guide us at the moment, it is difficult to predict how courts and tribunals will apply that test. Indeed, each employer's case for justification will differ depending on its own aims and the discriminatory impact of the scheme within its own organisation.

1 See reg 32(7).

(i) A scheme based on multiples of years of service but without any age bands

Many enhanced redundancy schemes are calculated purely on the basis of service, regardless of the age of the employee. Commonly, these schemes will pay an uncapped week's pay, or a multiple of a week's pay, for each year of employment (or SRP if this is more generous). Many others will pay a month's salary for each year of employment. These schemes are usually capped at say 12, 18, 20 or 24 months' salary. Some are uncapped. In some cases these enhanced payments are inclusive of notice pay.

Arguments in favour of the justification of service-related enhanced redundancy payments

- SRP is calculated by reference to service (albeit with age multiples) and the Government must, therefore, believe that there is a legitimate aim for the use of service in calculating redundancy pay.
- The House of Lords has accepted that, whilst the principal aim of a redundancy payment is ameliorating the financial impact of the job loss, rewarding loyalty is a legitimate secondary aim.[1]
- Service-related redundancy pay is an established element of UK employment conditions generally accepted as fair by employers, employees and unions.
- The ECJ in *Danfoss*[2] and *Cadman*[3] had little difficulty in accepting the legitimacy of service-related benefits under sex equality laws.

Arguments against the justification of service-related enhanced redundancy payments

- If the Government had believed these schemes to be inherently justified it would have widened the exceptions for enhanced payments in reg 33.

- The Government deliberately excluded enhanced redundancy payments from the exception in the Regulations for service-related benefits.[4]
- The Government's caution is, perhaps, understandable bearing in mind the established principal aim of redundancy payments relates to future losses and basing the calculation on service alone arguably insufficiently addresses the likely financial impact of the job loss on different employees of different ages.
- Just because enhanced redundancy pay has historically been calculated in this way does not necessarily equate it to a fair and justified calculation method.
- Why should a 40-year-old who was headhunted a year ago from a post she had filled for 20 years in a different organisation receive a small fraction of the redundancy pay a 45-year-old with 20 years' service with the employer would receive? The financial impact of unemployment is unlikely to differ greatly between the two.

It is difficult to predict confidently tribunals' approach to schemes based purely on a multiple of service. The justification of a service-related scheme could depend on the ease with which the employer could achieve its aim in a less discriminatory way. The justification of practices which follow closely the exceptions in the Regulations but do not satisfy all the criteria is considered in **Chapter 4**.[5]

An employer might understandably be reluctant to incorporate the SRP age bands into an existing scheme which does not currently take age into account. The result could be much lower redundancy payments for younger employees and much higher costs of making older employees redundant. On the other hand, the financial repercussions of an age discrimination claim arising out of an enhanced scheme which does not have age bands are significant and might be too much for some organisations.

The result of a successful challenge would be for all payments to be recalculated without the discriminatory factor ie on the basis of the maximum possible service.

Example:

An employer traditionally calculated enhanced redundancy pay based on one month's pay for each year of service with a cap of two years' pay (including pay in lieu of notice) (the Old Scheme).

The employer does not want to take the risk of having to objectively justify the scheme and so decides to bring the scheme within reg 33. It, therefore, reduces the cap to 20 months' pay after 20 years' service; pays in lieu of notice on top of the enhanced redundancy pay; and incorporates the SRP age bands. It still bases the payments on a month's actual pay rather than a week's pay subject to the statutory cap (the New Scheme).

We set out below how their redundancy pay would differ between the employer's old and new schemes.

It employs the following employees all of whom earn £36,000 per year.

Sally – she is 26, has worked for the Company for 10 years and is on 3 months' notice
Old Scheme – £30,000
New Scheme – £30,000

Henry – he is 63, has worked for the Company for 20 years and is on 6 months' notice
Old Scheme – £60,000
New Scheme – £108,000

Monazza – she is 45, has worked for the Company for 25 years and is on 3 months' notice which she will be required to work out.
Old Scheme – £72,000
New Scheme – £75,000

John – he is also 45, has worked for the Company for 3 years and is on one month's notice
Old Scheme – £9,000
New Scheme – £16,500.
Total payments

Old Scheme – £171,000
New Scheme – £229,500

If, however, the Company keeps its existing scheme (the Old Scheme) which is then successfully challenged, the payments would be increased to £72,000 each (based on each payment being levelled up to the maximum of 24 years' service) totalling £228,000 and an increased cost to the employer of £105,000 over the cost of the Old Scheme and £58,500 over the cost of having changed to the New Scheme.

This highlights the potential consequences of a discriminatory scheme being challenged.

An employer might also be nervous about changing its existing scheme to incorporate the SRP age bands as these may well be the subject of a future legal challenge as being incompatible with the Directive.[6] Further, if the Regulations have their desired effect of combating prejudice and discrimination in the job market, older workers will not find it so much harder than younger workers to find employment and the rationale for the age bands will be eroded. In that case the government would be forced to review their legitimacy in any event.

1 *Barry v Midland Bank* [1999] IRLR 581; see **11.5.1**.
2 [1989] IRLR 832.
3 [2006] IRLR 969.
4 See reg 32(7) and 'Notes on Regulations', DTI, March 2006, para 126, p 22.
5 **Chapter 4**, **4.7.8**.
6 **Chapter 2**.

(ii) A scheme which uses age bands which are different from those in the SRP scheme

Another common version of the enhanced redundancy scheme utilises age bands that are different from the age bands in the SRP scheme.

This type of scheme directly discriminates on the grounds of age. If the employer was unsuccessful in justifying it, all employees would be entitled to payments re-calculated without the age-discriminatory factor ie on the basis of the highest age multiples.

Example:

The employer calculates enhanced redundancy pay based on an uncapped week's pay for each year of service but applies a multiple of 1 in respect of years of service up to the age of 40; 1.5 between 40 and 50; and 5 from the age of 50. They cap service at 20 years.

Using our previous example, but giving each employee a weekly salary of £700, the payments would be as follows:

Sally – £7,000
Henry – £49,350
Monazza – £19,250
John – £3,150
Total payments – £78,750

If, however, the age bands were held to be discriminatory and the employer was forced to level upwards to a maximum (ie 20) years' service for each person, their claim would be for redundancy payments as follows:

Sally – £35,000
Henry – £70,000

Monazza £87,500
John – £10,500

A total liability of £203,000 (an additional liability of £124,250 over what they intended to pay).

Whilst the government clearly believes age bands are a legitimate way to address the increased financial impact of redundancy on older employees, an employer who operates a scheme with age bands which are different from those in the SRP scheme would have to justify the age discriminatory impact of its own bands. It would have to show that the bands addressed in a proportionate way the increased financial burden of job loss at particular ages in its industry and locality. Obtaining this evidence is likely to be difficult.

It is also likely to be difficult to show that increasing the multiple applied to past service is a better way of addressing the perceived increased financial impact on older employees than, say, applying age-related multiples to the total redundancy payment.

Most employees operating schemes of this kind would be well advised to change the age bands to those within the SRP scheme or remove them entirely. Neither of these routes is risk-free, however, since the SRP age bands are susceptible to legal challenge as being contrary to the Directive (see **11.5.2(b)**) and removing them entirely would prevent the scheme coming within the reg 33 exception leaving the employer exposed to a claim that taking service into account is age discriminatory (see **11.5.3(a)**).

(iii) A scheme which does not include the cap on 20 years service

To come within reg 33 the payment must be calculated on the basis set out in s 162 of the ERA 1996. Section 162(3) states that 'where twenty years of employment have been reckoned, no account shall be taken . . . of any year of employment earlier than those twenty years'. Any scheme which provides for a different (or no) cap on years' service would, therefore, need to be objectively justified.

Examples:

An employer calculates enhanced redundancy pay based on one month's pay for each year of service and incorporates the SRP age bands, but caps continuous employment for these calculations at 24 years' service.

Under this scheme:

- Beatrice, who is 50-years-old with 22 years' service and paid £2,000 per month would receive £53,000;
- Gawain, who is 40-years-old, with the same service and on the same pay would receive £40,000.

One might expect tribunals to accept that a scheme which so closely mirrors SRP is justified. However, the government saw fit to draft the enhanced redundancy pay exception very narrowly and it will be interesting to see what tribunals conclude from this.

Under the same scheme Ian, a 39-year-old employee who is a recent recruit to the same employer, claims that the use of continuous employment in calculating an enhanced redundancy payment indirectly discriminates against employees under 40. He argues that employees under 40 are less likely than those over 40 to have longer service and so be entitled to larger payments.

If the employer had capped service at 20 years rather than 24, Ian would not succeed with his claim as his employer would be able to rely on the reg 33 exception.

However, in this case, the employer could not rely on reg 33 as this scheme does not mirror SRP. Nor could it rely on reg 32 (which provides an exception for certain benefits based on length of service) as this exception does not apply to termination payments.[1] In order to avoid liability for age discrimination, it would have to seek to justify the indirect discrimination.

Again, one would probably expect tribunals to accept a scheme which so closely corresponds to SRP as justified, but this is not guaranteed.

Becky has 26 years' service and claims that the cap at 24 years discriminates against her as it does not take into account all of her service. It is difficult to see how this can amount to indirect age discrimination. If the cap had been 25 years the scheme would come within the exception and Becky could not claim.

The justification of such a scheme is also considered in **4.7.8**.

1 See reg 32(7).

(iv) A scheme which calculates a week's pay differently

In order to come within the reg 33 exception, the scheme must use as its base, the calculation of a week's pay for SRP.[1]

Example:

An employer includes an employee's last annual bonus in the calculation of a week's pay.

Since the employer in this example is using a different method for calculating a week's pay than applies for SRP purposes – by including the value of benefits in the calculation – the scheme would not come within the reg 33 exemption, so that any age discrimination would have to be justified.

Again, it may be that tribunals will accept as justified schemes which mirror SRP but with variations such as this. However, again, this cannot be guaranteed.

1 ERA 1996, s 162 and Ch II.

(v) A scheme which limits the payment to the salary the employee would have earned to retirement

Some enhanced schemes limit the redundancy payment to salary that the employee would have earned till retirement.

Example:

An employer pays one month for each year of service and incorporates the SRP age multiples. It limits the amount of the payment to the amount of salary the employee would have earned to retirement. The retirement age is 65.

Clare, who has 20 years' service, is made redundant on her 64th birthday. Although she would otherwise receive a redundancy payment of 30 months' pay (20×1.5), her redundancy pay is in fact limited to 12 months pay as she would have reached her retirement date in 12 months' time.

This enhanced scheme would not fall within the reg 33 exception because of this limit, so that any age discriminatory effect would have to be justified.

Bearing in mind the principal aim of redundancy payments is to ameliorate the financial implications of unemployment, one would expect this scheme, arguably, to satisfy the test of objective justification.

Clare might argue that she expected to work beyond retirement and it might even be the case that the employer customarily allowed many employees to do so. Nonetheless, the employer would have been free to retire Clare at 65. In any event, the financial risks of this scheme for the employer are limited, as a successful claim would only result in an award of the redundancy payment calculated without this limit.

Some support for a limit of this nature can be found in the government's attempts (which the EAT accepted) to justify the upper age limit (and tapering in the year prior to reaching the limit) which existed on the entitlement to receive statutory redundancy payments before the coming into force of the Regulations.

The government's justifications were:

- diminishing expectation of continued employment; and
- removing disincentive on employers to retain employees beyond retirement.

Stephen Walker[1] stated that:

> 'as employees approach state pension age, or the normal retirement age for their job if that is lower, their expectation of continued employment diminishes and eventually ceases and that, therefore, as they approach the age in question, their entitlement to compensation should similarly diminish and eventually cease.
>
> A secondary justification has been that the provisions remove a potential disincentive to employers keeping employees on beyond the age at which they would normally be expected to retire, ie 65 (or as the case may be) the lower normal retirement age for the job. In the absence of these provisions, employers would be faced with the prospect of having to make disproportionately large payments in the event of subsequent redundancy (given that age and length of service are factors in the calculation) if they kept such employees on rather than replacing them with younger ones.'[2]

His evidence continued 'The provisions can therefore be said to favour older employees, at least in this respect.'

Some caution should be expressed as the Regulations abolished the upper age limits and tapering of statutory redundancy payments. The government cannot, therefore, have believed very strongly in the force of these arguments.

This raises the question, can employers impose an upper age limit on their statutory redundancy payments?

The government's arguments in *Rutherford* above point to possible justification arguments.

If it is possible to cap redundancy payments for employees at pay to retirement, logically it should be possible to stop them beyond that age. Most employers will probably adopt the safer course of retiring employees over their retirement age rather than making them redundant.[3]

Employers might also consider a lower redundancy payment for employees beyond retirement age which took into account the reduced financial implications of redundancy and the lower expectation of continued employment but did not reduce this to nil.

In any event, it seems unlikely that many tribunals will agree with Mr Walker that an upper age limit on redundancy payments is a benefit to older employees.

1 Then assistant director, responsible for redundancy payments in the employment relations directorate of the DTI.
2 *Secretary of State for Trade and Industry v Rutherford (No 2)* [2003] IRLR 858 at [146], 877.
3 See commentary on entitlement to a redundancy payment in such circumstances – **11.5.4**.

(vi) A scheme in which the enhanced payment is inclusive of notice pay

In some schemes the enhanced redundancy payment is payable in addition to notice or notice pay but in others it includes notice pay. Of course, for a scheme to come within the enhanced redundancy exception it must be calculated exclusive of notice/notice pay. If the scheme is otherwise justifiable, the inclusion of notice pay is unlikely to affect this.

(c) Suggested model scheme

There are better, more 'proportionate', ways of rewarding loyalty whilst ensuring that the redundancy payment has the desired aim of ameliorating the financial impact of unemployment.

Example:

The employer pays a minimum payment of six months' pay. This is augmented by a further two weeks' pay for each year of service up to a maximum of 18 months' pay.

In the event the employer wishes to reflect the increasing difficulty that older workers face, it could multiply the total payment in a scheme like that set out in this example by a figure which would vary with the age of the employee and which the employer could review periodically based on available evidence of the varying difficulty redundant employees of different ages face in finding equivalent employment.

Alternatively, an employer wishing to avoid any risk of an age discrimination claim could base redundancy pay on a set proportion of salary (eg six months' salary – inclusive or exclusive of notice pay. If it includes notice pay, the employer must ensure that it is no less than notice pay plus SRP).

(d) Augmentation of benefits for those ineligible for enhanced pensions

As mentioned above, it is quite common for employers with occupational pension schemes to allow employees being made redundant over the age at which they can draw a pension (currently 50) to draw an enhanced pension which is not actuarially reduced on account of being drawn early.

Similar principles apply to enhanced pensions on compulsory redundancy as for enhanced pensions for those who take voluntary redundancy.[1]

However, some employers who provide for this valuable pension enhancement for redundant employees take it into account in the multiples they apply in calculating enhanced redundancy pay.

Example:

An employer calculates enhanced redundancy pay on an uncapped week's pay for each year of service and incorporates the SRP multiples. It allows employees over 50 to draw a nonactuarially reduced enhanced pension but multiplies the payment received by those being made redundant between 40 and 50 by 2 to compensate for their ineligibility for the enhanced payment.

Brent, Tamar and Sally will have 5 years' service and are paid £500 per week. Brent is 55-years-old; Tamar is 49-years-old; and Sally is 36-years-old. Brent would be entitled to a payment of £3,750; Tamar a payment of £7,500 and Sally £2,500. This would require objective justification.

If the employer could not justify the multiple applied to those between 40 and 50, all three would be able to 'level up' and claim payments of £7,500.

One can see the legitimate aim of cushioning the financial impact of unemployment. It would, however, probably be difficult to show that the application of the age multiples in this example was proportionate. How can the employer justify the differential treatment between the 39-year-old who receives no multiplier and the 40-year-old whose payment is doubled? Whilst the benefit to both 40- to 50-year-olds (the age-based multiples) and those over 50 (the enhanced pension) would both be largely dependent on service, would the employer be able to show that the multiple of two was the appropriate compensatory multiple to offset the benefit?

---

1 See **11.3.2**; **Chapter 8**.

(e) Timing of justification

One further question arises when an employer is faced with a long-standing enhanced redundancy scheme which will require objective justification to remain lawful under the Regulations.

Must the employer demonstrate:

- that it was objectively justified by reference to the aims of those who set it up?
- that the discriminating feature could be objectively justified by reference to the employer's current aims or, even if it cannot be shown, that these aims applied at the time it was established?
- that the employer must only objectively justify not changing the scheme to remove any discriminatory features?

The correct test would seem to be the employer's justification in not making changes to the scheme at the time of the challenge.[1] This is likely to be easier than justifying the discriminatory features of the scheme. Indeed, if it was necessary to refer to the aims of those who originally devised the scheme, many employers will be at a complete loss as no records will exist and the relevant employees will have long since left.

The employer can probably also take account of the impact of any change on the expectations of long-serving staff.[2]

1 **Chapter 4**, **4.7.7**.
2 See *Cross v British Airways* [2005] IRLR 423, discussed at **Chapter 4**, **4.7.5(a)**.

11.5.4 Retirement and redundancy payments

The Regulations establish a procedure which must be followed in order for a dismissal to be legally classified as a retirement. Briefly, this involves the employer notifying the employee in writing that his retirement is approaching and explaining that he has the right to request to stay on longer, should he wish to. If the retirement procedure is followed then for the purposes of unfair dismissal and age discrimination laws, the dismissal will be by reason of retirement.[1]

However, it is possible that a dismissal will satisfy the legal requirements of both a retirement and a redundancy under the EAR 1996.[2] New complicated provisions introduced into the ERA by the Regulations (s 98 ZB to ZE[3]) set out the circumstances in which dismissals at retirement age will be considered to be solely by reason of retirement. These complex provisions are considered in more detail in **Chapter 11**. Briefly, they give a set of various factual circumstances relating to the age of the employee, the timing of the dismissal and the normal retirement age in the employing organisation and say in each case whether retirement 'shall be taken to be the only reason for dismissal by the employer and any other reason shall be disregarded'.

There are two possible interpretations of this. Either it means that retirement should be taken to be the only reason for dismissal simply for the purpose of determining whether or not the dismissal is fair or unfair under s 98 of ERA; or it means that retirement is the only reason for all purposes which would include, for example, the entitlement to be paid a statutory redundancy payment in circumstances where the dismissal satisfies both the definition of retirement under s 98 and also of redundancy under s 135(1) (a) of ERA.

Since statutory redundancy payments are generally modest, many employers will be more concerned about a retirement dismissal giving rise to the right to an enhanced contractual redundancy payment. This would depend on the wording of the relevant scheme. Employers wishing to avoid the risk of having to make such payments should ensure that their enhanced redundancy policy clearly states that it does not apply where the redundancy also satisfies the definition of retirement.

Denying retiring employees a redundancy payment would, on the face of it, amount to age discrimination. However, excluding them from the right to such a payment could be legally justifiable on the following basis: the principal aim of redundancy payments is to cushion the employee against the financial implications of unexpected unemployment; unemployment is not unexpected for an employee who has reached retirement age, and who could legitimately be forced to retire. This argument is stronger where the employer tapers the redundancy payment for those close to retirement so that it does not exceed pay to retirement.[4]

Employers might elect to make employees over their retirement age redundant, particularly if part of a large-scale redundancy exercise. This may well be simpler and seen as fairer. As mentioned above, the employer will need to be clear whether it is retiring the employee or making him redundant as the processes are very different. One advantage of treating the employee as redundant and not retiring is that in a redundancy situation it is not necessary to give six months' notice of termination (though the employer will normally have to consult individually and possibly, collectively in a redundancy exercise which may mean that there is much less difference in timing in practice).

An advantage in retiring the employee and not making him redundant would exist. If the employer only just exceeds the threshold for collective consultation, treating the employee as retiring and not redundant might take the employer below that threshold.

1 **Chapter 12**, **12.6**.
2 See s 135(1)(a).
3 ERA 1996 introduced by Sch 8, Pt 1, para 23 of the Regulations.
4 See **11.5.3(b)(v)**.

Chapter 12

Retirement

12.1 Introduction

Retirement and age are inexorably connected. One of the greatest challenges for the government in shaping age discrimination laws was their impact on retirement.

In this chapter we cover:

- the meaning of retirement as the term has several different meanings depending on the context;
- the compatibility of the default retirement rules in the Regulations with the Directive;

- when a retirement might be unlawful;
- the meaning of the normal retirement age;
- the duty to consider requests to stay on procedure;
- issues for employers in extending employment beyond retirement age; and
- certain consequential issues relating to the employment contract.

The following issues are considered later in this book:

- recruitment close to and after retirement age[1];
- retirement and rights under share option and similar schemes[2];
- retirement gifts;[3]
- retirement and rights to redundancy payments.[4]

1 **Chapter 5, 5.3.2(c)** and **5.3.3(f)**.
2 **Chapter 6, 6.7.6.**
3 **Chapter 6, 6.7.**
4 **Chapter 11, 11.5.4.**

12.2 Meaning of retirement

The Oxford English dictionary defines retirement as 'Withdrawal from occupation, office, or business activity'.

The term 'retirement', nonetheless, is often used in many different ways. Retirement is customarily understood as an employee choosing to end his employment in order to stop working. However, an employee will often say that he is retiring if he is moving to part-time work, self-employment or a different, often less demanding, career.

Employees normally retire at or towards the end of their working lives. However, there is no defining age below which employees 'resign' and above which they 'retire'. As a consequence, differentiating between retirement and resignation is often far from straightforward.[1]

This chapter, however, predominantly deals with situations where the employee has not freely chosen to stop work but where the employment comes to an end because the employee has reached a particular age. Where the employer does not allow the employee to continue in employment beyond this age, the term used is 'mandatory' or 'compulsory' retirement.

Compulsory or mandatory retirement at a set age clearly represents the most obvious form of direct age discrimination. Age represents the grounds for the termination of the employment. However, it is widely accepted that there is a need to encourage employers to employ employees longer.[2] Some employers have abolished set retirement ages. In these cases, the employment cannot, on the face of it, be terminated by the employer by reason of retirement as the age of the employee cannot be the reason for the employer deciding to terminate the employment. There is no set age at which the employment terminates. Some other act must be the catalyst for the decision to dismiss.

As mentioned below,[3] in these cases and in cases where the employee has been allowed to work beyond his retirement age, the Regulations still permit the employer to 'retire' the employee (but not nonemployees) provided he has past his 65th birthday.

Where an employee chooses to 'retire' before any set retirement age, this is usually referred to as 'early retirement'.

Confusingly, the term 'retirement' is given a different meaning for partnerships. The removal or resignation of a partner is customarily referred to as retirement from the partnership whatever the age.

1 **Chapter 6**, **6.7.6**.
2 See **12.4**.
3 See **12.6**.

12.3 Distinguishing retirement age from pension age

Retirement ages should not be confused with pension ages. Nonetheless, unhelpfully, the media, politicians and union leaders often confuse the two.

The two are, of course, often closely connected. The term 'pension age' usually refers to the age at which an employee can draw a full pension from his employer's scheme.[1] Confusingly this can be referred to as the scheme's 'normal retirement date'.

Often the employer sets its pension age and retirement age at the same age. There is a certain logic to this. The employee is forced to stop work at the age at which he will be entitled to a full pension. The employee can normally choose to retire early but in these circumstances he will usually receive a reduced pension.

There is no reason in principle, however, why an employer cannot set different pension and retirement ages. Indeed, with the introduction of the default retirement age at 65,[2] many employers were forced to increase their retirement age to 65. Many are left with unchanged lower pension ages.

1 See **Chapter 8** on pensions generally.
2 See **12.4**.

12.4 Background

The trend in retirement ages and the future increase in state pension is explained in **Chapter 1**. As referred to in that chapter, the UK population is aging quickly and it is a healthy old age we are all living to.

There is considerable pressure to increase the working life of the workforce and it is untenable to expect workers to exit the workforce at age 60–65 (or even younger) with another 20 years or more of life expectancy, on average, ahead of them.[1]

The Pensions Commission in its recent report[2] concluded that 'an increase in average age in retirement must be one element of our response to the demographic challenge [of the pensions timebomb]'

Prior to the coming into force of the Regulations, it was, in practice, lawful to compulsorily retire employees. There were no laws which specifically addressed this. However, age discrimination laws were not yet in force, and unfair dismissal protection ceased at an employee's normal retirement age (or 65 if he did not have a normal retirement age). This essentially deprived an employee who was being retired of any legal basis to challenge his dismissal.

There was a concerted attempt to overturn this upper age limit by arguing that it unjustifiably indirectly discriminated against men who were more likely to work beyond retirement. *Secretary of State for Trade and Industry v Rutherford (No 2)*[3] went to the European Court of Justice (ECJ) and House of Lords before the claimants had finally to admit defeat. This case deals with important issues relating to comparisons in individual discrimination cases. Of more interest to age discrimination was the issue of whether, if the upper age limits did discriminate, the UK Government could justify them.

The government's policy justifications are set out in detail in the Employment Appeal Tribunal (EAT) decision.[4] The government's justifications for the upper age limit were threefold:

- (i) ensuring employers can meet the legitimate expectations of younger workers for advancement;
- (ii) predicting future recruitment needs; and
- (iii) allowing employees whose performance declines to an unsatisfactory level to leave with dignity.

The EAT accepted these arguments as 'reasonable policy objectives'.[5]

It is interesting to compare these with the policy justifications for the default retirement age.[6] The first two justifications from *Rutherford* are expanded in the justification of 'workforce planning' for the default retirement age.

However, wisely, the government had abandoned the leaving with dignity, justification which is predicated by ageist prejudices about the performance of older workers declining after 65.

With the impending coming into force, however, of age discrimination laws, the upper age limit on unfair dismissal rights was on borrowed time. The UK Government needed to decide its approach to retirement.

As mentioned above, requiring an employee to stop work merely because he has reached his employer's retirement age is, perhaps, the most obvious example of direct age discrimination. However, many British employers believed that requiring them to objectively justify retirement ages would be damaging to their businesses.

The government's original consultation paper in 2003[7] invited views on retirement but commented that:

> 'on the information we have at present we tend towards the view that legislation should: make retirement ages unlawful; but also provide for employers, exceptionally, to be able to justify mandatory retirement ages by reference to certain aims set out in the implementing legislation, and according to their own circumstances.'

It continued that the government was seeking views on whether 'employers should be able to retire their employees compulsorily at or after age 70 without having to justify their decision'.

Employers and employers' organisations like the Confederation of British Industry (CBI) were horrified by this proposal and campaigned vigorously for it to be changed.

The government's response was to set up a group under the chairmanship of Rita Donaghty of the Advisory, Conciliation and Arbitration Service (ACAS) and comprising representatives from the CBI, The Communications Workers' Union, the Third Age Employment Network, Age Concern, Employers Forum on Age, the TUC, Small Business Council and the Low Pay and Pensions Commission to seek a consensus. Ultimately and unsurprisingly, bearing in mind the widely differing viewpoints of this group, they reached deadlock.

The government responded with the proposal of a default retirement age of 65. As a sop to those who opposed this, they proposed a duty on employers to consider requests from employees to work beyond this age. Despite rumours at the time[8] that the default age would be subject to a sunset provision under which the default age would be abolished at a later date, the government merely committed to review the default after it had been in operation for five years in 2011.[9]

1 **Chapter 1, 1.2.1**.
2 'Pensions: Challenges and Choices', The first report of the Pensions Commission, Pensions Commission, 2004.
3 [2006] IRLR 551.
4 *Secretary of State for Trade and Industry (No 2) v Rutherford* [2003] IRLR 858 at [140]–[145], at 876 and 877.
5 See *Rutherford* [2003] IRLR 858 at [202], 883.
6 See **12.5**.
7 Equality and Diversity Age Matters, DTI, March 2003 para 4.24–4.31.
8 eg Personnel Today, 7 December 2006.
9 'Equality and Diversity: Coming of Age', DTI, July 2005, para 6.4, pp 71–73.

12.5 Mandatory retirement and the directive

In deciding its approach to mandatory retirement the government had to keep one eye on the Directive. If it were to make an exception for mandatory retirement in the United Kingdom it had to ensure that this was consistent with the Directive. The government made it clear in its first 2003 consultation paper that if it were to exempt mandatory retirement from the normal rules of age discrimination, it would have to justify this.[1]

Once it did decide to incorporate an exception in the Regulations for retirement, it relied on the aims of workplace planning and the potential adverse consequences for occupational pension schemes and other work-related benefits.[2]

The Department of Trade and Industry (DTI) guidance to the Regulations sets out the government's justification in more detail.[3]

> '99. This exception for retirement ages of 65 and over is considered to be within the exemption contained in article 6(1) of the Directive as being justified by reference to a legitimate aim of social policy in accordance with the test in *R v Secretary of State for Employment ex parte Seymour-Smith & Perez*.[4] The legitimate aim of social policy has two main elements – they are to meet the concerns of employers in relation to:
>
> (a) workforce planning; and
>
> (b) avoiding an adverse impact on the provision of occupational pensions and other work-related benefits.

100. What is meant by workforce planning in this context can be summarised as including the following:

- workforce planning means that a retirement age is a target age against which employers can plan their work and employees can plan their careers and retirement;
- for employers, being able to rely on a set retirement age allows the recruitment, training and development of employees, and the planning of wage structures and occupational pensions, against a known attrition profile. This is indirectly recognised in the Directive itself, where Article 6.1(c) lists as a justifiable difference of treatment: "the fixing of a maximum age for recruitment which is based on the training requirements of the post in question or the need for a reasonable period of employment before retirement." While other events may give rise to employees leaving the workforce, the age of retirement is nevertheless a significant element in employers' workforce planning;
- for both employers and employees, being able to rely on a set retirement age avoids the blocking of jobs (and often the more senior jobs) from younger workers;
- for employees, knowing there is a set retirement age means they cannot be certain that they will be in work after that time. This will encourage employees to save now and make provisions for their retirement, and avoid them putting off career and pension planning, on the assumption that they will be able to continue working indefinitely. This ties in with the Government's policy of encouraging employees to save more for retirement.

101. The need to avoid an adverse impact on the provision of occupational pensions and other work-related benefits stems from concern that if all employers only had the option of individually objectively justified retirement ages, this could risk adverse consequences for occupational pension schemes and other work related benefits. Some employers would instead simply reduce or remove benefits to offset the cost of providing them to all employees, including those over 65.'

The Directive does not contain any specific justifications for mandatory retirement. It does though, intriguingly state at recital 14 of the Preamble to the Directive that: 'This Directive shall be without prejudice to national provisions laying down retirement ages.' This is not, however, repeated in the substantive articles of the Directive.

Indeed, as mentioned earlier,[5] art 6(1) contains various examples of age-based treatment which might be justified and art 6(2) contains the specific example for admission or entitlement to retirement or invalidity benefits. Nowhere in this article, however, is there any suggestion that mandatory retirement ages might nonetheless remain justifiable.

There remains a body of opinion that the default retirement age exception in the Regulations fails properly to implement the Directive.

The Directive does contain a nonregression provision:

> 'The implementation of this Directive shall under no circumstances constitute grounds for a reduction in the level of protection against discrimination already afforded by Member States in the fields covered by this Directive.'[6]

However, as the United Kingdom did not previously have any limitations on retirement ages, it is difficult to see how the retirement exception in the Regulations infringes this provision.

Heyday, a UK charity linked to Age Concern, commenced judicial review proceedings to have the retirement exception declared unlawful.[7] In December 2006 the High Court referred this question to the ECJ. At the time of writing, it was reported that the parties were having difficulty in agreeing the questions to be asked to the ECJ.[8] A decision is not expected until 2008 or 2009.

In the meantime, two Spanish cases dealing with the compatibility of mandatory retirement ages in Spanish collective agreements with the Directive have been referred to the ECJ.[9] Advocate General Mazak's opinion in *Félix Palacios de la Villa* was delivered on 15 February 2007. The Advocate General's view was that the Spanish laws were not incompatible with the Directive. The court is not obliged to follow this opinion and, in fact, a departure from the Advocate General is not that rare, so care should be exercised in reading too much into the opinion.

Nonetheless, the opinion will certainly have been welcomed by the UK Government. The Madrid court had referred to Europe for a preliminary ruling of a claim by *Félix Palacios de la Villa* that his dismissal on the ground that he had reached the compulsory retirement age laid down in a collective agreement was unlawful. Spanish national law allowed compulsory retirement ages to be agreed in collective agreements provided certain conditions were fulfilled including the setting out in the collective agreement of the employment policy objectives which justify the retirement age and a requirement for the employee in question to have satisfied the minimum contribution period to draw a retirement pension.

If the Heyday challenge is successful then the UK Government will need to rethink its approach to mandatory retirement. In the meantime, employees who mandatorily retired may consider filing tribunal proceedings. At the time of writing, some employment tribunals are staying claims pending a decision in the Heyday challenge but there does not appear to be a consistent approach. In the meantime, public sector employees may be able to rely on the vertical direct effect[10]. of the Directive. In other words claimants can only rely directly on EU directives against 'emanations of the State' and only then where the directive in question is sufficiently clear, precise and unconditional.

1 'Equality and Diversity: Age Matters', DTI, July 2005, paras 4.11 and 4.12.
2 'Equality and Diversity: Coming of Age' DTI, July 2005, paras 6.1.14 and 6.1.15.
3 'Notes on Regulations', DTI, March 2006, paras 99 to 101.
4 [2000] 1 WLR 435.
5 **Chapter 4, 4.7.1**.
6 Article 8(2).
7 *R (on the application of Incorporated Trustees of the National Council of Ageing) v the Secretary of State for Trade and Industry* [2000] EWMC 5485. See **Chaper 2, 2.4.3(a)**; **Chapter 4, 4.7.3** and **4.7.5**.
8 Personnel Today, 5 June 2007.
9 *Félix Palacios de la Villa v Cortefiel Servicios SA* Case C-411/05; *Vincente Pascual Garcia v Confederación Hidrográfia del Duero* Case C-87/06.
10 **Chapter 2, 2.4.2(a)**.

12.6 When is a retirement lawful?

In considering whether or not the dismissal of a worker covered by the Regulations is unlawful, it is necessary to distinguish between employees and nonemployees.

12.6.1 Employees

Employees for this purpose are those within the meaning of s 230(1) of the Employment Rights Act (ERA) 1996[1] and not the broader definition in the Regulations.[2] Consequently, self-employed workers will not come within this definition. The only other categories of worker treated as employees for these purposes are those in Crown Employment and House of Commons and House of Lords' staff.

As mentioned earlier, before the introduction of the Regulations employers could safely compulsorily retire employees as age discrimination laws were not in force and employees lost unfair dismissal protection once they reached their normal retirement age.

The Regulations not only brought into force laws outlawing age discrimination, but also removed the upper age limit on unfair dismissal protection. Therefore, in order to permit employers still to retire employees safely, the retirement exception in the Regulations had to cover both unfair dismissal laws as well as the age discrimination laws being introduced by the same Regulations.

Once it had been decided that employers should be permitted to require employees to retire, at least from the default age of 65, it became necessary to define 'retirement' As mentioned above, this is not straightforward.[3]

The original draft regulations incorporated complex provisions to determine this. However, many commentators predicted that employees would not find it too difficult to show that the true reason for dismissal was, say, capability or redundancy and not retirement, particularly if some employees were selectively retained after the employer's retirement age.

The Regulations effectively now provide that the definition of 'retirement' is procedural.

1 Add definition.
2 **Chapter 3, 3.3.1**.
3 See **12.2**.

(a) Unfair dismissal

An employee dismissed by an employer by reason of retirement would, on the face of it, have claims for unfair dismissal[1] and age discrimination. The Regulations amend unfair dismissal laws to remove the upper age limit on the right to claim.[2]

The Regulations incorporate other amendments to the ERA 1996 to enable employers to retire employees without being guilty of unfair dismissal.

1 Under s 200 of the ERA 1996 police do not have unfair dismissal rights.
2 See para 25 of Sch 8 which removes s 109 of the ERA 1996.

(i) Retirement as a reason for dismissal

Section 98 of the ERA 1996 is amended by para 22 of Sch 8 to the Regulations by adding an additional potentially fair ground of dismissal – retirement.[1]

The meaning of retirement is then defined in the horribly complex additional s 98ZA to ZF of the ERA 1996. The relevant section depends on:

- (a) whether the employer has:
  - (i) no normal retirement age;
  - (ii) a normal retirement age at or above 65; or
  - (iii) a normal retirement age below 65; and
- (b) the date on which the retirement takes effect.[2]

There are three possible outcomes:

(i) Retirement shall be taken as the only reason for dismissal and any other reason shall be disregarded.[3]

(ii) Retirement shall not be taken as a reason for dismissal.

(iii) It will be up to the employer to show that retirement was the reason for dismissal.

In the latter case, the Regulations state that in determining whether or not retirement was the reason for dismissal particular regard must be had to the following:[4]

- whether or not the employer has notified the employee of his right to request at least 14 days before the intended retirement date;
- if so, how long before the intended retirement date notification was given; and
- whether or not the employee held the meeting and gave notice of his decision in accordance with para 7 of Sch 6 to the Regulations.

This is a strange clause. Presumably the intention is that the tribunal should be more likely to conclude that retirement was the real reason if the employer notified the employee of his right to request retirement some while before the 14-day deadline and then followed the procedure. However, the test remains whether or not the principal reason for dismissal was retirement. The procedure followed is likely in most cases to have little bearing on the employer's true reason.

In most cases, an employer who rarely allows employees to work beyond retirement is going to find it easier to show the real reason for dismissal was retirement than one who often grants requests to stay beyond the intended retirement date. If the employer is making value judgments about who can work beyond retirement and who can't, then it will be difficult to show that retirement was the reason for dismissal of those whose requests are not granted.

Example:

TechCo employs engineers. Since the Regulations came into force, six engineers have reached retirement age. All have requested to stay on. TechCo has granted two of the requests and declined the others. Amber is the seventh to reach retirement age. TechCo only notifies her four months before her intended retirement date because of an administrative error. Amber requests to stay on. This request is refused but the company refuses to give any reason. As the company failed to notify Amber at least six months beforehand of the intended retirement date but, nonetheless, will retire her on that intended retirement date, the dismissal is neither deemed to be by reason of retirement nor is it deemed not to be by retirement. The employer must, therefore, show a fair reason for dismissal, namely 'retirement' and the tribunal must take into account the extent to which the statutory procedure has been followed. In this case, it is likely to be difficult for TechCo to show the reason was retirement as it will have to explain why others have been allowed to work on and not Amber. If TechCo argues that the reason was the skills or demand for these employees, then Amber will argue that the reason she was refused was her lack of these skills (ie capability) or the TechCo's lack of need for her(ie redundancy).

In deciding which rule applies, it is necessary to consider the date on which the employment contract terminates:

(a) *If the contract terminates on the intended retirement date*[5]

(i) If the employer has notified the employee of the intended retirement date between six and twelve months before that date, then retirement is deemed to be the only reason for dismissal.

(ii) If the employer has not notified the employee of the intended retirement date between six and twelve months before the intended retirement date, then the reason for dismissal is neither deemed to be by reason of retirement or deemed not to be by reason of retirement (see above).

(b) *If the contract terminates before the intended retirement date*

Retirement cannot be the reason for dismissal.

In addition, retirement cannot be the reason for dismissal if:

(i) the employee has a normal retirement age and the dismissal takes place before that age;

(ii) the employee has no normal retirement age and the dismissal takes place before his 65th birthday; and

(iii) the employee has a retirement age under 65 which it cannot justify and at whatever age the dismissal takes place (even over 65).

If the employer attempts to retire the employee without giving at least the 14 days' notice required by para 4 of Sch 6 to the Regulations, then the dismissal cannot be deemed as being by reason of retirement. The factors listed above[6] will be taken into account in determining whether or not the dismissal was by reason of retirement. But, as mentioned below, even if it is considered to be a retirement, if 14 days' notice has not been given it will still be automatically unfair.

1 Now s 98 (ba) of the ERA 1996.
2 Introduced by para 23 of Sch 8 to the Regulations.
3 Though it is unclear whether this means that retirement shall be the only reason for unfair dismissal and age discrimination purposes or for all purposes. **See Chapter 11, 11.5.4**.
4 See s 98ZF of the ERA 1996 inserted by para 23 of Sch 8 to the Regulations.
5 Intended retirement date is defined in s 98ZH of the ERA 1996 as 'the date which, by virtue of paragraph 1(2) of Schedule 6 to the Regulations, is the intended date of retirement in relation to a particular dismissal'.
6

- whether or not the employer has notified the employee of his right to request at least 14 days before the intended retirement date;
- if so, how long before the intended retirement date notification was given; and
- whether or not the employee held the meeting and gave notice of his decision in accordance with para 7 of Sch 6 to the Regulations.

(ii) Reasonableness of dismissal

In order to be a fair dismissal, a retirement must not only satisfy the definition of retirement above but must also be procedurally fair. However, where the reason is retirement, the dismissal need not satisfy the normal test of reasonableness under the ERA 1996 nor must the statutory termination procedure be followed.

Section 98 of the ERA 1996 is amended by the introduction of a new subsection 3A.[1] This provides:

> 'In any case where the employer has fulfilled the requirements of subsection (1) by showing that the reason (or the principal reason) for the dismissal is retirement of the employee, the question whether the dismissal is fair or unfair shall be determined in accordance with subsection 98ZG.'

This subsection 98ZG states that a dismissal by reason of retirement will only be unfair (assuming the definition of retirement has been satisfied), if certain of the elements of the duty to consider requests to stay on procedure[2] have been breached by the employer. The relevant elements being:

- the employer has not notified the employee of his right to request to stay by 14 days before the retirement date;
- the employer fails to consider the request to stay on in the prescribed manner;[3] or
- the employer fails to allow the employee to appeal against a refusal to permit him to stay on, on the requested basis.

1 Introduced by para 22 (4) of Sch 8 to the Regulations.

2 See **12.9**.
3 A breach of the duty to permit the employee to be accompanied will only result in a financial award.

(iii) Failure to notify employee of right to stay on

It should be noted that if the employer fails to comply with its duty to notify the employee of his right to request to stay on before the first deadline of six months before the retirement date, this will not render the dismissal unfair provided the dismissal, nonetheless, satisfied the definition of retirement under the ERA 1996. It is only a continued failure to notify by the second deadline (14 days before date of retirement) that renders the dismissal automatically unfair.

(b) Age discrimination

As mentioned above, it is difficult to think of a more obvious example of direct age discrimination than requiring an employee to stop work, irrespective of his capability, merely because he has reached a set age.

Once the government decided to permit employers to retire employees free from legal challenge, it needed to introduce an appropriate exception in the Regulations.

Regulation 30 has this effect and states that the Regulations shall not 'render unlawful the dismissal of a person to whom this regulation applies[1] at or over the age of 65 where the reason for the dismissal is retirement'.

Regulation 30(3) then cross refers to the definition of retirement inserted into the ERA 1996 for unfair dismissal purposes (above). It states: 'For the purposes of this regulation, whether or not the dismissal is retirement shall be determined in accordance with ss 98ZA to 98ZF of the 1996 Act.'

1 Employees (as defined by the ERA 1996), person in Crown Employment or relevant member of House of Commons or House of Lords' staff.

(c) Other claims

Even if the retirement procedure is followed and the retired employee is unable to bring a claim for unfair dismissal or age discrimination, there is nothing to prevent him claiming another form of discrimination if he believes that, say, his gender, race or disability played a part in the decision to retire him.[1]

1 Cross refer to examples later in this chapter and **Chapter 9, 9.4.1**.

12.6.2 Non-employees

It should be noted that other categories of worker covered by the Regulations cannot benefit from the retirement exception. This would include the self-employed, contract workers, employment agency workers, police (not employed under contracts of employment), partners, office-holders and barristers. If an organisation wishes to retire a worker in one of these categories, it would have to rely on the defence of objective justification to defeat an age discrimination claim.

These workers are, of course, not covered by unfair dismissal laws in any event.

12.7 Concept of normal retirement age

It can be seen that the employee's 'normal retirement age' is important in determining whether or not a dismissal is by reason of retirement. If the employee's normal retirement age is below 65, this retirement age must be objectively justified in order for the reason for dismissal to be retirement.[1]

If the employee's normal retirement age is 65 or above, then for the dismissal to be by reason of retirement the retirement date must be on or after this normal retirement age.

Example:

Alphabet Ltd's employees have a normal retirement age of 70. Alphabet Ltd cannot dismiss them by reason of retirement until they reach 70. Betabet & Co's employees have no normal retirement age. Betabet & Co can dismiss them by reason of retirement once they reach 65.

If the employee has no normal retirement age the retirement must be on or after his 65th birthday.

Normal retirement age is a familiar concept from the ERA. Until removed by the Regulations, s 109(1) used to provide that an employee was precluded from bringing an unfair dismissal claim, if he had attained 'a normal retirement age for an employee holding the position held by the employee' which applied in the undertaking in which he was employed.

'Normal retirement age' was not statutorily defined but its meaning became clarified by a series of employment law cases (see below).

Importantly, an employee's normal retirement age is not necessarily the same as any contractual retirement age which may govern his employment.

Not all employees have a normal retirement age.

The relevant principles in determining what, if any, age represents an employee's normal retirement age were set out by the Court of Appeal in *Barclays Bank plc v O'Brien.*[2]

'(1) The social policy underlying [s 109(1)] is to secure fair treatment as regards compulsory retirement as between different employees holding the same or a similar "position"(in the statutory sense). (*Waite v Government Communications Headquarters*[3]). Such employees can conveniently be referred to collectively as "the group"(*Hughes v Dept of Health and Social Security*[4]).

(2) Where there is a contractual retirement age applicable to all or nearly all the employees in the group, there is a presumption that the contractual retiring age is the normal retiring age for the group (*Waite*).

(3) The presumption can be rebutted by evidence that there is in practice some higher age at which employees in the group are regularly retired and which they have reasonably come to regard as their normal retiring age (ibid).

(4) "Normal" in this context is not a synonym for "usual"and is not to be determined by a purely statistical approach (*Waite*).

(5) The question to be asked by the industrial tribunal is: what, at the effective date of termination of the applicant's employment and on the basis of the facts then known, was the age which employees of all ages in the group could reasonably regard as their normal retiring age? (*Brooks v British Telecommunications Plc*[5]).

(6) That some employees could reasonably expect to retire at different ages for special reasons does not entail that they and their group do not have a normal retiring age (*Waite*).

(7) The "position"of the applicant does not include the previous history of his employment (*Hughes*) nor his age (*Brooks*), but the fact that employees have different retirement ages as terms of their contracts of employment may be taken into account in determining whether the employees are in the same "position"(*Barber v Thames Television Plc*[6]).

(8) The test of reasonable expectation is an objective one, not dependent on what the applicant or any other individual in the group actually thought (*Hughes*).

(9) A normal retiring age is an aspect of an employer's employment policy which, once promulgated to the employees

concerned, will take effect as their normal retiring age unless it is a sham or has been abandoned (*Hughes*) or is never implemented (*Brooks*).

(10) If the contractual retiring age has been abandoned and employees retire at a variety of higher ages, there will be no normal retiring age and the statutory alternative of 65 will apply (*Waite*).'

In brief, the test was summarised by Lord Fraser in *Waite*[7] as follows: 'the proper test is . . . to ascertain what would be the reasonable expectation or understanding of the employees holding that position at the relevant time.'

The Regulations, however, introduce a statutory definition of normal retirement age[8], namely

> 'in relation to an employee, means the age at which employees in the employer's undertaking who hold, or have held, the same kind of position as the employee are normally required to retire'.

It seems likely that courts and tribunals will interpret this consistently with the body of case law that has developed on the meaning of 'normal retirement age' under the ERA 1996 before the introduction of the statutory definition (see above).

Employers should be alert to not inadvertently changing their normal retirement age or introducing one when they did not intend to do so.

Example:

ABC Ltd announces that its employees' retirement age will be 65. They introduce new employment contracts saying this. ABC wishes to embrace the new duty to consider procedure. All the employees who reach 65 request to stay on. ABC considers these requests and decides that as the employees all continue to have much to offer the company, they extend their employment for two years but decide, as a matter of policy, not to grant requests to stay beyond this two year extension. This means that employees are working till their 67th birthday. Billy approaches his 65th birthday. ABC Ltd recognises that it is overstaffed in Billy's department and so declines his request. As Billy's contractual retirement age is 65, ABC believes it is on safe ground in retiring him at this age. However, as the bulk of those reaching 65 have, in practice, been allowed to work on until their 67th birthday, this has become the age at which employee's holding 'the same kind of position as the employee are normally required to retire' and, hence, their normal retirement age. Billy's dismissal cannot, therefore, be by reason of retirement.

In this example, if ABC Ltd had granted all or the bulk of the requests to stay on, but ensured that the employees did not stay on until the same age then there would not have been an age at which the employees are normally required to retire and it would have been safe to retire Billy at 65.

---

1 See s 98ZE(2) introduced by para 23 of Sch 8 to the Regulations.
2 [1994] IRLR 580 at 583.
3 [1983] 2All ER 1013.
4 [1984] ICR 557.
5 [1992] ICR 414.
6 [1992] ICR 661.
7 [1983] 2All ER 1013 at 773 See p [724C].
8 s 98ZH of the ERA 1996 introduced by para 23 of Sch 8 to the Regulations.

12.8 Retirement age – options for employer

12.8.1 Retirement age under 65

Any employer that wishes to maintain a retirement age below 65 will have to objectively justify this. It will, therefore, have to point to a legitimate aim which is being addressed by this lower retirement age and also that the pre-65 retirement age is a proportionate means of achieving this aim.

It will be difficult for an employer to satisfy this test and very few employers have decided to attempt to do so.

(a) Legitimate aims

Possible legitimate aims might include:[1]

- Business/workforce planning;
- integrity of pensions or other employee benefit schemes;
- health and safety;
- legal or regulatory constraints;
- promoting diversity; and
- preserving employees' dignity.

The aims of business/workforce planning, health and safety, legal or regulatory constraints and promotion of diversity are covered in **Chapter 5**.[2]

1 **Chapter 4**, **4.7.5**.
2 **Chapter 5**, **5.3.3 (g)**, **(i)** and **(j)**.

(i) Integrity of pensions or other employee benefits

This aim is referred to in several sources:

- it is a supplemental aim on which British Airways relies on *Cross v British Airways*[1];
- the Government relies on it in support of the default retirement age[2]; and
- it has been used to support retirement ages under Canadian age discrimination laws.[3]

1 [2005] IRLR 423; **Chapter 4, 4.7.5(a)**.
2 See **12.5**.
3 *McKinney v University of Guelph* [1990] 3 CSR 229; see **12.8.1 (c)**; Connolly and Gough, 'Age Discrimination, The Default Retirement Age and Occupational Pensions: Experiences from Canada and Predictions for Britain' (2007) 1 Web JCLI.

(ii) Preserving Employees' Dignity

This is a much more contentious aim. It is referred to in the seminal Canadian Supreme Court decision on retirement ages[1] and in the *Rutherford* decision.[2] It does, however, appear to be an aim which is tainted by discriminatory prejudices, namely that if the employer was unable to retire the employee at the retirement age it would have to go through a performance review process, because by that age his performance is likely to be declining.

1 *McKinney* [1990] 3 CSR 229; see **12.8.1 (c)**.
2 See **12.4**.

(b) Professions with retirement ages under 65

A few sectors have retained retirement ages under 65.

(i) Police

The Home Office and Association of Chief Police Officers (ACPO) have set a retirement age of 60 for police between the ranks of constable and chief inspector. For higher ranks the retirement age is 65.

The Home Office/ACPO recognise that these retirement ages need to be objectively justified. To this end, they have published their justification.[1] This lists the legitimate aims behind the 60 retirement age as:

- providing operational resilience;
- ensuring public safety and assurance;
- ensuring health, welfare and safety; and

- encouraging diversity in the service through recruitment and retention.

The aims behind the 65 retirement age are listed as:

- facilitation of workforce planning and modernisation; and
- encouraging diversity in the service through recruitment and retention.

The justification note gives little explanation of why the ages are regarded as proportionate means of achieving these aims and it can only be a matter of time before they are challenged. It remains to be seen whether or not the nonapplication of the default retirement age to the police makes it easier to justify these ages. In other words, as the police authorities could not have used 65 safely as the retirement age for all its officers, will they be given more leeway in setting their own retirement age?

(ii) Pilots

The Civil Aviation Authority (CAA) has maintained a maximum age of 60 for solo pilots.[2] The CAA believes it can justify this limit with reference to the aim of health and safety. This has been challenged by Mr Evans who has commenced employment tribunal proceedings against the CAA arguing that its age limit is not proportionate as he has to undergo a medical check-up every six months and other countries such as Australia and New Zealand allow solo pilots to fly beyond 60. It is debatable whether terminating a solo pilot's employment at age 60 represents retirement or a dismissal justified by the aim of complying with a statutory requirement.[3] Unhelpfully, the procedures which the employer must follow will differ depending on the exceptions relied on.

The position of commercial pilots has been complicated by national rules in a few remaining countries (France, the United States, Columbia and Pakistan) restricting the overflying of their air space by captains of planes over 60. These are likely to be abolished before long and the retirement age of commercial pilots who do not fly solo is moving to 65.

In the United States there are pressures to increase the age limit which now only applies to US pilots and not overseas pilots. Joy Taylor at Stanford University recently published research that showed that declining physiological competence was more than compensated by the additional experience of older pilots. The US Federal Aviation Authority has indicated that the age 60 rule will be abolished but, at the time of writing, had not yet set a date for this.

(iii) Football referees

The retirement age for league football referees in the United Kingdom is currently 45.[4] Football referees' retirement ages have been the subject of age discrimination claims in Belgium and the Netherlands. In both cases, the retirement ages were held to be unlawful.[5]

1 'Compulsory Retirement Ages – Objective Justification' Home Office, December 2006.
2 **Chapter 5, 5.3.3(k); Chapter 10, 10.2.2.**
3 Agebusters News, 11 April 2007.
4 The FA has decided to remove age from decisions on promotion and renewal of referees up to Level 2.
5 **Chapter 9, 9.5.**

(c) Overseas laws

Other countries have also seen challenges to mandatory retirement ages. Perhaps the most celebrated of all cases on the point is the Canadian Supreme Court decision of *McKinney*.[1]

The majority of the Supreme Court held that the mandatory retirement age of 65 within the University was justified by the University's objectives of:

- enhancing the University's capacity to seek and maintain excellence by permitting flexibility in resource allocation and faculty renewal; and
- preserving academic freedom and the collegial form of association by minimizing intrusive modes of performance appraisal.

The Supreme Court continued that:

> 'Mandatory retirement . . . supports the tenure system by obviating the need for elaborate evaluation schemes, and ensures continuing faculty renewal by making spaces available in a closed system for new and younger faculty members.'

1 (1990) 13 CHRR D/171 (SCC).

12.8.2 Retirement age at 65

Most employers are likely to set their retirement age at 65.

The benefits of this approach include:

- It is the youngest age at which employers can safely compulsorily retire employees.

- It does not prevent the employer from retaining some or even all employees beyond this age.

The disadvantages include:

- The employer might lose talented experienced staff who prepare to stop work at 65.
- The employer might consider the potential issues in retaining staff beyond this age too risky or complex.
- It seems likely that the employer will need to alter this in 2011 when the default age comes up for review.

12.8.3 Retirement age above 65

Employers are free to set a normal retirement age higher than 65. In these cases, the higher retirement age is normally the age at which employees stop working with few employees retained beyond this age. This has proved rare but one example is Nationwide which has set a retirement age at 75.

The advantages over a retirement age of 65, particularly where requests to stay on are often granted, include:

- It removes much of the ill-will which can result from employees being selectively retained beyond a retirement age of 65.
- Less management time is taken up with requests to remain in employment after the age of 65.
- It creates certainty in the minds of employer and employee.
- Insured benefit and pensions schemes can be structured accordingly.
- It paints the employer in a positive and progressive light in its approach towards age diversity.
- It is less likely that it will need changing after the government's review in 2011.

The major disadvantage is that the employee cannot retire employees before this higher retirement age and so will be vulnerable to unfair dismissal (and possible age discrimination) claims from employees dismissed for health, capability or redundancy reasons.

The employee may also find it difficult or costly to extend insured benefits and defined benefit pension schemes to employees aged over 65.

12.8.4 No normal retirement age

More employers are abolishing retirement ages altogether than fixing a retirement age over 65. Examples include some government departments and many of the organisations which have been at the forefront of the age diversity agenda including B&Q, BT, Co-Operative, HBOS, Marks & Spencer and Sainsbury's.

There are two different approaches here. First, employers might abandon the use of retirement ages altogether. Employees will, therefore, continue in employment until they choose to retire or their employment is terminated for another reason.

Secondly, as employers with no set retirement age can retire employees at any age from 65, other employers without a retirement age will take advantage of this, retiring employees selectively from 65.

The advantage with this, over a retirement age above 65, is that the employer can still retire employees from 65. It is also the most robust approach as it will not need amending after the government's review in 2011. This approach also enables the employer to retain talented and experienced employees for as long as they can and wish to contribute. Even the employer with a retirement age of 70 will lose capable staff with much to contribute.

Examples of celebrated persons working very effectively beyond the age of 70 include, at the time of writing:

Jack Nicholson – age 70

Bobby Robson – was still managing Newcastle United at 71

Sepp Blatter – President of FIFA, age 71

The Dalai Lama – age 72

Judi Dench – age 73

Jacques Chirac – recently came to the end of his Presidency of France at age 74

Joan Collins – age 74

John McCain – US presidential candidate, age 75

Rupert Murdoch – age 76

Nelson Mandela – became President of South Africa at age 76

The Pope – age 80

The Queen – age 81

David Attenborough – age 81

Tony Benn – age 82

Robin Day – age 84

Humphrey Lyttelton – jazz musician, age 86

The disadvantages depend on which of the two approaches the employer adopts. The employer who selectively retires employees of age 65 has the potential to create uncertainty and ill-will. The employer who does not exercise any right to retire will face the same challenges as those listed above for employers with a retirement age higher than 65. In addition, without a long stop date, the financial exposure from successful discrimination claims from the workforce could be increased. Claimants might claim that they were planning to work till age 75 or older and should be compensated on lost earnings to such age.

12.8.5 Retirement age for nonemployees

As mentioned above[1], the default retirement age exception does not apply to nonemployees.[2]

'Employers' of these categories of workers must decide on what approach to take for retirement ages. The self-employed, contract and agency workers are rarely employed long-term (and if they were, their status as nonemployees would probably be questionable).

1 See **12.6.2**.
2 See eg self-employed, contract or agency workers, partners, office holders and barristers.

(a) Partners

The introduction of the Regulations without any default retirement age exception for partnership caused considerable consternation. Many wrongly assumed that it was an oversight.

Partnerships have, therefore, been left to justify their retirement age or remove it. Some have responded to the Regulations by raising the age.

Retirement

Partnerships which retain a retirement age should be aware of the prospect of a legal challenge and should think through their justification. Merely assuming that they will be able to rely on retirement at 65, like other organisations, will be very risky. The government did not extend the default age to partnerships as it did not think it would be able to justify doing so, particularly by reference to its stated aims for justifying retirement ages for employment.[1]

The most promising aim for partnerships is likely to be 'workplace planning'.[2] However, showing that the need for a retirement age is a proportionate means of achieving this aim will often be tricky. At least in professional partnerships, highly paid partners rarely work through to retirement age. In such a case, it will be very difficult to justify a set retirement age. Also, many partnerships plan to grow meaning that it is not necessary to force out departing partners to make way for new ones. Of course, each case will turn on its own facts.

In practice, with many partnerships, the need to retire partners is a reflection of their remuneration structure. With 'lockstep',[3] after a set number of years partners reach the top of lockstep (plateau). As pay is set on the basis of service as a partner and not performance, the plateau partners are paid disproportionately highly in comparison to their performance. There is, therefore, pressure after a time from other partners for these 'overpaid' partners to make way.

At first sight, it would seem unlikely that this pay structure would satisfy the justification test. It remains unclear to what extent tribunals will be prepared to take into account the difficulties in changing long-standard arrangements in considering their justification. Of course, partnerships are unlike companies and either unanimity or a set majority of partners will be required to agree to changes.[4]

In practice, many partnerships are adopting a wait and see approach to retirement age. They are hoping that others will be the first to be challenged before the approach of courts and tribunals is clarified.

1 See **12.5**.
2 **Chapter 4, 4.7.5**; **Chapter 5, 5.3.3(g)**; **12.8.1**.
3 **Chapter 6, 6.4.4(a)**.
4 **Chapter 4, 4.7.7**; *Broadley* (1991) 15 CHRR D/408.

(b) Directors

Executive directors have two relationships with the company:

(i) employment; and
(ii) as the holder of the office of director.

Nonexecutive directors only hold the office of director without being employees.

Companies do need to consider their approach to retirement ages for people who hold the office of director. Companies' with retirement ages for directors will need to justify these. It is difficult to see what aim a company might rely on to justify a retirement age for its directors. Until 6 April 2007, company law provided that no person over age 70 could be appointed a director of a public company or a subsidiary of a public company and that any director had to vacate their office at the AGM following their 70th birthday unless otherwise approved by general meeting of the shareholders.[1] This rule has now been repealed.

1 s 293 of the Companies Act 1985.

12.9 Duty to consider procedure

12.9.1 Overview

As mentioned above, in deciding to give in to representations to permit employers to retire employees free from legal claims, the government introduced a duty on employers to consider requests from employees to work beyond retirement. This duty is set out in Sch 6 to the Regulations.

As mentioned above, the duty arises if the employer wishes to show that the dismissal satisfies the definition of retirement. This is necessary if the employer wishes to establish both:

(a) a fair dismissal by reason of retirement (to avoid a claim of unfair dismissal); and

(b) that the dismissal comes within the retirement exception within the Regulations (to avoid an age discrimination claim).

The procedure is summarised in the flow charts set out in subsequent text (cross refer).

In summary:

Step 1 – the employer must inform the employee in writing at least six months but no more than 12 months before the intended retirement date:

(a) the date on which the employer intends the employee to retire; and

(b) the employee's right to request to stay on.

Fair Retirement Flowcharts

NRA = normal retirement age

IRD = intended retirement date

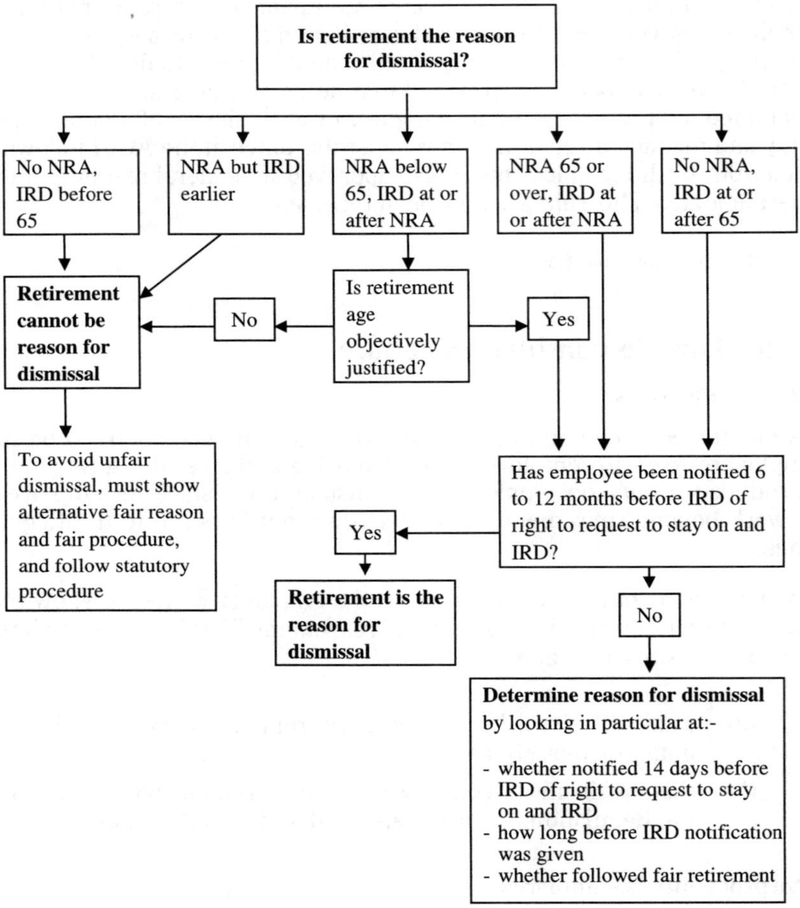

Step 2 – if the employee wants to stay on, he must make his request not to retire, in writing not more than six months but not less than three months before the retirement date. The request must state:

(a) that it is made under para 5 of Sch 6 to the Regulations; and

(b) whether the employee wishes his employment to continue:

(i) indefinitely;

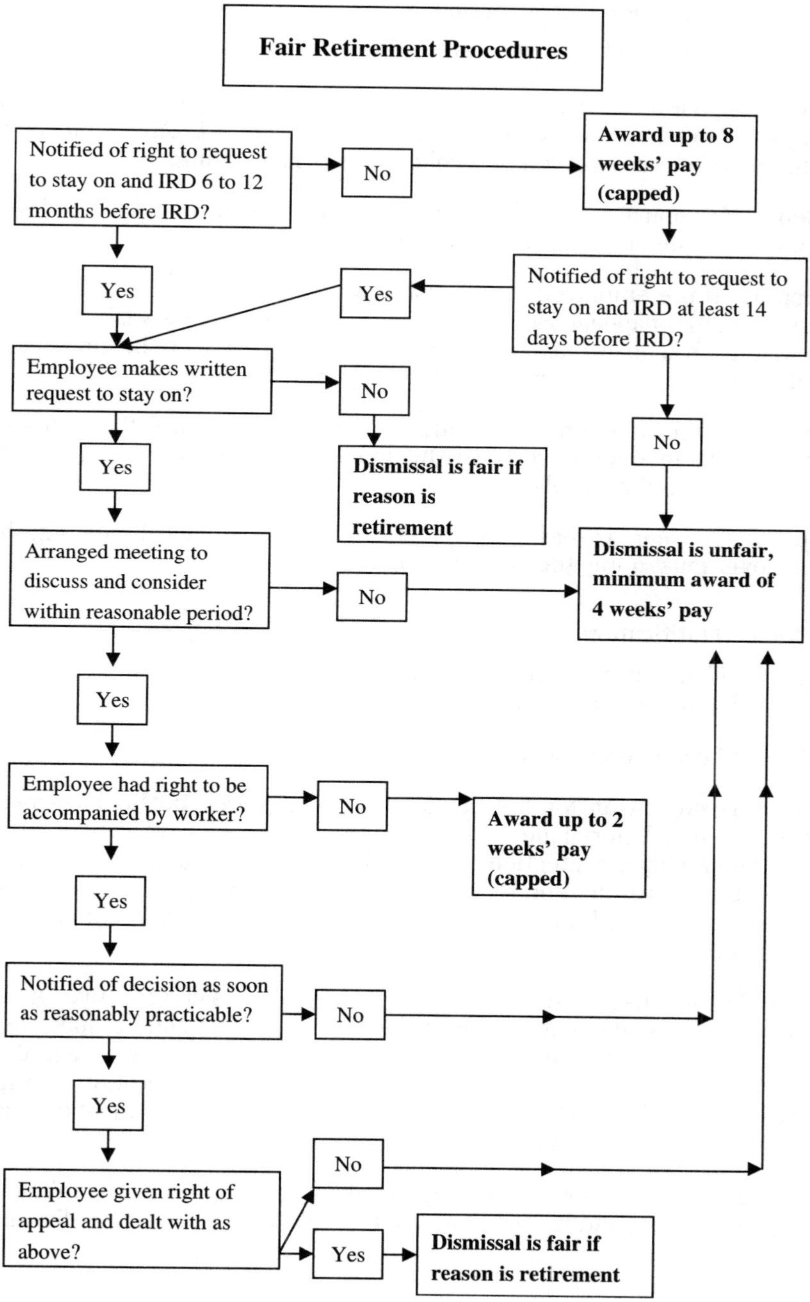
Fair Retirement Procedures
Notified of right to request to stay on and IRD 6 to 12 months before IRD?
No
Award up to 8 weeks' pay (capped)
Yes
Notified of right to request to stay on and IRD at least 14 days before IRD?
Yes
Employee makes written request to stay on?
No
Dismissal is fair if reason is retirement
Yes
No
Arranged meeting to discuss and consider within reasonable period?
No
Dismissal is unfair, minimum award of 4 weeks' pay
Yes
Employee had right to be accompanied by worker?
No
Award up to 2 weeks' pay (capped)
Yes
Notified of decision as soon as reasonably practicable?
No
Yes
Employee given right of appeal and dealt with as above?
No
Yes
Dismissal is fair if reason is retirement

(ii) for a stated period; or

(iii) until a stated date.

Step 3 – Within a reasonable period after receiving the request, the employer must hold a meeting to consider the request. The employee is entitled to be accompanied by a colleague to this meeting.

Step 4 – As soon as reasonably practicable after the meeting, the employer must notify the employee of its decision.

Step 5 – If the employee is dissatisfied with the employer's decision he has the right of appeal. He must notify the employer of his wish to appeal in writing as soon as reasonably practicable after receiving the employer's notice and must set out his grounds of appeal.

Step 6 – Within a reasonable period after receiving the appeal, the employer must hold a meeting to consider the appeal. The employee has a right to be accompanied by a colleague.

Step 7 – As soon as reasonably practicable after the appeal meeting, the employer must notify the employee of the outcome.

12.9.2 Notification

The detailed provisions governing the notification are set out in paras 2–4 of Sch 6 to the Regulations.

The notification must be dated.

There is no reason for the employer and employee not to have been in discussion beforehand about both the employee's retirement plans and the employer's intentions before giving the notification. Indeed, this will often represent good industrial relations practice. The employer needs to be clear, however, what constitutes the notification under this procedure.

The Regulations make clear that the duty applies irrespective of the term of the employment contract regarding retirement and irrespective of any other notification given by the employer to the employee regarding his retirement.[1] The interrelationship between this notification and the employer's obligation to give notice to terminate the employment contract is considered in the subsequent text.[2]

Of course, if the employer is happy to allow the employee to continue in employment beyond his retirement date then the employer can dispense with all or part of the procedure provided the employee's wish is not to remain for a longer period than the employer is prepared to agree to.

1 See para 2(2) of Sch 6 to the Regulations.
2 See **12.11.2**.

12.9.3 Employee's request

The detailed provisions governing the request are set out in para 5 of Sch 6 to the Regulations.

If the employer has not complied with its duty to inform the employee of his intended retirement date at least six months beforehand the employee can, nonetheless, still submit a request to stay on if he believes the employer intends to require him to retire. In this case the employee must state the date on which he believes the employer will require him to retire in his request.

If the employer fails to notify the employee at least six months before the retirement date and either subsequently notifies the employee or the employee elects, nonetheless, to submit a request, the employee's deadline for submitting the request is the intended date of retirement.

Whilst there is nothing to prevent the employee requesting to change the terms of his employment by, for example, changing his duties or reducing his hours of work, the employer is under no duty to agree to or, indeed, even consider the request provided, of course, the employee's age is not the reason for refusing the request if the employer is otherwise prepared to grant the request to stay on.

An employee may only make one request under this procedure in respect of an intended retirement date.

12.9.4 Meeting

The detailed provisions governing the meeting to consider the request are set out in paras 7 and 9 of Sch 6 to the Regulations.

Meeting is not defined. In today's technological world when employees are often based in different countries from those involved in conducting employment hearings, the issue of what constitutes a meeting can arise. There is no case law on the status of video conference meetings or meetings by conference call. It would seem more likely that a video conference would satisfy the definition than a conference call. However, to be safe, the employer should obtain the employee's agreement to any meeting which is not face to face in the same room.

The employer and employee must take all reasonable steps to attend the meeting. If it is not practicable to hold the meeting within a reasonable period, the employer may consider the request without holding a meeting provided that it considers any representations made by the employee.

12.9.5 Right to be accompanied

The employee has a right to be accompanied by a colleague to the meeting. This right is set out at para 9 of Sch 6. Unlike the right to be accompanied to disciplinary and grievance meetings this right is limited to colleagues and does not extend to trade union officials (unless that trade union official is also a colleague). This reflects the position on flexible working requests.[1]

It is for the employee to request to be accompanied. There is no duty on the employer to advise the employee of his right to be accompanied.

It is for the employee to choose the colleague to accompany him. However, if the time set for the meeting is inconvenient with the employee's colleague, the employee must propose an alternative time within the next seven days from the original time set for the meeting which is convenient with employer, employee and colleague.

The colleague is entitled to time off to attend the meeting and is protected from being subjected to a detriment for carrying out these duties.

At the meeting, the colleague can address the meeting and confer with the employee but is not entitled to answer questions on behalf of the employee.

1 Flexible Working (Procedural Requirements) Regulations 2002, SI 2002/3207, reg 14.

12.9.6 Notification of decision

The detailed provisions governing the notification of the employer's decision are set out in sub-paras 7(6) to (8) of Sch 6 to the Regulations.

The notification must be dated and must merely inform the employee of its decision. The employer can accept the request, reject the specific period requested by the employee but agree to a shorter period or reject the request and require the employee to retire on the intended retirement date. The employer need not give any reasons.

12.9.7 Giving reasons?

The duty to consider procedure was modelled on the right to request flexible working for parents of young children.[1] However, unlike the right to request flexible working, there is no obligation on the employer considering a request to stay on after retirement age to give any reasons.

There has been some debate over whether the safer course of action will, nonetheless, be for employers to give reasons.

The Advisory, Conciliation and Arbitration Service (ACAS) Guidance states:

> 'You are not required to give a reason for your decision as – if you have followed the retirement procedure correctly ... the reason for their dismissal will always be retirement.
>
> However, giving reasons and a more detailed explanation of your retirement policy may enable the employee to leave with dignity and respect and help you maintain good working relationships with other employees. This would be in line with normal good practice recommended by ACAS.'[2]

Employers should not generally be fearful that by giving reasons they might expose themselves to claims that retirement was not the true reason. As mentioned above, provided the employer follows the requisite procedure then the reason for the dismissal will be retirement. This concern of some employers may arise from commentary on the draft regulations published in July 2005 under which the employee could have challenged the reason for dismissal even where the employer had followed the procedure. However, as mentioned above,[3] this provision was removed when the final version of the Regulations was published.

Example:

Alf is denied the right to remain in employment after reaching 65, his retirement age. He does not believe that retirement was the true reason as all of his colleagues in similar situations have had their requests granted. Indeed, the employee has obtained an email from his boss through the HR Director in which his boss states that he thinks Alf's performance has declined and whilst this has not declined sufficiently to justify embarking on a performance management procedure, Alf's 65th birthday in seven months time represents an opportune moment to dismiss him safely. In such circumstances, Alf's boss states, the company could terminate his employment without making a costly severance payment and they could call it 'retirement'. In this case, provided the company follows the procedure set out in the Regulations, the dismissal will be deemed to be by retirement and Alf will not be able to bring either unfair dismissal or age discrimination proceedings.

Nonetheless, there are compelling legal and nonlegal reasons why prudent employers may want to give reasons for rejecting requests to remain in employment.

Whilst it is true that an employee who is dismissed by an employer who follows assiduously the retirement procedure in the Regulations cannot bring unfair dismissal or age discrimination claims, there seems no reason why he cannot pursue other claims, in particular discrimination claims on grounds other than age. Not only does there appear to be nothing in the Regulations preventing this (but see debate on retirement being only reason for dismissal),[4] but if the Regulations did purport to prevent someone from bringing other discrimination claims then this would surely breach the European directives governing those other forms of discrimination.

Example:

An employer only allows women to remain in employment beyond retirement age. A man denied the right to remain in employment could sue for sex discrimination even if the retirement procedure had been followed.

This might seem an unlikely scenario. However, indirect sex or race discrimination claims or disability discrimination claims might be more likely.[5]

Example:

Since the Regulations came into force, Bloggs & Co have had 20 requests to remain from female employees and accepted 16 of them. They have had 18 requests from men and accepted five of them. On the face of it this suggests that Bloggs & Co might have been indirectly discriminatory against the male employees. In order to defeat a sex discrimination claim, it would have to justify its actions. Being able to show why each request was accepted or rejected will help. The employer will be in a better position if it has reliable and contemporaneous evidence of these reasons.

Edith has had poor health over the two years preceding her retirement age. Her employer rejects a request to stay on. The employer follows the retirement procedure but does not give any reason for rejecting the request. Edith is suspicious as many of her contemporaries have had requests granted. There seems no reason why Edith could not pursue a disability discrimination claim in these circumstances. If Edith's health was not a factor in the employer's decision to reject her request, the employer would be in a better position if it had explained this at the time.

Notwithstanding the legal position, it surely makes sense from an industrial relations standpoint to give reasons to the employee who will often be a loyal long-serving member of staff. The employer should not want the relationship to end on such a defensive note. Not giving a reason also makes a mockery of the right of appeal against the rejection of a request.

Example:

Eric applies to remain after his retirement age. The employer rejects his request. Eric asks for the reason. The employer refuses to give one and replies saying he is not obliged to do so. He then asks Eric if he wishes to appeal. Eric says that he does. The employer asks Eric for his grounds of appeal and Eric responds saying he doesn't know as he doesn't know why his employer rejected his request.

The prudent employer who does give reasons, will be better placed if it can say that the reason for refusing the request was that there were no exceptional reasons to grant the request rather than focusing on, say, the rejected employee's failings. In granting requests the employer should then concentrate on the special reasons for saying yes, such as the employee's skills being in short supply or a difficulty in recruiting in that area.

1 'Equality and Diversity: Coming of Age', DTI, July 2005, para 6.3.3.
2 ACAS Guidance. *Age and the workplace: Putting the Employment Equality (Age) Regulations 2006 into practice* (ACAS), p 24.
3 See **12.61**.
4 **Chapter 11**, **11.5.4**.
5 **Chapter 9**, **9.4.1**.

12.9.8 Considering the request

As mentioned above, the employer should have little to fear from giving reasons for the refusal as the employee cannot challenge the employer's reasons unless they demonstrate that the employer has discriminated against the employee on grounds other than age.

The draft regulations originally included an obligation on the employer to consider requests to stay 'in good faith'. Commentators suggested that this would result in claims with employees denied the right to stay on challenging their employers' reasons and arguing that this demonstrated that the request had not been considered in 'good faith' and consequently the procedure had been breached by the employer.

The government clearly accepted theses arguments and in its determination to avoid litigation over retirement removed the duty to consider in good faith.

However, the question remains whether an employee can ever challenge the employer's consideration of his request. Paragraph 6 of Sch 6 to the Regulations states 'An employer to whom a request is made is under a duty to consider the request in accordance with . . . '. Arguably, this gives some scope to the employee to challenge an employer which he believes has not considered the request.

The concept of the employer having a 'duty to consider' a request is not a notion which we are particularly familiar with in employment law. However, there are some comparable concepts, which can give guidance as to how the tribunal might regard an employer's 'duty to consider' a request to continue working as part of the retirement procedures.

Perhaps the most obvious example of an employer having a 'duty to consider' a request arises when an employee makes a flexible working application pursuant to s 80F of the ERA 1996. However, the actual words 'duty to consider' does not appear in Pt VIIIA of the ERA 1996 or in the underlying Regulations.[1] In fact, the obligation on an employer when considering a flexible working request is much stricter than that set out in the Regulations. The ERA 1996, s 80G provides that an employer 'shall only refuse the application because he considers that one or more of the following grounds applies'. Section 80G then goes on to list eight grounds on which an employer can refuse a flexible working request. Regulation 5 of the Flexible Working (Procedural Requirements) Regulations 2002 also provides that where an employer makes the decision to refuse the flexible working application, it must give a notice in writing stating which of the grounds for refusal specified in s 80G it considers to be applicable and giving sufficient information as to why those grounds apply.

In the case of *Commotion v Rutty*,[2] the EAT considered whether the tribunal was entitled to assess objectively the employer's reasons for refusing a flexible working request. The EAT held that, although the tribunal is not entitled to see whether the employer acted fairly or reasonably in putting forward its rejection of the flexible working request, the tribunal is entitled to look at the grounds which the employer asserts were the reasons for refusing to grant the application, and to see whether they were factually correct. With flexible working requests, therefore, the tribunal is entitled to examine the evidence as to the circumstances surrounding the situation to which the application gave rise and enquire into what the effect of granting the application would have been. However, as mentioned above, the employer's obligations in considering a flexible working request are more onerous than in considering a request to stay on. It seems unlikely, therefore, that a tribunal will feel empowered by the Regulations to scrutinise a refusal of an application to stay on in the same way.

At first instance, in *Rutty*, the tribunal concluded that the manner in which the employer had dealt with Ms Rutty's request for flexible working amounted to a breach of the implied duty of trust and confidence allowing her to claim constructive unfair dismissal. However, this issue was not considered further on appeal.

When considering the question of the extent to which a tribunal can assess the employer's grounds for refusing a flexible working request, the EAT particularly emphasised the fact that the flexible working legislation provides a separate right of action if the employer fails to comply with its duty to properly consider their flexible working application, or if the employer's decision is based on incorrect facts. If an employee brings such a claim which is well-founded, the tribunal may make an order for reconsideration of the application and may also make an award of compensation of not more than eight weeks' pay.[3] However, in view of the low cap on compensation that can be recovered for failure to properly consider a flexible working request, most claims that arise as a result of a flexible working application are brought as indirect sex discrimination claims. There is no such separate right of action for failing properly to consider requests to stay on.[4]

Although not specifically referring to a 'duty to consider', an analogous scenario arises when an employer is obliged to consult:

(a) when contemplating dismissing 20 or more employees at one establishment[5]; or

(b) by virtue of the Transfer of Undertakings (Protection of Employment) Regulations 2006 (TUPE).

Regulation 13(7) of TUPE, for example, states that in the course of consultation, the employer should:

'(a) *consider any representations* made by the appropriate representatives; and

(b) reply to those representations and, if he rejects any of those representations, state his reasons.'

The employer must, therefore, 'consider' representations, and more importantly, reply to those representations, stating its reason for any rejection.

It is important to note that both Trade Unions and Labour Relations (Consolidation) Act 1992 and TUPE 2006 provide employees with a right to bring a claim for compensation of up to 13 weeks' pay if the employer fails in its obligations to inform and consult with representatives in relation to the redundancy/relevant transfer. Furthermore, it has been held that in both circumstances, the award should be punitive in nature, thereby imposing a penalty on the employer for failing in their duties.[6]

Returning to the Regulations, it is clear to see that, as compared with other areas of employment law, the 'duty to consider' obligation, contained in the retirement procedures, is a relatively simple obligation for the employer to comply with. The employer must simply convene a meeting to discuss the employee's request, ensure that the employee is offered the opportunity to be accompanied at that meeting, and provide notice of its decision to the employee, stating the employee's right to appeal where it refuses the request, or grants the request but for a shorter period than that proposed by the employee.

Unlike the flexible working application procedures, the employer can reject the employee's request on whatever grounds it wishes. Furthermore, in the Regulations, there is no obligation on the employer to provide written reasons explaining why it has refused the employee's request. Under the flexible working application procedures, an employer must provide a written notice setting out the grounds on which it has refused the request and providing 'sufficient' information as to why it considers those grounds apply. In addition, under TUPE, an employer must state his reasons for rejecting any representations made by the employee representatives during the consultation process. No such comparable provisions have been provided in the Regulations. Indeed, under the Regulations, it would seem to be sufficient simply to provide the employee with a bald written notice stating that their request has been refused and offering them the right to appeal.

There is no statutory obligation on the employer to do any more than comply with the purely procedural obligations as set out in Sch 6.

It is interesting to consider, however, whether the tribunal will take a more active approach in ensuring that, in reality, the employer has genuinely complied with its duty to consider the employee's request not to retire. By analogy with a redundancy scenario, where the tribunal particularly recognised the stressful nature of a redundancy process, and so imposed on the employer an obligation to consult genuinely with affected employees, will the tribunal also recognise the peculiar circumstances of a retirement scenario, where a person, who perhaps has been with an organisation for a considerable length of time, wishes to remain in employment beyond their normal retirement age? One can easily recognise that the very minimal duty to consider as set out in Sch 6, could be deemed to be too perfunctory in such circumstances.

In contrast, however, with other examples of consideration/consultation obligations discussed above, there are no equivalent requirements in the Regulations. Indeed, the employee has no right to know anything at all about the approach that the employer has taken in considering his request. As such, this may prevent the tribunal from feeling able to interfere with the decision of the employer in any way.

There is a possibility that, as in the *Rutty* case, an employee could claim constructive unfair dismissal on the grounds that the manner in which its employer had dealt with their request not to retire amounted to a breach of the implied duty of trust and confidence, entitling him to terminate his employment. However, as set out above, provided that the employer has complied with the basic procedure set out in Sch 6, there is no obligation on the employer to give any details whatsoever as to the manner in which it has considered its request. Accordingly, an employee might, quite legitimately on the part of the employer, have no evidence to demonstrate how the employer went about considering their request. In the event that an employer did reveal that it had considered the request in bad faith, or capriciously, then it is conceivable that the employee would be entitled to claim constructive unfair dismissal.

In such circumstances, presumably, it would however be open to the employer to argue that compensation should be limited as, had it refused to reveal its reasons for refusing the request, or had it considered the request in good faith and still decided to reject the request not to retire, then the employee's loss of earnings will be limited as until the originally intended date of retirement.

Some employers may be tempted to have a blanket policy to reject all requests. Would an employer who merely applied this policy every time be in breach of its duty to consider each employee's risk? Might the employee be able to claim constructive dismissal? Would he have to resign before the intended date of retirement?

At the very least, the prudent employer will ask (and keep a record of having asked) itself the question: 'Is there any reason in this case for me to depart from our normal policy of not permitting any employee to remain beyond retirement?'

1 Flexible Working (Procedural Requirements) Regulations 2002, SI 2002/3207; Flexible Working (Eligibility, Complaints and Remedies) Regulations 2002, SI 2002/3236.
2 [2006] IRLR 171.

3 Sees 80I of the ERA 1996; reg 7 of the Flexible Working (Eligibility, Complaints and Remedies) Regulations 2002.
4 See **12.9.9**.
5 Section 188 of the Trade Union and Labour Relations (Consolidation) Act 1992.
6 *GMB v Susie Radin Ltd* [2004] 2 EWCA Civ 180; *Sweetin v Coral Racing* [2006] IRLR 252.

12.9.9 Automatic extension of employment

If the retirement procedure remains uncompleted in that the employer has yet to give the employee notice of his decision following a meeting to consider a request to stay on, then the employee's employment shall continue automatically until the employer notifies the employee of his decision whereupon it shall terminate on the following day.[1]

The employment is not continued pending the outcome of any appeal.

The rules were also different during the transitional period.[2]

1 See para 10 of Sch 6 to the Regulations.
2 See **12.9.11**.

12.9.10 Consequences of breaching procedure

The consequence for the employer of breaching the procedure depends on the nature of the breach.

(a) Failure to give notification of intended retirement date between 12 and 6 months' notice of intended retirement but at least 14 days' notification given

In this case, an award of no more than eight weeks' capped pay[1] shall be made by an employment tribunal.

Also, the reason for dismissal is not deemed to be retirement (though the employer might still be able to show that the reason was retirement.[2])

1 To 1 February 2008 = £310 per week.
2 See **12.6.1(a)**.

(b) Right to be accompanied

If the employer denies the employee the right to be accompanied at the meeting at which his request or appeal is considered, an award of no more than two weeks' capped pay shall be made by an employment tribunal.

(c) Any other breach of the procedure

If the employer breaches the duty to consider requests to stay on procedure in any other way, including failing to give 14 days' notification of the intended retirement date, the dismissal will be automatically unfair.

12.9.11 Transitional Period

Transitional procedures set out in Sch 7 to the Regulations apply where the retirement date fell before 1 April 2007.

Schedule 7 covers four different scenarios:

(a) Notice of dismissal was given before 1 October 2006 and was at least four weeks in length (or the contractual notice if this was less than four weeks)

As soon as practicable after 1 October the employer must have notified the employee of his right to request to stay on.

(b) Notice of dismissal was given before 1 October 2006 and was less than four weeks in length (or less than contractual notice if this was shorter than four weeks)

The employer must have notified the employee of his right to request to stay on by the intended retirement date.

(c) Notice of dismissal was given on or after 1 October 2006 and was at least the length of the employee's contractual notice

The employer must have notified the employee of his right to request to stay on before or at the time of giving notice.

(d) Notice of dismissal was given on or after 1 October 2006 and is less than the employee's contractual notice

The employer must have notified the employee of his right to stay on by the intended retirement date.

In each case, the employee must have submitted his request four weeks before the intended retirement date or, if that was not reasonably practicable, as soon as reasonably practicable (although not more than four weeks after the termination). The employee cannot have made his request before having received the employer's notification.

Under the transitional provisions, but unlike the position subsequently, if the process was not completed by the intended retirement date, the process would have continued but the employment would have terminated.

12.10 Extending employment beyond retirement

If the employer is minded to allow the employee to work beyond retirement, it is necessary to consider:

- How long should this be for?
- What terms should be offered?

12.10.1 Duration of extension

The employer can extend the employment for a fixed period or to a set date or indefinitely. In each case, if the employment extends for longer than six months from the original intended date of retirement then the retirement procedure will need to be followed again.[1]

If the employment is extended for a fixed period, the employer is still free to dismiss the employee by reason of retirement before the expiry of the fixed period provided he goes through the retirement procedure. The major benefit of agreeing a fixed period is from an employee relations perspective rather than a legal one. It creates an expectation in the mind of the employee for which he can plan.

Employers should, however, be careful not inadvertently to change their normal retirement age by allowing a high number of employees to stay on to an age above their normal retirement age.[2]

1 See para 3(2)(a) of Sch 6 to the Regulations.
2 See **12.7**.

12.10.2 Terms of extension

There are no exceptions within the Regulations entitling employers to treat differently employees working beyond retirement age from those before retirement age. The exception regarding the recruitment of persons within six months of or over the employer's normal retirement age[1] only applies to:

- the arrangements made for the purpose of deciding to whom employment should be offered; or
- refusing to offer or deliberately not offering employment.

It does not apply to claims arising from the terms on which the employer offers a person employment.[2]

If an employer wishes, therefore, to employ a person working beyond retirement they must be able to objectively justify any different treatment. This is considered in more detail in **Chapter 6**.

Particular issues facing employers in these circumstances include:

- insured benefits such as medical cover, income protection, life assurance or critical illness cover[3]; and
- pensions.[4]

Before the introduction of the Regulations, employers would commonly re-engage retirees as self-employed consultants. The Regulations challenge this practice. If the employer has followed the retirement procedure, the individual in question cannot challenge a refusal to continue to employ him beyond retirement.

However, the individual might have claims in the following circumstance:

- he is offered part-time employment only;
- he is only offered an engagement on a self-employed basis;
- he is only offered a less senior position;
- he is not offered the same benefit package he enjoyed before retirement.

He could also bring these claims if he accepted an offer on one of the above bases, assuming that the offer of full-time employment in the same position was not open to him.

It is not straightforward to see the employer's legitimate aim in offering lesser terms to the post-retirement employee. The employer might be able to rely on the aim of the vocational integration of older workers – without being able to discriminate he would not have retained the employee post-retirement. This is not, however, a wholly attractive argument.

This will probably result in employers rejecting altogether requests to stay on beyond retirement rather than offering atypical working arrangements. This must be an unattractive unforeseen consequence of the Regulations.

Employers have also been looking at ways of retaining employees beyond retirement date without these risks. Employees will cooperate as otherwise they will not be allowed to remain. Nonetheless, it is not possible for an employee to agree to be discriminated against. Some employers are known to have entered into compromise agreements with employees being retained beyond retirement in which agreement they waive claims arising out of the terms on which they are retained. This will probably not be effective, as a compromise agreement cannot settle claims that have not yet arisen.[5] It is not as if women could be employed on less pay than men doing the same work as long as they enter into a compromise agreement first.

One risk for employers is that a retired employee applies to return to work on a self-employed basis. The exception for applicants close to or above an employer's retirement age only applies to employees and not the self-employed. There would be nothing, therefore, to prevent the applicant turned down for self-employment from suing for age discrimination. In most cases, the employer will be able to show that the reason was not age but that the job could not be done on a self-employed basis. However, the risks would increase for a company which engages many self-employed workers.

1 **Chapter 5, 5.3.2(c).**
2 Claims under reg 7(1)(b) as opposed to 7(1)(a) or (c).
3 **Chapter 6, 6.5.3.**
4 **Chapter 8, 8.6.1.**
5 *Lunt v Merseyside* [1999] IRLR 458.

12.11 Contractual issues

12.11.1 Changing retirement ages

With the coming into force of the Regulations, many employers reviewed their approach to retirement. Those with retirement ages under 65 were generally forced to increase them. Going forward, employers may decide that their current approach to retirement does not meet their organisation's needs. In particular, once the outcome of the government to its review of the default retirement age promised for 2011 becomes clear,[1] employers with a retirement age of 65 may be forced to review their policy once more.

In many cases, these retirement ages are contained in the employers' contracts of employment. Employers cannot unilaterally change these contractual terms. In practice, therefore, they have two options:

(i) seek agreement of all staff; or

(ii) inform staff that they can work on to the new retirement age without seeking all staff's agreement.

1 See **12.4**.

(a) Seek agreement

An employer who takes this option will introduce new contracts with the revised retirement date but with all other terms unchanged.

The downside with this option, particularly in larger organisations, will normally be ensuring all employees accept the new terms. This exercise will require all employees to confirm their agreement in writing. Employers cannot safely assume that having distributed the new contracts they will be deemed to have been accepted by any staff who have not objected to the change.[1]

The employer will be faced with the apathy of many employees who will not return their revised contracts and the suspicion of others who might confuse the increase in the retirement age with an obligation to work to a greater age.

Agreements will be particularly important and more difficult to obtain if employment terms change. An employer might decide that the increased cost of some benefits mean that it cannot afford to provide these beyond the old retirement age and is justified in doing so.[2] Employers with occupational pension schemes will need to decide whether to increase their pension age to match the new retirement. If they do and those who retire before the new pension age but at or after the old one suffer a discounted pension, employers might expect resistance form the workforce or their representatives. Employers who do not change their pension age will need to consider counting the additional service towards the employee's pension entitlement.[3]

Of course, a discriminatory term in a contract cannot be saved because an employer might have agreed to it. One cannot agree to be discriminated against.[4]

1 *Jones v Associated Tunnelling Co Ltd* [1981] IRLR 477; *Solectron Scotland Ltd v Roper* [2004] IRLR 4.
2 **Chapter 6, 6.5.3**.
3 **Chapter 8 8.9**.
4 See para 1 of Sch 5; **Chapter 14, 14.9.2**.

(b) Informing staff of change

An employer who takes this option will advise employees that they are free to work till the new retirement age (usually 65).

The advantage with this option is that the employer does not require any action from its employees. The downside, however, is that the contracts of employment will expire at the old retirement age and the employees will continue beyond that age without a written contract. In most cases this will have no practical impact as the parties will be considered to continue on the old terms.

An employer might find an employee arguing, say, that post-termination covenants in their old contract should not be implied into the contract which governs the relationship past the old retirement age. The employer will also have to give contractual notice to terminate at the new retirement age.[1]

A prudent employer will require employees working beyond the new retirement to enter into new contracts. This will, however, require considerable administrative resources.

1 See **12.11.2**.

12.11.2 Giving notice of termination

The notification of the intended retirement date is in accordance with the duty to consider procedure.[1]

Where an employee is employed under a contract of employment with a contractual retirement age, the employment is effectively employed on a very long fixed-term and no contractual notice is required to terminate the employment – the employment will expire on the retirement date. However, if notice has to be given, it must be given separately from notification (though it can be given at the same time).

Employers should be alert to cases where the retirement age has been raised but the contract of employment still refers to the old retirement age. Contractual notice should be given in this case.[2]

There is, however, no reason why an employer need await the outcome of any request to stay on procedure before giving any contractual notice to which the employee may be entitled.

1 See **12.9.2**.
2 See **12.11.1(b)**.

12.11.3 Pre-retirement wind down

Some employers allow employees approaching retirement to wind down in preparation for retirement. The employer's intentions are laudable as it enables the employee gradually to acclimatise to life post-work. However, such schemes are fraught with age discrimination issues.

In some schemes the reduction in working hours is accompanied by a reduction in pay. In others, however, the reduction does not affect pay.

Also, some schemes are only available to employees approaching their normal retirement age. Others are available to those retiring early. Many schemes require employees to have qualifying periods of employment.

Example:

Fizzo Ltd's retirement age is 65. It allows employees with at least two years' service to reduce their hours after their 64th birthday by up to 50 per cent with a consequential pay reduction.

This benefit clearly discriminates directly on grounds of age as employees under 64 do not have an absolute right to reduce their hours. Fizzo could seek to justify it by reference to the welfare of its employees. However, it might be open to challenge by a younger employee planning to retire early who would not be eligible to cut their hours under Fizzo's scheme.

The two-year qualifying period should be lawful. It would probably come within the exception for provision of certain benefits based on length of service[1] assuming it was not considered 'a benefit awarded to a worker by virtue of his ceasing to work for' Fizzo and taken outside the exception.[2] Even then, the service-related qualifying period is likely to be objectively justified.

Paxxo Ltd, Fizzo's major competitor, is more generous. It also has a retirement age of 65. Under its scheme all employees over 55 are eligible to reduce their hours in the year before retirement including those employees planning to retire early. Paxxo also allows the employee to remain on full pay.

Paxxo's scheme also directly discriminates on grounds of age as it is not available to those under 55 who are planning to retire. Paxxo also has the challenge of defining retirement. It does not want those benefiting from its scheme leaving and moving to Fizzo.[3] This is why it limited the scheme to those over 55. However, it again will be vulnerable to a challenge from a 54-year-old who wants to benefit from the scheme before his planned early retirement.

Paxxo will also be more vulnerable in practice to a claim. Those ineligible under Fizzo's scheme have not lost out financially and are likely to have limited claims for compensation. Fizzo is more exposed. It could face claims from departing employees arguing that they were paid less per hour than those over 55 who had reduced hours but unreduced pay.

1 See **Chapter 6, 6.7.5**.
2 See reg 32(7).
3 See reg 32; **Chapter 6, 6.3**.

These issues have been explored in two Dutch age discrimination cases.[1]

In the first case a policy of allowing employees aged over 60 to work reduced hours was held to be unjustifiable direct age discrimination. The Dutch Equal Treatment Commission took into account that few had taken up the entitlement as pointing towards it not meeting a real need of the employer.

In the second case, a policy of allowing employees aged over 57 with at least 10 years' service to work reduced hours and receive half pay for the lost hours was held to be unlawful.

However, the Canadian case of *Broadley v Steel Co of Canada Inc*[2] held that extended holiday for employees over 61 was justified by the aim of assisting the transition to retirement.

1 Cases CGB 2004–118; CGB – 150.
2 (1991) 15 CHRR D/408.

Chapter 13

Promoting and managing age equality

13.1 Introduction

The promotion and management of age equality involves putting the ideas behind age discrimination law into practice. In essence, this requires an employer to apply equality policies, practices and monitoring in order to ensure that an organisation does not contain inequalities based on age, and encourage under-represented age groups to participate fully in the workforce.

In this chapter, we look at the reasons why the promotion and management of age equality is important to all employers, and various practical strategies and recommendations for achieving best practice, including:

- Age equality policies – why are they important, and what should they contain?
- Action plans as recommended by the Advisory, Conciliation and Arbitration Service (ACAS) – what does this involve?
- Training – how and why should this be done?

- Monitoring – why is this important, and how should it be done in practice?
- Positive action – when is this allowed?

13.2 Why promote age equality?

There are a number of reasons why the promotion of age equality is important to an employer. The main ones are:

- Perhaps most obviously, the organisation will want to ensure that it complies with the law and does not discriminate. This will help to avoid legal claims and the attendant costs, damage to reputation and wasted management time.
- It is also a good practice that may help successful business. It is becoming increasingly common for organisations that put work out for tender to require evidence of compliance with discrimination laws and good equal opportunities practice, particularly in the public sector.
- Effective implementation of age equality at an organisational level may also help an employer to defend potential discrimination claims. First, it may be relevant for the purposes of reversal of the burden of proof. As explained in **Chapter 4**,[1] if an employee can show unfavourable treatment and a difference in age, together with other evidence that there may have been discrimination, the burden can shift to the employer to prove that it did not discriminate. A clear failure to implement or follow good age equality practices may be sufficient additional evidence to shift the burden in this way. Secondly, it may assist with claims that arise when one employee discriminates against another. As explained in more detail in **Chapter 3**,[2] an employer will generally be liable for the discriminatory acts of its employees. However, under reg 25(3), the employer has a defence if it can show that it took such steps as were reasonably practicable to prevent this from occurring. Evidence of good promotion and management of age equality will be a key part of such a defence.
- However, the most positive reason for promotion of age equality is the fact that this will help to ensure diversity within an organisation and the best workforce for the job. Much discrimination is irrational, and means that an employer will miss out on valuable skills and experience due to age-related prejudice and barriers to employment. Effective promotion of age equality will open up the workforce to all ages, so benefiting both business efficiency and society as a whole.

The promotion and management of age equality involves consideration of a number of different areas, which are discussed below. As yet, the Regulations do not have an associated statutory Code of Practice which provides specific guidance for employers. However, the Code of Practice on Racial Equality in Employment[3] (the 'Racial Equality Code') has been updated relatively recently, and much of its general guidance applies equally to age discrimination issues. In addition, ACAS has published a guide for employers on age in the workplace,[4] which includes some practical guidance on policies and strategies for promoting age equality. Both of these publications will be of assistance to employers who are trying to improve their age equality practices. There is also an organisation called the Employer's Forum on Age, which publishes guidance to assist employers in dealing with age equality issues.[5]

1 **Chapter 4, 4.6**.
2 **Chapter 3, 3.4.1**.
3 Commission for Racial Equality: Code of Practice on Racial Equality in Employment (2005).
4 ACAS Guidance, *Age and the Workplace: putting the Employment Equality (Age) Regulations 2006 into practice*.
5 See *www.efa.org.uk*.

13.3 Policies

A key part of an effective age equality strategy is an equal opportunities or diversity policy. Most organisations will already have a policy of this type which covers the other types of prohibited discrimination. It is essential that age discrimination is now specifically included in these policies, as otherwise an employer will risk accusations of not taking age equality as seriously as other types of discrimination.

So, why are policies so important?

- Most obviously, they are a very good way of demonstrating the organisation's ethos and commitment to equal opportunities. This is important in reassuring and encouraging existing staff and applicants, and will also be a key requirement for business partners that expect to see good equal opportunities practices.
- An employer that does not have a policy covering age equality will be particularly vulnerable if accused of age discrimination. As explained in **Chapter 4**,[1] inferences can be very important in discrimination cases, in recognition of the fact that direct evidence of discrimination can be difficult to find. An employer that does not even have a policy dealing with age discrimination may have a very difficult time in defending a claim. This may result in a shift of the burden of proof to the employer, and also make it difficult for the employer to prove that it did not discriminate if the burden of proof has already shifted.

- A policy will also set out the standards that those involved in the organisation are expected to adhere to, so helping to ensure that others do not discriminate and minimising the risk of claims.
- In addition, a clear policy that is implemented across the workforce will help an employer to defend itself in the event that one of its employees commits an unauthorised act of discrimination, by showing that it had taken reasonably practicable steps to prevent this from occurring. In fact, it is probably right to say that an employer that does not have such a policy would be unable to rely on this defence at all, because an equal opportunities policy is such an obvious practical step that can help to prevent discrimination in the workplace.

Both the Racial Equality Code and the ACAS guidance recommend that the introduction of or changes to such policies should be the subject of consultation with the workforce, whether with unions or other types of worker representatives such as a staff forum.[2] This will help to ensure that employees are aware of the content of the policy, and even have some input into its design. Such 'buy-in' from staff and management is important in ensuring that the policy is taken seriously in practice. As discussed later in the text, an equal opportunities policy is of little use if staff are not aware of what it means and not willing to adhere to its requirements.

In outline, an effective equal opportunities policy should cover the following key areas:

- A statement of the organisation's commitment to equal opportunities and opposition to discrimination on all applicable grounds, including age.
- An overview of types of discrimination, so that employees can understand what kind of behaviour is prohibited.
- An explanation of how the policy applies to the organisation's procedures and practices. This should cover the main aspects of the employment relationship – recruitment, terms and conditions, training and development, promotion, appraisals and performance, discipline and grievances, and termination.
- A specific explanation of harassment, including what it is and the fact that the organisation does not tolerate any form of harassment in the workplace. Some organisations choose to implement a separate harassment policy. This is not legally necessary, but it is important that employees understand how harassment may occur, and what can be done about it. This is particularly crucial in an area such as harassment on grounds of age, where 'ageist' jokes and banter may seem more socially acceptable than other forms of discrimination.

- Details of the complaints procedures that can be used if someone feels they have been discriminated against or harassed.
- Details of how the organisation will deal with any breaches of the policy. This is particularly important in showing how seriously the organisation takes its obligations and deterring staff from acting in breach of the policy.

Of course, a policy alone is not enough. It is essential that the policy is put into practice in an effective way. This involves promotion and training throughout the organisation, as discussed subsequently. It is also recommended that a named person is made responsible for overseeing the operation of the policy, in order to ensure that the policy is both seen and treated as being important and kept under review as the law develops.

1 **Chapter 4, 4.6.**
2 Commission for Racial Equality: Code of Practice on Racial Equality in Employment (2005), p 75; ACAS Guidance, *Age and the Workplace: Putting the Employment Equality (Age) Regulations 2006 into practice* (ACAS), p 10.

13.4 Action plans

Once a policy covering age equality is in place, the ACAS Guidance recommends that the employer develops an 'action plan' to put this into practice. Training and communication is a key part of this, as explored subsequently. The action plan should involve a review of various employment policies, to ensure compliance with the age discrimination legislation. In outline, this involves consideration of the following.[1]

1 ACAS Guidance, *Age and the Workplace: Putting the Employment Equality (Age) Regulations 2006 into practice* (ACAS),pp 10–29.

13.4.1 Recruitment

It is important to ensure that decisions about recruitment are based on the skills required to do the job, and not stereotyping based on age. This involves a review of recruitment documentation such as application forms, job descriptions and advertisements, to ensure that it does not contain any inappropriate language or requirements that may disadvantage a particular age group, and is accessible to a sufficiently wide audience of different ages. Shortlisting and interviewing should also be checked for any evidence of age-related bias.

13.4.2 Retention of staff

It is important to ensure that employees (and other types of worker) are treated fairly, regardless of their age. This involves checking for age bias in internal employment policies and procedures, such as performance appraisals, redundancy selection, sickness policies, and disciplinary and grievance policies. Annex 3 of the ACAS Guidance[1] provides a useful checklist for assessing age bias in workplace policies:

- What is the purpose of the policy or practice?
- What is it achieving?
- Do any age groups benefit and, if so, how?
- Do any age groups appear to lose out and, if so, how?
- Using this information, can any difference be justified? If not, should the policy be changed?

1 ACAS Guidance, *Age and the Workplace: Putting the Employment Equality (Age) Regulations 2006 into practice* (ACAS), p 46

13.4.3 Know your employees

Employers should use monitoring to produce an age profile of the workforce, and look for whether any remedial action is necessary, including positive action. Both monitoring and positive action are discussed in the subsequent text.

As this approach towards an action plan makes clear, it is important to take the principles of an age equality policy and apply them throughout the employment relationship, in order to identify and address any inequalities in practice. The remainder of this chapter looks in more detail at specific elements of an age equality strategy.

13.5 Training

Training is a crucial part of any age equality strategy. Policies and procedures alone are of very little use if the workforce has not been trained in why they are important, and how to apply them correctly.

Training is key to making sure that any age equality policy is actually meaningful in practice, and that employees understand and uphold the values of the organisation. This may be important in assisting the employer to defend discrimination claims if they do arise. A failure to train employees in age equality policies may amount to sufficient evidence of discrimination to shift the burden of proof to the employer to disprove discrimination. In addition, training of staff is essential if an employer may wish to rely on the reg 25(3)[1] defence to liability for discriminatory acts of its employees. If an employee has not been trained in age equality and the employer's policies, it will be virtually impossible for an employer to show that it took all reasonably practicable steps to prevent that employee from discriminating against others.

The starting point is that all employees in an organisation should be made aware of the equality policy, and the basics of what this means in practice. In particular, it is recommended that all employees should understand the meaning of the words 'discrimination' and 'harassment', and why these are unlawful and unacceptable.[2] In relation to ageist harassment, specific training for all employees is particularly important. Employees may well not realise that joking comments about age, which are regarded as generally socially acceptable, may actually be unlawful.

The Racial Equality Code suggests that basic equal opportunities training should cover the following[3]

- the law against discrimination and harassment;
- the organisation's equal opportunities policy, why it has been introduced, and how it will be put into practice;
- what is acceptable and unacceptable conduct in the workplace;
- workers' responsibilities under the policy; and
- how prejudice can affect the way an organisation functions, and the effects that discrimination and bias can have on others' chances.

An employer can choose to provide extensive training to all employees. However, it can be appropriate to provide different levels of training to different types of employee, with a focus on managers, as these are the employees with most scope to make potentially discriminatory decisions. The ACAS Guidance recommends that specific training should be provided to all of those who make decisions that may affect others – which include day-to-day decisions on matters such as work allocation and performance appraisals. It further recommends that supervisors and managers should have training in how to recognise and deal with bullying and harassment.[4]

A key element of successful training is to ensure that all employees actually attend the required sessions. Obviously, much of the point of the training is missed if a number of employees do not attend – and it might be assumed that those who miss the sessions are likely to be those most in need of the training. Questions about training of key decision makers are particularly common in discrimination questionnaires. A tribunal is likely to look unfavourably on an employer, or even go so far as to draw inferences of discrimination, if the individuals closely involved in an age discrimination case have failed to attend any appropriate age equality training.

Example:

An accountancy firm introduces a new equal opportunities policy, which specifically includes the new law on age discrimination. The policy is placed on the firm's intranet, but there is no general announcement. The firm organises one training session for everyone in the firm by sending out appointments to attend. Replies are not tracked, and the session is not repeated.

Alan does not attend the training session. Two months later, he does not include Judy in a promotion opportunity as he thinks she is unable to adapt to the new role. Judy is 53 years of age, and claims that Alan has assumed she cannot adapt because she is over 50.

The failure to include Judy in the promotion opportunity might be direct age discrimination, if Judy can show that Alan was influenced by assumptions about her age. The failure to organise training for Alan might cause the tribunal to infer that he did discriminate on grounds of age, in the absence of a good explanation for his view of Judy's abilities.

If Alan has been influenced by Judy's age, it is extremely unlikely that his assumption about Judy's abilities is a valid justification for this treatment, as it appears to be based on prejudice rather than fact. The firm will be vicariously liable for Alan's act of age discrimination.

It is unlikely that the firm will have a defence to this claim, by showing that it took all reasonably practicable steps to prevent the discrimination. It also risks the tribunal drawing inferences from its inadequate approach to implementing its policy, resulting in the firm having to prove that it did not discriminate against Alan and not vice versa. The firm has introduced a policy covering age. However, it did not do everything it reasonably could to ensure that all of the employees, including Alan, were aware of the policy and trained in what it means in practice.

There may be a number of other employees who did not attend the training, and remain unaware of the existence and content of the policy. In order to avoid discrimination claims and ensure that the firm's equality ethos is being upheld by its employees, the employer should publicise the policy and ensure that training is provided to everyone, with additional training for decision makers and managers.

---

1 Taking such steps as were reasonably practicable to prevent the discrimination from taking place.

2 ACAS Guidance, *Age and the Workplace: Putting the Employment Equality (Age) Regulations 2006 into practice* (ACAS), p 19.

3 Commission for Racial Equality: Code of Practice on Racial Equality in Employment (2005), p 33–34.
4 ACAS Guidance, *Age and the Workplace: Putting the Employment Equality (Age) Regulations 2006 into practice* (ACAS), p 19.

13.6 Monitoring

Even assuming that an equal opportunities policy and appropriate training is in place, monitoring of age equality in the workplace is extremely important. The main purpose of equality monitoring is to check whether there is any evidence of discrimination – and policies and procedures are of little use unless an employer is able to check that they are working in practice. This is especially important in relation to indirect discrimination, where a claim will be based on disadvantage to a particular age group, rather than prejudice or overt age barriers. Monitoring of the progress of different age groups is the best way to identify any patterns that suggest certain groups may be suffering from the effects of indirect age discrimination.

The ACAS Guidance provides an outline framework for age monitoring, which suggests the following[1]

- use of the following age bands – 16–21, 22–30, 31–40, 41–50, 51–60, 60–65, and 65+;
- keeping of records on how all employees fit into these age bands;
- collection of additional age data on:
  - job applicants, and who is successful;
  - employees who apply for training, and who is successful;
  - employees who apply for promotion, and who is successful;
  - employees who are subject to performance assessment;
  - employees who are involved in disciplinary and grievance processes, including the outcome; and
  - employees who leave the organisation.

The collection of all of this information should be capable of giving an employer a clear picture of any areas where there appears to be evidence of age bias, from recruitment through to departures from the organisation.

As noted in the Racial Equality Code,[2] it is important to set up the monitoring system carefully. In smaller organisations this may be something as simple as an annual questionnaire. It is recommended that trade unions or other worker representatives are consulted about any new monitoring systems, and understand the reasons why they are being introduced. It is also important to reassure people that the information will be treated in confidence. Although this may seem less important for age than for some other types of information, employees are more likely to participate if they feel that the information they provide will be treated carefully. In order to ensure that the data gives an accurate picture of the workforce, it is crucial to get as many people as possible to participate.

Some employers engage external specialists to collate the data. One advantage is that it maintains confidentiality.

It should also be noted that a person's age is not 'sensitive' personal data under the Data Protection Act 1998, unlike most of the other types of prohibited discrimination, and so this information is not subject to especially stringent rules on collection and use.[3] However, the information still constitutes 'personal data' and the basic provisions of the Data Protection Act should still be followed in relation to information about employees' ages.

Although age data may be collected anonymously, these principles will apply whenever an individual employee can be identified from the information. An employer is able to collect personal information about employees for legitimate business reasons, which would include monitoring equal opportunities. However, the collection and use of this information must follow specific principles and be 'proportionate'. In essence, this means that employees must be told in advance what information is being collected and what it will be used for. The information should be held securely with access limited to those who need it, and it should not be used for purposes other than those for which it was collected. Although a person's age may not fall within the legal definition of 'sensitive' information, it may still be regarded as a sensitive subject, so it is good practice to keep the information as confidential as possible.

Of course, it is not sufficient simply to collect information from equal opportunities monitoring – something must be done with the results. If the aim is to check that there is equality in practice, an employer should analyse the collated statistics for evidence of patterns of discrimination, or specific areas where certain age groups appear to be under-represented or losing out. Although under-representation of an age group does not necessarily mean that the employer has been discriminating, such evidence should at least be considered to make sure that the employer is unable to do anything to correct the situation.

It may be that the employer is already aware that it has some practices that do potentially indirectly discriminate on grounds of age, and this is confirmed by the statistics. However, considering the information in this way may also assist the employer to defend a claim of indirect discrimination, by showing that the practice is justified.

Part of the justification defence requires the employer to show that the impact is a proportionate means of achieving a legitimate aim.[4] If an employer has analysed the extent of the disadvantage, and considered whether there is any way of limiting this disadvantage while still achieving its business aims, it is more likely to be able to show that it has acted proportionately. In fact, the ACAS Guidance specifically mentions this as being one of the useful effects of monitoring – it can help employers to gather evidence that can be used by a tribunal in looking at objective justification of any type of age discrimination.[5]

It should be noted that monitoring may reveal data which suggests there is age discrimination within an organisation. This data would be disclosable in tribunal proceedings for age discrimination, and may assist the claimant's case. In addition, such information about the results of monitoring is often requested in discrimination questionnaires, and again would potentially assist the claimant's case. As there is no legal obligation as such to carry out monitoring, some employers might choose to avoid the issue rather than risk uncovering unhelpful data. For the reasons set out above, this would not be good practice, and monitoring is very important for an employer that is serious about age equality. However, this does mean that it is essential for an employer that carries out age equality monitoring to be committed to acting on the results both quickly and effectively.

1 ACAS Guidance, *Age and the Workplace: Putting the Employment Equality (Age) Regulations 2006 into practice* (ACAS),Annex p 47.
2 Commission for Racial Equality: Code of Practice on Racial Equality in Employment (2005), p 36.
3 Race, religion, sexual orientation and health are all 'sensitive' personal data under s 2 of the Data Protection Act 1998, which means that specific conditions under Sch 3 of the Act have to be satisfied before such information can be processed at all (although there are some limited exemptions for some types of equal opportunities monitoring).
4 **Chapter 4**, 4.7.13.
5 ACAS Guidance, *Age and the Workplace: Putting the Employment Equality (Age) Regulations 2006 into practice* (ACAS), p 47.

13.7 Positive action

Positive action allows limited discrimination to take place in favour of an under-represented group, in order to correct the effects of discrimination or disadvantage. This clearly goes against a general principle that everyone should be treated equally according to their merits, and so tends to be a controversial subject. Under UK discrimination law, most forms of positive discrimination are unlawful because they would amount to unlawful direct discrimination.[1] However, there are some specific circumstances where a very limited form of positive discrimination, called positive action, is allowed. Positive action is discussed in **Chapter 5**.[2]

Regulation 29 specifies that it is not unlawful to give people of a particular age group access to facilities for training to fit them for particular work, or to encourage people of a particular age group to take advantage of opportunities to do particular work. In both cases, it needs to reasonably appear that this will prevent or compensate for disadvantages linked to age.

This is a clear exception to the general principle that it would be unlawful direct discrimination to give a deliberate advantage to members of a particular age group. However, the exception is strictly limited to training and encouragement and does not extend to offering actual work – which includes 'on the job' training. So, an employer could offer a training course to individuals aged over 50 in a job that tends to be dominated by younger workers, or advertise roles in a youth-oriented magazine where the employer's current workforce tends to be older. However, an employer could not limit specific training opportunities in the workplace to existing employees of a specific age group, as this would potentially be unlawful direct discrimination (unless it is justified).

Example:

A web design company wants to place an advertisement for a role as a web designer. All web designers in the company at the moment are under 40, and the company wishes to attract some older candidates.

The company includes the following statements in its advertisement: 'We are looking for applicants aged 40 or over, and will provide the successful candidate with a one month paid trial period that will include intensive on-the-job training'.

This advertisement would signal an intention to act unlawfully. Limiting the job itself to those over 40 is direct age discrimination, which does not fall within the positive action exemption. It is very unlikely that this would be justified, as it is not a proportionate way of trying to address the existing age imbalance in the workforce. Although the offer of training might be covered, this is on-the job training, and so falls outside the exception as well.

The company places an alternative advert which includes the following statement: 'We would welcome applicants aged over 40, although candidates of any age may apply, and appointment will be on the basis of merit only'. The company also advertises a separate six-week training course in web design which is limited to people aged over 40.

The first advert is likely to be lawful positive action, as it is encouraging an under-represented age group to apply for specific work, but is makes it clear that all ages will be considered equally. The advertised training course is also likely to be lawful, as it is a stand-alone course for an under-represented age group, which is targeted at specific work.

Positive action ties in with age equality monitoring. Monitoring statistics can be used to back up a decision to implement positive action. In addition, although positive action may be relatively rare in practice, employers should consider it if the results of monitoring suggest that a particular age group is significantly under-represented and could be helped or encouraged to participate more in the workforce. This is recommended in the Racial Equality Code – although it also recognises that positive action can be controversial, and advises that workers should be informed in advance about the action and the fact that it is designed to create a level playing field rather than favour any particular group.[3]

Effective promotion and management of age equality involves a number of elements, the key points being implementation of a policy, training and monitoring. This is an essential part of an employer's strategy for avoiding and successfully defending claims of age discrimination, and organisations that do not take these issues seriously are likely to be regarded in a poor light by employment tribunals. However, perhaps more importantly, an effective age equality strategy is the best way to try and ensure that there is a diverse workforce and effective workers are not being sidelined due to prejudicial assumptions about age.

1 **Chapter 4**.
2 **Chapter 5, 5.3.2**.
3 Commission for Racial Equality: Code of Practice on Racial Equality in Employment (2005), p 40.

Chapter 14

Age discrimination claims in the employment tribunal

14.1 Introduction

At the time of writing (Spring 2007) no significant cases brought under the Regulations in the employment tribunal have yet been reported. Accordingly, we do not have the benefit of practical examples from which to observe how employment tribunals will handle claims brought under the Age Regulations. However, by considering the relevant provisions of the Regulations (particularly Pt 5, 'Enforcement') and the manner in which the tribunal deals with other discrimination claims, it is possible to draw out general principles which will govern the way in which claims of age discrimination will be handled by the tribunal.

In this chapter we consider:

- the jurisdiction of the employment tribunal;
- time limits and statutory dispute resolution procedures;
- conciliation and mediation;
- questionnaires;
- hearings; and
- remedies.

We also look at the pressures on both claimant and respondent to settle claims.

14.2 The jurisdiction of the employment tribunal

Regulation 36 provides that complaints under the Regulations should be presented to an employment tribunal. There are two exceptions to this general provision:

- in the case of qualification bodies, appeal proceedings can be brought against the relevant body by virtue of other statutory provisions.[1]
- if the complaint is being made by a student against an educational establishment,[2], the claim should be brought in the county court in England and Wales or in the sheriff court in Scotland.[3]

1 See reg 36(2)(a) of the Employment Equality (Age) Regulations 2006
2 See reg 36(2)(b) and (c). For the definition of 'educational establishment' see reg 23(4) and (5).
3 See reg 39.

14.3 Time limits and the statutory dispute resolution procedures

The starting point in relation to the relevant time limit within which to bring a claim of age discrimination in the employment tribunal is reg 42(1), which provides that complaints should be presented to the tribunal before the end of the three-month period beginning when the act complained of was done. However, reg 42(3) provides the tribunal with a wide discretion to consider a complaint which would otherwise be out of time if it considers it 'just and equitable to do so'. This reflects the other discrimination laws.

As confirmed in *Robertson v Bexley Community Centre*,[1] it is for the claimant to convince the tribunal that the strict time limit should be extended. In determining whether it is just and equitable to extend the time limit for presenting a complaint, the tribunal is likely to consider such factors as the reason for the delay, whether or not the claimant knew of their rights to bring a claim and/or the relevant time limits, and the likely prejudice that extending the time limit might have on the respondent, balanced as against the prejudice suffered by the claimant if they are unable to proceed with their claim. A key consideration will also be whether or not the delay will affect the tribunal's ability to conduct a fair trial.[2] In one notable case, the Court of Appeal upheld an extension of time of nearly nine years.[3] However, extensions of this considerable length would be very unusual as, in almost all cases, such a delay would adversely prejudice the respondent and make a fair hearing impossible.

As with almost all other employment claims, with employees (but not other workers such as partners) a complaint of age discrimination will also be affected by the statutory procedures, introduced by the Employment Act 2002. In order for the tribunal to have jurisdiction to hear their complaint, employees wishing to bring a claim of age discrimination must set out their grievance in writing and send the statement, or a copy of it, to their employer.[4]

This requirement must be complied with within the normal time limit for presenting a complaint to the tribunal or, if the claimant has presented a complaint to the tribunal within the normal time limit, within one month of the original time limit for making the complaint. The employee must then wait for a further period of 28 days before launching proceedings in the tribunal.[5] Following receipt of a grievance, the employer should (if the standard grievance procedure is being followed) meet with the employee in order to try to resolve the grievance in compliance with the statutory grievance procedures. Failure by either party to comply with the statutory grievance procedures may result in the award to the employee being increased by 10–50 per cent (if the failure was on the part of the employer) or decreased by 10–50 per cent (if the failure was on the part of the employee).[6]

In the case of discrimination on grounds of equal pay, sex, race, disability, religion or belief, or sexual orientation, if the employee's grievance concerns the fact that their employer is taking, or is contemplating taking, 'relevant disciplinary action'[7] against them, and such disciplinary action amounts to unlawful discrimination, the parties are not required to go through the full statutory grievance procedure (see reg 7 of the Employment Act 2002 (Dispute Resolution) Regulations 2004 (the Dispute Regulations). Instead, provided that the employee sets out their grievance in writing and presents this statement to the employer before the appeal meeting (under either the standard dismissal and disciplinary procedure or the modified procedure) or, if the procedures are not being followed, prior to presenting a complaint in the tribunal, then both parties shall be treated as having complied with the grievance procedure.

Initially, the Regulations failed to amend reg 7 to include claims of age discrimination. However, the recently published Employment Equality (Age) (Consequential Amendments) Regulations 2007, which came into force on 6 April 2007, have corrected this error. Accordingly, if an employee considers that they are being disciplined unfairly (for example, they are being disciplined for performance issues while similar performance issues are overlooked for older employees approaching retirement age) and that the disciplinary action is on the grounds of age, the employee need only present a written complaint to the employer, alleging age discrimination, before the appeal stage of the disciplinary process, in order for both parties to be held to have complied with the statutory grievance procedure. Both parties, therefore, avoid the adverse consequences of failing to follow the statutory grievance procedure, namely an uplift or reduction in compensation.

It is important to note, however, that if the employee is being dismissed, or the employer is contemplating dismissal, and the employee contends that such a dismissal is discriminatory, they are not required to follow the statutory grievance procedures at all.[8]

The Dispute Regulations also extend the normal time limit of three months in order to allow employees and employers to attempt to resolve disputes internally. Provided that the employee has either attempted to present a complaint in the tribunal within the normal time limit (but is prevented from doing so because they have not raised a written grievance with their employer and waited for 28 days) or have presented their employer with a written grievance within the normal time limit, the normal time limit is automatically extended by a period of three months, beginning with the day after the day on which it would otherwise have expired.[9]

In order to better explain how the statutory procedures impact upon the timeframes for commencing tribunal proceedings, two separate examples are set out below:

It should be noted that the DTI have recently published an independent review of the employment dispute resolution procedures,[10] which calls for the repeal of the current procedures, and recommends that they be replaced with new, less prescriptive guidelines promoting workplace settlement. It remains to be seen whether the government will follow these recommendations. However, amendments to the current regime will almost certainly come about in the near future.

Issues as to whether or not a party has complied with the statutory dispute resolution procedures or whether the claim has been brought within the prescribed time limits can be considered at a pre-hearing review (PHR). Alternatively, given that these issues are likely to be intrinsically linked with the detailed facts of the case, and bearing in mind the cost to the parties in attending lengthy preliminary hearings, the parties or the tribunal may conclude that it is better to consider these jurisdictional issues as part of the full hearing.

1 [2003] IRLR 434.
2 *DP v Marshall* [1998] ICR 518.
3 *Southwark London BC v Atolabi* [2003] ICR 800.
4 Employment Act 2002, Sch 2, para 6. Note that if the modified grievance procedure is being followed, the employee must not only set out their grievance in writing, but also 'the basis for it' and send a copy to the employer (para 9 of Sch 2).
5 See s 32 of the Employment Act 2002.
6 See s 31 of the Employment Act 2002.
7 As defined in reg 2 of the Employment Act 2002 (Dispute Resolution) Regulations 2004.
8 See reg 6(5) of the Employment Act 2002 (Dispute Resolution) Regulations 2004. See also *Lawrence v HM Prison Service* UKEAT/0630/06/CEA.
9 See reg 15 of the Employment Act 2002 (Dispute Resolution) Regulations 2004.
10 Gibbons 'Better Dispute Resolution; A review of employment dispute resolution in Great Britain' (DTI, March 2001).

14.4 Claims by nonemployees

As set out in **Chapter 3**, [1] claims of age discrimination can be made by nonemployees, such as job applicants, contract workers, office-holders or partners. However, the statutory procedures set out in Sch 2 to the Employment Act 2002 only apply to employees.[2] Accordingly, claims by nonemployees must be brought within the normal time limit of three months from the act complained of, unless the tribunal considers it 'just and equitable' to extend the time limit in accordance with reg 42(3).

1 **Chapter 3, 3.3.**
2 See s 40 of the Employment Act 2002.

14.5 ACAS conciliation and mediation

14.5.1 ACAS conciliation

The Employment Tribunals (Constitutions Rules of Procedure) Regulations 2004, Sch 1, paras 22, 23 and 24 provide that there should be a period within which the parties have the opportunity to reach an ACAS conciliated settlement. For the majority of claims, the ACAS conciliation period is for a fixed period of 13 weeks.[1] However, in the case of discrimination and whistle-blowing claims, the conciliation period is not for a limited period, but extends right up until the full hearing. As with certain provisions of the Dispute Resolution Regulations, the Age Regulations initially failed to amend the provisions of para 22 to include claims of age discrimination. This error has also now been rectified by virtue of the Employment Equality (Age) (Consequential Amendments) Regulations 2007, which came into force on 6 April 2007.

The practical implication of having an unlimited ACAS conciliation period is of course that the parties have a readily available forum through which to conduct 'without prejudice' discussions concerning settlement. In addition, if the case is settled through ACAS conciliation, by means of a COT3 agreement, there is no requirement for the claimant to enter into a compromise agreement or comply with the requirements to have received independent legal advice on the terms and effect of the agreement. This can be particularly helpful if the claimant is not represented.

1 Although in the case of certain claims (as listed in para 22(5) of Sch 1) the fixed conciliation period is for just seven weeks.

14.5.2 Mediation

Mediation is also offered by other organisations. Certain employment tribunals have been attempting a mediation service as part of the pre-hearing process. This has not applied to discrimination claims.

The Centre for Effective Dispute Resolution offers accredited mediators as do many solicitors' firms and barristers' chambers.

14.6 Age discrimination questionnaires

As with the other forms of discrimination, the legislation provides a questionnaire procedure by which an employee can request additional information from their employer, to assist them in bringing their claim.[1] Example questionnaires, together with a suggested form of reply from the respondent are set out at Schs 3 and 4 of the Regulations, although parties are not obliged to follow these example forms.

The purpose of the questionnaire procedure is to allow a would-be claimant to ask pertinent questions to the respondent in order to assess the merits of their claim prior to launching, or proceeding with, full tribunal procedures or having to wait for disclosure from the respondent. A discrimination questionnaire can also be used as a tactical tool by employees who consider launching a discrimination complaint. If an employer is served with a lengthy questionnaire, which includes questions that it will take considerable time and resources to answer, the employer may be more inclined to enter into early settlement negotiations with the claimant.

The questions contained in a discrimination questionnaire, together with any replies received from the respondent, are admissible as evidence in the tribunal proceedings. Accordingly, a respondent should be cautious in responding carelessly to a discrimination questionnaire. Similarly, if the tribunal concludes that the respondent deliberately, or without reasonable excuse, failed to reply to the questionnaire within the prescribed eight-week time limit, or concludes that their reply is evasive or equivocal, then the tribunal may draw such inferences as it considers 'just and equitable', including the possible inference that the respondent has committed an unlawful act or discrimination. Such an inference, together with a difference in age and a difference in treatment as between the claimant and other employees, may be sufficient to shift the burden of proof from the claimant to the respondent.[2]

Questionnaires are only admissible as evidence if they are served on the respondent within the specified time period. If the claimant serves the questionnaire before commencing tribunal proceedings, the questionnaires must be served within the period of three months, beginning when the last act complained of was done. If the questionnaire is served on the respondent after proceedings have commenced, then it should be served within 21 days of the complaint being presented (or, if leave is given for it to be served later, within such period as shall be specified by the tribunal).

A questionnaire, served under reg 41, does not constitute a grievance for the purposes of the statutory grievance procedures. Accordingly, an employee who has submitted an age discrimination questionnaire should also submit a written grievance to their employer.[3]

There are no specific provisions that extend the normal time limits for submitting age discrimination questionnaires in line with the extension of time provisions in the Dispute Resolution Regulations. However, if the normal time limit is extended by a further period of three months by virtue of the employee submitting a written grievance, it seems likely that the tribunal will permit the claimant to serve a discrimination questionnaire within the extended six-month time limit, particularly given that it is unlikely that the potential respondent will suffer any prejudice if the deadline for submitting the questionnaire is extended.

1 See reg 41.

2 **Chapter 4**, **4.6** on drawing inferences and shifting the burden of proof.

3 See reg 14 of the Dispute Resolution Regulations was, in error, not amended by the Age Regulations to include age discrimination questionnaires. Again, this has been amended by virtue of the Employment Equality (Age) (Consequential Amendments) Regulations 2007, coming into force 6 April 2007.

14.7 Procedures

A claim of age discrimination will, like all other claims in the tribunal, be conducted in accordance with the Employment Tribunals Rules of Procedure[1] (the Tribunal Rules). The Tribunal Rules include detailed provisions dealing with how to commence proceedings, how to respond to a claim and the possible consequences if a respondent fails to respond to a claim within the prescribed time limits or fails to respond in the prescribed form.

The Tribunal Rules also set out what case management powers the chairman of the tribunal can exercise; the manner in which parties should make applications for Orders from the Tribunal and rules relating to compliance with such Orders. Further the Tribunal Rules also deal with hearings, the judgment and the manner in which parties may request a review of the judgment. Finally, the Tribunal Rules also introduced new detailed provisions in relation to the possibility of parties applying for costs awards in the tribunal. However, a detailed examination of the Tribunal Rules is outside of the scope of this chapter.

1 See Sch 1 to the Employment Tribunals (Constitution and Rules of Procedure) Regulations 2004.

14.8 Hearings

In the majority of discrimination claims, the Tribunal is likely to order that the parties attend a case management discussion (CMD) in order to clarify the issues of the case, to agree a timetable for disclosure of documents and the exchange of witness statements, and to list dates for the full hearing. The parties might also agree a list of issues at the CMD or make requests for further information from the other party. A chairman will conduct a CMD sitting alone. The chairman is able to make standard Orders at a CMD (as listed in para 10(2) of the Tribunal Rules). However, certain Orders can only be made at a PHR. In particular, a chairman cannot make a judgment at a CMD.

A PHR shall, in the normal circumstances, be conducted by a chairman sitting alone. However, either party may request that the hearing be conducted by a full tribunal. The hearing will be conducted by a full tribunal if it is likely that substantive issues of fact will be determined at the PHR and a chairman orders that the PHR should be conducted by a full tribunal. As well as being able to make all the standard Orders that he might make at a CMD, a chairman may give judgment on preliminary issues of substance at a PHR. In particular, a chairman may strike out or dismiss a claim at a PHR.[1]

In addition, if a chairman considers that the contentions put forward by either party have little reasonable prospect of success, he can require that party to pay a deposit (of an amount not exceeding £500) as a condition of being permitted to continue to take part in the proceedings relating to that matter. An Order of this sort can only be made at a PHR. If the party fails to pay the deposit then the claim or response of that party will be struck out.[2]

The full tribunal hearing will be conducted by a chairman together with two other panel members. The chairman must have at least seven years of legal experience. The two other panel members are not legally qualified. One panel member will be a representative of an organisation or association of employees (such as a trade union organisation) while the other will be a representative of an organisation or association of employers (such as the Confederation of British Industry (the CBI)). Although it will, of course, depend on the facts of the case, and the number of witnesses called, a discrimination case will commonly last for several days. The chairman will direct how the hearing will be run. By way of example, the chairman may decide that each witness should read their witness statement in full as part of their evidence in chief. Alternatively, if he is concerned about time constraints, the chairman may decide that the witness statements will be taken as read, so that the tribunal can move swiftly on to the cross-examination of the witnesses.

In a case of age discrimination, the claimant will give their evidence first on the grounds that they bear the burden of proof. Note, however, that the burden of proof will shift from the claimant to the respondent, if the claimant is able to establish a prima facie case of discrimination (see **Chapter 4**). However, the question of the shifting burden of proof will not practically affect the way in which evidence is given by the parties in the tribunal. As Mummery LJ clarified in the recent case of *Madarassy v Nomura International Plc*,[3] although the tribunal is required to undertake a two-stage analysis of the evidence, the tribunal does not in practice hear the evidence and the argument in two stages. The tribunal will hear all of the evidence in the case before it embarks on the two-stage analysis to decide, first whether the burden of proof has moved to the respondent, and secondly whether the respondent has discharged the burden of proof.[4]

In all other respects, a hearing of a claim of age discrimination will be conducted in the same manner as any other claim within the tribunal; there are no specific provisions in the Regulations which in any way alter the standard procedure. Accordingly, parties shall be entitled to give evidence, call witnesses and address the tribunal,[5] although the tribunal has wide discretion to control how the proceedings are managed.

1 See r 18 of the Tribunal Rules.
2 See r 20 of the Tribunal Rules.
3 [2007] EWCA Civ 33.
4 **Chapter 4, 4.6**.
5 See r 27(3) of the Tribunal Rules.

14.9 Remedies

14.9.1 Declarations, compensation and recommendations

(a) Summary

If a claimant is successful in bringing a claim of age discrimination, the tribunal can provide the claimant with one or more of the following remedies:

- an Order declaring the rights of the claimant and the respondent in relation to the act to which the complaint relates;
- an Order requiring the respondent to pay the claimant compensation of an amount corresponding to any damages he could have been ordered by a county court or by a sheriff court to pay to the claimant if the complaint had fallen to be dealt with under the jurisdiction of the county court (see below for further details); or
- a recommendation that the respondent takes, within a specified period, action appearing to the tribunal to be practicable for the purpose of obviating or reducing the adverse effect on the claimant of any act of discrimination or harassment to which the complaint relates.[1]

1 See reg 38(1) of the Age Regulations 2006.

(b) Compensation

Compensation awards in discrimination claims are uncapped. The measure of loss is tortious, ie the claimant should, so far as is reasonably possible, be put back in the position that he would have been in, had the discrimination not happened. In cases in which the claimant is successful in claiming that their dismissal was discriminatory, the tribunal must consider what the claimant is entitled to by way of future loss of earnings. The tribunal should consider the question of whether it is possible that the claimant would have been dismissed in any event, or whether he would have remained in their employment.[1]

When assessing the issue of whether or not the claimant would have been dismissed, the tribunal should not ask what the 'reasonable' employer would have done – as it would in the case of a claim of unfair dismissal.

Instead, the tribunal should ask itself what this employer would have done.[2] This can be a difficult task for the tribunal as it requires it to forecast what might happen in the future. Based on the tribunal's decision on the likelihood of the claimant remaining in employment, which is often expressed as a percentage, the tribunal will then make an award for future loss of earnings. In cases of age discrimination involving older employees, it seems likely that the tribunal will often be inclined to find that the claimant would have remained with their employer until his retirement.

The claimant is of course required to mitigate his losses, by actively seeking alternative employment, and such efforts will be taken into account by the tribunal when assessing compensation. Here again, it seems likely that age claims may be treated slightly differently by the tribunal. An older employee who has been dismissed on discriminatory grounds may have greater difficulty in finding alternative work. By analogy to the case of *Cannock*, where the EAT recognised that women with young children have difficulty in finding work, it is likely that the tribunal will also take account of the fact that an older employee may have difficulty in finding a comparable position within a job market that is still intrinsically ageist.

As well as being entitled to compensation for future loss of earnings, the claimant may also claim that they are entitled to compensation for injury to feelings. As set out above, compensation should be determined on a tortious basis as if it were being brought as a civil claim in the county court. Regulation 39 contains provisions concerning the jurisdiction of the county court. Regulation 39(3) specifically states that damages may include compensation for injury to feelings in cases in which the county court has jurisdiction. Accordingly, it is inferred that tribunals are also entitled to make awards for injury to feelings.

The leading case on awards for injury to feelings is *Vento v Chief Constable of West Yorkshire Police*.[3] In this case, Mummery LJ sets three bands for the levels of compensation payable for injury to feelings. The top band, for the most serious cases, where for example, there has been a lengthy campaign of discriminatory harassment, should normally be between £15,000 and £25,000. Only in the most exceptional cases should awards for injury to feelings exceed £25,000. The middle band should be used for serious cases, which do not merit an award in the top band. In such cases, the claimant should receive an award for injury to feelings of between £5,000 and £15,000. Awards of £500 to £5,000 are appropriate for less serious cases where, for example, the act of discrimination is a one-off occurrence. Note of course that these sums should be increased to take account of the rate of inflation since the judgment was made in 2002.

The case of *HM Prison v Johnson*[4] has confirmed that aggravated damages are also available in discrimination cases. Such awards should be made where the respondent has behaved in such a way as to 'rub salt into the claimant's wounds', for example in the manner in which they have conducted their investigation into the complaint of discrimination.

In cases of indirect age discrimination, the tribunal's power to award compensation is limited to some extent. If the respondent is able to prove that the provision, criterion or practice was not applied with the intention of treating the claimant less favourably on grounds of age, then the tribunal is required to go through a two-stage consideration process. Essentially, the tribunal should first consider whether or not it would make an Order declaring the rights of the claimant or whether it would make a recommendation, as if it had no power to order compensation. If the tribunal decides that it would make such a declaration or recommendation then it should only make an Order for the respondent to pay compensation if it considers it 'just and equitable' to do so.[5]

1 *Ministry of Defence vCannock* [1994] IRLR 509.
2 *Abbey National Plc v Formoso* [1999] IRLR 222.
3 [2003] IRLR 102.
4 [1997] IRLR 162.
5 See reg 38(2) of the Age Regulations 2006.

(c) Recommendations

If a respondent, without reasonable justification, fails to comply with a recommendation made by the tribunal, then the tribunal can, if it considers it just and equitable to do so, either increase the amount of compensation which it has ordered that the respondent pay to the claimant or, if the respondent was not ordered to pay compensation, make such an Order. The tribunal cannot force the respondent to comply with a recommendation.

Recommendations are less common and of less use than awards of compensation particularly as there is no means of enforcing a recommendation.

14.9.2 Validity of contracts

Paragraph 1 of Sch 5 of the Regulations contains a strange provision which states:

> 'A term of a contract is void where –
>
> (a) the making of the contract is, by reason of the inclusion of the term, unlawful by virtue of these Regulations;
>
> (b) it is included in furtherance of an act which is unlawful by virtue of these Regulations;

(c) it provides for the doing of an act which is unlawful by virtue of these Regulations.'

This paragraph replicates identical provisions in other discrimination legislation.[1]

Sub-paragraph 1(2) of Sch 5 states that:

> 'Sub-paragraph (1) does not apply to a term, the inclusion of which constitutes, or is in furtherance of, or provides for, unlawful discrimination against, or harassment of, a party to the contract, but the term shall be unenforceable against that party.'

On the face of it is not easy to envisage a situation which does not fit within sub-para (2) reducing greatly the practical significance of this provision.

Discriminatory clauses in employment contracts will, therefore, be unenforceable against the party in respect of which it amounts to unlawful discrimination, namely the employee. The employer would not presumably want to enforce it against the employee. It is not, however, void.

The discriminated employee is then left with the remedy of financial compensation for the losses to which he has been subjected.

Example:

Corinne's employment contract states that she will receive health checks every three years until she is 45 from when she will receive them annually. She claims that this is discriminatory. It would, of course, be nonsensical if this term was void as Corinne would then not be entitled to any health checks. This term would, however, come within sub-para 1(2) as it is a term which provides for unlawful discrimination against a party to the contract (Corinne). This sub-paragraph goes on to say that it would be unenforceable against that party but this will be of no consequence as Corinne's employer's ability to enforce it against her is immaterial. Corinne is then left with the remedies of seeking a declaration and compensation.

Sub-paragraph 1(4) makes it clear that this provision applies equally to contracts entered into before the Regulations came into force but does not apply to periods before that date.

1 For example, s 72 of the Race Relations Act 1976 and s 77 of the Sex Discrimination Act 1975.

14.10 Costs

A further issue to consider in relation to claims of age discrimination in the employment tribunal is the question of costs. The tribunal's power to make costs awards against parties is not nearly as wide in scope as that of the civil courts. However, since changes made to the Tribunal Rules in 2001, and again in 2004, there are now wider circumstances in which a successful party may recover some of its costs in the tribunal.

There are three distinct types of costs awards that can be made to a successful party; a costs order (or expenses order in Scotland), a preparation time order, or a wasted costs order. A costs order may only be made in circumstances where the receiving party is legally represented either at a hearing or at the date when proceedings are determined.[1] The costs order is made to the receiving party and not to their representative. However, the costs award shall be in relation to fees, charges, disbursements or expenses incurred by the receiving party in relation to the proceedings.[2]

Costs orders may be awarded where a party makes an application to postpone or adjourn a hearing or a PHR, in relation to costs incurred or allowances paid as a result of the postponement or adjournment. Costs awards may also be made where, in the opinion of the tribunal or chairman:

> '... the paying party has in bringing the proceedings, or he or his representative has in conducting the proceedings, acted vexatiously, abusively, disruptively or otherwise unreasonably, or the bringing or conducting of the proceedings by the paying party has been misconceived.'[3]

Preparation time orders are made in circumstances where the receiving party is not legally represented either at a hearing or at the date when proceedings are determined.[4] The preparation time order will provide that the paying party should make a payment in respect of:

(a) time spent by the receiving party or his employees carrying out preparatory work directly relating to the proceedings; and/or

(b) time spent by the receiving party's legal advisers relating to the conduct of the proceedings, up to, but not including, the hearing.[5]

Preparation time orders may be made in the same circumstances as when a costs order might be awarded. Both a preparation time order and costs order cannot be made in favour of the same party in the same proceedings. However, in order to overcome this, if a tribunal or chairman wishes to make some sort of order concerning costs before the claim has been determined, he may make an order confirming that either a costs order or a preparation time order will be made to the receiving party, but that the question of which order it should be will be delayed until after the claim has been determined.[6]

Wasted costs orders may be made against a party's representative. The wasted costs order may disallow, or order the representative to meet the whole or part of any wasted costs of any party. This may include an order that the representative repay to his client any costs which have already been paid. In addition, the representative may also be ordered to pay the Secretary of State any allowances paid by him to a party or a witness.[7] Wasted costs are defined in the Tribunal Rules as any costs incurred by a party:

(a) as a result of any improper, unreasonable or negligent act or omission on the part of any representative; or

(b) which in the light of any such act or omission occurring after they were incurred, the tribunal considers it unreasonable to expect that party to pay.

It is difficult to determine whether the wider discretion granted to the tribunal in relation to the making of costs orders has impacted significantly on the manner in which litigants conduct tribunal claims. Certainly, the threat of an application for a costs order is used on a more widespread basis as a tactical tool by legal representatives seeking to encourage the withdrawal or settlement of a claim. However, the actual making of a costs order by the tribunal remains a relatively rare occurrence and is, of course, dependent on the particular facts of the case. In particular, the tribunal is likely to take into account the paying party's financial circumstances and whether they are able to make payment in accordance with the order. It seems likely that this pattern in relation to costs orders will continue in relation to claims of age discrimination.

1 See r 38(2) of the Tribunal Rules.
2 See r 38(3) of the Tribunal Rules.
3 See r 40 of the Tribunal Rules.
4 See r 42(2) of the Tribunal Rules.
5 See r 42(3) of the Tribunal Rules.
6 See r 46 of the Tribunal Rules.
7 See r 48(2) of the Tribunal Rules.

14.11 Why claims may be brought and pressures to settle

It does not require a crystal ball to envisage that many claims will be brought under the Regulations.[1] If the experience of other forms of employment law are anything to go by, the numbers will increase over time as people become aware of their rights and the impact of the Regulations becomes clearer.

Both claimant and respondent will face pressures to settle their dispute without proceeding to a full hearing. The pressures on the respondent include:

- the unpredictability of tribunals;
- the significant cost awards;
- the cost (normally unrecoverable) and management time spent in defending claims[2];
- the uncertainty of the new law; and
- the reputational damage with staff, prospective employees and customers.

The pressures on the claimant are similar:

- the unpredictability of tribunals;
- the uncertainty of the new law;
- damage to career prospects;
- cost (from taxed income and VAT on legal fees not recoverable);
- the stress and time spent on litigation;
- the conflict which often arises between the desire to get a new job and the impact of getting a new job on financial losses; and
- the need for money for day-to-day outgoings.

The dispute resolution procedures set out above were intended by the government to encourage the parties to resolve disputes informally. They have been a failure. In light of the Gibbons Report,[3] the government is consulting on changes which will almost certainly result in their withdrawal.[4]

In the meantime, official and unofficial alternative dispute resolution mechanism are growing in popularity.[5]

Practically, it seems likely that age discrimination claims will be treated in much the same way as other discrimination claims brought in the employment tribunal. However, it will be interesting to see how certain issues of age discrimination are handled by the tribunal. In particular, the question of the appropriate level of compensatory awards may vary from other forms of discrimination. As set out above, the tribunal may award more to an older employee in terms of future loss of earnings, particularly given that they may face serious difficulty in trying to mitigate their losses if they are in their late 50s or early 60s. However, the tribunal may be less inclined to make large awards for injury to feelings given that ageist comments and banter are not currently as socially unacceptable as making, for example, sexist or racist comments.

1 **Chapter 1**.
2 Research carried out by Lewis Silkin, Barclays Bank and the Centre for Effective Dispute Resolution showed that dealing with a disgruntled employee can typically cost up to £277,000 – of which £72,000 is management time. The study claimed that early mediation could reduce the costs to around £9,000.
3 Michael Gibbons, *Better Dispute Resolutions, A review of employment dispute resolution in Great Britain* (DTI, March 2007).
4 Success at Work, Resolving disputes in the Workplace', DTI, March 2007.
5 See **14.5**.

Appendix 1

Employment Equality (Age) Regulations 2006

Reproduced by kind permission of Westlaw.

No 1031

Part 1

General

1 Citation, commencement and extent

(1) These Regulations may be cited as the Employment Equality (Age) Regulations 2006, and shall come into force –

(a) subject to sub-paragraphs (b) and (c), on 1st October 2006;

(b) for the purposes of regulation 7 (Applicants and Employees) and regulation 24 (Relationships which have come to an end), in so far as either regulation relates to arrangements for –

(i) the payment of pension contributions;

(ii) admission to a pension scheme; and

(iii) the provision of any benefits relating to pensions,

on 1st December 2006, and

(c) for the purposes of regulation 11 (Pension Schemes) and Schedule 2 (Pension Schemes), on 1st December 2006].

(2) Any amendment, repeal or revocation made by these Regulations has the same extent as the provision to which it relates.

(3) Subject to that, these Regulations do not extend to Northern Ireland.

Amendment

Para (1): sub-paras (a) – (c) substituted by SI 2006/2408, reg 2(1), (2).

2 Interpretation

(1) In these Regulations, references to discrimination are to any discrimination falling within regulation 3 (discrimination on grounds of age), regulation 4 (discrimination by way of victimisation) or regulation 5 (instructions to discriminate) and related expressions shall be construed accordingly, and references to harassment shall be construed in accordance with regulation 6 (harassment on grounds of age).

(2) In these Regulations –

'1996 Act' means the Employment Rights Act 1996;

'act' includes a deliberate omission;

'benefit', except in regulation 11 and Schedule 2 (pension schemes), includes facilities and services;

'commencement date' means 1st October 2006;

'Crown employment' means –

(a) service for purposes of a Minister of the Crown or government department, other than service of a person holding a statutory office; or

(b) service on behalf of the Crown for purposes of a person holding a statutory office or purposes of a statutory body;

'detriment' does not include harassment within the meaning of regulation 6;

'employment' means employment under a contract of service or of apprenticeship or a contract personally to do any work, and related expressions (such as 'employee' and 'employer') shall be construed accordingly, but this definition does not apply in relation to regulation 30 (exception for retirement) or to Schedules 2, 6, 7 and 8;

'Great Britain' includes such of the territorial waters of the United Kingdom as are adjacent to Great Britain;

'Minister of the Crown' includes the Treasury and the Defence Council;

'proprietor', in relation to a school, has the meaning given by section 579 of the Education Act 1996;

'relevant member of the House of Commons staff' means any person who was appointed by the House of Commons Commission or who is a member of the Speaker's personal staff;

'relevant member of the House of Lords staff' means any person who is employed under a contract of employment with the Corporate Officer of the House of Lords;

'school', in England and Wales, has the meaning given by section 4 of the Education Act 1996, and, in Scotland, has the meaning given by section 135(1) of the Education (Scotland) Act 1980, and references to a school are to an institution in so far as it is engaged in the provision of education under those sections;

'service for purposes of a Minister of the Crown or government department' does not include service in any office mentioned in Schedule 2 (Ministerial offices) to the House of Commons Disqualification Act 1975;

'statutory body' means a body set up by or in pursuance of an enactment, and 'statutory office' means an office so set up; and

'worker' in relation to regulations 32 and 34 and to Schedule 2, means, as the case may be –

(a) an employee;

(b) a person holding an office or post to which regulation 12 (office-holders etc) applies;

(c) a person holding the office of constable;

(d) a partner within the meaning of regulation 17 (partnerships);

(e) a member of a limited liability partnership within the meaning of that regulation;

(f) a person in Crown employment;

(g) a relevant member of the House of Commons staff;

(h) a relevant member of the House of Lords staff.

(3) In these Regulations references to 'employer', in their application to a person at any time seeking to employ another, include a person who has no employees at that time.

3 Discrimination on grounds of age

(1) For the purposes of these Regulations, a person ('A') discriminates against another person ('B') if –

(a) on grounds of B's age, A treats B less favourably than he treats or would treat other persons, or

(b) A applies to B a provision, criterion or practice which he applies or would apply equally to persons not of the same age group as B, but –

(i) which puts or would put persons of the same age group as B at a particular disadvantage when compared with other persons, and

(ii) which puts B at that disadvantage,

and A cannot show the treatment or, as the case may be, provision, criterion or practice to be a proportionate means of achieving a legitimate aim.

(2) A comparison of B's case with that of another person under paragraph (1) must be such that the relevant circumstances in the one case are the same, or not materially different, in the other.

(3) In this regulation –

(a) 'age group' means a group of persons defined by reference to age, whether by reference to a particular age or a range of ages; and

(b) the reference in paragraph (1)(a) to B's age includes B's apparent age.

4 Discrimination by way of victimisation

(1) For the purposes of these Regulations, a person ('A') discriminates against another person ('B') if he treats B less favourably than he treats or would treat other persons in the same circumstances, and does so by reason that B has –

(a) brought proceedings against A or any other person under or by virtue of these Regulations;

(b) given evidence or information in connection with proceedings brought by any person against A or any other person under or by virtue of these Regulations;

(c) otherwise done anything under or by reference to these Regulations in relation to A or any other person; or

(d) alleged that A or any other person has committed an act which (whether or not the allegation so states) would amount to a contravention of these Regulations,

or by reason that A knows that B intends to do any of those things, or suspects that B has done or intends to do any of them.

(2) Paragraph (1) does not apply to treatment of B by reason of any allegation made by him, or evidence or information given by

him, if the allegation, evidence or information was false and not made (or, as the case may be, given) in good faith.

5 Instructions to discriminate

For the purposes of these Regulations, a person ('A') discriminates against another person ('B') if he treats B less favourably than he treats or would treat other persons in the same circumstances, and does so by reason that –

(a) B has not carried out (in whole or in part) an instruction to do an act which is unlawful by virtue of these Regulations, or

(b) B, having been given an instruction to do such an act, complains to A or to any other person about that instruction.

6 Harassment on grounds of age

(1) For the purposes of these Regulations, a person ('A') subjects another person ('B') to harassment where, on grounds of age, A engages in unwanted conduct which has the purpose or effect of –

(a) violating B's dignity; or

(b) creating an intimidating, hostile, degrading, humiliating or offensive environment for B.

(2) Conduct shall be regarded as having the effect specified in paragraph (1) (a) or (b) only if, having regard to all the circumstances, including in particular the perception of B, it should reasonably be considered as having that effect.

Part 2

Discrimination in Employment and Vocational Training

7 Applicants and employees

(1) It is unlawful for an employer, in relation to employment by him at an establishment in Great Britain, to discriminate against a person –

(a) in the arrangements he makes for the purpose of determining to whom he should offer employment;

(b) in the terms on which he offers that person employment; or

(c) by refusing to offer, or deliberately not offering, him employment.

(2) It is unlawful for an employer, in relation to a person whom he employs at an establishment in Great Britain, to discriminate against that person –

(a) in the terms of employment which he affords him;

(b) in the opportunities which he affords him for promotion, a transfer, training, or receiving any other benefit;

(c) by refusing to afford him, or deliberately not affording him, any such opportunity; or

(d) by dismissing him, or subjecting him to any other detriment.

(3) It is unlawful for an employer, in relation to employment by him at an establishment in Great Britain, to subject to harassment a person whom he employs or who has applied to him for employment.

(4) Subject to paragraph (5), paragraph (1)(a) and (c) does not apply in relation to a person –

(a) whose age is greater than the employer's normal retirement age or, if the employer does not have a normal retirement age, the age of 65; or

(b) who would, within a period of six months from the date of his application to the employer, reach the employer's normal retirement age or, if the employer does not have a normal retirement age, the age of 65.

(5) Paragraph (4) only applies to a person to whom, if he was recruited by the employer, regulation 30 (exception for retirement) could apply.

(6) Paragraph (2) does not apply to benefits of any description if the employer is concerned with the provision (for payment or not) of benefits of that description to the public, or to a section of the public which includes the employee in question, unless –

(a) that provision differs in a material respect from the provision of the benefits by the employer to his employees; or

(b) the provision of the benefits to the employee in question is regulated by his contract of employment; or

(c) the benefits relate to training.

(7) In paragraph (2) (d) reference to the dismissal of a person from employment includes reference –

(a) to the termination of that person's employment by the expiration of any period (including a period expiring by reference to an event or circumstance), not being a termination immediately after which the employment is renewed on the same terms; and

(b) to the termination of that person's employment by any act of his (including the giving of notice) in circumstances such that he is entitled to terminate it without notice by reason of the conduct of the employer.

(8) In paragraph (4) 'normal retirement age' is an age of 65 or more which meets the requirements of section 98ZH of the 1996 Act.

8 Exception for genuine occupational requirement etc

(1) In relation to discrimination falling within regulation 3 (discrimination on grounds of age) –

(a) regulation 7(1) (a) or (c) does not apply to any employment;

(b) regulation 7(2) (b) or (c) does not apply to promotion or transfer to, or training for, any employment; and

(c) regulation 7(2) (d) does not apply to dismissal from any employment,

where paragraph (2) applies.

(2) This paragraph applies where, having regard to the nature of the employment or the context in which it is carried out –

(a) possessing a characteristic related to age is a genuine and determining occupational requirement;

(b) it is proportionate to apply that requirement in the particular case; and

(c) either –

(i) the person to whom that requirement is applied does not meet it, or

(ii) the employer is not satisfied, and in all the circumstances it is reasonable for him not to be satisfied, that that person meets it.

9 Contract workers

(1) It is unlawful for a principal, in relation to contract work at an establishment in Great Britain, to discriminate against a contract worker –

(a) in the terms on which he allows him to do that work;

(b) by not allowing him to do it or continue to do it;

(c) in the way he affords him access to any benefits or by refusing or deliberately not affording him access to them; or

(d) by subjecting him to any other detriment.

(2) It is unlawful for a principal, in relation to contract work at an establishment in Great Britain, to subject a contract worker to harassment.

(3) A principal does not contravene paragraph (1) (b) by doing any act in relation to a contract worker where, if the work were to be done by a person taken into the principal's employment, that act would be lawful by virtue of regulation 8 (exception for genuine occupational requirement etc).

(4) Paragraph (1) does not apply to benefits of any description if the principal is concerned with the provision (for payment or not) of benefits of that description to the public, or to a section of the public to which the contract worker in question belongs, unless that provision differs in a material respect from the provision of the benefits by the principal to his contract workers.

(5) In this regulation –

'principal' means a person ('A') who makes work available for doing by individuals who are employed by another person who supplies them under a contract made with A;

'contract work' means work so made available; and

'contract worker' means any individual who is supplied to the principal under such a contract.

10 Meaning of employment and contract work at establishment in Great Britain

(1) For the purposes of this Part ('the relevant purposes'), employment is to be regarded as being at an establishment in Great Britain if the employee –

(a) does his work wholly or partly in Great Britain; or

(b) does his work wholly outside Great Britain and paragraph (2) applies.

(2) This paragraph applies if –

(a) the employer has a place of business at an establishment in Great Britain;

(b) the work is for the purposes of the business carried on at that establishment; and

(c) the employee is ordinarily resident in Great Britain –

(i) at the time when he applies for or is offered the employment, or

(ii) at any time during the course of the employment.

(3) The reference to 'employment' in paragraph (1) includes –

(a) employment on board a ship only if the ship is registered at a port of registry in Great Britain, and

(b) employment on an aircraft or hovercraft only if the aircraft or hovercraft is registered in the United Kingdom and operated by a person who has his principal place of business, or is ordinarily resident, in Great Britain.

(4) Subject to paragraph (5), for the purposes of determining if employment concerned with the exploration of the sea bed or sub-soil or the exploitation of their natural resources is outside Great Britain, this regulation has effect as if references to Great Britain included –

(a) any area designated under section 1(7) of the Continental Shelf Act 1964 except an area or part of an area in which the law of Northern Ireland applies; and

(b) in relation to employment concerned with the exploration or exploitation of the Frigg Gas Field, the part of the Norwegian sector of the Continental Shelf described in Schedule 1.

(5) Paragraph (4) shall not apply to employment which is concerned with the exploration or exploitation of the Frigg Gas Field unless the employer is –

(a) a company registered under the Companies Act 1985;

(b) an oversea company which has established a place of business within Great Britain from which it directs the exploration or exploitation in question; or

(c) any other person who has a place of business within Great Britain from which he directs the exploration or exploitation in question.

(6) In this regulation –

'the Frigg Gas Field' means the naturally occurring gas-bearing sand formations of the lower Eocene age located in the vicinity of the intersection of the line of latitude 59 degrees 53 minutes North and of the dividing line between the sectors of the Continental Shelf of the United Kingdom and the Kingdom of Norway and includes all other gas-bearing strata from which gas at the start of production is capable of flowing into the above-mentioned gas-bearing sand formations;

'oversea company' has the same meaning as in section 744 of the Companies Act 1985.

(7) This regulation applies in relation to contract work within the meaning of regulation 9 as it applies in relation to employment; and, in its application to contract work, references to 'employee', 'employer' and 'employment' are references to (respectively) 'contract worker', 'principal' and 'contract work' within the meaning of regulation 9.

11 Pension schemes

(1) It is unlawful, except in relation to rights accrued or benefits payable in respect of periods of [pensionable service] prior to the coming into force of [this Regulation], for the trustees or managers of, [or any employer in relation to], an occupational pension scheme to discriminate against a member or prospective member of the scheme in carrying out any of their functions in relation to it (including in particular their functions relating to the admission of members to the scheme and the treatment of members of it).

(2) It is unlawful for the trustees or managers of, [or any employer in relation to], an occupational pension scheme, in relation to the scheme, to subject to harassment a member or prospective member of it.

(3) Schedule 2 (pension schemes) shall have effect for the purposes of –

(a) defining terms used in this regulation and in that Schedule;

(b) exempting certain rules and practices in or relating to pension schemes from Parts 2 and 3 of these Regulations;

(c) treating every occupational pension scheme as including a non-discrimination rule;

(d) giving trustees or managers of an occupational pension scheme power to alter the scheme so as to secure conformity with the non-discrimination rule;

(e) making provision in relation to the procedures, and remedies which may be granted, on certain complaints relating to occupational pension schemes presented to an employment tribunal under regulation 36 (jurisdiction of employment tribunals).

Amendment

Para (1): words 'pensionable service' in square brackets substituted by SI 2006/2931, regs 2, 3(b).

Para (1): words 'this Regulation' in square brackets substituted by SI 2006/2408, reg 2(1), (3).

Paras (1), (2): words ', or any employer in relation to,' in square brackets inserted by SI 2006/2931, regs 2, 3(a).

12 Office-holders etc

(1) It is unlawful for a relevant person, in relation to an appointment to an office or post to which this regulation applies, to discriminate against a person –

(a) in the arrangements which he makes for the purpose of determining to whom the appointment should be offered;

(b) in the terms on which he offers him the appointment; or

(c) by refusing to offer him the appointment.

(2) It is unlawful, in relation to an appointment to an office or post to which this regulation applies and which is an office or post referred to in paragraph (8)(b), for a relevant person on whose recommendation (or subject to whose approval) appointments to the office or post are made, to discriminate against a person –

(a) in the arrangements which he makes for the purpose of determining who should be recommended or approved in relation to the appointment; or

(b) in making or refusing to make a recommendation, or giving or refusing to give an approval, in relation to the appointment.

(3) It is unlawful for a relevant person, in relation to a person who has been appointed to an office or post to which this regulation applies, to discriminate against him –

(a) in the terms of the appointment;

(b) in the opportunities which he affords him for promotion, a transfer, training or receiving any other benefit, or by refusing to afford him any such opportunity;

(c) by terminating the appointment; or

(d) by subjecting him to any other detriment in relation to the appointment.

(4) It is unlawful for a relevant person, in relation to an office or post to which this regulation applies, to subject to harassment a person –

(a) who has been appointed to the office or post;

(b) who is seeking or being considered for appointment to the office or post; or

(c) who is seeking or being considered for a recommendation or approval in relation to an appointment to an office or post referred to in paragraph (8) (b).

(5) Paragraphs (1) and (3) do not apply to any act in relation to an office or post where, if the office or post constituted employment, that act would be lawful by virtue of regulation 8 (exception for genuine occupational requirement etc); and paragraph (2) does not apply to any act in relation to an office or post where, if the office or post constituted employment, it would be lawful by virtue of regulation 8 to refuse to offer the person such employment.

(6) Paragraph (3) does not apply to benefits of any description if the relevant person is concerned with the provision (for payment or not) of benefits of that description to the public, or a section of the public to which the person appointed belongs, unless –

(a) that provision differs in a material respect from the provision of the benefits by the relevant person to persons appointed to offices or posts which are the same as, or not materially different from, that which the person appointed holds; or

(b) the provision of the benefits to the person appointed is regulated by the terms and conditions of his appointment; or

(c) the benefits relate to training.

(7) In paragraph (3) (c) the reference to the termination of the appointment includes a reference –

(a) to the termination of the appointment by the expiration of any period (including a period expiring by reference to an event or circumstance), not being a termination immediately after which the appointment is renewed on the same terms and conditions; and

(b) to the termination of the appointment by any act of the person appointed (including the giving of notice) in circumstances such that he is entitled to terminate the appointment without notice by reason of the conduct of the relevant person.

(8) This regulation applies to –

(a) any office or post to which persons are appointed to discharge functions personally under the direction of another person, and in respect of which they are entitled to remuneration; and

(b) any office or post to which appointments are made by (or on the recommendation of or subject to the approval of) a Minister of the Crown, a government department, the [Welsh Ministers, the First Minister for Wales, the Counsel General to the Welsh Assembly Government] or any part of the Scottish Administration,

but not to a political office or a case where regulation 7 (applicants and employees), 9 (contract workers), 15 (barristers), 16 (advocates) or 17 (partnerships) applies, or would apply but for the operation of any other provision of these Regulations.

(9) For the purposes of paragraph (8) (a) the holder of an office or post –

(a) is to be regarded as discharging his functions under the direction of another person if that other person is entitled to direct him as to when and where he discharges those functions;

(b) is not to be regarded as entitled to remuneration merely because he is entitled to payments –

(i) in respect of expenses incurred by him in carrying out the function of the office or post; or

(ii) by way of compensation for the loss of income or benefits he would or might have received from any person had he not been carrying out the functions of the office or post.

(10) In this regulation –

(a) appointment to an office or post does not include election to an office or post;

(b) 'political office' means –

(i) any office of the House of Commons held by a member of it;

(ii) a life peerage within the meaning of the Life Peerages Act 1958, or any office of the House of Lords held by a member of it;

(iii) any office mentioned in Schedule 2 (Ministerial offices) to the House of Commons Disqualification Act 1975;

(iv) the offices of Leader of the Opposition, Chief Opposition Whip or Assistant Opposition Whip within the meaning of the Ministerial and other Salaries Act 1975;

(v) any office of the Scottish Parliament held by a member of it;

(vi) a member of the Scottish Executive within the meaning of section 44 of the Scotland Act 1998, or a junior Scottish Minister within the meaning of section 49 of that Act;

(vii) any office of the National Assembly for Wales held by a member of it;

(viia) [a member of the Welsh Assembly Government],

(viii) in England, any office of a county council, a London borough council, a district council, or a parish council held by a member of it;

(ix) in Wales, any office of a county council, a county borough council, or a community council held by a member of it;

(x) in relation to a council constituted under section 2 of the Local Government etc (Scotland) Act 1994 or a community council established under section 51 of the Local Government (Scotland) Act 1973, any office of such a council held by a member of it;

(xi) any office of the Greater London Authority held by a member of it;

(xii) any office of the Common Council of the City of London held by a member of it;

(xiii) any office of the Council of the Isles of Scilly held by a member of it;

(xiv) any office of a political party;

(c) 'relevant person', in relation to an office or post, means –

(i) any person with power to make or terminate appointments to the office or post, or to determine the terms of appointment,

(ii) any person with power to determine the working conditions of a person appointed to the office or post in relation to opportunities for promotion, a transfer, training or for receiving any other benefit, and

(iii) any person or body referred to in paragraph (8) (b) on whose recommendation or subject to whose approval appointments are made to the office or post;

(d) references to making a recommendation include references to making a negative recommendation; and

(e) references to refusal include references to deliberate omission.

Amendment

Para (8): in sub-para (b) words from 'Welsh Ministers, the' to 'Welsh Assembly Government' in square brackets substituted by SI 2007/1388, art 3, Sch 1, paras 153, 154(1), (2).

Para (10): sub-para (viia) inserted by SI 2007/1388, art 3, Sch 1, paras 153, 154(1), (3).

13 Police

(1) For the purposes of this Part, the holding of the office of constable shall be treated as employment –

(a) by the chief officer of police as respects any act done by him in relation to a constable or that office;

(b) by the police authority as respects any act done by it in relation to a constable or that office.

(2) For the purposes of regulation 25 (liability of employers and principals) –

(a) the holding of the office of constable shall be treated as employment by the chief officer of police (and as not being employment by any other person); and

(b) anything done by a person holding such an office in the performance, or purported performance, of his functions shall be treated as done in the course of that employment.

(3) There shall be paid out of the police fund –

(a) any compensation, costs or expenses awarded against a chief officer of police in any proceedings brought against him under these Regulations, and any costs or expenses incurred by him in any such proceedings so far as not recovered by him in the proceedings; and

(b) any sum required by a chief officer of police for the settlement of any claim made against him under these Regulations if the settlement is approved by the police authority.

(4) Any proceedings under these Regulations which, by virtue of paragraph (1), would lie against a chief officer of police shall be brought against the chief officer of police for the time being or in the case of a vacancy in that office, against the person for the time being performing the functions of that office; and references in paragraph (3) to the chief officer of police shall be construed accordingly.

(5) A police authority may, in such cases and to such extent as appear to it to be appropriate, pay out of the police fund –

(a) any compensation, costs or expenses awarded in proceedings under these Regulations against a person under the direction and control of the chief officer of police;

(b) any costs or expenses incurred and not recovered by such a person in such proceedings; and

(c) any sum required in connection with the settlement of a claim that has or might have given rise to such proceedings.

(6) Paragraphs (1) and (2) apply to a police cadet and appointment as a police cadet as they apply to a constable and the office of constable.

(7) Subject to paragraph (8), in this regulation –

'chief officer of police' –

(a) in relation to a person appointed, or an appointment falling to be made, under a specified Act, has the same meaning as in the Police Act 1996;

(b) in relation to a person appointed, or an appointment falling to be made, under the Police (Scotland) Act 1967, means the chief constable of the relevant police force;

(c) in relation to any other person or appointment means the officer or other person who has the direction and control of the body of constables or cadets in question;

'police authority' –

(a) in relation to a person appointed, or an appointment falling to be made, under a specified Act, has the same meaning as in the Police Act 1996;

(b) in relation to a person appointed, or an appointment falling to be made, under the Police (Scotland) Act 1967, has the meaning given in that Act;

(c) in relation to any other person or appointment, means the authority by whom the person in question is or on appointment would be paid;

'police cadet' means any person appointed to undergo training with a view to becoming a constable;

'police fund' –

(a) in relation to a chief officer of police within sub-paragraph (a) of the above definition of that term, has the same meaning as in the Police Act 1996;

(b) in any other case means money provided by the police authority; and

'specified Act' means the Metropolitan Police Act 1829, the City of London Police Act 1839 or the Police Act 1996.

(8) In relation to a constable of a force who is not under the direction and control of the chief officer of police for that force, references in this regulation to the chief officer of police are references to the chief officer of the force under whose direction and control he is, and references in this regulation to the police authority are references to the relevant police authority for that force.

(9) This regulation is subject to regulation 14.

14 Serious Organised Crime Agency

(1) For the purposes of this Part, any constable or other person who has been seconded to SOCA to serve as a member of its staff shall be treated as employed by SOCA.

(2) For the purposes of regulation 25 (liability of employers and principals) –

(a) the secondment of any constable or other person to SOCA to serve as a member of its staff shall be treated as employment by SOCA (and not as employment by any other person); and

(b) anything done by a person so seconded in the performance, or purported performance, of his functions shall be treated as done in the course of that employment.

(3) In this regulation 'SOCA' means the Serious Organised Crime Agency established under section 1 of, and Schedule 1 to, the Serious Organised Crime and Police Act 2005.

15 Barristers

(1) It is unlawful for a barrister or barrister's clerk, in relation to any offer of a pupillage or tenancy, to discriminate against a person –

(a) in the arrangements which are made for the purpose of determining to whom the pupillage or tenancy should be offered;

(b) in respect of any terms on which it is offered; or

(c) by refusing, or deliberately not offering, it to him.

(2) It is unlawful for a barrister or barrister's clerk, in relation to a pupil or tenant in the set of chambers in question, to discriminate against him –

(a) in respect of any terms applicable to him as a pupil or tenant;

(b) in the opportunities for training, or gaining experience, which are afforded or denied to him;

(c) in the benefits which are afforded or denied to him; or

(d) by terminating his pupillage, or by subjecting him to any pressure to leave the chambers or other detriment.

(3) It is unlawful for a barrister or barrister's clerk, in relation to a pupillage or tenancy in the set of chambers in question, to subject to harassment a person who is, or has applied to be, a pupil or tenant.

(4) It is unlawful for any person, in relation to the giving, withholding or acceptance of instructions to a barrister, to discriminate against any person by subjecting him to a detriment, or to subject him to harassment.

(5) In this regulation –

'barrister's clerk' includes any person carrying out any of the functions of a barrister's clerk;

'pupil', 'pupillage' and 'set of chambers' have the meanings commonly associated with their use in the context of barristers practising in independent practice; and

'tenancy' and 'tenant' have the meanings commonly associated with their use in the context of barristers practising in independent practice, but also include reference to any barrister permitted to work in a set of chambers who is not a tenant.

(6) This regulation extends to England and Wales only.

16 Advocates

(1) It is unlawful for an advocate, in relation to taking any person as his pupil, to discriminate against a person –

(a) in the arrangements which he makes for the purpose of determining whom he will take as his pupil;

(b) in respect of any terms on which he offers to take any person as his pupil; or

(c) by refusing to take, or deliberately not taking, a person as his pupil.

(2) It is unlawful for an advocate, in relation to a person who is his pupil, to discriminate against him –

(a) in respect of any terms applicable to him as a pupil;

(b) in the opportunities for training, or gaining experience, which are afforded or denied to him;

(c) in the benefits which are afforded or denied to him; or

(d) by terminating the relationship, or by subjecting him to any pressure to terminate the relationship or other detriment.

(3) It is unlawful for an advocate, in relation to a person who is his pupil or taking any person as his pupil, to subject such a person to harassment.

(4) It is unlawful for any person, in relation to the giving, withholding or acceptance of instructions to an advocate, to discriminate against any person by subjecting him to a detriment, or to subject him to harassment.

(5) In this regulation –

'advocate' means a member of the Faculty of Advocates practising as such; and

'pupil' has the meaning commonly associated with its use in the context of a person training to be an advocate.

(6) This regulation extends to Scotland only.

17 Partnerships

(1) It is unlawful for a firm, in relation to a position as partner in the firm, to discriminate against a person –

(a) in the arrangements they make for the purpose of determining to whom they should offer that position;

(b) in the terms on which they offer him that position;

(c) by refusing to offer, or deliberately not offering, him that position; or

(d) in a case where the person already holds that position –

(i) in the way they afford him access to any benefits or by refusing to afford, or deliberately not affording, him access to them; or

(ii) by expelling him from that position, or subjecting him to any other detriment.

(2) It is unlawful for a firm, in relation to a position as partner in the firm, to subject to harassment a person who holds or has applied for that position.

(3) Paragraphs (1)(a) to (c) and (2) apply in relation to persons proposing to form themselves into a partnership as they apply in relation to a firm.

(4) Paragraph (1) does not apply to any act in relation to a position as partner where, if the position were employment, that act would be lawful by virtue of regulation 8 (exception for genuine occupational requirement etc).

(5) In the case of a limited partnership references in this regulation to a partner shall be construed as references to a general partner as defined in section 3 of the Limited Partnerships Act 1907.

(6) This regulation applies to a limited liability partnership as it applies to a firm; and, in its application to a limited liability partnership, references to a partner in a firm are references to a member of the limited liability partnership.

(7) In this regulation, 'firm' has the meaning given by section 4 of the Partnership Act 1890.

(8) In paragraph (1) (d) reference to the expulsion of a person from a position as partner includes reference –

(a) to the termination of that person's partnership by the expiration of any period (including a period expiring by reference to an event or circumstance), not being a termination immediately after which the partnership is renewed on the same terms; and

(b) to the termination of that person's partnership by any act of his (including the giving of notice) in circumstances such that he is entitled to terminate it without notice by reason of the conduct of the other partners.

18 Trade organisations

(1) It is unlawful for a trade organisation to discriminate against a person –

(a) in the terms on which it is prepared to admit him to membership of the organisation; or

(b) by refusing to accept, or deliberately not accepting, his application for membership.

(2) It is unlawful for a trade organisation, in relation to a member of the organisation, to discriminate against him –

(a) in the way it affords him access to any benefits or by refusing or deliberately omitting to afford him access to them;

(b) by depriving him of membership, or varying the terms on which he is a member; or

(c) by subjecting him to any other detriment.

(3) It is unlawful for a trade organisation, in relation to a person's membership or application for membership of that organisation, to subject that person to harassment.

(4) In this regulation –

'trade organisation' means an organisation of workers, an organisation of employers, or any other organisation whose members carry on a particular profession or trade for the purposes of which the organisation exists;

'profession' includes any vocation or occupation; and

'trade' includes any business.

19 Qualifications bodies

(1) It is unlawful for a qualifications body to discriminate against a person –

(a) in the terms on which it is prepared to confer a professional or trade qualification on him;

(b) by refusing or deliberately not granting any application by him for such a qualification; or

(c) by withdrawing such a qualification from him or varying the terms on which he holds it.

(2) It is unlawful for a qualifications body, in relation to a professional or trade qualification conferred by it, to subject to harassment a person who holds or applies for such a qualification.

(3) In this regulation –

'qualifications body' means any authority or body which can confer a professional or trade qualification, but it does not include –

(a) a governing body of an educational establishment to which regulation 23 (institutions of further and higher education) applies, or would apply but for the operation of any other provision of these Regulations, or

(b) a proprietor of a school;

'confer' includes renew or extend;

'professional or trade qualification' means any authorisation, qualification, recognition, registration, enrolment, approval or certification which is needed for, or facilitates engagement in, a particular profession or trade;

'profession' and 'trade' have the same meaning as in regulation 18.

20 The provision of vocational training

(1) It is unlawful, in relation to a person seeking or undergoing training, for any training provider to discriminate against him –

(a) in the arrangements he makes for the purpose of determining to whom he should offer training;

(b) in the terms on which the training provider affords him access to any training;

(c) by refusing or deliberately not affording him such access;

(d) by terminating his training; or

(e) by subjecting him to any other detriment during his training.

(2) It is unlawful for a training provider, in relation to a person seeking or undergoing training, to subject him to harassment.

(3) Paragraph (1) does not apply if the discrimination concerns training that would only fit a person for employment which, by virtue of regulation 8 (exception for genuine occupational requirement etc), the employer could lawfully refuse to offer the person seeking training.

(4) In this regulation –

'professional or trade qualification' has the same meaning as in regulation 19;

'registered pupil' has the meaning given by section 434 of the Education Act 1996;

'training' means –

(a) all types and all levels of training which would help fit a person for any employment;

(b) vocational guidance;

(c) facilities for training;

(d) practical work experience provided by an employer to a person whom he does not employ; and

(e) any assessment related to the award of any professional or trade qualification;

'training provider' means any person who provides, or makes arrangements for the provision of, training, but it does not include –

(a) an employer in relation to training for persons employed by him;

(b) a governing body of an educational establishment to which regulation 23 (institutions of further and higher education) applies, or would apply but for the operation of any other provision of these Regulations; or

(c) a proprietor of a school in relation to any registered pupil.

21 Employment agencies, careers guidance etc

(1) It is unlawful for an employment agency to discriminate against a person –

(a) in the terms on which the agency offers to provide any of its services;

(b) by refusing or deliberately not providing any of its services; or

(c) in the way it provides any of its services.

(2) It is unlawful for an employment agency, in relation to a person to whom it provides its services, or who has requested it to provide its services, to subject that person to harassment.

(3) Paragraph (1) does not apply to discrimination if it only concerns employment which, by virtue of regulation 8 (exception for genuine occupational requirement etc), the employer could lawfully refuse to offer the person in question.

(4) An employment agency shall not be subject to any liability under this regulation if it proves that –

(a) it acted in reliance on a statement made to it by the employer to the effect that, by reason of the operation of paragraph (3), its action would not be unlawful; and

(b) it was reasonable for it to rely on the statement.

(5) A person who knowingly or recklessly makes a statement such as is referred to in paragraph (4) (a) which in a material respect is false or misleading commits an offence, and shall be liable on summary conviction to a fine not exceeding level 5 on the standard scale.

(6) For the purposes of this regulation –

(a) 'employment agency' means a person who, for profit or not, provides services for the purpose of finding employment for workers or supplying employers with workers, but it does not include –

(i) a governing body of an educational establishment to which regulation 23 (institutions of further and higher education) applies, or would apply but for the operation of any other provision of these Regulations; or

(ii) a proprietor of a school; and

(b) references to the services of an employment agency include guidance on careers and any other services related to employment.

22 Assisting persons to obtain employment etc

(1) It is unlawful for the Secretary of State to discriminate against any person by subjecting him to a detriment, or to subject a person to harassment, in the provision of facilities or services

under section 2 of the Employment and Training Act 1973 (arrangements for assisting persons to obtain employment).

(2) It is unlawful for Scottish Enterprise or Highlands and Islands Enterprise to discriminate against any person by subjecting him to a detriment, or to subject a person to harassment, in the provision of facilities or services under such arrangements as are mentioned in section 2(3) of the Enterprise and New Towns (Scotland) Act 1990 (arrangements analogous to arrangements in pursuance of the said Act of 1973).

(3) This regulation does not apply in a case where –

(a) regulation 20 (the provision of vocational training) applies or would apply but for the operation of any other provision of these Regulations, or

(b) the Secretary of State is acting as an employment agency within the meaning of regulation 21 (employment agencies, careers guidance etc).

23 Institutions of further and higher education

(1) It is unlawful, in relation to an educational establishment to which this regulation applies, for the governing body of that establishment to discriminate against a person –

(a) in the terms on which it offers to admit him to the establishment as a student;

(b) by refusing or deliberately not accepting an application for his admission to the establishment as a student; or

(c) where he is a student of the establishment –

(i) in the way it affords him access to any benefits,

(ii) by refusing or deliberately not affording him access to them, or

(iii) by excluding him from the establishment or subjecting him to any other detriment.

(2) It is unlawful, in relation to an educational establishment to which this regulation applies, for the governing body of that establishment to subject to harassment a person who is a student at the establishment, or who has applied for admission to the establishment as a student.

(3) Paragraph (1) does not apply if the discrimination concerns training that would only fit a person for employment which, by virtue of regulation 8 (exception for genuine occupational requirement etc), the employer could lawfully refuse to offer the person in question.

(4) This regulation applies to the following educational establishments in England and Wales, namely –

(a) an institution within the further education sector (within the meaning of section 91(3) of the Further and Higher Education Act 1992);

(b) a university;

(c) an institution, other than a university, within the higher education sector (within the meaning of section 91(5) of the Further and Higher Education Act 1992).

(5) This regulation applies to the following educational establishments in Scotland, namely –

(a) a college of further education within the meaning of section 36(1) of the Further and Higher Education (Scotland) Act 1992 under the management of a board of management within the meaning of Part I of that Act;

(b) a college of further education maintained by an education authority in the exercise of its further education functions in providing courses of further education within the meaning of section 1(5)(b)(ii) of the Education (Scotland) Act 1980;

(c) any other educational establishment (not being a school) which provides further education within the meaning of section 1 of the Further and Higher Education (Scotland) Act 1992;

(d) an institution within the higher education sector (within the meaning of Part 2 of the Further and Higher Education (Scotland) Act 1992);

(e) a central institution (within the meaning of section 135 of the Education (Scotland) Act 1980).

(6) In this regulation –

'education authority' has the meaning given by section 135(1) of the Education (Scotland) Act 1980;

'governing body' includes –

(a) the board of management of a college referred to in paragraph (5)(a), and

(b) the managers of a college or institution referred to in paragraph (5)(b) or (e);

'student' means any person who receives education at an educational establishment to which this regulation applies; and 'university' includes a university college and the college, school or hall of a university.

24 Relationships which have come to an end

(1) In this regulation a 'relevant relationship' is a relationship during the course of which an act of discrimination against, or harassment of, one party to the relationship ('B') by the other party to it ('A') is unlawful by virtue of any preceding provision of this Part.

(2) Where a relevant relationship has come to an end, it is unlawful for A –

(a) to discriminate against B by subjecting him to a detriment; or

(b) to subject B to harassment;

where the discrimination or harassment arises out of and is closely connected to that relationship.

(3) In paragraph (1), reference to an act of discrimination or harassment which is unlawful includes, in the case of a relationship which has come to an end before [the date on which the act of discrimination or harassment became unlawful by virtue of these Regulations], reference to an act of discrimination or harassment which would, after [that date], be unlawful.

Amendment

Para (3): words from 'the date on' to 'of these Regulations' in square brackets substituted by SI 2006/2408, reg 2(1), (4)(a).

Para (3): words 'that date' in square brackets substituted by SI 2006/2408, reg 2(1), (4)(b).

Part 3

Other Unlawful Acts

25 Liability of employers and principals

(1) Anything done by a person in the course of his employment shall be treated for the purposes of these Regulations as done by his employer as well as by him, whether or not it was done with the employer's knowledge or approval.

(2) Anything done by a person as agent for another person with the authority (whether express or implied, and whether precedent or subsequent) of that other person shall be treated for the purposes of these Regulations as done by that other person as well as by him.

(3) In proceedings brought under these Regulations against any person in respect of an act alleged to have been done by an employee of his it shall be a defence for that person to prove that he took such steps as were reasonably practicable to prevent the employee from doing that act, or from doing in the course of his employment acts of that description.

26 Aiding unlawful acts

(1) A person who knowingly aids another person to do an act made unlawful by these Regulations shall be treated for the purpose of these Regulations as himself doing an unlawful act of the like description.

(2) For the purposes of paragraph (1) an employee or agent for whose act the employer or principal is liable under regulation 25 (or would be so liable but for regulation 25(3)) shall be deemed to aid the doing of the act by the employer or principal.

(3) A person does not under this regulation knowingly aid another to do an unlawful act if –

(a) he acts in reliance on a statement made to him by that other person that, by reason of any provision of these Regulations, the act which he aids would not be unlawful; and

(b) it is reasonable for him to rely on the statement.

(4) A person who knowingly or recklessly makes a statement such as is referred to in paragraph (3) (a) which in a material respect is false or misleading commits an offence, and shall be liable on summary conviction to a fine not exceeding level 5 on the standard scale.

Part 4

General Exceptions from Parts 2 and 3

27 Exception for statutory authority

(1) Nothing in Part 2 or 3 shall render unlawful any act done in order to comply with a requirement of any statutory provision.

(2) In this regulation 'statutory provision' means any provision (whenever enacted) of –

(a) an Act or an Act of the Scottish Parliament;

(aa) [a Measure or Act of the National Assembly for Wales;]

(b) an instrument made by a Minister of the Crown under an Act;

(c) an instrument made under an Act or an Act of the Scottish Parliament by the Scottish Ministers or a member of the Scottish Executive.

(d) [an instrument made after the end of the initial period under an Act, or under a Measure or Act of the National Assembly for Wales, by the Welsh Ministers, the First Minister for Wales or the Counsel General to the Welsh Assembly Government].

(3) [In paragraph (2)(d) 'the initial period' has the same meaning as in the Government of Wales Act 2006 (see section 161(6) of that Act)]

Amendment

Para (2): para (aa) inserted by SI 2007/1388, art 3, Sch 1, paras 153, 155(1), (2).

Para (2): sub-para (d) inserted by SI 2007/1388, art 3, Sch 1, paras 153, 155(1), (3).

Para (3): inserted by SI 2007/1388, art 3, Sch 1, paras 153, 155(1), (3).

28 Exception for national security

Nothing in Part 2 or 3 shall render unlawful an act done for the purpose of safeguarding national security, if the doing of the act was justified by that purpose.

29 Exceptions for positive action

(1) Nothing in Part 2 or 3 shall render unlawful any act done in or in connection with –

(a) affording persons of a particular age or age group access to facilities for training which would help fit them for particular work; or

(b) encouraging persons of a particular age or age group to take advantage of opportunities for doing particular work;

where it reasonably appears to the person doing the act that it prevents or compensates for disadvantages linked to age suffered by persons of that age or age group doing that work or likely to take up that work.

(2) Nothing in Part 2 or 3 shall render unlawful any act done by a trade organisation within the meaning of regulation 18 in or in connection with –

(a) affording only members of the organisation who are of a particular age or age group access to facilities for training which would help fit them for holding a post of any kind in the organisation; or

(b) encouraging only members of the organisation who are of a particular age or age group to take advantage of opportunities for holding such posts in the organisation,

where it reasonably appears to the organisation that the act prevents or compensates for disadvantages linked to age suffered by those of that age or age group holding such posts or likely to hold such posts.

(3) Nothing in Part 2 or 3 shall render unlawful any act done by a trade organisation within the meaning of regulation 18 in or in connection with encouraging only persons of a particular age or age group to become members of the organisation where it reasonably appears to the organisation that the act prevents or compensates for disadvantages linked to age suffered by persons of that age or age group who are, or are eligible to become, members.

30 Exception for retirement

(1) This regulation applies in relation to an employee within the meaning of section 230(1) of the 1996 Act, a person in Crown employment, a relevant member of the House of Commons staff, and a relevant member of the House of Lords staff.

(2) Nothing in Part 2 or 3 shall render unlawful the dismissal of a person to whom this regulation applies at or over the age of 65 where the reason for the dismissal is retirement.

(3) For the purposes of this regulation, whether or not the reason for a dismissal is retirement shall be determined in accordance with sections 98ZA to 98ZF of the 1996 Act.

31 Exception for the national minimum wage

(1) Nothing in Part 2 or 3 shall render it unlawful for a relevant person ('A') to be remunerated in respect of his work at a rate which is lower than the rate at which another such person ('B') is remunerated for his work where –

(a) the hourly rate of the national minimum wage for a person of A's age is lower than that for a person of B's age, and

(b) the rate at which A is remunerated is below the single hourly rate for the national minimum wage prescribed by the Secretary of State under section 1(3) of the National Minimum Wage Act 1998.

(2) Nothing in Part 2 or 3 shall render it unlawful for an apprentice who is not a relevant person to be remunerated in respect of his work at a rate which is lower than the rate at which an apprentice who is a relevant person is remunerated for his work.

(3) In this regulation –

'apprentice' means a person who is employed under a contract of apprenticeship or, in accordance with regulation 12(3) of the National Minimum Wage Regulations 1999, is to be treated as employed under such a contract;

'relevant person' means a person who qualifies for the national minimum wage (whether at the single hourly rate for the national minimum wage prescribed by the Secretary of State under section 1(3) of the National Minimum Wage Act 1998 or at a different rate).

32 Exception for provision of certain benefits based on length of service

(1) Subject to paragraph (2), nothing in Part 2 or 3 shall render it unlawful for a person ('A'), in relation to the award of any benefit by him, to put a worker ('B') at a disadvantage when compared with another worker ('C'), if and to the extent that the disadvantage suffered by B is because B's length of service is less than that of C

(2) Where B's length of service exceeds 5 years, it must reasonably appear to A that the way in which he uses the criterion of length of service, in relation to the award in respect of which B is put at a disadvantage, fulfils a business need of his undertaking (for example, by encouraging the loyalty or motivation, or rewarding the experience, of some or all of his workers).

(3) In calculating a worker's length of service for these purposes, A shall calculate –

(a) the length of time the worker has been working for him doing work which he reasonably considers to be at or above a particular level (assessed by reference to the demands made on the worker, for example, in terms of effort, skills and decision making); or

(b) the length of time the worker has been working for him in total;

and on each occasion on which he decides to use the criterion of length of service in relation to the award of a benefit to workers, it is for him to decide which of these definitions to use to calculate their lengths of service.

(4) For the purposes of paragraph (3), in calculating the length of time a worker has been working for him –

(a) A shall calculate the length of time in terms of the number of weeks during the whole or part of which the worker was working for him;

(b) A may discount any period during which the worker was absent from work (including any period of absence which at the time it occurred was thought by A or the worker to be permanent) unless in all the circumstances (including the way in which other workers' absences occurring in similar circumstances are treated by A in calculating their lengths of service) it would not be reasonable for him to do so;

(c) A may discount any period of time during which the worker was present at work ('the relevant period') where –

(i) the relevant period preceded a period during which the worker was absent from work, and

(ii) in all the circumstances (including the length of the worker's absence, the reason for his absence, the effect his absence has had on his ability to discharge the duties of his work, and the way in which other workers are treated by A in similar circumstances) it is reasonable for A to discount the relevant period.

(5) For the purposes of paragraph (3)(b), a worker shall be treated as having worked for A during any period during which he worked for another if –

(a) that period is treated as a period of employment with A for the purposes of the 1996 Act by virtue of the operation of section 218 of that Act; or

(b) were the worker to be made redundant by A, that period and the period he has worked for A would amount to 'relevant service' within the meaning of section 155 of that Act.

(6) In paragraph (5) –

(a) the reference to being made redundant is a reference to being dismissed by reason of redundancy for the purposes of the 1996 Act;

(b) the reference to section 155 of that Act is a reference to that section as modified by the Redundancy Payments (Continuity of Employment in Local Government, etc) (Modification) Order 1999.

(7) In this regulation –

'benefit' does not include any benefit awarded to a worker by virtue of his ceasing to work for A; and

'year' means a year of 12 calendar months.

33 Exception for provision of enhanced redundancy payments to employees

(1) Nothing in Part 2 or 3 shall render it unlawful for an employer –

(a) to give a qualifying employee an enhanced redundancy payment which is less in amount than the enhanced redundancy payment which he gives to another such employee if both amounts are calculated in the same way;

(b) to give enhanced redundancy payments only to those who are qualifying employees by virtue of sub-paragraph (a) or (c) (i) of the definition of qualifying employee below.

(2) In this regulation –

'the appropriate amount', 'a redundancy payment' and 'a week's pay' have the same meaning as they have in section 162 of the 1996 Act;

'enhanced redundancy payment' means a payment of an amount calculated in accordance with paragraph (3) or (4);

'qualifying employee' means –

(a) an employee who is entitled to a redundancy payment by virtue of section 135 of the 1996 Act;

(b) an employee who would have been so entitled but for the operation of section 155 of that Act;

(c) an employee who agrees to the termination of his employment in circumstances where, had he been dismissed –

(i) he would have been a qualifying employee by virtue of sub-paragraph (a) of this definition; or

(ii) he would have been a qualifying employee by virtue of sub-paragraph (b).

(3) For an amount to be calculated in accordance with this paragraph it must be calculated in accordance with section 162(1) to (3) of the 1996 Act.

(4) For an amount to be calculated in accordance with this paragraph –

(a) it must be calculated as in paragraph (3);

(b) however, in making that calculation, the employer may do one or both of the following things –

(i) he may treat a week's pay as not being subject to a maximum amount or as being subject to a maximum amount above the amount laid down in section 227 of the 1996 Act;

(ii) he may multiply the appropriate amount allowed for each year of employment by a figure of more than one;

(c) having made the calculation as in paragraph (3) (whether or not in making that calculation he has done anything mentioned in sub-paragraph (b)) the employer may increase the amount thus calculated by multiplying it by a figure of more than one.

(5) For the purposes of paragraphs (3) and (4), the reference to 'the relevant date' in section 162(1)(a) of the 1996 Act is to be read, in the case of a qualifying employee who agrees to the termination of his employment, as a reference to the date on which that termination takes effect.

34 Exception for provision of life assurance cover to retired workers

(1) Where a person ('A') arranges for workers to be provided with life assurance cover after their early retirement on grounds of ill health, nothing in Part 2 or 3 shall render it unlawful –

(a) where a normal retirement age applied in relation to any such workers at the time they took early retirement, for A to arrange for such cover to cease when such workers reach that age;

(b) in relation to any other workers, for A to arrange for such cover to cease when the workers reach the age of 65.

(2) In this regulation, 'normal retirement age', in relation to a worker who has taken early retirement, means the age at which workers in A's undertaking who held the same kind of position as the worker held at the time of his retirement were normally required to retire.

Part 5

Enforcement

35 Restriction of proceedings for breach of Regulations

(1) Except as provided by these Regulations no proceedings, whether civil or criminal, shall lie against any person in respect of an act by reason that the act is unlawful by virtue of a provision of these Regulations.

(2) Paragraph (1) does not prevent the making of an application for judicial review or the investigation or determination of any matter in accordance with Part 10 (investigations: the Pensions Ombudsman) of the Pension Schemes Act 1993 by the Pensions Ombudsman.

36 Jurisdiction of employment tribunals

(1) A complaint by any person ('the complainant') that another person ('the respondent') –

(a) has committed against the complainant an act to which this regulation applies; or

(b) is by virtue of regulation 25 (liability of employers and principals) or 26 (aiding unlawful acts) to be treated as having committed against the complainant such an act;

may be presented to an employment tribunal.

(2) This regulation applies to any act of discrimination or harassment which is unlawful by virtue of any provision of Part 2 other than –

(a) where the act is one in respect of which an appeal or proceedings in the nature of an appeal may be brought under any enactment, regulation 19 (qualifications bodies);

(b) regulation 23 (institutions of further and higher education); or

(c) where the act arises out of and is closely connected to a relationship between the complainant and the respondent which has come to an end but during the course of which an act of discrimination against, or harassment of, the complainant by the respondent would have been unlawful by virtue of regulation 23, regulation 24 (relationships which have come to an end).

(3) In paragraph (2)(c), reference to an act of discrimination or harassment which would have been unlawful includes, in the case of a relationship which has come to an end before [the date on which the act of discrimination or harassment became unlawful by virtue of these Regulations], reference to an act of discrimination or harassment which would, after [that date], have been unlawful.

(4) In this regulation, 'enactment' includes an enactment comprised in, or in an instrument made under, an Act of the Scottish Parliament.

Amendment

Para (3): words from 'the date on' to 'of these Regulations' in square brackets substituted by SI 2006/2408, reg 2(1), (4)(a).

Para (3): words 'that date' in square brackets substituted by SI 2006/2408, reg 2(1), (4)(b).

37 Burden of proof: employment tribunals

(1) This regulation applies to any complaint presented under regulation 36 to an employment tribunal.

(2) Where, on the hearing of the complaint, the complainant proves facts from which the tribunal could, apart from this regulation, conclude in the absence of an adequate explanation that the respondent –

(a) has committed against the complainant an act to which regulation 36 applies; or

(b) is by virtue of regulation 25 (liability of employers and principals) or 26 (aiding unlawful acts) to be treated as having committed against the complainant such an act, the tribunal shall uphold the complaint unless the respondent proves that he did not commit, or as the case may be, is not to be treated as having committed, that act.

38 Remedies on complaints in employment tribunals

(1) Where an employment tribunal finds that a complaint presented to it under regulation 36 is well-founded, the tribunal shall make such of the following as it considers just and equitable –

(a) an order declaring the rights of the complainant and the respondent in relation to the act to which the complaint relates;

(b) an order requiring the respondent to pay to the complainant compensation of an amount corresponding to any damages he could have been ordered by a county court or by a sheriff court to pay to the complainant if the complaint had fallen to be dealt with under regulation 39 (jurisdiction of county and sheriff courts);

(c) a recommendation that the respondent take within a specified period action appearing to the tribunal to be practicable for the purpose of obviating or reducing the adverse effect on the complainant of any act of discrimination or harassment to which the complaint relates.

(2) As respects an unlawful act of discrimination falling within regulation 3(1)(b) (discrimination on the grounds of age), if the respondent proves that the provision, criterion or practice was not applied with the intention of treating the complainant unfavourably on grounds of age, an order may be made under paragraph (1)(b) only if the employment tribunal –

(a) makes such order under paragraph (1)(a) (if any) and such recommendation under paragraph (1)(c) (if any) as it would have made if it had no power to make an order under paragraph (1)(b); and

(b) (where it makes an order under paragraph (1)(a) or a recommendation under paragraph (1)(c) or both) considers that it is just and equitable to make an order under paragraph (1)(b) as well.

(3) If without reasonable justification the respondent to a complaint fails to comply with a recommendation made by an employment tribunal under paragraph (1)(c), then, if it thinks it just and equitable to do so –

(a) the tribunal may increase the amount of compensation required to be paid to the complainant in respect of the complaint by an order made under paragraph (1)(b); or

(b) if an order under paragraph (1)(b) was not made, the tribunal may make such an order.

(4) Where an amount of compensation falls to be awarded under paragraph (1)(b), the tribunal may include in the award interest on that amount subject to, and in accordance with, the provisions of the Employment Tribunals (Interest on Awards in Discrimination Cases) Regulations 1996.

(5) This regulation has effect subject to paragraph 6 of Schedule 2 (pension schemes).

39 Jurisdiction of county and sheriff courts

(1) A claim by any person ('the claimant') that another person ('the respondent') –

(a) has committed against the claimant an act to which this regulation applies; or

(b) is by virtue of regulation 25 (liability of employers and principals) or 26 (aiding unlawful acts) to be treated as having committed against the claimant such an act,

may be made the subject of civil proceedings in like manner as any other claim in tort or (in Scotland) in reparation for breach of statutory duty.

(2) Proceedings brought under paragraph (1) shall –

(a) in England and Wales, be brought only in a county court; and

(b) in Scotland, be brought only in a sheriff court.

(3) For the avoidance of doubt it is hereby declared that damages in respect of an unlawful act to which this regulation applies may include compensation for injury to feelings whether or not they include compensation under any other head.

(4) This regulation applies to any act of discrimination or harassment which is unlawful by virtue of –

(a) regulation 23 (institutions of further and higher education); or

(b) where the act arises out of and is closely connected to a relationship between the claimant and the respondent which has come to an end but during the course of which an act of discrimination against, or harassment of, the claimant by the respondent would have been unlawful by virtue of regulation 23, regulation 24 (relationships which have come to an end).

(5) In paragraph (4)(b), reference to an act of discrimination or harassment which would have been unlawful includes, in the case of a relationship which has come to an end before [the date on which the act of discrimination or harassment became unlawful by virtue of these Regulations], reference to an act of discrimination or harassment which would, after [that date], have been unlawful.

Amendment

Para (5): words from 'the date on' to 'of these Regulations' in square brackets substituted by SI 2006/2408, reg 2(1), (4)(a).

Para (5): words 'that date' in square brackets substituted by SI 2006/2408, reg 2(1), (4)(b).

40 Burden of proof: county and sheriff courts

(1) This regulation applies to any claim brought under regulation 39 in a county court in England and Wales or a sheriff court in Scotland.

(2) Where, on the hearing of the claim, the claimant proves facts from which the court could, apart from this regulation, conclude in the absence of an adequate explanation that the respondent –

(a) has committed against the claimant an act to which regulation 39 applies; or

(b) is by virtue of regulation 25 (liability of employers and principals) or 26 (aiding unlawful acts) to be treated as having committed against the claimant such an act,

the court shall uphold the claim unless the respondent proves that he did not commit, or as the case may be, is not to be treated as having committed, that act.

41 Help for persons in obtaining information etc

(1) In accordance with this regulation, a person ('the person aggrieved') who considers he may have been discriminated against, or subjected to harassment, in contravention of these Regulations may serve on the respondent to a complaint presented under regulation 36 (jurisdiction of employment

tribunals) or a claim brought under regulation 39 (jurisdiction of county and sheriff courts) questions in the form set out in Schedule 3 or forms to the like effect with such variation as the circumstances require; and the respondent may if he so wishes reply to such questions by way of the form set out in Schedule 4 or forms to the like effect with such variation as the circumstances require.

(2) Where the person aggrieved questions the respondent (whether in accordance with paragraph (1) or not) –

(a) the questions, and any reply by the respondent (whether in accordance with paragraph (1) or not) shall, subject to the following provisions of this regulation, be admissible as evidence in the proceedings;

(b) if it appears to the court or tribunal that the respondent deliberately, and without reasonable excuse, omitted to reply within eight weeks of service of the questions or that his reply is evasive or equivocal, the court or tribunal may draw any inference from that fact that it considers it just and equitable to draw, including an inference that he committed an unlawful act.

(3) In proceedings before a county court in England or Wales or a sheriff court in Scotland, a question shall only be admissible as evidence in pursuance of paragraph (2) (a) –

(a) where it was served before those proceedings had been instituted, if it was so served within the period of six months beginning when the act complained of was done;

(b) where it was served when those proceedings had been instituted, if it was served with the leave of, and within a period specified by, the court in question.

(4) In proceedings before an employment tribunal, a question shall only be admissible as evidence in pursuance of paragraph (2) (a) –

(a) where it was served before a complaint had been presented to the tribunal, if it was so served within the period of three months beginning when the act complained of was done;

(b) where it was so served when a complaint had been presented to the tribunal, either –

(i) if it was served within the period of twenty-one days beginning with the day on which the complaint was presented, or

(ii) if it was so served later with leave given, and within a period specified, by a direction of the tribunal.

(5) A question and any reply thereto may be served on the respondent or, as the case may be, on the person aggrieved –

(a) by delivering it to him;

(b) by sending it by post to him at his usual or last-known residence or place of business;

(c) where the person to be served is a body corporate or is a trade union or employers' association within the meaning of the Trade Union and Labour Relations (Consolidation) Act 1992, by delivering it to the secretary or clerk of the body, union or association at its registered or principal office or by sending it by post to the secretary or clerk at that office;

(d) where the person to be served is acting by a solicitor, by delivering it at, or by sending it by post to, the solicitor's address for service; or

(e) where the person to be served is the person aggrieved, by delivering the reply, or sending it by post, to him at his address for reply as stated by him in the document containing the questions.

(6) This regulation is without prejudice to any other enactment or rule of law regulating interlocutory and preliminary matters in proceedings before a county court, sheriff court or employment tribunal, and has effect subject to any enactment or rule of law regulating the admissibility of evidence in such proceedings.

(7) In this regulation 'respondent' includes a prospective respondent.

42 Period within which proceedings to be brought

(1) An employment tribunal shall not consider a complaint under regulation 36 unless it is presented to the tribunal before the end of the period of three months beginning when the act complained of was done.

(2) A county court or a sheriff court shall not consider a claim brought under regulation 39 unless proceedings in respect of the claim are instituted before the end of the period of six months beginning when the act complained of was done.

(3) A court or tribunal may nevertheless consider any such complaint or claim which is out of time if, in all the circumstances of the case, it considers that it is just and equitable to do so.

(4) For the purposes of this regulation and regulation 41 (help for persons in obtaining information etc) –

(a) when the making of a contract is, by reason of the inclusion of any term, an unlawful act, that act shall be treated as extending throughout the duration of the contract; and

(b) any act extending over a period shall be treated as done at the end of that period; and

(c) a deliberate omission shall be treated as done when the person in question decided upon it,

and in the absence of evidence establishing the contrary a person shall be taken for the purposes of this regulation to decide upon an omission when he does an act inconsistent with doing the omitted act or, if he has done no such inconsistent act, when the period expires within which he might reasonably have been expected to do the omitted act if it was to be done.

Part 6

Supplemental

43 Validity of contracts, collective agreements and rules of undertakings

Schedule 5 (validity of contracts, collective agreements and rules of undertakings) shall have effect.

44 Application to the Crown etc

(1) These Regulations apply –

(a) to an act done by or for purposes of a Minister of the Crown or government department; or

(b) to an act done on behalf of the Crown by a statutory body, or a person holding a statutory office,

as they apply to an act done by a private person.

(2) These Regulations apply to Crown employment as they apply to employment by a private person, and shall so apply as if

references to a contract of employment included references to the terms of service and references to dismissal included references to termination of Crown employment.

(3) Paragraphs (1) and (2) have effect subject to paragraph (4) and regulations 13 (police) and 14 (Serious Organised Crime Agency).

(4) These regulations do not apply to service in any of the naval, military or air forces of the Crown.

(5) Regulation 10(3) (meaning of employment and contract work at establishment in Great Britain) shall have effect in relation to any ship, aircraft or hovercraft belonging to or possessed by Her Majesty in right of the government of the United Kingdom as it has effect in relation to a ship, aircraft or hovercraft specified in regulation 10(3)(a) or (b).

(6) The provisions of Parts 2 to 4 of the Crown Proceedings Act 1947 shall apply to proceedings against the Crown under these Regulations as they apply to proceedings in England and Wales which by virtue of section 23 of that Act are treated for the purposes of Part 2 of that Act as civil proceedings by or against the Crown, except that in their application to proceedings under these Regulations section 20 of that Act (removal and transfer of proceedings) shall not apply.

(7) The provisions of Part 5 of the Crown Proceedings Act 1947 shall apply to proceedings against the Crown under these Regulations as they apply to proceedings in Scotland which by virtue of the said Part are treated as civil proceedings by or against the Crown, except that in their application to proceedings under these Regulations the proviso to section 44 of that Act (proceedings against the Crown in the Sheriff Court) shall not apply.

45 Application to House of Commons staff

(1) Subject to paragraphs (2) and (3), these Regulations apply in relation to employment as a relevant member of the House of Commons staff as they apply in relation to other employment.

(2) These Regulations apply to employment as such a member as they apply to employment by a private person, and shall so apply as if references to a contract of employment included references to the terms of employment of such a member and references to dismissal included references to termination of such employment.

(3) In relation to employment as such a member, subsections (6) to (12) of section 195 of the 1996 Act (person to be treated as employer of House of Commons staff) apply, with any necessary modifications, for the purposes of these Regulations.

46 Application to House of Lords staff

(1) These Regulations apply in relation to employment as a relevant member of the House of Lords staff as they apply in relation to other employment.

(2) Section 194(7) of the 1996 Act (continuity of employment) applies for the purposes of this regulation.

47 Duty to consider working beyond retirement

Schedule 6, which sets out the procedure to be followed if an employee (within the meaning of that Schedule) is to be retired, shall have effect.

48 Duty to consider working beyond retirement – transitional provisions

Schedule 7, which sets out transitional provisions in relation to the duty to consider working beyond retirement, shall have effect.

49 Amendments, transitionals, repeals and revocations

(1) Schedule 8, which contains amendments to and repeals of legislation and related transitional provisions, shall have effect.

(2) Schedule 9, which contains repeals and revocations, shall have effect.

Gerry Sutcliffe

Parliamentary Under-Secretary of State for Employment Relations and Consumer Affairs

Department of Trade and Industry

3rd April 2006

SCHEDULE 1

Norwegian Part of the Frigg Gas Field

Regulation 10(4)

1 The part of the Norwegian sector of the Continental Shelf described in this Schedule is the area defined by –

(a) the sets of lines of latitude and longitude joining the following surface co-ordinates –

Longitude	Latitude
02 degrees 05 minutes 30 seconds E	60 degrees 00 minutes 45 seconds N
02 degrees 05 minutes 30 seconds E	59 degrees 58 minutes 45 seconds N
02 degrees 06 minutes 00 seconds E	59 degrees 58 minutes 45 seconds N
02 degrees 06 minutes 00 seconds E	59 degrees 57 minutes 45 seconds N
02 degrees 07 minutes 00 seconds E	59 degrees 57 minutes 45 seconds N
02 degrees 07 minutes 00 seconds E	59 degrees 57 minutes 30 seconds N
02 degrees 07 minutes 30 seconds E	59 degrees 57 minutes 30 seconds N
02 degrees 07 minutes 30 seconds E	59 degrees 55 minutes 30 seconds N
02 degrees 10 minutes 30 seconds E	59 degrees 55 minutes 30 seconds N
02 degrees 10 minutes 30 seconds E	59 degrees 54 minutes 45 seconds N
02 degrees 11 minutes 00 seconds E	59 degrees 54 minutes 45 seconds N
02 degrees 11 minutes 00 seconds E	59 degrees 54 minutes 15 seconds N
02 degrees 12 minutes 30 seconds E	59 degrees 54 minutes 15 seconds N
02 degrees 12 minutes 30 seconds E	59 degrees 54 minutes 00 seconds N
02 degrees 13 minutes 30 seconds E	59 degrees 54 minutes 00 seconds N
02 degrees 13 minutes 30 seconds E	59 degrees 54 minutes 30 seconds N
02 degrees 15 minutes 30 seconds E	59 degrees 54 minutes 30 seconds N
02 degrees 15 minutes 30 seconds E	59 degrees 53 minutes 15 seconds N
02 degrees 10 minutes 30 seconds E	59 degrees 53 minutes 15 seconds N
02 degrees 10 minutes 30 seconds E	59 degrees 52 minutes 45 seconds N
02 degrees 09 minutes 30 seconds E	59 degrees 52 minutes 45 seconds N
02 degrees 09 minutes 30 seconds E	59 degrees 52 minutes 15 seconds N
02 degrees 08 minutes 30 seconds E	59 degrees 52 minutes 15 seconds N
02 degrees 08 minutes 30 seconds E	59 degrees 52 minutes 00 seconds N
02 degrees 07 minutes 30 seconds E	59 degrees 52 minutes 00 seconds N
02 degrees 07 minutes 30 seconds E	59 degrees 51 minutes 30 seconds N
02 degrees 05 minutes 30 seconds E	59 degrees 51 minutes 30 seconds N
02 degrees 05 minutes 30 seconds E	59 degrees 51 minutes 00 seconds N
02 degrees 04 minutes 00 seconds E	59 degrees 51 minutes 00 seconds N

Longitude	Latitude
02 degrees 04 minutes 00 seconds E	59 degrees 50 minutes 30 seconds N
02 degrees 03 minutes 00 seconds E	59 degrees 50 minutes 30 seconds N
02 degrees 03 minutes 00 seconds E	59 degrees 50 minutes 00 seconds N

(b) a line from the point 02 degrees 03 minutes 00 seconds E 59 degrees 50 minutes 00 seconds N west along the parallel of latitude 59 degrees 50 minutes 00 seconds N until its intersection with the Dividing Line;

(c) a line from the point of intersection specified in sub-paragraph (b) along the Dividing Line until its intersection with the parallel of latitude 60 degrees 00 minutes 45 seconds N;

(d) a line from the point of intersection specified in sub-paragraph (c) east along the parallel of latitude 60 degrees 00 minutes 45 degrees N until its intersection with the meridian 02 degrees 05 minutes 30 seconds E.

2 In this Schedule, the 'Dividing Line' means the dividing line as defined in an Agreement dated 10th March 1965 and made between the government of the United Kingdom of Great Britain and Northern Ireland and the government of the Kingdom of Norway as supplemented by a Protocol dated 22nd December 1978.

SCHEDULE 2

Pension Schemes

Regulation 11(3)

Part 1

Pension Schemes – General

Interpretation

1 (1) In this Schedule, subject to sub-paragraphs (2) and (3), 'occupational pension scheme' means an occupational pension scheme within the meaning of section 1(1) of the Pension Schemes Act 1993.

(2) In relation to rules, practices, actions and decisions identified at paragraph 7(a), 'occupational pension scheme' means an occupational pension scheme within the meaning of section 1(1) of the Pension Schemes Act 1993 under which only retirement-benefit activities within the meaning of section 255(4) of the Pensions Act 2004 are carried out.

(3) In relation to rules, practices, actions and decisions identified at [paragraphs 3A, 7(b), 9, 15A, 17 to 21, 23, 24, 25, 25A and 30], 'occupational pension scheme' means an occupational pension scheme within the meaning of either section 1(1) of the Pension Schemes Act 1993 or section 150(5) of the Finance Act 2004.

(4) In this Schedule, 'scheme' means an occupational pension scheme, construed in accordance with sub-paragraphs (1) to (3).

(5) In this Schedule, in relation to a scheme –

'active member' has the meaning given by section 124(1) of the Pensions Act 1995, but in paragraph 13 also includes an active member within the meaning of section 151(2) of the Finance Act 2004;

['additional state retirement pension' means the additional pension in the Category A retirement pension within the meaning of sections 44 and 45 of the Social Security Contributions and Benefits Act 1992;]

'age related benefit' means benefit provided from a scheme to a member –

(a) on or following his retirement (including early retirement on grounds of ill health or otherwise),

(b) on his reaching a particular age, or

(c) on termination of his service in an employment;

['basic state retirement pension' means the basic pension in the Category A retirement pension within the meaning of section 44 of the Social Security Contributions and Benefits Act 1992;]

['block transfer' means a transfer in a single transaction or a series of transactions from a scheme of all the sums and assets held for the purposes of, or representing, or derived from –

(i) all accrued rights under a scheme,

(ii) contracted-out rights, or

(iii) rights which are not contracted-out rights,

relating to a period of continuous pensionable service (or pensionable service which is treated as continuous) or one or more of a number of separate periods of such pensionable service which relate to a member and at least one other member;]

'contracted-out rights' are such rights, under or derived from an occupational pension scheme or an appropriate personal pension scheme as fall within the following categories –

(a) entitlement to payment of, or accrued rights to, guaranteed minimum pensions;

(b) protected rights; or

(c) section 9(2B) rights,

but not safeguarded rights (within the meaning of section 68A of the Pension Schemes Act 1993);

'death benefit' means benefit payable from a [scheme], in respect of a member, in consequence of his death;

'deferred member' has the meaning given by section 124(1) of the Pensions Act 1995;

'defined benefits arrangement' has the meaning given by section 152(6) of the Finance Act 2004, but the reference in that section to an arrangement shall be read as referring to an arrangement in respect of a member under a scheme as defined in section 1(1) of the Pension Schemes Act 1993 rather than in respect of a member under a pension scheme as defined in section 150(1) of the Finance Act 2004;

'dependant' means [a widow, widower or surviving civil partner or a] dependant as defined in the scheme rules;

['early retirement pivot age' means, in relation to age related benefit provided under a scheme, an age specified in the scheme rules (or otherwise determined) as the earliest age at which entitlement arises –

(a) without consent (whether of an employer, the trustees or managers of the scheme or otherwise), and

(b) without an actuarial reduction,

but disregarding any special provision as to early payment on grounds of ill health or otherwise;]

'employer' has the meaning given by section 318(1) of the Pensions Act 2004;

. . .

'employment' includes any trade, business, profession, office or vocation, whether or not a person is employed in it under a contract of employment or is self employed;

['guaranteed minimum pension' has the meaning given in section 8(2) of the Pension Schemes Act 1993;]

'late retirement pivot age' means an age specified in the scheme rules [(or otherwise determined)] above which benefit becomes payable with actuarial enhancement;

['lower earnings limit' means the amount specified for the tax year in question in regulations made under section 5(1)(a)(i) of the Social Security Contributions and Benefits Act 1992 (earnings limits and thresholds for Class 1 contributions);]

'managers' has the meaning given by section 124(1) of the Pensions Act 1995;

'member' means any active member, deferred member or pensioner member, but in paragraph 12 includes any active, deferred or pensioner member within the meaning of section 151(2) to (4) of the Finance Act 2004;

. . .

'money purchase arrangement' has the meaning given by section 152(2) of the Finance Act 2004, but the reference in that section to an arrangement shall be read as referring to an arrangement in respect of a member under a scheme as defined in section 1(1) of the Pension Schemes Act 1993 rather than in respect of a member under a pension scheme as defined in section 150(1) of the Finance Act 2004;

'non-discrimination rule' means the rule in paragraph 2(1);

'normal pension age' has the meaning given by section 180 of the Pension Schemes Act 1993;

'normal retirement age', in relation to a member, means the age at which workers in the undertaking for which the member worked at the time of his retirement, and who held the same kind of position as the member held at his retirement, were normally required to retire;

. . .

'pensionable pay' means that part of a member's pay which counts as pensionable pay under the scheme rules;

'pensionable service' has the meaning given by section 124(1) of the Pensions Act 1995;

'pensioner member' has the meaning given by section 124(1) of the Pensions Act 1995; and 'prospective member' means any person who, under the terms of his employment or the scheme rules or both –

(a) is able, at his own option, to become a member of the scheme,

(b) shall become so able if he continues in the same employment for a sufficient period of time,

(c) shall be so admitted to it automatically unless he makes an election not to become a member, or

(d) may be admitted to it subject to the consent of any person.

['protected rights' has the meaning given in section 10 of the Pension Schemes Act 1993;]

['redundancy' means being dismissed by reason of redundancy for the purposes of the Employment Rights Act 1996;]

['relevant transfer' has the meaning given in –

(a) regulation 2(1) of the Transfer of Undertakings (Protection of Employment) Regulations 1981 (a relevant transfer), or as the case may be,

(b) regulation 2(1) of the Transfer of Undertakings (Protection of Employment) Regulations 2006 (a relevant transfer);]

['section 9(2B) rights' are –

(a) rights to the payment of pensions and accrued rights to pensions (other than rights attributable to voluntary contributions) under a scheme contracted-out by virtue of section 9(2B) of the Pension Schemes Act 1993, so far as attributable to an earner's service in contracted-out employment on or after 6th April 1997; and

(b) where a transfer payment has been made to such a scheme, any rights arising under the scheme as a consequence of that payment which are derived directly or indirectly from –

   (i) such rights as are referred to in sub-paragraph (a) under another scheme contracted-out by virtue of section 9(2B) of that Act; or

   (ii) protected rights under another occupational pension scheme or under a personal pension scheme attributable to payments or contributions in respect of employment on or after 6th April 1997;]

['upper earnings limit' means the amount specified for the tax year in question in regulations made under section 5(1) (a) (iii) of the Social Security Contributions and Benefits Act 1992 (earnings limits and thresholds for Class 1 contributions)].

(6) . . .

(7) In this Schedule –

'personal pension scheme' has the meaning given by section 1(1) of the Pension Schemes Act 1993;

'registered pension scheme' has the meaning given by section 150(2) of the Finance Act 2004; and

references to contributions under a money purchase arrangement shall be construed as including amounts credited to a member's account whether or not they reflect payments actually made under the scheme.

(8) Any term used in regulation 11 (pension schemes) shall have the same meaning in that regulation as it has in this Schedule [and 'occupational pension scheme' shall mean an occupational pension scheme within the meaning of either section 1(1) of the Pension Schemes Act 1993 or section 150(5) of the Finance Act 2004].

Non-discrimination rule

2 (1) Every scheme shall be treated as including a provision ('the non-discrimination rule') containing a requirement that the trustees or managers of the scheme refrain from doing any act which is unlawful by virtue of regulation 11.

(2) The other provisions of the scheme are to have effect subject to the non-discrimination rule.

(3) The trustees or managers of a scheme may –

(a) if they do not (apart from this sub-paragraph) have power to make such alterations to the scheme as may be required to secure conformity with the non-discrimination rule, or

(b) if they have such power but the procedure for doing so –

(i) is liable to be unduly complex or protracted, or

(ii) involves the obtaining of consents which cannot be obtained, or can only be obtained with undue delay or difficulty,

by resolution make such alterations to the scheme.

(4) Alterations made by a resolution such as is referred to in sub-paragraph (3) –

(a) may have effect in relation to a period before the alterations are made (but may not have effect in relation to any time before [1st December 2006]), and

(b) shall be subject to the consent of any employer in relation to the scheme whose consent would be required for such a modification if it were to be made under the scheme rules.

Exception for rules, practices, actions and decisions relating to occupational pension schemes

3 Nothing in Part 2 or 3 of these Regulations shall render it unlawful for an employer, or for trustees or managers, to maintain or use, in relation to a scheme, any of the rules, practices, actions or decisions set out in Part 2 of this Schedule.

Length of service exemptions

3A (1) Subject to sub-paragraph (2), nothing in Part 2 or 3 of these Regulations shall render it unlawful for –

(a) any rule, practice, action or decision of the trustees or managers ('A') of a scheme regarding –

(i) admission to the scheme ('admission terms'); or

(ii) the accrual of, or eligibility for, any benefit under the scheme ('benefit terms'),

where the admission terms or the benefit terms put a member ('B') of the scheme at a disadvantage when compared with another member ('C') if and to the extent that the disadvantage suffered by B is because B's length of service with an employer ('D') in relation to the scheme is less than that of C;

(b) any rule, practice, action or decision of an employer ('E') in relation to a scheme regarding the admission terms or benefit terms where it puts a member ('F') of the scheme at a disadvantage when compared with another member ('G') if and to the extent that the disadvantage suffered by F is because F's length of service with E is less than that of G; or

(c) any rule, practice, action or decision of an employer ('H') regarding payment of contributions in respect of a worker ('I') to a personal pension scheme or to a money purchase arrangement ('contribution terms') where it puts I at a disadvantage when compared with another worker ('J') if and to the extent that the disadvantage suffered by I is because I's length of service with H is less than that of J.

(2) Where B's, or as the case may be, F's or I's length of service exceeds 5 years and a length of service criterion in the admission terms or as the case may be, the benefit terms or contribution terms puts B or F or I at a disadvantage –

(a) where sub-paragraph (1) (a) applies, A –

(i) must ask D to confirm whether the length of service criterion reasonably appears to D to fulfil a business need of D's undertaking (for example by encouraging the loyalty or motivation, or rewarding the experience, of some or all of his workers), and

(ii) may rely on D's confirmation;

(b) for the purposes of paragraph (a) (i), D must –

(i) calculate B's length of service;

(ii) provide A with details of B's length of service; and

(iii) respond to A's request within a reasonable time;

(c) where sub-paragraph (1) (a) or (b) or (c) applies, it must reasonably appear to D or, as the case may be, E or H that the length of service criterion applies in such a way that it fulfils a business need of his undertaking (for example by encouraging the loyalty or motivation, or rewarding the experience, of some or all of his workers).

(3) When calculating B's or, as the case may be, F's or I's length of service D or, as the case may be, E or H shall calculate –

(a) the length of time the member or worker has been working for him doing work which he reasonably considers to be at or above a particular level (assessed by reference to the demands made on the member or worker, for example, in terms of effort, skills and decision making), or

(b) the length of time the member or worker has been working for him in total,

and it is for D or, as the case may be, E or H to decide which of paragraphs (a) or (b) to use.

(4) For the purposes of sub-paragraph (3), D or, as the case may be, E or H shall calculate the length of time a member or worker has been working for him in accordance with paragraphs (4) to (7) of regulation 32 (exception for provision of certain benefits based on length of service) and any reference in those paragraphs to –

(a) 'A' shall be read as if it were a reference to 'D' or, as the case may be, 'E' or 'H'; and

(b) 'worker' shall, where sub-paragraph (1)(a) or (b) applies, be read as if it were a reference to 'member'.

(5) For the purposes of this paragraph, a 'member' shall include a 'prospective member'.]

Exception for rules, practices, actions and decisions relating to contributions by employers to personal pension schemes

4 Nothing in Part 2 or 3 of these Regulations shall render it unlawful for an employer, in relation to the payment of contributions to any personal pension scheme in respect of a worker, to maintain or use any of the rules, practices, actions or decisions set out in Part 3 of this Schedule.

Unlawfulness of rules, practices, actions or decisions relating to Part 2 or Part 3 of Schedule 2

4A (1) The inclusion of a rule, practice, action or decision in Part 2 of this Schedule (excepted rules, practices, actions and decisions relating to occupational pension schemes) shall not be taken to mean that, but for the exemption in Part 2, the use or maintenance by an employer, trustees or managers of a scheme of the rule, practice, action or decision in relation to the scheme, would be unlawful.

(2) The inclusion of a rule, practice, action or decision in Part 3 of this Schedule (excepted rules, practices, actions and decisions relating to contributions by employers to personal pension schemes) shall not be taken to mean that, but for the exemption in Part 3, the use or maintenance by an employer of the rule, practice, action or decision in relation to the payment of contributions to a personal pension scheme in respect of a worker, would be unlawful.

Procedure in employment tribunals

5 Where under regulation 36 (jurisdiction of employment tribunals) a member or prospective member of a scheme presents to an employment tribunal a complaint that the trustees or managers of the scheme –

(a) have committed against him an act which is unlawful by virtue of regulation 11 (pension schemes) or 24 (relationships which have come to an end); or

(b) are by virtue of regulation 25 (liability of employers and principals) or 26 (aiding unlawful acts) to be treated as having committed against him such an act,

the employer in relation to the scheme shall, for the purposes of the rules governing procedure, be treated as a party and be entitled to appear and be heard in accordance with those rules.

Remedies in employment tribunals

6 (1) This paragraph applies where –

(a) under regulation 36 (jurisdiction of employment tribunals) a member or prospective member of a scheme ('the complainant') presents to an employment tribunal a complaint against the trustees or managers of the scheme or an employer;

(b) the complainant is not a pensioner member of the scheme;

(c) the complaint relates to the terms on which persons become members of the scheme, or the terms on which members of the scheme are treated; and

(d) the tribunal finds the complaint to be well-founded.

(2) Where this paragraph applies, the employment tribunal may, without prejudice to the generality of its power under regulation 38(1)(a) (power to make order declaring rights of complainant and respondent), make an order declaring that the complainant has a right –

(a) where the complaint relates to the terms on which persons become members of the scheme, to be admitted to the scheme;

(b) where the complaint relates to the terms on which members of the scheme are treated, to membership of the scheme without discrimination.

(3) An order under sub-paragraph (2) –

(a) may be made in respect of such period as is specified in the order (but may not be made in respect of any time before [1st December 2006]);

(b) may make such provision as the employment tribunal considers appropriate as to the terms on which, or the capacity in which, the complainant is to enjoy such admission or membership.

(4) Where this paragraph applies, the employment tribunal may not make an order for compensation under regulation 38(1)(b), whether in relation to arrears of benefits or otherwise, except –

(a) for injury to feelings;

(b) by virtue of regulation 38(3).

Amendment

Para 1: in sub-para (3), words 'paragraphs 3A, 7(b), 9, 15A, 17 to 21, 23, 24, 25, 25A and 30' in square brackets substituted by SI 2006/2931, regs 2, 4(1).

Para 1: in sub-para (5) definition 'additional state retirement pension' inserted by SI 2006/2931, regs 2, 4(2)(e).

Para 1: in sub-para (5) definition 'basic state retirement pension' inserted by SI 2006/2931, regs 2, 4(2)(e).

Para 1: in sub-para (5) definition 'block transfer' inserted by SI 2006/2931, regs 2, 4(2)(e).

Para 1: in sub-para (5) definition 'contracted-out rights' inserted by SI 2006/2931, regs 2, 4(2)(e).

Para 1: in sub-para (5) in definition 'death benefit' word 'scheme' in square brackets substituted by SI 2006/2931, regs 2, 4(2)(a).

Para 1: in sub-para (5) in definition 'dependant' words 'a widow, widower or surviving civil partner or a' in square brackets inserted by SI 2006/2931, regs 2, 4(2)(b).

Para 1: in sub-para (5) definition 'early retirement pivot age' substituted by SI 2006/2931, regs 2, 4(2)(c).

Para 1: in sub-para (5) definition 'employer contribution' (omitted) revoked by SI 2006/2931, regs 2, 4(2)(f).

Para 1: in sub-para (5) definition 'guaranteed minimum pension' inserted by SI 2006/2931, regs 2, 4(2)(e).

Para 1: in sub-para (5) in definition 'late retirement pivot age' words '(or otherwise determined)' in square brackets inserted by SI 2006/2931, regs 2, 4(2)(d).

Para 1: in sub-para (5) definition 'lower earnings limit' inserted by SI 2006/2931, regs 2, 4(2)(e).

Para 1: in sub-para (5) definition 'member contribution' (omitted) revoked by SI 2006/2931, regs 2, 4(2)(f).

Para 1: in sub-para (5) definition 'pensionable age' (omitted) revoked by SI 2006/2931, regs 2, 4(2)(f).

Para 1: in sub-para (5) definition 'protected rights' inserted by SI 2006/2931, regs 2, 4(2)(e).

Para 1: in sub-para (5) definition 'redundancy' inserted by SI 2006/2931, regs 2, 4(2)(e).

Para 1: in sub-para (5) definition 'relevant transfer' inserted by SI 2006/2931, regs 2, 4(2)(e).

Para 1: in sub-para (5) definition 'section 9(2B) rights' inserted by SI 2006/2931, regs 2, 4(2)(e).

Para 1: in sub-para (5) definition 'upper earnings limit' inserted by SI 2006/2931, regs 2, 4(2)(e).

Para 1: sub-para (6) revoked by SI 2006/2931, regs 2, 4(3).

Para 1: in sub-para (8) words from 'and 'occupational pension scheme" to 'the Finance Act 2004' in square brackets inserted by SI 2006/2931, regs 2, 4(4).

Para 2: in sub-para (4)(a) words '1st December 2006' in square brackets substituted by SI 2006/2408, reg 2(1), (5)(a).

Para 3A: inserted by SI 2006/2931, regs 2, 5.

Para 4A: inserted by SI 2006/2931, regs 2, 6.

Para 6: in sub-para (3)(a) words '1st December 2006' in square brackets substituted by SI 2006/2408, reg 2(1), (5)(a).

Part 2

Excepted Rules, Practices, Actions and Decisions Relating to Occupational Pension Schemes

Admission to schemes

7 In relation to admission to a scheme –

(a) a minimum or maximum age for admission, including different ages for admission for different groups or categories of worker;

(b) a minimum level of pensionable pay for admission where that minimum –

(i) does not exceed one and a half times the lower earnings limit;

(ii) does not exceed an amount calculated by reference to the lower earnings limit where the aim is more or less to reflect the amount of the basic state retirement pension; or

(iii) does not exceed an amount calculated more or less to reflect the amount of the basic state retirement pension plus the additional state retirement pension.

The use of age criteria in actuarial calculations

8 The use of age criteria in actuarial calculations [in a scheme], for example in the actuarial calculation of –

(a) any age related benefit commencing before any early retirement pivot age or enhancement of such benefit commencing after any late retirement pivot age;

(b) member or employer contributions [by or in respect of a member] to a scheme; or

(c) any age related benefit commuted in exchange for the payment of any lump sum.

Contributions

9 Any difference in the rate of member or employer contributions, [to a scheme], by or in respect of different members to the extent that this is attributable to any differences in the pensionable pay [or, where paragraph 19A applies, different accrual rates] of those members.

Contributions under money purchase arrangements

10 Under a money purchase arrangement –

(a) different rates of member or employer contributions according to the age of the members by or in respect of whom contributions are made where the aim in setting the different rates is –

(i) to equalise [amount of age related benefit in respect of comparable aggregate periods of pensionable service] to which members of different ages who are otherwise in a comparable situation will become entitled under the arrangement, or

(ii) to make more nearly equal the amount of the age related benefit, in respect of comparable aggregate periods of pensionable service, to which members of different ages who are otherwise in a comparable situation will become entitled under the arrangement;

(b) equal rates of member or employer contributions irrespective of the age of the members by or in respect of whom contributions are made;

(c) any limitation on any employer contributions in respect of a member or member contributions by reference to a maximum level of pensionable pay.

Contributions under defined benefits arrangements

11 Under a defined benefits arrangement, different rates of member or employer contributions according to the age of the members by or in respect of whom contributions are made, to the extent that –

(a) each year of pensionable service entitles members in a comparable situation to accrue a right to defined benefits based on the same fraction of pensionable pay, and

(b) the aim in setting the different rates is to reflect the increasing cost of providing the defined benefits in respect of members as they get older.

11A Any limitation on employer contributions in respect of a member or member contributions to a defined benefit arrangement by reference to a maximum level of pensionable pay.

Age related rules, practices, actions and decisions relating to benefit

12 (1) Subject to sub-paragraph (4), a minimum age for any member of a scheme to be entitled to a particular age related benefit that is paid in accordance with sub-paragraph (2) and is paid –

(a) either with or without consent (whether of an employer, the trustees or managers of the scheme or otherwise), and

(b) before the early retirement pivot age relevant to that age related benefit.

(2) The age related benefit must –

(a) be actuarially reduced on the basis that the aim is to reflect that it is paid on a date before the applicable early retirement pivot age; and

(b) not be enhanced by crediting the member with any additional periods of pensionable service or additional benefits.

(3) Sub-paragraph (1) shall also apply to different minimum ages for different groups or categories of members.

(4) Sub-paragraph (1) shall not apply to any member who retires on the grounds to which paragraph 13, 13A or 15 apply.

13 (1) A minimum age for any active or prospective members of a scheme for payment of or entitlement to a particular age related benefit before the early retirement pivot age relevant to that age related benefit where –

(a) the entitlement to the age related benefit at a minimum age applies to a member who is an active or prospective member of the scheme on 1st December 2006;

(b) the age related benefit may be paid, at a minimum age, to the active or prospective member either with or without consent (whether of an employer, the trustees or managers of the scheme or otherwise); and

(c) the age related benefit is enhanced in one or more of the ways specified in sub-paragraph (2).

(2) For the purposes of sub-paragraph (1) (c) the specified ways are the enhancement of any age related benefit payable to or in respect of the member calculated in one or more of the following ways –

(a) by reference to some or all of the years of prospective pensionable service a member would have completed if he had remained in pensionable service until normal pension age;

(b) by reference to a fixed number of years of prospective pensionable service;

(c) by making an actuarial reduction which is smaller than if early retirement had been on grounds to which paragraph 12 applies; or

(d) by not making any actuarial reduction for early retirement.

(3) Sub-paragraph (1) shall also apply to different minimum ages for different groups or categories of active or prospective members.

13A Paragraph 13 shall continue to apply to any member who after 1st December 2006 –

(a) joins a scheme as a result of a block transfer or relevant transfer;

(b) joins a scheme as a result of a block transfer or relevant transfer from a scheme to which paragraph (a) applied; or

(c) joins a scheme on the basis that it will provide the same benefits as those provided by the scheme to which paragraph 13 applied.

13B (1) A minimum age for any member of a scheme for payment of or entitlement to a particular age related benefit on the grounds of redundancy where it is enhanced in accordance with sub-paragraph (2) and paid either with or without consent (whether of an employer, the trustees or managers of the scheme or otherwise).

(2) The enhancement of any age related benefit payable to or in respect of a member on the grounds of redundancy where the enhancement is calculated in one or more of the following ways –

(a) by reference to the years of prospective pensionable service a member would have completed if he had remained in pensionable service until normal pension age;

(b) by reference to a fixed number of years of prospective pensionable service;

(c) by making an actuarial reduction which is smaller than if early retirement had been on grounds to which paragraph 12 applied; or

(d) by not making any actuarial reduction for early retirement.

(3) Sub-paragraph (1) shall also apply to different minimum ages for different groups or categories of members.

14 An early retirement pivot age or a late retirement pivot age including –

(a) different such ages for different groups or categories of member, and

(b) any early retirement pivot age or late retirement pivot age for deferred members which is different than for active members.

15 (1) A minimum age for any member of a scheme for payment of or entitlement to a particular age related benefit on the grounds of ill health where the age related benefit is enhanced in accordance with sub-paragraph (2) and paid either with or without consent (whether of an employer, the trustees or managers of the scheme or otherwise).

(2) The enhancement of any age related benefit payable to or in respect of a member on the grounds of ill health where the enhancement is calculated in one or more of the following ways –

(a) by reference to some or all of the years of prospective pensionable service a member would have completed if he had remained in pensionable service until normal pension age;

(b) by reference to a fixed number of years of prospective pensionable service;

(c) by making an actuarial reduction which is smaller than if early retirement had been on the grounds to which paragraph 12 applied; or

(d) by not making any actuarial reduction for early retirement.

(3) Sub-paragraph (1) shall also apply to different minimum ages for different groups or categories of members.

15A (1) The calculation of any death benefit payable in respect of a member –

(a) by reference to some or all of the years of prospective pensionable service a member would have completed if he had remained in service until normal pension age; or

(b) by reference to a fixed number of years of prospective pensionable service.

(2) Payment after a member's death of a death benefit calculated by reference to the period remaining in a pension guarantee period.

(3) For the purposes of sub-paragraph (2), a pension guarantee period means a fixed period specified in or permitted by the scheme rules beginning on –

(a) the date on which the payment of pension to or in respect of the member began, or

(b) if specified in the scheme rules, the date of the member's death on or after normal pension age where payment of pension to or in respect of him had not begun.

(4) Any difference between the death benefits payable in respect of deferred members who die before normal pension age and the death benefits payable in respect of deferred members who die on or after normal pension age.

16 (1) Any rule, practice, action or decision where –

(a) the rate of pension to which a pensioner member is entitled is reduced at any time between age 60 and 65 ('the reduction date'), by either –

(i) an amount not exceeding the relevant state retirement pension rate at the reduction date, or

(ii) the rate of the pension in payment where on the reduction date the relevant state retirement pension rate is greater than the rate of that pension;

(b) from the date a member is entitled to present payment of a pension from a scheme he is entitled to an additional amount of pension which does not exceed the amount of the basic state retirement pension plus the additional state retirement pension that would be payable at state pension age; or

(c) a member who reaches his state pension age is not entitled to, or no longer entitled to, an additional amount of pension which does not exceed the amount of the basic state retirement pension plus the additional state retirement pension that would be payable at state pension age.

(2) For the purposes of paragraph (1) –

'relevant state retirement pension rate' has the same meaning as in paragraph 2(5) of Schedule 28 to the Finance Act 2004;

'state pension age' means the pensionable age specified in the rules in paragraph 1 of Schedule 4 to the Pensions Act 1995.]

17 The [actuarial] reduction of any pension payable [from a scheme] in consequence of a member's death to any dependant of the member where that dependant is more than a specified number of years younger than the member.

18 In relation to pensioner members who have retired [from a scheme] on ill health grounds. . ., discontinuation of any life assurance cover once any such members reach the normal retirement age which applied to them at the time they retired, or in relation to members to whom no such normal retirement age applied, once such members reach the age of 65.

Other rules, practices, actions and decisions relating to benefit

19 Any difference in the amount of any age related benefit or death benefit payable under a [scheme] to or in respect of members with different lengths of pensionable service to the extent that the difference in amount is attributable to their differing lengths of service, provided that, for each year of pensionable service, members in a comparable situation are entitled to accrue a right to benefit based upon the same fraction of pensionable pay.

19A (1) Any differences in –

(a) the fraction of pensionable pay at which any age related benefit accrues, or

(b) the amount of death benefit,

to or in respect of active or prospective members of a scheme where the differences are attributable to the aim specified in sub-paragraph (2).

(2) The aim referred to in sub-paragraph (1) is that members in a comparable situation will have the right to age related benefit or death benefit equal to the same fraction, proportion or multiple of pensionable pay –

(a) without regard to each member's length of pensionable service under the scheme, and

(b) provided that each member continues in pensionable service under the scheme until normal pension age.

(3) Any differences in age related benefits which accrue, or entitlement to any death benefits which arises, to or in respect of active or prospective members of a scheme who are in a comparable situation where –

(a) those differences are attributable to the aim specified in sub-paragraph (2), and

(b) the member's pensionable service under the arrangement ceases before normal pension age.

(4) Where sub-paragraph (1) applies, any limitation on the amount of any age related benefit or death benefit payable from a scheme where the limitation arises from imposing one or both of the following –

(a) a maximum amount on the age related benefit or death benefit which is equal to a fraction, proportion or multiple of the member's pensionable pay, or

(b) a minimum period of pensionable service.

19B Where paragraph 19A applies, different rates of member or employer contributions according to the age of the members by, or in respect of whom, contributions are made, where for each year of pensionable service members in comparable situations accrue different fractions of pensionable pay.

20 Any difference in the amount of any age related benefit or death benefit payable from a scheme to or in respect of different members to the extent that the difference in amount is attributable to differences over time in the pensionable pay of those members.

21 (1) Any limitation on the amount of any age related benefit or death benefit payable from a scheme where either or both sub-paragraphs (2) and (3) apply.

(2) The limitation results from imposing a maximum number of years of pensionable service by reference to which the age related benefit or death benefit may be calculated.

(3) The limitation arises from imposing a maximum amount on the age related benefit or death benefit which is equal to a fraction, proportion or multiple of a member's pensionable pay.

22 Any rule, practice, action or decision where any age related benefit or death benefit is only payable from a scheme where a member is entitled to short service benefit under section 71 of the Pension Schemes Act 1993 (basic principles as to short service benefit).

23 When determining a member's pensionable pay by reference to which any age related benefit or death benefit payable to or in respect of a member is calculated, to exclude from the member's remuneration an amount which –

(a) does not exceed one and a half times the lower earnings limit;

(b) does not exceed an amount calculated by reference to the lower earnings limit where the aim is more or less to reflect the amount of the basic state retirement pension; or

(c) does not exceed an amount calculated more or less to reflect the amount of the basic state retirement pension plus the additional state retirement pension.

23A Any difference in the amount of age related benefit or death benefit payable under a scheme to or in respect of members where the difference is attributable to accrual of age related benefit at a higher fraction of pensionable pay for pensionable pay over the upper earnings limit (and a lower fraction of pensionable pay for pensionable pay under the upper earnings limit) where the aim is to reflect the additional state retirement pension.

24 Any limitation on the amount of any age related benefit or death benefit payable from a scheme where the limitation –

(a) relates to –

(i) all members who joined, or who became eligible to join the scheme on, after or before a particular date; or

(ii) any group or category of members who joined, or who became eligible to join the scheme on, after or before a particular date; and

(b) results from imposing a maximum level of pensionable pay by reference to which the age related benefit or death benefit may be calculated.

Closure of schemes

25 The closure of a scheme, from a particular date, to workers who have not already joined it.

Closure of sections of schemes

25A (1) The closure of any section of a scheme, from a particular date, to workers who have not already joined it.

(2) For the purposes of paragraph (1) –

(a) a scheme may be divided into two or more sections, and

(b) a section of a scheme shall mean any of the groups in sub-paragraph (3).

(3) A section of a scheme shall mean any of the following –

(a) any group of members who became eligible to join, or who joined, the scheme on, after or before a particular date on the basis that particular benefits will be provided to or in respect of those members or that a particular level of contributions will be paid in respect of those members; or

(b) any group of members who became eligible to join, or who joined, the scheme as a result of a block transfer or relevant transfer.

Other rules, practices, actions and decisions

26 Increases of pensions in payment which are made to members over 55 but not to members below that age.

27 Any difference in the rate of increase of pensions in payment for members of different ages to the extent that the aim in setting the different rates is to maintain [or more nearly maintain] the relative value of members' pensions.

28 Any difference in the rate of increase of pensions in payment for members whose pensions have been in payment for different lengths of time to the extent that the aim in setting the different rates is to maintain [or more nearly maintain] the relative value of members' pensions.

29 The application of an age limit for transfer of the value of a member's accrued rights into or out of a scheme, provided that any such age limit is not more than one year before the member's normal pension age.

Registered pension schemes

30 (1) . . . Any rules, practices, actions or decisions relating to entitlement to or payment of benefits under a [scheme which is a] registered pension scheme insofar as compliance is necessary to secure any tax relief or exemption available under Part 4 of the Finance Act 2004 or to prevent any charge to tax arising under that Part of that Act, whoever is liable in relation to such charge.

(2) . . .

Amendment

Para 7: sub-para (b) substituted by SI 2006/2931, regs 2, 7(1).

Para 8: words 'in a scheme' in square brackets inserted by SI 2006/2931, regs 2, 8(1)(a).

Para 8: in sub-para (b) words 'by or in respect of a member' in square brackets inserted by SI 2006/2931, regs 2, 8(1)(b).

Para 9: words ', to a scheme,' in square brackets inserted by SI 2006/2931, regs 2, 8(2)(a).

Para 9: words 'or, where paragraph 19A applies, different accrual rates' in square brackets inserted by SI 2006/2931, regs 2, 8(2)(b).

Para 10: in sub-para (a)(i) words from 'amount of age' to 'of pen sionable service' in square brackets substituted by SI 2006/2931, regs 2, 9(a).

Para 10: sub-para (a)(ii) substituted by SI 2006/2931, regs 2, 9(b).

Para 10: sub-para (c) inserted by SI 2006/2931, regs 2, 9(c).

Para 11A: inserted by SI 2006/2931, regs 2, 10.

Para 12: substituted by SI 2006/2931, regs 2, 11(1).

Paras 13, 13A, 13B: substituted, for para 13 as originally enacted, by SI 2006/2931, regs 2, 11(2).

Para 14: substituted by SI 2006/2931, regs 2, 12.

Para 15, 15A: substituted, for para 15 as originally enacted, by SI 2006/2931, regs 2, 13(1).

Para 16: substituted by SI 2006/2931, regs 2, 14(1).

Para 17: word 'actuarial' in square brackets inserted by SI 2006/2931, regs 2, 15(a).

Para 17: words 'from a scheme' in square brackets inserted by SI 2006/2931, regs 2, 15(b).

Para 18: words 'from a scheme' in square brackets inserted by SI 2006/2931, regs 2, 16(a).

Para 18: words omitted revoked by SI 2006/2931, regs 2, 16(b).

Para 19: word 'scheme' in square brackets substituted by SI 2006/2931, regs 2, 17.

Paras 19A, 19B: inserted by SI 2006/2931, regs 2, 18.

Para 21: substituted by SI 2006/2931, regs 2, 19.

Para 22: substituted by SI 2006/2931, regs 2, 20.

Para 23: substituted by SI 2006/2931, regs 2, 7(2).

Para 23A: inserted by SI 2006/2931, regs 2, 7(3).

Para 24: substituted by SI 2006/2931, regs 2, 21.

Para 25A: inserted by SI 2006/2931, regs 2, 22.

Para 27: words 'or more nearly maintain' in square brackets inserted by SI 2006/2931, regs 2, 23.

Para 28: words 'or more nearly maintain' in square brackets inserted by SI 2006/2931, regs 2, 23.

Para 30: in sub-para (1) words omitted revoked by SI 2006/2931, regs 2, 24(a)(i).

Para 30: in sub-para (1) words 'scheme which is a' in square brackets inserted by SI 2006/2931, regs 2, 24(a)(ii).

Para 30: sub-para (2) revoked by SI 2006/2931, regs 2, 24(b).

Part 3

Excepted Rules, Practices, Actions and Decisions Relating to Contributions by Employers to Personal Pension Schemes

Contributions by employers

31 Different rates of contributions by an employer [to a personal pension scheme] according to the age of the workers in respect of whom the contributions are made where the aim in setting the different rates is –

(a) to equalise [amount of age related benefit, derived from contributions made each year by the employer,] to which workers of different ages who are otherwise in a comparable situation will become entitled under their personal pension schemes, or

(b) to make more nearly equal the amount of the age related benefit, derived from contributions made each year by the employer, to which workers of different ages who are otherwise in a comparable situation will become entitled under their personal pension schemes.

32 Any difference in the rate of contributions by an employer [to a personal pension scheme] in respect of different workers to the extent that this is attributable to any differences in remuneration payable to those workers.

33 Any limitation on any contributions by an employer, to a personal pension scheme, by reference to a maximum level of remuneration.

34 A minimum age for commencement of payment of contributions by an employer to a personal pension scheme in respect of a worker.

35 Different minimum ages for commencement of payment of contributions by an employer to a personal pension scheme in respect of different groups or categories of workers.

36 Equal rates of contributions by an employer to a personal pension scheme irrespective of the age of the workers in respect of whom contributions are made.

Amendment

Para 31: words 'to a personal pension scheme' in square brackets inserted by SI 2006/2931, regs 2, 25.

Para 31: in sub-para (a) words from 'amount of age' to 'by the employer,' in square brackets substituted by SI 2006/2931, regs 2, 26(a).

Para 31: sub-para (b) substituted by SI 2006/2931, regs 2, 26(b).

Para 32: words 'to a personal pension scheme' in square brackets inserted by SI 2006/2931, regs 2, 25.

Paras 33–36: inserted by SI 2006/2931, regs 2, 27.

SCHEDULE 3

Questionnaire of Person Aggrieved

Regulation 41(1)

To .... *(name of person to be questioned)*

of ....

.... *(address)*

1 (1) I .... *(name of questioner)*

of ....

.... *(address)*

consider that you may have discriminated against me [subjected me to harrassment] contrary to the Employment Equality (Age) Regulations 2006.

(2) *(Give date, approximate time and a factual description of the treatment received and of the circumstances leading up to the treatment.)*

(3) I consider that this treatment may have been unlawful because .....

....

....

.... *(complete if you wish to give reasons, otherwise delete)*.

2 Do you agree that the statement in paragraph 1(2) above is an accurate description of what happened? If not, in what respect do you disagree or what is your version of what happened?

3 Do you accept that your treatment of me was unlawful discrimination [harrassment]? If not –

(a) why not,

(b) for what reason did I receive the treatment accorded to me, and

(c) how far did considerations of age affect your treatment of me?

4 *(Any other questions you wish to ask.)*

5 My address for any reply you may wish to give to the questions raised above is [that set out in paragraph 1(1) above] [the following address....

....]

.... *(signature of questioner)*

.... *(date)*

NB – By virtue of regulation 41 of the Employment Equality (Age) Regulations 2006 this questionnaire and any reply are (subject to the provisions of that regulation) admissible in proceedings under the Regulations. A court or tribunal may draw any such inference as is just and equitable from a failure without reasonable excuse to reply within eight weeks of service of this questionnaire, or from an evasive or equivocal reply, including an inference that the person questioned has committed an unlawful act.

SCHEDULE 4

Reply by Respondent

Regulation 41(1)

To .... *(name of questioner)*

of ....

.... *(address)*

1 (1) I .... *(name of person questioned)*

of ....

.... *(address)*

hereby acknowledge receipt of the questionnaire signed by you and dated

which was served on me on .... *(date)*.

2 [I agree that the statement in paragraph 1(2) of the questionnaire is an accurate description of what happened.]

[I disagree with the statement in paragraph 1(2) of the questionnaire in that ....

....]

3 I accept/dispute that my treatment of you was unlawful discrimination [harrassment].

[My reasons for so disputing are ....

....

The reason why you received the treatment accorded to you and the answers to the other questions in paragraph 3 of the questionnaire are...

....]

4 *(Replies to questions in paragraph 4 of the questionnaire.)*

5 [I have deleted (in whole or in part) the paragraph(s) numbered..... above, since

I am unable/unwilling to reply to the relevant questions in the correspondingly numbered paragraph(s) of the questionnaire for the following reasons..

....]

.... *(signature of questioner)*

.... *(date)*

SCHEDULE 5

Validity of Contracts, Collective Agreements and Rules of Undertakings

Regulation 43

Part 1

Validity and Revision of Contracts

1 (1) A term of a contract is void where –

(a) the making of the contract is, by reason of the inclusion of the term, unlawful by virtue of these Regulations;

(b) it is included in furtherance of an act which is unlawful by virtue of these Regulations; or

(c) it provides for the doing of an act which is unlawful by virtue of these Regulations.

(2) Sub-paragraph (1) does not apply to a term the inclusion of which constitutes, or is in furtherance of, or provides for, unlawful discrimination against, or harassment of, a party to the contract, but the term shall be unenforceable against that party.

(3) A term in a contract which purports to exclude or limit any provision of these Regulations is unenforceable by any person in whose favour the term would operate apart from this paragraph.

(4) Sub-paragraphs (1), (2) and (3) shall apply whether the contract was entered into before or after the date on which any term of the contract became unlawful by virtue of these Regulations, but in the case of a contract made before the date on which a term became unlawful, those sub-paragraphs do not apply to that term in relation to any period before that date.

2 (1) Paragraph 1(3) does not apply –

(a) to a contract settling a complaint to which regulation 36(1) (jurisdiction of employment tribunals) applies where the contract is made with the assistance of a conciliation officer within the meaning of section 211 of the Trade Union and Labour Relations (Consolidation) Act 1992;

(b) to a contract settling a complaint to which regulation 36(1) applies if the conditions regulating compromise contracts under this Schedule are satisfied in relation to the contract; or

(c) to a contract settling a claim to which regulation 39 (jurisdiction of county or sheriff courts) applies.

(2) The conditions regulating compromise contracts under this Schedule are that –

(a) the contract must be in writing;

(b) the contract must relate to the particular complaint;

(c) the complainant must have received advice from a relevant independent adviser as to the terms and effect of the proposed contract and in particular its effect on his ability to pursue a complaint before an employment tribunal;

(d) there must be in force, when the adviser gives the advice, a contract of insurance, or an indemnity provided for members of a profession or professional body, covering the risk of a claim by the complainant in respect of loss arising in consequence of the advice;

(e) the contract must identify the adviser; and

(f) the contract must state that the conditions regulating compromise contracts under this Schedule are satisfied.

(3) A person is a relevant independent adviser for the purposes of sub-paragraph (2)(c) –

(a) if he is a qualified lawyer;

(b) if he is an officer, official, employee or member of an independent trade union who has been certified in writing by the trade union as competent to give advice and as authorised to do so on behalf of the trade union; or

(c) if he works at an advice centre (whether as an employee or a volunteer) and has been certified in writing by the centre as competent to give advice and as authorised to do so on behalf of the centre.

(4) But a person is not a relevant independent adviser for the purposes of sub-paragraph (2) (c) in relation to the complainant –

(a) if he is employed by, or is acting in the matter for the other party, or is a person who is connected with the other party;

(b) in the case of a person within sub-paragraph (3) (b) or (c), if the trade union or advice centre is the other party or a person who is connected with the other party; or

(c) in the case of a person within sub-paragraph (3) (c), if the complainant makes a payment for the advice received from him.

(5) In sub-paragraph (3) (a) 'qualified lawyer' means –

(a) as respects England and Wales, a barrister (whether in practice as such or employed to give legal advice), a solicitor who holds a practising certificate, or a person other than a barrister or solicitor who is an authorised advocate or authorised litigator (within the meaning of the Courts and Legal Services Act 1990; and

(b) as respects Scotland, an advocate (whether in practice as such or employed to give legal advice), or a solicitor who holds a practising certificate.

(6) A person shall be treated as being a qualified lawyer within sub-paragraph (5) (a) if he is a Fellow of the Institute of Legal Executives employed by a solicitors' practice.

(7) In sub-paragraph (3) (b) 'independent trade union' has the same meaning as in the Trade Union and Labour Relations (Consolidation) Act 1992.

(8) For the purposes of sub-paragraph (4) (a) any two persons are to be treated as connected –

(a) if one is a company of which the other (directly or indirectly) has control; or

(b) if both are companies of which a third person (directly or indirectly) has control.

(9) An agreement under which the parties agree to submit a dispute to arbitration –

(a) shall be regarded for the purposes of sub-paragraphs (1) (a) and (b) as being a contract settling a complaint if –

(i) the dispute is covered by a scheme having effect by virtue of an order under section 212A of the Trade Union and Labour Relations (Consolidation) Act 1992, and

(ii) the agreement is to submit it to arbitration in accordance with the scheme, but

(b) shall be regarded as neither being nor including such a contract in any other case.

3 (1) On the application of a person interested in a contract to which paragraph 1(1) or (2) applies, a county court or a sheriff court may make such order as it thinks fit for –

(a) removing or modifying any term rendered void by paragraph 1(1), or

(b) removing or modifying any term made unenforceable by paragraph 1(2);

but such an order shall not be made unless all persons affected have been given notice in writing of the application (except where under rules of court notice may be dispensed with) and have been afforded an opportunity to make representations to the court.

(2) An order under sub-paragraph (1) may include provision as respects any period before the making of the order (but after [the date on which the inclusion of any term which is the subject of the order becomes unlawful by virtue of these Regulations]).

Amendment

Para 1: sub-para (4) substituted by SI 2006/2408, reg 2(1), (6) (a).

Para 3: in sub-para (2) words from 'the date on' to 'of these Regulations' in square brackets substituted by SI 2006/2408, reg 2(1), (6) (b).

Part 2

Collective Agreements and Rules of Undertakings

4 (1) This Part of this Schedule applies to –

(a) any term of a collective agreement, including an agreement which was not intended, or is presumed not to have been intended, to be a legally enforceable contract;

(b) any rule made by an employer for application to all or any of the persons who are employed by him or who apply to be, or are, considered by him for employment;

(c) any rule made by a trade organisation (within the meaning of regulation 18) or a qualifications body (within the meaning of regulation 19) for application to –

(i) all or any of its members or prospective members; or

(ii) all or any of the persons on whom it has conferred professional or trade qualifications (within the meaning of regulation 19) or who are seeking the professional or trade qualifications which it has power to confer.

(2) Any term or rule to which this Part of this Schedule applies is void where –

(a) the making of the collective agreement is, by reason of the inclusion of the term, unlawful by virtue of these Regulations;

(b) the term or rule is included or made in furtherance of an act which is unlawful by virtue of these Regulations; or

(c) the term or rule provides for the doing of an act which is unlawful by virtue of these Regulations.

(3) Sub-paragraph (2) shall apply whether the agreement was entered into, or the rule made, before or after the date on

which any term of the agreement or rule became unlawful by virtue of these Regulations; but in the case of an agreement entered into, or a rule made, before the date on which a term, or rule, became unlawful, that sub-paragraph does not apply to that term or rule in relation to any period before that date.

5 A person to whom this paragraph applies may present a complaint to an employment tribunal that a term or rule is void by virtue of paragraph 4 if he has reason to believe –

(a) that the term or rule may at some future time have effect in relation to him; and

(b) where he alleges that it is void by virtue of paragraph 4(2)(c), that –

(i) an act for the doing of which it provides, may at some such time be done in relation to him, and

(ii) the act would be unlawful by virtue of these Regulations if done in relation to him in present circumstances.

6 In the case of a complaint about –

(a) a term of a collective agreement made by or on behalf of –

(i) an employer,

(ii) an organisation of employers of which an employer is a member, or

(iii) an association of such organisations of one of which an employer is a member, or

(b) a rule made by an employer within the meaning of paragraph 4(1)(b),

paragraph 5 applies to any person who is, or is genuinely and actively seeking to become, one of his employees.

7 In the case of a complaint about a rule made by an organisation or body to which paragraph 4(1)(c) applies, paragraph 5 applies to any person –

(a) who is, or is genuinely and actively seeking to become, a member of the organisation or body;

(b) on whom the organisation or body has conferred a professional or trade qualification (within the meaning of regulation 19) which the organisation or body has power to confer; or

(c) who is genuinely and actively seeking such a professional or trade qualification which the organisation or body has power to confer.

8 (1) When an employment tribunal finds that a complaint presented to it under paragraph 5 is well-founded the tribunal shall make an order declaring that the term or rule is void.

(2) An order under sub-paragraph (1) may include provision as respects any period before the making of the order (but after [the date on which the inclusion of the term or rule became unlawful by virtue of these Regulations]).

9 The avoidance by virtue of paragraph 4(2) of any term or rule which provides for any person to be discriminated against shall be without prejudice to the following rights (except in so far as they enable any person to require another person to be treated less favourably than himself), namely –

(a) such of the rights of the person to be discriminated against; and

(b) such of the rights of any person who will be treated more favourably in direct or indirect consequence of the discrimination,

as are conferred by or in respect of a contract made or modified wholly or partly in pursuance of, or by reference to, that term or rule.

10 In this Schedule 'collective agreement' means any agreement relating to one or more of the matters mentioned in section 178(2) of the Trade Union and Labour Relations (Consolidation) Act 1992 (collective agreements and collective bargaining), being an agreement made by or on behalf of one or more employers or one or more organisations of employers or associations of such organisations with one or more organisations of workers or associations of such organisations.

Amendment

Para 4: sub-para (3) substituted by SI 2006/2408, reg 2(1), (6)(c).

Para 8: in sub-para (2) words from 'the date on' to 'of these Regulations' in square brackets substituted by SI 2006/2408, reg 2(1), (6)(d).

SCHEDULE 6

Duty to Consider Working beyond Retirement

Regulation 47

Interpretation

1 (1) In this Schedule –

'dismissal' means a dismissal within the meaning of section 95 of the 1996 Act;

'employee' means a person to whom regulation 30 (exception for retirement) applies and references to 'employer' shall be construed accordingly;

'intended date of retirement' has the meaning given by sub-paragraph (2);

'operative date of termination' means (subject to paragraph 10(3)) –

(a) where the employer terminates the employee's contract of employment by notice, the date on which the notice expires, or

(b) where the employer terminates the contract of employment without notice, the date on which the termination takes effect;

'request' means a request made under paragraph 5; and

'worker' has the same meaning as in section 230(3) of the 1996 Act.

(2) In this Schedule 'intended date of retirement' means –

(a) where the employer notifies a date in accordance with paragraph 2, that date;

(b) where the employer notifies a date in accordance with paragraph 4 and either no request is made or a request is made after the notification, that date;

(c) where,

(i) the employer has not notified a date in accordance with paragraph 2,

(ii) a request is made before the employer has notified a date in accordance with paragraph 4 (including where no notification in accordance with that paragraph is given),

(iii) the request is made by an employee who has reasonable grounds for believing that the employer intends to retire him on a certain date, and,

(iv) the request identifies that date,

the date so identified;

(d) in a case to which paragraph 3 has applied, any earlier or later date that has superseded the date mentioned in paragraph (a), (b) or (c) as the intended date of retirement by virtue of paragraph 3(3);

(e) in a case to which paragraph 10 has applied, the later date that has superseded the date mentioned in paragraph (a), (b) or (c) as the intended date of retirement by virtue of paragraph 10(3)(b).

Duty of employer to inform employee

2 (1) An employer who intends to retire an employee has a duty to notify the employee in writing of –

(a) the employee's right to make a request; and

(b) the date on which he intends the employee to retire,

not more than one year and not less than six months before that date.

(2) The duty to notify applies regardless of –

(a) whether there is any term in the employee's contract of employment indicating when his retirement is expected to take place,

(b) any other notification of, or information about, the employee's date of retirement given to him by the employer at any time, and

(c) any other information about the employee's right to make a request given to him by the employer at any time.

3 (1) This paragraph applies if the employer has notified the employee in accordance with paragraph 2 or 4 or the employee has made a request before being notified in accordance with paragraph 4 (including where no notification in accordance with that paragraph is given), and –

(a) the employer and employee agree, in accordance with paragraph 7(3)(b) or 8(5)(b), that the dismissal is to take effect on a date later than the relevant date;

(b) the employer gives notice to the employee, in accordance with paragraph 7(7)(a)(ii) or, where the employee appeals, paragraph 8(9)(a)(ii), that the dismissal is to take effect on a date later than the relevant date; or

(c) the employer and employee agree that the dismissal is to take effect on a date earlier than the relevant date.

(2) This Schedule does not require the employer to give the employee a further notification in respect of dismissal taking effect on a date –

(a) agreed as mentioned in sub-paragraph (1)(a) or notified as mentioned in sub-paragraph (1)(b) that is later than the relevant date and falls six months or less after the relevant date; or

(b) agreed as mentioned in sub-paragraph (1)(c) that is earlier than the relevant date.

(3) If –

(a) a date later than the relevant date is agreed as mentioned in sub-paragraph (1)(a) or notified as mentioned in sub-paragraph (1)(b) and falls six months or less after the relevant date, or

(b) a date earlier than the relevant date is agreed as mentioned in sub-paragraph (1)(c),

the earlier or later date shall supersede the relevant date as the intended date of retirement.

(4) In this paragraph, 'the relevant date' means the date that is defined as the intended date of retirement in paragraph (a), (b) or (c) of paragraph 1(2).

Continuing duty to inform employee

4 Where the employer has failed to comply with paragraph 2, he has a continuing duty to notify the employee in writing as described in paragraph 2(1) until the fourteenth day before the operative date of termination.

Statutory right to request not to retire

5 (1) An employee may make a request to his employer not to retire on the intended date of retirement.

(2) In his request the employee must propose that his employment should continue, following the intended date of retirement –

(a) indefinitely,

(b) for a stated period, or

(c) until a stated date;

and, if the request is made at a time when it is no longer possible for the employer to notify in accordance with paragraph 2 and the employer has not yet notified in accordance with paragraph 4, must identify the date on which he believes that the employer intends to retire him.

(3) A request must be in writing and state that it is made under this paragraph.

(4) An employee may only make one request under this paragraph in relation to any one intended date of retirement and may not make a request in relation to a date that supersedes a different date as the intended date of retirement by virtue of paragraph 3(3) or 10(3)(b).

(5) A request is only a request made under this paragraph if it is made –

(a) in a case where the employer has complied with paragraph 2, more than three months but not more than six months before the intended date of retirement, or

(b) in a case where the employer has not complied with paragraph 2, before, but not more than six months before, the intended date of retirement.

An employer's duty to consider a request

6 An employer to whom a request is made is under a duty to consider the request in accordance with paragraphs 7 to 9.

Meeting to consider request

7 (1) An employer having a duty under paragraph 6 to consider a request shall hold a meeting to discuss the request with the employee within a reasonable period after receiving it.

(2) The employer and employee must take all reasonable steps to attend the meeting.

(3) The duty to hold a meeting does not apply if, before the end of the period that is reasonable –

(a) the employer and employee agree that the employee's employment will continue indefinitely and the employer gives notice to the employee to that effect; or

(b) the employer and employee agree that the employee's employment will continue for an agreed period and the employer gives notice to the employee of the length of that period or of the date on which it will end.

(4) The duty to hold a meeting does not apply if –

(a) it is not practicable to hold a meeting within the period that is reasonable, and

(b) the employer complies with sub-paragraph (5).

(5) Where sub-paragraph (4)(a) applies, the employer may consider the request without holding a meeting provided he considers any representations made by the employee.

(6) The employer shall give the employee notice of his decision on the request as soon as is reasonably practicable after the date of the meeting or, if sub-paragraphs (4) and (5) apply, his consideration of the request.

(7) A notice given under sub-paragraph (6) shall –

(a) where the decision is to accept the request, state that it is accepted and –

(i) where the decision is that the employee's employment will continue indefinitely, state that fact, or

(ii) where the decision is that the employee's employment will continue for a further period, state that fact and specify the length of the period or the date on which it will end,

(b) where the decision is to refuse the request, confirm that the employer wishes to retire the employee and the date on which the dismissal is to take effect,

and, in the case of a notice falling within paragraph (b), and of a notice referred to in paragraph (a) that specifies a period shorter than the period proposed by the employee in the request, shall inform the employee of his right to appeal.

(8) All notices given under this paragraph shall be in writing and be dated.

Appeals

8 (1) An employee is entitled to appeal against –

(a) a decision of his employer to refuse the request, or

(b) a decision of his employer to accept the request where the notice given under paragraph 7(6) states as mentioned in paragraph 7(7)(a)(ii) and specifies a period shorter than the period proposed by the employee in the request,

by giving notice in accordance with sub-paragraph (2) as soon as is reasonably practicable after the date of the notice given under paragraph 7(6).

(2) A notice of appeal under sub-paragraph (1) shall set out the grounds of appeal.

(3) The employer shall hold a meeting with the employee to discuss an appeal within a reasonable period after the date of the notice of appeal.

(4) The employer and employee must take all reasonable steps to attend the meeting.

(5) The duty to hold a meeting does not apply if, before the end of the period that is reasonable –

(a) the employer and employee agree that the employee's employment will continue indefinitely and the employer gives notice to the employee to that effect; or

(b) the employer and employee agree that the employee's employment will continue for an agreed period and the employer gives notice to the employee of the length of that period or of the date on which it will end.

(6) The duty to hold a meeting does not apply if –

(a) it is not practicable to hold a meeting within the period that is reasonable, and

(b) the employer complies with sub-paragraph (7).

(7) Where sub-paragraph (6)(a) applies, the employer may consider the appeal without holding a meeting provided he considers any representations made by the employee.

(8) The employer shall give the employee notice of his decision on the appeal as soon as is reasonably practicable after the date of the meeting or, if sub-paragraphs (6) and (7) apply, his consideration of the appeal.

(9) A notice under sub-paragraph (8) shall –

(a) where the decision is to accept the appeal, state that it is accepted and –

(i) where the decision is that the employee's employment will continue indefinitely, state that fact, or

(ii) where the decision is that the employee's employment will continue for a further period, state that fact and specify the length of the period or the date on which it will end,

(b) where the decision is to refuse the appeal, confirm that the employer wishes to retire the employee and the date on which the dismissal is to take effect.

(10) All notices given under this paragraph shall be in writing and be dated.

Right to be accompanied

9 (1) This paragraph applies where –

(a) a meeting is held under paragraph 7 or 8, and

(b) the employee reasonably requests to be accompanied at the meeting.

(2) Where this paragraph applies the employer must permit the employee to be accompanied at the meeting by one companion who –

(a) is chosen by the employee;

(b) is a worker employed by the same employer as the employee;

(c) is to be permitted to address the meeting (but not to answer questions on behalf of the employee); and

(d) is to be permitted to confer with the employee during the meeting.

(3) If –

(a) an employee has a right under this paragraph to be accompanied at a meeting,

(b) his chosen companion will not be available at the time proposed for the meeting by the employer, and

(c) the employee proposes an alternative time which satisfies sub-paragraph (4),

the employer must postpone the meeting to the time proposed by the employee.

(4) An alternative time must –

(a) be convenient for employer, employee and companion, and

(b) fall before the end of the period of seven days beginning with the first day after the day proposed by the employer.

(5) An employer shall permit a worker to take time off during working hours for the purpose of accompanying an employee in accordance with a request under sub-paragraph (1)(b).

(6) Sections 168(3) and (4), 169 and 171 to 173 of the Trade Union and Labour Relations (Consolidation) Act 1992 (time off for carrying out trade union duties) shall apply in relation to sub-paragraph (5) above as they apply in relation to section 168(1) of that Act.

Dismissal before request considered

10 (1) This paragraph applies where –

(a) by virtue of paragraph 6 an employer is under a duty to consider a request;

(b) the employer dismisses the employee;

(c) that dismissal is the contemplated dismissal to which the request relates; and

(d) the operative date of termination would, but for sub-paragraph (3), fall on or before the day on which the employer gives notice in accordance with paragraph 7(6).

(2) Subject to sub-paragraph (4), the contract of employment shall continue in force for all purposes, including the purpose of determining for any purpose the period for which the employee has been continuously employed, until the day following that on which the notice under paragraph 7(6) is given.

(3) The day following the day on which that notice is given shall supersede –

(a) the date mentioned in sub-paragraph (1)(d) as the operative date of termination; and

(b) the date defined as the intended date of retirement in paragraph (a), (b) or (c) of paragraph 1(2) as the intended date of retirement.

(4) Any continuation of the contract of employment under sub-paragraph (2) shall be disregarded when determining the operative date of termination for the purposes of sections 98ZA to 98ZH of the 1996 Act.

Complaint to employment tribunal: failure to comply with paragraph 2

11 (1) An employee may present a complaint to an employment tribunal that his employer has failed to comply with the duty to notify him in paragraph 2.

(2) A tribunal shall not consider a complaint under this paragraph unless the complaint is presented –

(a) before the end of the period of three months beginning with –

(i) the last day permitted to the employer by paragraph 2 for complying with the duty to notify, or

(ii) if the employee did not then know the date that would be the intended date of retirement, the first day on which he knew or should have known that date; or

(b) within such further period as the tribunal considers reasonable in a case where it is satisfied that it was not reasonably practicable for the complaint to be presented before the end of that period of three months.

(3) Where a tribunal finds that a complaint under this paragraph is well-founded it shall order the employer to pay compensation to the employee of such amount, not exceeding 8 weeks' pay, as the tribunal considers just and equitable in all the circumstances.

(4) Chapter 2 of Part 14 of the 1996 Act (calculation of a week's pay) shall apply for the purposes of sub-paragraph (3); and in applying that Chapter the calculation date shall be taken to be the date on which the complaint was presented or, if earlier, the operative date of termination.

(5) The limit in section 227(1) of the 1996 Act (maximum amount of a week's pay) shall apply for the purposes of sub-paragraph (3).

Complaint to employment tribunal: denial of right to be accompanied

12 (1) An employee may present a complaint to an employment tribunal that his employer has failed, or threatened to fail, to comply with paragraph 9(2) or (3).

(2) A tribunal shall not consider a complaint under this paragraph in relation to a failure or threat unless the complaint is presented –

(a) before the end of the period of three months beginning with the date of the failure or threat; or

(b) within such further period as the tribunal considers reasonable in a case where it is satisfied that it was not reasonably practicable for the complaint to be presented before the end of that period of three months.

(3) Where a tribunal finds that a complaint under this paragraph is well-founded it shall order the employer to pay compensation to the worker of an amount not exceeding two weeks' pay.

(4) Chapter 2 of Part 14 of the 1996 Act (calculation of a week's pay) shall apply for the purposes of sub-paragraph (3); and in applying that Chapter the calculation date shall be taken to be the date on which the relevant meeting took place (or was to have taken place).

(5) The limit in section 227(1) of the 1996 Act (maximum amount of a week's pay) shall apply for the purposes of sub-paragraph (3).

Detriment and dismissal

13 (1) An employee has the right not to be subjected to any detriment by any act by his employer done on the ground that he exercised or sought to exercise his right to be accompanied in accordance with paragraph 9.

(2) A worker has the right not to be subjected to any detriment by any act, or any deliberate failure to act, by his employer done on the ground that he accompanied or sought to accompany an employee pursuant to a request under paragraph 9.

(3) Section 48 of the 1996 Act shall apply in relation to contraventions of sub-paragraph (1) or (2) above as it applies in relation to contraventions of certain sections of that Act.

(4) Sub-paragraph (2) does not apply where the worker is an employee and the detriment in question amounts to dismissal (within the meaning of Part 10 of the 1996 Act).

(5) An employee who is dismissed shall be regarded for the purposes of Part 10 of the 1996 Act as unfairly dismissed if the reason (or, if more than one, the principal reason) for the dismissal is that he –

(a) exercised or sought to exercise his right to be accompanied in accordance with paragraph 9, or

(b) accompanied or sought to accompany an employee pursuant to a request under that paragraph.

(6) Sections 128 to 132 of the 1996 Act (interim relief) shall apply in relation to dismissal for the reason specified in sub-paragraph (5)(a) or (b) above as they apply in relation to dismissal for a reason specified in section 128(1)(b) of that Act.

SCHEDULE 7

Duty to Consider Working Beyond Retirement – Transitional Provisions

Regulation 48

1 In paragraphs 2 to 6 –

(a) 'the expiry date' means the date on which notice of dismissal given by an employer expires; and

(b) words and expressions shall have the same meanings as they do in Schedule 6.

2 (1) This paragraph applies in a case where –

(a) an employer has given notice of dismissal to the employee before the commencement date of –

(i) at least the period required by the contract of employment; or

(ii) where the period required by the contract exceeds four weeks, at least four weeks;

(b) the expiry date falls before 1st April 2007; and

(c) the employer has made the employee aware, before the commencement date, that the employer considers that the employee is being retired on the expiry date.

(2) Where this paragraph applies and the employer on or as soon as is practicable after the commencement date notifies the employee in writing of the employee's right to make a request under paragraph 5 of Schedule 6 –

(a) the employer shall be treated as complying with the duty in paragraph 2 of Schedule 6;

(b) a request shall be treated as being a request made under paragraph 5 of Schedule 6 provided it –

(i) is made after the employer notified the employee of his right to make a request;

(ii) satisfies the requirements of sub-paragraphs (2) and (3) of paragraph 5 of Schedule 6; and

(iii) is made –

(aa) where practicable, at least four weeks before the expiry date; or

(bb) where that is not practicable, as soon as reasonably practicable (whether before or after the expiry date) after the employer notified the employee of his right to make a request, but not more than four weeks after the expiry date.

(3) Where this paragraph applies and the employer does not, on or as soon as is practicable after the commencement date, notify the employee in writing of the employee's right to make a request under paragraph 5 of Schedule 6 –

(a) the duty to notify in accordance with paragraph 2 of Schedule 6 does not apply;

(b) the duty to notify in accordance with paragraph 4 of Schedule 6 applies as if –

(i) the employer had failed to notify in accordance with paragraph 2 of that Schedule; and

(ii) the duty was one to notify at any time before the expiry date;

(c) a request shall be treated as being a request made under paragraph 5 of Schedule 6 if it satisfies the requirements of sub-paragraphs (2) and (3) of that paragraph and is made –

(i) before any notification given in accordance with paragraph 4 of Schedule 6; or

(ii) after such notification and –

(aa) where practicable, at least four weeks before the expiry date; or

(bb) where that is not practicable, as soon as reasonably practicable (whether before or after the expiry date) after the employer notified the employee of his right to make a request, but not more than four weeks after the expiry date.

3 (1) This paragraph applies in a case where the employer has given notice of dismissal to the employee before the commencement date and –

(a) the expiry date falls before 1st April 2007, but

(b) the period of notice given is shorter than the minimum period of notice required by paragraph 2(1)(a) or the employer has not complied with paragraph 2(1)(c).

(2) Where this paragraph applies –

(a) the duty to notify in accordance with paragraph 2 of Schedule 6 does not apply;

(b) the duty to notify in accordance with paragraph 4 of Schedule 6 applies as if –

(i) the employer had failed to notify in accordance with paragraph 2 of that Schedule; and

(ii) the duty was one to notify at any time before the expiry date;

(c) a request shall be treated as being a request made under paragraph 5 of Schedule 6 if it satisfies the requirements of sub-paragraphs (2) and (3) of that paragraph and is made –

(i) before any notification given in accordance with paragraph 4 of Schedule 6; or

(ii) after such notification and –

(aa) where practicable, at least four weeks before the expiry date; or

(bb) where that is not practicable, as soon as reasonably practicable (whether before or after the expiry date) after the employer notified the employee of his right to make a request, but not more than four weeks after the expiry date.

4 (1) This paragraph applies in a case where –

(a) notice of dismissal is given on or after the commencement date of at least –

(i) the period required by the contract of employment; or

(ii) if longer, the period required by section 86 of the 1996 Act; and

(b) the expiry date falls before 1st April 2007.

(2) Where this paragraph applies and the employer notifies the employee in writing of the employee's right to make a request under paragraph 5 of Schedule 6 before, or on the same day as, the day on which notice of dismissal is given –

(a) the employer shall be treated as complying with the duty in paragraph 2 of Schedule 6;

(b) a request shall be treated as being a request made under paragraph 5 of Schedule 6 provided it –

(i) is made after the employer notified the employee of his right to make a request;

(ii) satisfies the requirements of sub-paragraphs (2) and (3) of paragraph 5 of Schedule 6; and

(iii) is made –

(aa) where practicable, at least four weeks before the expiry date; or

(bb) where that is not practicable, as soon as reasonably practicable (whether before or after the expiry date) after the employer notified the employee of his right to make a request, but not more than four weeks after the expiry date.

(3) Where this paragraph applies but the employer does not notify the employee in writing of the employee's right to make a request under paragraph 5 of Schedule 6 before, or on the same day as, the day on which notice of dismissal is given –

(a) the duty to notify in accordance with paragraph 2 of Schedule 6 does not apply;

(b) the duty to notify in accordance with paragraph 4 of Schedule 6 applies as if –

(i) the employer had failed to notify in accordance with paragraph 2 of that Schedule; and

(ii) the duty was one to notify at any time before the expiry date;

(c) a request shall be treated as being a request made under paragraph 5 of Schedule 6 if it satisfies the requirements of sub-paragraphs (2) and (3) of that paragraph and is made –

(i) before any notification given in accordance with paragraph 4 of Schedule 6; or

(ii) after such notification and –

(aa) where practicable, at least four weeks before the expiry date; or

(bb) where that is not practicable, as soon as reasonably practicable (whether before or after the expiry date) after the employer notified the employee of his right to make a request, but not more than four weeks after the expiry date.

5 (1) This paragraph applies in a case where –

(a) notice of dismissal is given on or after the commencement date and is for a period shorter than –

(i) the period required by the contract of employment; or

(ii) if longer, the period required by section 86 of the 1996 Act; and

(b) the period of notice expires on a date falling before 1st April 2007.

(2) Where this paragraph applies –

(a) the duty to notify in accordance with paragraph 2 of Schedule 6 does not apply;

(b) the duty to notify in accordance with paragraph 4 of Schedule 6 applies as if –

(i) the employer had failed to notify in accordance with paragraph 2 of that Schedule; and

(ii) the duty was one to notify at any time before the expiry date;

(c) a request shall be treated as being a request made under paragraph 5 of Schedule 6 if it satisfies the requirements of sub-paragraphs (2) and (3) of that paragraph and is made –

(i) before any notification given in accordance with paragraph 4 of Schedule 6; or

(ii) after such notification and –

(aa) where practicable, at least four weeks before the expiry date; or

(bb) where that is not practicable, as soon as reasonably practicable (whether before or after the expiry date) after the employer notified the employee of his right to make a request, but not more than four weeks after the expiry date.

6 In every case to which paragraph 2, 3, 4 or 5 applies –

(a) paragraph 10 of Schedule 6 does not apply; and

(b) the employer is under a duty to consider any request which complies with the requirements of paragraph 2 (2) (b), 2 (3) (c), 3 (2) (c), 4 (2) (b), 4 (3) (c) or 5 (2) (c) in accordance with paragraphs 7 to 9 of Schedule 6.

SCHEDULE 8

Amendments to Legislation and Related Transitional Provisions

Regulation 49 (1)

Part 1

Primary Legislation

The Mines and Quarries Act 1954

1 The Mines and Quarries Act 1954 is amended as follows.

2 (1) In section 42 (1) (charge of winding and rope haulage apparatus when persons are carried) omit the words 'who has attained the age of twenty-two years'.

(2) In section 43(2) (charge of winding and rope haulage apparatus when persons are not carried) omit the words 'who has attained the age of eighteen years'.

(3) In section 44 (charge of conveyors at working faces) omit the words 'who has attained the age of eighteen years'.

The Parliamentary Commissioner Act 1967

3 The Parliamentary Commissioner Act 1967 is amended as follows –

4 (1) Section 1 (appointment and tenure of office) is amended in accordance with this paragraph.

(2) In subsection (2) omit the words from ', and any person' to 'during good behaviour'.

(3) After subsection (2) insert –

'(2A) A person appointed to be the Commissioner shall hold office until the end of the period for which he is appointed.

(2B) That period must be not more than seven years.

(2C) Subsection (2A) is subject to subsections (3) and (3A).'.

(4) For subsection (3) substitute –

'(3) A person appointed to be the Commissioner may be –

(a) relieved of office by Her Majesty at his own request, or

(b) removed from office by Her Majesty, on the ground of misbehaviour, in consequence of Addresses from both Houses of Parliament.'.

(5) After subsection (3A) insert –

'(3B) A person appointed to be the Commissioner is not eligible for re-appointment.'.

5 (1) Section 3A (appointment of acting Commissioner) is amended in accordance with this paragraph.

(2) After subsection (1) insert –

'(1A) A person appointed to act as the Commissioner ('an acting Commissioner') may have held office as the Commissioner.

(1B) A person appointed as an acting Commissioner is eligible for appointment as the Commissioner unless he has already held office as the Commissioner.'.

(3) In subsection (2) for the words 'under this section' substitute 'as an acting Commissioner'.

(4) For subsection (3) substitute –

'(3) A person appointed as an acting Commissioner shall, while he holds office, be treated for all purposes, except for the purposes of section 1 and 2, and this section of this Act, as the Commissioner.'.

6 The amendments made to the Parliamentary Commissioner Act 1967 apply in relation to appointments made on or after the commencement date.

The Pilotage Act 1987

7 (1) The Pilotage Act 1987 is amended in accordance with this paragraph.

(2) In section 3(2) (authorisation of pilots) omit the word 'age,'.

The Social Security Contributions and Benefits Act 1992

8 The Social Security Contributions and Benefits Act 1992 is amended as follows.

9 (1) Section 163(1) (interpretation of Part 11 and supplementary provisions) is amended in accordance with this paragraph.

(2) In the definition of 'employee' omit paragraph (b) and the word 'and' preceding it.

(3) For the definition of 'employer' substitute –

"employer', in relation to an employee and a contract of service of his, means a person who –

(a) under section 6 above is liable to pay secondary Class 1 contributions in relation to any earnings of the employee under the contract, or

(b) would be liable to pay such contributions but for –

(i) the condition in section 6(1)(b), or

(ii) the employee being under the age of 16:'.

10 (1) Section 171(1) (interpretation of Part 12 and supplementary provisions) is amended in accordance with this paragraph.

(2) In the definition of 'employee' omit paragraph (b) and the word 'and' preceding it.

(3) For the definition of 'employer' substitute –

"employer', in relation to a woman who is an employee, means a person who –

(a) under section 6 above is liable to pay secondary Class 1 contributions in relation to any of her earnings; or

(b) would be liable to pay such contributions but for –

(i) the condition in section 6(1)(b), or

(ii) the employee being under the age of 16;'.

(4) This paragraph applies in relation to any case where the expected week of confinement begins on or after 14th January 2007.

11 (1) Section 171ZJ (Part 12ZA: supplementary) is amended in accordance with this paragraph.

(2) In subsection (1) for the definition of 'employer' substitute –

"employer', in relation to a person who is an employee, means a person who –

(a) under section 6 above is, liable to pay secondary Class 1 contributions in relation to any of the earnings of the person who is an employee; or

(b) would be liable to pay such contributions but for –

(i) the condition in section 6(1)(b), or

(ii) the employee being under the age of 16;'.

(3) In subsection (2) omit paragraph (b) and the word 'and' preceding it.

(4) This paragraph applies in relation to an entitlement to –

(a) statutory paternity pay (birth) in respect of children whose expected week of birth begins on or after 14th January 2007;

(b) statutory paternity pay (adoption) in respect of children –

(i) matched with a person who is notified of having been matched on or after the commencement date; or

(ii) placed for adoption on or after the commencement date.

12 (1) Section 171ZS (Part 12ZB: supplementary) is amended in accordance with this paragraph.

(2) In subsection (1) for the definition of 'employer' substitute –

"employer', in relation to a person who is an employee, means a person who –

(a) under section 6 above is liable to pay secondary Class 1 contributions in relation to any of the earnings of the person who is an employee; or

(b) would be liable to pay such contributions but for –

(ii) the condition in section 6(1)(b), or

(ii) the employee being under the age of 16;'.

(3) In subsection (2) omit paragraph (b) and the word 'and' preceding it.

(4) This paragraph applies in relation to an entitlement to statutory adoption pay in respect of children –

(a) matched with a person who is notified of having been matched on or after the commencement date; or

(b) placed for adoption on or after that commencement.

13 (1) In Schedule 11 omit paragraph 2(a) (period of entitlement not to arise if at the relevant date the employee is over 65).

(2) Sub-paragraph (1) applies in relation to a period of incapacity for work which –

(a) begins on or after the commencement date, or

(b) begins before and continues on or after the commencement date.

(3) But in a case falling within sub-paragraph (2)(b), sub-paragraph (1) does not affect the application of paragraph 1 of Schedule 11 to the 1992 Act in relation to the part of the period of incapacity for work that falls before the commencement date.

The Health Service Commissioners Act 1993

14 The Health Service Commissioners Act 1993 is amended as follows.

15 (1) Schedule 1 (the English Commissioner) is amended in accordance with this paragraph.

(2) For paragraph 1 (appointment of Commissioners) substitute the following new paragraphs –

'1 Her Majesty may by Letters Patent appoint a person to be the Commissioner.

1A Subject to paragraphs 1C and 1D a person appointed to be the Commissioner shall hold office until the end of the period for which he is appointed.

1B That period must be not more than seven years.

1C A person appointed to be the Commissioner may be relieved of office by Her Majesty at his own request.

1D A person appointed to be the Commissioner may be removed from office by Her Majesty, on the ground of misbehaviour, in consequence of Addresses from both Houses of Parliament.

1E A person appointed to be the Commissioner is not eligible for re-appointment.'.

(3) In paragraph 2 (appointment of acting Commissioners) –

(a) after sub-paragraph (1) insert –

'(1A) A person appointed to act as the Commissioner ('an acting Commissioner') may have held office as the Commissioner.

(1B) A person appointed as an acting Commissioner is eligible for appointment as the Commissioner unless he has already held office as the Commissioner.';

(b) in sub-paragraph (2) for the words 'under this paragraph' substitute 'as acting Commissioner,'; and

(c) for sub-paragraph (3), substitute –

'(3) A person appointed as an acting Commissioner shall, while he holds office, be treated for all purposes, except for the purposes of paragraphs 1, 4 to 10 and this paragraph, as the Commissioner.'.

16 The amendments made to the Health Service Commissioners Act 1993 apply in relation to appointments made on or after the commencement date.

The Statutory Sick Pay Act 1994

17 (1) The Statutory Sick Pay Act 1994 is amended in accordance with this paragraph.

(2) In section 1(2) omit the words after paragraph (b).

The Employment Tribunals Act 1996

18 The Employment Tribunals Act 1996 is amended as follows.

19 (1) Section 18(1) (conciliation) is amended in accordance with this paragraph.

(2) At the end of paragraph (p), omit 'or'.

(3) After paragraph (q), insert

'or

(r) under regulation 36 of the Employment Equality (Age) Regulations 2006.'.

20 (1) Section 21(1) (jurisdiction of Appeal Tribunal) is amended in accordance with this paragraph.

(2) At the end of paragraph (q), omit 'or'.

(3) After paragraph (r) insert –

'or

(s) the Employment Equality (Age) Regulations 2006.'.

The Employment Rights Act 1996

21 The 1996 Act is amended as follows.

22 (1) Section 98 (fairness of dismissal: general) is amended as follows.

(2) In subsection (2), after paragraph (b) insert –

'(ba) is retirement of the employee,'.

(3) After subsection (2) insert –

'(2A) Subsections (1) and (2) are subject to sections 98ZA to 98ZF.'.

(4) After subsection (3) insert –

'(3A) In any case where the employer has fulfilled the requirements of subsection (1) by showing that the reason (or the principal reason) for the dismissal is retirement of the employee, the question whether the dismissal is fair or unfair shall be determined in accordance with section 98ZG.'.

(5) In subsection (4) for 'Where' substitute 'In any other case where'.

23 After section 98 insert –

'Retirement

98ZA No normal retirement age: dismissal before 65

(1) This section applies to the dismissal of an employee if –

(a) the employee has no normal retirement age, and

(b) the operative date of termination falls before the date when the employee reaches the age of 65.

(2) Retirement of the employee shall not be taken to be the reason (or a reason) for the dismissal.

98ZB No normal retirement age: dismissal at or after 65

(1) This section applies to the dismissal of an employee if –

(a) the employee has no normal retirement age, and

(b) the operative date of termination falls on or after the date when the employee reaches the age of 65.

(2) In a case where –

(a) the employer has notified the employee in accordance with paragraph 2 of Schedule 6 to the 2006 Regulations, and

(b) the contract of employment terminates on the intended date of retirement,

retirement of the employee shall be taken to be the only reason for the dismissal by the employer and any other reason shall be disregarded.

(3) In a case where –

(a) the employer has notified the employee in accordance with paragraph 2 of Schedule 6 to the 2006 Regulations, but

(b) the contract of employment terminates before the intended date of retirement,

retirement of the employee shall not be taken to be the reason (or a reason) for dismissal.

(4) In a case where –

(a) the employer has not notified the employee in accordance with paragraph 2 of Schedule 6 to the 2006 Regulations, and

(b) there is an intended date of retirement in relation to the dismissal, but

(c) the contract of employment terminates before the intended date of retirement,

retirement of the employee shall not be taken to be the reason (or a reason) for dismissal.

(5) In all other cases where the employer has not notified the employee in accordance with paragraph 2 of Schedule 6 to the 2006 Regulations, particular regard shall be had to the matters in section 98ZF when determining the reason (or principal reason) for dismissal.

98ZC Normal retirement age: dismissal before retirement age

(1) This section applies to the dismissal of an employee if –

(a) the employee has a normal retirement age, and

(b) the operative date of termination falls before the date when the employee reaches the normal retirement age.

(2) Retirement of the employee shall not be taken to be the reason (or a reason) for the dismissal.

98ZD Normal retirement age 65 or higher: dismissal at or after retirement age

(1) This section applies to the dismissal of an employee if –

(a) the employee has a normal retirement age,

(b) the normal retirement age is 65 or higher, and

(c) the operative date of termination falls on or after the date when the employee reaches the normal retirement age.

(2) In a case where –

(a) the employer has notified the employee in accordance with paragraph 2 of Schedule 6 to the 2006 Regulations, and

(b) the contract of employment terminates on the intended date of retirement,

retirement of the employee shall be taken to be the only reason for the dismissal by the employer and any other reason shall be disregarded.

(3) In a case where –

(a) the employer has notified the employee in accordance with paragraph 2 of Schedule 6 to the 2006 Regulations, but

(b) the contract of employment terminates before the intended date of retirement,

retirement of the employee shall not be taken to be the reason (or a reason) for dismissal.

(4) In a case where –

(a) the employer has not notified the employee in accordance with paragraph 2 of Schedule 6 to the 2006 Regulations, and

(b) there is an intended date of retirement in relation to the dismissal, but

(c) the contract of employment terminates before the intended date of retirement,

retirement of the employee shall not be taken to be the reason (or a reason) for dismissal.

(5) In all other cases where the employer has not notified the employee in accordance with paragraph 2 of Schedule 6 to the 2006 Regulations, particular regard shall be had to the matters in section 98ZF when determining the reason (or principal reason) for dismissal.

98ZE Normal retirement age below 65: dismissal at or after retirement age

(1) This section applies to the dismissal of an employee if –

(a) the employee has a normal retirement age,

(b) the normal retirement age is below 65, and

(c) the operative date of termination falls on or after the date when the employee reaches the normal retirement age.

(2) If it is unlawful discrimination under the 2006 Regulations for the employee to have that normal retirement age, retirement of the employee shall not be taken to be the reason (or a reason) for dismissal.

(3) Subsections (4) to (7) apply if it is not unlawful discrimination under the 2006 Regulations for the employee to have that normal retirement age.

(4) In a case where –

(a) the employer has notified the employee in accordance with paragraph 2 of Schedule 6 to the 2006 Regulations, and

(b) the contract of employment terminates on the intended date of retirement,

retirement of the employee shall be taken to be the only reason for dismissal by the employer and any other reason shall be disregarded.

(5) In a case where –

(a) the employer has notified the employee in accordance with paragraph 2 of Schedule 6 to the 2006 Regulations, but

(b) the contract of employment terminates before the intended date of retirement,

retirement of the employee shall not be taken to be the reason (or a reason) for dismissal.

(6) In a case where –

(a) the employer has not notified the employee in accordance with paragraph 2 of Schedule 6 to the 2006 Regulations, and

(b) there is an intended date of retirement in relation to the dismissal, but

(c) the contract of employment terminates before the intended date of retirement,

retirement of the employee shall not be taken to be the reason (or a reason) for dismissal.

(7) In all other cases where the employer has not notified the employee in accordance with paragraph 2 of Schedule 6 to the 2006 Regulations, particular regard shall be had to the matters in section 98ZF when determining the reason (or principal reason) for dismissal

98ZF Reason for dismissal: particular matters

(1) These are the matters to which particular regard is to be had in accordance with section 98ZB(5), 98ZD(5) or 98ZE(7) –

(a) whether or not the employer has notified the employee in accordance with paragraph 4 of Schedule 6 to the 2006 Regulations;

(b) if the employer has notified the employee in accordance with that paragraph, how long before the notified retirement date the notification was given;

(c) whether or not the employer has followed, or sought to follow, the procedures in paragraph 7 of Schedule 6 to the 2006 Regulations.

(2) In subsection (1) (b) 'notified retirement date' means the date notified to the employee in accordance with paragraph 4 of Schedule 6 to the 2006 Regulations as the date on which the employer intends to retire the employee.

98ZG Retirement dismissals: fairness

(1) This section applies if the reason (or principal reason) for a dismissal is retirement of the employee.

(2) The employee shall be regarded as unfairly dismissed if, and only if, there has been a failure on the part of the employer to comply with an obligation imposed on him by any of the following provisions of Schedule 6 to the 2006 Regulations –

(a) paragraph 4 (notification of retirement, if not already given under paragraph 2),

(b) paragraphs 6 and 7 (duty to consider employee's request not to be retired),

(c) paragraph 8 (duty to consider appeal against decision to refuse request not to be retired).

98ZH Interpretation

In sections 98ZA to 98ZG –

'2006 Regulations' means the Employment Equality (Age) Regulations 2006;

'intended date of retirement' means the date which, by virtue of paragraph 1(2) of Schedule 6 to the 2006 Regulations, is the intended date of retirement in relation to a particular dismissal;

'normal retirement age', in relation to an employee, means the age at which employees in the employer's undertaking who hold, or have held, the same kind of position as the employee are normally required to retire;

'operative date of termination' means –

(a) where the employer terminates the employee's contract of employment by notice, the date on which the notice expires, or

(b) where the employer terminates the contract of employment without notice, the date on which the termination takes effect.

Other Dismissals'.

24 In section 108 (qualifying period of employment) in subsection (3) (cases where no qualifying period of employment is required) –

(a) at the end of paragraph (l) omit 'or'; and

(b) after paragraph (m) insert –

'or

(n) paragraph (a) or (b) of paragraph 13(5) of Schedule 6 to the Employment Equality (Age) Regulations 2006 applies.'.

25 Omit section 109 (upper age limit on unfair dismissal right).

26 (1) Section 112 (remedies for unfair dismissal: orders and compensation) is amended as follows.

(2) In subsection (5)(a) after 'section' insert '98ZG or'.

27 (1) Section 119 (basic award) is amended as follows.

(2) Omit subsections (4) and (5).

28 (1) Section 120 (basic award: minimum in certain cases) is amended as follows.

(2) In subsection (1A) after 'section' insert '98ZG or'.

29 In section 126(1) (acts which are both unfair dismissal and discrimination), for paragraph (b) substitute –

'(b) any one or more of the following –

(i) the Sex Discrimination Act 1975;

(ii) the Race Relations Act 1976;

(iii) the Disability Discrimination Act 1995;

(iv) the Employment Equality (Sexual Orientation) Regulations 2003;

(v) the Employment Equality (Religion or Belief) Regulations 2003;

(vi) the Employment Equality (Age) Regulations 2006.'.

30 Section 156 (upper age limit) is repealed.

31 Section 158 (pension rights) is repealed.

32 (1) Section 162 (amount of a redundancy payment) is amended in accordance with this paragraph.

(2) Subsections (4), (5) and (8) are repealed.

(3) In subsection (6), for the words 'Subsections (1) to (5)' substitute 'Subsections (1) to (3)'.

33 In relation to any case where the date that is the relevant date by virtue of section 153 of the 1996 Act falls before the commencement date, paragraphs 30 to 32 do not apply.

34 (1) Section 209 (powers to amend Act) is amended as follows.

(2) In subsection (5) omit '109(1),'.

35 (1) Section 211 (period of continuous employment) is amended in accordance with this paragraph.

(2) In paragraph (a) of subsection (1) for the words 'subsections (2) and' substitute 'subsection'.

(3) Subsection (2) is repealed.

The Employment Act 2002

36 (1) The Employment Act 2002 is amended in accordance with this paragraph.

(2) At the end of each of the following Schedules –

(a) Schedule 3 (tribunal jurisdictions to which section 31 applies for adjustment of awards for non-completion of statutory procedure);

(b) Schedule 4 (tribunal jurisdictions to which section 32 applies for complaints where the employee must first submit a statement of grievance to employer); and

(c) Schedule 5 (tribunal jurisdictions to which section 38 applies in relation to proceedings where the employer has failed to give a statement of employment particulars),

insert –

'Regulation 36 of the Employment Equality (Age) Regulations 2006 (discrimination in the employment field)'.

The Equality Act 2006

37 The Equality Act 2006 is amended as follows.

38 (1) Section 14(1) (codes of practice) is amended in accordance with this paragraph.

(2) At the end of paragraph (g) omit 'and'.

(3) After paragraph (h) insert –

'and

(i) Parts 2 and 3 of the Employment Equality (Age) Regulations 2006.'.

39 (1) Section 27(1) (conciliation) is amended in accordance with this paragraph.

(2) At the end of paragraph (f) omit 'or'.

(3) After paragraph (g) insert –

'or

(h) regulation 39 of the Employment Equality (Age) Regulations 2006 (Jurisdiction of County and Sheriff Courts).'.

40 (1) Section 33(1) (equality and human rights enactments) is amended in accordance with this paragraph.

(2) At the end of paragraph (g) omit 'and'.

(3) After paragraph (h) insert –

'and

(i) the Employment Equality (Age) Regulations 2006.'.

Part 2

Other Legislation

41 (1) The Coal and Other Mines (Locomotives) Regulations 1956, Schedule 1 to the Coal and Other Mines (Locomotives) Order 1956 is amended in accordance with this paragraph.

(2) In regulation 17(1) (drivers of locomotives) omit the words 'and no appointed driver shall operate a locomotive hauling persons in vehicles unless he has attained the age of –

(a) in the case of a mine of shale, eighteen years;

(b) in the case of any other mine, twenty-one years'.

42 (1) The Stratified Ironstone, Shale and Fireclay Mines (Explosives) Regulations 1956 are amended in accordance with this paragraph.

(2) In regulation 3 (qualification of shot firers) omit the words 'he has attained the age of twenty-one years; and'.

43 (1) The Miscellaneous Mines (Explosives) Regulations 1959 are amended in accordance with this paragraph.

(2) Omit regulation 6(2).

(3) In regulation 8(2) (control of issue of detonators) omit the words 'has attained the age of eighteen years and'.

44 (1) The Lynemouth Mine (Diesel Vehicles and Storage Battery Vehicles) Special Regulations 1961 are amended in accordance with this paragraph.

(2) In regulation 15 after the words 'Regulations 17' insert 'as amended by the Employment Equality (Age) Regulations 2006'.

45 (1) The South Crofty Mine (Locomotive) Special Regulations 1965 are amended in accordance with this paragraph.

(2) In regulation 11(2) omit the words 'has attained the age of twenty-one years and'.

46 (1) The Glebe Mine (Locomotives and Diesel Vehicles) Special Regulations 1967 are amended in accordance with this paragraph.

(2) In regulation 15(2) omit the words 'has attained the age of eighteen years and'.

47 (1) The Winsford Rock Salt Mine (Diesel Vehicles and Storage Battery Vehicles) Special Regulations 1971 are amended in accordance with this paragraph.

(2) In regulation 14(2) omit the words 'is under the age of twenty-one years and'.

48 (1) The Thoresby Mine (Cable Reel Load-Haul-Dump Vehicles) Special Regulations 1978 are amended in accordance with this paragraph.

(2) In regulation 17 after the words 'Regulations 17' insert 'as amended by the Employment Equality (Age) Regulations 2006'.

49 The Statutory Sick Pay (General) Regulations 1982 are amended as follows.

50 (1) Regulation 16 (meaning of 'employee') is amended in accordance with this paragraph.

(2) In paragraph (1) –

(a) at the beginning insert the words 'Subject to paragraph (1ZA),', and

(b) omit the words 'over the age of 16'.

(3) After paragraph (1) insert –

'(1ZA) Any person under the age of 16 who would have been treated as an employed earner or, as the case may be, would have been treated otherwise than as an employed earner by virtue of the Social Security (Categorisation of Earners) Regulations 1978 had he been aged 16 or over, shall be treated as if he is aged 16 or over for the purposes of paragraph (1).'.

51 (1) Regulation 17(2) (meaning of 'earnings') is amended in accordance with this paragraph.

(2) At the end of sub-paragraph (a) insert '(or would have been so excluded had he not been under the age of 16)'.

(3) At the end of sub-paragraph (b) insert '(or where such a payment or amount would have been so excluded and in consequence he would not have been entitled to statutory sick pay had he not been under the age of 16)'.

52 The Statutory Maternity Pay (General) Regulations 1986 are amended as follows.

53 (1) Regulation 17 (meaning of 'employee') is amended in accordance with this paragraph.

(2) In paragraph (1) –

(a) at the beginning insert the words 'Subject to paragraph (1A),', and

(b) omit the words 'over the age of 16'.

(3) After paragraph (1) insert –

'(1A) Any woman under the age of 16 who would have been treated as an employed earner or, as the case may be, would have been treated otherwise than as an employed earner by virtue of the Social Security (Categorisation of Earners) Regulations 1978 had she been aged 16 or over, shall be treated as if she is aged 16 or over for the purposes of paragraph (1).'.

54 (1) Regulation 20(2) (Meaning of 'earnings') is amended in accordance with this paragraph.

(2) At the end of sub-paragraph (a) insert '(or would have been so excluded had she not been under the age of 16)'.

(3) At the end of sub-paragraph (b) insert '(or where such a payment or amount would have been so excluded and in consequence she would not have been entitled to statutory maternity pay had she not been under the age of 16)'.

(4) This paragraph applies in relation to any case where the expected week of confinement begins on or after 14th January 2007.

55 (1) The Coal and Other Safety-Lamp Mines (Explosives) Regulations 1993 are amended in accordance with this paragraph.

(2) In regulation 4(4) (appointment of shotfirers and trainee shotfirers) omit the words 'he is at least 21 years of age and'.

56 (1) The Employment Tribunals (Interest on Awards In Discrimination Cases) Regulations 1996 are amended in accordance with this paragraph.

(2) In sub-paragraph (b) of the definition of 'an award under the relevant legislation' in regulation 1(2) (interpretation) –

(a) after 'regulation 30(1)(b) of the Employment Equality (Sexual Orientation) Regulations 2003' omit 'or'; and

(b) after 'regulation 30(1)(b) of the Employment Equality (Religion or Belief) Regulations 2003' insert –

'or regulation 38(1)(b) of the Employment Equality (Age) Regulations 2006'.

57 (1) The Employment Protection (Continuity of Employment) Regulations 1996 are amended in accordance with this paragraph.

(2) In regulation 2 (application) –

(a) omit the word 'or' at the end of paragraph (e); and

(b) after paragraph (f) insert –

', or

(g) a decision taken arising out of the use of the statutory duty to consider procedure contained in Schedule 6 to the Employment Equality (Age) Regulations 2006.'.

58 (1) The National Minimum Wage Regulations 1999 are amended in accordance with this paragraph.

(2) Omit regulation 12(2)(a).

(3) Omit paragraphs (2) to (6) of regulation 13.

(4) In regulation 13(7) for the words 'Paragraphs (1) and (2) do' substitute 'Paragraph (1) does'.

(5) In relation to any case where, before the commencement date, a worker within the meaning of regulation 12(2) has attained the age of 26, sub-paragraph (2) does not apply.

59 The Statutory Paternity Pay and Statutory Adoption Pay (General) Regulations 2002 are amended as follows.

60 (1) Regulation 32 (Treatment of persons as employees) is amended in accordance with this paragraph.

(2) In paragraph (1) –

(a) at the beginning insert the words 'Subject to paragraph (1A),', and

(b) omit the words 'over the age of 16'.

(3) After paragraph (1) insert –

'(1A) Any person under the age of 16 who would have been treated as an employed earner or, as the case may be, would have been treated otherwise than as an employed earner by virtue of the Social Security (Categorisation of Earners) Regulations 1978 had he been aged 16 or over, shall be treated as if he is aged 16 or over for the purposes of paragraph (1).'.

61 (1) Regulation 39(2) (Meaning of 'earnings') is amended in accordance with this paragraph.

(2) At the end of sub-paragraph (a) insert '(or would have been so excluded had he not been under the age of 16)'.

(3) At the end of sub-paragraph (b) insert '(or where such a payment or amount would have been so excluded and in consequence he would not have been entitled to statutory paternity pay or, as the case may be, statutory adoption pay had he not been under the age of 16)'.

62 (1) Schedule 1A (occupational pension schemes) to the Employment Equality (Religion or Belief) Regulations 2003 is amended in accordance with this paragraph.

(2) In paragraph 1(1) –

(a) in the definition of 'active member', 'deferred member', 'managers', 'pensioner member' and 'trustees or managers', omit the words 'as at the date of the coming into force of these Regulations', and

(b) in the definition of 'occupational pension scheme' omit the words 'as at the date of the coming into force of these Regulations'.

(3) In paragraph 1(2) omit the words 'as at the date of the coming into force of these Regulations'.

63 (1) Schedule 1A (occupational pension schemes) to the Employment Equality (Sexual Orientation) Regulations 2003 is amended in accordance with this paragraph.

(2) In paragraph 1(1) –

(a) in the definition of 'active member', 'deferred member', 'managers', 'pensioner member' and 'trustees or managers', omit the words 'as at the date of the coming into force of these Regulations', and

(b) in the definition of 'occupational pension scheme' omit the words 'as at the date of the coming into force of these Regulations'.

(3) In paragraph 1(2) omit the words 'as at the date of the coming into force of these Regulations'.

64 (1) The Employment Act 2002 (Dispute Resolution) Regulations 2004 are amended in accordance with this paragraph.

(2) In regulation 4(1) (dismissals to which the dismissal and disciplinary procedures do not apply) –

(a) omit the word 'or' at the end of sub-paragraph (f); and

(b) after sub-paragraph (g) insert –

', or

(h) the reason (or, if more than one, the principal reason) for the dismissal is retirement of the employee (to be determined in accordance with section 98ZA to 98ZF of the 1996 Act)'.

SCHEDULE 9

Repeals and Revocations

Regulation 49(2)

(1) Repeals	
Short title and chapter	Extent of repeal
Marriage (Scotland) Act 1977 (c 15)	In section 9(1) the proviso, In section 12 the proviso, and In section 17 the proviso
Education (Scotland) Act 1980 (c 44)	Section 89
Solicitors (Scotland) Act 1980 (c 46)	Section 6(1)(a)
Weights and Measures Act 1985 (c 72)	Section 73(3)
Electricity Act 1989 (c 29)	In Schedule 10, paragraph 9(3)
Judicial Pensions and Retirement Act 1993 (c 8)	In Schedule 6, paragraph 66
Scottish Public Services Ombudsman Act 2002 (asp 11)	In Schedule 1, paragraph 4(1)(c) In Schedule 1, in paragraph 4(3), the words in brackets
Freedom of Information (Scotland) Act 2002 (asp 13)	Section 42(4)(b) In section 42(5), the words in brackets

(2) Revocations	
Title and reference	Extent of revocation
Coal and Other Mines (Sidings) Regulations 1956, Schedule to the Coal and Other Mines (Sidings) Order 1956 (SI 1956/1773)	Regulation 21 In regulation 22, the definition of locomotive
The Management and Administration of Safety and Health in Mines Regulations 1993 (SI 1993/1897)	Regulation 17(2)

Appendix 2

COUNCIL DIRECTIVE 2000/78/EC

Reproduced by kind permission of Westlaw.

27 November 2000 - establishing a general framework for equal treatment in employment and occupation

THE COUNCIL OF THE EUROPEAN UNION

Having regard to the Treaty establishing the European Community, and in particular Article 13 thereof,

Having regard to the proposal from the Commission,[1]

Having regard to the Opinion of the European Parliament,[2]

Having regard to the Opinion of the Economic and Social Committee,[3]

Having regard to the Opinion of the Committee of the Regions,[4]

Whereas:

(1) In accordance with Article 6 of the Treaty on European Union, the European Union is founded on the principles of liberty, democracy, respect for human rights and fundamental freedoms, and the rule of law, principles which are common to all Member States and it respects fundamental rights, as guaranteed by the European Convention for the Protection of Human Rights and Fundamental Freedoms and as they result from the constitutional traditions common to the Member States, as general principles of Community law.

(2) The principle of equal treatment between women and men is well established by an important body of Community law, in particular in Council Directive 76/207/EEC of 9 February 1976 on the implementation of the principle of equal treatment for men and women as regards access to employment, vocational training and promotion, and working conditions.[5]

(3) In implementing the principle of equal treatment, the Community should, in accordance with Article 3(2) of the EC Treaty, aim to eliminate inequalities, and to promote equality between

men and women, especially since women are often the victims of multiple discrimination.

(4) The right of all persons to equality before the law and protection against discrimination constitutes a universal right recognised by the Universal Declaration of Human Rights, the United Nations Convention on the Elimination of All Forms of Discrimination against Women, United Nations Covenants on Civil and Political Rights and on Economic, Social and Cultural Rights and by the European Convention for the Protection of Human Rights and Fundamental Freedoms, to which all Member States are signatories. Convention No 111 of the International Labour Organisation (ILO) prohibits discrimination in the field of employment and occupation.

(5) It is important to respect such fundamental rights and freedoms. This Directive does not prejudice freedom of association, including the right to establish unions with others and to join unions to defend one's interests.

(6) The Community Charter of the Fundamental Social Rights of Workers recognises the importance of combating every form of discrimination, including the need to take appropriate action for the social and economic integration of elderly and disabled people.

(7) The EC Treaty includes among its objectives the promotion of coordination between employment policies of the Member States. To this end, a new employment chapter was incorporated in the EC Treaty as a means of developing a coordinated European strategy for employment to promote a skilled, trained and adaptable workforce.

(8) The Employment Guidelines for 2000 agreed by the European Council at Helsinki on 10 and 11 December 1999 stress the need to foster a labour market favourable to social integration by formulating a coherent set of policies aimed at combating discrimination against groups such as persons with disability. They also emphasise the need to pay particular attention to supporting older workers, in order to increase their participation in the labour force.

(9) Employment and occupation are key elements in guaranteeing equal opportunities for all and contribute strongly to the full participation of citizens in economic, cultural and social life and to realising their potential.

(10) On 29 June 2000 the Council adopted Directive 2000/43/EC[6] implementing the principle of equal treatment between persons irrespective of racial or ethnic origin. That Directive

already provides protection against such discrimination in the field of employment and occupation.

(11) Discrimination based on religion or belief, disability, age or sexual orientation may undermine the achievement of the objectives of the EC Treaty, in particular the attainment of a high level of employment and social protection, raising the standard of living and the quality of life, economic and social cohesion and solidarity, and the free movement of persons.

(12) To this end, any direct or indirect discrimination based on religion or belief, disability, age or sexual orientation as regards the areas covered by this Directive should be prohibited throughout the Community. This prohibition of discrimination should also apply to nationals of third countries but does not cover differences of treatment based on nationality and is without prejudice to provisions governing the entry and residence of third-country nationals and their access to employment and occupation.

(13) This Directive does not apply to social security and social protection schemes whose benefits are not treated as income within the meaning given to that term for the purpose of applying Article 141 of the EC Treaty, nor to any kind of payment by the State aimed at providing access to employment or maintaining employment.

(14) This Directive shall be without prejudice to national provisions laying down retirement ages.

(15) The appreciation of the facts from which it may be inferred that there has been direct or indirect discrimination is a matter for national judicial or other competent bodies, in accordance with rules of national law or practice. Such rules may provide, in particular, for indirect discrimination to be established by any means including on the basis of statistical evidence.

(16) The provision of measures to accommodate the needs of disabled people at the workplace plays an important role in combating discrimination on grounds of disability.

(17) This Directive does not require the recruitment, promotion, maintenance in employment or training of an individual who is not competent, capable and available to perform the essential functions of the post concerned or to undergo the relevant training, without prejudice to the obligation to provide reasonable accommodation for people with disabilities.

(18) This Directive does not require, in particular, the armed forces and the police, prison or emergency services to recruit or maintain in employment persons who do not have the required

capacity to carry out the range of functions that they may be called upon to perform with regard to the legitimate objective of preserving the operational capacity of those services.

(19) Moreover, in order that the Member States may continue to safeguard the combat effectiveness of their armed forces, they may choose not to apply the provisions of this Directive concerning disability and age to all or part of their armed forces. The Member States which make that choice must define the scope of that derogation.

(20) Appropriate measures should be provided, ie effective and practical measures to adapt the workplace to the disability, for example adapting premises and equipment, patterns of working time, the distribution of tasks or the provision of training or integration resources.

(21) To determine whether the measures in question give rise to a disproportionate burden, account should be taken in particular of the financial and other costs entailed, the scale and financial resources of the organisation or undertaking and the possibility of obtaining public funding or any other assistance.

(22) This Directive is without prejudice to national laws on marital status and the benefits dependent thereon.

(23) In very limited circumstances, a difference of treatment may be justified where a characteristic related to religion or belief, disability, age or sexual orientation constitutes a genuine and determining occupational requirement, when the objective is legitimate and the requirement is proportionate. Such circumstances should be included in the information provided by the Member States to the Commission.

(24) The European Union in its Declaration No 11 on the status of churches and non-confessional organisations, annexed to the Final Act of the Amsterdam Treaty, has explicitly recognised that it respects and does not prejudice the status under national law of churches and religious associations or communities in the Member States and that it equally respects the status of philosophical and non-confessional organisations. With this in view, Member States may maintain or lay down specific provisions on genuine, legitimate and justified occupational requirements which might be required for carrying out an occupational activity.

(25) The prohibition of age discrimination is an essential part of meeting the aims set out in the Employment Guidelines and encouraging diversity in the workforce. However, differences in treatment in connection with age may be justified under

certain circumstances and therefore require specific provisions which may vary in accordance with the situation in Member States. It is therefore essential to distinguish between differences in treatment which are justified, in particular by legitimate employment policy, labour market and vocational training objectives, and discrimination which must be prohibited.

(26) The prohibition of discrimination should be without prejudice to the maintenance or adoption of measures intended to prevent or compensate for disadvantages suffered by a group of persons of a particular religion or belief, disability, age or sexual orientation, and such measures may permit organisations of persons of a particular religion or belief, disability, age or sexual orientation where their main object is the promotion of the special needs of those persons.

(27) In its Recommendation 86/379/EEC of 24 July 1986 on the employment of disabled people in the Community,[7] the Council established a guideline framework setting out examples of positive action to promote the employment and training of disabled people, and in its Resolution of 17 June 1999 on equal employment opportunities for people with disabilities,[8] affirmed the importance of giving specific attention inter alia to recruitment, retention, training and lifelong learning with regard to disabled persons.

(28) This Directive lays down minimum requirements, thus giving the Member States the option of introducing or maintaining more favourable provisions. The implementation of this Directive should not serve to justify any regression in relation to the situation which already prevails in each Member State.

(29) Persons who have been subject to discrimination based on religion or belief, disability, age or sexual orientation should have adequate means of legal protection. To provide a more effective level of protection, associations or legal entities should also be empowered to engage in proceedings, as the Member States so determine, either on behalf or in support of any victim, without prejudice to national rules of procedure concerning representation and defence before the courts.

(30) The effective implementation of the principle of equality requires adequate judicial protection against victimisation.

(31) The rules on the burden of proof must be adapted when there is a prima facie case of discrimination and, for the principle of equal treatment to be applied effectively, the burden of proof must shift back to the respondent when evidence of such discrimination is brought. However, it is not for the respondent to prove that the plaintiff adheres to a particular religion or

belief, has a particular disability, is of a particular age or has a particular sexual orientation.

(32) Member States need not apply the rules on the burden of proof to proceedings in which it is for the court or other competent body to investigate the facts of the case. The procedures thus referred to are those in which the plaintiff is not required to prove the facts, which it is for the court or competent body to investigate.

(33) Member States should promote dialogue between the social partners and, within the framework of national practice, with non-governmental organisations to address different forms of discrimination at the workplace and to combat them.

(34) The need to promote peace and reconciliation between the major communities in Northern Ireland necessitates the incorporation of particular provisions into this Directive.

(35) Member States should provide for effective, proportionate and dissuasive sanctions in case of breaches of the obligations under this Directive.

(36) Member States may entrust the social partners, at their joint request, with the implementation of this Directive, as regards the provisions concerning collective agreements, provided they take any necessary steps to ensure that they are at all times able to guarantee the results required by this Directive.

(37) In accordance with the principle of subsidiarity set out in Article 5 of the EC Treaty, the objective of this Directive, namely the creation within the Community of a level playing-field as regards equality in employment and occupation, cannot be sufficiently achieved by the Member States and can therefore, by reason of the scale and impact of the action, be better achieved at Community level. In accordance with the principle of proportionality, as set out in that Article, this Directive does not go beyond what is necessary in order to achieve that objective.

1 OJ C 177 E, 27.6.2000, p. 42.
2 Opinion delivered on 12 October 2000 (not yet published in the Official Journal).
3 OJ C 204, 18.7.2000, p. 82.
4 OJ C 226, 8.8.2000, p. 1.
5 OJ L 39, 14.2.1976, p. 40.
6 OJ L 180, 19.7.2000, p. 22.
7 OJ L 225, 12.8.1986, p. 43.
8 OJ C 186, 2.7.1999, p. 3.

HAS ADOPTED THIS DIRECTIVE:

CHAPTER I

GENERAL PROVISIONS

Article 1

Purpose

The purpose of this Directive is to lay down a general framework for combating discrimination on the grounds of religion or belief, disability, age or sexual orientation as regards employment and occupation, with a view to putting into effect in the Member States the principle of equal treatment.

Article 2

Concept of discrimination

1. For the purposes of this Directive, the 'principle of equal treatment' shall mean that there shall be no direct or indirect discrimination whatsoever on any of the grounds referred to in Article 1.
2. For the purposes of paragraph 1:
   (a) direct discrimination shall be taken to occur where one person is treated less favourably than another is, has been or would be treated in a comparable situation, on any of the grounds referred to in Article 1;
   (b) indirect discrimination shall be taken to occur where an apparently neutral provision, criterion or practice would put persons having a particular religion or belief, a particular disability, a particular age, or a particular sexual orientation at a particular disadvantage compared with other persons unless:
      (i) that provision, criterion or practice is objectively justified by a legitimate aim and the means of achieving that aim are appropriate and necessary, or
      (ii) as regards persons with a particular disability, the employer or any person or organisation to whom this Directive applies, is obliged, under national legislation,

to take appropriate measures in line with the principles contained in Article 5 in order to eliminate disadvantages entailed by such provision, criterion or practice.

3. Harassment shall be deemed to be a form of discrimination within the meaning of paragraph 1, when unwanted conduct related to any of the grounds referred to in Article 1 takes place with the purpose or effect of violating the dignity of a person and of creating an intimidating, hostile, degrading, humiliating or offensive environment. In this context, the concept of harassment may be defined in accordance with the national laws and practice of the Member States.
4. An instruction to discriminate against persons on any of the grounds referred to in Article 1 shall be deemed to be discrimination within the meaning of paragraph 1.
5. This Directive shall be without prejudice to measures laid down by national law which, in a democratic society, are necessary for public security, for the maintenance of public order and the prevention of criminal offences, for the protection of health and for the protection of the rights and freedoms of others.

Article 3

Scope

1. Within the limits of the areas of competence conferred on the Community, this Directive shall apply to all persons, as regards both the public and private sectors, including public bodies, in relation to:
   (a) conditions for access to employment, to self-employment or to occupation, including selection criteria and recruitment conditions, whatever the branch of activity and at all levels of the professional hierarchy, including promotion;
   (b) access to all types and to all levels of vocational guidance, vocational training, advanced vocational training and retraining, including practical work experience;
   (c) employment and working conditions, including dismissals and pay;
   (d) membership of, and involvement in, an organisation of workers or employers, or any organisation whose members carry on a particular profession, including the benefits provided for by such organisations.
2. This Directive does not cover differences of treatment based on nationality and is without prejudice to provisions and conditions

relating to the entry into and residence of third-country nationals and stateless persons in the territory of Member States, and to any treatment which arises from the legal status of the third-country nationals and stateless persons concerned.

3. This Directive does not apply to payments of any kind made by state schemes or similar, including state social security or social protection schemes.
4. Member States may provide that this Directive, in so far as it relates to discrimination on the grounds of disability and age, shall not apply to the armed forces.

Article 4

Occupational requirements

1. Notwithstanding Article 2(1) and (2), Member States may provide that a difference of treatment which is based on a characteristic related to any of the grounds referred to in Article 1 shall not constitute discrimination where, by reason of the nature of the particular occupational activities concerned or of the context in which they are carried out, such a characteristic constitutes a genuine and determining occupational requirement, provided that the objective is legitimate and the requirement is proportionate.
2. Member States may maintain national legislation in force at the date of adoption of this Directive or provide for future legislation incorporating national practices existing at the date of adoption of this Directive pursuant to which, in the case of occupational activities within churches and other public or private organisations the ethos of which is based on religion or belief, a difference of treatment based on a person's religion or belief shall not constitute discrimination where, by reason of the nature of these activities or of the context in which they are carried out, a person's religion or belief constitute a genuine, legitimate and justified occupational requirement, having regard to the organisation's ethos. This difference of treatment shall be implemented taking account of Member States' constitutional provisions and principles, as well as the general principles of Community law, and should not justify discrimination on another ground.

Provided that its provisions are otherwise complied with, this Directive shall thus not prejudice the right of churches and other public or private organisations, the ethos of which is based on religion or belief, acting in conformity with national constitutions and laws, to require individuals working for them to act in good faith and with loyalty to the organisation's ethos.

Article 5

Reasonable accommodation for disabled persons

In order to guarantee compliance with the principle of equal treatment in relation to persons with disabilities, reasonable accommodation shall be provided. This means that employers shall take appropriate measures, where needed in a particular case, to enable a person with a disability to have access to, participate in, or advance in employment, or to undergo training, unless such measures would impose a disproportionate burden on the employer. This burden shall not be disproportionate when it is sufficiently remedied by measures existing within the framework of the disability policy of the Member State concerned.

Article 6

Justification of differences of treatment on grounds of age

1. Notwithstanding Article 2(2), Member States may provide that differences of treatment on grounds of age shall not constitute discrimination, if, within the context of national law, they are objectively and reasonably justified by a legitimate aim, including legitimate employment policy, labour market and vocational training objectives, and if the means of achieving that aim are appropriate and necessary.
   Such differences of treatment may include, among others:
   (a) the setting of special conditions on access to employment and vocational training, employment and occupation, including dismissal and remuneration conditions, for young people, older workers and persons with caring responsibilities in order to promote their vocational integration or ensure their protection;
   (b) the fixing of minimum conditions of age, professional experience or seniority in service for access to employment or to certain advantages linked to employment;
   (c) the fixing of a maximum age for recruitment which is based on the training requirements of the post in question or the need for a reasonable period of employment before retirement.
2. Notwithstanding Article 2(2), Member States may provide that the fixing for occupational social security schemes of ages for admission or entitlement to retirement or invalidity benefits, including the fixing under those schemes of different ages for employees or groups or categories of employees, and the use,

in the context of such schemes, of age criteria in actuarial calculations, does not constitute discrimination on the grounds of age, provided this does not result in discrimination on the grounds of sex.

Article 7

Positive action

1. With a view to ensuring full equality in practice, the principle of equal treatment shall not prevent any Member State from maintaining or adopting specific measures to prevent or compensate for disadvantages linked to any of the grounds referred to in Article 1.
2. With regard to disabled persons, the principle of equal treatment shall be without prejudice to the right of Member States to maintain or adopt provisions on the protection of health and safety at work or to measures aimed at creating or maintaining provisions or facilities for safeguarding or promoting their integration into the working environment.

Article 8

Minimum requirements

1. Member States may introduce or maintain provisions which are more favourable to the protection of the principle of equal treatment than those laid down in this Directive.
2. The implementation of this Directive shall under no circumstances constitute grounds for a reduction in the level of protection against discrimination already afforded by Member States in the fields covered by this Directive.

CHAPTER II

REMEDIES AND ENFORCEMENT

Article 9

Defence of rights

1. Member States shall ensure that judicial and/or administrative procedures, including where they deem it appropriate conciliation procedures, for the enforcement of obligations under this

Directive are available to all persons who consider themselves wronged by failure to apply the principle of equal treatment to them, even after the relationship in which the discrimination is alleged to have occurred has ended.

2. Member States shall ensure that associations, organisations or other legal entities which have, in accordance with the criteria laid down by their national law, a legitimate interest in ensuring that the provisions of this Directive are complied with, may engage, either on behalf or in support of the complainant, with his or her approval, in any judicial and/or administrative procedure provided for the enforcement of obligations under this Directive.
3. Paragraphs 1 and 2 are without prejudice to national rules relating to time limits for bringing actions as regards the principle of equality of treatment.

Article 10

Burden of proof

1. Member States shall take such measures as are necessary, in accordance with their national judicial systems, to ensure that, when persons who consider themselves wronged because the principle of equal treatment has not been applied to them establish, before a court or other competent authority, facts from which it may be presumed that there has been direct or indirect discrimination, it shall be for the respondent to prove that there has been no breach of the principle of equal treatment.
2. Paragraph 1 shall not prevent Member States from introducing rules of evidence which are more favourable to plaintiffs.
3. Paragraph 1 shall not apply to criminal procedures.
4. Paragraphs 1, 2 and 3 shall also apply to any legal proceedings commenced in accordance with Article 9(2).
5. Member States need not apply paragraph 1 to proceedings in which it is for the court or competent body to investigate the facts of the case.

Article 11

Victimisation

Member States shall introduce into their national legal systems such measures as are necessary to protect employees against dismissal or other adverse treatment by the employer as a reaction to a complaint within the undertaking or to any legal proceedings aimed at enforcing compliance with the principle of equal treatment.

Article 12

Dissemination of information

Member States shall take care that the provisions adopted pursuant to this Directive, together with the relevant provisions already in force in this field, are brought to the attention of the persons concerned by all appropriate means, for example at the workplace, throughout their territory.

Article 13

Social dialogue

1. Member States shall, in accordance with their national traditions and practice, take adequate measures to promote dialogue between the social partners with a view to fostering equal treatment, including through the monitoring of workplace practices, collective agreements, codes of conduct and through research or exchange of experiences and good practices.
2. Where consistent with their national traditions and practice, Member States shall encourage the social partners, without prejudice to their autonomy, to conclude at the appropriate level agreements laying down anti-discrimination rules in the fields referred to in Article 3 which fall within the scope of collective bargaining. These agreements shall respect the minimum requirements laid down by this Directive and by the relevant national implementing measures.

Article 14

Dialogue with non-governmental organisations

Member States shall encourage dialogue with appropriate non-governmental organisations which have, in accordance with their national law and practice, a legitimate interest in contributing to the fight against discrimination on any of the grounds referred to in Article 1 with a view to promoting the principle of equal treatment.

CHAPTER III

PARTICULAR PROVISIONS

Article 15

Northern Ireland

1. In order to tackle the under-representation of one of the major religious communities in the police service of Northern Ireland, differences in treatment regarding recruitment into that service, including its support staff, shall not constitute discrimination insofar as those differences in treatment are expressly authorised by national legislation.
2. In order to maintain a balance of opportunity in employment for teachers in Northern Ireland while furthering the reconciliation of historical divisions between the major religious communities there, the provisions on religion or belief in this Directive shall not apply to the recruitment of teachers in schools in Northern Ireland in so far as this is expressly authorised by national legislation.

CHAPTER IV

FINAL PROVISIONS

Article 16

Compliance

Member States shall take the necessary measures to ensure that:

(a) any laws, regulations and administrative provisions contrary to the principle of equal treatment are abolished;

(b) any provisions contrary to the principle of equal treatment which are included in contracts or collective agreements, internal rules of undertakings or rules governing the independent occupations and professions and workers' and employers' organisations are, or may be, declared null and void or are amended.

Article 17

Sanctions

Member States shall lay down the rules on sanctions applicable to infringements of the national provisions adopted pursuant to this Directive and shall take all measures necessary to ensure that they are applied. The sanctions, which may comprise the payment of compensation to the victim, must be effective, proportionate and dissuasive. Member States shall notify those provisions to the Commission by 2 December 2003 at the latest and shall notify it without delay of any subsequent amendment affecting them.

Article 18

Implementation

Member States shall adopt the laws, regulations and administrative provisions necessary to comply with this Directive by 2 December 2003 at the latest or may entrust the social partners, at their joint request, with the implementation of this Directive as regards provisions concerning collective agreements. In such cases, Member States shall ensure that, no later than 2 December 2003, the social partners introduce the necessary measures by agreement, the Member States concerned being required to take any necessary measures to enable them at any time to be in a position to guarantee the results imposed by this Directive. They shall forthwith inform the Commission thereof.

In order to take account of particular conditions, Member States may, if necessary, have an additional period of 3 years from 2 December 2003, that is to say a total of 6 years, to implement the provisions of this Directive on age and disability discrimination. In that event they shall inform the Commission forthwith. Any Member State which chooses to use this additional period shall report annually to the Commission on the steps it is taking to tackle age and disability discrimination and on the progress it is making towards implementation. The Commission shall report annually to the Council.

When Member States adopt these measures, they shall contain a reference to this Directive or be accompanied by such reference on the occasion of their official publication. The methods of making such reference shall be laid down by Member States.

Article 19

Report

1. Member States shall communicate to the Commission, by 2 December 2005 at the latest and every five years thereafter, all the information necessary for the Commission to draw up a report to the European Parliament and the Council on the application of this Directive.

2. The Commission's report shall take into account, as appropriate, the viewpoints of the social partners and relevant non-governmental organisations. In accordance with the principle of gender mainstreaming, this report shall, inter alia, provide an assessment of the impact of the measures taken on women and men. In the light of the information received, this report shall include, if necessary, proposals to revise and update this Directive.

Article 20

Entry into force

This Directive shall enter into force on the day of its publication in the Official Journal of the European Communities.

Article 21

Addressees

This Directive is addressed to the Member States.

Done at Brussels, 27 November 2000.

For the Council

The President

E. GUIGOU

Index

Register classification

05200500 – General social provisions

Subject

Approximation of laws; Provisions under Article 235 EEC; Social provisions; Free movement of workers

Keywords

employment policy; equal treatment; anti-discriminatory measure; social policy

Year (Dates)

Date of Publication

2000/12/02

Date of document

2000/11/27

Date of entry into force

2000/12/02 = EV

Date of end of validity

9999/99/99

Transposition date

2003/12/02

Date overview

of document: 27/11/2000

of effect: 02/12/2000; Entry into force Date pub. See Art 20

end of validity: 99/99/9999

of transposition: 02/12/2003; At the latest See Art 18

References

Celex number

300L0078

Legal base

EC Treaty Article 13 [197E013]

Legal citations

EC Treaty Article 6 [197E006]

Directive 1976/207 [376L0207]

EC Treaty Article 3 [197E003]

Directive 2000/43 [300L0043]

386X0379

399Y0702(01)

EC Treaty Article 5 [197E005]

Modifies

COM(1999) 565 [599PC0565] Adoption

Modified by

Corrected by corrigendum [300L0078R(01)]

Corrected by corrigendum [300L0078R(02)]

Preparatory Acts

PR;COMM;CO 99/0565 FIN

PCONS;PARL;RENDU 12/10/2000

PCONS;CDR;JO C 226/2000 P 1

PCONS;CES;JO C 204/2000 P 82

Bibliographic Information

Authoring institution

Council

Basic treaty

European Community

Legal instrument

Directive

Document type

DIRECTIVE

Addressee

The Member States

Additional Information

CNS 92025

Publication reference

Official Journal L 303, 02/12/2000, p. 0016–0022 (ES, DA, DE, EL, EN, FR, IT, NL, PT, FI, SV)

CS.ES Chapter 5 Volume 04 P. 79–85

ET.ES Chapter 5 Volume 04 P. 79–85

HU.ES Chapter5 Volume 04 P. 79–85

LT.ES Chapter 5 Volume 04 P. 79–85

LV.ES Chapter 5 Volume 04 P. 79–85

MT.ES Chapter 5 Volume 04 P. 79–85

PL.ES Chapter 5 Volume 04 P. 79–85

SK.ES Chapter 5 Volume 04 P. 79–85

SL.ES Chapter 5 Volume 04 P. 79–85

Countries (National Measures)

Austria:

1. Gleichbehandlungsgesetz – GlBG und Anderung des Bundesgesetzes uber die Gleichbehandlung von Frau und Mann im Arbeitsleben (Gleichbehandlungsgesetz)
2. Bundesgesetz uber die Gleichbehandlung
3. Gesetz, mit dem die Dienstordnung 1994 (18. Novelle zur Dienstordnung 1994), die Vertragsbedienstetenordnung 1995 (18. Novelle zur Vertragsbedienstetenordnung 1995) unddas Wiener Verwaltungssenat-Dienstrechtsgesetz 1995 (6. Novelle zum Wiener Verwaltungssenat-Dienstrechtsgesetz 1995) geandert werden (Antidiskriminierungsnovelle)
4. Anderung des Bundes-Gleichbehandlungsgesetzes
5. Gesetz vom 21. Oktober 2004, mit dem die Karntner Landesverfassung geandert und ein Gesetz uber das Verbot der

Diskriminierung auf Grund der ethnischen Zugehorigkeit, der Religion, der Weltanschauung, einer Behinderung, des Alters, der sexuellen Ausrichtung und des Geschlechts (Karntner Antidiskriminierungsgesetz – K-ADG) erlassen werden

6. NO Landarbeitsordnung 1973
7. Gesetz vom 6. Juli 2004, mit dem ein Gesetz uber die Gleichbehandlung im Bereich des Landes, der Gemeinden und Gemeindeverbande (Landes-Gleichbehandlungsgesetz L-GBG) erlassen und das Landes-Dienstrecht und Besoldungs¬recht geandert wird
8. Anderung des NO Gleichbehandlungsgesetzes
9. Gesetz vom 17. November 2004 uber die Gleichbehandlung im Landesdienst (Landes-Gleichbehandlungsgesetz2005 – L-GlBG 2005)
10. Gesetz vom 17. November 2004 uber die Gleichbehandlung im Dienst der Gemeinden und der Gemeindeverbande (Gemeinde-Gleichbehandlungsgesetz 2005 – G-GlBG 2005)
11. Tiroler Gesetz vom 1. Februar 2005 uber das Verbot von Diskriminierungen (Tiroler Antidiskriminierungsgesetz 2005 – TADG 2005)
12. Karntner Landarbeitsordnung 1995; Anderung
13. NO Antidiskriminierungsgesetz
14. OO. Antidiskriminierungsgesetz
15. Gesetz uber das Verbot der Diskriminierung (Antidiskriminierungsgesetz – ADG)
16. Oberosterreichische Landarbeitsordnungs-Novelle 2005
17. Gesetz, mit dem die Landarbeitsordnung 2000 geandert wird
18. Behinderteneinstellungsgesetz
19. Burgenlandisches Antidiskriminierungsgesetz
20. Wiener Antidiskriminierungsgesetz
21. Gesetz, mit dem das Wiener land- und forstwirtschafltiche Gleichbehandlungsgesetz umgesetz wird

Belgium:

1. Decret relatif a la mise en oeuvre du principe de l'egalite de traitement
2. Dekret bezuglich der Sicherung der Gleichbehandlung auf dem Arbeitsmarkt.Decret relatif a la garantie de l'egalite de traitement sur le marche du travail.

3. Loi du 25 fevrier 2003 tendant a lutter contre la discrimination et modifiant la loi du 15 fevrier 1993 creant un Centre pour l'egalite des chances et la lutte contre le racisme MB du 17/03/2003 p. 12844 (C – 2003/12105)
4. Decret du 08 mai 2002 relatif a la participation proportionnelle sur le marche de l'emploi MB du 26/07/2002 p. 33267 (C – 2002/35892)
5. Ordonnance du 26 juin 2003 relative a la gestion mixte du marche de l'emploi dans la Region de Bruxelles-Capital MB du 29/07/2003 p. 39629 (C – 2003/31362)
6. Besluit van 30/01/2004 van de Vlaamse regering tot uitvoering van het decreet van 8/5/2002 houdende evenredige participatie op de arbeidsmarkt wat betreft de beroepskeuzevoorlichting, beroepsopleiding, loopbaanbegeleiding en arbeidsbemiddeling MB du 04/03/2004 p. 12050 (C – 2004/35293) (SG(2004)A/3766 du 05/04/2004)
7. Arrete du 17/02/2004 du Gouvernement de la Communaute française modifiant l'arrete du Gouvernement de la Communaute française du 15/07/2003 fixant la repartition des competences entre les ministres du Gouvernement de la Communaute française MB du 04/03/2004 p. 12055 (C – 2004/29065) (SG(2004)A/3766 du 05/04/2004)

Denmark:

1. Lov om aendring af lov om forbud mod forskelsbehandling pa arbejdsmarkedet m. v.
2. Lov om forbud mod forskelsbehandling pa arbejdsmarkedet m. v.
3. Lov om Wndring af lov om forbud mod forskelsbehandling pa arbejdsmarkedet mv.
4. Lov om Wndring af lov om forbud mod forskelsbehandling pa arbejdsmarkedet mv.
5. Lov om Wndring af lov om forbud mod forskelsbehandling pa arbejdsmarkedet mv.
6. Lov om Wndring af lov om forbud mod forskelsbehandling pa arbejdsmarkedet m.v.

Finland:

1. Yhdenvertaisuuslaki SSK no 21 tethy 20/1/2004 p. 49

France:

1. Loi no 2005-102 du 11/2/2005 pour l'egalite des droits et des chances, la participation et la citoyennete des personnes handicapees.
2. Loi no 2005-843 du 26/7/2005 portant diverses mesures de transposition du droit communautaire a la fontion publique.

Germany:

NO REFERENCE AVAILABLE

Greece:

1. ,,,, .

Ireland:

NO REFERENCE AVAILABLE

Italy:

1. Decreto Legislativo 9/7/2003,n. 216 – Attuazione della direttiva 2000/78/CE pe rla parita di trattamento in materia di occupazione e di condizioni di lavoro. GURI no 187 del 13/8/2003 p. 3

Luxembourg:

NO REFERENCE AVAILABLE

Netherlands:

1. Besluit van 23 februari 2004, houdende vaststelling van de datum van inwerkingtreding van de Wet gelijke behandeling op grond van leeftijd bij de arbeid
2. Wet van 17 december 2003, houdende gelijke behandeling op grond van leeftijd bij arbeid, beroep en beroepsonderwijs (Wet gelijke behandeling op grond van leeftijd bij de arbeid)
3. Besluit van 11 maart 2004, houdende vaststelling van het tijdstip van inwerkingtreding van de Wet van 21 februari 2004 tot wijziging van de Algemene wet gelijke behandeling en enkele andere wetten ter uitvoering van richtlijn nr. 2000/43/EG en richtlijn nr. 2000/78/EG (EG-implementatiewet Awgb)

4. Wet van 3/4/2003 tot vaststelling van de Wet gelijke behandeling op grond van handicap of chronische ziekte. ref: Staatsblad no 206 van 22/5/2003
5. Besluit van 11/8/2003, houdende vaststelling van het tijdstip van inwerkingtreding van de Wet geljike behandeling op grond van handicap of chronische ziekte. re: Staatsblad no 329 van 28/8/2003

Portugal:

1. Decreto-Lei no 99 de 27/8/2003 Diario da Republica I Serie A no 197 de 27/8/2003 p. 5558

Spain:

1. Ley 62/2003 de 30/12, de medidas fiscales, administrativas y del orden social. BOE no 313 de 31/12/2003 p. 46874
2. LEY 54 de 12/12/2003, de reforma del marco normativo de la prevencion de riesgos laborales. BOE no 298 de 13/12/2003 p. 44408 (SG(2004)A/01739 du 16/02/2004)
3. LEY 53 de 10/12/2003, sobre empleo publico de discapacidados. BOE no 296 de 11/12/2003 p. 44082 (SG(2004)A/01740 du 16/02/2004)
4. Correccion de errores y errata de la Ley 62 de 30/12/2003, de medidas fiscales administrativas y de orden social. BOE no 79 de 01/04/2004 p. 13787 (SG(2004)A/03937 du 13/04/2004)

Sweden:

NO REFERENCE AVAILABLE

Great Britain:

1. The Employment Equality (Sexual Orientation) Regulations 2003 SI no 1661 of 26/06/2003
2. The Employment Equality (Religion or Belief) Regulations 2003 SI no 1660 of 26/06/2003
3. The Disability Discrimination Act 1995 (Amendment) Regulations 2003 SI no 1673 of 02/07/2003
4. The Employment Equality (Sexual Orientation) (Amendment) Regulations 2003 SI no 2827 of 06/11/2003

5. The Employment Equality (Religion or Belief) (Amendment) Regulations 2003 SI no 2828 of 06/11/2003
6. The Disability Discrimination Act 1995 (Pensions) Regulations 2003 SI no 2770 of 01/11/2003
7. The Independent Schools (Employment of Teachers in Schools with a Religious Character) Regulations 2003 SI no 2037 of 05/08/2003
8. School Standards and Framework Act 1998 – Chapter 31 School Standards and Framework Act 1998
9. The Industrial Tribunals (Interest on Awards in Discrimination Cases) Regulations 1996 SI no 2803 of 05/11/1996
10. Disability Discrimination Act 1995 – Chapter 50 Disability Discrimination Act 1995
11. Disability Rights Commission Act 1999 – Chapter 17 Disability Rights Commission Act 1999
12. Special Educational Needs and Disability Act 2001 – Chapter 10 Special Educational Needs and Disability Act 2001
13. Education (Scotland) Act 1980 – Chapter 44 Education (Scotland) Act 1980
14. The Fair Employment and Treatment (Northern Ireland) Order 1998 SI no 3162 (N.I. 21) of 16/12/1998
15. Employment Equality (Sexual Orientation) Regulations (Northern Ireland) 2003 SI no 497 of 01/12/2003 (SG(2004)A/01932 du 19/02/2004)
16. Industrial Tribunals (Interest on Awards in Sexual Orientation Discrimination Cases) Regulations (Northern Ireland) 2003 SI no 498 of 02/12/2003 (SG(2004)A/01932 du 19/02/2004)
17. Fair Employment and Treatment Order (Amendment) Regulations (N. Ireland) 2003 SI no 520 of 9/12/2003 (SG(2004)A/01932 du 19/02/2004)

[illegible] (NORTHERN IRELAND) 2007/[illegible]

Index

[all references are to paragraph number]